- "Congress' Secret Comm___ the forerunner of the State Department.

- Lafayette's crest: "cur non" ("why not")

PJ 58 - Lafayettes feelings about America's virtue.

FOR LIBERTY AND GLORY

ALSO BY JAMES R. GAINES

Wit's End: Days and Nights of the Algonquin Round Table
The Lives of the Piano
Evening in the Palace of Reason

FOR LIBERTY AND GLORY

Washington, Lafayette, and Their Revolutions

JAMES R. GAINES

W. W. Norton & Company

NEW YORK · LONDON

For information about permission to reproduce selections from this book,
write to Permissions, W. W. Norton & Company, Inc.,
500 Fifth Avenue, New York, NY 10110

For information about special discounts for bulk purchases, please contact
W. W. Norton Special Sales at specialsales@wwnorton.com or 800-233-4830

Manufacturing by R.R. Donnelley, Harrisonburg
Book design by Brooke Koven
Production manager: Anna Oler

Library of Congress Cataloging-in-Publication Data

Gaines, James R.
For liberty and glory : Washington, Lafayette, and their revolutions / James R. Gaines. — 1st ed.
p. cm.
Includes bibliographical references and index.
ISBN 978-0-393-06138-3 (hardcover)
1. Washington, George, 1732–1799. 2. Washington, George, 1732–1799—Influence.
3. United States—History—Revolution, 1775–1783. 4. United States—History—Revolution,
1775–1783—Biography. 5. Presidents—United States—Biography. 6. Lafayette, Marie Joseph Paul
Yves Roch Gilbert Du Motier, marquis de, 1757–1834. 7. Lafayette, Marie Joseph Paul Yves Roch
Gilbert Du Motier, marquis de, 1757–1834—Influence. 8. France—History—Revolution,
1789–1799. 9. France—History—Revolution, 1789–1799—Biography.
10. Statesmen—France—Biography. I. Title.
E312.25.G35 2007
973.4'1092—dc22
[B]

2007022449

W. W. Norton & Company, Inc., 500 Fifth Avenue, New York, N.Y. 10110
www.wwnorton.com

W. W. Norton & Company Ltd., Castle House, 75/76 Wells Street, W1T 3QT

1 2 3 4 5 6 7 8 9 0

For Karen

Contents

I think continually of those who were truly great. . . .
The names of those who in their lives fought for life,
  Who wore at their hearts the fire's center.
Born of the sun they traveled a short while towards the sun,
  And left the vivid air signed with their honor.

—STEPHEN SPENDER

A quote for heroes !

PART ONE

The Quest for Glory

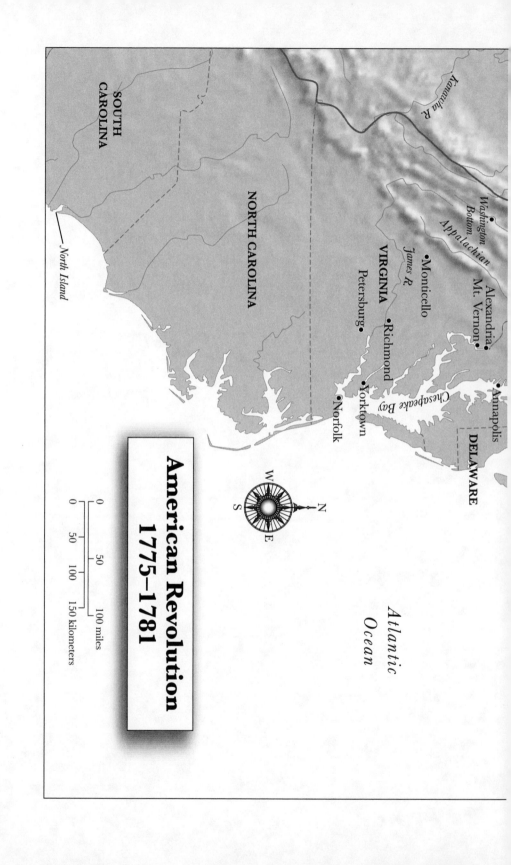

American Revolution
1775–1781

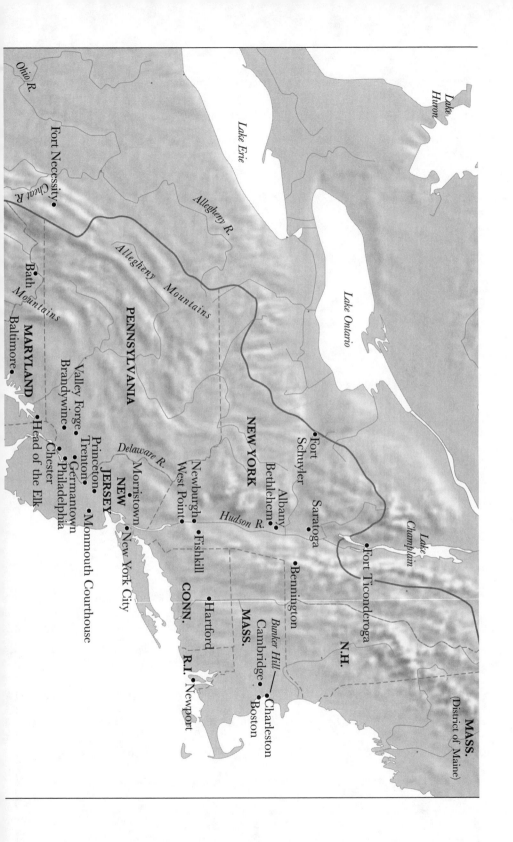

I

Introductions

THANKS TO A RICH historical record, we do not have to imagine the reaction of General George Washington when, on July 31, 1777, he was introduced to the latest French "major general" to be foisted on him by the Continental Congress, this one a rich aristocrat not yet out of his teens. Virtually ever since Washington had taken command of the colonial army, he had been trying to sweep back a tide of counts, chevaliers, and lesser foreign volunteers, many of whom brought with them enormous self-regard, no English, and less interest in the American cause than in motives ranging from martial vanity to sheriff-dodging. As the chaplain of one French regiment put it, the first volunteers were "men crippled with debts and without reputation at home, who gave themselves assumed titles and false names, received distinguished ranks and considerable advances and promptly disappeared." Later candidates were of a somewhat higher caliber, but there were simply too many of them. In early 1776, the Continental Congress had sent a representative to Paris in search of experienced military engineers, and now their recruiter, Silas Deane, seemed to be handing out high commissions to all comers, "wild conduct" that was about to result in his recall.

Washington had long been pleading that the flow of foreign volunteers be stopped. In October 1776, he wrote one of his congressional supervisors, "I am under no small difficulties on account of the French gentlemen that are here." At the turn of the year, he was still complaining: "You cannot conceive what a weight these kind of people are upon the service . . .

entirely useless." Two months after that, he wrote an old friend and fellow Virginian in Congress, "I shall be much obliged to you to stop the shoals of French men [who] are coming on . . . in swarms." The reply ignored his request and asked Washington to welcome several others, including one Tronson du Coudray, on whom Deane had bestowed the rank of major general, the highest commission below Washington's. That had led to a fierce protest from three of Washington's other generals, one of whom threatened to quit. Since then, though, during his five months' service, Coudray had been found so pretentious, self-absorbed, and generally loathsome that, when he accidentally drowned, John Adams considered it a stroke of luck that "will save us much altercation."

The French "major general" presenting himself now to George Washington was the nineteen-year-old marquis de Lafayette, who was in America principally because he was enormously rich. A Currier & Ives print commemorates the meeting, which took place at a dinner in the colonial capital, at Philadelphia's City Tavern (see illustration following page 150). The decor and decorous company in that rendering represent something of an improvement on the original scene, which was very late and men-only, but the body language seems right: a young officer, eager to impress, leaning hopefully into the presence of a grave and imposing general, who is plainly if ever so slightly leaning away. Washington saw immediately in the young marquis that terrible combination of very little military experience with grand and excited ideas about his prospects in the American army. Though Congress had told Washington that Lafayette's commission was purely honorific, no one seemed to have told the young marquis, and two weeks after that first meeting Washington shot off a letter to Benjamin Harrison, another fellow Virginian in Congress, complaining that his latest French import expected command of a division! "What line of conduct I am to pursue, to comply with [Congress's] design and his expectations, I know no more than the child unborn and beg to be instructed. If Congress meant that this rank should be unaccompanied by command I wish it had been sufficiently explained to him. If on the other hand, it was intended to vest him with all powers of a major-general, why have I been led into a contrary belief? This difficulty adds no small embarrassment to a command, which, without it, is abundantly perplexed."

So it was. At the time Washington met Lafayette, the success of the

Revolution was very much in doubt. For more than a year, apart from two militarily insignificant but symbolically critical victories in Trenton and Princeton, Washington's army had succeeded only at evasion and retreat. His depleted forces were riddled with smallpox and jaundice, there was not enough money to feed or pay them, and part of the reason Washington was in Philadelphia was that the British, emboldened by their victories to dream of an early end to the war, were on their way toward the capital with a fleet of more than two hundred fifty ships carrying eighteen thousand British regulars, news that Washington had received with that morning's breakfast. At the dinner where he met Lafayette, Washington had to address the urgent fear of congressmen that Philadelphia itself could fall to the British, and he had nothing of much comfort to tell them, having long since admitted to them and to himself the "melancholy truths" that his colonial soldiers were no match for redcoats and that their one saving asset was how well they ran away.

Against this backdrop, a pushy French teenager would seem to have been the last problem Washington needed, and eventually he was told that he was free to do as he liked with the impetuous young marquis. How then to explain the fact that before the month of August was out, Lafayette was living in Washington's house, with his very small "family" of top military aides; that in a matter of weeks he was riding at Washington's side on parade; that by early September he was riding with Washington into battle; that after he was wounded at the Battle of Brandywine Creek (a defeat that did indeed lead to the fall of Philadelphia), he was attended by Washington's personal physician and watched over anxiously by the general himself? Three months after his twentieth birthday, Lafayette had his division, and perhaps somewhat to his own surprise, he became one of Washington's most successful generals, distinguishing himself at the Battle of Monmouth Court House and, in command of an army in the South, managing to corner the much greater force of the Earl Cornwallis at Yorktown, which set up the victorious siege that would be the last battle of the American Revolution.

After the war, separated by an ocean, the two men wrote and sent each other presents. Washington sent hams, live birds, and silver shoe buckles to Paris; Lafayette sent hounds and mules to Mount Vernon, as well as a key to the Bastille after he had ordered its demolition. Lafayette's role as founding father of the French Revolution was a continual source of anxiety to Washington during his first term as president; and his second term was shadowed by Lafayette's imprisonment, after the Revolution had turned violently against him. For reasons of state, there was little Washington could do to help, but he did take in Lafayette's only son, a teenager named George Washington Lafayette.

Everyone who saw them together was struck by the closeness and open affection between Washington and Lafayette. In 1779, two months after Lafayette had returned for a hiatus in France, the French minister to the United States witnessed an extraordinary outburst when he paid the marquis a compliment at dinner. Suddenly, "tears fell from [Washington's] eyes," the diplomat recalled. "He clasped my hand and could hardly utter the words: 'I do not know a nobler, finer soul, and I love him as my own son.'" Lafayette called Washington, with typical effusion, "the admiration of the universe." Washington called Lafayette "the man I love."

"Never during the Revolution was there so speedy and complete a conquest of the heart of Washington," his biographer Douglas Southall Freeman wrote. "How did [Lafayette] do it? History has no answer."

In fact, biographers of both men actually do seem to agree on a straightforward explanation of their relationship: that Washington saw in Lafayette the son he never had, and that Lafayette found in Washington his long-lost father—a conclusion that, even if true, is so widely and briskly postulated as almost to suggest a wish to avoid the question. In any case, it is unsatisfying in several ways. Lafayette's respect for Washington is diminished by reducing it to a sort of benign neurosis, as is Lafayette himself. Though only nineteen when they met, he had been married for three years, he was a father, he had been in the military since the age of thirteen, and as the descendant of a family whose military service to the king stretched back seven centuries, he was a certified member of France's *noblesse d'épée* (nobility of the sword). Washington, who was exactly the age Lafayette's father would have been, obviously makes for a very tempting father figure—though childless, he was after all the "father of his country," a phrase first applied to him in 1776—but he rarely expressed regret at not having a son or daughter of his own, and though he had many young military aides, he hardly treated them with fatherly tenderness. One of them, his young adjutant Alexander Hamilton, who like Lafayette had lost his father in infancy, found Washington so peremptory and demanding he quit.

Perhaps most discouraging of all to the father-son model is the fact that the relationship between Washington and Lafayette was not one of unalloyed affection. The elaborate eighteenth-century courtesies in their correspondence may be easily misread as signs of warmth. They could also disguise the opposite. Washington and Lafayette differed on many things, and are sometimes found to be working against each other in secret, each to his own ends. Their relationship in this way reflects the always problematic relations between their two countries, an alliance of which they were also the founding fathers.

A supposedly friendly bilateral relationship fraught with more tension than that of France and the United States is difficult to imagine. In 1800, when Napoleon brought years of outrageous French attacks on American shipping to an end with a new commercial treaty, he dismissed the long, acrimonious, and costly conflict as a "family spat." In 2003, during their bitter confrontation over war in Iraq, Secretary of State Colin Powell reassured France's distraught ambassador to the United Nations, among others, by reminding him that America and France had been through "two centuries of marriage counseling, and the marriage is . . . still strong," an analysis that was widely appreciated and that brought not the shortest pause in the exchange of diplomatic fire.

Others have described the French-American relationship as that of siblings, as "sister republics" that were born during "sister revolutions." If so, it is not hard to find the source of Franco-American conflict, since the parents of these siblings deeply despised one another. No national rivalry was more spiteful than the one between the Old Regime of the Bourbons and Hanoverian England, who did however share a belief in the profound insignificance of the American colonies. As colonial overlords, Washington's mother country and the *patrie* of Lafayette's father saw North America as mainly a tempting place to poach and plunder, a potential chip in their war with each other, and a small but easy market of primitives and misfits who lived in forests and dressed in animal skins. One of the colonies' most devoted advocates in Britain, Edmund Burke, protested in

March 1775 that America "at this day serves for little more than to amuse you with stories of savage men, and uncouth manners," and that is in fact all that many of his fellow parliamentarians and most French scientists felt it would ever be. Though he had never crossed the Atlantic, France's most renowned naturalist, the comte de Buffon, declared that the North American climate could produce only "degenerate, small, cowardly" animals that were "a thousand times less dangerous than those of Asia and Africa." Native Americans, he said, were "sexually frigid and perverted, unprolific . . . devoid of the most basic moral sense." A Dutch colleague, Corneille de Pauw, helpfully explained that this was probably because America had had its Flood later than Europe, so that when first discovered there, "men had just climbed down from the rocks and elevations . . . into vast prairies still covered with sloughs and slime. . . . The heavy and fetid vapors that rise from [flooded lands] engender chronic maladies. . . . We now perceive the reason why they were all found in a state of savagery. . . . The valleys and meadows had to dry out more. . . ." De Pauw had not been to America either.

Closer observation did little to improve the French view of America, whose colonists were discovered to be a bunch of sharp-dealing money-grubbers, a nation of merchants, hawkers, and thieves. Nor did familiarity much improve American settlers' opinion of the French, who were seen as prancing, light-minded land-grabbers sent by the Pope to incite Indian massacres.

Given these and later stereotypes and the sharp-pointed jokes they have long inspired in both countries, one may well wonder why there is a statue of George Washington in Paris's place d'Iéna and what Lafayette's is doing on Pennsylvania Avenue across from the White House, in Lafayette Park. At a time when Western civilization itself faces a geopolitical challenge that requires more than casual Franco-American cooperation, the question is not frivolous.

The answer begins with the fact that the French and American revolutions were less like sisters than like distant cousins, and that the French Revolution was incomparably more important to the United States than American independence was to France. Three dozen or so of the first- and second-rank leaders of the French Revolution and many more of its foot soldiers were veterans of the war in America and carried home to their tottering monarchy the ideal of an Arcadian society free from want and despotism, but America was otherwise irrelevant to the revolutionary governments of France except as a debtor. In America, on the other hand, the French Revolution dominated both domestic and foreign affairs throughout Washington's two terms as president. Especially after the execution of Louis XVI and France's declaration of war on England, it became one of the most divisive and defining elements of American politics, at just the time when the newly united states were struggling toward consensus on forms of government and their common character as a nation. It was in the crucible of debate over whether to go the way of Britain or France that the citizens of the United States would discover what it was to be American.

The friendship of Washington and Lafayette seems in many ways about as unlikely as the French-American one, almost a joke: What does a Virginia frontiersman and grade-school dropout have in common with a rich French aristocrat who learned to ride with three future kings? Or, what do you call a bumptious optimist whose best friend is a moody loner? Lafayette threw his arms around people and kissed them on both cheeks. Alexander Hamilton once offered to buy Gouverneur Morris dinner if he would clap Washington on the shoulder and say how great it was to see him again. When he did, Washington simply, without a word, removed Morris's hand from the sleeve of his coat and froze him with a stare.

Washington and Lafayette shared one characteristic of overriding importance, however: They were aristocrats in a monarchy, links in a chain of favor and patronage that depended ultimately from a king, in a world where status could not be earned but had to be conferred.

Washington achieved that status by working hard to pull himself into the class of a Virginia gentleman. After leaving school he placed himself under the patronage of the powerful Fairfax family, whose seat at Belvoir was in sight of Mount Vernon. To help map the Fairfaxes' 5-million-acre land grant and as the first step toward being the huge landowner he would eventually become, he learned the craft of surveying—an honorable, indeed prestigious profession at a time of widespread settlement in a new country. He also began a rigorous course in self-improvement. At sixteen, he started to read Addison's *Spectator* and wrote a 150-word memorandum to himself on a coat he wished to have made. In the next few years he bought Henry Fielding's *Tom Jones*, Daniel Defoe's *Tour throughout the Whole Island of Great Britain,* and Caesar's *Commentaries.* With the help of James Greenwood's *English Royal Grammar,* his early correspondence shows constant attention to improvement in spelling and syntax. He worked on his handwriting. He took lessons from a dancing master, hired a fencing instructor, and famously copied out a book of etiquette titled *Rules of Civility and Decent Behavior in Company and Conversation.* Many of its one hundred and ten maxims are eminently practical—Number 12 is "Bedew no mans face with your spittle, by approaching too near him when you speak"—but they are also full of remarkable advice about proper deportment in an aristocratic society of minute distinctions.

> 57. In walking up and Down in a House, only with One in Company if he be Greater than yourself, at the first give him the Right hand and Stop not till he does and be not the first that turns, and when you do turn let it be with your face toward him, if he be a Man of Great Quality, walk not with him Cheek by Joul but Somewhat behind him; but yet in Such a Manner that he may easily Speak to you.

Unlike Washington, of course, Lafayette was born and raised to be a courtier. He was proud to tell the story of how he spurned the offer of a position at court, and he complained of the cringing, fawning behavior he saw there, but that was his world and his background.

In the pre-revolutionary world of Washington and Lafayette, the notion of equality was almost literally unthinkable. Lafayette's early opposition to slavery was as prescient as it was commendable, but neither he nor Washington considered slaves or Native Americans (or most other people) as even remotely their equals, whatever their stated principles. Distinctions of rank were implicit in the unspoken language of everyday life, imbedded too deep to be much remarked on even when they were pointedly felt, as they often were. Freedom, too, was a strange concept. In both the colonies and France, the word "liberty" usually referred to a traditional or newly granted privilege, such as an exemption from tax. Among the French aristocracy's greatest complaints against Louis was the loss of such special considerations, or "liberties." The model of "independence" that Washington held before him was that of the Virginia gentleman, whose property and wealth liberated him from the need to be dependent on anyone, even powerful friends. To declare one's independence was to declare oneself an aristocrat.

That this would change so dramatically and so thoroughly was due in part to the eighteenth century's enchantment with the republican ideals of ancient Rome, what has been called the revolutionary period's "cult of antiquity." Most leaders of the American and French revolutions were educated in the Latin classics written in the last century BC and the first century AD. Most of their schoolboy texts were by Virgil, Cicero, Horace, Plutarch, Livy, Ovid, Tacitus, and others of their time and place. (Plutarch, whose *Parallel Lives* of Greek and Roman heroes was perhaps the work most widely read, was Greek, but at a time when Greece was Roman.) Washington's foreshortened education was an exception among the founders (though many of them were the first generation in their families to attend university), but his favorite work of literature was also perhaps the most popular English-language play of the eighteenth century, Addison's *Cato*, based on Plutarch's *Life of Cato the Younger*. Some of the great lines of the revolutionary period were not merely inspired by but were taken almost whole from *Cato*. Patrick Henry's great moment in the Virginia legislature, when he broke the imaginary shackles from his wrists and said, "give me liberty or give me death," came straight from Act II, Scene V, when Cato says: "It is not now a time to talk of aught/But chains or conquest, liberty or death." Nathan Hale could "regret that I have but one life to give for my country" because he had heard Cato observe, "what pity is it /That we can die but once to serve our country."

During the winter of Valley Forge, to distract his men from their misery with an appeal to principle, Washington put on a production of *Cato* using officers and enlisted men as actors. As Addison makes clear in his prologue, *Cato* is meant to present models of good behavior. "[T]o make mankind in conscious virtue bold," Addison says, his audience should "live o'er each scene and be what they behold." To copy exemplary models from classical Greece and Rome was a popular method of self-improvement

particularly in the North American colonies, and Addison's play acknowl-
edges this essential project of the Enlightenment in the lives of ordinary
people.

> *A Roman soul is bent on higher views:*
> *To civilize the rude unpolished world,*
> *And lay it under the restraint of laws;*
> *To make Man mild, and sociable to Man;*
> *To cultivate the wild licentious Savage*
> *With Wisdom, discipline, and liberal arts*
> *Th' embellishments of life: Virtues like these*
> *Make human nature shine, reform the soul*
> *And break our fierce barbarians into men.*

Virtue was learned like anything else, according to Yale president Ezra
Stiles, and as the president of Princeton put it to young James Madison,
one achieved it only by intense self-study, by "recalling the lost images of
virtue, contemplating them, and using them as motives of action, till they
overcome those of vice again and again until after repeated struggles and
many foils they at length acquire the habitual superiority." In other words,
one became one's chosen ideal by acting the part.

America's founding fathers used no metaphor more commonly to
describe themselves than that of actors on a stage in the theater of revolution. Washington was perhaps the supreme example of such studied
self-creation, which is one reason why his behavior can seem so opaque, so
relentlessly intentional, so disconnected from any urge of personality. As
the eminent historian Gordon Wood put it, "It was as if he was always
onstage, acting a part." (The same was said by Talleyrand of Lafayette.)
When his friend Henrietta Liston, the wife of the British minister,
remarked one day in 1796 how relaxed Washington looked as he prepared
finally to leave office, he pulled her up short. "You are wrong!" he blurted
out. "My countenance never yet betrayed my feelings." This, Liston said,
was "the only weak or vain thing I ever heard Washington utter." That he
disclosed himself in an apparently reflexive denial of being knowable
speaks to just how important the fixed mask was to him and how hard he
worked to keep it in place.

The transformation that the founding fathers most desired for themselves was not private, inward, or truly characterological but rather a function of public perception, and the test of their success was what they called their "fame," "glory," and "character"—words that did not signify either celebrity or moral courage but referred to a person's public reputation, which was also called his "honor." Thomas Jefferson characterized Washington as "panting for glory" and chastised Lafayette for a "canine appetite for popularity and fame," but wherever he went Jefferson carried a picture of Francis Bacon, one of his three great heroes (the others were Newton and Locke). For Bacon, honors from contemporaries were a measure of "virtue and worth," and he compiled a taxonomy of glory in which there were five levels, the penultimate being that of legislators, "the great law givers . . . also called *perpetui principes* or perpetual rulers, because they govern by their ordinances after they are gone." He reserved the highest place for "*conditores imperiorum*, FOUNDERS OF STATES AND COMMONWEALTHS."

The sort of fame the founders sought was not a cheap popularity divorced from achievement, as it would be to an age when people could become "famous for being well known." Fame, glory, and its synonyms meant in the eighteenth century an illustrious eminence, a stature achieved by having led a consequential (though not necessarily a conventionally virtuous) life; and this sort of fame found its consummation not only in praise by contemporaries but even more so in the pages of history, the collective memory of those "unborn millions" whom Washington considered the people he ultimately served.

As the historian Douglas Adair pointed out, the pursuit of acclaim was not particularly Christian—it called for self-assertion rather than self-abnegation, competition rather than humility—but neither the founding fathers nor Lafayette were Christians in practice, even if they were by denomination. Though Washington was for many years a regular churchgoer, he quit the vestry when he left the army and stopped going to church when he left the presidency. His letters speak about Providence and Fate, not about God, and the words "Jesus Christ" occur exactly once in the many volumes of his correspondence, in a speech he made to the chiefs of the Delaware Indians. The word "honor" comes up 3,952 times.

Washington, Lafayette, and others like them foreswore religious faith not from reading or thinking deeply about the matter (asked why the

Constitution did not invoke God, Hamilton supposedly said, "We forgot") but in the spirit of the times, which was characterized by the Enlightenment's confidence in observation, empirical experiment, and the rigorous application of reason grounded in fact rather than abstraction. Abandoned along with faith and metaphysics was the certainty of an afterlife, and without the prospect of spiritual immortality, the best hope of defying oblivion was to secure a place in history. For America's founding fathers and for the leaders of the French Revolution as well, fame was the closest thing to heaven.

Unlike Lafayette, who was quite open about how driven he was by *l'amour de la gloire*, Washington rarely let his ambition show, but it did once, in a letter to Lafayette at a critical moment for both of them in 1788. As Lafayette took his place as a leader in the momentous tumult of pre-revolutionary Paris, only a few more states were needed for ratification of the U.S. Constitution, after which there would be a presidential election that everyone knew Washington would win. Clearly sensing that he and his friend were going into history together, Washington wrote to introduce Lafayette to Joel Barlow, a second-rate poet he described as "one of those bards who hold the keys of the gate by which patriots, sages and heroes are admitted to immortality. Such are your ancient bards who are both the priest and doorkeepers to the temple of fame. And these, my dear Marquis, are no vulgar functions. . . . In some instances by acting reciprocally, heroes have made poets, and poets heroes." Caesar and Alexander had great poets to celebrate them, Washington reminded Lafayette, and Augustus, "the professed and magnificent rewarder of poetical merit, did [not] lose the return of having his achievements immortalized in song. . . . Perhaps," he coyly concluded, "we shall be found, at this moment, not inferior to the rest of the world in the performances of our poets and painters."

Read with the dictionary of another age, such open, overriding concern with public acclaim can make Washington and Lafayette seem shamelessly self-regarding at times. Thanks to Washington's great achievements, this tends to be explained away as a sort of unfortunate eighteenth-century twitch, but it has been more costly to Lafayette's reputation, particularly in France. His most comprehensive biography was the life's work of the eminent historian Louis Gottschalk, who died before it could be finished. The sixth volume ends in July 1790, at the first anniversary of the fall of the Bastille, with Lafayette at the height of his power and popularity. Gottschalk saw Lafayette, in part because of his apparently overweening concern with image and reputation, as a person of low self-esteem, and he located the source of Lafayette's courage and commitment—in keeping with a psychological theory popular among historians of the 1930s—in a psychic compensation for repressed frustration. To the extent it is true, this diagnosis could apply to Washington as well, but what motivated them seems clearly to have been more than that, if it was that at all.

To point out similarities between them should not suggest an equivalency. The two men were separated in age by more than a generation, Washington was the shrewder, tougher, and wiser man, and thanks to their different characters and circumstances he was a far more important historical figure than Lafayette was. Still, an account of their friendship opens a window on many things that their story as individuals does not, including the first act in the great psychodrama of French-American relations, as well as the perennially tempting mystery of how struggles for the same noble and universal principles could have had such wildly different outcomes. Most of all, it is a way to witness the creation of a new order, an idea of government that would sweep away the oppressive rule of monarchs and oligarchs to which humanity had submitted itself from time immemorial and that would lead the way to a perhaps even more profound reorientation in human relations, which followed from the declaration that "all men are created equal." This applied only to men and only white men at first, but it embraced everyone in principle and eventually would do so by precedent and statute.

As Washington and Lafayette set out on their public lives, they did not understand the world in these terms. They understood themselves then to be in a class of men "above the common run," as Washington put it. Only superior men could hope to achieve glory, honor, and fame, just as only men of such uncommon virtue as theirs could be trusted to govern. They were a new brotherhood, what Addison called the great "Fraternity of Spectators," made up of "every one that considers the World as a Theatre, and desires to form a right Judgment of those who are the Actors on it." If those in this gentlemanly elect were a new sort of self-made aristocracy, at least it was not an estate born of courtly patronage: It was a distinction that could be worked for and won, certified not by the favor a hereditary king but by a peerage of merit. This was a start.

Finding themselves leading the struggle for the basic human right to become something other than what we are born to be, Washington and Lafayette, in their very different ways, had to fight for their own independence, and to watch them as they did that—making their way from courtier-subjects in a hierarchy of blood and privilege to patriot-citizens in a commonwealth of equals—is one way to see a radically new world being born, a world in which the value of a life is not extrinsic and bestowed but grounded in self-respect, something that can be earned by one's own effort and that might be lost but cannot be taken away. In this sense both the American and French revolutions were psychological as well as political upheavals. Only on the basis of self-respect could people imagine themselves capable of self-government; and once such a basis was established, the experiment of self-government, if not its success, was inevitable.

Like other founding fathers of this new world, Washington and Lafayette started out by striving to create for themselves the image of the people they wished to be, in a lifelong endeavor to act well. If their motives for doing that were mixed, their commitment to doing it was not, and somewhere along the way, in a kind of moral and political alchemy, the urgings of fame and glory were transmuted into finer stuff, and their lives became enactments of high principle. They lived such a life, did such deeds, even remained friends in part to stake their claim to immortality, which meant to have their story told; and the audience they cared most to hear it was posterity, which is us.

II

Lexington and Versailles

THE REBELLION IN NORTH AMERICA had very few partisans in France in early 1775. Apart from the foreign office at Versailles and some far-sighted *philosophes*, very few people gave it any thought at all. One of those who did was a forty-three-year-old entrepreneur, inventor, architect, spy, and playwright named Pierre-Augustin Caron de Beaumarchais, whose new comedy, *The Barber of Seville*, had just opened to loud catcalls at the Comédie Française. His sympathy with the plight of the American colonists did not necessarily throw the cause in a great light. Everything about Beaumarchais was stagy and a bit dubious, like the best part of his name, "de Beaumarchais," which he had managed to filch from the previous husband of his first dead wife, who was just as rich and died after a marriage just as suspiciously short as his second one. The charming Pierre-Augustin was chronically short of funds, but Voltaire, for one, discounted the rumors: Beaumarchais, he said, was entirely "too *drôle*" to be a wife-killer.

Before appropriating from his first dead wife's previous husband the pseudo-noble "de," Beaumarchais was known simply as the "*fils* Caron," son of the dashing André-Charles Caron, favorite clock- and watchmaker of the king's favorite mistress. Since in the spoken French of eighteenth-century Paris, the "s" in *fils* was almost silent and the "on" in Caron not as nasal as it would become (more like "oh"), Beaumarchais's real name was pronounced, roughly, *fee-karo*, so when the character Figaro made his debut in *The Barber of Seville*, his self-consciously savvy audience knew exactly who they were watching on the stage.

Beaumarchais was the perfect advertisement for himself: His art pla-giarized his life, which was a frantic blur—*Figaro here, Figaro there*—of rehearsals, deals, lover-juggling, and scandal-quashing. He was forever having to get himself out of some new jam. More than once he won his reprieve by undertaking a secret mission to clean up some problem for the king, as he was doing right now, along with closing a big commodities deal and fixing up *Barber*, which would go on to become one of the hits of the season. Before the year was out, Beaumarchais would become a central fig-ure in supplying critical French aid to the American Revolution, a man without whom there might never have been a United States. Before he could become a revolutionary hero, though, he would have to persuade a certain former French spy to spend the rest of his life dressed as a woman.

As improbable as it may seem that a playwright and a transvestite dra-goon would play any role at all in the unfolding of the American Revolu-tion, 1775 was going to be that kind of year, a time as busy and slippery as a Beaumarchais. As the year began, Europe was not at war and it was not at peace. Paris and London were aswarm with spies, but there was as yet no settled truth or plot to ferret out. Britain's colonies in North America, though up in arms, could not yet see the King and Mother Country as the enemy, nor could they see France, so recently the enemy, as a friend. In the colonies, in England, and in France, most people had no intention of put-ting the end to an old order or starting a new one, even as they were very effectively doing both. History seemed to stumble forward accident by accident in 1775, the year when everything began except for a clear under-standing of exactly what that was.

History tends to date revolutions from a definitive outbreak of violence, by which standard the "first year of the American Revolution"* began on the day of Lexington and Concord, and the French Revolution began at the gates of the Bastille. In fact, of course, the French Revolution started

---

*In my used copy of Allen French's *The First Year of the American Revolution*, I found a letter the author had sent in 1938 to a reader who took issue with him for beginning with the day of Lexington and Concord. French explained: "I committed myself, unconsciously but quite sincerely, to the theory that the active Revolution began when the fighting began,—fighting, that is, that did not stop. . . . In fact, however, I suppose the Revolution began with the Stamp Act opposition—unless, of course, we wish to begin with John Winthrop."

long before July 14, 1789, and good arguments have been made that the American Revolution was over by 1775 and that it did not really begin until the Constitutional Convention of 1787. With such fungible birthdays, the American and French revolutions may also be treated as roughly simultaneous, in part because two of their leaders' lives converged here and in part because they actually were.

April 18, 1775, was a Tuesday, which was market day in Dijon, the capital city of Burgundy. The day before, a miller named Janty had paraded through town with large sacks of flour in a wheelbarrow and almost boastfully said he would refuse to sell any of it for less than the going rate, which was high and going higher. The price of a four-pound loaf of bread had recently almost tripled, to 8 sous, or about $1.80, at a time when the average family consumed five loaves a week ($9), and the peasant's average weekly wage was $15.* Soon it would rise to 14 sous, meaning the average peasant family would have to spend more than its entire income to keep itself in bread, their diet staple. Instead, of course, they went hungry. People were already going hungry, which is why, that market day, a riot broke out over the price of flour. A mob led by fishwives brandishing sticks and dead carp began by breaking down the door of a lawyer who was hiding a certain M. Carré, the richest flour mill owner in town. M. Carré managed to make his escape scrambling over rooftops, but the crowd then laid waste to the house and all its furniture before destroying his mill. Their rampage slowed at a cave of wine barrels, with which they amused themselves until they fell asleep, but the king's highest local lawman on duty, taking no chances, spent the night in hiding, awaiting reinforcements.

Late that night, on the other side of the Atlantic, Paul Revere rode through the Massachusetts countryside warning that the British were coming, and at a tavern near Lexington Green Captain John Parker and a few dozen of his militiamen stayed up all night waiting for them. Finally, at dawn, a detachment of royal troops showed up as expected, heading for Concord to seize the ammunition depot there. Captain Parker and his men did not plan to stop them. They were only planning to form ranks as a show of strength on the Green, staying off the road and out of the way. In the event, for reasons unknown, the British charged them. Captain

---

*For a note on currency values, see p. 23 below.

Parker instantly ordered his men to disperse, but some did not, and some-one on one side or the other fired a shot, and the British officers lost control of their men. When it was over, eight Americans were dead and eleven wounded; the only British casualty was one officer's horse. As the British proceeded to Concord and news of the engagement spread, however, villagers and farmers turned out by the hundreds, then by the thousands, bringing their muskets and fowling pieces. Two British soldiers and four Americans were killed during a tense standoff in Concord, and on the regulars' brutal sixteen-mile march back to Boston—outnumbered by a factor of two, exhausted by midday heat, and taking constant fire from behind trees and stone walls on both sides of their line of march—another sixty-five of them were killed. Only the slow loading and famously wild trajectory of musket balls prevented a massacre.

All told, forty-nine "insurrectionists" gave their lives that day, which ended with thousands of colonists holding the high ground around Boston, the British army virtually captive below, the fleet subject to bombardment in the harbor.

England's King George III was eerily sanguine, almost giddy after Lexington and Concord, even though he knew that his forces were under siege. "Nothing can equal the ease, composure and even gaiety of the great disposer of all in this lower orb," wrote Edmund Burke, a member of Parliament who was much troubled by this and every other effect of Britain's colonial policy. "It is too much, if not real, for the most perfect King-craft."

Louis XVI was similarly unruffled by the outbreak in Dijon of what would come to be called the Grain War, which pointed in a long but almost straight line to the fall of the Bastille fourteen years later. He dealt with the disturbance as his grandfather Louis XV would have done, with a couple of exemplary hangings in Paris's place de Grève. The scapegoats were a twenty-eight-year-old market porter and an even younger apprentice gauzemaker whose crime was having "kicked the door of a bakeshop to demand that it be opened." The scaffold for their execution was built unusually high, eighteen feet, so that everyone could watch the hangmen cinch the slip knots tight against their necks and then "with their knees, kick the victims off the ladders. . . . Then the executioners, each holding fast to the beam of a gibbet, [stepped] onto the bound hands of the dying men and, by jabbing them in the stomach with their knees and jerking them, put an end to their agony."

All very distasteful, so Louis turned his attention to a long overdue and entirely unnecessary coronation in Rheims. A good measure of the cognitive dissonance at this historic moment is the fact that Louis thought a fine way to distract and win back his famished countrymen would be a coronation costing 760,000 livres (more than $5 million),* "covering robes for the king, peers of the realm, major officials of the crown, the chancellor, and others, as well as adornments for the cathedral of Rheims, embellishments for the reliquary of St. Marcoul, the canopy surmounting the crown at Aix-la-Chapelle, lace and linens, royal offerings, medals, remuneration of ceremonial officials, church fees, the cost of transporting monks from the Abbey of Saint-Denis to escort the crown and sword of Charlemagne . . . expenses and wages of the king's officers and musicians, lighting, construction costs in the archbishop's palace and the cathedral as well as the covered walkway between them." There were to be new clothes for every royal servant down to the pages.

His minister of finance, Anne-Jacques-Robert de Turgot, whose job was to bring some order to the king's disastrous finances, tried to talk Louis out of having a coronation, then tried to convince him at least to spare some expense by moving it to Paris; but Louis was adamant, and in a way he turned out to be right. The peasants who made their way through the Champagne district just to catch a glimpse of the king at his coronation, awed by the pageantry of it, were moved to tears for love of the king their master. Marie-Antoinette, who was not so crass as to say, "let them eat cake," but could be fairly crass, had the decency to observe the strangeness of the crowd's reaction. "It is both a surprise and a relief," she wrote to her mother, Empress Maria Theresa of Austria, "to be so

---

*Current value of old currency is an impossible calculation, because there is no "right" answer. There are many legitimate measures—inflation statistics, relative buying power, the historic price of gold, etc. One common estimate is that the British pound of 1770 was worth about 24 livres, and according to another calculation £5,000 in 1770 would have been worth approximately £444,000 at the end of 2005. This would suggest that one eighteenth-century livre would be worth roughly seven twenty-first-century U.S. dollars. Readers wishing more information can do their own calculations at eh.net and measuringworth.com.

well received just two months after the [Grain War began] and despite the high cost of bread."

On June 15, 1775, three days after Louis's coronation, George Washington had dinner at Peg Mullen's Beefsteak House in Philadelphia with several members of the Continental Congress, which had just elected him commander in chief of an army that did not yet officially exist. The thirty-two-year-old Thomas Jefferson was there, as was Benjamin Franklin, who was almost seventy. The coincidence of timing is evocative, but this was no coronation dinner. Dr. Benjamin Rush, congressman from Pennsylvania, remembered that when someone raised the first after-dinner toast to "the Commander in Chief of the American armies":

> General Washington rose from his seat and with some confusion thanked the company for the honor they did him. The whole company instantly rose and drank the toast standing. This scene, so unexpected, was a solemn one. A silence followed it, as if every heart was penetrated with the awful but great events which were to follow. . . .

No one's heart seemed to be penetrated with that sensation more sharply than Washington's. Earlier in the day, notified of his unanimous election, he had thanked his colleagues for the honor they bestowed on him but warned them that their confidence might prove to be misplaced: "I beg it may be remembered by every gentleman in the room that I this day declare with the utmost sincerity I do not think myself equal to the command I am honored with."

This was more than the rhetoric of false modesty, but it was that too. He had, after all, worn his military uniform every day of the convention, he had taken his place on every military committee, and he was the obvious candidate. As a Virginian when the battle and the army were in New England, and at a time when knitting the Northern and Southern colonies together was critical, he was politically perfect; and as the only delegate who could claim anything close to the status of a war hero, thanks to his service in the French and Indian War, he was the clear military choice as well. Beyond that, there was the argument of his bearing: The way he looked and commanded a room inspired attention and respect. At something over six feet two inches, he was a head taller than everyone around him, and though he seemed to be composed of damaged spare parts— a nose too large for his pockmarked face, eyes too small for their sockets, a mouth slammed shut over decayed teeth, enormous hands and feet and outsized hips—the effect of George Washington in motion was by every account one of profound grace. Benjamin Rush credited him with "so much martial dignity . . . that there is not a king in Europe but would look like a valet de chambre by his side."

On the other hand: He had not been in active service for fifteen years, he had never led more than a few hundred men or won an important battle, he had had little acquaintance with strategy except in books, and his character was not molded for conflict. Behind his famous, carefully managed calm, he was hotheaded and extremely sensitive to criticism, and never more obviously so than during his early years in the military. The history of his first engagement might have given the delegates pause had the subject come up, because while touted by Washington as a victory, it was in fact a flagrant failure of command, a military debacle, and a political disaster of global proportions.

As a twenty-two-year-old lieutenant colonel in the Virginia militia, Washington had been given a small detachment charged with fortifying a British garrison at the meeting of the Allegheny and the Monongahela rivers, "the Forks of the Ohio." When he got there, he found that it had already been occupied by a large and well-armed French force. While awaiting instructions, he and his men, led by a band of friendly Indians and their chief, came upon a small encampment of French forces they thought had been sent out against them. The brief but bloody engagement (fifteen minutes, ten French soldiers killed; one colonial casualty) gave Washington his first acclaim in the colonial press, whose accounts featured the young officer's adrenal response to first blood. "I hear bullets whistle," he was quoted as saying, "and believe me there is something charming in the sound."

The truth was not glorious at all. Having caught the French by surprise in early morning, Washington's men fired first. All of the musket wounds had to have been inflicted in the first two volleys, because at that the

French commander, Joseph Coulon de Villiers, sieur de Jumonville, who was shot as he called for quarter, got Washington to cease firing. Reading from a prepared statement, he said he was on a diplomatic mission to all British troops in the area, who were ordered to leave this territory immediately or face eviction by French armed forces. Jumonville had an English translator with him, but accounts differ as to who read the summons. If Jumonville was reading it in French, Washington would have had no idea what he was saying. The Indian chief with him, however, spoke very good French, so he was in no confusion when he walked over to the wounded commander, who was lying on the ground. "*Tu n'est pas encore mort, mon père* [Thou art not dead yet, my father]," he said. Then he buried his hatchet in Jumonville's skull. With that the Indians killed some of the wounded and scalped the dead, while their chief "took out [Jumonville's] brains and washed his hands in them." In the first battle of his military career, Washington presided over a massacre, and if his report of it was not technically a lie, which is debatable, it was a great deal less than the whole truth. Making the best of a horrible incident—and demonstrating the side of his character that had been toughened by his time in the frontier—Washington suggested that the French scalps be sent to Delaware and Iroquois villages as arguments for joining the American/English cause.

A few weeks later, a punitive expedition led by Jumonville's brother killed a third of Washington's troops and forced him to surrender his ineptly positioned, badly constructed, but well-named Fort Necessity. Beyond that, one of the articles of capitulation that Washington signed stipulated that he had "assassinated" a diplomat (a word that Washington's Dutch fencing instructor, who had been brought along to translate, apparently botched). Washington's signature on a document that one contemporary writer called "the most infamous a British subject ever put his hand to" gave the French the ability to fix on Britain the responsibility for firing the first shot in what became Europe's Seven Years' War, known in America as the French and Indian War. Voltaire's famous remark—"Such was the complication of political interests that a cannon shot fired in America could give the signal that set Europe in a blaze"—may be an exaggeration of more than the ordnance involved, but the Jumonville affair began an escalation that did in fact end in a general European war.

If Washington can be blamed for that, he can be given responsibility for both the French and American revolutions as well, because by the time the Treaty of Paris ended the Seven Years' War, both France and England were virtually bankrupt. Britain's need to raise taxes to pay for that war resulted in the Stamp Act, the "Intolerable Acts," the Boston Tea Party, and all that followed, just as the attempt to raise revenue in France would lead eventually, if by a more circuitous route, to the storming of the Bastille and the execution of Louis XVI. None of this of course could have been foreseen in 1754, and when Washington marched his men out of Fort Necessity on July 4, that surely would not have struck him as a date he would ever celebrate.

This was not the Washington of marble coolness and self-mastery; this was an undisciplined young officer who would cover up a failure in order to prevent damage to his reputation, a man whose temper and temperament were as yet untamed. With a couple of weeks to think about what had happened, he apparently realized this about himself, because he asked "ardently" to be placed "under the command of an experienced officer."

Given the greatness of his later accomplishments, the letters of his early military career show somewhat more than one wants to see of Washington, but they also explain the man he would become. Other than reports of actions in the field, his most notable official communications in these years are personal pleadings filled with frustration, humiliation, and rage. One persistent and increasingly sharp complaint was about the inequality between militia officers and those of the British regular army, one of whom he desperately wanted to be. That second-class status was an issue so important to him that his report to Virginia governor Robert Dinwiddie on the Jumonville disaster was preceded by a very long passage complaining that his pay as a militia colonel did not equal that of a British captain. He had written to the governor and others several times before about this, and Dinwiddie had obviously had enough of it, because Washington's letter, an unsuccessful mix of flattery, fault-finding, and self-regard, began with a kind of apology: "I am much concerned that your Honour should seem to charge me with ingratitude, for I assure you, Honorable Sir, nothing is a greater stranger to my breast, or a sin that my soul abhors, than that black and detestable one Ingratitude." He then repeated his complaint and supported it by reminding Dinwiddie what a valuable officer he was: "I have a constitution hardy enough to encounter and undergo the most severe trials, and, I flatter myself, resolution to face what any man durst, as shall be proved when it comes to the test. . . ." All of which was true, but there were eight paragraphs of that before Washington got around "to acquaint you with what has happened" in the place now called Jumonville Glen. He gives the incident two sentences before spending several paragraphs warning Dinwiddie not to believe whatever contrary stories he might hear later.

After Jumonville, Dinwiddie broke the Virginia Regiment into companies that were to be headed by militia captains reporting to captains in the regular army. Effectively demoted, Washington angrily resigned, and when he was offered an honorary commission if he would lead a company in the next campaign, he blew up: "If you think me capable of holding a commission that has neither rank nor emolument annexed to it, you must entertain a very contemptible opinion of my weakness, and believe me more empty than the commission itself." Rather than deal with the issue again, he signed up as an unpaid volunteer with the next expedition to the Forks, a much larger one led by British General Edward Braddock, whom he ended up burying after a bloody defeat there. Washington's cool leadership of that retreat saved many lives, earning him rightful praise and a new measure of renown, but a few months later he virtually came apart over the decision to build a new road to the Ohio Valley, this time from Pennsylvania rather than Virginia. He had written to the authorities that if they undertook such "a new road to the Ohio . . . all is lost! All is lost, by Heavens!" His complaints were so hysterical that a British general wondered aloud whether Washington was actually fit to lead men, given behavior that was "in no ways like a soldier." When they decided to build the road despite this warning of apocalypse, Washington wrote in desolation to John Robinson, then speaker of the Virginia House of Burgesses: "That appearance of glory once in view, that hope, that laudable ambition of serving our country and meriting its applause, is now no more!" His "country" was still Virginia, not yet colonial America.

When he set out the first time for the Forks of the Ohio, Washington described his mission as an enactment of "the heroic spirit of every freeborn Englishman to attest the rights and privileges of the King . . . and rescue from the invasion of a usurping enemy our Majesty's property, his dignity and land." A little more than a year later, he wrote to his brother about the same mission: "I was employed to go on a journey in the winter (when I believe few or none would have undertaken it) and what did I get by it? My expenses borne!"

During his five years in the Virginia militia, Washington threatened four times to return his commission, decided three times to resign from the militia, and did so twice.

Now, as commander in chief, he would report to every member of the Continental Congress in theory, and to several of them in fact; and for as long as there was a war there would be a world of second-guessers all around him. In the intervening years, though, Washington had studied himself closely; and however loudly he disclaimed any ambition for it, he had worked steadily toward and finally achieved the position that would give him either the glory he so desperately sought or the disgrace he so abjectly feared.

Three days after his election as commander in chief, he wrote to explain himself to Martha, who was expecting him home any day. In that letter, he disclaimed any wish for the Continental command and any effort to get it: "You may believe me, my dear Patsy, when I assure you, in the most solemn manner, that, so far from seeking this appointment, I have used every endeavor in my power to avoid it. . . . It was utterly out of my power to refuse this appointment, without exposing my character to such censures, as would have reflected dishonor upon myself, and given pain to my friends." On the other hand, he enclosed a will that he said he had been too busy to finish before he left home. Why would he have thought to start drafting a will before a journey to Philadelphia that he had made before? For that matter, when he left Mount Vernon for the Second Continental Congress, why did he bring his uniform?

That day too he closed a diary that he had been keeping for fifteen years, in which he had made a daily note of the weather: "Very warm in the forenoon but cooler much afterwards," he wrote. "Wind shifting northerly."

.   .   .

In New York, on the way to Cambridge, Washington broke the seal on an urgent message from Massachusetts authorities to Congress. It reported on the battle that would come to be known as Bunker Hill, an all-out British attack on colonial entrenchments above Boston. "Though this scene was almost horrible, and altogether new to most of our men," the report read, "yet many stood and received wounds by swords and bayonets before they quitted their lines." There had been sixty or seventy Americans killed and a hundred wounded, the authorities reported, but more among the enemy.

In fact, British losses were enormous. They had to make three assaults before they overcame the colonists' resistance, and more than 1,000 out of the 2,400 British regulars engaged in the battle were killed or wounded. Washington would have been pleased to know that colonial soldiers could stand up so well against regulars and may have shared this news with his hosts in New York, but he would not have passed on what he read in the next paragraph: "As soon as an estimate can be made of public and private stocks of gunpowder in this Colony it shall be transmitted without delay, which we are well assured will be small, and by no means adequate to the exigence of our case."

When he arrived in Cambridge, he was relieved to hear that the store of gunpowder was 308 barrels, or about 16 tons, and he was pleased by the placement of American fortifications, if not by their quality. On the other hand, the army he found was a tent city with a floating population that lacked any semblance of martial discipline. In a letter to his fellow Virginian Richard Henry Lee, he complained of "an unaccountable kind of stupidity in the lower class of these people which, believe me, prevails but too generally among the officers of the Massachusetts part of the Army. . . . [T]here is no such thing as getting officers of this stamp to exert themselves in carrying orders into execution." He had been predisposed against New England officers and soldiers in part by an old friend Major Thomas Gage, who had written to militia colonel George Washington in 1756 that New Englanders were "the greatest boasters and worst soldiers on the continent . . . I never saw any in my life as infamously bad." Gage was now on the other side of Washington's field glasses, in command of the British fleet in Boston Harbor.

A worse problem by far than inferior officers, Washington's force was outnumbered—there were fewer than fourteen thousand Continentals fit for duty, as opposed to the eighteen thousand he had been promised—and his blindness and impotence on the water without a naval force meant Gage could deliver a devastating surprise attack virtually any time and anywhere up and down the coast. "Between you and me," Washington wrote Richard Henry Lee a week after he arrived, "I think we are in an exceedingly dangerous situation."

On August 1, he found out just how dangerous it was. When he had asked for an accounting of all the gunpowder on hand, he had been given the total number of barrels that had been sent to the troops headquartered at Cambridge, including all that was used at Bunker Hill. Instead of 308 barrels, there were only 36, enough for fewer than nine rounds per man (British troops carried sixty). Someone with Washington when he heard the news said, "For half an hour, he did not utter a word."

While Benjamin Franklin talked up the virtues of bows and arrows, Washington quietly ordered his men to begin sharpening spears. He also began America's first campaign of disinformation, putting out the word that despite an almost embarrassing oversupply of gunpowder, the men should stop shooting off their weapons in camp, whether for sport or to keep them clean, since such signs of amateurism would only give comfort to the enemy. Arriving troops of riflemen helped for a while by picking off British sentries from a distance, which had a terrorist effect while using minimal ammunition, but in time the riflemen became restive and demanding and Washington wished they had never come. Some of them, he grumbled, "know no more of a rifle than my horse."

In those first weeks and months in Cambridge, Washington had every reason to remember his prophecy to Patrick Henry the day he was chosen commander in chief. "Remember, Mr. Henry, what I now tell you. From the day I enter into command of the American armies I date my fall and the ruin of my reputation."

III

Endgames of the Old Regime

I N THE SUMMER OF 1775, while Washington tried to bring discipline
and gunpowder to the Continental Army in Cambridge, the
seventeen-year-old marquis de Lafayette and his young fellow officers
could be found having a fine time with local girls during the annual
maneuvers in Metz, a frontier garrison town 150 miles east of Paris. In the
afterglow of Louis's coronation, with the peasantry temporarily pacified,
the French nobility went on with what they later recalled as the best years
of their lives. "Bliss was it in that dawn to be alive," William Wordsworth
wrote, "But to be young was very heaven!"

Wordsworth was writing about the early days of the French Revolution and would come to regret the error, but his observation applies perfectly well to the decade before that dawn, at least for France's young
aristocrats. If you never lived in that time and station, Talleyrand once
said, you can never know what it is like to be really happy. By getting the
pox and dying, the despised Louis XV had finally ridded the court of his
even more hated mistress, the ex-courtesan Mme du Barry, and now the
court enjoyed a kind, well-meaning king and his lively young queen,
Marie-Antoinette, whose full social calendar of masquerade balls, gambling parties, and nights at the opera drew around her a brilliant new court
of young nobles.

At the center of this new crew was the self-styled *Société de l'Epée de
Bois* (Society of the Wooden Sword), a floating cast of young aristocrats
named for their favorite cabaret and famed for heavy drinking, light gam-

bling, and avid skirt-chasing. Most of them were married, of course, but at this time and place, marriage and romance were understood to be wholly distinct; finding them under the same roof suggested a lack of imagination. One of the odd ones in this set, who actually seemed fond of his wife, was the marquis de Lafayette. Summer maneuvers were known to be fairly raucous, combining all the privileges of aristocracy with some newly dignified, proto-republican slumming. Strangely, Lafayette seemed driven to tell his wife, Adrienne, all about it, or almost all. "The women here are pretty, and good company," he wrote her once. "We dance all night."

Lafayette was something of a misfit in the *Épée de Bois* set, as he had been at school. His military pedigree was serious: His ancestors and family name figured in battlefield histories from the Crusades to the Hundred Years' War. Family legend had it that it was a Lafayette, during the Sixth Crusade, who rescued the Crown of Thorns, and Gilbert de Lafayette III was a marshal of France who led the army of Joan of Arc at Orléans in 1428. In 1759, a month after Lafayette's second birthday, his father, a colonel in the French Grenadiers, was killed by an English cannonball at the Battle of Minden, and with that the little boy, who was baptized "the very high and mighty lord Monseigneur Marie-Joseph-Paul-Yves-Roch-Gilbert du Motier de La Fayette," added "baron de Vissac, lord of Saint Romain, Fix and other places" to his name. The two paternal aunts who raised him in Chavaniac, his ancestral château, called him Gilbert.

His childhood was privileged but somewhat austere. In part to preserve the special privileges of the *noblesse présentée* for her son, his mother had gone to Paris to be presented at court when he was still an infant; and after his father died she rarely came back, staying in Paris at the family apartments in the Luxembourg Palace, where she lived with her father and grandfather. His closest friend was an older female cousin who also lived at Chavaniac. His rank discouraged other playmates. From the time he was able to venture into the village, all the men and boys in the forty families who lived there were expected to doff their caps to the young marquis, the women and girls to give a curtsy. He remembered spending long days exploring the forests surrounding the château and often said he drew strength from the ancient volcanic mountains that he could see from the tower room where he was born, and where his father was born before him.

He traced both his impetuosity and his courage under fire to those mountains. "In my blood is the hot lava, in my bones the solid granite which formed the homeland of my youth," as he put it. "The whole New World would . . . not make me renounce that part of the old one where I had the good fortune to be born . . . an Auvergnat."

When he was eleven, his mother sent for him to come to her in Paris. There, he would have been recognized by his more urbane peers as a provincial noble from the "cadet" side of his family (i.e., lineage through other than the eldest sons). On the other hand, he would soon be wealthier than almost all of them.

His mother enrolled him in what was then the most prestigious school in Paris, the Collège du Plessis. One wonders what his teachers and those at other schools in Paris at the time thought they were doing when they taught Cicero, Virgil, and Tacitus, anti-authoritarians who idealized the Roman Republic, excoriated the Empire, and extolled Brutus as a saviour, but perhaps it should not be surprising that most leaders of the French Revolution were educated that way. A gifted Latin scholar, Lafayette might have won the *prix d'université* except that he dropped a whole sentence and was marked one point off for each missing word. (Some things have not changed in French education since the eighteenth century.) The lessons of the Roman Republic having clearly been internalized, Lafayette's most vivid memory from school was of scandalizing one of his masters with a writing assignment: Asked to describe the perfect horse, he wrote about one that, when threatened with a whip, threw his rider and bolted.

In April 1770, his mother died, and her father died of heartbreak a few weeks later. With that, at the age of twelve, Lafayette became an orphan in the care of his great-grandfather. He had at least the consolation of a fortune large enough to give him an income of 120,000 livres, the equivalent of more than $800,000, which exceeded that of most of the aristocrats in Paris. He became a member of the King's Black Musketeers, in which his great-grandfather had been a captain. At the same time, he began attending the *Grande Ecurie* and *Manège* (riding school) of Versailles, which were reserved for only the highest-ranking princes and sons of the king's most highly placed courtiers. At the *Ecurie* his study of Le Blond's *Treatise on Artillery* and other military texts would have been leavened with lessons in fencing and dancing, even music and drawing; but students spent barely ten hours a week with their professors, their main education being physical, and their most important sport being horsemanship. Every morning was spent at the *Manège*, the best riding school in Europe, renowned for the perfection of its horses and the excellence of its riding masters.

His social and military careers were acutely vertical. In 1772, he was chosen to marry the second daughter of Jean-Paul-François de Noailles, the duc d'Ayen, scion of one of the first families of France. Once negotiations of the marriage and dowry were completed between the Noailles family and Lafayette's great-grandfather, the comte de la Rivière, he was given a sublieutenancy in the Noailles Regiment, and d'Ayen began seeing that Lafayette got private lessons with one of the top officers in his company of the king's bodyguards. At the wedding, the bride, Adrienne de Noailles, was fourteen, and she would have her first miscarriage before her first communion. (Though early to the altar, earnest attention to spiritual doubts delayed her confirmation.) A month after the wedding, at sixteen, Lafayette was given a captaincy in the Noailles regiment over a company of his own, although he was not permitted to command it until the age of eighteen.

The young Adrienne de Noailles and marquis de Lafayette now joined the effervescent court of Marie-Antoinette, whose signal events were her weekly balls. Adrienne loved them as much as her husband did not. Lafayette felt entirely unsuited for court life. Once, when Marie-Antoinette chose him as her dancing partner for a quadrille, he was so clumsy she actually laughed at him.

Lafayette's best friends were his brother-in-law the vicomte de Noailles, who had married Adrienne's older sister, and the comte de Ségur, who for the moment was a bachelor. Both of them attended the court balls with him and were fellow officers at Metz. Unlike Noailles and Ségur, who gloried in life at court and passed their garrison time as pleasantly as most officers did, spending as little time on their military education as possible, Lafayette seems to have learned his lessons well, and he could only have done so by training hard in the ring, paying close attention to his texts on tactics and strategy, and leading his men in maneuvers.

He never enjoyed the heavy drinking that went with *Epée de Bois* evenings, whether on duty or at court. He bragged about the only recorded occasion in his life when he had too much—"Remember to tell Noailles how much I drank," he said before friends tucked him in—and his philandery seemed forced, for effect. His one apparently sincere attempt in these years was a notorious failure. Mme Aglaé d'Hunolstein was the mistress of the duc de Chartres (her husband was a colonel in Chartres's regiment) and one of the most beautiful women in Paris. To make a play for the mistress of a prince of the blood* (which Chartres was, as the son of the duc d'Orléans) was just short of insane, especially since Chartres was gallant, charming, and handsome. Lafayette's sandy red hair seemed already to be receding from a very high forehead, an effect italicized by a long pointed nose and bad chin, and a certain birdlike aspect combined with his arrhythmic dancing to produce a not especially erotic effect, at least on Mme d'Hunolstein. Thinking that his friend Ségur had been more successful with her than he, Lafayette challenged him to a duel, and it took Ségur several hours to convince him he had no relation with her at all. Given that his inextinguishable passion for the unattainable Mme d'Hunolstein had reached the point of homicidal jealousy, Ségur could only laugh when, a few days later, "the duc de Noailles and other members of his family [begged] me to use my influence to melt [Lafayette's] reserve . . . to put some fire in his spirit."

Lafayette himself explained his deceptively quiet demeanor as the result of an observant nature and "disguised vanity," a feeling that he was superior to the people and above the conversations around him. He would say later that he had never heard anything in the *Epée de Bois* crowd that he thought worth remembering. This quality defined him in opposition to the inconsequence of life at court: "My awkward manner made it impossible for me to bend to the graces of the court or to the charms of a supper in the capital," as he put it, but he found the same diffidence to be "not out of place during great events." Manly gracelessness was not among the virtues prized in Paris society, however, and especially infuriated his father-in-law the duc d'Ayen, who compared Lafayette unfavorably to his other son-in-law, the worldlier Noailles.

---

*A paternal descendant in the royal family, directly related to the king, as distinguished from a conferred title.

At one point, d'Ayen tried to give Lafayette a way ahead in civil as well as military service by getting him a position in the household of the king's brother the comte de Provence, but Lafayette would have none of it. He managed to sabotage the appointment at a masked ball when Provence, in a green domino, began showing off his good memory. "Everyone knows that memory is a fool's substitute for wit," Lafayette cracked, and later, when Provence asked him if he had known who he was talking to, Lafayette said defiantly that he had. The position was of course not offered, and his father-in-law was even more furious with him, seeing in the move not self-assertion but ill-mannered ineptitude.

Lafayette always said he decided to join the American cause after a dinner in Metz given in honor of the Duke of Gloucester, brother but no supporter of England's George III. On August 8, 1775, the week after Washington found out just how little powder was left at headquarters in Cambridge, Gloucester extolled the American cause at a dinner given by Lafayette's commanding officer, the comte Charles-François de Broglie. Lafayette was one of several young officers at that dinner, and he obviously listened closely; he pointed to this dinner as the turning point in his life. Gloucester thought that his brother's policy toward the colonies was disastrous and self-defeating, that the king should simply stop the fighting and give Americans their independence, thus protecting a bond that would grow stronger through mutual trade and mutual respect. In resisting British efforts to suppress them, the colonists were fighting for the rights of all humankind, in the view of ultra-Whigs like Gloucester, an opinion then more advanced than all but the most radical thinking in the colonies, not to mention France. "When I first heard of [the colonists'] quarrel, my heart was enlisted," Lafayette said in his memoirs, "and I thought only of joining my colors to those of the revolutionaries."

After that summer's maneuvers he returned to the Noailles mansion in Paris, with its Watteaus and old masters on the wall and the Old Regime in its bones, back to the social rounds at Versailles and masquerade balls at the Opéra, back to the carousing of the *Epée de Bois* crowd. Before the next year's maneuvers, however, he and some of his fellow officers were placed on reserve. Lafayette and Noailles went to their father-in-law to ask permission to sign on with the American cause, as other young officers were doing. D'Ayen said he would take it up with the prime minister, but only in behalf of Noailles, not Lafayette. Noailles, after all, was "suffi-ciently strong, energetic, and determined to undertake anything," he explained to Lafayette. "What on earth would *you* find to do over there?"

As Lafayette went back to the social whirl of Paris, Beaumarchais was finally coming to terms with the chevalier d'Eon in London. Even for a smooth-tongued character like Beaumarchais, getting one of the King's Dragoons into drag would ordinarily have been something of a challenge; but for the chevalier d'Eon, a life sentence to cross-dressing was not much of a sentence. He had lived as a woman during more than one period in his life and had been doing so to great effect in London for quite some time now. D'Eon had platinum blond hair (and beard), delicate fea-tures, and claimed to have served in his first covert mission as a lady's maid in St. Petersburg. He was rewarded for his espionage work with a cap-taincy in the King's Dragoons, a seat in the Parlement of Paris, and the Order of St. Louis. Among his other attributes, d'Eon was a renowned duelist, so despite his indefinite gender he was not lightly mocked.

The secret service of Louis XV had grown steadily in size and impor-tance after 1763, when France's humiliation by England in the Seven Years' War was certified by the degrading Treaty of Paris. The party at Versailles became only more scandalous and fun after that, but Louis settled down to plot revenge in the daytime, faithfully attended by his spymaster, the scheming cutthroat comte de Broglie (who would become Lafayette's commander at Metz). In furtherance of the king's fondest ambition—an invasion of England and restoration of the Catholic Stuarts—Louis XV sent undercover agents far and wide. The chevalier d'Eon, for the moment in pants, was placed in the London embassy, where his job was to throw bribes at all sides of the British political scene and to do reconnaissance for the coming invasion, reporting directly to the king and the comte de Broglie.

After a few years in London, he got into a very ugly catfight with the ambassador, which he took clamorously public. The ambassador and his family swore vengeance for d'Eon's various insults, which they would doubtless have extracted had the chevalier returned to France. D'Eon was publicly rebuked and dismissed but privately kept on retainer and told to stay in London. Soon, though, without an official role, and resentful of his enforced obscurity, d'Eon began very noticeably . . . changing. He started telling his most well placed old associates, always with copious tears and pleading for deepest secrecy, that his life as a man had been a brave but—*how could I not have seen this before?*—shameful front. He had not been undercover in his work as a woman, he claimed now, but more himself, or rather herself, than at any other time. He even wrote a letter of confession to Broglie and collaborated in a memoir titled *Military, Political and Private Life of Mademoiselle d'Eon*, which explained that she had been baptized a boy so that the family would have a male heir. There were many doubters, however, and during the past several years in London large bets had been placed on the chevalier's sex—bets that lay on the table until his death in 1810, when an autopsy discovered "male organs of generation perfectly formed in every respect."

Louis kept the chevalier on his pension throughout this gender drama because d'Eon had stashed under the floorboards of his flat several crates of highly sensitive memoranda to and from the king about his "grand project" and other aspects of Anglo-French diplomacy. D'Eon had begun referring to these documents in his applications to spymaster Broglie and the king for more money and for the right to come home. Broglie sent two intermediaries to d'Eon to no effect. One of them apparently proposed marriage.

Enter Beaumarchais, who had done work for Louis XV for several years, stopping a leak here, threatening reprisals there. In fact, he had been expecting help with a pending court case in return for having quieted an extortionate journalist in London when Louis XV died, leaving the realm to his grandson, now Louis XVI. Knowing he would have to start all over again with the new king, Beaumarchais wrote his best contact at Versailles: "All the king wishes to know alone and promptly, here I am: I have at his service a head, a heart, arms, and no tongue."

London was a very good place to be a spy in 1775. The Treaty of Paris and the peace of Europe had for years been hanging by a thread, as the foreign ministry at Versailles focused increasingly on North America as the best venue for revenge. Opinion in Britain had been bitterly divided for years on the king's repressive colonial policy, and Beaumarchais had highly placed sources on both sides of the argument. "I can give [the king] the most accurate estimate of the action of the mother country, on her colonies and the effect of colonial disorder on England; what the result may be on both sides; the extreme importance that these events have for the interests of France; what we can hope or fear for our possessions in the West Indies; what can bring us peace and what war, etc." Instead, the new king gave him a couple of problems that seemed more pressing at the time, including the case of the chevalier d'Eon.

Predictably, Beaumarchais was smitten, and so was d'Eon. ("We met," the chevalier explained, "owing, no doubt, to a curiosity on the part of extraordinary animals to see one another.") Taking up the chevalier's cause with sympathy and vigor, Beaumarchais wrote to the king at one point: "When it is thought that this creature, so much persecuted, is of *a sex to which everything is forgiven*, the heart becomes moved with pity." Emphasis added: This was the key. No one would visit serious vengeance on a woman—even female spies were exempt from execution—so if d'Eon would agree to remain in the dress of her sex, she could return to France without fear of the ambassador's family, and the king could have his papers back. As Beaumarchais started to work out that bargain with d'Eon, his comic sense apparently began to overtake his ardor. "Everyone tells me that this mad woman is mad about me," he wrote to his handler in the Foreign Office. "I am far from despising her, but who the devil would ever have imagined that to serve the king I would have to play the gallant knight to a captain of dragoons? This adventure is so absurd that it is all I can do to stay serious enough about it to finish this note." Fortunately for the course of American history, he kept a straight face and persevered.

Attitudes in France toward the American colonies began to change dramatically only late in 1775, once the standoff in Boston became widely known and understood as the possible prelude to a glorious, underdog victory. Louis XVI noticed that Marie-Antoinette's set had a new favorite card game called "Boston." There was also greater urgency to his briefings on the subject with his wily and hardworking foreign minister Charles Gravier, comte de Vergennes, who followed events in the colonies with a predatory hunger that was fed conscientiously by his best source in

London, who simply could not bring himself to concentrate only on the case of the chevalier d'Eon. During their early acquaintance, Beaumarchais had been introduced by d'Eon into one particularly ardent Whig circle and to Arthur Lee, an American agent. Lee had been asked by the revolutionary Congress's Committee on Secret Correspondence (forerunner to the U.S. State Department) to sound out foreign governments for aid. In no time Lee and Beaumarchais were telling their respective governments exactly what they wanted to hear. Lee told the Secret Committee that France was ready to commit $5 million worth of arms to the cause (on the basis of nothing but Beaumarchais's imagination or his own). Beaumarchais told Vergennes and others at Versailles that the colonists' victory was only a matter of time (based on bad intelligence or nothing at all).

Vergennes did not need to be persuaded that France should take the opportunity to humiliate Britain in North America, but he needed to convince his young king, which first required getting him off his horse (he spent most of his time at the hunt) and then to concentrate on his history lessons. "The humiliating peace of 1763," Vergennes wrote in one such paper for Louis XVI, "was bought at the price of our possessions, of our commerce, and of our credit." This was the "sad and humiliating" position in which France found itself when Louis took the throne. France now owed it "to its honor, its dignity, and its position before men, to free itself as soon as it is able. If it neglects this and allows fear to turn it from its duty, it but adds degradation to disgrace, and makes itself an object of contempt in its own day and in time to come."

Vergennes took every occasion to bring Louis's attention to the rebellion in the colonies. In his regular reports on progress in the case of the chevalier d'Eon, he included the intelligence Beaumarchais was turning up on the extent to which the American rebels were embarrassing the British in Boston. He even encouraged a direct channel from Beaumarchais to the king, which began with a letter that was presented sealed to Louis on September 21, when Washington had been in Cambridge for two months and still counted a total of fourteen thousand soldiers fit for duty. According to Beaumarchais, the Americans had "thirty-eight thousand armed and determined men beneath the walls of Boston" and "forty-thousand more defending the rest of the country." This was either fantasy or the result of disinformation. On the same date as this letter to the king,

Washington wrote to Congress's president, John Hancock, that the situation of the Continental Army was "inexpressibly distressing." Winter was coming, enlistments were expiring, and there was no money to pay the men, who were becoming mutinous. "I am of opinion [that] if the evil is not immediately remedied and more punctuality observed in the future, the Army must absolutely break up."

As useful as Vergennes found Beaumarchais's "intelligence" to be, he prudently sent his own spy to find out what was actually happening in the colonies, one Archard de Bonvouloir, who sailed in September and was to report back as soon as possible.

A few weeks later, the chevalier d'Eon had agreed provisionally to dress as a woman and give up his trunks full of documents. There were just a few small issues to be worked out, and for guidance on how to deal with them, Beaumarchais the courtier wrote another letter to the king, whose reply must have been received by Beaumarchais the writer with great comic delight:

> Essential points . . . to be replied to in the margin:—
> Does the king grant to Mademoiselle d'Eon permission to wear the cross of St. Louis on her woman's clothes?
> *Answer of the king*—Only in the provinces.
> Does His Majesty approve of the gratuity of 200 écus that I have made to the lady for her trousseau?
> *Answer of the king*—Yes.
> If so, is she free to do as she likes with her civilian [man's] clothes?
> *Answer of the king*—She must sell them.

And so on. What must be among the oddest state papers in history was signed on November 4, 1775, by the "special private envoy of the King of France" and "Mlle Charles-Geneviève-Louis-Auguste-Andrée-Timothée d'Eon, spinster." In it the chevalier agreed to "retake and wear the costume of his chosen sex to the time of his death," a clause to which d'Eon insisted on adding, in his own handwriting, "which I have already worn on divers occasions known to His Majesty."

For all the incident's piquant quality, Beaumarchais had solved a major problem in bringing the chevalier d'Eon to heel, because at a time when

France and England were pretending to uphold their legal alliance but were in reality poised for war, the papers under the chevalier's floorboards had the potential for a diplomatic explosion of the first magnitude. Beaumarchais's greatest reward for this service was his relationship with the king, which allowed him to end the letter that contained these final questions of the d'Eon case with a matter much closer to his heart.

"If ever a question was important, it is this one," he wrote. "I answer on my head . . . for the most glorious success of this operation . . . without [the king's] person, or that of his ministers, or his interests being in the least compromised."

This "operation" that would leave no fingerprints was the arming of the American rebels through a trading house to be run by Beaumarchais that would be secretly funded by the French government. Beaumarchais pressed this idea on the king relentlessly, even recklessly, and if Vergennes was not advising him to do so, he was clearly a happy accessory. When Vergennes told him Louis was worried that helping the colonial rebellion would be a violation of the Treaty of Paris, Beaumarchais actually gave the king a lecture on international law, citing Montesquieu to tell the king that he had a "strict and rigorous duty" to do whatever necessary to punish the English by whatever means necessary for the "humiliating" terms of the Treaty of Paris, a "humiliation which would have made Louis XIV *eat his arms* [rather] than not atone for . . . humiliation that makes the heart of every Frenchman bleed . . ." (emphasis in the original).

As 1775 drew to a close, there was no longer room for doubt in Washington's mind that this was a war to the finish. He had laid the bloodshed of Lexington and Concord to "the Ministerial Troops (for we do not, nor cannot yet prevail upon ourselves to call them the King's Troops)," but he could no longer exempt George III from responsibility after the burning to ashes of the entire town of Falmouth, Massachusetts (now Portland, Maine), and especially after the king's opening speech at the latest session of Parliament, a copy of which had reached him only recently. "Those who have too long successfully labored to inflame my people in America," the king intoned, "now openly avow their revolt, hostility, and rebellion. . . . It is now become the part of wisdom, and (in its effects) of clemency, to put a speedy end to these disorders by the most decisive exertions." Along the way he mentioned "the most friendly offers of foreign assistance," which confirmed a rumor Washington had heard that many shiploads of Hessian mercenaries (thirty thousand of them, in fact) were coming.

The king also mentioned the eventual possibility of pardon for "such persons as [local authorities] shall see fit," but Washington would certainly not be one of those. His letters never refer to this fact, which suggests he did not dwell on it, but all of his fellow founders thought and talked about what defeat would bring, particularly in the summer of the following year, when they put their signatures on the Declaration of Independence. This is the sentence one British judge gave to some Irish revolutionaries: "You are to be drawn on hurdles to the place of execution, where you are to be hanged by the neck, but not until you are dead, for while you are still living your bodies are to be taken down, your bowels torn out and burned before your faces, your heads then cut off, and your bodies divided each into four quarters, and your heads and quarters to be then at the King's disposal; and may the Almighty God have mercy on your souls."

Washington's most pressing problem as 1775 drew to a close was recruitment. The enlistments of virtually his entire force expired in December 1775, and they were not signing up for new tours without hard bargaining. Many appeared unwilling to reenlist under any terms.

Writing to his former close aide and friend Joseph Reed, as a heavy snowfall buried the American encampment, Washington said he was having "many an uneasy hour when all around me are wrapped in sleep. Few people know the predicament we are in, on a thousand accounts; fewer still will believe, if any disaster happens to these lines, from what cause it flows." For one concerned with glory, this position was exquisitely painful: He could let no one know the weakness of his army because that intelligence would surely cause the British to attack, so his failure to act forcefully would be laid to personal reticence. He would have been even more pained to learn that his old friend Reed, a newly elected legislator in Pennsylvania, reacted to this letter not with sympathy but with concern that Washington was not, after all, equal to his task.

.   .   .

Beaumarchais responded to every rejection of his plan to help the Americans with a new argument in a new letter to the king. In early 1776, he pleaded with Vergennes for "fifteen minutes with the king alone," and two weeks later apologized for pressing on the king a plan he had already discarded, but "there are plans of such supreme importance . . . that a zealous servant may deem it right to present them more than once. . . . When this paper is read to you, my duty is done." It was read to Louis again and was again turned down.

The report from Vergennes's spy Bonvouloir could have upset everything had it addressed the actual strength of the Continental Army, but Washington's obfuscation worked to avert that, as did Vergennes's suddenly narrowing Bonvouloir's instructions just before he left. The spy was to confine himself to two projects: to give "a faithful account of events and the general feeling of America"; and to reassure Americans that "we admire the grandeur and nobleness of their efforts." As a result, Bonvouloir's report went into no discouraging details and concluded that the colonies were preparing for all-out war in the spring, which was all Vergennes really wanted to know. Referring to his meetings with Congress's Secret Committee, Bonvouloir wrote: "They asked me if France would help them, and at what price. I replied that I believed France *wished them well*. Whether she would help them? That that *might very well be*" (emphasis in the original).

The Secret Committee eventually boiled its questions for Bonvouloir down to three, and they asked for his answers in writing: (1) How might they be assured of France's friendship in their cause? (2) Could France send them experienced military officers? and (3) Could they exchange colonial goods for French arms and munitions and safely do so using French ports? Speaking only for himself as an "inquisitive traveler," Bonvouloir told Vergennes he had replied: (1) You should ask them yourselves; (2) Yes; and (3) Yes. "I shall give you the address of certain good correspondents. . . . That the Government might close its eyes to it . . . is all you require." Clearly, Vergennes's spy had been briefed, if only generally, on the plan that Beaumarchais was pushing on the king.

· · ·

On February 27, 1776, Washington issued a chilling set of General Orders: "As the season is fast approaching, when every man must expect to be drawn into the field of action, it is highly necessary that he should prepare his mind . . . [and] if any man in action shall presume to skulk, hide himself, or retreat from the enemy . . . he will be instantly shot down as an example of cowardice."

Two days later, Beaumarchais sent another missive to the king, this one a several thousand word essay entitled "Peace or War" which began: "Today, when the moment of violent crisis is rapidly approaching. . . ." Beaumarchais had no idea that a "moment of violent crisis" was "rapidly approaching"—news of such a thing would not reach France for two months—but in fact it was. Washington and his council of generals had settled on a plan to besiege the British from fortifications to be erected suddenly, in the dead of night, above Boston Harbor, on Dorchester Heights.

While that siege was underway, Vergennes presented to Louis's council a memo entitled "*Considérations*," which was a conflation of Bonvouloir's report, Vergennes's own thinking, and Beaumarchais's sophistry. "Peace or War" was by all accounts critical to Louis's eventual decision, which speaks most of all to the king's lack of experience and judgment. Beaumarchais's argument for aiding the American rebellion considered the four possible outcomes of the war:

1. England successfully suppresses the colonies (unlikely but theoretically possible, in Beaumarchais's view). In this case, England would seize the French sugar islands in the West Indies to compensate itself for the war effort, in which case France would be obliged to declare war anyway.
2. Americans win the war. In this case, the English would strike out at France to redeem their honor.
3. England peacefully accepts Americans' independence (in his opinion the likeliest outcome). In this case, the colonies would only have emerged from the conflict in an even better position to take the French islands in the West Indies.
4. America peacefully decides to reconcile itself to the status of a British colony. In this case, the Americans would be so angry with

France for refusing to help them in their hour of need they would *join* Britain to take the islands, so giving France two enemies in the war rather than one. "Be assured, sire," Beaumarchais wrote, "that the necessary preparations for the first campaign alone [in such a war] will cost you more than all the aid they ask you for today."

Louis was not yet twenty-two years old; his grandfather Louis XV had given him exactly no knowledge of kingship, not to mention high-stakes diplomacy; and despite the wish to be a good and popular king, he would rather have been hunting than thinking about any of this. As he looked around for some way out short of war, he found himself inside a neatly wrapped strategic box.

The only minister at the meeting about Vergennes's *Considérations* who objected to the plan was the finance minister, Turgot, whose argument posed the problem that would lead by a series of sidesteps to the French Revolution. Since Louis XVI took the throne, he said (though by no means only since then), the payments of the government had exceeded its receipts every year. When he took office in July 1774, the shortfall was almost 50 million livres against expenses of 325 million. Since then Turgot had managed to bring costs under control with a program of reform, but should there be a major new draw on resources, there were only three things that could be done: raise taxes, declare some cosmetically improved version of bankruptcy in order to suspend payments, or reduce other expenses dramatically. The first two were problematic, and he had looked everywhere for economies already. "The first gunshot," he warned, "will drive the state to bankruptcy."

Turgot actually supported the republican ideals of the American Revolution—as Vergennes, a supporter of royal authority, did not—but Turgot also had a broad, ambitious program of reform at stake: He aimed to dismantle monopolies, abolish internal customs duties, establish a banking system to regulate credit, lift price controls, and revoke a great hodgepodge of old financial concessions—all laudable measures, each with opposition that was powerful and devout. Nevertheless, earlier in the year, he had got Louis to sign off on what were known as his Six Edicts, one of which abolished the hated *corvée*, which forced peasants to work on the country's roads or pay for an exemption, another that defanged the guilds, which protected trades from competition. The other edicts were less important but almost as controversial, and in late February 1776 the Parlement of Paris had issued a remonstrance against them, meaning they exercised their exclusive power to put aside the king's edicts. The only way for a king to overcome a remonstrance by the Paris Parlement was to nullify it in a so-called *lit de justice* or "bed of justice," so named for the couch high above the magistrates' heads from which the king pronounced such a fiat. On the very day of Vergennes's meeting on the *Considérations*, Louis had to preside over just such a ceremony in the Great Guards' Hall at Versailles, at the end of which something unprecedented and once unthinkable had happened: There was protest at his decision, some of it submitted in written form, some of it audible in a stony silence, and, worst of all, some of it actually spoken, and by the king's own brothers. There was even applause for the critics! Clearly shaken, Louis withdrew with the promise that "if experience brings to light certain drawbacks in these provisions, I shall take care to correct them."

A few weeks later Turgot was fired, as perhaps Vergennes knew that day he would be, eventually to be replaced by Jacques Necker, who would declare the royal treasury to be in perfectly fine shape and make a lot of speculators like himself very rich by putting the French monarchy deeper and deeper into high-interest debt. After that the French Revolution was still years in the future but just one tax hike away, the one made necessary by France's aid to the American Revolution.

Two weeks after Vergennes's meeting and Louis's *lit de justice*, Washington had the profound satisfaction of watching the British leave the city of Boston as the fleet sailed out of the harbor. An operation that was intrepid, well executed, and very lucky, the siege from Dorchester Heights finally gave Washington something to boast about, which he did in a letter to his younger brother John Augustine Washington that summed up the war to date: "We have maintained our ground against the enemy under the . . . want of powder—and we have disbanded one army and recruited another within musket shot of two and twenty regiments, the flower of the British army. . . . [N]o man perhaps since the first institution of armies ever commanded one under more difficult circumstances than I have done." The worst part was that he could tell no one about his army's weaknesses "to conceal them from the enemy . . . thereby subjecting my conduct to interpretations unfavorable to my character." Happily, he found that his reputation had apparently survived, he told his brother, "which, in retirement, will afford many comfortable reflections."

If anyone could have been happier than Washington about the British evacuation of Boston, it was Beaumarchais. When the word of it reached him, he wrote Vergennes from London, "the opposition and the ministry are openly tearing out each other's eyes about it."* Six days later he said reports of the siege's outcome had arrived in mail on a ship from Virginia, "but [the news] was so bad that it was thought advisable to say that the chest containing the mail was washed overboard in a storm. Admirable ruse! Effort of superior genius!"

When still no approval of his plan was forthcoming ("Are we going to let them perish?"), Vergennes sent Beaumarchais a suggestively veiled letter dated May 2: "Do not suppose that because your plans are not immediately acted on, that they are rejected. . . . Think well and you will find that I am nearer to you than you imagine."

Vergennes could not say so, but on that date Louis approved the plan to send covert aid to the American rebels in North America. A month later Beaumarchais got his first million livres, to be followed by the same amount from Louis's Bourbon cousin the king of Spain. With that he set up a trading company under the name Hortalez Rodrigue et Cie and

---

*In fact, at least one British minister seemed not too worried about it. In a letter to his friend MP William Strachan on May 10, David Hume wrote that he had just run into the First Lord of the Admiralty, Lord Sandwich, who was on a trout-fishing trip with a few fellow lords and a matching number of ladies of the evening. "Sandwich . . . had passed five or six days there and intended to pass all this week and the next in the same place," Hume wrote with deep disdain. He was just putting the final changes to a new edition of his six-volume *History of England*, which may explain his view of this spectacle as one of historic depravity: "I do not remember in all my little or great knowledge of history . . . such another instance . . . that the first lord of the admiralty . . . should, at a time when the fate of the British Empire is in dependence, and in dependence on him, find so much leisure, tranquility, presence of mind, and magnanimity. . . . *What a ornament would it be in a future history to open the glorious events of the ensuing year with the narrative of so singular an incident.*"

began buying clothing, weapons, ammunition, and other supplies, much of it from royal stores. His plan was to keep the shipments going with cash flow provided by return shiploads of tobacco and other American produce.

On June 16, he wrote to Arthur Lee in London, alias Miss Mary Johnston, that he was about to have a ship loaded with supplies worth £25,000 sterling. "On your part, do not fail to send a ship loaded with good Virginia tobacco. . . ."

Miss Johnston replied: ". . . we ought to do all in our power, without insisting on a certain and immediate return." In cipher, Lee asked Beaumarchais to remember that "we are not transacting a mere mercantile business."

Beaumarchais replied to Miss Johnston that he would "send out the supplies . . . depending, in the mean time, upon remittances in tobacco." Obviously, they had different ideas of the terms of their agreement, which would lead in no time at all to a world of grief.

One week after Beaumarchais got his first million, the defeated and now unemployed finance minister Turgot could at least take a measure of satisfaction from another quarter. On June 11, a new, economy-minded minister of war, as part of a general program of reform, placed on reserve many of the unblooded bluebloods who had made venal offices of high military rank and a mockery of the French officer corps. One of the officers put at ease was Lafayette, a failed courtier and now a captain without a command. With his military career at a dead end and having disqualified himself for a place at court, the marquis de Lafayette was suddenly and quite unexpectedly a man without a future.

IV

La Victoire

ON JULY 6, 1776, an agent of Congress's Secret Committee named Silas Deane arrived in Paris, having no idea that two days earlier his nation had declared its independence from Great Britain. That would have been no great surprise, but it would have been nice to know; and for months thereafter Deane would write to the Secret Committee in growing frustration for some official confirmation of what was all over the newspapers in Europe. (Every mailbag from Congress to its representatives abroad was filled with weights and labeled with instructions to "throw overboard in the event of capture," and so full of such mailbags were British ships and the Atlantic Ocean in 1776 that Deane did not receive official notice of the Declaration of Independence—or any other word from Congress—until November 7.) In response to Bonvouloir's clear message that the French stood ready to give as much covert aid as the Americans could want, Deane came, under cover of a merchant, with instructions to obtain an array of armament as well as supplies for twenty-five thousand men and some experienced military engineers. In a three-hour meeting at Versailles just a few days after he arrived in Paris, Vergennes promised Deane nothing but steered him with a wink to Beaumarchais, who on seeing Deane's bona fides dropped the cagey Arthur Lee and negotiated an agreement with Deane that was clear and in writing. Infected by Beaumarchais's zeal, Deane began to see beyond his instructions, imagining how wonderful it would be to recruit disciplined and experienced French officers to the colonial cause. In no time, especially for displaced officers like Lafayette, the name "Silas Deane" would become a code word for military adventure.

So too would the name of the comte de Broglie, the former spymaster who had become Lafayette's commander at Metz. Restive in this consolation command and inspired by the same dinner with the Duke of Gloucester to which Lafayette attributed his political awakening, Broglie had begun to form a plan by which he would replace Washington as commander in chief of the Continental Army and become the American head of state himself. As hard as it would later be to see this as a plausible ambition even for a megalomaniac, everyone at the time assumed there would just be a different sort of monarch for the colonies at the end of the war— maybe something like the Dutch Stadtholder—and at a time when nobles of various nationalities were proposed and proposing themselves as heads of state all over Europe, Broglie's idea was not completely delusional.

London may actually have known of his scheme before anyone at Versailles did, thanks to a spy they had placed very close to Silas Deane, a former student of Deane's named Edward Bancroft, who served as his secretary. Just a month after Deane's arrival, Bancroft began stuffing notes written in invisible ink into sealed bottles—copies of correspondence, notes on meetings, reports of conversations. Every Tuesday evening after nine thirty, he left a bottle in the hole of a tree on the southern terrace of the Tuileries Gardens for his British go-between. Bancroft knew everything, and he was never caught, so France's pretense not to be helping the Americans would always be known to London for the charade it was, though to protect their source and quality of information, they could never protest with the ferocity that the facts justified. Not long after Deane arrived, Bancroft had already told his handlers that Beaumarchais was to "supply the Congress with such . . . goods and commodities as they might want," and that Vergennes had assured Deane "that Beaumarchais would be properly supported."

Deane, on the contrary, had very little support and by late fall was at his wit's end. He had received no word about the Declaration of Independence, he had received no response to his contract with Beaumarchais, no payment for Beaumarchais's shipments was forthcoming, he had had no instructions since he sailed from America in March, and he was "wellnigh harassed to death with applications of officers to go to America."

Foremost among these applicants were the protégés and would-be agents of Broglie. Deane not only knew very well what Broglie's ambition was, he had even pitched the Secret Committee on the idea as if it were his own. "My aim is simply to find a man whose name and reputation alone will demoralize the enemy," Deane wrote. "Such a man is available, and I believe I have found him. . . . The question is to win his confidence, which can only be done by heaping sufficient honors upon him to gratify his ambition, as, for instance, naming him commander-in-chief. . . ." This of course went quite a bit beyond Deane's instructions and was reason enough for his later recall.

Broglie was stunningly explicit about his plot to replace Washington in a letter he wrote to the seniormost officer he proposed to send to the colonies, the self-styled "Baron" Johann de Kalb. He told Kalb to describe him as "a man fitted to carry the weight of authority in the colony. . . . [Y]*ou must of course not appear to know whether he entertains any wish for such a position*; but you must intimate that nothing but the most favorable stipulations would induce him to make the sacrifices expected of him . . . all the appropriate honors, dignities, and powers over subordinate functionaries; in short, with a well ordered power" (emphasis in the original). Deane promised Kalb the rank of major general and gave Broglie's other men inflated commissions as well.

About the only person who had no idea what Broglie intended was the marquis de Lafayette. When he first approached Broglie about going to America, the count affected to dissuade him: "No. I watched your uncle die in Italy. I was commander-in-chief when your father was killed at Minden. In my opinion your first duty is to your family. . . . I will have nothing to do with jeopardizing your life unnecessarily." But later, when his father-in-law so adamantly refused to take his case to the ministry, Lafayette vented his fury with Broglie and met with a very different response. "Good!" Broglie said. "Get even—be the first to go to America. I will take care of it." Broglie promptly introduced him to Kalb, with whom Lafayette met virtually every day throughout the month of November.

By the end of that month Beaumarchais was almost finished loading his first three ships, which were at anchor in Le Havre, and Broglie's men were set to leave with them, Lafayette included. But on December 7, the day he signed his contract with Deane, Noailles was refused permission to go. Thanks to the loud (and well-informed) protests of the British ambassador, the prime minister had told the duc d'Ayen that no French officers would be permitted to go, especially those from the first families of France. Lafayette was ready to go without permission from his father-in-law or the court, but the fact that Noailles would not be going with him made him hesitate, and that evening he wrote to Broglie for advice.

On the same day, a ship carrying Benjamin Franklin arrived in France. Congress had appointed him as one of three commissioners to France—the other two being Silas Deane and Arthur Lee, though they did not know it yet—to negotiate for an official treaty of alliance with France. After a night's sleep, Franklin wrote to John Hancock that he liked what he saw at the port: "I find several vessels here laden with military stores for America just ready to sail. On the whole, there is the greatest prospect that we shall be well provided for another campaign, and much stronger than we were last."

He had not yet met the man responsible for those ships. When Franklin left for Paris, Beaumarchais was about to arrive in Le Havre to watch the embarkation. He was rightfully proud of what he had accomplished: In addition to tents and clothes for thirty thousand men, "I have procured for you about two hundred pieces of brass cannon," he wrote to the Secret Committee under the fictitious cover of his trading company, "two hundred thousand pounds of cannon powder, twenty thousand excellent fusils, some brass mortars, bombs, cannon balls, bayonet . . . and lead for musket balls." In fact, according to the invoice he enclosed in a subsequent letter to Congress, the *Amphitrite* alone carried "52 pieces of brass cannon with all the apparatus, 6,132 stand of arms, 255,000 gun flints, 952 tents, 21 bales and one case cloths, serges, linens, &c. five bales blankets, 62 packages of tin plates, a large quantity of iron and lead balls, intrenching tools, grenades, 1,029 bls. of powder, &c." as well as "22 commissioned officers of the train, &c. also a number of workmen and artificers." And *Amphitrite* was just the first of three that were ready to sail. By March 1777, Beaumarchais would have seen ten ships off to America.

His wish to see off his first ships was understandable if a bit risky, since his association with the shipments was supposed to be a closely held secret. To avoid detection, he assumed the nom de guerre of "M. Durand" for the occasion. The British of course knew very well that he was there and why, thanks to their spy in Deane's office, but they would have had a hard time explaining how they knew and so could not very well protest. But then Beaumarchais, displeased with a local production of *The Barber of Seville*, could not resist rehearsing the actors himself, which blew his cover and gave the British government the opportunity for a fiercely vociferous protest. One of Beaumarchais's ships, the *Amphitrite*, had already left the dock by then, with Tronson du Coudray and many fellow officers aboard; but the other two ships were being held in port, leaving Kalb and Broglie's other men stranded. Lafayette was still awaiting advice from Broglie when Vergennes ordered the chief of police in Paris to arrest, "with plenty of publicity and severity," any officer who even talked about going to America.

He did this in part because he had just received word of the disastrous Battle of Long Island, when Washington barely managed to save his army from complete destruction with a clever and lucky retreat by night into dense fog. On December 21, Vergennes sent one of the most breathtakingly duplicitous of the many such messages he had sent the British ambassador in Paris: "I am deeply touched by the attention of Your Excellency in permitting me to share with you the joy you feel at the happy news of the successes of the British arms in . . . New York."

Had Lafayette been a happy courtier, had his father-in-law thought better of him, had he been left with his command at Metz, had he been a bit less rich, who knows what might have happened? In the event, he determined to put all his resources to the purpose of severing his fate from the whims of state, family, and the French port authority. "Before this you have only seen my enthusiasm," he wrote Silas Deane. "Perhaps it will now become useful: I shall buy a ship to transport your officers." Possibly realizing how foolhardy this might seem to the American agent, he added, "Be confident. I want to share your fortune in this time of danger."

The brother of Broglie's secretary helpfully offered to go to Bordeaux for him and in no time had arranged to purchase *La Bonne Mère*, a 22-ton ship with a crew of thirty, which Lafayette rechristened *La Victoire*. Over the next few months, the ship was secretly outfitted, rigged with cannon, provisioned with food, and loaded with a commercial cargo, for all of which Lafayette paid 112,000 livres, 40,000 on the contract of sale, the rest due when the ship returned with fresh cargo.

It was at about this time that Lafayette decided to change the motto on his coat of arms. It had been "*Vis sat contra fatum*" (Determination is enough to overcome destiny). He made it simpler and took fate out of it. His sword would henceforth read "*Cur non?*" (Why not?)

Lafayette continued to talk about going to America, but he told no one in his family about *La Victoire*, and the only friends he told were his co-conspirators. He was ordered not to go to America in several different ways by several different people, and one order forbidding his departure was even signed by the king himself, but he was not to be deterred. Concerned that the ship could be confined to port in Bordeaux, he had it sailed to a small port in Spain. Not long before his departure, in part to cover his plan, he made a trip to London, where he actually attended an opera with General Henry Clinton, soon to command the British forces in America. Clearly, hatred of the English was not uppermost in his mind on that trip. ("London is a delightful city," he wrote Adrienne. "I am overwhelmed with kindnesses. . . . We dance, we dine, we always stay up late.") After that he returned only briefly to Paris, where he secretly visited his old *Epée de Bois* comrades to tell them he was going and to glory in their envy and admiration for his daring. There followed a couple of false starts and what Lafayette chose to interpret as conflicting signals from Versailles; but finally, on April 20, 1777, barely dodging the king's order to desist, Lafayette ordered *La Victoire* out to sea, little imagining that he carried a shipful of officers whose mission was to replace George Washington. "Don't worry," he wrote a concerned friend, "once I am victorious everyone will applaud my enterprise."

His family, some of whom were on their way to Italy when he cast off and were waiting for him to join them in Marseilles, found out he was gone only when they opened letters that he had left behind for them. "You will be astonished, my dear papa, by what I am about to tell you," he wrote to the duc d'Ayen. "I am a general officer in the army of the United States of America. My zeal for their cause and my sincerity have won their confidence. . . . Farewell, my dear Papa, I hope to see you again soon. Keep your affection for me, for I want very much to deserve it."

To Adrienne—the sixteen-year-old mother of their two-year-old daughter Henriette and now pregnant with another child—he wrote a letter so scattered it reads as if he was actually considering the implications of what he was doing for the first time:

> I am too guilty to vindicate myself. . . . Do not be angry with me.
> Believe that I am sorely distressed. I had never realized how much
> I loved you—but I shall return soon, as soon as my obligations are
> fulfilled. Good-bye, good-bye, write to me often, every day.
> Embrace our dear Henriette. And, moreover, you are pregnant, all
> of which adds to my torment. If you knew how painful this is. . . .
> Farewell, I have saved this letter for last; I finish my good-byes with
> you. They are going to take me far away. It is terribly hard for me
> to tear myself away from here, and I do not have the courage to
> speak to you longer of a man who loves you with all his heart, and
> who cruelly reproaches himself for the time he will spend without
> seeing you.

A letter he sent to Adrienne the day before he sailed at least tracked a bit better. "My heart is broken," he wrote. "Tomorrow is the moment of cruel departure." Less than wholly credible, no doubt, but not a great deal less so than Washington's letter to Martha from the Continental Convention; just a callow, younger man's version. Like Washington, he simply could not do otherwise and keep his honor: "[H]aving to choose between the slavery that everyone believes he has the right to impose upon me, and liberty, which called me to glory, I departed. . . ."

Never a good sailor, Lafayette was seasick for some time, possibly for weeks. He suggests as much in a long, fervid shipboard letter to Adrienne that is dated May 30, a bit past the halfway point of their fifty-four days at sea. In the first installment, he wrote of "so many griefs and so many worries . . . added to the intense grief of leaving everything that is most dear to me. . . . Your grief, that of my friends, Henriette—all came to my mind with a terrifying vividness and I could find no more excuses for myself. . . . If you knew how deeply I have suffered . . . in flight from all I love best in the world! Must I add to this the unhappiness of learning that you do not forgive me?"

One day, someone sighted a gull. *La Victoire* was still a very long way from shore, but hope that the journey might soon be over apparently revived his memory of where he was going and why. In the last installment of his shipboard letter to Adrienne, he wrote: "Coming as a friend to offer my services to this most interesting republic, I bring there only my sincerity and my goodwill, and no personal ambition or selfish interest. In striving for my own glory, I work for their happiness."

A statement of revolutionary principle follows this declaration of his motives' purity, and though it may sound somewhat hollow given the clarity of the ambition he bends to deny and the practical need to cover himself with his wife, it must be noted, more than incidentally, that he would be saying the same thing fifty years later:

America's happiness is intimately linked to that of mankind; she will become the respectable and safe asylum of virtue, integrity, tolerance, equality, and a peaceful liberty.

V

To Brandywine

IN THE EIGHTEENTH CENTURY, the vagaries of weather and celestial navigation made it impossible to predict how long any transatlantic crossing would take, particularly going westbound, against the prevailing winds. Such voyages could last six weeks or six months. On long crossings, food and fresh water frequently became scarce or contaminated. Some captains actually counted on that so they could sell provisions to passengers from the ships' stores at inflated prices; on one particularly hard-struck voyage, ship rats sold for a shilling sixpence, and mice went for sixpence each. Disease and death among passengers were so common there was a commercial convention by which the halfway mark determined the fare: If a passenger died after that point, the family still had to pay for the passage; before that, it was the captain's loss. Storms, mutinies, and shipwrecks kept many vessels from ever reaching their destinations. The fate of *La Victoire* was specifically haunted by the specter of British ships. She had only two cannon, so interception would almost certainly mean capture. Lafayette had determined to blow up the vessel rather than allow it to be taken.

For all that, the most taxing feature of most such passages was a special kind of boredom amplified by despair, a state of mind sharpened by the suspicion that there could be no end to it. "I have been in the most tedious of regions; the sea is so dismal, and I believe we sadden each other, she and I," Lafayette wrote to Adrienne. "[O]ne day follows another here, and, what is worse, they are all alike. Always the sky, always the water, and again the next day the same thing. . . ." The deck was too small for a walk. Lafayette and his men spent most of their time in tiny cabins being pitched about by the sea.

Among the ways that Lafayette and some of his shipmates steadied themselves against the waves and waves of ennui was to think about the glamour of the cause they had joined. The "shots heard round the world" on Lexington Green rang out with special force in France, eventually raising what had been a vague awareness of the colonial cause to broad and exuberant support. An intellectual foundation for such a response had been laid by the *philosophes*, who saw in America a place where the ideals of the Enlightenment—religious liberty, freedom from tyranny, respect for "natural rights"—were being enacted and not simply argued. Even the abbé Raynal, whose *Histoire des Deux Indes* popularized the theory that its extremes of temperature would forever stunt the growth of North American creatures, commerce, and culture, finally retracted that idea and heralded "a new Olympus, a new Arcady, a new Athens, a new Greece" that would give birth to "new Homers. . . . Perhaps there will arise another Newton in New England. It is in British America, let there be no doubt on this, that the first rays of knowledge are to shine, if they are at last to dawn under this long obscured sky."

Lafayette had read Raynal before he came to America, as had others on *La Victoire*, but for most of the volunteers, lofty aims were secondary at best. In the French military even the young officers who had not been placed in reserve could look forward only to the unglamorous routine of garrison duty. A war between France and England, though deeply wished, was a distant dream, and so therefore was hope of finding "glory" in the French military. In America, there was the prospect not only of fighting the British but also of military adventure and advancement. The most common motivation on board *La Victoire* was that of Kalb and the other officers who had signed on to the cause of the comte de Broglie, among them the vicomte de Mauroy, a noble without a fortune who was distinctly pragmatic about going to America. "I was in no position to be choosy," as he put it. "I thought I would at least get credit for my willingness to serve, and that the least favorable result I could expect would be to receive a position when I returned to France."

Though Mauroy's opportunism was far more common than Lafayette's idealism, Broglie's men and everyone else onboard gave at least lip service to the higher cause—all except for Mauroy. It seemed to Mauroy at times that he was the only sane man on board, certainly the only one who would tell Lafayette the truth. "My fellow passengers were in a laughable state of enthusiasm," he wrote in a memoir of the journey some time later. "I certainly had no intention of trying to cure them of it, but the Marquis de Lafayette really interested me." He liked Lafayette—his charming optimism, his obvious devotion to the American cause, his spunk in sweeping away every obstacle in his path to get to North America—but he was quite sure the marquis was going to be let down. "While everyone else around him flattered his fondest hopes," as he put it, "I wanted to prepare him for the disappointments he could experience."

So Mauroy treated Lafayette to his own theory of why people were flocking to America. "Fanaticism, the insatiable desire to get rich, and misery," he said. "Those are, unfortunately, the three sources from which flow that nearly uninterrupted stream of immigrants who, sword in hand, go to cut down . . . forests more ancient than the world, watering a still virgin land with the blood of its savage inhabitants and fertilizing with thousands of scattered cadavers the fields they conquered through crime. In this tableau," he asked Lafayette, "do you see any less horror than you see in the continent we are leaving?"

Apparently over time Mauroy had the desired effect, because he remembered Lafayette finally turning to him one day with shocked disbelief and demanding: "Don't you believe that the [Americans] are united by the love of virtue and liberty? Don't you believe that they are simple, good, hospitable people who prefer beneficence to all our vain pleasures, and death to slavery?' "

In a way, Mauroy and Lafayette defined the spectrum of interests that brought French officers to America, and though Mauroy's vision was rather bleak, he was right that Lafayette's utopian expectations would be dramatically challenged by his American experience, and in short order. Before the year was out, he would know what it is actually like to fight a war with an inferior and underequipped force of non-soldiers. Just a few months from now, as he took up winter quarters at Valley Forge, he would be forced to define the limits of his wish for martial glory, his dedication to the American revolutionary cause, and even his affection for Washington.

·   ·   ·

At midnight on Friday, June 13, Lafayette and a party of his officers touched dry land for the first time in almost eight weeks. He had hoped they could sail directly into Charleston, where *La Victoire*'s cargo was to be unloaded and sold, but two British frigates were blocking the harbor (they sighted Lafayette's ship but could not give chase thanks to a northerly wind). After some time spent searching for a safe harbor, the captain finally anchored off North Island, South Carolina, then lowered the ship's launch so that Lafayette, Kalb, and a few others could go ashore for a pilot who knew the bars and shallows of the coast.

They rowed for hours, and it was pitch-dark when they finally came upon a group of slaves in an oyster boat who did not know a pilot but offered to take them to their master, an American officer whose summer house was on the shore nearby. As they approached, they woke the dogs at the house of Benjamin Huger, a major in the South Carolina militia who, after assuring himself that they were who they said they were, gave them a first, very welcome taste of American hospitality, including clean beds that did not rock and something more to eat than salted fish and hard tack. Next day he found them a pilot for *La Victoire* and even came up with three horses so some of them at least could ride to Charleston ahead of the ship. A boat happened to be waiting to leave for France, so Lafayette hastily scribbled a note to Adrienne: "The manners of the people here are simple, honest, and altogether worthy of the country where everything re-echoes the beautiful name of *liberty*." He had yet to sleep his second night in an American bed, but between Lafayette and America, as his biographer Louis Gottschalk would write, "it was love at first sight."

The party that undertook the long overland hike to Charleston had been advised to go well armed to protect themselves from fugitive slaves, so to make room for guns and ammunition they left behind their changes of clothes. After trekking for three days and two nights through pathless forests and burning sands, they arrived in Charleston looking "like beggars and brigands," and they were received accordingly. "The people of Charleston detest the French and heap abuse on them," wrote one of Lafayette's party, Charles-François Dubuysson, who kept a journal of the trip. Charleston was a common waypoint for French volunteers from the island of Martinique, many of whom had tried to pass themselves off as aristocrats and high officers in order to get a place for themselves in the colonial militia, but among Americans memories of fighting the French were still fresh. One of the French volunteers wrote that in America he was told "that an Englishman could beat three Frenchmen; that the French were a poor, meager, puny, little, dark-colored and almost dwarfish nation; that they fed on *soupe maigre* and frogs; that they wore wooden shoes and ruffles without shirts, to which popery and slavery being added, the French nation was represented as sufficiently contemptible.... I was often complimented with the observation that I did not look like a Frenchman."

The spectacle of Lafayette's ship sailing into port next day brought a distinct change in Charleston's reception of his party. Particularly the French officers and enlisted men in town, "who had been the first to jeer at us," Dubuysson wrote, "came in crowds to fawn upon the Marquis de Lafayette and try to join his party."

In the days that followed, restored to respectability by *La Victoire* and its provisions, Lafayette enjoyed a tour of the local battle sites, met with the president of the provincial assembly, and enjoyed a five-hour dinner with heroes of the successful defense of Charleston the year before, including the illustrious General William Moultrie, to whom he donated clothing and arms for a hundred men in honor of his defense of Fort Moultrie.

In letters home, Kalb complained to his wife about Charleston's high prices and the "unsupportable" heat. Another of Lafayette's party complained about "horrible lodgings" and "detestable water" and said the women were "very sullen." Lafayette loved everyone and everything. In the afterglow of his dinner with Moultrie, after all of six days in North America, he wrote to Adrienne that Americans were

> as likable as my enthusiasm has led me to picture them.... A sim-
> plicity of manners, a desire to please, the love of country and of lib-
> erty, and an easy equality prevail everywhere here.... What charms
> me here is that all the citizens are brothers. In America there are no
> paupers, or even the sort of people we call peasants. Every individ-

ual has an adequate amount of property, [a considerable number of negroes,]* and the same rights as the most powerful proprietor in the land.

He was in such a swoon he could even overlook slavery.

During their five days in Charleston, Lafayette sold his cargo and arranged a loan to provision the 800-mile hike to Philadelphia that was ahead of them. They left Charleston in three parties, one of which was to take its chances with a trip to Philadelphia by water, the other two on foot. Lafayette's group started out grandly in four carriages, himself and Kalb in the first one, two lesser officers in the second, three aides-de-camp in the next, and a cart for the baggage in the rear. In a few days the carriages had fallen apart and the old workhorses for which they had overpaid in Charleston had gone lame or died in the heat. They left behind baggage to lighten their load, and some of what they kept was stolen. Sleeping in the woods, short on food, prostrated by the heat, they were plagued by fevers and dysentery, and occasionally someone had to be left behind to recuperate. "On the whole, people are not very obliging," one of the party wrote, "and we have been able to find assistance only by paying for it. . . . I do not know whether the future will prove to be better for us, but things are not at all as they were described to us in France." Even the usually upbeat Dubuysson had to admit along the way, "no campaign in Europe could be more difficult than this journey."

Lafayette was in bliss. He saw only "vast forests and immense rivers . . . [the] youth and majesty" of North America. "The farther I advance toward the north," he wrote Adrienne three weeks after leaving Charleston, "the more I like both this country and its people."

A week later they made it to Annapolis, Maryland, where they could go by boat to Baltimore. Finally, on the morning of July 27, after thirty-two days' travel, Lafayette's party walked into Philadelphia—exhausted, filthy, and very much relieved that the ordeal of getting there was over. They arrived on a Sunday, when Congress would not be meeting, but they wanted to waste no time letting the Americans know they had arrived, so after finding rooms and brushing themselves off, Lafayette, Kalb, and

*Phrase in brackets was later stricken out but is in the letter Adrienne received.

Dubuysson bundled up their contracts from Silas Deane and those of *La Victoire*'s twelve other officers and presented themselves proudly at the home of John Hancock, then the president of Congress. He received them politely and sent them to see Robert Morris, now head of the Secret Committee, who accepted their papers for review and told them to meet him at the door of Carpenters' Hall the next morning, when Congress would be in session.

They turned up right on time that Monday morning, and then they waited . . . and waited. Unnervingly late, Morris finally came out with James Lovell, congressman from Massachusetts and head of the Committee on Foreign Applications. As Dubuysson remembered it, Morris told them, "This gentleman speaks French very well . . . deal with him from now on," then turned his back on them and went inside. "The other gentleman received us in the street," Dubuysson wrote, "where he left us, after calling us adventurers—in very good French." They were dismissed without even a boilerplate sendoff like the best wishes of Congress for their future happiness. They were just left open-mouthed on Chestnut Street, fifteen French officers who had risked an ocean crossing and spent the worst three months of their lives for the pleasure of this moment.

Their misfortune was that they were preceded by so many conniving, demanding, and useless countrymen. Silas Deane's recruits were models of military excellence compared to those who had come before, like some of the French volunteers they had met in Charleston. The problem with Deane was that he had, with better intentions than judgment, recruited too many men and made too many inflated promises. He had been authorized by Congress to recruit only four engineers, but on the *Amphitrite* alone, which was just Beaumarchais's first ship to leave France, there were men representing twenty-two officers' commissions from Deane, including a general, a colonel-commandant, ten captains, nine lieutenants, and a surgeon major. Not all of these would receive the commissions they were promised—as most of Lafayette's group would not— but before he was recalled, Deane would manage to insert no fewer than fifty-seven French officers into Washington's army, including three generals, five brigadier generals, seven colonels, sixteen lieutenant colonels, twelve majors, and twelve captains. They were known best for bad English, great military vanity, obsession with rank and pay, condescension to the officers of the Continental Army, and contempt for its soldiers. Washington complained frequently and loudly to Congress that Deane's commissions were demoralizing to those American officers who would be outranked and who had been serving faithfully all along (and who could speak English, and who were not arrogant, demanding, and contemptuous). But as the president of Congress explained in one letter, there was a potentially critical alliance with France in the balance, and summarily rejecting Deane's recruits could "injure our cause abroad where we would wish it to stand well. As you put it, Sir, the affair requires great delicacy."

Congress and the Secret Committee were no happier with the French recruits than Washington. About the time Lafayette left Paris to join *La Victoire* in Spain, they had been so overwhelmed with complaints and appeals that they formed the Committee on Foreign Applications and put James Lovell in the chair, knowing him to be suspicious of French aid generally and specifically hostile to Deane. "Ought not this weak or *roguish* man be recalled?" he stormed to one correspondent two days before he met with Lafayette and his men, and on the same day he wrote to commiserate with Washington, who had lodged yet another complaint: "No one has been more backward than I in desiring to see foreigners in our service, to the slight of my countrymen.... Your Excellency would doubtless smile if you should ever hear that even a number of peasants disputed three days about the difference between the consequences of a man's being Colonel in chief, or First Colonel, or Colonel to take rank & command of all heretofore appointed, or Colonel Commandant of Engineers."

With that as background, Lafayette and the fourteen other officers commissioned by Deane who stood before Lovell outside Congress that morning were not at all likely to be well received.

Still, Lafayette was not any other applicant, and Lovell obviously recognized that, because the next day he and a fellow congressman, William Duer of New York, came to see him and apologized for the rude reception. Deane's letter of recommendation was as explicit as it could be without insulting Lafayette by admitting that he was hired only for his diplomatic and publicity value. Not failing to mention "his high birth, his alliances, the great dignities which his family holds at this court, his considerable estates in this realm," Deane had written diplomatically that he based Lafayette's commission "above all [on] his zeal for the liberty of our provinces." But Lafayette knew exactly what his claim on a general's commission was—"When I presented myself to Mr. Deane . . . I spoke more of my enthusiasm than of my experience. I dwelt much upon the effect my departure would excite in France"—and he was not above a little deceit in the pursuit of glory: He told Deane that he could only persuade his father-in-law to let him go if he had a general's commission, and Deane used that: "Not thinking that he can obtain leave of his family . . . till he can go as a general officer," Deane had "thought I could not better serve my country . . . than by granting to him . . . the rank of major general."

Deane was right. A second letter recommending Lafayette was signed by Benjamin Franklin, himself the best possible publicity for the American cause in France. His letter also put a fine point on Lafayette's potential effect on public opinion and suggested that he be handled with kid gloves: "[W]e are satisfy'd that the civilities and respect that may be shown him will be serviceable to our affairs here. . . . [W]e hope that his bravery and ardent desire to distinguish himself will be a little restrained by . . . prudence; so as not to permit his being hazarded much but on some important occasion."

By then what had come to be known as the "*brillante folie* de La Fayette" was the talk of Paris. At a party, the aged Voltaire sought out Adrienne and dramatically knelt before her in homage to Lafayette's service to the cause of human rights. Mme de Deffand wrote to Horace Walpole that, though his expedition was no doubt foolish, "it does not do him discredit. More people praise than blame him," and Gibbon reported that Lafayette's flight to America was the main topic of conversation in London. Very close to home, the duc d'Ayen was warned that if he continued to criticize his son-in-law's behavior, he would have a hard time finding matches for his unmarried daughters. "All he seeks is glory," Deane wrote to Robert Morris, whom he asked to look after Lafayette's finances and protect him from his excessive generosity, "and everyone here says he has taken the most noble method to procure it. . . . [I]t makes a great noise in Europe, & . . . well managed it will greatly help us."

Three days after the chilly reception from Lovell, Lafayette got his major general's sash and was taken to meet General Washington, for whom this had been a very bad day. That morning, after finding out that the British were on their way toward Philadelphia in force, he sent orders to his generals to "cross the Delaware with all possible dispatch" and march to the defense of Philadelphia, but he knew he was in no position to fight a conventional war with the British. Dinner with the congressmen at the City Tavern that night was just a replay at high volume of a dialogue that had been going on with Congress virtually since the day he took command of the Continental Army. To their insistence that he fortify the city against attack, he would have explained calmly, as he had done so many times before, that his strategy would not allow him to defend any particular post or territory, especially a large city. Trying to fortify the city was useless. If he could defeat the British army in a fight, the fortifications would be unnecessary, and if he could not they would only be used by the British against the Americans after they had occupied the city. America's only hope was simply to keep its army in the field, taking advantage of opportunities as they arose and making the highest priority merely to survive in the hope of outlasting the enemy's will. This was a hard lesson for the congressmen, especially for those who had already begun to question Washington's ability and put their hopes in General Horatio Gates, commander of the (so far) separate Northern Army. Gates's ambition to replace Washington as commander in chief was becoming increasingly obvious and his behavior increasingly insubordinate. He had recently, "in a most extraordinary manner," appropriated uniforms meant for Washington's army and had accused Washington of trying to horde "every tent upon the continent." When Lafayette met him, Washington had had a very long day indeed.

Not surprisingly, given Lafayette's every other reaction to America and Americans, his first impression of Washington was awestruck: "Although he was surrounded by officers and citizens, it was impossible to mistake for a moment his majestic figure and deportment. . . ." Washington, so often described as coldly distant, struck Lafayette as open and warm. The general had of course been briefed on Lafayette and on his symbolic value for French-American diplomacy (most of the recipients of Lafayette's letters of recommendation were at that night's dinner). This may explain his courtesy in taking Lafayette aside after dinner and inviting him to come along for the next day's tour of defenses along the Delaware River, where the British navy was expected at any moment.

The fact that he invited Lafayette so quickly into his small military "family," though, may suggest that he also saw something of himself in this ambitious young general with no battlefield experience who harbored dreams of his own division. When he was Lafayette's age, with only his wilderness skills and a powerful patron to recommend him, he too had gone after a position for which he was completely unqualified, riding around the Virginia countryside presenting an outrageously presumptuous request—to become an adjutant general in the Virginia militia—to influential men in the colonial government whom he had never met. The military disaster that had attended his success in getting that adjutancy was reason enough for Washington to keep Lafayette close beside him in the first few months.

The fact is too that, by every account, Lafayette was enormously likable, immediately appealing even to his fellow generals, who had every reason to resent the presence of one so young at their councils of war. He had of course been trained from birth in the elegant social manner of the French nobility, and if he was less polished than was called for by the exquisitely elaborate etiquette of Versailles, he had a behavioral vocabulary of flattery and ease that would only have been leavened by his winning effort to use his very poor English.

Lafayette had two other qualities that recommended him to Washington and his fellow officers, qualities that were not often found in combination: a conscientious devotion to his success and reputation, and the willingness to acknowledge his limits and mistakes. "The first rule [in choosing officers]," Washington once said, "is to determine whether the candidate is truly a gentleman, whether he has a genuine sense of honor and a reputation to risk." For many officers, that risk often resulted in a desire to hide weakness or ignorance, and nowhere more so, it seemed to Washington, than among the French officers he had known. Lafayette was in this way different: For him, the solution to weakness was to become stronger, and the cure for ignorance was study and experience. Some time later, Washington would write his friend Gouverneur Morris, "I do most devoutly wish that we had not a single foreigner among us except the Marquis de Lafayette, who acts upon very different principles from those which govern the rest."

About a week after he met Washington, Lafayette was invited to a

review of the troops. There he saw what he later described as "eleven thousand men poorly armed and even more poorly clothed." Washington must
have seen his army through Lafayette's eyes that day, because as they
reviewed the troops together he said, "we should be embarrassed to show
ourselves to an officer who has just left the French army." Lafayette later
wrote that his response to this observation cemented their relationship. "I
am here to learn," he told Washington, "not to teach."

As winning as Lafayette may have been, though, he would never have
gained Washington's trust and a division of the Continental Army had he
not proved himself in battle. Under the influence of what he always called
his "lucky star," he would be given the opportunity to do that after only a
few weeks in Washington's camp and only five days after his twentieth
birthday.

A major battle had long seemed imminent. "The times are critical," as
Washington put it in late July, "big with important events." The
British were enacting a grand strategy to end the war during the summer
1777 campaign, attempting to divide the colonies by taking control of the
Hudson River, which would sever the supply line from New England to
Washington's army and the revolutionary capital of Philadelphia. A large
army led by General John Burgoyne was to push down from Canada, to
be supported by a converging force from the main army in New York City.
If all went according to plan, the heartland of the rebellion would be
choked off, and victory would be in reach.

The plan, which was Burgoyne's idea, had begun brilliantly, with the
stunning capture of Fort Ticonderoga on the southern end of Lake Champlain in early July. Fortunately for American history, the British colonial
secretary of state Lord George Germain was either negligent or not very
bright or both: He had also approved another plan, which called for Sir
William Howe, now the British commander in chief, to move from New
York against Philadelphia and leave Burgoyne to make his own way south.
These two plans were never reconciled, and both were allowed to play out
as if the other did not exist. As a result, Washington could make no sense
of what he saw. He was sure that Burgoyne's and Howe's armies would
attempt to converge and take control of the Hudson, but in early July Howe

loaded the British army aboard the fleet in New York Harbor and since then had been taking it everywhere but to the aid of General Burgoyne—a fact "so unaccountable," Washington wrote on July 30, that "I cannot help casting my eyes continually behind me." For most of July, Washington had been marching his army from one place to another as Howe ordered the fleet now here and now there, leading Washington on what he described as "a very disagreeable dance."

The dance was hard on every side. By mid-August, Washington's men were exhausted by all their futile marches, and the fourteen thousand soldiers on board Howe's two hundred fifty ships were drowning in their own sweat, their horses dying in a heat so intense "the pitch [was] melting off the seams of the vessels." Meanwhile, Burgoyne's army continued a doomed march southward toward Washington's Army of the Northern Department under the command of General Gates. Only in late August, when the fleet was clearly committed to disembark at Head of Elk, the northernmost point accessible from the Chesapeake Bay, could Washington finally position his army against the assault on Philadelphia.

On August 24, as a show of strength, he issued orders for a parade through the city. The men, he said, should "appear as decent as circumstances permit," and the drums and fifes should play "a tune for the quickstep . . . but with such moderation that the men may step to it with ease, and without *dancing* along. . . ." In lieu of a common uniform, the men all put green sprigs in their hats, and by Lafayette's newly adjusted standards they made "a fine appearance." Washington led on his huge white horse, Lafayette rode by his side, and they were followed by other high officers and members of Washington's entourage, including Lafayette's new friends the young Alexander Hamilton and John Laurens, son of the next president of Congress. The lineup after that was by regiment, each one led by its field artillery and accompanied by its own fife and drum corps. During the two hours it took the fifteen-thousand-man army to pass through the city, every sidewalk and window was filled with spectators who were not so much cheering a martial spectacle as sizing up their future. As the army marched from Front Street onto Chestnut and past Carpenters' Hall, members of Congress also came out to look. John Adams for one was not entirely pleased with what he saw. "Our soldiers have not yet quite the air of soldiers. They don't step exactly in time. They don't hold up their heads quite erect, nor turn out their toes exactly as they ought."

He did notice, on the other hand, that they were "extremely well-armed." There was a great deal wrong with the Continental Army then: Disease was rife, the currency with which soldiers were paid was depreciating fast, and for those reasons and others desertion was epidemic. But there was one bright spot in that summer of 1777, for which thanks were due almost entirely to the diligence of a certain playwright in Paris.

After the parade the army continued its march south, and the next day Howe's army disembarked and prepared for the march north to Philadelphia. Directly between the two armies, running northwest to southeast, was Brandywine Creek, which Howe would have to cross and where Washington would make his stand. By September 10, Washington's men were arrayed along the northern bank, and Howe's force was encamped six miles south of the other.

There were seven obvious places where the Brandywine could be crossed before it forked off several miles upstream. Washington was told—wrongly, and fatally so—that there were no crossing points above the forks. He massed troops around the southernmost fords but covered all seven, placing himself at the head of troops at the likeliest of them, which was called Chadd's Ford.

On the morning of September 11, the Hessian general von Knyphausen was stopped by a Quaker woman as he led his troops toward Chadd's Ford. "Dear man," she said, "George Washington is on the other side, and he has all the men in this world with him."

"Never mind, Madam," Knyphausen said, "I have all the men in the other world with me."

In fact, he had only 6,800 of them. Unseen by Washington's spies and unthinkable according to his intelligence, 8,200 more British troops, led by Lieutenant General Charles, 2nd Earl Cornwallis, were marching north toward unguarded crossings above the forks, planning to carve an arc into Washington's side.

By eleven o'clock in the morning, Washington began to get intelligence that there was a second column of British troops moving north. Thinking that Howe had split his army, he prepared to use his numerical superiority against Knyphausen. Then, just before his men were to charge across the Brandywine, a message arrived saying there was no British march to the north, and Washington rescinded his order to attack.

A few hours later a farmer named Thomas Cheyney came riding into Washington's camp shouting that they were being surprised from the north by a huge British force. Aides tried to quiet him, but Washington heard the commotion and came outside. Suspecting he was a spy, Washington informed him of the penalty for treason, at which point Cheyney leaped off his horse and drew a map in the dirt of where he had seen them and where they might be attacked. When Washington still seemed dubious, Cheyney burst out, "My life for it, you're mistaken, General! By hell it's so! . . . I have this day's work as much at heart as e'er a blood of you!" Just then another dispatch came from General John Sullivan saying that two British brigades "are in the rear of my right about two miles, coming down" and that there was "dust back in the country for above an hour." At four thirty, bursts of artillery in Sullivan's direction told Washington what he most feared: He had been outflanked.

Lafayette, who had been at headquarters all day, asked if he could join Sullivan, and Washington, with other things to think about, sent him on his way. Then, before riding off to join the battle himself, Washington dictated a letter to Congress, as he had promised to do periodically throughout the day:

> At half after four o'clock, the enemy attacked General Sullivan at the ford next above this, and the action has been very violent since. It still continues. A very severe cannonade has began here too, and I suppose we shall have a very hot evening.

Three divisions were arrayed to face the British advance by the time Lafayette arrived, and he rode toward the center, where the Third Pennsylvania Brigade was led by French officers under Brigadier Thomas Conway, an Irishman but a longtime veteran of the French army who had come over on Beaumarchais's first ship, the *Amphitrite*. Almost as soon as the enemy engaged, both right and left flanks folded, and the battle moved to the center. Lafayette helped rally Conway's brigade to fix bayonets and charge, but the British advance was withering. Lafayette did not even notice when a ball went through his left leg below the calf until sometime later, when blood began seeping from his boot.

Cornwallis's assault was the signal for Knyphausen's force to charge across Chadd's Ford, and the Americans fought valiantly on both fronts. Hessian captain Friedrich von Münchhausen, who was at Chadd's Ford, said that even two hours after the battle began, "our left wing still had not been able to advance. Here the rebels fought very bravely. . . ." Captain Johann Ewald, with Cornwallis's forces, said the Continentals put up "a steady, stubborn fight from hill to hill and from wall to wall." Private Elisha Stevens recorded the view from the midst of battle: "cannons roaring muskets cracking drums beating bombs flying all round. Men a dying woundeds horred grones which would greave the heardist of hearts to see such a dollful sight as this to see our fellow creators slain in such a manner as this."

Finally, despite their bravery, the Americans were outgeneraled and outfought, and all that saved them from a massacre was falling darkness. The retreat was chaotic as men fumbled their way through a pitch-black night, each man following the one in front of him. More than three hundred men took the occasion to desert. Twelve miles from the battlefield, at a stone bridge across a creek near headquarters in Chester, Lafayette established a control point that brought some order to the army's flight. Not until Washington and Greene relieved him did he go to headquarters in Chester to have his wound properly bandaged.

When Washington and others finally arrived at the house where Lafayette was being treated, he was lying on the dining-room table. He said they looked awfully hungry, and he hoped they would not mistake him for dinner. Washington's spirits were not quite so buoyant.

"Congress must be written to, gentlemen," he said, "and one of you must do it, for I am too sleepy."

Adjutant General Thomas Pickering wrote the draft, which, after Washington approved it, was sent to the president of Congress, datelined "At midnight, Chester, September 11, 1777."

Sir: I am sorry to inform you, that in this day's engagement, we have been obliged to leave the enemy masters of the field. Unfortunately the intelligence received of the enemy's advancing up the

Brandywine, and crossing at a ford about six miles above us, was uncertain and contradictory, notwithstanding all my pains to get the best. This prevented my making a disposition adequate to the force with which the enemy attacked us on the right; in consequence of which the troops first engaged were obliged to retire before they could be reinforced. . . . Notwithstanding the misfortune of the day, I am happy to find the troops in good spirits; and I hope another time we shall compensate for the losses now sustained.

In the next sentence he reported, "the marquis de Lafayette was wounded in the leg," which was Lafayette's first battlefield citation, but not his last.

Washington's letter described his losses as "not . . . very considerable, I believe much less than the enemy's." In fact, losses were more than considerable on both sides. The British counted 89 dead, 488 wounded, and 6 missing in action. The Americans, by the best current estimate, had the same number wounded but twice as many dead, a tribute to superior British training, and they left behind 400 prisoners. Howe called for Washington to send surgeons to treat the wounded, and one of them who went was Dr. Benjamin Rush, the Pennsylvania congressman, who afterward wrote an entry in his journal comparing the rigid discipline and security of the British camp with the "disorders of the American army . . . the troops undisciplined and ragged, guns fired a hundred a day, pickets left five days and sentries twenty-four hours without relief; bad bread, no order, universal disgust."

That was just the beginning. So widespread was the criticism of Washington after Brandywine that his own adjutant Pickering called Washington's behavior there more that of "a passive spectator than the commanding general," and he felt comfortable remarking to General Nathanael Greene that while he came into the army with a high opinion of Washington, "I have since seen nothing to enhance it." Greene said he had to agree; "the General does want decision."

As Congress fled Philadelphia eight days later in advance of the British occupation, John Adams wrote: "Oh! Heaven grant us one great soul! One leading mind would extricate the best cause, from the ruin which seems to await it. . . . One active, masterly capacity would bring order out of this confusion and save this country." He was not alone in thinking so.

Four days after the Battle of Brandywine Creek, one of Congress's last acts before leaving Philadelphia was to grant a major general's commission to Baron Johann de Kalb, just as he was about to return to France with several of the other officers who had come over on *La Victoire* in service to the cause of the comte de Broglie. No evidence but this coincidence of timing suggests that Congress was looking to Broglie as the American saviour, but some members at least were clearly entertaining candidates. Many years later John Jay told his son William that since the revolutionary Congress did not publish its debates, no one would ever know the true history of the American Revolution, because they would never know about the heated and bitter debate over Washington's leadership that went on "from first to last." Still, in the correspondence of the congressmen at this time, which was carefully archived, and in the correspondence of Washington and others, there are more than occasional glimpses of a ferocious, very personal battle over the head if not the heart of the Revolution, a battle in which Lafayette would be forced to take sides.

VI

Another Kind of Crucible

ODDLY, THE FIRST OFFICERS to renounce a challenge to Washington were the ones who thought of it first, Broglie's men of *La Victoire*. In a letter of September 24, in which Kalb reported to Broglie on the fiasco at Brandywine Creek, he drew a portrait of Washington whose candor, given his recent commission, verged on disloyalty: "He is the most amiable, kind-hearted, and upright of men; but as a general he is too slow, too indolent, and far too weak. . . . In my opinion whatever success he may have will be owing to good luck and to the blunders of his adversaries [rather] than to his abilities." Perhaps he was only trying to soften the blow he was about to deliver to Broglie's ambitions: Kalb declared it "impossible to execute the great design I have so gladly come to serve." As one of his returning officers would explain in more detail, he said, trying to replace Washington was "totally impracticable; it would be regarded no less as an act of crying injustice against Washington than as an outrage on the honor of the country."

Some congressmen were not so sure of that, particularly after the British marched into Philadelphia on September 26 (Congress's flight had been a bit premature), and even more so after the Battle of Germantown a week later, a defeat that left more wounded and almost as many killed and captured as Brandywine. Germantown was actually thought by some (most important, by the French) to be a moral victory, proof that Washington's troops were sufficiently self-confident and disciplined to take on the same army that had routed them so recently. But Germantown was followed closely and suggestively by an unalloyed American victory: the surrender of General Burgoyne's entire army to General Gates at Saratoga. The victory actually belonged to his second in command, Benedict Arnold—Gates never even took the field—but Gates's friends in Congress did not know that, since he gave Arnold no credit in his reports.

After Brandywine, the loss of Philadelphia, the Battle of Germantown, and the very different example of Saratoga, Gates's stock in Congress was high and rising, while Washington's sank to a new low. Benjamin Rush, in a letter describing Gates's army as "a well-regulated family," called Washington's "an unformed mob" and went on to compare the two men—one "on the pinnacle of military glory," an exemplar of "vigor and bravery," the other "outgeneraled and twice beaten . . . forced to give up a city the capital of a state. . . . If our Congress can witness these things with composure and suffer them to pass without an inquiry, I shall think we have not shook off monarchical principles. . . ." Henry Laurens wrote to his son John, who was at Washington's headquarters, "I know the cruelty of tongues speaking the fullness of designing hearts. Nevertheless I am afraid there may be some ground for some of these remarks."

One of Gates's most outspoken partisans and Washington's fiercest critics was Brigadier Thomas Conway, with whom Lafayette had fought at Brandywine. After Germantown, Conway began to campaign actively against Washington, cultivating a relationship with Rush and like-minded congressmen and making a sharp contrast between his own intrepid performance in battle and Washington's "passive . . . miserable" command. Conway did in fact lead the first charge at Germantown, but Washington actually thought of court-martialing him afterward, because he attacked at the center instead of the flank and because he was "a considerable time separated from his brigade." In any case, Conway began to pursue a major general's commission shortly after Kalb got his ("It is with exquisite concern that I find myself slighted and forgot," he wrote to Congress, claiming falsely that he had outranked Kalb in France), and his letters in pursuit of a promotion became increasingly demanding and rude. Only Gates's patronage and Conway's talent for self-promotion can explain Congress's benign and even warm reaction to his pleadings, especially after he threatened to resign if the promotion were not immediately forthcoming. "For

God's sake, do not suffer him to resign!" Rush exclaimed. "He is . . . the idol of the whole army."

Against that backdrop, one can only imagine Washington's reaction when he opened the first letter he ever received from Lafayette, who was recuperating at a settlement of the Moravian Brotherhood in Bethlehem, Pennsylvania, and still very much working on his English. "My dear general . . . I do not do myself the honor of writing to you as many times as I would choose, because I fear to disturb your important occupations—but I indulge now that pleasure to me on the occasion of the two nominations of Congress [the other was that of Kalb]. General Connay [*sic*] is a so brave, intelligent, and active officer that he schall, I am sure, justify more and more the esteem of the army and your approbation. . . ." He went on to say how happy he was to hear about Gates's victory at Saratoga. Lafayette had had nothing much to do but write letters for the past several weeks, and in his restlessness and boredom he stumbled into trouble with his correspondence several times. The same day he wrote Washington, he sent congratulations to Gates for the "happy and glorious success" of Saratoga, which "add some thing yet to your glory and to the gratefulness of every one who loves the cause we fight for." A few days later he wrote the president of Congress to second Conway's promotion.

These letters may have been prompted by Conway himself, since he had by no means got a promotion yet, he was still campaigning for it, and by this time he had visited Lafayette more than once. In deference to his Noailles connection at court, Conway was as obsequious to Lafayette as he was insolent to Washington, calling himself "Lafayette's soldier." He knew of Lafayette's respect and affection for Washington, and so his recruitment of Lafayette to Gates's cause was subtle and indirect. Lafayette had begun to think out loud about various military adventures besides the American rebellion that could promote the cause of France against England, excursions that Lafayette would lead and/or finance himself. He talked with Conway about mounting offensives to seize British territory in the West Indies, or Mauritius, or India, or all of them. During his recuperation, Lafayette actually wrote about his ambitions in the West Indies to the governor of Martinique (who happened to be a cousin and who thought to remind him that France and England were at the moment not at war). He even shared some of his ideas with Versailles, where Prime Minister

Maurepas remarked that Lafayette "will one day end up selling the furniture of Versailles for the service of his American cause, because once he gets something in his head no one can stop him."

Conway fanned Lafayette's ambition with flattery and turned it to his use, saying he should really get to know General Gates, another intrepid general like himself, the man who had so triumphantly lifted the gloom of recent defeats by giving the colonies the military victory they so needed and deserved. Gates had spoken well of Lafayette, he said, and Lafayette, never one to turn aside a compliment, wrote Gates effusively, "I am very desirous, sir, to convince you how I wish to cultivate your friendship." In reply, Gates assured him the feeling was mutual. "I . . . can but gratefully remember the valuable offer you have tendered me of your friendship." Conway must have thought he had an ally for Gates in Lafayette, if not an enemy of Washington.

Lafayette had no idea how politically dangerous his courtship of Gates and his friendship with Conway was, of course, but his letter about Conway and Gates actually helped Washington by alerting him to the possibility of a promotion for Conway—a prospect that inspired the most heated letter Washington would ever send to a member of Congress. He may have thought he cushioned it by sending it to a friend since childhood, Richard Henry (then "Dickie") Lee, but if so he was misguided; along with Rush and John Adams, Lee had become one of Washington's severest critics.

> [I]f there is any truth in a report . . . that Congress . . . are about to appoint Brigadier Conway a Major General in this army, it will be as unfortunate a measure as ever was adopted . . . a fatal blow to the existence of the army. Upon so interesting a subject I must speak plain: General Conway's merit . . . as an officer, and his importance in this army exists more in his own imagination than in reality: For it is a maxim with him to leave no service of his own untold. . . .

The burden of Washington's argument was what promoting Conway would do to his officer corps.

> I am very well assured of (though I have not directly, nor indirectly, exchanged a word with any one of the brigadiers on the subject . . .)

that they will not serve under him. I leave you to guess, therefore, at the situation this army would be in at so important a crisis, if this event should take place. These gentlemen have feelings as officers, and . . . almost all our officers are tired out: Do not, therefore, afford them good pretexts for retiring: No day passes over my head without application for leave to resign; within the last six days, I am certain, twenty commissions, *at least*, have been tendered to me. I must, therefore, conjure you to conjure Congress to consider this matter well, and not . . . incur a train of evils unforeseen and irremediable.

At the end of the letter, Washington did something that, as commander of the Continental Army, he had never done before and would never do again: He threatened to resign.

To sum up the whole, I have been a slave to the service: I have undergone more than most men are aware of, to harmonize so many discordant parts; but it will be impossible for me to be of any further service if such insuperable difficulties are thrown in my way.

Issuing such a threat was risky, since he knew very well that Gates was at his heels. After Burgoyne's surrender, Gates had not even bothered to notify him about it but wrote to Congress directly, a pointed snub that was widely noted. Hoping to end the campaign of 1777 with a victory of his own, Washington had requested reinforcements from Gates, expecting at the very least to get back those troops he had sent to reinforce the Northern Army before their confrontation with Burgoyne; but with the exception of sending back Daniel Morgan's company of riflemen, Gates ignored the request. In a letter of October 30 that gently chastised Gates for writing to Congress directly about Burgoyne, Washington said he was sending his young aide Alexander Hamilton to explain why he needed more men. Hamilton carried Washington's authority to order two of Gates's three regiments to march, but, with a discretion that must have been a bit shocking to the commander in chief, he decided not to press too hard on Washington's request for troops, explaining later that he thought it would be "dangerous" to issue a direct order when Gates's "successes have raised him into the highest importance . . . [and] the entire confidence of the eastern states" as well as "influence and interest elsewhere." Hamilton thought Gates's preference would have been to send no one, and he felt lucky to get one brigade out of him.

Four days after Washington's letter to Gates, he received one from a loyal general that contained truly shocking news: One of Gates's aides, after a bit too much to drink, had talked about a letter that Conway wrote to Gates which listed more than a dozen reasons why Brandywine was a disaster, many of them derogating Washington. Worse, Gates had reportedly read the letter to fellow officers. One line from Conway's letter to Gates was quoted directly: " 'Heaven has been determined to save your country, or a weak general and bad councilors would have ruined it.' "

The news in this letter was not even so much Conway's treachery or Gates's indiscretion as the fact that they knew each other at all. For the first time, Washington saw Conway's insubordinate ambition and Gates's independence, which he had thought were separate problems, as links in a conspiracy to bring him down: Gates by withholding men to undermine his battlefield initiative, Conway by a promotion that would cost him what loyal officers he had.

After taking a day to consider his response, Washington wrote Conway the briefest possible statement of fact:

> Sir,
>   A letter I received last night contained the following paragraph: "In a letter from General Conway to General Gates, he says, 'Heaven has been determined to save your country, or a weak general and bad councilors would have ruined it.' "
>   I am, sir, your humble servant,
>   George Washington

In his reply two days later, Conway was very far from apologizing. He was able to deny truthfully having written the sentence Washington quoted to him, but what he actually wrote, which Washington discovered only months later, was scarcely any better: "What pity there is but one General Gates! but the more I see of this Army the less I think it fit for general action under its actual chiefs. I . . . wish I could serve under you."

Conway admitted to Washington that in the letter to Gates, "I spoke my mind freely [and] found fault with several measures pursued by this army." His opinion of Washington, he said patronizingly, was that he was a strong man who allowed himself to be rule by weak ones: "[Y]ou are a brave man, an honest man, a patriot, and a man of great sense . . . [but] you have often been influenced by men who were not equal to you in point of experience, knowledge or judgment." He then gave Washington a lesson on military etiquette from his vastly greater experience (Conway never lost an opportunity to say that he had once served with Frederick the Great). "Correspondence between general officers in all army's is encouraged rather than discountenanced, because from this intercourse of ideas something useful might arise." He likened Washington's accusatory letter to an "inquisition" undertaken by "despotic and tyrannical governments."

The clearest message in this letter was that Conway felt exactly no fear of Washington, presumably thanks to the support of Gates and other friends in high places. On November 14, as copies of the Washington-Conway correspondence circulated in Congress, Conway wrote again to argue for his major general's commission, in the process slighting his "friend" Lafayette as one of those generals "who had never seen a line of battle . . . before Brandywine, as it too well appeared."

In response to Washington's *cri du coeur* about Conway, Richard Henry Lee assured him that Conway would not be promoted "whilst it is likely to produce the evil consequences you suggest," but he admitted that the idea had a good deal of support ("it has been affirmed, that it would very agreeable to the army, whose favorite Mr. Conway was asserted to be"). In the same letter, Lee dropped the news that Congress was about to create a new Board of War to supervise Washington and the Continental Army, this one composed not of congressmen but of general officers. They were thinking of putting Washington's adjutant Thomas Pickering on the new board (the man who had called Washington a "passive spectator" at Brandywine), and they thought a good replacement at Washington's headquarters would be Conway. Lee actually said he wanted to know Washington's opinion of that idea.

Venturing ever further into Washington's zone of disfavor, Lee said that another proposed member of the board was General Thomas Mifflin, the army's fatefully incompetent quartermaster general, whom Washington had always suspected of using his power of procurement to feather his nest and who recently, seeing his end coming, had resigned that job and moved to York, where he could politick against Washington full time. On November 17, Mifflin wrote to Gates: "[Y]ou have saved our Northern Hemisphere, and in spite of our consummate & repeated blundering you have changed the constitution of the southern campaign on the part of the enemy from offensive to defensive." The day before Mifflin wrote that letter, the Continental Army suffered another defeat with the loss of a fort on the Delaware that had been one of only two positions from which they could harass the fleet's supply of Philadelphia. Two days later, the other one fell to the British as well.

A week after that, on November 23, Richard Henry Lee wrote Sam Adams, "Gen. Mifflin has been here, and he urges strongly the necessity of having Gen. Gates to be president of the new Board of War. He thinks the military knowledge and authority of Gates necessary to procure the indispensable changes in our army. I believe he is right." Four days later, Gates was elected to the board and to its presidency.

No one had the nerve to tell Washington directly. He got the news when he received from Henry Laurens, as president of Congress, a list of documents that were being forwarded to him, congressional orders relating to "the appointment of three additional members to the Board of War & Major General Gates President." The next document on the list bore news that may have been even more infuriating, an order "of the 28th appointing a Committee of three Members of Congress to confer with your Excellency for enquiries into the cause of losses & failures & for divers other matters."

Among those "divers other matters" was "to consider of the best and most practicable means for carrying on a winter's campaign with vigor and success, an object which Congress has much at heart." The idea was to call out a huge army of militia for an assault to retake Philadelphia. This of course flew in the face of Washington's strategy of avoiding direct confrontation in a "war of posts," for which he had been frequently compared to the Roman general Fabius Maximus, who eventually won acclaim for defensive tactics that were at first thought cowardly. When some of Washington's generals urged caution against trying to retake the capital, James Lovell exploded in a letter to Gates: "Good God! What a situation we are in! [O]ur affairs are fabiused into a very disagreeable posture. . . . Many spirited officers are discouraged by an overbalance of languid counselors." When Congress made a formal request for the assault on Philadelphia, Washington put the question to all of his generals and asked for their responses in writing. They were unanimous in the opinion that such an operation would be suicide. General Sullivan pointed out that a third of the army was already confined to tents for lack of clothing. General Varnum said the commissary was having difficulty keeping up with the army's daily needs: How could it possibly handle a huge influx of militia?

Lafayette, who had returned to camp several weeks before this with a bad limp, wrote the most detailed and robust opinion on the winter campaign. Despite his naturally aggressive enthusiasm, he demonstrated the depth of his military education in a strongly cautionary opinion. "The project . . . seems to me attended with so many difficulties, inconveniences and bad chances," his memo began, "that if it is not looked upon as a necessary and almost desperate enterprise, though it is a very shining and highly pleasing idea . . . I can not think it is a prudent and reasonable one." What followed was a mature, clearheaded assessment of the tactical and practical contingencies of such an operation: the need for solid ice or bridges across the river, the problem of disposing both militia and regular forces to storm deeply entrenched fortifications, the states' difficulty recruiting militia in winter, the problems associated with their equipage and subsistence, and finally the diplomatic fallout that would attend a defeat:

> Europe has a great idea of our being able to raise when we please an immense army of militia, and it is looked upon as our last but certain resource. If we fall this phantom will fall also and you know that the American interest has always been since the beginning of this war to let the world believe that we are stronger than we can ever expect to be. . . .

His memo ended where it began: "[W]e must not let a shining appearance and the pleasing charms of a bold fine enterprise deceive us upon the inconveniences and dangers. . . ."

There was nothing political in Lafayette's assessment. He seemed to have been unaware of any politics in the air at all. Two days before writ-

ing this memo, he had written to Gates with "a thousand tender compliments." In any case, he could have done little to stop the moves against
Washington in Congress even if he had been aware of the backstabbing
by Mifflin and Conway. There had been great "losses and failures," after
all, and Congress had a responsibility for due diligence. Beyond that, however, there was a deeper, fundamental issue at stake, and one which would
be debated not only throughout the American Revolution but even more
pointedly in the nation-building period that followed: the issue of how a
nation of free people should best be led. In addition to doubts about
Washington's prosecution of the war, congressmen like Adams, Rush, and
Lee were deeply suspicious of the power he had drawn to himself as commander in chief. When Congress was thrown into turmoil by the British
occupation of Philadelphia, he had been temporarily given nearly dictatorial powers to fill the potential leadership vacuum, and though it is hard
to imagine any general being more fastidious about yielding to civilian
control than Washington was even then, he had protested loudly and
often about the necessity of long-term enlistment, which to Adams, Lee,
and others of like mind was just another description of a standing army,
the very fount of tyranny.

People like Conway and Mifflin, of course, played to such fears, casting Washington and his generals as the "reigning cabal" who were driving
from the army those deserving officers and men who were less than willing to "worship the image & pay an undeserved tribute of praise & flattery to the great & powerful," as Mifflin put it in his letter to Gates. At
the time, Washington was being accused of rushing to winter quarters, in
effect of abandoning both Pennsylvania and New Jersey to Howe's venge-
ful plundering, and Mifflin used that to recruit Gates and undermine
Washington. "The list of our disgusted patriots is long and formidable,"
he wrote to Gates, "their resentments . . . and their powers of opposition
not despicable. . . . [I]f our troops are obliged to retire to Lancaster, Reading, Bethlehem &c for winter quarters & the country below is left open
to the enemy's flying parties—great & very general will be the murmur—
so great and so general that nothing inferior to a Commander in Chief
will be able to resist the mighty torrent of public clamor & public
vengeance. . . . In short, this army will be totally lost unless you come down
& collect the virtuous band who wish to fight under your banner. Prepare

yourself for a jaunt to this place. Congress must send for you. I have ten thousand things to tell."

Washington would be accused of indecision and excessive consultation to the end of the war, but often what was being complained of was the virtue of restraint. In the opening week of December, Howe's army ventured out of Philadelphia in the direction of Washington's camp, and he would have mounted an attack if a spy had not prepared the Americans for it. Howe continued to feint, in what he described later as an effort to tempt the enemy into battle, but Washington's refusal to engage in more than isolated skirmishes was seen by Congress as another example of supine leadership. Writing to Sam Adams about "a subject very sickening to even a strong stomach," James Lovell declared: "It was evident, among friends I say it, that our army was not inclined to fight."

In its report of December 10, the committee appointed by Congress concluded that Washington was right to resist fighting Howe and to go into winter quarters (Howe had done so two days before), but its members still expressed the wish that "a reform may take place in the army, and proper discipline be introduced." In a resolution of the same date, Congress chided Washington for taking provisions from a distance instead of simply foraging from local farms, attributing it to his "delicacy in exerting military authority on the citizens of these states," which was proving "destructive to the army and prejudicial to the general liberties of America." Washington said in his reply that he had taken his supplies from counties close by to the point that they were exhausted, but it was true that he was loath to do it, not wishing to undermine the support of faithful fellow Americans.

Three days later, on December 13, in a move it deemed "essential to the promotion of discipline in the American army, and to the reformation of the various abuses which prevail in the different departments," Congress created the post of Inspector General, whose task would be to propagate and enforce "the practice of the best disciplined European armies." To that end, the new inspector was to review "the behavior, capacity and assiduity of every individual [and] . . . make this review minutely, man by man, attending to the complaints and representations of both soldier and officer, and transmitting to Congress what petitions and grievances he shall think worthy of notice." To fill this post, Congress named none other than

Thomas Conway, who was thus not only promoted to the rank of major general but in effect became Washington's judge and jury. Washington was never informed of this decision by Congress and would not learn of it until two weeks later, on December 29, when Conway himself would come to winter quarters at Valley Forge to present his new orders and declare victory to Washington's face.

Congress had long before declared December 18 to be a national day of Thanksgiving this year.* Now that it was here, as Lieutenant Colonel Henry Dearborn wrote in his journal, no one could quite remember what they were giving thanks for, "this being the third day we have been without flour or bread—& are living on a high uncultivated hill, in huts & tents laying on the cold ground, upon the whole I think all we have to be thankful for is that we are alive & not in the grave. . . ." The next day they were to march to winter quarters at Valley Forge, and in this day's General Orders, after wishing everyone a happy Thanksgiving, Washington ordered the regiments to be divided into squads of twelve, each of which was to build itself a hut: They were being ordered to erect on the two great hillsides of Valley Forge a small city for more than ten thousand men, and they were to build it out of standing trees. Washington offered twelve dollars to the squad that finished its hut first, and a hundred dollars to anyone who could figure out the best way to cover them without using up precious planks of wood. Another soldier remembered of that Thanksgiving, "We had neither bread nor meat 'till just before night when we had some fresh beef, without any bread or flour, the beef wou'd have answer'd to have made minced pis if it cou'd been made tender enough, but it seem'd Mr. Commissary did not intend that we shou'd keep a day of rejoicing—but however we sent out a scout for some fowls and by night he return'd with one dozen: we distributed five of them among our fellow sufferers three we roasted two we boil'd and borrowed a few potatoes[:]

*The first Thanksgiving Day celebrated by all the colonies was in October of the previous year. The last Thursday in November was the date chosen by Abraham Lincoln in 1863.

upon these we supp'd without any bread or anything stronger than water to drink!"

On December 19, the day the American army officially took up residence at Valley Forge, Congress asked Washington to send specific plans for the defense of eastern Pennsylvania and New Jersey. At the time he received it, he was writing a letter begging Congress for supplies. Those responsible for the shortage, such as Clothier General James Mease and Commissary General of Purchases William Buchanan—names that should live forever in American memory—were congressional appointees; and so, in addition to being corrupt and lazy, they could ignore Washington's orders with virtual impunity. The plea of General James Mitchell Varnum, three days after "Thanksgiving," was typical:

> Three days successively we have been destitute of bread. Two days we have been intirely without meat. . . . Whenever we procure beef, it is of such a vile quality as to render it a poor [substitute] for food. . . . The complaints are too urgent to pass unnoticed. It is with pain that I mention this distress. I know it will make your Excellency unhappy; but if you expect the exertions of virtuous principles while your Troops are deprived of the essential necessaries of life, your final disappointment will be great. . . .

Washington received Varnum's plea just before Congress's letter arrived telling him to move his army to the defense of Pennsylvania and New Jersey. In the circumstances, his reply was more than generous. "It would give me infinite pleasure to afford protection to every individual and to every spot of ground in the whole of the United States," he responded. "Nothing is more my wish. But this is not possible with our present force."

The next day he had to respond to a strong denunciation from the Pennsylvania Assembly for his decision to go into winter quarters, a particularly galling criticism since the state had ignored his call for supplies and clothing, leaving his troops miserably ill-equipped for any season, much less winter. In his letter to Congress, Washington was clearly not yet in the Christmas spirit: "I can assure those gentlemen that it is a much easier and less distressing thing to draw remonstrances in a comfortable

room, by a good fire-side, than to occupy a cold bleak hill, and sleep under
frost and snow without clothes or blankets: however, although they seem
to have little feeling for the naked and distressed soldiers, I feel super-
abundantly for them, and from my soul, pity those miseries which it is not
in my power either to relieve or to prevent." A canvassing of his men that
day, he wrote, found that almost three thousand were "unfit for duty because
they are bare foot and otherwise naked." If provisions were not soon forthcoming, he was convinced "beyond a doubt" that "this Army must inevitably
be reduced to one or other of these three things. Starve, dissolve, or disperse,
in order to obtain subsistence in the best manner they can."

Washington's Christmas dinner for his generals and aides that year was
suitably and necessarily spartan—a little mutton, some potatoes, some
cabbage, and nothing more, because there was nothing more: only water
to drink, no sugar, no bread, no dessert, not even enough knives and forks.
Washington had lost his baggage and was down to eating with a single
spoon.

Four days later, Conway came to Valley Forge and rode straight to
Washington's headquarters, where he presented Washington the resolution of Congress announcing his promotion and his responsibilities.
Washington's exact words are not recorded, but from what Conway wrote
later it is clear that Washington minced no words: He said he found it
remarkable that Congress would promote someone who spoke so little at
war councils before operations and criticized so often afterwards, someone
so low as to conspire against his commander in chief with his friends Mifflin and Gates and to promote himself as a battlefield hero when he had
been on the verge of court-martial. Searching for some technically acceptable way to tell Conway what he could do with his resolution, Washington fixed on Congress's resolve to send along instructions as to how the
troops were to be trained. Did Conway have those instructions with him?
He did not. Until he did, Washington said, he could hardly function in his
new role, and now he was free to show himself out.

Remarkably, Conway went away hurt. "Greatly disappointed and chagrined," he wrote Gates, "I am stopped in functions, cannot be useful. . . .
I wish I could be sent somewhere else." He may also have run for solace
to Lafayette, but by now, better late than never, Lafayette had begun to see
what was going on behind Washington's back. As recently as December 14

he had told Gates he could "depend upon my attachment forever," yet two days later, something had changed. In a long letter to his father-in-law the duc d'Ayen, his first since arriving in America, after filling him in on the war to date, Lafayette talked about his love of Washington ("a man made for this revolution"); he argued his "superiority over General Gates" despite the appearance of his defeats and Gates's victory; and he referred to certain "jealous intriguers" who "would like to tarnish [Washington's] reputation. . . . There are many important matters I cannot put on paper." Lafayette was the only one of his officers with whom Washington had yet discussed Conway's disloyalty, and Lafayette's change of sentiment suggests that he did so between these two letters of mid-December.

Hearing about the confrontation with Conway almost as soon as it happened, Lafayette rushed to Washington's quarters. Told that the general was too busy to see him, he then wrote a long letter whose eloquence, despite his poor English, plainly derived from its sincerity. "I don't need telling you how I am sorry for all what happens since some time," he began. "When I was in Europe I thought that here almost every man was a lover of liberty . . . at that time I believed that all good Americans were united together, that the confidence of Congress in you was unbounded." He could not have been more astonished, he said, when he discovered that there were "open dissentions in Congress . . . stupid men who without knowing a single word about war undertake to judge you . . . who want to push you in a moment of ill humor to some rash enterprise upon the lines or against a much stronger army."

It was a remarkable letter, and a remarkable step for Lafayette to take. Courage on the battlefield was one thing—that way lay glory, honor, and fame. Courage in taking a position that put one's reputation at risk was quite another. In making the choice to write this letter and declare his fidelity to Washington so openly and so decisively, Lafayette placed himself in direct opposition to some of Congress's most powerful leaders, not to mention the entire Board of War, including General Gates. In doing so, Lafayette had plainly confronted not only the anti-Washington "cabal" but also himself. "Conway had done all [in h]is power by cunning maneuvers to take off my confidence and affection for you. . . . [He] had engaged me by entertaining my head with ideas of glory and shining projects, and I must confess for my shame that it is a too certain way of deceiving me."

Now that he had learned the truth, he declared, "My desire of deserving your satisfaction is stronger than ever, and every where you'll employ me you can be certain of my trying every exertion in my power to succeed. I am now fixed to your fate, and I shall follow it and sustain it as well by my sword as by all means in my power."

The "Conway Cabal" was far from over—the *cabaleurs* had not even dreamed up their most dramatic attempt to win over Lafayette—but Washington was appropriately moved by the expression of support, and he replied to it with one of the most emotionally open, wise, and grateful letters he ever wrote: open in its description of "dirty arts and low intrigues" of the people who had tried to hurt him; wise in its restrained commitment to "steady and uniform conduct, which I shall invariably pursue while I have the honour to command"; and grateful to his friend Lafayette, with whom he hoped, at the end of the war,

> if you will give me your company in Virginia, we will laugh at our past difficulties and the folly of others; [and] where I will endeavor by every civility in my power to show you how much and how sincerely, I am, your affectionate and obedient servant,

> G. WASHINGTON

VII

Enter France

ANY YEARS LATER, during his last visit to the United States, in 1824, Lafayette said that during his first months in America, despite the intimacy with Washington he claimed in his first letters home, he had the uneasy feeling that the commander in chief for some reason did not really trust him. "This thought was an obsession," he remembered, "and it made me very unhappy." That had ended, he said, only during the winter of Valley Forge, when he joined the American Union Lodge of Freemasons, with Washington presiding as Master Mason. After that, "I never had reason to doubt his entire confidence, and soon thereafter I was given a very important command-in-chief." Much has been written about the role of Freemasonry in the American Revolution. Clearly it was a venue for the discussion of principles (and possibly, in the case of the St. Andrews Lodge and Green Dragon Tavern in Boston, of tea parties). It was also in certain respects a model of the new society the Revolution was to create, one based not on a social hierarchy but on merit and mutual respect in a brotherhood of equals. But Lafayette's attribution of a command to Freemasonry is misremembered history, because he had actually got his command of a division before the army came to Valley Forge. If the "very important command-in-chief" he meant was the offer that winter to lead an elaborate and costly expedition to Canada, he may have wished to change history, because it was a work of treachery by Conway *cabaleurs* that once again exploited Lafayette's weakness for "glory" in an attempt to bring Washington down.

Lafayette was given his division shortly after returning to camp from his convalescence after Brandywine, when he proved himself again in battle as well as in command. He had joined General Greene and his army in New Jersey, where Greene was attempting to interfere with Cornwallis as his men foraged for the supply of Philadelphia. On November 25, 1777, Lafayette left Greene's camp with four hundred men to reconnoiter, and that afternoon happened on an advance force of four hundred Hessians. He immediately attacked, pressing them back for at least a mile. Reinforcements from Cornwallis began arriving as night fell, and Lafayette fell back under cover of darkness, having killed fifty or sixty enemy troops, including at least three officers, wounding many more, capturing fourteen prisoners, and losing only one man of his own. It was a small victory, but it was a victory, and at Greene's request Lafayette wrote Washington immediately to commend the "bravery and alacrity" of his troops. "The conduct of our soldiers is above all praise: I never saw men so merry, so spirited." It was Lafayette's fearless but prudent execution that impressed Greene, who wrote approvingly to Washington, "The marquis is determined to be in the way of danger." After reading Greene's report, Washington wrote to Congress commending Lafayette's "military ardor" and recommending him for a divisional command, which was promptly granted.

In late January 1778, Lafayette heard that Congress was planning a new expedition to Canada. (The first had been in 1775–76, a cruel winter campaign courageously led by Brigadier Generals Benedict Arnold and Richard Montgomery that ended with the former wounded and the latter dead.) Expelling the British to bring Canada into the union—like the single, decisive military thrust that would bring American independence—was among the most compelling delusions of the Revolutionary Congress, and Lafayette was among its most determined adherents, in part because Canada had been among France's most costly and humiliating losses in the Seven Years' War. Even after what would be a very cautionary experience in early 1778, Lafayette continued to propose assaults on Canada—at the end of this year, and again in 1779, in 1780, 1782, and 1783.

Lafayette's only distress in hearing about the expedition now was the rumor that Conway was to be in command of it. This would not have come as wholly bad news to Washington, of course, since it would mean

Conway would not be returning to his army in the role of Inspector General, but for Lafayette the prospect of anyone but himself in charge of such a campaign was exquisitely painful. He and Conway had actually talked about the idea during his convalescence after Brandywine. In a letter to Washington about Conway and Canada, Lafayette's tone of mockery masked an obvious sense of injury: "They will laugh in France when they'll hear that he is chosen upon such a commission out of the same army where I am, principally as he is an Irishman . . . when the project should be to show to the Frenchmen of that country a man of their nation." He disclosed just how conflicted he was with a sentence that was both illogical and false: "I do not entertain myself any idea of leaving your army . . . but I would not lose a moment to write your Excellency of [Conway's] journey towards Congress." Conway had gone to York, but that was not the subject of Lafayette's letter; and an expedition to Canada would obviously involve leaving Washington's army.

Though no other letters on the subject survive, this one may have been part of a correspondence campaign by Lafayette to retrieve the command for himself. If so, it was successful. Three days after he wrote it, Congress authorized the expedition and, without consulting or even directly informing Washington, they put Lafayette in charge of it, with Conway as second in command. On January 27, 1778, Lafayette received the news of his appointment directly from Gates as president of the Board of War; and as Gates made clear, this was a separate command in which he would report to the board, not to Washington.

Gates's letter came to headquarters along with a bundle of other correspondence from the board addressed to Washington, including a pro forma, obviously belated request for his thoughts about the expedition to Canada. Washington's response was remarkably generous. He said that since he knew nothing about the operation, he could not give an opinion, but added, "I can only sincerely wish, that success may attend it, both as it may be advancive of the public good and on account of the personal honor of the Marquis de la Fayette, for whom I have a very particular esteem and regard."

Washington's reaction may have sprung less from warmth toward Lafayette than from a weary fatalism. He was never so besieged in battle as he was at Valley Forge. The bloody footprints in the snow that form the signal image of those dark days represent what was a true nightmare, in which more than two thousand men died of starvation, exposure, and disease. Committeemen from Congress came and went all winter, each of them seconding Washington's view that the army's provisions were pathetically, indeed lethally insufficient; and despite all of Congress's advice and committees, America's merchants and farmers, facing the choice between worthless Continental paper money and British silver, continued to trade with the enemy, leaving their army to starve within sight of some of the most fertile fields in the colonies, in the winter after a rich harvest. As the surgeon Albigence Waldo described in his justly famous journal:

> Poor food—hard lodging—Cold Weather—fatigue—Nasty Cloaths—nasty Cookery—Vomit half my time—smoak'd out my senses—the Devil's in't—I can't Endure it. . . . There comes a Soldier, his bare feet are seen thro' his worn out Shoes, his legs nearly naked from the tatter'd remains of an only pair of stockings, his Breeches not sufficient to cover his nakedness, his Shirt hanging in Strings, his hair dishevell'd, his face meagre; his whole appearance pictures a person forsaken and discouraged. He comes, and crys with an air of wretchedness and despair, I am Sick, my feet lame, my legs are sore, my body cover'd with this tormenting Itch—my Cloaths are worn out, my Constitution is broken, my former Activity is exhausted by fatigue, hunger and Cold, I fail fast I shall soon be no more! and all the reward I shall get will be— "Poor Will is dead."

Officers' conditions at Valley Forge were far better than the men's. Washington was not the only general to have his wife in camp, and as the historian Charles Royster has written, the temptation to feel sorry for officers wrapped in blankets for lack of overcoats must be balanced by the picture of them among men without even blankets. Still, no creature comfort could insulate Washington from the human tragedy he saw around him every day, for which he was given the blame and felt the responsibility. "The General is . . . well worn with fatigue and anxiety," Martha wrote to a friend. "I never knew him to be so anxious as now."

Washington's allies made matters worse by loyally passing on every criticism they heard. Dr. James Craik, who was with Washington during his earliest campaign of the French and Indian War and would be beside him at his deathbed, wrote in the first week of January 1778 to warn him of "secret enemies . . . base and villainous men [who] are endeavoring to lessen you in the minds of the people and taking underhanded methods to traduce your character." Craik named names and said he had multiple sources who testified that "the new board of war is composed of such leading men as will throw such obstacles and difficulties in your way as to force you to resign." Patrick Henry, governor of Virginia, forwarded an anonymous letter he had received and warned Washington, "there may possibly be some scheme or party forming to your prejudice." Henry said he hoped he wasn't causing alarm unnecessarily; he had no idea whose handwriting it was, he said, adding that it may have been written by someone of no importance. The letter read in part:

> The northern army [under Gates] has shown us what Americans are capable of doing with a general at their head. The spirit of the southern army is no ways inferior to the spirit of the northern. A Gates, a Lee or a Conway would in a few weeks render them an irresistible body of men.

Washington was stricken when he recognized, as perhaps Henry had as well, the handwriting of Dr. Benjamin Rush, whom he had thought to be a friend.

At about the same time an anonymous memo, "Thoughts of a Freeman," was found on stairs in the building where Congress met. Addressed to all members of Congress and sent to Washington by then president Henry Laurens, it was a catalogue of Washington's errors and faults to date. A small sampling of its allegations:

> That the proper methods of attacking conquering and beating the enemy have never as yet been adopted by the commander in c-f. That more men will die this winter than it would have cost lives to have conquered the enemy last summer and fall. That it is better to die honorably in the field than in a stinking hospital. . . . That the

people of America have been guilty of idolatry by making a man their god—and that the god of heaven and earth will convince them by woeful experience that he is only a man.

Among the more transparent efforts by the new Board of War to restrict Washington's power was Lafayette's independent command. Lafayette knew that, of course, and attempted to mitigate the slight, but his efforts were ineffective and seem in retrospect to have been half-hearted. He declared that he would refuse to lead the expedition if Conway had any part in it, but he backed down when the board ignored the threat. He successfully insisted that his command be under the authority of the commander in chief, but later he reported to the board and to Congress directly, occasionally apologizing to Washington before doing so again. He recorded proudly in his memoirs that before he left on the expedition, at a dinner of Gates and his supporters, he forced them to drink an embarrassed toast to Washington, but one has to wonder what he did not write about his dealings with Gates and Congress.

In any case, the expedition was doomed; and Lafayette was fortunate that that became obvious so quickly, because if it had not been aborted it would have become a disaster. After a tough winter journey from Valley Forge to Albany that wore down even Lafayette's irrepressible spirits ("I go on very slowly sometimes pierced by rain, sometimes covered with snow. . . . I am angry against the roads, against my horse, against everything"), neither the supplies nor the men nor the money that had been promised were at the staging point, and the season was too advanced to wait for them. Gates's aide-de-camp Robert Troup said the fault was Lafayette's own and suggested he be sent back to Washington's army (where "the blunders of his youth & inexperience will pass as maneuvers"), but in fact four generals warned him against undertaking the expedition as it was then provisioned. Even Conway advised against it.

The aftermath of this debacle was not Lafayette's finest hour. "Men will have the right to laugh at me," he fumed to Henry Laurens after calling off the operation. "No, sir, this expedition will certainly reflect a little upon my reputation . . . but it will reflect much more upon the authors of such blunders. I'll publish the whole history. I'll publish my instructions *with notes* through the world, and I'll loose [*sic*] rather the honor of twenty

Gates's and twenty boards of war than let my own reputation be hurt in the least thing." He pleads with Laurens to send him anything written about this embarrassment in the newspapers. He also suggests that perhaps if Congress were to give him something glorious to do—say, for example, the command of a full-scale assault on New York—he might be persuaded *not* to return with all his fellow French officers to France, where to protect his reputation he would "go and laugh [about] the new American ministry of war. . . . I am reduced to wish to have never put the foot in America."

Such histrionics make his appeals for support to Washington in this "distressing, ridiculous, foolish, and indeed nameless situation" especially unpleasant to witness. "I confess, my dear general, that I find myself of very quick feelings whenever my reputation and glory are concerned in anything. It is very hard indeed that such a part of my happiness . . . would depend upon the schemes of some fools." Perhaps remembering his own rage in similar circumstances and at the same age, Washington wrote back to "dispel those fears respecting your reputation, which are excited only by an uncommon degree of sensibility. . . . [I]t will be no disadvantage to you to have it known in Europe that you had received so manifest a proof of the good opinion and confidence of Congress as an important detached command—and I am persuaded that everyone will applaud your prudence. . . . However sensibly your ardour for glory may make you feel this disappointment, you may be assured that your character stands as fair as ever it did, and that no new enterprise is necessary to wipe off this imaginary stain." That "new enterprise" was the idea of an assault on New York, which Lafayette had suggested in his letters to Washington as well as Laurens as a proper consolation for him. For a variety of overwhelmingly sensible reasons, however, Washington deemed the idea "unadvisable in our present circumstances. . . ."

Lafayette's sense of humiliation was compounded by a report that he was going to be recalled to Valley Forge and that Conway would inherit the Northern Army. "I am very far from making complaints," he wrote Laurens, "but as I hope Congress returns me some of the warm attachment I have showed for their country, they will permit and approve my going to France immediately. . . . Don't believe, Sir, that I speak here out of any particular ambition of supreme command [but] after a chief command is given to one of my officers when I am directed to repair to the main army. . . . [h]ow do you think such a treatment will look? How can I agree to it?" He had no choice (though Congress did agree not to give Conway the Northern Army). On March 20, a month after arriving in Albany, Lafayette was recalled to the main army by Washington on the order of Congress.

Fortunately, perhaps as much for Lafayette as for Washington and certainly for their relationship, the so-called Conway Cabal had almost run its course by then. For all the backstage angling, Gates had never mounted a serious threat to Washington, whose officers grew increasingly furious at the denigration of their commander in chief; and the perfidy of Gates's allies finally took its rightful toll on them. The next time Conway threatened to hand in his resignation, it was accepted. One of General Greene's aides suggested that a good way to put an end to all the sniping would be "a few ounces of gunpowder diffused through proper channels," and some of Washington's men seemed to be taking his advice. A civilian member of the Board of War found himself being stalked menacingly by the legendary and very large rifleman Daniel Morgan, and General John Cadwalader finally called out Conway and put a musket round through his mouth. Standing over him, Cadwalader said, "I have stopped the damned rascal's lying anyway."

Conway eventually recovered, and before leaving for France he wrote a letter of apology to Washington. Mifflin began calling Washington, much to general amusement, "the best friend he ever had in his life." At length Washington told Gates he would let the whole matter drop "as far as future events will permit." From then on, those who worried about Washington becoming too powerful would simply have to keep worrying. Although his opponents would continue to contend and complain to the end of the war and beyond, his position as commander in chief was never again remotely assailable.

The transatlantic news cycle of the late eighteenth century was at least three months—six weeks one way and six weeks back. So it was that the fortunes of war in late 1777 were unknown in France until December of that year and that the world-changing results of that news would not reach America until spring was coming to Valley Forge.

On the morning of December 4, 1777, the American commissioners were meeting with Beaumarchais at their headquarters outside Paris when, just before noon, the sound of hoofbeats brought them all out to the courtyard. The rider was a messenger from America whom John Paul Jones had deposited at Nantes the day before and who had been riding hard ever since. By the rider's obvious excitement, Franklin assumed he was there to tell them that Philadelphia had fallen to the British, which they had already heard. No, the rider said, "I have bigger news than that—General Burgoyne and his whole army are prisoners!"

Ecstatic over a victory he knew would have been impossible without the arms he had supplied to Washington's army, Beaumarchais rushed off to Paris with the news. In his excitement, he pushed his driver so hard that his carriage overturned, leaving Beaumarchais with a broken arm and cuts all over his hands and face from broken glass. Franklin, who was equally thrilled but more composed, wrote a story for the newspapers:

> Mail arrived from Philadelphia at Dr. Franklin's house in Passy [saying that on] October 14th General Burgoyne was forced to lay down his arms, 9200 men killed or taken prisoner. . . . General Howe is in Philadelphia, where he is imprisoned. All communication with his fleet is cut off.

He was more careful with his facts when he wrote to Versailles, which two days later replied to this news with a letter on the gilded stationery that Louis XVI used for his private correspondence. It was an invitation to the Americans to resubmit their request for treaties of friendship and commerce, which of course meant that the long-sought French alliance was as good as fact.

Beaumarchais's accident got more play than Franklin's press release or the colonists' victory over Burgoyne. Among his other jobs, Vergennes supervised the censors who supervised the French press, and he was not ready to upset the British ambassador with stories crowing about an American victory. But he was almost ready. Not knowing how fast events were moving along without him, Beaumarchais began to pummel Vergennes with memos; and the degree to which Vergennes listened to him is suggested by two letters dated December 11. Beaumarchais to Vergennes: ". . . [T]he first who recognizes American independence will alone gather from it all the fruits." Vergennes to his ambassador in Spain: "The power that will first recognize the independence of the Americans will be the one that will reap the fruits of this war." In any case, everyone—Vergennes, the American commissioners, the king, and Beaumarchais—was finally in agreement. The treaties, which were negotiated and signed in only two months, called for France to recognize American independence, for the two nations to become favored trading partners, and for neither country, in the event of war between France and England, to make a separate peace. At the same time, France renounced any claim to Canada, and America promised to defend French territories in the West Indies. The treaty terms were exceedingly generous on the part of France, in the interest, Louis insisted with all apparent sincerity, of a true and lasting alliance.

The treaties were to be kept secret until ratified by Congress, but by the second week in March it became apparent that such a long wait was inexpedient, so the French ambassador delivered to the British Foreign Office a copy of the treaties, which of course they had already seen and which they could now denounce as the de facto declaration of war that they were. At that, both countries withdrew their ambassadors, and a week later Franklin was formally presented at court as the representative of the "United Provinces of North America." Despite some argument on the point with more hardheaded colleagues, Franklin always chose to see France's alliance with America as a reflection of Louis's principles and friendship for America. Some of his American colleagues, including John Adams, found this notion credulous, but Franklin's warm expressions of gratitude endeared him to the court and to the French. At his presentation, with his usual talent for the grand gesture but also with tears in his eyes, Franklin said to Louis, "If all monarchies were governed by the principles which are in your heart, Sire, republics would never be formed."

VIII

The Beauty of a Draw

I N THE SIX WEEKS that elapsed before news of the alliance reached Washington, another kind of miracle was taking place at Valley Forge. Out of the depths of despair, just as spring was breaking through the snow, came an army. The miracle was man-made, and the man who made it was the Baron Friedrich Wilhelm August Heinrich Ferdinand von Steuben. He had adopted these names for their sonority, and he had been made a baron by the prince of Hohenzollern-Hechninger just before both of them fled the country as bankrupts. In the interest of a recommendation from Silas Deane and a loan from Beaumarchais, von Steuben also gave himself a fictional promotion from his rank of captain in the army of Frederick the Great to lieutenant general. He came over with one of the last shipments of Beaumarchais's "secret" aid, in February 1778, and when he offered himself as a volunteer, Washington gave him the job, without the title, that Conway had been given: to train his troops to the standards of a European army.

Washington always said that the book from which he learned most about training an army was *Instructions to His Generals* by Frederick the Great, the ultimate handbook for the management of an army with officer-aristocrats. In such an army, soldiers were cannon fodder. Frederick considered that for him as for other monarchs, "hardworking people" should be "the apple of one's eye," to be kept at their commerce and industry in wartime. Soldiers would therefore have to be mercenaries, criminals, and ne'er-do-wells. Officers were expected to work for the love of glory and loyalty to the king, but their men were not to think about the cause they were fighting for, or anything else, because thinking was the road to insubordination. Maintaining sharp social distinctions was considered not only appropriate but also necessary for an army whose men would go to battle only if they feared their officers more than they feared the enemy. Not surprisingly, then, Frederick's manual begins with fourteen rules for preventing desertion: "By not encamping too near a wood . . . calling the roll frequently . . . doubling the cavalry posts at dusk . . . avoiding night marches," and so on. Frederick's famous battle cry to his troops was the altogether unvarnished, "Dogs! Would you live forever?"

From the beginning of the war, Washington adopted Frederick's attitude both toward his officer corps and toward the rank and file. "A coward," he said, "when taught to believe that if he breaks his ranks [he] will be punished with death by his own party, will take his chance against the enemy." Even his most inspiring orders before battle almost always included the warning that cowards would be shot. But Washington's army, officers and men alike, proved stubbornly resistant to Frederick's brand of regimentation.

What Steuben found when he arrived at Valley Forge was an army in which there was "no regular formation. . . . Each colonel had a system of his own. . . . No captain kept a book. Accounts were never furnished or required. . . . When I asked a colonel the strength of his regiment, the usual reply was 'Something between two and three hundred men.'" The men's muskets were covered with rust, many of them could not even be fired, and many more had no bayonets. "The American soldier, never having used this arm, had no faith in it, and never used it but to roast his beefsteak"—except that there was no beefsteak. "The men were literally naked, some of them in the fullest sense of the word. The officers who had coats had them of every color and make. I saw officers, at a grand parade at Valley Forge, mounting guard in a sort of dressing-gown. . . . With regard to their military discipline, I may safely say no such thing existed."

Steuben wrote a manual for the Continental Army while he was at Valley Forge, which came to be known as the Blue Book. Steuben proudly called his *Regulations for the Order and Discipline of the Troops of the United States* "my rhapsody," and the strangest recurrent theme in it, one that would no doubt have surprised even Steuben when he first landed in

America, was love: love of the soldier for his fellow soldier, love of the officer for his men, love of country, and love of his nation's ideals. Steuben had not been taught to train soldiers this way, of course—he was a creature of Frederick's army—but he obviously intuited before many Continental officers that a people's army, a force of citizen-soldiers fighting for freedom from oppression by a monarch or anyone else, would be motivated most powerfully not by fear but, as he put it, by "love and confidence"—love of their cause, confidence in their officers and in themselves. Punishment for most offenses was to be "mild," the military equivalent of staying after school, and the officers were to be "patient" with their men in the interest of inspiring their respect and loyalty. "The genius of this nation," Steuben explained in a letter to the French minister of war, "is not in the least to be compared with that of the Prussians, Austrians, or French. You say to your soldier, 'Do this,' and he does it; but I am obliged to say, 'This is the reason why you ought to do that,' and then he does it."

Before Steuben, the Southern officers in particular had disdained parade-ground duty, thinking it below the work of "gentlemen." After the example of Steuben—certifiably a gentlemen, after all, as an officer of the Holy Roman Empire of the German Nation, but one who turned up on the parade ground at dawn before everyone else—officers learned the importance of drill, and the effect their attention to it would have on the performance of their men. When Washington first arrived at Cambridge, he was shocked at the egalitarian behavior of New England officers and men: they actually fraternized! "[O]fficers of the Massachusetts part of the Army," he wrote in disbelief to a fellow Virginian, "are *nearly* of the same kidney with the Privates." He had moved aggressively to put a stop to that. Now, though, under Steuben's influence, Washington's attitude toward his men began to soften, and while there was still insubordination, perhaps more than there would have been otherwise, there was also a new pride in the ranks, a sense of dignity. The change in Washington was reflected in a new policy announced six weeks after Steuben began his training: Henceforth, Washington declared, officers would ride when their men marched only when absolutely necessary, it being important for every officer to "share the fatigue as well as danger to which his men are exposed." Fortunately for his officers and himself, Washington came to feel this way only when spring—and food—had come to Valley Forge.

Steuben did not train the Continental Army in every Prussian drill and maneuver—"I should have been pelted had I attempted it, and should inevitably have failed"—but his simplified system was good enough for the American army for eighty-five years, until the Civil War, and many procedures and terms of the Blue Book were still in use more than two centuries later. Motivating soldiers through affection and idealism had important practical advantages. With less danger of desertion, the Continental forces could be broken into the smaller units necessary for guerrilla fighting. Steuben's methods also encouraged longer enlistments. During inspections, one of his instructors would ask each man his term of enlistment. When the term was limited, he would continue his usual inspection, "but to every soldier who exclaimed when called upon by name, 'for the war!' he respectfully bowed, and raising his hat said, 'you, Sir, are a gentleman I perceive, I am happy to make an acquaintance with you.'"

A *soldier* and a gentleman? This was a new concept for a new kind of military, an army with which George Washington, for one, was entirely unfamiliar. One night at Valley Forge, when spring and a new quartermaster had finally brought provisions to camp, Steuben hosted a dinner. The only qualification for attendance was that a man could not own a whole pair of breeches. "The guests clubbed their rations," as one of the baron's French attachés put it, "and we feasted sumptuously on tough beef steaks and potatoes, with hickory nuts for our dessert. In lieu of wine we had some kind of spirits, with which we made salamanders; that is to say: after filling our glasses we set the liquor on fire and drank it up, flame and all. Such a set of ragged and the same time merry fellows were never brought together. The baron loved to speak of that dinner, and of his *sans-culottes*, as he called us . . . at a time when it could not be foreseen that the name which honored the followers of Washington would afterward be assumed by the satellites of Marat and Robespierre."

When Washington broke the still unofficial news to his officers that France had signed a formal treaty of alliance and recognized the independence of the "United Provinces of North America," Lafayette grabbed him and kissed him on both cheeks, which may have been a first for him, though perhaps not an unwelcome one: witnesses said Washington was himself nearly crying for joy. The general elation was somewhat constrained for the moment by the fact that the news was unconfirmed; and, in a cruel accident of timing, Lafayette's celebration ended later the same day, when he received a letter from Adrienne telling him that their daughter Henriette had died. Lafayette's letters are quite unusual for his time, not only in their over-the-top ebullience and exaggeration ("I have had no news of anyone for millions of centuries") but also in their open affection, particularly for "my poor little Henriette; kiss her a thousand times for me, talk to her of me; but do not tell her all the ill of me that I deserve. . . . I am sure I will find my poor little Henriette very gentle and attractive when I return. . . . My daughter will always be, I hope, the best friend I have. I shall want to be a father only in the sense of loving her." In every one of his letters home so far, he had spoken in such loving terms of Henriette, and because his letters from Adrienne had been intercepted and otherwise delayed, he had been saying such things for eight months after she died. Several days after receiving the news of her death, official notice arrived at camp that his dream had come true— treaties of alliance had in fact been ratified—but Lafayette could celebrate only halfheartedly at the elaborate ceremony Washington organized to mark the occasion.

At nine o'clock on Wednesday, May 6, 1778, a cannon shot at Valley Forge called the men to their brigades, where they were read a summary of the treaties and given a sermon by their chaplain. Another roar of cannon sounded at ten thirty, calling the men to arms. Washington specified that and everything to follow in that day's General Orders, no doubt aided in the task by the officer who was now known simply as "the Baron" and who was the same day officially given the title of Inspector General in the Continental Army. Washington could never have issued orders for such precise parade-ground maneuvers three months before.

> The Brigade Inspectors will . . . inspect their Dress and Arms, form the Battalions according to instructions given them and announce to the Commanding Officers of Brigades that the Battalions are formed. The Brigadiers or Commandants will then appoint the Field Officers to command the Battalions, after which each Battalion will be ordered to load and ground their Arms. At half after

eleven a second Cannon will be fired as a signal for the march upon which the several Brigades will begin their march by wheeling to the right by Platoons and proceed by the nearest way to the left of their ground in the new Position; this will be pointed out by the Brigade Inspectors.

What followed was a *feu de joie* (literally, "fire of joy"), which began when Washington's guard fired their muskets. One by one, thirteen cannon were fired, followed by a running fire of muskets, one quickly following another, all the way around the lines. Another cannon shot signaled the first huzzah, "Long Live the King of France!" Then all the guns were reloaded, another round of rapid fire filled Valley Forge, and then another, followed by "Long live the friendly European Powers!" Finally guns were reloaded for one more rapid-fire salute, this one dedicated "To the American States!" Through it all, John Laurens wrote to his father, Washington "wore a countenance of uncommon delight."

Afterward, the men were dismissed with "an allowance of brandy," and there was a "cold collation" for the officers, who marched to it arm-in-arm, thirteen abreast. "Fat meat, strong wine, and other liquors" were served, according to Kalb, who wrote the comte de Broglie all about it. In another account of the day, which he sent to his wife, Kalb clearly demonstrated that Washington had won him over. "It was a fine day for us and a great day for Washington," he wrote. "Let me say that no one could be more worthy of this good fortune. His integrity, humanity, and love for the just cause of his country . . . receive and merit the veneration of all men." When Washington took his leave, according to another officer, "there was a universal clap, with loud huzzas, which continued till he had proceeded a quarter of a mile, during which time there were a thousand hats tossed in the air. His Excellency turned round with his retinue and huzzaed several times."

The *Pennsylvania Gazette* based its coverage of the event on an anonymous letter: "We were favored with a day as serene and delightful as if it had been commanded for the purpose. . . . The exact order in which the columns marched to their ground—the celerity and precision with which the lines were formed—the regularity of the fire—the pillars of fleecy smoke ascending in rapid succession—the continued sound of the musketry, not unlike the rolling of distant thunder—the martial appearance of the troops—[all] conspired to exhibit a magnificent scene of joy, worthy of the great occasion." The Continental Army had never put on—had never seen—a military spectacle quite like it, and the *Gazette* report ended, appropriately, with a tribute to the man responsible: "For the military part of our entertainment, we are much indebted to Baron de Steuben, Inspector General of the American Army."

After he had given Steuben the money and the transatlantic passage to join the American army, Beaumarchais wrote to his aide Thomas Francey, who was on the same ship, that he was "proud to put a man of honor in his true place." In December 1778, on a bit longer than usual news cycle, Beaumarchais wrote Francey, "I hear that [Steuben] is the inspector general of all the American troops. Bravo!"

When George III heard about the French alliance with his American colonies, he wrote his war minister that it would be "a joke to think of keeping Pennsylvania, for we must form from the army now in America a corps sufficient to attack the French islands." (Beaumarchais had at least had that right.) Accordingly, orders were drawn up directing that five thousand of the British troops in America be sent to the Caribbean, and three thousand more be devoted to defending control of the Floridas; the rest of the British army was to be withdrawn to New York to assume a defensive posture, wreaking revenge along the coastline for privateering, which had already cost them several hundred British ships. If New York could not be held, the British fleet and army were to consolidate in Newport, and if that fell they should move to Halifax. The orders included news that a commission empowered to negotiate for terms of peace with the colonies was on its way. "I now look upon the contest as at an end," Howe's secretary wrote when these orders were received. "Nothing remains for [the king] but to attempt a reconciliation with what I may now venture to call the United States of America. . . . O Thou righteous God, where will all this villainy end?"

At a council of war two days after the *feu de joie*, Washington's generals agreed to defer offensive plans for the coming campaign until they could get some sense of Britain's next move. For the moment, the British seemed quite content to stay in Philadelphia, where their officers had spent a most enjoyable winter, being entertained in Philadelphia's best parlors and warmed by its best wine and most beautiful women. (Howe was an inveterate playboy, a heavy gambler, and an amiable if not terribly aggressive commander in chief.) Within ten days of Washington's war council, convincing intelligence suggested that the British were preparing to move from Philadelphia, though their strategy and destination remained unclear. Some thought they could be planning to spread their occupation deeper into Pennsylvania, if only to send Congress running again; others thought they might try once more for control of the Hudson River. On May 18, to reconnoiter and to harass whatever early movements they might undertake, Washington sent out Lafayette with a party of twenty-two hundred troops, placing him under strict instructions to avoid unnecessary risk and specifically warning him to keep moving his camp, not to settle in any one place. "You will remember, that your detachment is a very valuable one, and that any accident happening to it would be a very severe blow to this army."

At three o'clock the same afternoon, a lavish party began at a British fortification on the Delaware just outside Philadelphia. Howe had just been recalled to answer for his failure to attack Washington at Valley Forge and elsewhere; and after a winter like the last one his officers, very sorry to see him go, decided to see him off with an appropriately elaborate fête they called a *Mischianza*, a "variety of entertainments . . . to exhibit a something before unknown to the New World, perhaps to the Old." Twenty-two of Howe's officers contributed more than £3,000 for the occasion, which began when the assembled guests were "embarked in flat-boats and passed down the Delaware River with musical accompaniment." They disembarked at the expropriated estate of a rebel exile and filed through lines of grenadiers toward a triumphal arch guarded by two girls with swords drawn. Beyond were fourteen young women in turbans and long white dresses, wearing variously colored sashes: some pink with silver spangles, others white with gold. The ones with pink and silver were known as the Ladies of the Blended Rose, the others as Ladies of the Burning Mountain. What followed was a "joust" with fourteen corresponding Knights, wherein, as the evening's impresario, Captain John Andre, described it, the Knights of the Blended Rose and those of the Burning

Mountain would vie to defend the honor and unparalleled excellence of their respective ladies "by the ancient laws of chivalry." After the "joust," there were "cooling liquors."

That night, Lafayette may have been close enough to see some of the handiwork of Captain John Montresor, a long and elaborate display of fireworks. His scouts could even have got close enough to hear the music at the ball that followed, which, after a midnight supper, broke up at four o'clock in the morning. Had Lafayette been struck by such frivolity undertaken by men supposedly at war, he would not have been alone. One British artillery major was quoted as saying, "The Knights of the Burning Mountain are tomfools, and the Knights of the Blended Rose are damned fools!"

As the British officers and their ladies recovered from the *Mischianza* next day, word came that Lafayette and a sizable force had established a camp close by (the one thing Washington had told Lafayette not to do). Howe could not believe his good luck. That evening, after telling the ladies to come back the next day for dinner with the marquis, he sent out more than five thousand men; and after a night's rest, Howe himself followed at the head of almost six thousand more. His brother, Admiral Richard Howe, came along to enjoy the show, as did his replacement, Sir Henry Clinton. Howe must have been salivating at the prospect: What could be better to cap his career and silence his critics than to bring home the man whose military glory had done so much to consecrate and who himself symbolized the Franco-American alliance?

Though Lafayette had ignored Washington's advice by establishing a stationary camp, he had disposed his men well to protect it—if only the six hundred militia under General James Potter had actually protected his left flank as they were assigned to do. Why they bungled that job remains unclear; but because they did, only a series of accidents and missteps on the part of the British that day prevented Lafayette from losing his entire force and becoming a prisoner of war or a corpse, in either instance a footnote in history. Lafayette was very lucky to face an indecisive British general who waited for reinforcements that were late arriving; but he also showed remarkable cunning, throwing out his men in small detachments made to look like the heads of columns, and making his snipers move between shots to create the appearance of a larger force, while his army made its way to safety. Though it should not have been necessary, Lafayette made good his escape with great agility and without casualties, and Howe sailed back to England without his prize.

Not long after that, the peace commissioners from George III arrived in Philadelphia, and almost immediately Washington began to hear rumors that the British were preparing to evacuate the city. In fact, Clinton had been planning to do so for weeks, because those were his instructions and because he knew that a French fleet was on its way which, when it arrived, could bottle up his own fleet in Chesapeake Bay. For Washington, the clinching intelligence came on June 16, when a spy told him that the commissioners had asked for all their laundry to be returned to them immediately, clean or not.

In the early morning of June 18 the British "didn't leave—they vanished" from Philadelphia. The fleet, filled with stores and troops, sailed for New York, and the army, now led by Clinton and trailing fifteen hundred wagons and hundreds of Tory exiles, began the march across New Jersey to join them. In a few days Washington had an advance force of five thousand troops behind them, with Lafayette in command.

His enthusiasm rather than his seniority recommended him for the post. It had been declined by General Charles Lee, who was not only the most senior but arguably the most experienced officer in the American service, one who might have been given command of the entire Continental Army except for the fact that he was a native of Britain and had been a high British army officer. Released in a POW exchange only a few weeks before this, Lee had been captured in December 1776 and had spent sixteen months in a not terribly confining prison. He was held in the council chamber at New York's City Hall, "one of the genteelest public rooms in the city," where he was daily provided candles and firewood by his "captors." Each night, at British army expense, a nearby tavern delivered dinner for himself and six guests of his choosing, along with suitable wines and liquors. No one on the American side knew at the time that he had advised Howe on a strategy for winning the war; only in 1857 was a document labeled "Mr. Lee's Plan, 29 March, 1777" found among Howe's private papers. Nor did anyone make much of the fact that when he was released to Valley Forge and Washington gave him the new oath of loyalty, in which he had to swear to "support, maintain and defend the said United States against King George the Third, his heirs and successors," he twice withdrew his hand from the Bible. Asked why, he joked that while he did not mind giving up George III, he was not sure about the Prince of Wales, and everyone laughed. Washington also did not know that Lee had begun almost immediately upon his release to criticize the commander in chief behind his back, saying he was "weak . . . ruining the whole cause . . . ignorant."

In every war council he attended after arriving at Valley Forge, Lee advised extreme caution, arguing from the vast superiority of British troops and the danger of bringing on an all-out battle; and his opinion carried weight because of his experience and seniority. But by June 24, it was clear from Clinton's route that his army was going to spread itself out along a single road, burdened by all his civilians and a baggage train that alone was twelve miles long, which left his rear plainly vulnerable to attack. Arguing still that "it would be the most criminal madness to hazard a general action at this time," Lee narrowly carried a close vote of the war council, a meeting that Hamilton said "would have done honor to the most honorable society of midwives, and to them only." Afterward several of the officers who had been at the council—Steuben, Greene, Hamilton, and Lafayette—agreed that its conclusion was wrong: They should strike immediately and with force. Lafayette spoke for all of them in a letter to Washington. "I would lay my fortune," he said, that if a sizable detachment were sent forward to attack, "some good effect and no harm shall arise of it. . . . I saw my dear General that you were rather inclined to follow the same path I so ardently wish for, and I wish a council of war would never have been called." Beyond that, he gave Washington his firm opinion that such councils were fundamentally flawed as a way of making tactical decisions. "Such a council is a school of logic [that] will never be a means of doing what is consistent with the good of the service, the situation at hand, or in fact the authority of the commander-in-chief."

Lafayette was right about Washington's inclination: He responded to his generals' appeals by ordering out almost three thousand men, then another thousand, and then another. He did Lee the courtesy of asking if he wanted to command the force, and when Lee demurred gave the command to Lafayette.

Lee went back to Washington's tent later to say he had changed his mind, but when Washington brought up Lee's doubts about the mission those doubts returned, and Lee once more agreed to step aside. Not long after that Lee returned and "recanted again," Hamilton recalled, "and became very importunate." At that, Washington "grew tired of such fickle behavior and ordered the marquis to proceed." Lafayette, of course, was thrilled—this was the largest army he had ever commanded—and his aide Dr. James McHenry recorded in his diary for June 25: "The young Frenchman . . . moves toward the enemy . . . in raptures with his command and burning to distinguish himself." Hamilton went along as Washington's liaison officer.

Lee was not finished. Next day, one of his aides brought Washington a letter in which Lee said if he were not given the command of so large and important a force he would be "disgraced." This was an appeal too great for Washington or even Lafayette to ignore, and it was followed by a remarkable military kabuki carried out in correspondence on the eve of battle. Lee had already gone to Lafayette in person to, as he put it, "place my fortune and my honor in your hands." The next day, Lafayette wrote to Washington:

> [I]f it is believed necessary or useful to the good of the service and the honour of General Lee . . . I will cheerfully obey and serve him, not only out of duty, but out of what I owe to that gentleman's character.

In reply, Washington thanked him for his courtesy and laid out for him an elaborate compromise.

> At the same time that I felt for General Lee's distress of mind, I have had an eye to your wishes and the delicacy of your situation; and have, therefore, obtained a promise from him, that when he gives you notice of his approach and command, he will request you to prosecute any plan you may have already concerted for the purpose of attacking, or otherwise annoying the enemy; this is the only expedient I could think of to answer the views of both. . . .

On June 26, when Washington was marching the entire Continental Army through thunderstorms and hundred-degree heat to be in position to support the advance force—a day when the fifteen households around

Monmouth Court House felt sufficiently threatened to bundle up their belongings and leave for the duration, along with the sheriff and the prisoners in his jail—on this day, the commander in chief found time to write an even more detailed letter of understanding to General Lee: "Your uneasiness . . . fills me with concern, as it is not in my power fully to remove it without wounding the feelings of the Marquis de Lafayette. I have thought of an expedient. . . ."

Taking the time to think through such a problem of protocol under such conditions is remarkable enough, but especially so since Washington was changing command on the eve of battle in favor of a general who was plainly overwrought, who had never commanded an important battle in this war, and who did not believe in the mission. Furthermore, when it became clear on the 27th that the battle would take place the following morning, Washington gave Lee only the most general orders: simply to attack when the British began to move out of their encampment near Monmouth Court House—not whether the object of the attack was to capture the baggage train or to slow the redcoats' march, not even whether a harassment or a general action was intended. As Edward Lengel points out in his close study of Washington the general, he that day "abdicated much of his responsibility as commander-in-chief."

Given such a welter of indecision, the result was predictably chaotic. At the hour when Washington expected to hear the roar of cannon and the steady crack of musket fire, he heard only a few sparse shots, and as he rode toward what was supposed to be the battlefield, a fifer he found going in the opposite direction said the army was in full retreat. Incredulous, Washington had the man placed under arrest to stop the spread of such a demoralizing story. Nevertheless, as he rode on, more and more men passed him, and by the time he galloped up to General Lee, he was sputtering with rage. An eyewitness reported the exchange.

"My God, General Lee, what are you about?" Lee looked stunned. "Sir," he stuttered, "sir . . ." When he tried to explain, Washington silenced him with a wave of his hand and barked, "Go to the rear, sir." An officer said later that he actually heard Washington swearing.

Yes, sir, he swore on that day till the leaves shook on the trees. Charming! Delightful! Never have I enjoyed such swearing, before or since. Sir, on that memorable day, he swore like an angel from Heaven.

With so many units retreating at their own initiative, Lafayette did well just to keep his men together as they moved toward a more secure position.

Washington was about to turn the army around to chase the British, who he assumed would have resumed their march, when an aide rode up to tell him the British were coming toward him and were only fifteen minutes away. Anticipating an attack on his rear guard, Clinton had put picked troops there and determined to mount a counterattack. Instead of forming up for a march, therefore, Washington disposed his men to make a stand. As he did so, Hamilton recalled later, "I never saw the general to so much advantage. His coolness and firmness was admirable. . . . A general rout, dismay, and disgrace would have attended the whole army in any other hands but his." Characteristically, Lafayette was even more effusive: "General Washington seemed to arrest fortune with one glance. . . . His presence stopped the retreat. His graceful bearing on horseback, his calm and deportment which still retained a trace of displeasure . . . were all calculated to inspire the highest degree of enthusiasm. . . . I thought then as now that I had never beheld so superb a man."

This was the battle in which Washington reaped the first harvest of Steuben's training. As he wrote to Congress later, "the officers of the army . . . seemed to vie with each other in manifesting their zeal and bravery"; and the troops, "after they recovered from the first surprise occasioned by the retreat of the advanced corps, was such as could not be surpassed." They fought until nightfall, when Washington ordered his men to get some rest. The British had ended the day arrayed for battle, and Washington intended to attack them at first light. He slept among his men that night. Spreading his cloak under an apple tree, he talked with Lafayette about the bizarre behavior of General Lee* until they both fell asleep.

---

*A court-martial convicted Lee of disobeying orders in not attacking, of "misbehavior before the enemy" by leading a chaotic retreat, and of "disrespect to the Commander-in-chief" in letters he sent after the event. The sentence was that he be suspended from the army for one year. Virtually all who studied the case later concluded that the sentence was unjust: He had in fact launched an attack, and the retreat left the American

In the morning the British were gone, apparently having decided to cut their losses. The weather alone had taken an awful toll. Of the 72 Americans killed, 37 died from heatstroke, which accounted for perhaps 60 of Britain's 294 dead. Washington might have pushed his troops to march after the British that day, and as burdened and exhausted as they were he might have done a great deal of damage. But it was another hundred-degree day, his own men were as weary as the British, and draws were all he needed anyway.

Later that summer, with the British back in New York and his Continentals free to roam upstate New York, as well as New Jersey, Pennsylvania, and all New England, Washington wrote to Brigadier General Thomas Nelson from his old headquarters in White Plains: "It is not a little pleasing, nor less wonderful to contemplate, that after two years maneuvering and undergoing the strangest vicissitudes that perhaps ever attended any one contest since the creation, both armies are brought back to the very point they set out from. . . . The hand of Providence has been so conspicuous in all this that he must be worse than an infidel that lacks faith, and more than wicked that has not gratitude enough to acknowledge his obligations, but it will be time enough for me to turn preacher when my present appointment ceases. . . ."

---

army in a better position from which to defend itself. He was clearly guilty of "disrespect" for Washington, however; and when he was similarly obnoxious in a letter to Congress, he was dismissed outright. He spent his last three years spewing vituperation about Washington, and when he died in 1782, of lung disease, he requested burial away from any churchyard or other cemetery—"I have kept so much bad company while living that I do not choose to continue it when dead." His request unheeded, he was buried at Christ Church in Philadelphia.

IX

Showing Their Colors

AFTER THE BATTLE of Monmouth Court House, Lafayette was in one of those interstitial periods that always resulted in a wave of correspondence, much of it lobbying for promotions and commissions on behalf of his fellow Frenchmen. On July 6, 1778, he sent three such letters of recommendation to the president of Congress, "one I could not refuse to Major Du Bois, the second in behalf of the [Marquis de] Vienne, the third for . . . the worthy Mr. Touzard." Before these three were letters for a Mr. de Lesser, Mr. Capitaine, chevaliers de Fayolles and de Cambray, Mr. de Noirmont, Colonels Failly and Armand, Messers. de Luce, de Second, de Valfort, and so on, and so on. Lafayette sent dozens of such requests, repeated as necessary, to Henry Laurens, other friends in Congress, and Washington, who was perhaps his least receptive audience. Having recently received several of them, Washington wrote a friend in Congress that he was at the end of his patience with "the appointment of so many Foreign officers of high rank. . . . Men, who in the first instance tell you that they wish for nothing more than the honour of serving in so glorious a cause, as Volunteers—The next day solicit Rank without pay— the day following want money advanced them—and in the course of a Week want further promotion and are not satisfied with anything you can do for them." Like all the recipients of Lafayette's recommendations, Washington wished they would stop. He wrote sympathetically to Henry Laurens, on whose desk Lafayette's letters usually ended up: "His Countrymen soon find access to his heart, and he is but too apt afterwards to

interest himself in their behalf. . . . I am sure you have been severely punished by their importunities as well as myself."

The arrival of the French fleet on July 9 at least arrested the flow of
mail. It did not do much else. In command of its twelve ships of the line
and fourteen frigates was comte Charles-Henri-Théodat d'Estaing, who
spoke no English but had the perfect interlocutor in Lafayette, a fellow
Auvergnat and a relative by marriage. His arrival stirred Lafayette to a
high pitch of patriotic and anti-British fervor: "May you defeat them, sink
them to the bottom, lay them *as low as they have been insolent;* may you
begin the great work of their destruction by which we shall trample upon
their nation; may you prove to them at their expense what a Frenchman,
and a Frenchman from Auvergne, can do. . . ." Unfortunately, however, the
fleet was of little use that campaign season; and if working with d'Estaing
and his own service again brought Lafayette a longed-for taste of home, it
also provided him an unwelcome reminder of how very far away from
home he was.

Historians have not been kind to d'Estaing, but he was burdened by a
command that was problematical from the start. An army general, he had
been named a vice admiral for the occasion, but his naval officers always
called him "General" and never gave him their complete confidence. He
was also cursed by bad intelligence, bad timing, and, bad luck. After a
crossing that had taken nearly three months, he arrived very short of fresh
water and with a scurvy-ridden crew, only to discover that his warships
drew too much water to make it over the bar outside New York Harbor,
making an attack on the greatest part of the British fleet impossible.

Washington and d'Estaing agreed instead to mount an assault on the
British in Newport. The general on the spot, John Sullivan, was ordered to
call up as many militia as he could, and Lafayette was sent to Rhode Island
with two thousand Continentals—which, after another contortion of protocol, Washington then split with the more senior General Nathanael
Greene, a native of Rhode Island. Lafayette readily agreed, because by then
d'Estaing had suggested a command for him whose glory went beyond any
number of troops: He proposed that Lafayette head an American detachment to join his infantrymen in a combined Franco-American force. At
the thought of serving as a general officer among French troops,
Lafayette's heart leaped up. He had already written excitedly about the

idea to Washington before he heard Greene would be taking half his troops. Washington was plainly relieved at Lafayette's response to that. "I . . . was a little uneasy lest you should conceive, that it was intended to lessen your command," he wrote, congratulating him on the prospect of a joint French-American command. "I am persuaded that the supporters of each [France and America] will be emulous to acquire honor & promote your glory upon this occasion."

In the context of "glory," Washington's letter continued with the awkward request that Lafayette find out what Marie-Antoinette had said about him, deflecting any suspicion that he would be interested in the answer himself by saying that if the story were true it would reflect well on his wife:

> Apropos, can you, my dear Marquis, through the medium of your lovely lady (if she is at the court of Versailles) or by any other indirect means, discover whether there is any truth in the information . . . that your amiable Queen had honored Mrs. Washington with an elegant testimonial of her approbation of my conduct. . . . [A]lthough it was too great an honor to be expected, I could not forbear giving credence to the report. . . .

Six weeks later, Lafayette replied that none of his officers knew anything about it, which seems to have slightly annoyed Washington ("The information, my dear Marquis . . . was not, I am persuaded, to be had through the channel of the officers of the French fleet, but by application to your fair lady"), but by then both men had much bigger problems to worry about: The French-American alliance was dangerously close to falling apart.

In the delicate negotiations between Sullivan and d'Estaing over plans for the assault, Lafayette was supposed to represent the American position, but he agreed less often with the American general than the French one and represented no interests better than his own. Even his comrade John Laurens said later "his private views withdrew his attention wholly from the general interest." His keenest wish was to gain the joint French-American command, and nothing—not the critical shortage of senior Continental officers, not the disapproval of Generals Sullivan and Greene, nor that of his friend Laurens—could dissuade him from the notion. He even gave d'Estaing elaborate advice on how he could diplomatically but firmly insist on it. There was the further matter of who attacked first. Sullivan and Greene had thought it advisable for tactical reasons that the Americans move from their positions first, but apparently for reasons of national pride d'Estaing would not hear of it, and Lafayette agreed with him.

All such questions became irrelevant when the British, anticipating an assault, began to consolidate their troops around Newport. Sullivan, seeing an opportunity to cut off an isolated outpost, moved in without consulting d'Estaing or his officers, which infuriated them and him, and resulted in a row that sounded to Laurens "like women disputing precedence in a country dance, instead of men engaged in pursuing the common interest of two great nations."

The catfight was interrupted when sails began appearing on the horizon, which turned out to be British warships. Fearing that his fleet could be trapped in the harbor, d'Estaing hoisted sail with all his troops aboard and took the fleet out to meet them, subjecting himself to British land batteries along the way. Lafayette said he had "never been so proud" as he was at the sight of the French fleet on its way to meet the long unchallenged "mistress of the seas."

The British ships sailed away in the face of d'Estaing's aggression, but in pursuing them d'Estaing ran straight into a violent and relentless storm that scattered both fleets and left his heavily damaged. For three days the storm raged, wreaking havoc on land and sea alike and teaching one eyewitness in the American camp that "men are more hardy than horses," since he saw horses simply sinking and dying in the ocean of mud. After the storm abated, Lafayette, Sullivan, and Greene waited five days for some sign of the French fleet, which finally came limping into port on August 19. Two of the largest ships had been dismasted, including d'Estaing's flagship, which had also lost its rudder. A 74-gun ship of the line was lost at sea. D'Estaing sent word to Sullivan that though he had promised to come back and help in the assault, he had no choice but to take the fleet to Boston for repairs. He offered to take Sullivan's men from their staging point back to the mainland, but that was all he could do.

The next morning, Lafayette and Greene went to d'Estaing's flagship to see if they could change his mind. Greene left with the distinct feeling that the general would have stayed and had been overruled by his officers, but even some American pilots aboard were said to agree that staying there was dangerous. A new British fleet under command of Admiral John Byron (the poet's grandfather) was long overdue, and when they arrived the French would be outnumbered, as would whatever force remained on the island.* Nevertheless, Lafayette and Greene declined d'Estaing's offer to withdraw their men, and a few hours after they left, despite an unfavorable wind, the French weighed anchor and sailed away.

Greene was concerned with what to do next. "To evacuate the Island is death; to stay may be ruin." Sullivan was simply livid, and he unwisely vented his anger in a strong letter of protest listing nine ways in which d'Estaing's decision was "derogatory to the honor of France." Next day he issued general orders that made the French decision sound duplicitous and cowardly, which of course sent Lafayette into a furious spin. The Tory newspapers were thrilled, reporting a rumor that "the renowned Don Quixoto, Drawcansiro de Fayetto," was going to take on Sullivan and the entire U.S. Congress. By then, Lafayette had already made himself somewhat ridiculous (as Washington warned him he would) by challenging the head of the British peace commission to a duel over an alleged insult to France. The commissioner had responded archly that he found it "hard to make a serious reply" to Lafayette's demand for satisfaction and suggested that the matter might "best be decided when Admiral Byron meets the Count d'Estaign," whose name the British seemed habitually to misspell.

The fight between Sullivan and d'Estaing obviously presented a clear and critical threat to the French-American alliance, without which the Revolution could well have been lost, and Lafayette did what he could do in good conscience to span the breach. When he visited d'Estaing with Greene, Lafayette had genuinely tried to get him to stay in Newport for the assault. "The Marquis' great thirst for glory and national attachment often run him into errors," Greene wrote Washington. "However, he did everything to prevail on the admiral to cooperate with us that man could

---

*Byron's fleet did appear off Newport ten days later, only a day after Sullivan, with Lafayette's help, had taken his force back to the mainland. Had they waited twenty-four hours, they could have been destroyed.

do." Once the fleet was gone, though, Lafayette felt it his duty to defend the honor of his countryman, who was indignant at Sullivan's assault on his honor but too proud to defend himself. Lafayette wrote repeated apologies to d'Estaing and long screeds to Congress and to Washington, complaining how "Frenchmen of the highest characters" had been slandered, "and me, yes, myself, the friend of America, the friend of General Washington, I am more upon a warlike footing in the American lines than when I come near the British lines at Newport."

Washington was plainly upset by d'Estaing's failure to stay and fight, but he advised Sullivan to "put the best face upon the matter and, to the world, attribute the removal to Boston to necessity. The reasons are too obvious to need explaining." He made clear just how urgent he felt the situation to be in another letter he wrote on the same day, in which, by way of telling him to calm down, Washington begged Lafayette to "afford a healing hand" to the French-American rift. "I feel every thing that hurts the sensibility of a gentleman; and, consequently, upon the present occasion, feel for you & for our good & great allies the French. . . . [But] in a free & republican government . . . every man will speak as he thinks, or more properly without thinking. . . . I, your friend, have no doubt but that you will use your utmost endeavors to restore harmony." For good measure, he signed this letter, for the first time, "your affectionate friend."

By mid-September, the diplomatic crisis was past, and Lafayette was plotting next steps with d'Estaing. As it had during his recuperation from the wound at Brandywine, his ambition spanned the globe. In one letter alone, he proposed missions to Bermuda, the West Indies, Newfoundland, Florida, and Canada, as well as New York and Georgia. In letters to Washington and Hamilton, among others, he casts these ideas as d'Estaing's, but d'Estaing had clear instructions: After leaving North America he was to take the fleet to the West Indies. In any case, just as Lafayette had thought about going home after his humiliating non-invasion of Canada, the assault on his country's honor and by extension on his own prompted him to think about it again. At his darkest moment in the crisis, he wrote a friend, "I begin to see that, seduced by a false enthusiasm, I made a mistake to leave everything and run to America."

Finally, all of these ideas—the memory of Canada, the idea of going home, the desire to see his nation's honor avenged, and the thrill he had felt at the prospect of fighting alongside d'Estaing's men—seem to have combined into one: He would go home and convince Versailles to give him an expeditionary force for a joint Franco-American invasion of Canada! First, of course, he would have to convince Congress that this was a good idea.

Perhaps recalling Washington's doubts about a Canadian expedition earlier that year, Lafayette was more than vague when he floated the idea of lobbying Congress about Canada again, but Washington got the drift immediately, and his response, though clothed in ornate syntax, was blunt: "If you have entertained thoughts my dear Marquis of paying a visit to your court, to your lady, and to your friends this winter, but waver on acct. of an expedition into Canada, friendship induces me to tell you that I do not conceive that the prospect of such an operation is so favorable at this time as to cause you to change your views."

As always, though, there were strong advocates for the idea in Congress, particularly among some of those who had given comfort to the Conway *cabaleurs*, notably Richard Henry Lee, James Lovell, and Sam Adams. These men and others were named to a committee to interview Lafayette and to come up with a recommendation on Canada.

Congress was deeply riven just then on several issues, none of them more bitterly divisive than the recall of Silas Deane (who had been brought home on d'Estaing's flagship) and the American debt to Beaumarchais. Both disputes showed the malicious handiwork of Deane's former co-commissioner Arthur Lee, the brother of Congressman Richard Henry Lee. Virtually ever since Beaumarchais had stopped working with him in favor of Deane, Arthur Lee had been trying with his brother's help to convince Congress that Deane was a thief and Beaumarchais's aid was supposed to have been a free gift from France, this despite two important facts: Deane and Beaumarchais had a signed contract, which Congress had ratified; and the French government had always denied and would continue to deny giving any aid at all before the alliance was official. Knowing of Lee's campaign, Franklin wrote a letter to Congress supporting Deane, which had the effect of raising questions about himself more than it allayed suspicions about Deane. The debate over Deane became so divisive that Congress was at times literally unable to deal with it, making Deane stay in the capital for long months waiting to testify at hearings that were always adjourned prematurely and inconclusively, leaving Deane in limbo and Beaumarchais in debt. No fewer than ten of Beaumarchais's ships had reached America just in the month before the Treaty of Alliance did.

Congress's deliberations over exactly what was owed to Beaumarchais would continue for decades after he was dead. Deane, whose reputation was never reliably impugned and never clearly vindicated, would end up in ruin.*

Just about the only person who was liked by everyone in that deeply conflicted Congress was the marquis de Lafayette. So perhaps it should come as no surprise that Lafayette took no part in the debate about the man who had given him a major general's commission in the Continental Army when he was nineteen years old.

Lafayette's political deftness and personal charm can have no better testament than this: By the time the hearings on an expedition to Canada were finished, he had been identified as the key player in it; both Franklin and Washington were instructed to work with him on furthering the effort; he was able plausibly to insist the idea had been Congress's in the first place; he had made friends on both sides of the question; and he had confused generations of historians. The two American scholars whose work on Lafayette is definitive, Stanley Idzerda of Cornell and Louis Gottschalk of

---

*Burdened with debts he could not repay and by unresolved suspicions of self-dealing after months of inconclusive congressional hearings, Deane moved to Britain. Unable to find work there, he settled ever deeper into obscurity and privation. His brother told him in 1788 that it was safe for him to come home to Connecticut, because "your creditors . . . have already taken all the property you have in this country; they can take no more." Deane wrote to Washington in the summer of 1789 that he was "reduced to the extremes of poverty," but he received no reply. He died penniless in September of that year onboard the ship that was to take him home to America. One of his last friends was the spy Edward Bancroft, who was a chemist of some ability and a specialist in poisons. The distinguished historian Julian Boyd theorized that Bancroft started the rumor that Deane had committed suicide in order to cover up the fact that he had been poisoned, and Boyd suggested that Bancroft had a plausible motive for murder: Deane had vowed to make a final effort to clear his name, and a careful examination of his papers might have incriminated Bancroft. The likelihood, however, is that Deane died of natural causes from one or a mix of the several illnesses that had been afflicting him for years. Bancroft's work as a double agent remained secret until the British government released its file on him in 1891. Having won the French and British patents to import yellow-oak bark, Bancroft died a rich man.

the University of Chicago, represent the poles on this moment in Lafayette's life. Gottschalk argued that Lafayette ignored, indeed tried to steamroll Washington in order to ram his project down Congress's throat. Idzerda supports Lafayette's claim to Washington that "the idea was not suggested by me and I acted in the affair a passive part." Even the first French minister to the United States, Vergennes's former secretary Conrad-Alexandre Gérard, who must have warned Lafayette that the French actually had no interest in joining a Canadian expedition, praised his "wisdom and dexterity" on the issue. The pro-expedition forces in Congress, Gérard wrote, "had warmly solicited his return with troops sent by the king. He responded with a correct sensibility and showed himself completely resigned to the king's will. . . ." In the cover letter he sent to Washington with the plan, Gouverneur Morris, who was agnostic on Canada but chaired the committee and drafted the proposal, simply threw up his hands and told Washington to deal with Lafayette directly: "He could say more than I can write in a week, and you know more of the subject than all of us together."

Washington was having none of it. When he complied with Congress's requests that he review the proposed plan, send his thoughts to Congress, and copy Lafayette, he began his response by asking to be excused from including Lafayette because he had to get into details of "our wants and our weaknesses [that] ought only to be known to ourselves." What followed was a long, detailed, and devastating logistical critique of the plan. He put his deeper concerns in a private letter to Henry Laurens. If France helped America to wrest Canada from Britain, why would she not wish to keep it? Anticipating his own bulwark principle of American foreign policy (and plainly taking exception with Franklin's more sentimental view of France's motives), Washington wrote that, much as he valued the French alliance, no country acted out of friendship; nations acted only from self-interest. It was even possible, he said, that Lafayette's idea was a plant. "As the Marquis disclosed his proposition when he spoke of it to me, it would seem to originate wholly with himself; but it is far from impossible that it had its birth in the cabinet of France and was put into this artful dress, to give it the readier currency. I fancy that I read in the countenances of some people on this occasion more than the disinterested zeal of allies. I hope I am mistaken. . . ."

As Washington wrote this letter, Lafayette was in a sickbed in Fishkill, New York, fifteen miles from Washington's headquarters, where he had been for more than a week. He had already been running a fever when he rode out of Philadelphia for Boston, where he was to meet the ship that would take him home and where he was to receive his final instructions from Congress. Along the way, he tried to fight his illness with tea, rum, and Madeira, until, at Fishkill, he realized he could go no further. He was confined to bed for three weeks, attended by Washington's physician Dr. John Cochran, and for some time he was thought to be critically ill. At least he thought so, as he wrote in his third-person memoir: "General Washington came every day to ask for news of his friend"—a thirty-mile round trip every day?—"but, fearing to disturb him, he spoke only with the doctor and returned to his camp with a heavy heart and tears in his eyes."

There were no tear stains on Washington's letter to Henry Laurens. How to explain that? Lafayette was the man of the moment, the hero for all tastes, friend alike to Conway *cabaleurs* and Washington's best friends. "No one but himself has known how to reconcile the clashing parties of this Continent to his own views," the commissioners' former secretary wrote to Franklin from Philadelphia. "By this you may judge not only of his amiable character, but of his discretion. The resolves in the letters of Congress in his favor will show you their sense of his merit, and I do assure you, that the sentiments of the people at large, and of the army are the same." It was true. Congress commended him lavishly in letters to Versailles and in resolutions, and it ordered Franklin to have made for him an "elegant sword with proper devices" to commemorate his service. Gérard almost apologized for reporting the depth of American sentiment for Lafayette in one of his dispatches to Vergennes at the end of 1778. "You know, Monseigneur, how far I am from adulation [of Lafayette]," he wrote, "but I would be lacking in justice if I did not transmit to you the testimonials which here are in every one's mouth without an exception."

But there was an exception: the man who said he loved Lafayette more than any friend he had ever had, the man to whom Lafayette had given almost puppylike adoration, the man in whose service he had shed blood and faced death. If Washington could have suspected Lafayette of smuggling a French plot to regain Canada into the American alliance, and lying about it to his face, how could he befriend him? And why continue to trust him as he did, as an advocate for American interests in France, and, later, as the general he would pick to send to the rescue of his home state of Virginia and to the aid of General Nathanael Greene in the South, the command that would allow Lafayette to prepare the way for the ultimate American victory at Yorktown?

There is surely more than one answer to those questions, but among them was the matter of glory: Washington expected the pursuit of personal and national honor to be the attribute of every honorable officer and every respectable man, which was one of the reasons he did not much love foreign officers in his service unless they clearly had something important and personal to lose in the cause. Of course Lafayette would put his country and his reputation there first—he had said exactly that to Sullivan and Greene when they tried to involve him in the protest against d'Estaing, and he proudly repeated this to Washington, knowing that Washington would never have expected him to take the American side against France. "I am sure you will approve the part I have taken in [the conflict]," Lafayette wrote at the time, "which was to stay much at home with all the French gentlemen who are here, and declare in the same time that anything thrown before me against my nation I would take as the most particular affront."

That lively sense of honor was exactly what Lafayette had to lose in an American defeat on the battlefield—the honor of his country, his own honor, and his place of honor in the eyes of the countrymen who had so warmly adopted him. He had worked hard for their approval. One of the many letters of praise that reached Versailles before Lafayette did was from d'Estaing, who said he thought the most remarkable thing about Lafayette was not just that he gave up so much for such rigors at such a young age, nor that he could acclimate himself to so different a life.

One becomes accustomed to using a knife as a spoon, doing without napkins, drinking to the health of ten persons with each drop one swallows . . . drinking from the same enormous goblet from which many have just wet their uninviting lips. But one must also fawn, to the height of insipidity, over every little republican who regards flattery as his sovereign right (this same behavior that our master formerly banished from Versailles), hold command over captains who are not good enough company to be permitted to eat with their general officers . . . and have some colonels who are innkeepers at the same time. It is [Lafayette's] knowing how to turn all that to advantage, to put it in his place and remain in his own that has most impressed me.

When his country's honor was not at issue, Lafayette was as devoted to the American cause as any Continental officer. His response to one of the many encomia Congress gave him before he returned home (on a ship it had placed at his disposal) showed that neither the wrangling over Canada nor anything else had dimmed the ardor he could feel for the cause of "my new country," which perhaps was sharpened for him at the moment by the knowledge that he was leaving it: "The moment I heard of America I loved her. The moment I knew she was fighting for freedom, I burnt with the desire of bleeding for her—and the moment I shall be able to serve her in any time or any part of the world, will be among the happiest ones in my life." He identified America's honor with his own.

By the time Lafayette reached Boston, Washington's memo to members of Congress about Canada had been read and all but dismissed: They said that instead of simply listing his logistical concerns, he should find ways of addressing them, at which point Washington decided he would have to go to the capital and argue the matter in person. Lafayette had decided by that time that he could no longer wait for his final instructions in Boston, and he took his leave of Congress with one last appeal: "May I beg leave to recommend Mr. Colombe, who desires to solicit the commission of Major."

The harder letter was the one to Washington. He began by apologizing for leaving before everything had been decided, then assured his friend that his health was completely restored. He promised to be back for the campaign in spring and begged Washington for letters—long letters, please, and as often as possible.

Farewell, my most beloved General, it is not without emotion I tell you this last adieu before so long a separation. Don't forget an absent friend and believe me for ever and ever with the highest respect and tenderest affection, dear General,

Your most obedient. servant and affectionate friend

LAFAYETTE

Five days later, aboard ship, he could not resist tearing open the letter to write one more good-bye. "Every body as well as myself is of opinion that I would be wrong to wait any longer. I hope I am right and hope to hear soon from you. Adieu, my dear and for ever beloved friend, adieu."

Another day, another ripped-open envelope: "All agree to be certain that Congress think I am gone—and that the sooner I'll go will be the better. Farewell, my dear general . . . I hope I shall soon see you again, and tell you myself with what emotion I now leave the coast you inhabit. . . ."

On January 12, 1779, the day after Lafayette sailed, letters arrived in Boston from Congress and from Washington giving him the news that the Canada expedition "has been laid aside," as Washington put it. He enclosed a letter of recommendation to Franklin, perhaps in part because without the collaboration on Canada, Franklin would now have no official business with Lafayette. He wrote a longer good-bye later, after he received Lafayette's. He said he would only expect to share "fresh toils and dangers with you in the plains of America" if war continued. If he could not hold out the prospect of military glory, he said,

I can entertain little hopes that the rural amusements of an infant world, or the contracted stage of an American theatre can withdraw your attention and services from the gaieties of a court, and the active part which you will more than probably be called upon to share in the administration of your government. The soldier will then be transformed into the statesman, and your employment in this new walk of life will afford you no time to revisit this continent, or think of friends who lament your absence. . . . I have now, I think, complied with your request in writing you a long letter. . . .

Adieu, my dear Marquis. My best wishes will ever attend you.

X

The Ally and the Traitor

ORE THAN A YEAR LATER, as the spring of 1780 began to thaw winter quarters in Morristown, New Jersey, Washington's army was emerging from the grimmest four months of the war, a season in some ways worse than Valley Forge. The army was down to barely more than three thousand fit for service, which included those who had not succumbed to starvation and exposure in the cruelest winter then on record, when six feet of snow fell on one day and a person could not stay outside without risking death from the subzero cold. For lack of food some of the men had been reduced to cooking and eating their shoes, and by the end of that winter, when a majority of the army's enlistments expired, some of the infantry companies had fewer than five men. Congress had long since stopped paying the soldiers, but paper money was worthless now anyway. In Continental currency, the twenty dollars that a soldier was supposed to receive each month was worth exactly 1.6 cents. There had been a mutiny in January, and there would be more of them. At least Washington could be sure that the fault did not lie this time with his quartermaster general, who was Nathanael Greene, perhaps the angriest and most frustrated man in camp. "A country once overflowing with plenty," he wrote to a friend that winter, "are now suffering an army, employed for the defense of everything that is dear and valuable, to perish for want of food."

Washington needed some good news when, on May 6, 1780, he opened the first letter from Lafayette he had received in five months. Postmarked Boston, it could have been written by no one else. It began, "Here I am."

Washington had several reasons to be pleased that Lafayette was back. Despite the distance and difference in age between them, their correspondence over the past year suggested a real sense of kinship. Beneath the florid professions characteristic of eighteenth-century letters, Washington actually unburdened himself to Lafayette as he did to none but his closest relations, which is to say relatively little rather than not at all. Still, Washington was a deeply passionate man, one not ashamed of crying openly, and despite his careful, reticent manner and the self-conscious dignity of his writing, it was plain he missed Lafayette, if not with quite the adolescent fervor with which Lafayette missed him. The previous fall, Washington was pained to learn that many of his earlier letters to Lafayette had gone astray, and he tried to make up for that by composing one of the longest personal letters he ever wrote, saying he had written to Lafayette so often to show that he "kept you constantly in remembrance" and from "a desire of giving you proofs of it." His affection, he said, had "ripened . . . into perfect love & gratitude that neither time nor absence can impair." He told Lafayette about the visit that the French ambassador La Luzerne and his secretary had made to headquarters not long before. He did not say what had happened at dinner that night, when the secretary paid Lafayette a compliment and Washington's eyes suddenly filled with tears.

Toward the end of this letter Washington virtually leaped out of character in referring to the compliments Lafayette forwarded from his wife. "Tell her . . . that I have a heart susceptible of the tenderest passion," he wrote, "and that it is already so strongly impressed with the most favorable ideas of her, that she must be cautious of putting love's torch to it, as you must be in fanning the flame. . . . I hear you say, 'I am not apprehensive of danger—my wife is young—you are growing old & the Atlantic is between you.' All this is true, but know my good friend that no distance can keep *anxious* lovers long asunder." Casual flirtation was not unusual for Washington, but at least in his letters he almost never made a joke or spoke of an intimate relationship in this way. For such odd flights from the norm, his letters to Lafayette from this time forward are unique in his correspondence.

Beyond a renewal of their friendship, Lafayette's arrival held out the possibility of what Washington had been waiting most to hear: that the French were coming back to restore American supremacy at sea. Without that, he had long since realized, there was no hope of winning the war; and after the disastrous failure of a joint attempt to regain Savannah the previous fall, d'Estaing had sailed back to France without instructions to return. Since then, Washington had been encouraging Lafayette in his efforts to rally support at Versailles for a new expeditionary force, and the reason that his friend had not returned until now, as his letters had made clear, was that he did not wish to return with empty hands.

With the hope that Lafayette had succeeded came a less pleasant thought: how his new French comrades would react when they took the measure of his sick and depleted army. Americans seemed to have stopped caring about the war in the past year or two, as small victories matched by small defeats and a series of inconclusive "actions" falling short of full-scale battles failed to inspire much public cheer or notice. The depreciated currency made raising funds to pay for the war increasingly difficult even as it paradoxically created a spending-driven economic boom: People bought today fearing the currency would fall further tomorrow, and so far they had been right. The luxuries people had sacrificed early in the war effort once again came into high demand, including British luxuries, and as Americans traded with the enemy, their army became an easy touch for profiteers. Purchasing agents embezzled through self-dealing. American merchants routinely sold the army rotten meat and bad gunpowder, clothing and shoes that fell apart; and even some of Washington's own officers and soldiers took part in the free-for-all—quartermasters bought their own equipment at inflated prices, discharges were sold for bribes, rations turned up for sale outside camp. Still, the intramural graft was relatively small time. The worst of the profiteering was committed by American civilians, and it began to turn the Continental Army, particularly its officers, against the people for whom they were fighting. Lieutenant Colonel Ebenezer Huntington was down to rags for clothes when he wrote to his brother in Connecticut: "The rascally stupidity which now prevails in the country at large is beyond all descriptions. . . . Why don't you reinforce your army, feed them, clothe and pay them? . . . I despise my cowardly countrymen who flinch at the very time when their exertions are wanted and hold their purse strings as though they would damn the world rather than part with a dollar to their Army. . . . I wish I could say I was not born in America. I once gloried in it, but now I am ashamed of it."

Civilian apathy led to the most dismal recruitment levels since the war began. In February 1780, Washington figured that even counting men unfit for service he was short of his objective of a 22,000-man army by 14,436 men. That summer he would report that the year's recruiting efforts had so far brought in fewer than thirty men. This was a fact Washington told no one but a few senior members of Congress and the Board of War, of course. He certainly would not have told someone who was trying to encourage the French to send reinforcements and aid. In any case he did not tell Lafayette.

Four days after his "Here I am" letter, there he was. First came his delight in a very happy reunion with Washington and his "family" siblings John Laurens and Alexander Hamilton. Then came shock, as Lafayette saw before him what he described to Joseph Reed, now governor of Pennsylvania, as "an Army that is reduced to nothing, that wants provisions, that has not one of the necessary means to make war. . . . I confess I had no idea of such an extremity." As Washington had done, Lafayette decided to say nothing of this in his letters home or to Versailles.

Lafayette had been working for American interests in France virtually from the moment he returned home the year before, even before he first set foot in Paris. On the way there, with the dust of the ride from the port at Brest covering his American uniform, he had stopped for rest at Versailles at two o'clock in the morning and found himself in the midst of a ball hosted by his cousin the prince de Poix. The party stopped to heap him with praise and questions, and next morning the prince took him for his first official meeting with Vergennes and with the king's first minister, Maurepas, with whom he spent two hours discussing the situation in America.

Because Lafayette had left France two years before in the face of a royal order to desist, Maurepas could not let him see the king before going on to Paris.* For show, Maurepas confined him to "house arrest" in Paris for the next eight days, during which time he could see only relatives; but the place of detention was the Noailles mansion, and Lafayette was related somehow to nearly everyone at court, so it was a busy and triumphant confinement. Lafayette wrote Louis a contorted letter of apology (he only did it to humiliate France's enemies; he thought Louis's order to stay in France was a diplomatic ruse; and he supposed his patriotic zeal had overcome his judgment). Finally, after giving Lafayette an audience for a "*réprimande douce*," Louis congratulated him on his success in America.

Adrienne might actually have taken his brief house arrest as a gift, since she would otherwise have completely lost her husband again in the tide of adulation. She lost him soon enough. Mme Aglaé d'Hunolstein, mistress of the duc de Chartres and the object of his unrequited passion, had warmed up in his absence. She was among his first stops after confinement, and soon they were known to be having an affair. Lines were written into a popular play about them, and she wrote to discourage another lover: "I see much of [Lafayette], and consider myself very lucky to have some place in his esteem." As Lafayette put it in his memoirs, "When I arrived [in France], I had the honor of being consulted by all the ministers and, what is much more worth while, of being kissed by all the ladies." Still, Adrienne obviously got some of his attention too, because within a month of his return she was pregnant again, with a daughter they would name Anastasie.

Thanks in part to the intervention of Marie-Antoinette, he was returned to active service and given a promotion to *mestre-de-camp*. The king, meaningfully, invited him to his levee, the elaborately ritualistic scene at which he arose in the morning and was attended by those select courtiers who had been given the high honor of getting him dressed. The king also asked Lafayette to go hunting with him, a more pleasant if not more prestigious invitation. He even gave Lafayette the right to purchase, for 80,000 livres (the equivalent of more than half a million

---

*Marie-Antoinette was not permitted to receive Lafayette officially for the same reason, but it was arranged that her once laughable dancing partner, now hailed as the "hero of two worlds," would be at a certain spot in the palace gardens as she passed by in her carriage so that they could meet "accidentally."

dollars) a regiment of the King's Dragoons. Lafayette had hoped to lead them in an attack on England that had been meticulously planned in his absence, but eventually the invasion came to nothing, and his ambition turned full time to the prospect of leading a French expeditionary force to America.

For persistence and fervor, Lafayette's lobbying effort at Versailles on behalf of a new expeditionary force for America could have been matched only by Beaumarchais. There are no fewer than nineteen letters from Lafayette to Maurepas and Vergennes on the subject, some of them quite long; and there were others to the minister of war and the minister of the marine. When the letters failed to produce the desired response, he turned up at their offices without appointments. Twice Maurepas declined to see him, pleading the press of other business. So Lafayette wrote to him again, with a flourish of underlinings that left no doubt of his sense of urgency: "By the *end of February* we must be ready," he wrote on January 25, 1780, a year after his return to France, "in *two weeks* we must write to America, and *in four days* I would like to see the *preparations* . . . undertaken with vigor." Since d'Estaing had recently returned and had no doubt reported candidly to Maurepas on the rough edges of the French-American relationship, Lafayette cleverly used that to argue for what he most devoutly wished: to be placed in command of the expedition himself. "[I]n supposing that I should command the land detachment *I vow that my head shall answer* for avoiding even a shadow of jealousy or of dispute."

He knew he was very young for such a command, and so did Maurepas and Vergennes. On March 5, Vergennes finally handed Lafayette instructions to leave as soon as possible—a frigate was waiting—to resume his command in the American army. He was to tell Washington that a large French fleet and thousands of troops were on the way. They would be under command of one of the most distinguished and experienced officers in the French military, the comte Jean-Baptiste-Donatien de Vimeur de Rochambeau, a fifty-five-year-old veteran of the Seven Years' War who had held the rank of major general in the French service virtually since Lafayette was born. He was promoted for this occasion to lieutenant general, a rank which had no American equivalent and which would therefore make him senior to all of the American generals except Washington. If

Lafayette had any doubts about Rochambeau's appointment, he kept them to himself.

The French fleet reached Newport on July 10, 1780, two months after Lafayette told Washington they were coming, but they brought a great deal less aid than Washington or Lafayette expected. In order to depart before a new British fleet was scheduled to set sail, Rochambeau had made the difficult decision to leave behind two regiments and the ships necessary to transport them. Fifteen thousand tons of powder and 100,000 stands of arms had been left behind to make room for the servants and plush accoutrements befitting Rochambeau's top officers, who were among the most notable men in France, including Lafayette's brother-in-law the vicomte de Noailles; Marie-Antoinette's lover Count Axel de Fersen; the renowned *bon vivant* duc de Lauzun, with "Lauzun's Legion"; the comte de Deux Ponts with his eponymous regiment; and many others, including, with the rank of major general, the estimable François-Jean de Beauvoir, chevalier de Chastellux, an intellectual whose works were known and approved by the *philosophes*. One of the "immortals" of the French Academy, Chastellux had to his credit that most precious badge of cultural authority, a Voltaire anecdote featuring himself. At what was supposed to be his last Academy appearance, Voltaire had exhorted the members to contribute to a new dictionary and himself took responsibility for the letter "A." Taking his leave, Voltaire exclaimed: "Gentlemen, I thank you in the name of the Alphabet!" to which Chastellux shot back, "And we, Sir, thank *you* in the name of Letters!"

Chastellux would serve as Rochambeau's translator. Washington used Lafayette, whom he sent to greet the French fleet on its arrival in Rhode Island, along with a letter of recommendation to Rochambeau: "As a general officer I have the greatest confidence in [Lafayette]," he wrote. "As a friend he is perfectly acquainted with my sentiments and opinions; he knows all the circumstances of our army and the country at large; all the information he gives and all the propositions he makes, I entreat you will consider as coming from me."

This was a bad start. Rochambeau had had his fill of courtier-officers, and he knew that Lafayette had wanted his command. For those reasons and because of Lafayette's age and relative inexperience, Rochambeau resented being asked to receive him as an equal; but having no choice, he had to satisfy himself with the occasional barbed aside. "I embrace you, my dear Marquis, most heartily," he replied to Lafayette's first letter, "and don't make me any more compliments, I beg of you."

The report that Lafayette made to Rochambeau was unrelievedly bad. Washington's army was gravely undermanned and underequipped, so much so that Clinton had felt free to send a major detachment from New York to the South; and on May 12, Charleston, South Carolina, had fallen to a British siege. Rochambeau, of course, had a grim report of his own to deliver, since many of the supplies, ships, and men that Washington had been counting on were now prevented from sailing by a British blockade.

All that having been said, Washington had a fairly simple proposal for Lafayette to present to Rochambeau: If and when the French were able to establish naval superiority, they should collaborate on an assault on New York, Britain's most concentrated and most strategically important stronghold, and one now weakened by the British offensive in the South. Rochambeau agreed in principle, but he pointed out that two days after he arrived at Newport, a British fleet under Admiral Thomas Graves had arrived in New York, so superiority would have to await the arrival of the rest of the fleet.

Since both generals' insistence on naval superiority clearly implied inaction for the present, Lafayette, ever impetuous, put forward a plan of his own, which at first he allowed Rochambeau to believe was Washington's: The French naval forces would be used only to keep the British navy occupied, while combined French and American land forces undertook the assault on New York. This to Rochambeau was so preposterous that he assumed Lafayette was getting ahead of his commander in chief, as he was. Washington had already told Lafayette that even assuming the British navy could be distracted, "there are only two things that would hinder us from taking New York . . . the want of men and arms to do it with."

Rochambeau was willing to make allowances for Lafayette's youth, at least for the moment. In a letter to the French minister La Luzerne, he praised Lafayette's zealousness and chided him only gently for impatience

("He now proposes . . . taking Long Island and New York without a navy"). Lafayette was at least straightforward in his report to Washington, saying that Rochambeau was "of opinion that nothing could be undertaken unless we had a naval superiority, and as I know it is your opinion also (though it is not mine) I durst not insist on that article."

Typically, he insisted anyway. In a letter to Rochambeau and the admiral of the French fleet, Lafayette went quite a bit beyond the role of interpreter. "From an intimate knowledge of our situation," he wrote, "I assure you, Sirs (as an individual and in my own name), that it is important for us to act during the present campaign, and that all the troops which you may expect from France next year will not repair the fatal consequences of our inaction now." He added that unless they took the action he suggested, "you will be able to accomplish nothing in America for the common good." It sounded almost like Sullivan to d'Estaing, and ran the same risk as Sullivan's peremptory judgment had done. In a brief reply, Rochambeau simply referred Lafayette to an earlier letter that set forth his views and asked again for a meeting soon with "our general." He also wrote to Washington asking that they deal with each other directly.

Lafayette was stung by Rochambeau's dismissive reply and wrote back defending his position. Fortunately, regaining his good sense and political judgment, he also invoked his long admiration for Rochambeau and finally just apologized: "If I have offended you, I ask your pardon."

The old general was now able to place Lafayette upon what he considered the proper footing. "Permit an old father, my dear Marquis, to answer you as he would an affectionate son whom he loves and prizes very much." After explaining the tactical problems with Lafayette's plan, he added,

> I am going to tell you a big secret derived from forty years' experience. There are no troops more easily beaten than when they have once lost confidence in their leader; and they lose it immediately when they have been exposed to danger through private and personal ambition. If I have been fortunate enough to retain their confidence until now, I owe it to the most scrupulous examination of my conscience that, of the 15,000 men or thereabouts who have been either killed or wounded under me in the different grades and

in the most bloody engagements, I have not to reproach myself with having caused the death of a single man for my own personal advantage.

Having plunged in the knife, he tried to withdraw it as gently as possible, with a more generous explanation for Lafayette's impetuosity: "[T]he warmth of your heart and mind . . . somewhat overheated the evenness and wisdom of your judgment. Preserve the latter quality for the council, and keep all the former for the moment of execution. This is still old Papa Rochambeau talking to his dear son La Fayette, whom he loves, and will continue to love and to esteem until his last breath."

Perhaps one of the reasons Lafayette so treasured his time in America was that no one (until Rochambeau) condescended to him there. He was treated as a man of substance, as he had earned the right to be. For this campaign season Washington had given him command of a corps of light infantry, two thousand picked troops from companies of the New York, Connecticut, Massachusetts, and Pennsylvania lines. Lafayette was justifiably proud of the assignment not only because it was an elite group, the equivalent of the French *chasseurs*, but because the missions of Washington's "flying army" would appeal to his wish for action. Those two thousand men were joined by a hundred riflemen and the three hundred–man cavalry of "Light-Horse Harry" Lee. So that they would be recognized as the elite troops they in fact were, Lafayette immediately set about outfitting them, writing Noailles that they were "distinguished by a black-and-red feather." Other units being covetous of such finery, the feathers began disappearing, and Lafayette had to tell Washington that unless the black-and-red feathers were restricted to his Light Division, "we will loose all our feathers, some of them have been already stolen a way."* Later he made arrangements for the officers to buy good uniforms at cost from a French merchant, and he gave them all good swords as well as cockades, epaulets,

*Washington's General Orders for August 29, 1780, declared: "As black and red feathers have been furnished the Division of Light Infantry to distinguish it from the rest of the Army they are not to be worn by any officers or soldiers but those who belong to it."

and other accessories to distinguish them. For himself, he asked the French consul in Philadelphia to find him a horse "of a perfect whiteness and the greatest beauty."

After giving each regiment its own elegant standard, he trained them to impeccable, parade-ground standards and inspired in them an esprit de corps that came to be known as the best in the army. When Chastellux visited the headquarters of the American forces, which was then on the New Jersey side of the Hudson River, Washington took him to see Lafayette's camp. A heavy rain was falling, so Chastellux was especially grateful for Lafayette's "large bowl of grog, which is a fixture on his table and is presented to every officer who enters. . . . We found all his troops in order of battle . . . and himself at their head, expressing by his bearing and countenance that he was happier in receiving me here than at his estate in Auvergne. The confidence and attachment of the troops are to him priceless possessions, hard-won riches . . . but what I think is even more flattering for one so young is the influence and stature he is accorded in political and military circles."

To Lafayette's dismay, the parade-ground finery of his Light Division would remain just that. In August, a letter from Vergennes told Washington that because of the British blockade the second division would not be coming until late fall at the earliest, effectively eliminating the year's campaign season. August brought worse news still. Congress had entrusted the increasingly critical Southern command to General Gates (Washington had preferred Greene but was not consulted). Now, only three weeks after taking over the army, Gates had been routed by Cornwallis at Camden, South Carolina. Most of his army had run away at the first sign of battle, the rest had been killed or taken prisoner, and Gates had allowed himself to be swept from the battlefield with the first fleeing militia, saying over his shoulder that he would "bring the rascals back into line." He never came back. Someone saw him riding away at a gallop. At the end of that day he was sixty miles from the battlefield, with no part of his army, and he kept going. "Was there ever an instance of a general running away . . . from his whole army?" Hamilton wrote to a friend. "One hundred and eighty miles in three days and a half. It does admirable credit to the activity of a man at his time of life [he was fifty-two]. But it disgraces the general and the soldier." The defeat also left the South open to the British, whose conquest of Virginia would put only Philadelphia between them and their army in New York.*

After Camden only Washington could have remained hopeful, as of course he did, holding out the possibility that the French fleet in the West Indies would respond to his plea for help. In a letter to its admiral, he put the worst possible face on the situation from which his army and his cause now desperately needed rescue: "The government without finances; its paper credit sunk, and no expedients it can adopt capable of retrieving it; the resources of the country much diminished by a five years war, in which it has made efforts beyond its ability; Clinton . . . in possession of one of our capital towns and a large part of the state to which I belong . . . Lord Cornwallis . . . in complete possession of two states, Georgia and South Carolina; a third, North Carolina, by recent misfortunes at his mercy. . . ." Washington had never made a more abject appeal.

The French fleet from the West Indies never came, but a new fleet did arrive from Britain—thirteen warships under command of the legendary Admiral George Rodney. Washington received this news as he was setting out with Lafayette for his first face-to-face meeting with Rochambeau, at Hartford, Connecticut. Since they now lacked naval superiority or any prospect of it, the conference at Hartford produced very little apart from a joint appeal to Versailles for more money, troops, and ships. Rochambeau sent his son to France to deliver their letter to Versailles and make their argument in person.

On the way back to camp, Washington suffered what was in some

---

*Gates left the battle in the hands of his second in command, Lafayette's friend the Baron de Kalb, who led the diehards with him past the point of valor. His head slashed by a saber, he was dressed with a handkerchief and fought on, taking three musket balls and eight bayonet wounds before he fell. His aide the chevalier Dubuysson, another veteran of *La Victoire*, was with him to the end. Sheltering him from further bayonet and saber blows while screaming that he was a general, Dubuysson sustained injuries to his arms and hands but survived. Kalb was carried from the field by British troops and after his death three days later was buried by his last enemies with full honors. Congress passed a resolution for a memorial, but there was no money for it, and the promise was filed away, along with many others. Lafayette himself finally laid the cornerstone of a monument to Kalb in Camden, South Carolina, during his last visit to America, in 1825.

ways the most shocking setback of the war, for him and for his fellow Americans as well. He had decided to make an inspection of West Point, the most important Continental position in the North. Comprising the fort on the river as well as a daunting complex of mountaintop batteries and redoubts and the virtually impregnable Fort Putnam at the summit, with its unimpeded view for miles in every direction, West Point guarded access to the Hudson. Its biggest guns were trained on an enormous barricade—a twelve-inch-thick iron chain resting on logs sixteen feet long—at an elbow in the river. Standing between the British and control of the Hudson, West Point was the masterpiece of the Continental army's forts, a tour de force of engineering and a testament to years of hard labor. Not long before this time, he had given command of the post to one of his most trusted officers, General Benedict Arnold.

On the morning of September 25, Washington sent two aides ahead to warn Arnold that he and his entourage, including Lafayette, Hamilton, and General Henry Knox, would be arriving for breakfast. On the way there, Washington inspected some redoubts on the east bank of the Hudson, so that the party did not arrive at Arnold's headquarters until ten o'clock. By then, according to the aide de camp who welcomed them, Arnold had been called to West Point by an urgent message, but breakfast was waiting for them. General Arnold's barge would take them to West Point when they were finished, and Arnold would be there to greet them. But of course Arnold would not be there.

Washington found West Point in an advanced state of disrepair. One entire wall of Fort Putnam had collapsed, decay was spreading everywhere, and there were no maintenance crews at work. After a two-hour inspection, Washington returned furious to Arnold's house, only to be even angrier and more mystified to find that Arnold was not there either. He discovered why as he rested in his room before dinner, when Hamilton brought him some papers that had just been found in the boot of a British spy who was carrying a pass signed by Arnold. Among the papers were details of artillery placement and troop strength at West Point, as well as detailed descriptions of the fort: "Redoubt No. 3, a slight Wood Work 3 Feet thick, very Dry . . . easily set on fire—no cannon." Enclosed too were notes from a council of war that Washington had sent to Arnold. Unable to believe what he was seeing but seeing it clearly nevertheless, he sent off Hamilton and one of Lafayette's aides with orders to find Arnold and place him under arrest.

Lafayette was dressing for dinner when the aide rushed into their room to get his revolver and told him what had happened. When Lafayette next saw him, Washington was sitting with his head in his hands, saying, "Who can we trust now?"

XI

Into Virginia

WASHINGTON'S REACTION to Arnold's betrayal was the common one. The fall of Charleston in May, the ignominious defeat of "the hero of Saratoga" at Camden in August, and now this. What was one to make of the fact that one of the certified heroes of the Revolution—the man who had really defeated Burgoyne's army, with brilliant leadership and stunning bravery on the battlefield, the man who had tried to storm Quebec in the middle of winter, one of the generals whose skill and bravery Washington most admired—could sell himself and West Point and the cause of American independence for £6,300? Even more unsettling, he had actually schemed with the British for the capture of the commander in chief himself. On some level, Arnold's treason led Americans to suspect themselves. A week after the betrayal became public, Colonel Alexander Scammel wrote: "Treason! Black as hell! . . . We were all astonishment, each peeping at his next neighbor to see if any treason was hanging about him: nay, we even descended to a critical examination of ourselves." An aide to General Knox said simply, "Somehow or other, I cannot get Arnold out of my head."

The suspicion of collective guilt was far more acute among civilians. Arnold's defection reminded Americans of the vulnerability of their army and their cause, for which "they"—those sharp-minded, money-grubbing farmers and merchants and all those shortsighted, tightfisted politicians—were responsible. The "we" went unspoken but was deeply felt. Dr. Benjamin Rush discovered a disease among people who either befriended

Great Britain or that larger number who simply did not take an active part in the war. He called it "Revolutiana," and classified it as a form of hypochondria, "tristimania." The disease, which was commonly known as "tory rot" and "protection fever," was found in people disturbed by "the real or supposed distresses of [their] country." Its symptoms included impotence, alcoholism, and "the most awful symptom ... DESPAIR." Rush's prescribed treatment was "to avoid reading newspapers, and conversing upon political subjects, and thereby to acquire a total ignorance of public events." The only other cure he knew of was to "take a part in the disputes which divide his fellow citizens."

Pillorying Arnold became a popular form of the latter during that winter of 1780–81, and it was therapeutic even for those without full-blown cases of Revolutiana. The shock at his betrayal, which threatened belief in American virtue and the virtue of the cause itself, was mitigated in direct proportion as Arnold was demonized, his character defined as uniquely evil. Gradually, as that was accomplished, his treason actually came to have a galvanizing effect on the war effort; and when he turned up in the first days of January 1781 as a brigadier general at the head of fifteen hundred British troops laying waste to Virginia, neither Washington nor Rochambeau needed the clamor of an outraged public to stir them to action.

Just then a providential storm scattered the British fleet that had for months blockaded the French ships in Rhode Island, allowing at least a temporary window of operation. Emboldened by the idea of capturing Arnold and his army, which was attempting to establish a sea base at Portsmouth, Rochambeau and the fleet's Admiral Charles Destouches determined to send the entire fleet to Virginia to participate in an allied attack by land and sea. "The great importance which it has seemed to me that your Excellency attaches to the gaining of a foothold by Arnold," Rochambeau wrote to Washington, "has determined M. Destouches to sacrifice everything with that in view." In turn, Washington dispatched Lafayette with twelve hundred men, many of them drawn from his beloved Light Divison. His orders, on the happy chance that Arnold was captured, called on Lafayette to "execute the punishment due to his treason and desertion in the most summary way."

·   ·   ·

On March 2, 1781, three days ahead of schedule after a very fast march south through mud and freezing rain, Lafayette's troops reached Head of Elk. Washington's orders were to stay there until Lafayette was sure the fleet would be in Virginia to meet him: A French convoy was to escort his men south through Chesapeake Bay. Lafayette knew enough to wonder about that. A few days after arriving at Head of Elk, he received a letter from Washington saying that Admiral Destouches "seems to make a difficulty, which I do not comprehend, about protecting the passage of your detachment down the Bay." On March 8, Lafayette began his reply diplomatically, "I very much apprehend that the winds will not permit," but then explained that in fact they were simply not interested in having Lafayette and his American troops share the glory of capturing Arnold and his army. "Count de Rochambeau thinks his troops equal to the business," Lafayette wrote, "and wishes that they alone may display their zeal." After sealing this letter, to be sure he and his men would not be left out of the action, Lafayette violated Washington's orders and began to embark his men to Annapolis before he knew the fleet had left Newport. He then went south ahead of his men in an open, lightly armed boat so that he could meet Destouches and demand the escort in person. For good measure, he brought a friend with him who had been visiting at camp. "I have clapped on board my boat," he wrote Washington gleefully, "the only son of the minister of the French Navy, whom I shall take out to speak if circumstances require it."

In the end, there was no need. Destouches took too long in preparations for leaving Rhode Island, and the delay proved fatal to the plan. By the time they sailed, British intelligence knew of their plan, the British ships were repaired, and ordered out to sea in hot pursuit. The French and British fleets found each other on March 16, and a sea battle, with eight ships of the line on each side but superior armament in Britain's favor, left the British in control of Chesapeake Bay. This allowed Clinton to dispatch twenty-six hundred troops to reinforce Arnold from New York under command of General William Phillips, the same officer whose artillery unit killed Lafayette's father at the Battle of Minden almost twenty years before. (There is no evidence that Clinton knew that, and Lafayette's only mention of it at the time was in a letter to Greene in which he spoke of the connection and confessed, with an understatement that was suggestively atypical, that it inspired in him a wish to "contract the latitude of [Phillips's] plans.")*

Lafayette learned that the French fleet had been beaten and had returned to Newport only when he reached Williamsburg and was told that the warships he had been assured were in the harbor were not French but British. This of course required telling Washington exactly how it was that he came to be in Virginia and his troops came to be in Annapolis when he had been told to stay in Head of Elk until his French escort arrived. Lafayette said it was partly the wind and mentioned other vaguely described "essential reasons," but then gave himself up, saying he was concerned mainly for "the glory of the troops under my command." He then scurried back to his troops as quickly as possible to execute Washington's order that they join the rest of the army in the North.

The order was welcome in any case, since Lafayette assumed that the focus of the war would once again be New York. He was wrong, but he could not have known that. Washington himself would not realize for some time that the war in the North was already over.

Even before Lafayette and his army began to march back toward Head of Elk, the Southern Army had a delicious victory; and before the final, decisive campaign of the war began in Virginia later that summer, they would have a profitable defeat as well. In mid-January 1781, Daniel Morgan, now with the brigadier generalship he had long since earned at the head of his intrepid riflemen, had humiliatingly routed the superior army of the much-feared British cavalry leader Banastre Tarleton in the Battle of Cowpens, South Carolina, a work of tactical ingenuity in which Morgan combined militia with regular troops to greater effect than had ever been done before. He did that in part by placing a river at his army's back, which prevented the militia from running away but also cut off the possibility of retreat. Cornwallis, still stinging from Tarleton's defeat, decided to take his revenge on Greene's army in North Carolina, but by

*Although some biographers have passed along the more emotionally satisfying story that Phillips was killed by a cannon ball at the Battle of Yorktown, in fact he died of typhus a month after joining Arnold in Virginia.

the time he did Greene had led him on such a debilitating chase that after the British "victory" at the Battle of Guilford Court House, Cornwallis's army was exhausted. Greene then turned his army south to try to retake South Carolina from British forces under Lord Rawdon, and Cornwallis's army slowly made its way north to join forces with Arnold in Virginia.

The 3,500 to 4,000 regulars in the combined force of Generals Phillips and Arnold were already enjoying free rein in Virginia, burning Continental ships and barracks and destroying all the stores of weapons and supplies they could find. At the same time that Lafayette began making his way back to his troops, Greene was appealing to Washington either to reinforce his army in case Phillips and Arnold came south to reinforce Cornwallis, or to reinforce Baron Steuben, who was in command of what forces there were to face Cornwallis and Arnold in Virginia, almost all of them militia. Knowing that the British clearly had committed themselves to the South, Washington had to oblige him, and so ordered the Pennsylvania troops under General "Mad Anthony" Wayne to march to Virginia. He also told Lafayette, the day after ordering him to march north, to take his men south after all.

Both Wayne and Lafayette promptly faced mutinies. When Lafayette's army left camp, they had been told not to bring much gear since they would be gone only for a short time. They had now been on the march for six weeks. Their clothes were in tatters, and many had worn out their shoes. Most of them were moreover from New England and had a dislike verging on dread of the Southern climate. This dovetailed nicely with Lafayette's disappointment about being asked to go south, since in his opinion the concentration of forces there only made his "grand and decisive object"—meaning an attack on New York—more feasible. "Many men have already deserted; many more will," Lafayette wrote Washington. ". . . While I was writing this, accounts have been brought to me that a great desertion had taken place last night." Among the deserters were some of the best men in the Rhode Island line.

General Wayne's men had not been paid for months and were even more poorly clothed and equipped than Lafayette's. In a similar situation earlier, Wayne had been able to end the defiance by negotiating with the men for their back pay, but he could raise no such aid this time and felt he had no alternative to using force. A quick court-martial ended with six ringleaders sentenced to death, and Wayne ordered the sentences to be carried out immediately. "The particular messmates of the culprits were their executioners," Wayne wrote later. "While the tears rolled down their cheeks in showers, they silently and faithfully obeyed their orders." A regimental fifer never forgot the scene: "The distance that the platoons stood from [the condemned men] at the time they fired could not have been more than ten feet. So near did they stand that the handkerchiefs covering the eyes of some of them were set on fire . . . The fence and even the heads of rye for some distance within the field were covered with the blood and brains." The entire brigade was then made to file past the corpses. The next morning, they marched south, "mute as fish."

Lafayette tried something else. He told his men they were free to go. Ahead of them, he said, lay a hard road, great danger, and a superior army determined on their destruction. He for one meant to face them, but anyone who did not wish to fight could avoid the crime of desertion by simply applying for leave to return to camp in Morristown, which would be granted. Given the option of fighting or declaring themselves to be unpatriotic cowards, Lafayette's men stopped deserting, and several of the deserters returned remorsefully and were allowed to stay. One who did not return was later caught and hanged. Lafayette rewarded his men for their loyalty by spending £2,000 on his own credit to buy desperately needed clothing, shorts, shoes, hats, and blankets; but it was his appeal to their pride that stopped the desertions, an appeal that would never have worked in the French army, at least not until several years later.

Even before he received Washington's emphatic reply to his letter about New York, which told Lafayette to forget his "great and decisive object" and report to Greene as soon as possible, he had already left Head of Elk and started south. On the way he received orders from Greene to march straight to Virginia, where the British appeared to be mounting a full-scale offensive.

Two weeks before, Congress had decided to send its own representative to Versailles to reinforce the plea from Rochambeau's son, who had got nowhere with Vergennes. The king could never accede to the Americans' "immense demands," he had said, "and if he did he would

Lafayette set sail for America aboard *La Victoire* on April 20, 1777. This depiction notwithstanding, his departure drew no congratulatory crowd. He left in secret, just ahead of an order to desist.

An engraving by Currier and Ives commemorates the moment when Lafayette was introduced to Washington, at the City Tavern in Philadelphia, on the night of July 31, 1777.

Commander in Chief George Washington, in an engraving based on the drawing by Louis-Charles-Auguste Couder.

A nineteenth-century artist's rendering of the young marquis de Lafayette.

In November 1776, the self-styled "baron" Johann de Kalb introduced Lafayette to the Continental Congress's recruiter in Paris, Silas Deane.

London bookies were confounded and the playwright Caron de Beaumarchais (top left) was smitten by Louis XV's gender-bending spy Charles-Geneviève-Louis-Auguste-André-Timothée d'Eon, who was equally improbable as (from top right) ingénue, swashbuckler, and dowager. Thousands of pounds were won and lost when, at death, d'Eon was found to have been a man.

Lafayette and Washington at Valley Forge.

At the Battle of Monmouth Court House, Lafayette said, Washington "seemed to arrest fortune with one glance. . . . I thought then as now that I had never beheld so superb a man."

At a sitting for the American painter Benjamin West, George III asked what he thought Washington would do when the war was over. "They say he will return to his farm," West said. The king was incredulous. "If he does that, he will be the greatest man in the world." On December 3, 1783 (above), Washington appeared before Congress, resigned his commission as commander in chief, and retired to Mount Vernon, though not for long.

A gallery in Philadelphia hails the preeminent figures of the Federal Convention of 1787, the aging Benjamin Franklin and the presiding officer, George Washington.

On a balcony of Federal Hall in lower Manhattan, Washington swore the oath of office on a Bible borrowed for the occasion from a local Masonic lodge, and his fellow Freemason Robert Livingston swore him in. Cheering crowds in the streets below could still be heard as Washington gave his First Inaugural Address in the Senate chamber.

ALEXANDER HAMILTON, Secy of the Treasury.

GEORGE WASHINGTON.   GEN'L HENRY KNOX, Secy. of War.   THOMAS JEFFERSON, Secy of State.   EDMUND RANDOLPH, Attorney General.

WASHINGTON AND HIS CABINET.

All the most incendiary issues in American politics were fought out among the most trusted members of Washington's administration, sometimes forthrightly in private, more often anonymously and in public.

surely ruin France!" Congress's emissary was young John Laurens, who came recommended not only for his closeness to Washington, for his European education, and for his fluency in French, but also for what was equally important in France, a distinguished family name. Before Laurens arrived, appeals came to Benjamin Franklin from both Lafayette and Washington to do everything in his power to help, and Franklin did. In a letter dated February 13, quoting urgent appeals from both Lafayette and Washington ("it is impossible to conceive . . . the distress which the troops have suffered"), Franklin delivered a masterpiece of rhetoric, a relentless crescendo of arguments that ranged from the dire ("there is some danger lest the . . . whole system of the new government in America may be shaken") to the horrifying ("if the English are suffered once to recover that country, such an opportunity of effectual separation as the present may not occur again in the course of ages") to the catastrophic:

> The possession of these fertile and extensive regions and that vast seacoast will afford [England] so broad a basis for future greatness . . . as will enable them to become the *terror of Europe*, and to exercise with impunity that insolence which is so natural to their nation, and which will increase enormously with the increase of their power.

He even appealed to personal pity. "I am grown old. I feel myself much enfeebled by my late long illness, and it is probable I shall not long have any more concern in these affairs. . . ."

Vergennes loved Franklin, but even that was not enough to allay his fury when he learned that a new American emissary was coming with a demand for an additional 25 million livres. "This is already the fourth campaign that has been opened for [the Americans]," he fumed in a letter to his American ambassador on February 19. "The expenses of the last one . . . called for an extraordinary outlay of one hundred and fifty millions! The King is obliged to have recourse to retrenchments and to loans for his own service, and he was justified in expecting that the United States would at least provide for the expenses of their army." Pointing out that they had only recently given in to Franklin's plea for 5 million livres, Vergennes said the Americans' request for 25 million more was simply outrageous: "We shall be grieved to refuse . . . but Congress must be notified of this refusal, in order that it may not be taken by surprise."

Just then, in fact on the very day Vergennes wrote that letter, a publication without precedent hit France with revolutionary force. For the first time ever, the king's minister of finance published an accounting of the royal finances, titled *Compte Rendu au Roi*. The intention of its author, Jacques Necker, was to create confidence in the royal balance sheet, which was drawn up to show a modest surplus. This was extraordinary, and Necker was proclaimed a financial genius: Only a wizard could have managed to finance the entire war effort in America without raising taxes. The fact is, however, that he had done it by borrowing. Over the four years leading up to 1781, he had solicited loans of no less than 520 million livres, most of it for terms of less than twenty years and at interest rates of up to 10 percent. These funds went into accounts that were not covered in the *Compte Rendu*, but few people noticed, perhaps because they wished not to.*

The *Compte Rendu* bore many children. One could argue—and some historians have—that it started the French Revolution. Certainly it relaxed fiscal vigilance at Versailles, at a time when the royal treasury was already on the verge of bankruptcy; and Necker's banker friends in Amsterdam became even richer when the king, relieved by his surprisingly sound financial standing, decided to borrow another 10 million livres for the American cause, to make an outright grant of another 6 million in

---

*Historians differ on the extent to which Necker's presentation was deceptive. Some defend Necker as only trying to show that the king's budget balanced in normal times, specifically excluding wartime, and others believe that Necker's approach was purposefully evasive. The balance of the evidence points to an intentional ambiguity. In his biography of Louis XVI, for example, John Hardman points to a memorandum from the keeper of the royal treasury to Necker's successor which demonstrated a deficit even in the ordinary account of 15 million livres rather than a surplus of 10, and pointed out that if the king wanted to repay his debt according to its terms (another function of the ordinary account), the deficit would be 52 million livres. This memo did not reach the king until Necker had resigned some time after the next round of financing for the American war.

cash and goods, and, costliest of all, to continue spending what was necessary to keep his large naval force in North America.

Laurens and the vicomte de Rochambeau were sent back to America with the 16 million livres in hand, but thanks to Vergennes's opposition (neither he nor chief minister Maurepas were fooled by Necker's legerdemain), there would be no more ships or troops, not even the "second division" that had been promised earlier but held back by the British blockade. Sometime in late summer, though, a French fleet that was just now sailing for the West Indies would be available for a short period to join the fleet already in America for action wherever Washington deemed most promising. That was the best Versailles would do. Luckily, it was just enough.

By late May, when Washington and Rochambeau met in Wethersfield, Connecticut, to discuss this development, Lafayette had been in Virginia for a month. Though he had spent not one day on the offensive, he had managed to defend Richmond, which had been virtually burned to the ground in Arnold's previous assault, against a second attack by both Arnold and Phillips, who outnumbered his army by more than two to one. He did that, however, at the cost of allowing the British to pillage freely elsewhere. Outside Richmond, every military storage facility and every cache of provisions the British could find that could conceivably be of use to the Continental Army was plundered or destroyed. Plantations and warehouses full of tobacco went up in flames. Barrels of flour, livestock, wagons, clothing, shoes, horses, even saddles and bridles were taken or destroyed. After Phillips's death from typhus on May 13, all the regulars in Virginia came under Arnold's sole command. A week later, Cornwallis converged with his 1,500 men, and then came 2,000 reinforcements from New York, bringing the British total to roughly 7,200. Lafayette was down to only 900 of the 1,200 Continentals who had come with him, and somewhat more than that number of Virginia militiamen. He would be outnumbered even after Wayne joined him, and that was still almost three weeks away.

He now knew how Washington had felt for the past six years. "So here I am prescribed by that triumvirate [Arnold, Phillips, and Cornwallis],"

Lafayette wrote in late May, before he knew that Phillips had died. "I can not help smiling at the ridiculous figure . . . our militia dragoons without pistols, swords, saddles, bridles, and boots. . . . What annoys me most is the shortage of everything, the total want of resources, the slowness in filling orders that we are forced to put up with in this region." He was maintaining his sense of humor, but his predicament was anything but amusing. "I shall now proceed to dislodge La Fayette from Richmond," Cornwallis wrote to Clinton at the end of May, "and with my light troops to destroy any magazines or stores in the neighborhood." At least until Wayne arrived, the best Lafayette could do was to minimize his casualties through evasion; and like Washington facing the empty powder casks at Cambridge, Lafayette feared that his flight from the enemy would be attributed to personal reticence. Despite the commander in chief's deep familiarity with that situation, Lafayette was so concerned about the accusation of timidity that he wrote Washington on May 24, almost by way of apology: "Had I followed the first impulse of my temper, I would have risked some thing more. But I have been guarding against my own warmth; and this [possibility] of a general defeat . . . has rendered me extremely cautious in my movements." Thanks to the shortage of men and supplies, he added, "I am not strong enough even to get beaten."

Not surprisingly, some of Virginia's leading citizens implored Washington to come to the aid of his native state, or at least send them someone more seasoned than Washington's youngest general. Lafayette probably never read the letter Washington wrote to foreclose such complaints, which was an unqualified declaration of faith in his friend: "The command of the troops in that state cannot be in better hands than the Marquis's. He possesses uncommon military talents, is of quick and sound judgment, persevering, and enterprising without rashness, and besides these, he is of a very conciliating temper and perfectly sober, which are qualities that rarely combine in the same person." Washington added that Lafayette had learned as much in "three or four years as some others will in ten or a dozen."

The commander in chief's judgment was more than vindicated only a few weeks later. Cornwallis and his army, having given up on trapping Lafayette and having done a satisfying amount of damage otherwise, were already tired of slogging through inland Virginia when new orders came through Clinton from the war ministry in London: His assignment was to build a deep-water port on the Chesapeake for eventual operations against Philadelphia. As Cornwallis marched his men toward the coast, Lafayette—in what was probably the most tactically clever course of action he ever undertook—simply followed him, staying far enough away that he would be in no danger of running into Cornwallis's rear guard. He had not yet actually made his rendezvous with Wayne (at which point "we shall be in a position to be beaten more decently"), but the rumor spread along his route that the two Continental armies had already joined forces: Why else would Lafayette be so bold as to be chasing Cornwallis? This was precisely the impression Lafayette wanted to create to embolden citizens of the state, and it worked: More militia began to turn out every day, including gentlemen on thoroughbreds who paid their own expenses to join his cavalry. Farmers who had previously hidden what they had against impressment now came forward with provisions. Lafayette was still far from strong enough to face Cornwallis on the battlefield, but the contrary belief among Virginians represented a formidable weapon in itself.

For virtually the entire month of June, Lafayette followed Cornwallis on his way south through Virginia, picking up strength along the way— Wayne and his Pennsylvania line finally arrived, then Steuben and his militia, who had been called away to support Greene in North Carolina. By the time he celebrated the Fourth of July, 1781, with a *feu de joie*, he boasted three brigades representing more than two thousand Continentals, as well as fifty dragoons, sixty cavalrymen, and three hundred artillerymen. What's more, he was credited with driving Cornwallis's army from most of Virginia, a feat attributed by his aide Dr. James McHenry to "sorcery . . . a very necessary science for an American general at this moment." This feat of magic was deft enough to fool even the first historians of the Revolution, who attributed Cornwallis's "retreat" to Lafayette's superior tactical movements.

By the first week of August, Cornwallis had settled on Yorktown as the site for the British deep-water port and had begun to work on the fortifications for it. With that, the sorcery was complete: While Lafayette had done little more than follow along and watch, Cornwallis had painted himself into the corner from which he would be forced to make Britain's last stand in America.

XII

Yorktown

On August 14, 1781, Washington received the word he had long awaited: that the promised French fleet, under command of Admiral François-Joseph-Paul, comte de Grasse, was on its way to America. The fact that he was sailing to the Chesapeake instead of New York was distressing, because Washington had hoped to mount his offensive against New York; but Rochambeau and his officers did not believe de Grasse's force would be sufficient to tip the scales there, and Rochambeau had actually encouraged de Grasse to focus on the Chesapeake despite knowing of Washington's contrary view. After learning of de Grasse's plan, Washington admitted in his diary that the fight was moving to Virginia because of the narrow window of time and the preference of the French, but he was still convinced that by the time they got there, Cornwallis would be gone. He also knew that after a march which would be so long and so fast, both the French and American armies would arrive exhausted.

The next day, he wrote Lafayette to let him know that de Grasse and the fleet were coming and that the combined armies would soon be on the march. By the time they arrived, he was convinced that Cornwallis, having established the coastal port, would "detach part of his force to New York and go with the residue to South Carolina." In any case, he gave Lafayette his orders: "Whether the enemy remain in force or whether they have only a detachment left, you will immediately take such a position as will best enable you to prevent their retreat . . . which I presume they will attempt the instant they perceive so formidable an armament."

Two days later, Washington had cause to be a bit more optimistic: A letter from Lafayette told him that Cornwallis was using his entire army to fortify and build the port at Yorktown, apparently still unaware that he was in any danger. Now Washington began to worry less about Cornwallis leaving than that the convergence of forces would somehow be delayed or derailed. Marching his men quickly toward the rendezvous with Rochambeau's land force—"we have not a moment to lose"—he arrived only to find that the French were days behind in crossing the Hudson River, slowed by too much equipage and too few pack animals. Beyond that, the comte de Barras, who was in charge of bringing the heavy siege artillery and salt provisions but was still in Rhode Island, was balking at serving under de Grasse, who was in rank his inferior. Though Barras had reluctantly agreed to do so, getting to the scene of battle meant sailing past the British in New York, which he had never been willing to do before.

There was also word that another British fleet was about to arrive on the American coast. With his artillery and food supplies in the balance, timing critical, and no further word of either Barras or de Grasse, Washington's fabled calm failed him. In a letter to Lafayette on September 2, he confessed to being "distressed beyond expression to know what is become of the Count de Grasse and for fear the English fleet by occupying the Chesapeake (to which my last accounts say they were steering) should frustrate all our flattering prospects in that quarter. I am also not a little solicitous for the Count de Barras, who was to have sailed from Rhode Island on the 23rd ulto, and from whom I have heard nothing since that time. . . . If you get anything new from any quarter send it, I pray you, *on the spur of speed*, for I am almost all impatience and anxiety."

Three days later, as Rochambeau's ships drifted into port below Philadelphia at Chester, they beheld on the dock something never seen before or after: Washington, the austere commander in chief whom the French had found to be "of a natural coldness and of a serious and noble approach," was jumping up and down and waving his arms in great, wide arcs, his hat in one hand and handkerchief in the other, a great smile on his face, and he was screaming at them: De Grasse was in the Chesapeake! At this moment, Washington appeared to one of Rochambeau's officers like "a child whose every wish had been gratified," as indeed they had been: De Grasse had arrived with twenty-eight ships of the line equipped with some two thousand cannon, along with three frigates, many transports, and almost twenty thousand men. Cornwallis and his army, trapped by Lafayette ashore, were now cut off from the sea and as good as captive. Another French officer said of Washington that he had "never seen a man more overcome with great and sincere joy. . . ." When Rochambeau came ashore, Washington actually embraced him.

Two days after Washington learned that de Grasse was in the Chesapeake, reports reached him that the fleet had left it again, for unknown reasons. Several days passed before he learned that de Grasse had sailed out to meet the threat of a British fleet and after a sea battle had sent them back to New York, sealing Cornwallis's fate. A few days later, after a short diversion for his first visit to Mount Vernon in six years, Washington rode into the American camp at Williamsburg with Rochambeau and the marquis de Chastellux. By then he had heard the other news he most needed to know, that the fleet under Barras had arrived from Newport with the heavy siege weapons.

Hearing that Washington had arrived, Lafayette rode toward Williamsburg at a gallop, jumped off his horse, ran to him with open arms, and, "with an ardour not easily described," as one interested French observer put it, kissed Washington on both cheeks. As they parted, Washington may have noticed that Lafayette's hair had got noticeably thinner and that his face wore the pallor of a high fever, which he had ignored to enjoy the happiness of this moment.

Lafayette had undergone several tests of character since they had last seen each other, the latest quite recently. As soon as de Grasse arrived in the Chesapeake, he had virtually commanded Lafayette not to wait for Washington and Rochambeau but to begin the assault on Yorktown immediately: Cornwallis could not escape, he argued, and their combined forces were at least equal to those of the British. This was a hard order to turn aside. De Grasse was after all Lafayette's senior in the French military by several ranks and decades, and his proposal promised a lion's share of glory for what was to be the decisive victory of the war. Once the main American army arrived, moreover, Lafayette knew he would be outranked by General Benjamin Lincoln and could only hope for a secondary command, after having spent the entire summer successfully overcoming impossibly long odds to bring Cornwallis to the point of surrender and keep him there.

Choosing to rebuff de Grasse and insist on waiting for Washington was out of character for the man who had arrived in America four years before, but Lafayette had changed. Blooded in battle, bonded with his men, sobered by the demands of leadership, and devoted not only to the principles of the Revolution but also to its leader, he had apparently come to recognize that there was more at stake than his personal glory, or that glory was a more complex alloy than he had known before. That knowledge had made him more thoughtful and less impetuous, as both his letters and his behavior showed. As he had written to Greene during one trying time in the field late that summer: "To speak truth I become timid in the same proportion as I become independent. Had a superior officer been here, I could have proposed half a dozen schemes." Cornwallis's very captivity in Yorktown was attributable to virtues that hardly characterized the younger Lafayette: discretion rather than boldness, caution more than intrepidity, and a regard for his men that mitigated his desire for acclaim. To Washington's news that Benjamin Lincoln would have command of the American wing of the allied army, Lafayette asked only that "the division I will have under him may be composed of the troops which have gone through the fatigues and dangers of the Virginia campaign. . . . I confess the strongest attachment to those troops."

He got what he asked for and more. The allied army arrayed itself before Yorktown with the French on the left and Americans on the right. The three Continental divisions were commanded by Lincoln, Steuben, and Lafayette. One of Lafayette's two brigades was the force he had brought with him from New York. The other contained two regiments that Washington had recently designated "the Light Corps," one commanded by Alexander Hamilton, the other by John Laurens—all of them under command of Lafayette, whose force was given the place of honor at the right side of the front line. Lafayette would end his American Revolution at the heart of the battle, at the head of his beloved light infantry, and with his two closest American comrades.

Preparations for it took several weeks, but the siege of Yorktown lasted only ten days. By the time Cornwallis surrendered his army on October 19, the British had lost 236 men, the Americans 53, the French 60; but de Grasse's defeat of the British fleet in the Battle of the Capes had long since put the British defeat beyond doubt. Outnumbered almost two to one (thanks to Lafayette's decision to wait for Washington and Rochambeau), Cornwallis held out as long as he did only because he had been promised that a second fleet would come to his rescue. That fleet did not leave New York until the day of his surrender, two weeks late.

At Lafayette's urging, the British were denied full battlefield honors, to compensate for the same indignity visited on Americans at the surrender of Charleston. As they marched in dress uniform between the American and French armies, they made a point at first of looking only to the French on the left—all of them in spotless white uniforms, the Bourdonnais regiment with their crimson lapels and pink collars, the Soisonnais with their light blue collars and yellow buttons, Lauzun's cavalry in their scarlet- and yellow-striped sashes. This clearly intended affront to the bedraggled Continentals on the right gave Lafayette, who stood with his American regiments, the chance to show his colors: He ordered his drum major to strike up "Yankee Doodle," and that was the tune to which the British marched as they made their way to an open field, where they gave up their weapons and themselves.

Next day Lafayette gave himself the pleasure of writing to Maurepas: "The play is over, Monsieur le Comte; the fifth act has just ended."

Within the month Lafayette was on his way back to France, and Washington returned to the task that had occupied most of his last two thousand days and would occupy him for the next two years as well: trying to provision the army and keep it together. That job was never more difficult than it was in the face of widespread jubilation at the prospect of victory and the end of war. Washington, of course, could not afford to share in the celebratory mood. His ruling assumption was, as it had to be, that peace talks would break down and that rumors of a breakthrough in the talks could be enemy disinformation, meant to encourage the American military to disband prematurely. At the same time, continually sounding that alarm raised the suspicion in some circles that Washington was simply trying to hold on to his base of power.

If the American public had been reluctant in its generosity toward the Continental Army before, it was even more ungenerous now that the war seemed almost over. As Charles Royster has observed, many American civilians were bruised by a sense of their own inaction or insufficient patriotism during the war—like sufferers from Rush's "Revolutiana"—and so embraced the wishful belief that it was less the soldiers' sacrifice than Americans' common patriotic fervor that had won America its independence. The army's pride was felt as a kind of rebuke to the people's patriotism and war effort, and public resentment focused in particular on the pensions and back pay that had been promised to officers by Congress in the thick of the war.

By early 1783, the government was indebted to its officers for between $4 million and $5 million, and when there was no response to many polite but persistent requests for payment, the officer corps at camp in Newburgh, New York, very nearly dissolved in mutiny. Letters signed only "a fellow soldier" circulated among them, lambasting an ungrateful nation that "tramples on your rights, disdains your cries and insults your distresses," and warning ominously: "The army has its alternative." Washington sympathized with his officers' demand for what they had been promised; but the suggestion that the army should refuse to disarm when peace came, or that it should refuse to fight a renewed war, leaving the government helpless, was more than he could bear.

At a meeting he called to quiet the rising anger, Washington denounced the anonymous writer ("My God! . . . Can he be a friend to this country?"). He told the men he supported their monetary claims and cited the difficulty of getting anything through Congress because of its competing interests. At last, he made a stirring appeal to their courage and devotion to high principle. By standing against this "fellow soldier," he said, "you will give one more distinguished proof of unexampled patriotism and patient virtue . . . And you will, by the dignity of your conduct, afford occasion for posterity to say . . . 'had this day been wanting, the world [would] never [have] seen the last stage of perfection to which human nature is capable of attaining.' "

That was the end of his prepared speech, but after gauging its effect, he apparently felt it was not enough. In his pocket he had a letter from Virginia congressman Joseph Jones that tried to explain the complications of getting the officers' pay through Congress, and he began to read it to the men, but after a few sentences he reached into his vest pocket for a pair of glasses. This was new to Washington's officers, who had never seen him in spectacles. Washington had got them from the manufacturer not long before, having said he needed a pair that would "magnify properly & show those objects very distinctly which at first appear like a mist blended together & confused." Hearing a rustle in the audience as he put them on, he thought to say, "Gentlemen, you must pardon me. I have grown gray in the service of my country and now find myself growing blind."

Washington had a gift for the dramatic, but there is no indication this was anything but what it seemed, a slightly rueful moment of self-effacement that unintentionally yet movingly reminded his audience that every day of the past eight years had required of their commander in chief great personal sacrifice, relentless dedication to the cause, and unremitting hard work. He went on to read the letter from Congressman Jones, which was most certainly not the reason, after Washington left the room, that some of his officers were discreetly drying their eyes. Before the meeting adjourned, Washington's officers unanimously passed a resolution declaring their gratitude toward him and their commitment to continued negotiations with Congress. Once again, Washington had held the Continental Army together with nothing but a demonstration of his own belief in and commitment to the righteousness of the American cause.

This was clearly a new kind of officer corps, indeed a new kind of person, this Continental soldier. Johann Ewald, captain of a company of German jaegers, was among those who tipped his hat to his ill-fed, barefoot enemies. "With what soldiers in the world could one do what was done by these men. . . . Deny the best disciplined soldiers of Europe what is due them and they will run away in droves. . . . But from this one can perceive what an enthusiasm—which these poor fellows call 'Liberty'—can do."

Like Ewald, Baron von Steuben came from a military tradition in which officers fought for military "glory," and martial discipline was maintained by hierarchy and fear. He too had emerged from Valley Forge and finished his American Revolution as a different officer and a changed man, convinced of the motive power of comradeship and shared ideals. As he put it in his farewell to the New Jersey line in July 1783:

A desire of fame was my ruling motive for visiting America, but when I saw so many brave, so many good men encountering every species of distress for the cause of their country, the course of my ambition was changed, and my only wish was to be linked in the chain of friendship . . . and to render that country which had given birth to so many patriots, every service in my power.

Washington of course had learned the same lesson, in part from Steuben. But from the public's strange resentment of their victorious military—from its reluctant support all along—he had learned another lesson as well: As good as a well-led force of men could be, the public, badly governed, could be as faithless and dangerous as a mob, potentially fatal to the best of causes. He enshrined this concern in his final Circular to the States, in June 1783, when peace was finally a fait accompli and he was bound for what he swore would be his final retirement from public life. In one of the most subtle and carefully crafted statements of his career, he began by paying flowery tribute to all the fruits of the Revolution—"absolute freedom and Independency . . . a fairer opportunity for political happiness, than any other nation has ever been favored with." Then, noting Americans' good fortune that this had been attempted not "in the gloomy age Ignorance and Superstition, but at an epoch when the rights of mankind were better understood and more clearly defined than at any former period," he brought down the hammer:

> At this auspicious period, the United States came into existence as a nation, and if their citizens should not be completely free and happy, the fault will be entirely their own. . . . It is in their choice, and depends upon their conduct, whether they will be respectable and prosperous or contemptible and miserable as a nation. . . . [It] is yet to be decided, whether the Revolution must ultimately be considered as a blessing or a curse. . . .

What a strange farewell that must have seemed. Its burden, of course, was to convince the states of the wisdom of a strong central government, and of the alternative danger, "that unless the States will suffer Congress to exercise [its] prerogatives, every thing must very rapidly tend to anarchy and confusion. . . ." He had seen what weak governance could do, and he had seen the ingratitude and shortsightedness of a feckless people. His officers were paying for both with their pensions.

Lafayette, like many of the French soldiers and officers, took back to France a less nuanced, entirely enthusiastic vision of the American Revolution, the story of a great-hearted people's triumph over despotic power in the cause of their inalienable human rights, the creation of a new society based on equality and civil liberty. Almost as soon as he was home, Lafayette wrote Washington to express his enthusiasm for more movements of human liberation. He suggested that they jointly buy an estate somewhere in America as the site of a grand experiment: "to free the Negroes and use them only as tenants. Such an example as yours might render it a general practice, and if we succeed in America I will cheerfully devote a part of my time to render the method fashionable in the West Indies. If it be a wild scheme, I had rather be mad that way, than to be thought wise on the other tack." The suggestion was both admirably idealistic and, if not mad, oblivious of political reality in the American South. Washington responded that the plan "is a striking evidence of the benevolence of your heart" and said he would be happy to join him but preferred for the moment to defer a discussion of details until their next meeting. As good as his word, Lafayette eventually proceeded with the plan, buying a plantation for the purpose in French Guyana. Washington wrote nothing more about it and took no part.

Always sympathetic to Lafayette and his idealism, Washington was never tempted to depart from what he knew to be realistically possible. In the same letter in which he talked about ending slavery, Lafayette told Washington he would like to be the person who carried the Treaty of Paris to London for signature, and in a letter to Congress's secretary of foreign affairs Washington seconded his request. When the secretary objected, though, Washington immediately conceded: "There is no man upon earth I have a greater inclination to serve than the Marquis La Fayette; but I have no wish to do it in matters that interfere with . . . our national policy, dignity or interest."

Deprived of its context, construed only as the victory of high ideals over corrupt power, the American Revolution turned out not to travel well. Years later John Adams tried to explain in a letter to the abbé de Mably, who was threatening to write a history of the glorious War of Independence, that Americans had been well prepared for their revolution by colonial institutions. Only by implication did he observe that these pre-conditions were entirely missing in France. The American people, he said, had long been knit together by their towns, schools, congregations, and militia. Public issues had always been subject to debate. Every turn of the revolutionary movement had been argued—as everything from grazing rights to local ordinances had always been argued—in town meetings (in other words, not decided elsewhere and dictated from above, as in France). Public education was the right of every American child and required in every town with sixty families or more, and these schools (not a social hierarchy) were responsible for turning out the community's future leaders. The church's congregations (not Rome, not hereditary wealth) determined who would preach in every pulpit, and church leaders (instead of having mistresses and barely if ever visiting their parishes) were held to practice what they preached. Finally, the core of the American military was its militia, a citizens' army charged to protect citizens' rights and public safety (not to enforce the king's absolute rule or protect the privileges of an aristocracy).

After Yorktown, the marquis de Chastellux continued the tour of America that he had begun the year before, and he too sounded caution-ary notes about the fate of the American idea in France. Revisiting Lex-ington and Concord, Bunker Hill, and Dorchester Heights, he reflected on how odd it was that a Virginian, a man who had never seen Boston before, came to be its liberator. He was struck by the great differences among the states and their citizens, which prompted a reflection that the leaders of the French Revolution might have done well to take to heart: "States, like individuals, are born with a temperament of their own . . . which can never be entirely changed. Thus, legislators, like doctors, ought never presume to believe that they can bestow, at will, a particular tem-perament on bodies politic, but should attempt to understand the temper they already have, while striving to combat the disadvantages and increase the advantages resulting from it."

Chastellux had a premonition that his country would be going through a radical transition, one that perhaps had already begun. In Philadelphia, an old Quaker asked him why, given the admonishments of the *philosophes*, there was still such intolerance in France. Chastellux said the man was right to have faith in the power of Enlightenment thinking in France, explaining only half facetiously that although they were still richly rewarded, prejudice and persecution increasingly faced the ultimate French rebuke: "They are no longer fashionable."

Clearly, however, Chastellux was under no illusion that the American experience could be simply transplanted. Two weeks before sailing back to France, he was in Boston with a group of twenty other returning French officers when they visited with the Reverend Samuel Cooper, the eloquent, Francophile pastor of Boston's Brattle Square Church. When the officers spoke eagerly about the triumph of liberty, Cooper cut them short. "Take care, young men," he said. "You carry home with you the seeds of liberty, but if you attempt to plant them in a country that has been corrupt for so long, you will face obstacles far more formidable than we did. We spilled a great deal of blood to win our liberty, but to establish it in the old world, you will shed it in torrents."*

Chastellux, a distant relative, became one of Lafayette's most outspoken admirers, beginning the day they met in his camp. In light of events soon to unfold, Chastellux's initial estimation of Lafayette achieved the force of prophecy: "Fortunate his country if she knows how to avail herself of [his talents]. More fortunate still should she stand in no need of them!"

Though he lived to see Lafayette rise to prominence in France's early reform movement, Chastellux would never know how great was the role Lafayette would be called upon to play in their country, or just how horribly the zeal for liberation would play out there; because long before Lafayette found himself at the head of the French Revolution, long before the blood began to flow in earnest, Chastellux was dead. So was Vergennes; and Maurepas, the last man who was ever in control of Louis's

---

*Perhaps this was Cooper's genuine opinion, but we cannot be sure. The Reverend Cooper had been paid for years to promote the interests of France in America by none other than Charles Gravier de Vergennes, who knew very well that by supporting America's independence France had contributed to a cause whose spread could represent a threat to monarchy itself.

increasingly rebellious parlements, died just after he heard about the victory at Yorktown.

Vergennes hoped for a time that he could be Maurepas's replacement, but Louis would never designate another chief minister, as much as he would need one. The day after Maurepas's death, Louis called a meeting of his ministers, one of whom recorded in his journal afterward that the king had talked much more than usual that day, "as one saying to himself, 'I want to reign.'"

PART TWO

The Dark Side of Liberty

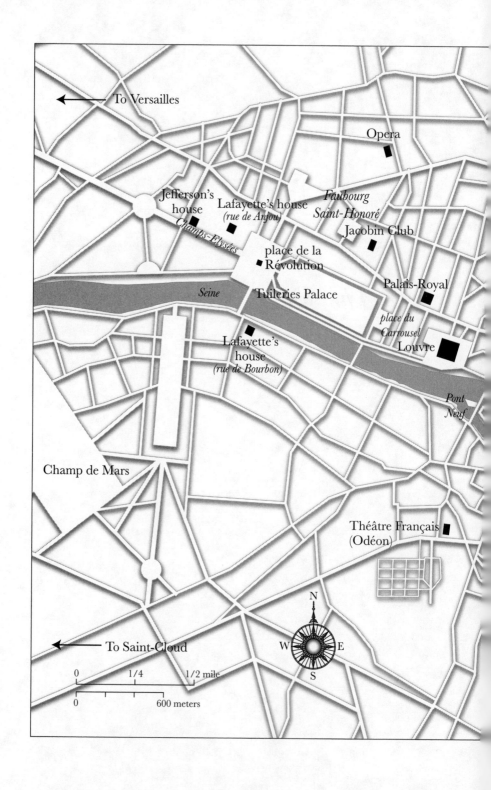

To Versailles

Opera

Jefferson's house

Lafayette's house
(rue de Anjou)

Faubourg Saint-Honoré

Champs-Elysées

Jacobin Club

place de la Révolution

Seine

Tuileries Palace

Palais-Royal

place du Carrousel

Louvre

Lafayette's house
(rue de Bourbon)

Pont Neuf

Champ de Mars

Théâtre Français (Odéon)

To Saint-Cloud

0   1/4   1/2 mile

0   600 meters

N
W   E
S

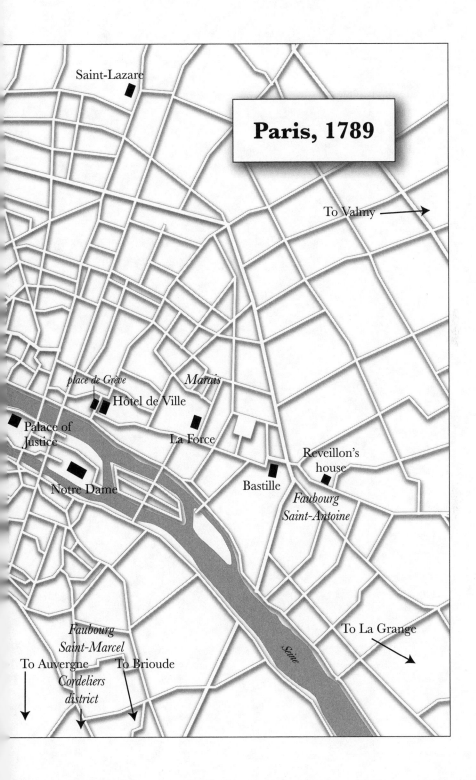

Saint-Lazare

Paris, 1789

To Valmy →

place de Grève   *Marais*
Hôtel de Ville

Palace of
Justice   La Force

Reveillon's
house

Notre Dame   Bastille

*Faubourg
Saint-Antoine*

To La Grange

*Faubourg
Saint-Marcel*

To Auvergne   To Brioude

Seine

*Cordeliers
district*

XIII

Entr'acte

On December 8, 1783, a remarkable notice appeared in the *Journal de Paris* from a man claiming he could walk on water. A watchmaker, identified only as "D . . . ," said he had discovered a new force, which had something to do with ricochets, on the basis of which he had devised a pair of what he called "elastic shoes." In these, he declared, he would walk across the Seine near the Pont Neuf on New Year's Day, provided that his demonstration would by then be subscribed in the amount of 200 gold louis, or about 4,000 livres. More than 3,000 livres arrived at the journal's offices within the week, from some of the most prominent citizens of Paris. One of the most beneficent contributors was Lafayette. Of course it was. He was rich, he was enthusiastic, and, thanks to his legendary feats in America, he was prominent in all things: a force in Paris society among aristocrats and *philosophes* alike, a favorite of both the king and the queen, and one of Paris's few bona fide popular celebrities, at a time when the concept of "popular" would have excluded the vast majority of French people (the peasantry and most townsfolk) but embraced an expanding circle of merchants, business owners, civic officials, academics, writers, physicians, advocates, and other professionals, otherwise known as *bourgeois*.

Among this new popular culture's most riveting fascinations was popular science, whose extravagant promise had begun to reach the imagination of the common man. Even people who would not have read Voltaire's popularization of Newton, even people who could not read at all, had heard of Franklin's experiment with a kite and key in lightning, and then there had come a feat that trumped both electricity and gravity.

On September 19, 1783, a sixty-foot-high taffeta balloon of azure blue, painted with gold fleurs-de-lys and filled with hot air, was released from the ministers' courtyard of Versailles and rose unsteadily but surely above the earth. On board, in addition to a duck and a rooster, was a sheep, the first of God's unfeathered creatures to spend any time at all above the earth. When further balloon flights with humans aboard confirmed that man had indeed penetrated the mystery of flight, no further proof was needed that the age of omniscience had dawned. One courtier-cynic observed drily that the spectacle of manned flight had "given such a shock to the French that it has restored vigor to the aged, imagination to the peasants, and constancy to our women." But the more common reaction was open-mouthed awe. When one balloon landed in the French countryside, a group of astonished peasants are said to have asked the pilots, "Are you men or gods?" Far more sophisticated observers asked the same thing, likening balloon pilots to "the gods of antiquity carried on clouds. . . . Myths have come to life in the marvel of physics." Witnesses to balloon flights described them almost as secular Assumptions: "It is impossible to describe that moment, the women in tears, the common people raising their hands toward the sky in deep silence; the passengers leaning out of the gallery, waving and crying out in joy. . . . No one said anything but, 'Great God, how beautiful!' "

On December 3, not long before he made his contribution to the elastic shoe maker, Lafayette attended the latest aeronaut to astonish his fellow Parisians. The scientist J.-A.-C. Charles, in a silk balloon filled with hydrogen, had just piloted a two-hour flight from the Tuileries to a touchdown twenty-seven miles away. Before a crowd of admiring aristocrats, *bourgeois*, and equally awestruck lessers, Charles ducked into Lafayette's carriage for the ride back to Paris and a congratulatory reception at the Palais-Royal. A few days later, Lafayette wrote his first (and only) scientific treatise, "An authentic narrative of experiments lately made in France with air balloons."

In France, in 1783, everybody was a scientist. "In all our gatherings," a contemporary observer wrote, "at all our suppers, at the toilettes of our lovely women as in our academic lyceums, we talk of nothing but experiments, atmospheric air, inflammable gas, flying chariots, journeys in the air." Small wonder science was the rage, since it seemed to be at the brink of telling all the world's secrets. After enumerating the "incredible discoveries" of the past decade, the *Journal de Bruxelles* asked, "Who knows how far we can go? What mortal would dare set limits to the human mind?" At a time when the suspension of disbelief seemed commonsensical, of course, credulity could not be far behind.

Happily for his subscribers, D's elastic shoes were exposed as a hoax several days before January 1, 1784, and so took their place among many other such "findings" of popular science. Less than a month after purveying the ricochet theory behind walking on water, the *Journal de Paris* dusted itself off and published a letter from someone who had found a way to see perfectly well in pitch-black darkness. Other journals reported on "styptic water" that would stanch all hemorrhages, a mill that created its own power, and a method for traveling and breathing underground. They also featured scientific explications of such former mysteries as dancing eggs and talking dogs.

The most widely discussed of the popular sciences was Mesmerism, which could also claim Lafayette as an early proselyte. The German physician Franz Anton Mesmer had arrived from Vienna in Paris in 1778, and by the time Lafayette returned from America in 1782, his theory of "animal magnetism" had utterly captivated French society, including Marie-Antoinette. Mesmer's theory, which roughly comported with other, more scientific thinking, was that an ethereal fluid pervaded the universe and was not only the medium of action for light, heat, gravity, and electricity but was also the fount of human health and the source of all disease, which was nothing more nor less than an obstacle to the flow of this mesmeric fluid, a blockage also known as a lack of natural "harmony." The restoration of harmony was accomplished by reorienting—"mesmerizing"—the body's magnetic poles. The important north and south poles at head and feet, which received the mesmeric fluid from stars and the earth respectively, were not to be disturbed. Rather, Mesmer and his assistants worked on the many smaller poles that were located all around the body. These were constantly changing positions, and so the patient had to be felt about for them by skilled and busy fingers, which made for interesting scenes and torrid gossip.

The best proof that harmony was being restored was a convulsive "crisis," which a later age would diagnose as an hysterical fit. The historian Robert Darnton, in his brilliant and bemused study *Mesmerism and the End of Enlightenment in France*, draws a vivid picture of the atmosphere at Mesmer's clinic, where everything

> was designed to produce a crisis in the patient. . . . Heavy carpets, weird astrological wall-decorations, and drawn curtains shut [the patient] off from the outside world and muffled the occasional words, screams, and bursts of hysterical laughter that broke the habitual heavy silence. Shafts of fluid struck him constantly in the somber light reflected by strategically placed mirrors. Soft music, played on wind instruments, a pianoforte, or the glass "harmonica" that Mesmer helped to introduce in France, sent reinforced waves of fluid deep into his soul. Every so often fellow patients collapsed, writhing on the floor, and were carried by Antoine, the mesmerist-valet, into the crisis room; and . . . Mesmer himself would approach, dressed in a lilac taffeta robe, and drill fluid into the patient from his hands, his imperial eye, and his mesmerized wand.

Professional scientists and physicians began attacking Mesmer for charlatanism almost as soon as they noticed him; and thus began, as early as 1779, a war of words that resulted in at least two hundred books and pamphlets on the Mesmerist side alone, more than were written on any single subject in the next decade (which, lest we forget, led up to a violent social and political revolution). Mesmer's army of amateur scientists adopted a posture of wounded innocence, of misunderstood genius, which only further inflamed their critics in the universities, at the Royal Society of Medicine, and in the Academy of Sciences. When some of the faculty of the University of Paris medical school joined in Mesmer's defense, they were summarily fired. Protest over these dismissals, which were said to be a symptom of the "most absolute despotism of opinion," inaugurated the rhetorical link between Mesmerism and the French Revolution, but of course no one made the connection between Mesmer and political dissent at the time. How could they? Among Mesmer's defenders was Marie-Antoinette, who intervened to get him a life pension of 20,000 livres a year. In a grand-standing public letter to the queen, he refused the offer, citing "the austerity of my principles," but at the same time suggesting that a country estate might do, and what was a few hundred thousand francs to the royal treasury? The revolutionary current in Mesmerism was, for the moment, deeply submerged.

The Society of Universal Harmony (*Société de l'Harmonie Universelle*), a secretive, crypto-Masonic group which eventually had chapters in every major city in France, was founded in Paris by the lawyer Nicolas Bergasse and the banker Guillaume Kornmann to spread the faith of Mesmerism but also to fund a hospital and a home base for Mesmer. Their goal was to raise 30,000 louis d'or from three hundred subscribers, so they naturally turned to the wealthy aristocrats who were clamoring for membership from the start. Among them were such veterans of the American Revolution as the duc de Lauzun, the comte de Ségur, the marquis de Chastellux, and, of course, the marquis de Lafayette. In theory, at least, nobles were treated without favor in the group. Each member took his place in order, regardless of rank: Lawyer Bergasse was Member No. 1, banker Kornmann No. 2, the marquis de Lafayette No. 91. Mesmer proudly proclaimed his indifference to titles and his contempt for all forms of social hierarchy. Prominent in his treatment facility were four wide tubs, where patients sat in shallow water and exposed themselves to an apparatus filled with iron filings in order to restore the magnetic flow to their afflicted areas. One of these tubs, reserved for the poor, was rarely occupied; another, for ladies of rank, was set off by flowers; and the doorman at Mesmer's quarters at the Hôtel de Coigny was said to have three different whistles to distinguish arrivals by class. Still, even the illusion of class-mixing was oddly titillating. The ideas of freedom and equality were quite pleasing to the aristocracy of Paris, so long as they were not taken seriously. As Ségur put it in his memoirs, "There is a satisfaction in descending from a high rank, as long as the resumption of it is thought to be free and unobstructed. . . . We enjoyed our patrician advantages together with the sweets of a plebian philosophy."

The trouble came when mingling got out of hand, for which, in certain circles, the Americans were held responsible. In 1783, a collection of the states' constitutions was published in Paris. Even Benjamin Franklin, who supervised the edition, was surprised the censors had let it through.

As summarized approvingly in the conservative *Année littéraire,* the constitutions declared categorically "that it is in the people that all power
originally resides . . . [and] it is from the people that all power emanates."
In pleasure seemingly mixed with shock, the journal article named the
rights given, for example, to the citizens of Massachusetts: ". . . liberty,
equality, the full enjoyment of one's property, the rendering to God the
worship dictated by conscience." In a nation with neither civil liberty nor
equality nor full property rights nor freedom of religion, these were incendiary ideas, and by 1783 they were coming from all sides. Despite warnings
from the likes of the Reverend Samuel Cooper, thousands of returning
French officers and troops were bringing home tales of a society governed
by principles of freedom, equality, and popular sovereignty, and no one
brought them back with quite so much uproar as Lafayette.

L afayette arrived at the Hôtel de Noailles for the first time since Yorktown on January 19, 1782, during a banquet given by the city of Paris
to celebrate the long-awaited delivery of the king's first child (whose failure to appear sooner had raised questions about the royal couple's sex life).*
News of Lafayette's homecoming would have reached the gathering at the
Hôtel de Ville very quickly, but he could not expect Adrienne to be home
for some time: Etiquette forbade her from leaving the party before the
king and queen, and after that would follow the usual long procession
behind them to their quarters, which tonight would be the Château de la
Muette near the Bois de Boulogne. Soon after Lafayette arrived home,
though, the clatter of carriages brought him to the front door, where a
large crowd had already gathered to cheer the return of their "hero of two
worlds." They shared his shock when the carriage of Marie-Antoinette
pulled up in front of his house at the head of the royal procession, and
doubly so when it became apparent that Adrienne was riding beside her,

*To check on things the emperor Joseph himself visited and reported to his brother
Leopold, "This is the secret: in bed, he has good hard erections; he injects his organ,
remains there motionless for two minutes or so, then withdraws, still stiff, without
discharging, and drops off to sleep. It makes no sense . . . he needs to be beaten like
an ass to get him to discharge his spunk. With all this, my sister has little appetite for
the whole business, and together they make a hopelessly clumsy pair."

an astonishing breach of protocol that was also a mark of great favor—for Adrienne and for Lafayette. So was the queen's insistence, after warmly praising Lafayette for his glorious American service, that Adrienne get out of the carriage and stay behind with him. At that the crowd burst into applause, and Adrienne, altogether overcome, fainted into her husband's arms.

So, metaphorically, did France. "The reception I have met from the nation at large, from the King and from my friends . . . surpassed my utmost ambition," he wrote Washington a few days later. Poems and pamphlets about him appeared in the bookstalls, his face was engraved on porcelain pieces, artists came to paint his portrait, and King Gustavus III invited him to Sweden. Back in his box at the Opéra, he saw that a bust of himself had been set up on stage in place of Achilles, and he accepted the audience's cheers as the star soprano crowned it with a laurel wreath. (Actors were doing this sort of thing at the time. The same was done for pioneer balloonists.)

At about the same time, the Virginia Assembly ordered a bust to be made and presented to Lafayette in Paris. In a letter informing him of the honor, Washington said he was glad to be the one "through which the just and grateful plaudits of my native state are communicated to the man I love." A few days later, though, he thought to write a member of the Assembly about it: "I am not a judge of the etiquette on these occasions, but it really does seem odd to me to present a man with his own likeness."

Lafayette, of course, was thrilled with the honor, this one and all the many others. Three weeks after his homecoming, he was the first person ever admitted by acclamation to the Masonic Lodge of Saint-Jean d'Ecosse du Contrat Social, whose members included Chastellux and de Grasse. Being elected without a vote was an honor "reserved for heroes," he was told, "of which there have been no previous examples." Climbing aboard the Lafayette bandwagon, Louis XVI made him a *maréchal-de-camp* (at all of twenty-four, which caused grumbling among more senior officers), and only a few months later gave him the even more coveted Cross of the Order of St. Louis. At a ball in Versailles's Hall of Mirrors for the visiting czarevitch Paul of Russia, Marie-Antoinette, by the light of five thousand candles, danced with Lafayette again, and this time he did not stumble.

Fortune's smile on Lafayette seemed almost giddy. Despite the expense of his American adventure, which eventually cost him more than a million livres, Lafayette was richer than he had ever been: His great-grandfather the comte de La Rivière had died while he was in America, leaving him a huge estate in Brittany. He was such a soft touch for people and causes in need that his trustee began to complain of his profligacy, but as of that fall he no longer had to listen. On September 6, 1782, he turned twenty-five, then the legal age of majority in France. Two weeks later, Adrienne gave birth to their fourth child, a daughter whom they named Virginie. With Anastasie now five and George Washington almost four, they bought and lavishly furnished a home of their own on the rue de Bourbon, which quickly became a center of gravity in Paris society, known for its "Monday dinners," also dubbed "American dinners." Benjamin Franklin, long ailing with "the gravel" (kidney stones), came to Paris from Passy only rarely, but John Adams and John Jay, who had been sent to Paris to negotiate treaties of commerce and friendship with all the nations of Europe, were frequent guests. So were such veterans of the American Revolution as Chastellux and Noailles, and some of Lafayette's friends from more recent enthusiasms, such as Mesmerism, ballooning, and the abolition movement.

Lafayette, with and without Adrienne, was a prominent fixture in other Paris salons as well, notably those of the circle of the prince de Conti, where he often found his friends Ségur and the prince de Poix, and where he had met Aglaé d'Hunolstein. That relationship resumed with his return to France, but within a few months her family complained that her connection with Lafayette had become an embarrassment to her husband (though they made no recorded complaint when she was mistress of the duc d'Orléans). In early 1783 she asked Lafayette to release her, and in a letter that made much of how resistant she had been to him, as if for public or family consumption, he made a great show of giving her up. In fact, however, he had met someone else by then, the comtesse de Simiane, who was twenty-two years old and said to be an even greater beauty than Aglaé d'Hunolstein had been. Lafayette's relationship with Mme de Simiane would continue for decades, long outlasting whatever romantic infatuation there might have been—perhaps because, as some of his friends thought, he was actually more interested in politics than romance. Far more of Lafayette's correspondence with Mme de Simiane is about their ideological differences than their relationship, and in politics they were not bedfellows at all. Resolutely, defiantly aristocratic, she became one of the people who would most vigorously challenge his liberal principles.

Lafayette was actually better known among his friends for his domestic attachment than for his extramarital affairs. Perhaps because he had felt comforted by the hand of fate all his life, he seemed impervious to most of the usual temptations that attend fame and fortune. Visitors to the "American dinners" took special note of two things. One was how much Lafayette and Adrienne doted on their children—"the more remarkable," as young Abigail Adams noted in her diary, "in a country where the least trait of such a disposition is scarce known." The other was the presence of George Washington, whose portrait dominated the drawing room and whose influence was constant, palpable, and frequently invoked. "My little family," Lafayette wrote to his "adopted father," "are taught before all to revere and to love General Washington. . . . I hope you will approve my conduct, and in every thing I do I first consider what your opinion would be had I an opportunity to consult it."

L afayette was certifiably a celebrity, no less a popular hero than the Montgolfier brothers or their fellow balloonists, and as an aristocrat wrapped in the flag of equality he was also among the signal figures of a social revolution that predated and set the scene for the political one.

The society of Paris had been conflating for more than a decade by the early 1780s, when the convergent aristo-rabble found a kind of capital within the capital in the open quadrangle and covered promenade of the new Palais-Royal. "There," wrote the Paris chronicler Louis-Sébastien Mercier, "you can see everything, learn everything. . . ." Formerly Cardinal Richelieu's palace, it belonged now to the duc d'Orléans, who converted it into a day-and-night commercial carnival of shops, cafés, billiard parlors, gambling dens, and bordellos. The masses had rarely teemed into central Paris before, but now, hard by the Louvre and the Tuileries, pouring into the very heartland of the court, came a steady stream of orators and pickpockets, sidewalk poets and streetwalkers, slumming aristocrats and seedy social climbers. Especially after dark, the Palais-Royal was a kind of pedigree-free zone: Was that a great lady passing by, or a well-dressed courtesan? (Sometimes, of course, the difference was technical.) That somber fellow across the way, was he a parlementarian or a pimp? Everything was for sale at the Palais-Royal, from lemonade to sex to subsidized diatribes by literary lowlife. Police rarely invaded property of the king's relatives, so everything forbidden was safe here, censored truths and scurrilous *libelles* alike. Some would say later that d'Orléans knew exactly what he was doing when he built "this enchanted place," as Mercier called it, where one could see "the confusion of estates, the mixture, the throng." In any case, the Palais-Royal was an exciting place where things could get even more exciting very quickly.

These days, the rowdy public were invading all the best places. Crowds had never been invited to gather at Versailles, for example, until the balloon launch of Jacques-Etienne Montgolfier brought out more than a hundred thousand not altogether ruly spectators, most of whom walked from Paris. The result was perhaps only symbolic, but Versailles was all about symbolism. It had been built by Louis XIV so that the spectacle of absolutism could be minutely choreographed and all power would be shown to emanate from Himself. As the *mise en scène* for a balloon launch, however, Versailles was demystified, the eyes of the crowd were lifted above the majesty of the king, and the results were suggestive. The *Journal de Bruxelles*, for instance, reported on an odd scene that took place around another balloon launch, when, just after the release, a commoner named Fontaine jumped aboard, startling several nobles who had earlier refused him a place. "On earth I respected you," he explained, "but here we are equals!"

Placing the birth of the French Revolution is a parlor game everybody wins: Was it born in the gondola of a balloon, or in the courtyard of the Palais-Royal, or with the Declaration of Independence, or at the outbreak of the Grain War in Dijon? Yes. It was also born in the theater.

Our man Beaumarchais was a pioneer at these blurred social borders, twenty-five years ahead of Lafayette: Was he a man of the people or an aristocrat? It depended when you asked the question, and who asked it. In 1783, one could have an interesting discussion about that; ten years later, the answer meant life or death. At the moment, Beaumarchais could have given whatever answer he wanted. He had made enough money at commerce to buy his way into the nobility twenty years ago, and as the sometime recipient of covert royal funds and a well-known if informal adviser at Versailles, he was certifiably one of the king's men. But he was also famous (thanks to his pamphleteering for himself) for being the first person ever to have won a judgment against a nobleman before the parlement of Provence, a victory celebrated in an all-night outpouring of joy and disbelief: Could it be that the double standard of justice was at an end? So Beaumarchais and his partisans profoundly wished. He was writing *The Marriage of Figaro* at the time. This lyric did not make it past the censors:

> *Soldier stealing a bracelet*
> *Gets hung without remission;*
> *But as for the contribution*
> *That a general puts in his pocket*
> *It's thought a noble deed.*

Louis was among the play's first readers, and he forbade its performance, seeing it instantly for the subversion it was. "This man mocks everything that must be respected in a government," he said, adding the unwitting prophecy that were he to allow it an audience, he might as well "tear down the Bastille." Napoleon would come to agree with him. "If I had been the king, [Beaumarchais] would have been locked up," he said. "With *The Marriage of Figaro*, the Revolution had already begun."

The Marriage of Figaro was the best play Beaumarchais had ever written, the best one he would ever write, and he was not about to allow it to become a casualty of absolutism. Fortunately for him, the king felt that the monarchy and France were much in Beaumarchais's debt. With the peace treaty of 1783, France was resurgent. Its African colonies were restored, and Dunkirk was freed from its occupation, one of the most poignant humiliations visited by defeat in the Seven Years' War. Beaumarchais's triumphant initiative on American policy had given him standing at the highest levels of government and the court, so when the battle over *Figaro* was joined, the playwright had his own highly placed advocates. He could play the honest man up against a corrupt despotism because one of the people who wanted to see his play was Marie-Antoinette.

He gave private readings, but always under elaborate protest and always to an audience whose rank would protect him from the king's wrath. Marie-Antoinette's closest friends, the princesse de Lamballe and Mme de Polignac, eventually ordered readings, as did the maréchal de Richelieu. Even the king's brothers were divided over whether a perform-ance of *Figaro* should be allowed, the older Provence against it, d'Artois outspokenly for; and so the readings continued. Mme de Campan, secre-tary to Marie-Antoinette, wrote in her journal, "Every day you could hear people saying, 'I have been or I am going to a reading of Beaumarchais's play.'"

Finally, the comte d'Artois succeeded in getting the king to allow a single performance for the court by the actors of the Théâtre Français. It was to take place on the evening of June 13, 1783, in Versailles's Théâtre des Menus-Plaisirs. Drawn by what promised to be one of the spectacular events of the season, guests began arriving hours early to claim the best seats. Some minutes before the curtain, however, there arrived a *lettre de cachet* from the king banning the production "on pain of His Majesty's indignation," which meant the price of defiance would be prison. The audience were beyond enraged: Their reaction was downright revolution-ary. "This prohibition by the King," wrote Mme de Campan, "seemed an attack on the public liberty. So many disappointed hopes excited dissatis-faction to such a point that the words 'oppression' and 'tyranny' were never pronounced with more passion and vehemence. . . ." Beaumarchais, who was of course livid, affected obedience. "I again patiently replace the piece in my portfolio," he wrote to M. Breteuil, a senior member of the queen's party, "waiting until another event shall draw it forth."

That fall, again at the urging of his brother d'Artois, Louis lifted his ban to permit another of the queen's friends, the comte de Vandreuil, to host a single performance at a small theater in his home. Cleverly, Beau-marchais insisted that before any such performance the play would have to win the censors' approval, which he knew would be forthcoming for any performance patronized by a brother of the king. The verdict was as he expected: The censor deemed the play to be the amusing but benign story of one of those "intriguers of the lower class, whose examples are not dangerous for any man of the world." And so one afternoon in late September, a long procession of carriages, including those of d'Artois, Mme de Polignac, and the princesse Lamballe, left Versailles bound for Vaudreuil's home in Gennevilliers. Marie-Antoinette had said she was going as well, but at the last minute she canceled, pleading illness. To banish the heat of an Indian-summer day, Beaumarchais bashed out the windows of the theater with his cane. Then he went to work on his audience.

What they saw (and all that Mozart chose to make of it in his opera, in deference to his audience) was a drawing-room comedy—"the most trifling of plots," as Beaumarchais himself described it, "a Spanish nobleman in love with a girl whom he wishes to seduce; and the efforts that the girl, the man to whom she is betrothed, and the nobleman's wife make together to thwart an absolute master whose rank, fortune, and profligacy make him all-powerful. That's all, nothing more." Nothing more indeed. Inside that "most trifling of plots," Beaumarchais smuggled the most powerful attack on hereditary power ever to hit a public stage. Everything in the play—everything in Beaumarchais's life and career—leads up to the third scene of the fifth act, when Figaro delivers one of the longest soliloquies in the history of the theater, sometimes speaking as if directly to Count Almaviva, at other times to himself.

> No, Count, you shall not have her! You shall not have her! Because you're a great noble man you think you are a great genius! Nobility, fortune, rank, status: so much to glory in! But what did you do to get where you are? You took the trouble to be born, and that's all.

One can see Louis's problem, and even more clearly so as Beaumarchais elaborates on the fate of a playwright in a world of noble boors. As one of the great moments in the theater of dissent (one could argue that this was the moment of its birth), the speech in which Beaumarchais tears apart the royal censors bears reading at length.

> FIGARO: I reckoned I could lampoon Mahomet without treading on anyone's corns. But an envoy from . . . somewhere promptly complains that my play has offended the Ottoman Empire, part of the Indian subcontinent, the whole of Egypt. . . . And my comedy

goes up in flames. . . . I did my best to survive. Views were being aired on the nature of wealth. You don't have to own something to be able to discuss it, so, without a penny to my name, I wrote an essay on the value of money and its net earnings. At once I saw, from the depths of my carriage, the drawbridge of a castle being lowered for me; at its gate I left behind hope and liberty. [*Rising to his feet*] How I'd like to get my hands on one of those four-day potentates, those blithe issuers of warrants for evil. . . . I'd tell him— that printed trifles don't matter a jot, except in places where their circulation is restricted—that without freedom to censure there can be no praise and no flattery—and that only little men are afraid of little books.

Figaro's speech continues for several minutes after that, plunging deeper and deeper into political blasphemy, until all that is left is for Almaviva's cruel lust to be decisively foiled and the innocent lovers to be happily united in marriage. In the seventh verse of the final song, Figaro thinks over what he has learned during this Day of Madness, and sinks his knife into monarchy itself:

> *By the hazard of gestation,*
> *One's a shepherd, the other's a king;*
> *Chance caused this separation;*
> *Wit alone can change everything.*
> *Scores of kings held in veneration*
> *Pass on and unadorned lie;*
> *And Voltaire will never die.*

One of life's lesser mysteries is with what passionate enthusiasm some of the the noblest nobles in Louis's court loved *The Marriage of Figaro*. Could they really not have seen themselves as the worthless, born-lucky boobs who were the objects of Figaro's contempt? Could they not see how threatening was the notion that hereditary power is by definition corrupt? "Strange blindness!" as one audience member had the wisdom to observe in her journal of the pre-revolutionary years. For whatever reason, the audience at the comte de Vandreuil's home theater in Gennevilliers interrupted *Figaro* so many times with applause that the play lasted more than five hours.

When Louis finally relented and allowed the piece to open at the new home of the Théâtre Français (later the Odéon), it ran longer than any play had ever done, sixty-eight performances back to back, eventually bringing in 350,000 livres at the box office and 40,000 livres in royalties, much of that from the cheap seats in the raucous *parterre*. No other play in the history of French theater had ever made its author rich.

This success of course did not endear Beaumarchais to the king, and one night, in a fit of pique during a card game, Louis ordered Beaumarchais's arrest. On the back of a seven of spades, he wrote out an order to have him sent, pointedly, to Saint-Lazare—not to a toney depot for nobles and intellectuals like Vincennes or the Bastille but a place reserved for lesser forms of life, including pimps, lepers, and juvenile delinquents. Paris was shocked to awaken to that news, and Louis, thinking better of his tantrum the night before, ordered Beaumarchais's immediate release.

Beaumarchais, however, refused to leave his cell, insisting that he deserved not a pardon but the king's open approbation of the playwright and his play. To mollify him, Louis sent one of his most senior ministers, the controller-general of finance, to reason with Beaumarchais, and their negotiation led to the following fairly remarkable terms: By order of the king and as a sign of his favor, his entire cabinet would be ordered to attend a performance of *Figaro* the very next night, and a month later there would be a gala performance of *The Barber of Seville* at Versailles, with the royal family themselves performing the lead roles, d'Artois appearing as Figaro, Marie-Antoinette as Rosina.

The night of that performance Beaumarchais sat at the king's right hand, no doubt trying not too obviously to gloat over Figaro's victory, in life as in art. But fate is a trickster, and, as several people on stage and in the hall that night would learn, the crowd can turn.

The man who negotiated Beaumarchais's delicious if not ultimate vindication, Charles-Alexandre de Calonne, had been controller-general for only a few months, and he had bigger problems than Beaumarchais. His predecessor (the second controller-general since

Necker) had taken on the Farmers-General, the powerful and vastly profitable cartel that, among other things, "farmed" the king's taxes, deploying
its own armed force and meting out rough justice to would-be tax dodgers
throughout the kingdom. Advancing revenues to the royal treasury, the
Farmers-General spared the king the unseemly side of tax enforcement
and the embarrassment of a lumpy cash flow. Paris was in the midst of a
building boom when Calonne took over as controller-general, and the
most evident new construction was a wall that ran round the entire city
linking forty-seven elaborate customs gates, the Farm's tollbooths for all
goods entering and leaving. To the citizens of Paris, the wall represented
the stranglehold of the Farm, an "infernal machine," as Mercier called it,
"that seizes each citizen by the throat and pumps out his blood." They had
seized Calonne's reform-minded predecessor by the throat as well, which
brought Calonne into office.

Calonne was not a fool. He adopted a more generous view of the Farm
and of its customs wall, telling the architect that he should think of the
tollhouses as temple-like "gateways to the capital of the world [that]
announce the grandeur of an opulent city." To secure his power base,
Calonne also paid off d'Artois's personal debt to the state of 56 million
livres, added 100,000 livres to the allowance of the queen's friends the
Polignacs, and returned to the powerful minister of the marine all that his
predecessor's economies had taken away, including funding for a huge new
port at Cherbourg. He knew very well that the Farm's monopolistic grip
on the French economy had to be relaxed, but he had seen what happened
when his predecessor had been too plain in the attempt. Calonne acted the
part of the Farm's best friend but was in fact only a more careful enemy.

In that double game he found a useful ally in the marquis de Lafayette,
who from the time of his return from America had been using his prestige nowhere more effectively than as a lobbyist at Versailles for the American cause. Calonne's predecessor had been too distracted by efforts for
general financial reform to pay much attention to Lafayette's pleas to lift
duties on American goods and ships; but Calonne saw in Lafayette's campaign a way to attack the Farm's control of markets without fear of
reprisal. Accordingly, at the end of 1783, he encouraged Lafayette to put
his thoughts on paper. So did Benjamin Franklin, who sent Lafayette a
letter he had recently received in which Robert Morris set forth his

thoughts on the same subject. Lafayette would "make a proper use of them," Franklin promised Morris, "and perhaps they may have more weight, as appearing to come from a Frenchman, than they would have if it were known that they were the observations of an American."

In fact, though, Lafayette did not make use of Morris's thinking. This fight was to be his own. His wrote his "Observations on the Commerce of the United States with France and the French Colonies" in December 1783, the same month as his report on ballooning and his donation to the watchmaker's elastic shoes, but this document was based more on study than enthusiasm. Drawing on current economic theory as well as the practical experience of American merchants trying to do business in France, his "Observations" made a powerful case for lowering trade barriers, arguing from the French national interest. In a several thousand word treatise that ranged knowledgeably over all the most important imports and exports—codfish, salted provisions, lumber, livestock, rum, molasses, flour, whale oil, and especially tobacco—he demonstrated in concrete terms the general case for duty-free ports and freer markets. "In a word," he wrote, "if we wish the Americans to buy from us, we must multiply their means of selling." The trouble, he declared forthrightly, was the Farm, whose monopolistic privileges allowed it to set prices arbitrarily, effectively destroying, for example, the French market for America's tobacco, its best export. "While it brings only nine sous in our ports, it yields sixteen sous in London and Amsterdam," he noted, adding dryly that business "does not appear to me to be a matter of sentiment." No matter what political relationship there might be between France and the colonies, American exports would follow market prices, he wrote, and if France failed to accommodate itself to this fact, it would not only strengthen British commerce, it would also lose the commercial advantage that would otherwise have been its best reward for supporting the American Revolution.

In mid-December, he took the "Observations" to Versailles, giving copies to the minister of the marine, to Vergennes, and to Calonne, who would eventually take it to the king. He also sent a copy to Robert Morris, who, as events would prove, was more interested in cooperating with the Farm's monopoly in his private interest than in opening French markets to American commerce. Morris had been Lafayette's friend, but this was business, and business was "not a matter of sentiment."

.   .   .

At about the same time, Lafayette received three letters from Washington. Carried by a returning French officer, all three had been
written in October. In the first, Washington apologized for not having
written sooner, thinking that Lafayette would be arriving in person at
any moment. (Every letter from Lafayette to Washington for the past
six months had been giving a new date for departure and a new reason
why the last one had come and gone, mostly having to do with the
unfinished negotiation of Franco-American trade concessions.) In
Washington's second letter he enclosed a document describing the new
"Society of the Cincinnati," an honorary organization for officers who
had served with distinction in the war for at least three years. As president pro tem of the society, Washington appointed Lafayette to field
applications from the French officers who had served in the Continental Army, leaving Rochambeau to determine the eligibility of his own
officers.

The strangest letter was the third, in part because he wrote it as he was
concerned with all the details attendant to ending the Revolutionary War:
the orderly breakup of the Continental Army; the deployment and supply
of a residual force; wrapping up his own business as commander in chief,
including the disposition of his papers; a last round of promotions; letters
of farewell to Rochambeau and other senior French officers; plans for a
farewell to his own officers in New York once the British had evacuated;
and how properly to resign his commission and take his formal leave of
Congress. In the midst of all this, Washington wrote Lafayette to ask if he
would be so kind as to purchase a silver tea set, a project to which he
seemed to give the same sense of urgency he had expressed for the rendezvous of armies at Yorktown. He wanted the set

as soon as possible, by the first vessel which may sail after they are
ready either to Alexandria, Baltimore, Philadelphia or New York,
the last, on account of the packets which are to sail twice in every
month, might be the readiest conveyance to this country, though it
would not be so convenient for me afterwards. Nevertheless, (as I
am desirous of getting the plate, as soon as may be) I would rather

have them sent to that place than wait for a conveyance to either of the others. . . . I have only to wish, in the last place, that they may be packed in a proper (permanent) case, that will bear transportation in the first instance, and will be a proper repository afterwards when not in use, if it should be found more convenient to keep them there.

Washington explained that he wanted a French set because he did not want to buy anything from England if he could avoid doing so.

A few weeks later, though, he had become so impatient that he decided to buy English silver after all, since it was available right away. "I have made a purchase of . . . plated ware, as to render it unnecessary for you to comply with the request of my letter of the 30th . . . and have to beg the favor of you to take no steps in consequence thereof."

Unquiet, the General was going home.

XIV

Movements West and Left

O N CHRISTMAS DAY, 1783, when Lafayette visited Versailles to
try to get a response to his "Observations," George Washington
had nothing to do. For the first time in almost eight years, he
found himself a private citizen again at Mount Vernon, where he had
arrived the day before, just in time for the fall of a winter freeze that would
keep him housebound for almost two months. He had no visitors for
weeks and wrote few letters. After a month of that, he wrote Lafayette
manfully: "At length, my dear Marquis, I am become a private citizen on
the banks of the Potomac, and under the shadow of my own vine and my
own fig-tree,* free from the bustle of a camp and the busy scenes of public life. . . . I am not only retired from all public employments, but I am
retiring within myself. . . . Envious of none, I am determined to be pleased
with all; and this my dear friend, being the order for my march, I will
move gently down the stream of life, until I sleep with my fathers."

Given his sudden inaction, Washington was perhaps fortunate that,
after years of war and neglect, Mount Vernon needed work. He decided
to build a greenhouse. He chose paving stones for the piazza. He noticed

---

*The reference is to the fourth chapter of Micah: "And he shall judge among many
people, and rebuke strong nations afar off; and they shall beat their swords into plow-
shares, and their spears into pruning hooks: nation shall not lift up a sword against
nation, neither shall they learn war any more. But they shall sit every man under his
vine and under his fig tree; and none shall make them afraid: for the mouth of the
Lord of hosts hath spoken it."

the cupola was leaking and started planning a new roof for it. He devised a better way to keep ice in the summer. He thought about how to collect past-due rents on his western lands with as little unpleasantness as possible. After a few more weeks of cold and quiet, though, he plainly hungered for meatier stuff. On March 3, he wrote plaintively to his fellow Virginian Thomas Jefferson, now a congressman in Philadelphia: "If you have any news that you are at liberty to impart, it would be charity to communicate a little of it to a body."

Jefferson had more than news. "I suppose the crippled state of Congress is not new to you," he wrote on March 15, 1784. "We have only nine states present"—better than the seven they had had for months until then, but unanimity of the thirteen states was required on all questions of importance, and Jefferson was frustrated: "We are wasting our time." He told Washington he had busied himself in the meantime trying to find some way to open the Potomac to the Ohio River and so encourage trade from the western territories to come south through Virginia rather than north through Pennsylvania and New York. He must have known this was a longtime dream of Washington's as well (see the young militia officer on page 28, wailing, "all is lost!" when he found out a new road was going to the western territories through Pennsylvania instead of Virginia). "This is the moment," Jefferson wrote, ". . . if ever we mean to have it. All the world is becoming commercial." Jefferson had tried to convince the Virginia legislature to raise a tax for the project, but the proposal had foundered on the suspicion that public projects were always badly managed and ran wildly over-budget. He thought this objection would be overcome, however, if Washington himself would agree to supervise the work. Jefferson said he knew such a project might "break in too much on the sweets of retirement & repose," but added: "What a monument to your retirement would it be!"

Washington answered at once. He frankly confessed that he had huge tracts of land in the West whose value would rise dramatically with their proximity to markets (not to mention that, if the plan succeeded, all of the western goods would float to market past Mount Vernon). He said he too believed strongly in the value of the project to the public weal. He reminded Jefferson that he had tried before the war to get a similar project underway, and the problem then had been Maryland, whose merchants were understandably concerned that the Potomac would carry commerce away from Baltimore to Georgetown. He also worried that it would be impossible to raise taxes at a moment when public credit was so weakened by war debt. In any case, he left no doubt that he fully shared Jefferson's enthusiasm for the project. "I am satisfied that not a moment ought to be lost, for I *know* the Yorkers will delay no time to remove every obstacle in the way of the other communication, so soon as the posts at Oswego and Niagara are surrendered [by the British]." As for his own participation, he was coy, but he conceded that "the immense advantages which this country would derive from the measure would be no small stimulus to the undertaking; if that undertaking could be made to comport with that line of conduct with which I meant to glide gently down the stream of life. . . ." Jefferson must have known he was hooked on the idea, as indeed he was. No one who knew Washington expected him to glide gently anywhere.

The issues that Washington and Jefferson thus joined—the weakness of Congress, the overhang of state and national war debt, the critical need to resolve the states' commercial conflicts in the interest of all, the general tension between loyalty to the states and commitment to the union—defined the tangle from which would emerge, in the next four years, either a coherent American nation or a vaguely allied group of competing sovereignties.

In that spring of 1784, the outcome was anything but certain. Washington was right about New York, which even as he wrote Jefferson was delivering an ultimatum to Congress: The Continental Congress would be given exactly nine months to get the British to evacuate its five garrisons in western New York, which were strangling off the fur trade; after that time, the state would "be compelled to consider herself as left to pursue her own councils, destitute of the protection of the United States."

Few state governments were much more committed to union than that; at least for the moment, the appeal of nationalism was roughly aligned with their various self-interests. Speaking very generally indeed: New Jersey and Delaware were nationalistic out of weakness relative to New York and Pennsylvania; Maryland's nationalism arose from the need for a counterbalance to Virginia; Georgia and North Carolina seemed indifferent to the idea of an American nation, at least when times were flush; Connecticut was nationalistic out of economic desperation. In other words, with the possible exception of Rhode Island and New Hampshire, which had little tolerance for any government at all, it was the weak states that felt the benefits of nationhood most palpably. Apart from political theory and principle—the arguments on which Washington based his last Circular to the States—very little seemed to favor union, and the centrifugal forces were powerful.

In 1784, virtually the only national institution other than the Congress—which was in shambles for lack of money and because few people were prepared to take long leaves from homes and livelihood in exchange for the salary of a legislator—was the Society of the Cincinnati, which was under ferocious attack for the provision that gave membership to the members' firstborn sons, raising the specter of an hereditary aristocracy. In April 1784, Washington asked Jefferson for his opinion on the Society, and Jefferson was delighted to have the chance to eviscerate everything about it, especially its provision for hereditary membership, which he found to be "against the letter of some of our constitutions;—against the spirit of all of them. . . . [T]he foundation on which all these are built is the natural equality of man, the denial of every preeminence but that annexed to legal office, & particularly the denial of a preeminence by birth. . . ." He cited the "anguish of the mind" he had sensed in some of his congressional colleagues about the Society (he did not say so, but it was mostly among those who, like Jefferson, had not served in the military). He believed that such a military organization would inevitably become a political force and that any organization which set out to create an exclusive military caste was inherently dangerous. Only Washington's personal "moderation & virtue . . . prevented this revolution from being closed as most others have been, by a subversion of that liberty it was intended to establish," he wrote, adding that such virtue was less common than the absence of it.

In early May, on his way to the society's first annual meeting in New York, Washington stopped in Annapolis, where Congress was meeting, and discussed the issue with Jefferson by candlelight until midnight. Understandably, he could not accept the notion that his officers should be deprived of their distinction, but Jefferson and others—including Lafayette—persuaded him that the dangers were real.

At the meeting, a few days after leaving Jefferson, he insisted that either the bylaws and character of the organization be radically changed or he would resign the presidency and give up his membership in the Society. "Strike out every word, sentence, and clause which has a political tendency," he demanded. "Discontinue the hereditary part in all its connections, *absolutely*. . . . Admit no more Honorary members. . . . Abolish the General Meetings altogether."

Washington and Jefferson would not see each other again for more than five years. A week after they met, Congress appointed Jefferson minister to Paris to take the place of John Jay, who was coming home to take up the long-vacant post of secretary of foreign affairs. It was the second time Congress had tried to post Jefferson to France. The first was three years before, when he was asked to join a peace delegation. He had regretfully declined, since he was then facing charges that as governor of Virginia in 1781 he had led the state government in an unnecessarily brisk retreat before advancing British forces. Though he was eventually acquitted of the charge, he was never entirely freed of it, despite the fact that both Washington and Lafayette, the general who had come to the state's aid at the time, felt the accusation was unfair. Thoroughly embittered by the assault on his character, Jefferson was plunged into despair by the death of his wife a year later, after which he desperately needed some reason to leave Monticello. That wish was answered with his election to Congress; but after less than a year in that inert body he was delighted with another opportunity to go to Paris, this time to help John Adams and Benjamin Franklin negotiate treaties of commerce and friendship in Europe. Leaving his two-year-old daughter Lucy behind with an aunt, he took his older daughter Patsy with him to Boston, and at four o'clock on the morning of July 4, 1784, a fair wind carried the Jeffersons out to sea.

Several weeks later, somewhere in the mid-Atlantic, they passed Lafayette going the other way. Not all the trade concessions he had lobbied for were in his pocket, but he had done all he could for the moment, and his visit to Washington in Mount Vernon had been postponed for too long.

On August 4, two days before Jefferson saw Paris for the first time, Lafayette sailed into New York Harbor and had his first view of the city he had so desperately wanted to wrest from the British by force. His first impressions are not recorded, nor are many details of the receptions and reunions with friends that delayed his departure from the city and continued to delay him on his journey south. In his first letter to Paris, which he wrote to Adrienne a few days after his landing, he expressed pleasure at seeing old comrades, at seeing the ruins of war cleared away and everywhere a new bustle of peacetime commerce; but he also expressed acute frustration at his slow progress toward Virginia: "What concerns me now is seeing General Washington again," he told Adrienne. "In three days I shall be at Mount Vernon, and I leave you to imagine with what impatience I await that moment."

He delayed the trip only once himself, to attend a meeting of the American Philosophical Society in Philadelphia, at which he touted Mesmerism and "the wonderful effects of a certain invisible power in nature called *animal magnetism*." In his speech, he reported matter-of-factly that during his ocean voyage a cabin boy had fallen off a rope and "died" of his injuries. Lafayette, through the power of animal magnetism, had brought the boy back to life.* Unfortunately, Mesmer had made all of his disciples promise not to disclose his secrets, Lafayette said, so he could not tell them how he had done it, which must have somewhat dampened the reception for his talk. (He made an exception for Washington. In his last letter before leaving Paris he had promised to "get leave to let you into the secret of Mesmer," but there is no evidence that Washington ever took him up on the offer.)

On the same stop, Lafayette delivered a more serious message to the Pennsylvania legislature, which had invited him to speak: He pleaded with the lawmakers to support a strong federal union, one which "as it supports . . . the commercial wealth of America . . . will show to the greatest advantage the blessings of a free government."

During the four event-filled months he spent in America, he repeated that message wherever he went. He had experienced firsthand the difficulty of negotiating commercial agreements with separate and competing states; and a fractionated America was a weaker ally for France than a true

---

*He did not mention it, but before he left, Mesmer gave him some not-exactly-revolutionary advice for avoiding seasickness through polarity: Hug the mast.

United States would be. But he also seemed to intuit a national destiny that some with a closer perspective could not see, perhaps precisely because he was not American. Every citizen of America was first the citizen of one of its states, but as a man with no loyalty to state or region he belonged equally everywhere. He had fought in the North, in the middle states, and in the South; he had visited every state but Georgia; and everywhere he went, he represented that collective patriotic spirit which had been so critical during the war and was now so palpably absent. The French chargé d'affaires, François de Barbé-Marbois, sensed that when he wrote Vergennes on August 15: "The reception given by the magistrates and the people to M. le marquis de La Fayette is surpassing anything that has been done before on this kind of occasion. . . . All classes of citizens are equally ardent in giving him the proof of their affection. . . . No more has been done for General Washington himself." Even Washington was still a Virginian first, although that was about to change.

After two days' more excited receptions in Baltimore, Lafayette finally reached Mount Vernon on August 17 and saw Washington for the first time in three years. No one recorded the moment, but Washington's correspondence, which had been extensive in the weeks leading up to Lafayette's arrival, all but stopped. Apart from brief responses to the letters Lafayette brought for him from France, he wrote nothing at all for the next ten days—nothing of course about whatever his emotional response might have been to seeing Lafayette again, though Lafayette was typically effusive about it. "Our meeting was very tender and our satisfaction completely mutual," he wrote to Adrienne three days after he arrived. "I am not just turning a phrase when I assure you that in retirement General Washington is even greater than he was during the Revolution. His simplicity is truly sublime. . . ."

In letters to Adrienne and to friends, the marquis described the course of their days together: long talks at breakfast, after which Washington attended to the business of Mount Vernon and left Lafayette with "things to read that have been written in my absence." Conversation at midday dinner, which included Mrs. Washington and guests, turned to wartime reminiscences. Evenings were spent with the family, which included two of Martha's children from her first marriage. "The General has adopted them and loves them with great tenderness," he assured Adrienne, adding that Washington took particular pleasure in reading the letter from their daughter Anastasie, now seven years old.

> Dear Washington, I hope that papa whill come back son here. I am verry sorry for the loss of him, but I am verry glade for you self. I wich you a verry good health and I am whith great respect, Dear Sir, your most objedient servent. Anastasie de la Fayette

At the same time, Lafayette let it be known to his friends that not all their time together was quite so innocent. During a brief trip to Alexandria, it was said "the general and I got a little tipsy," he wrote the prince de Poix, "but that's an abominable slander." He also said that he and Washington had spent some "very sweet hours . . . speaking of the past and the present, and talking a bit of politics about the future." No doubt that conversation centered on the precarious state of the nation.

At the same time, Washington was preparing for a long-planned trip to visit his land in the trans-Appalachian West. So far, because of wartime neglect, the 40,000 or so acres he had accumulated there had not yielded him enough income to justify the accounting. He needed to clear off squatters, enforce his titles, collect past-due rents, and come to terms with a disreputable "partner" named Gilbert Simpson, custodian of one of his most valuable pieces of property. The 1,600-acre tract known as Washington's Bottom featured 150 acres of fenced meadow, an apple orchard, a house, barn, stable and other outbuildings, and a large stone gristmill on which he had spared no expense; but he had never made a shilling from the entire parcel. One of Washington's first acts after returning to Mount Vernon was to demand from Simpson "a full & complete settlement of our Partnership accounts. . . . The world does not scruple to say that you have been much more attentive to your own interest than to mine," he wrote. "But I hope your accounts will give the lie to these reports." When Simpson's response suggested that the world's opinion was probably right, Washington determined to dissolve the partnership. On June 24, before he knew that Lafayette had this time actually sailed for America when he said he would, Washington placed an advertisement announcing that on September 15 he would hold an auction at which Washington's Bottom would be leased to the highest bidder.

More important than such practical necessities, the dream that Jefferson had helped to revive in him greatly increased his sense of urgency about the trip and about the search for the elusive passage between navigable sections of the Ohio and Potomac rivers, which would do more to increase the value of his holdings than any amount of diligence as a landlord. Lafayette too had business elsewhere, though none so pressing. He had promised Sam Adams a visit to Boston, for example, and as he sped by disappointed well-wishers on his trip south toward Mount Vernon, he had promised to revisit them when he had more time. So, agreeing to a reunion at Mount Vernon in the fall, Lafayette headed north again on August 28; and three days later, Washington, accompanied by his friend and physician Dr. James Craik, headed west, where, in a way, Washington discovered America.

He knew the way well. He had not been to the Ohio territories for a dozen years, but he had been along this route several times, first as a teenaged surveyor for Lord Fairfax, later during his ignominious return from Fort Necessity and then the even bloodier Braddock campaign. Proceeding behind three servants and horses bearing the baggage, he and Dr. Craik made twenty-five miles the first day (Washington's usual pace on such woodland treks being a fairly brisk five miles an hour), along the way checking on 275 acres he had bought in 1763 to serve as a way station on the route to his "Bullskin" plantation further west. The next morning before lunch they made thirty-six miles to Leesburg. Washington set out before sunrise the day after that in his haste to deal with the tenants on the Bullskin plantation, who were deeply in arrears and whom he had warned that he was coming to collect. In fact, though, he spent more time there talking about the inland navigation of the Potomac with his old comrade Daniel Morgan than he did with his tenants, from whom he received little satisfaction. He spent the whole next day talking on the same subject with one Captain Stroads, arriving the day after that at Bath (now Berkeley Springs, West Virginia), "after traveling the whole day through a drizzling rain, 30 Miles."

At Bath, his mind was again on personal business. To protect title to two lots, he engaged a local contractor to build a log cabin on each one.

Passing next day by another of his "very valuable" tracts, he engaged a local man to offer it for lease, "the Tenant not to remove any of the walnut timber . . . as I should reserve that for my own use," after which he rode on until he reached the settlement of Colonel Thomas Cresap. Washington was a sixteen-year-old surveyor when he first met Colonel Cresap, who was already a well-known frontiersman. On that visit, thirty Indians in a war party had arrived at Cresap's trading post, disconsolate at having only a single scalp to show for their latest foray. Fortified by Cresap's spirits, they had treated young Washington to his first experience of an Indian dance, every detail of which the wide-eyed boy noted carefully in his diary. Times had changed since then. Cresap, now ninety years old, lived in a county that not long before had been renamed Fayette, and just a few days' ride to the west lay a county named Washington.

The next day being rainy again, Washington rested, but the day after, he began to make his way across the Alleghenies on Braddock's Road, several days' hard going through rain, through Shades of Death (two stretches so called for the density of the woods and overgrowth), and past some bad memories. Two days after leaving Cresap's, he made Great Meadow, the site of Fort Necessity. He had not been back since that awful July 4, 1754, but a decade later, he had purchased a 234-acre tract there sight unseen. If he reflected on his history with the place on this visit he did not say so in his diary, where he noted only that his parcel would be "a very good stand for a Tavern" and "Much Hay may be cut here . . . & the Upland, East of the Meadow, is good for grain." He would offer a ten-year lease on the place at his auction of Washington's Bottom five days later.

When he reached Washington's Bottom, perhaps he should not have been surprised to find the mill without water, the dam in rubble, the land fallow, and the buildings in a dismal state of disrepair. "I never hear of the Mill under the direction of Simpson," he had written his cousin Lund Washington nine years before, "without a degree of warmth & vexation at his extreme stupidity."

The auction brought out a large number of people, but many of them must have come just to see George Washington, because it raised almost no cash. The auctioneer collected a grand total of £3 6 shillings in actual currency, though bonds and notes may have brought the theoretical take to almost £150. Despite offering fifteen months rent-free, he got no bids at all for the mill, which he had spent upwards of £1,200 to build. The best offer he got for anything was from Gilbert Simpson, to whom he ended up renting 500 acres for a yield of 500 bushels of wheat per year, which not surprisingly he could never collect.

Things went no better for him at Miller's Run, which fronted a tributary whose source was at the conjunction of the Ohio and Allegheny rivers. Squatters had been living on his 2,800 acres there for the past ten years, and now, George Washington or no George Washington, these residents of Washington County unanimously refused to recognize his title, forcing him to start legal action to have them ejected forcibly.

Washington had intended to go on to his larger and more remote holdings—by 1784 he had accumulated almost 35,000 acres on the Ohio and Kanawha rivers, more elsewhere—but he was reliably warned of hostile Indians (it later turned out that at least one party of them was lying in wait). His last act as a landlord on this trip was to turn over all his rent collection and other land management activity to a local agent, at which point he was free to concentrate on the search for a navigable route from there to the Potomac. Knowing this would involve several days of hard riding and rough living, he left some of his baggage for Dr. Craik to take back to Mount Vernon and left more with Gilbert Simpson, making a careful inventory of it in his diary: some Madeira, port, and "cherry bounce," a drink made by steeping cherries in brandy with sugar, as well as some camp kettles and fishing tackle. He then rode southeast toward Cheat River, a tributary of the Monongahela that ran close to the North Branch of the Potomac. If there was a navigable route by portage and canal from the Ohio, he now believed, this would be it.

About the time Washington reached the Cheat River, Lafayette was on his way through the Mohawk Valley toward Fort Schuyler in western New York State, where a peace treaty was to be negotiated between the United States and the Six Nations,* who until then had been

---

*The Six Nations were also known as the Iroquois Confederacy (though some of them considered the term "Iroquois" derogatory) and comprised the Mohawks, Oneida, Onandaga, Cayuga, Seneca, and Tuscarora tribes.

allies of Britain. Here he would be no less a salesman for America as a nation than he had been at earlier stops. Since the British had yet to evacuate their forts there (the subject of New York's recent ultimatum to Congress), the result of this conference was anything but certain. Lafayette had no official role in the negotiations but was probably convinced to go along by the French chargé Barbé-Marbois, who hoped to get French merchants, through the Americans, back into the fur trade. Lafayette, in turn, brought along the young James Madison, a protégé of his fellow Virginian Thomas Jefferson and lately a member of the Continental Congress, where he was earning the reputation as a knowledgeable and ardent advocate of strong central government.

Their progress toward Fort Schuyler was no more comfortable than Washington's journey, taking them through white settlements that grew sparser as the charcoal remains of stockades and the ruins of log cabins gave evidence of brutal Indian-settler violence. The five barrels of brandy they carried with them gave little comfort against the advance of a deep winter cold; and since their carriage had proved unequal to the all but trackless wilderness, they were riding workhorses with blankets for saddles. Not for the first time, the only one in good sprits, in an increasingly miserable party, was Lafayette, "who appears to be proof against heat, cold, drought, moisture, and the intemperance of the weather," Barbé-Marbois noted in a journal of the trip that he later sent to Vergennes. Lafayette's main defense against the cold was a coat made of gummed taffeta that he had brought to America packed in newspapers. Since they had got stuck to the gum and Lafayette had never bothered to peel them off, Marbois joked that watching Lafayette get dressed in the morning gave him a chance to catch up on the latest headlines from Europe.

Like Washington on his trip west, Lafayette had been down this road before in unhappier times. While he was licking his wounds from the abortive assault on Canada in 1778, he had left Albany and passed through this same Indian country by sleigh toward another contentious meeting with the Six Nations. On that occasion, the Iroquois, many more of whom spoke French than English, had so warmed to Lafayette that they inducted him into the tribe and gave him the name of their late great warrior Kayeheanla. He had been known by this name among the tribes of the Six Nations ever since. The Indians at Fort Schuyler now were allied with

Britain mainly because of their distrust of the United States, but they had always been closer to the French than the British, and their fellow feeling toward Kayeheanla made them even more so. The governor of Canada, for one, was very worried that Lafayette would be able to cement American-Indian relations: "I know the character of the Marquis to be enterprising."

Despite his unofficial role, Lafayette opened and set the tone for the talks, having been introduced superfluously by one of the American commissioners as "one of the head warriors of the great Onontio [Louis XVI] . . . who comes with his friends to . . . give you the advice of a father." An interpreter translated for the commissioners—the Indians understood Lafayette's French perfectly well—and except for such odd but customary diplomatic forms of rhetoric as the address of a "father" to his "children," Lafayette's message was clear and straightforward, combining an appeal for trust in the Americans with a pitch for commerce with the French.

After an elaborate greeting, he began by reminding them that everything he had told them in 1778 had come to pass, that the Americans had defeated the British and that the French had stood with them. While stressing the French-American alliance, he made very clear that France's support of the Six Nations depended on their support of America: "The great Onontio gives his hand forever to your brothers [the Americans], who offer you theirs, and by this means we shall form a great chain." When the Oneida chief Great Grasshopper rose to thank Kayeheanla for his wisdom, he offered Lafayette a wampum belt that he had received from a French officer years before. With great deference, Lafayette gave it back to him, saying he was pleased to see it had been so lovingly preserved, and promising that France would be ready to hold one end of it as long as America held the other, once more conveying the message that America was the necessary link between "the French and their children."

Lafayette's American audience seemed to be as taken by his performance as the chiefs of the Six Nations. Marbois wrote Vergennes afterwards that Lafayette's speech demonstrated "the grace and nobility that you know in him," and Madison wrote to Jefferson that the speech inspired in the audience "the greatest reverence. . . . The commissioners were eclipsed." It is worth remembering that Lafayette had just turned twenty-six.

Madison was sufficiently intrigued by his new friend to try to sum up his character for Jefferson. His conclusion was neither generous nor mean, and yet it was both. Lafayette had admitted to having "three hobby-horses," Madison wrote, namely, the French-American alliance, a strong federal union for the states, and the abolition of slavery. "The first two are dearer to him," Madison concluded, "as they are connected with his personal glory. The last does him real honor, as it is a proof of his humanity. In a word, I take him to be as amiable a man as his vanity will admit." Jefferson of course agreed with him, but several months later Madison seemed to have changed his mind. "Though his foibles did not disappear . . . if he is ambitious it is rather of the praise which virtue dedicates to merit than of the homage which fear renders to power."

The day Lafayette gave his speech to the Six Nations, Washington rode up to Mount Vernon after a journey of thirty-five days and some 680 miles that had yielded little in the way of hard cash or clear titles but a great deal more than that. Less than a week after his return he wrote a 2,000-word argument—which he sent to both Benjamin Harrison, then governor of Virginia, and George Plater, a senior legislator and future governor of Maryland—arguing that the time had come to open a way to trade with the western territories, not only because of the effect it would have on local economies but also in the national interest. "The flanks and rear of the United States are possessed by other powers, and formidable ones too," he wrote, referring to Spanish control of the Mississippi to the south and Britain's continuing presence at the Great Lakes to the north. Holding out the possibility that the settlers might choose to ally themselves with one or both, he added, "The Western settlers, (I speak now from my own observation) stand as it were upon a pivot; the touch of a feather, would turn them any way. . . . The more communications are opened to [them], the closer we bind that rising world (for indeed it may be so called) to our interests and the greater strength shall we acquire by it. . . ." The "we" in that sentence clearly referred to an entity and a cause greater than Virginia, even if what had driven Washington toward his vision of an American nation were the practical requirements of commerce and a common defense.

Whether to give Washington a forum for his argument or for some other reason, Harrison invited him to come to Richmond, where the assembly was in session. Washington readily accepted, and since Lafayette had already written that that would be his first Southern destination, he proposed that they meet there and return to Mount Vernon together.

By now Lafayette had left the Six Nations conference* for what amounted to a victory tour that by this time had led him from Albany to Hartford to Worcester to Boston, accompanied everywhere he went by cannon salutes and banquets ending with Lafayette's pitch for a stronger federal union. The tour's high point came in Boston on October 19, the third anniversary of Cornwallis's surrender at Yorktown. After a parade in his honor down State Street, he was escorted by artillery and accompanied by several thirteen-gun salutes to a banquet being given for him at Faneuil Hall. Seated under a giant flower arrangement in the shape of a fleur-de-lys, he was startled when a curtain on the wall behind him was pulled away to reveal a large, handsome portrait of Washington, which was Boston's gift to him. He received it "with a countenance mingled with pleasure and surprise, and a tear of friendship starting in his eye," one of the guests wrote. "Many were the friendly tears that involuntarily started from the company." It is possible that the after-dinner toasts had contributed to the emotionalism of the occasion. Tonight there were thirteen of them, which began with "the United States" and went on to include "Louis XVI, Washington, Massachusetts, France, Saratoga, Yorktown, justice, the rights of man, the arts and sciences and other worthy subjects." That night there were fireworks, and the next day at Harvard, Lafayette became the Marquis de Lafayette, LL.D.

He was having so much fun, he arrived in Richmond three days after Washington, who had used the time to lobby legislators in the Virginia Assembly for his plan to link the western settlers to America rather than Spain or Britain. When Lafayette arrived, they lobbied together—Washington for the Potomac project, Lafayette for the strong central government that would facilitate commercial relations and make a stronger ally for France.

By the time they reached Mount Vernon, the two men had only three more days together before Lafayette had to leave to catch a frigate that was waiting for him in New York. Washington accompanied him as far as

---

*It took three more weeks to arrive at a settlement that was soon broken.

Annapolis, where they lobbied the Maryland legislature. On December 1, they left together, but riding in separate carriages on a road that soon branched off north and south. When he got home, Washington wrote Lafayette that when they separated, he could not shake a premonition. In one of the most darkly sentimental letters he ever wrote, he said that he could not help wondering

> whether that was the last sight I ever should have of you? And though I wished to say no, my fears answered yes. I called to mind the days of my youth, and found they had long since fled to return no more; that I was now descending the hill I had been 52 years climbing, and that though I was blessed with a good constitution, I was of a short lived family and might soon expect to be entombed in the dreary mansions of my fathers. These things darkened the shades and gave a gloom to the picture, consequently to my prospects of seeing you again; but I will not repine, I have had my day.

Washington never had a reputation for prophecy, and this letter would not have given him one. He was not close at all to the dreary mansions of his fathers, nor did he act it for longer than it took him to write this letter.

As soon as he got home, he continued his jawboning correspondence with Maryland and Virginia legislators in behalf of a bilateral committee that would draft a bill setting up a Potomac–James River development scheme. To blunt the issues of new taxes and weak public credit, he also proposed setting up a private company that could issue stock to supplement government appropriations.

His renewed efforts were not needed, as it turned out. Only two weeks after he reached Mount Vernon, a courier from Richmond brought him two resolutions the Virginia Assembly had passed a week before, one commending the idea of the development project, the other establishing a bilateral commission with Maryland to get the project started. By then, Maryland had passed the same legislation. Washington, who was to serve on the commission for Virginia, instantly took charge and sent off a message calling for a first meeting of the commission in just four days, on the day before Christmas Eve, in Annapolis.

Though he had made a point of arriving home at Mount Vernon by

Christmas Eve the year before, Christmas in Annapolis came and went without comment in his diary or letters. He wrote only two letters after he arrived there, both of them on December 28. One was to the Assembly of Virginia, reporting that the committee had drafted a bill that "meets our entire approbation." The other was to James Madison: "It is now near 12 at night, and I am writing with an aching head, having been constantly employed in this business since the 22nd, without assistance from my colleagues." One of his fellow committeemen from Virginia had been sick throughout, the other had simply left.

In the first week of January 1785, both Maryland and Virginia passed the bill virtually as the committee had drafted it, perhaps in part simply because the prestige of Washington was behind the plan, but also thanks to his energy, drive, and vision. That, at least, was Madison's view. "The earnestness with which he espouses the undertaking is hardly to be described," he wrote Jefferson, "and shows that a mind like his, capable of grand views, and which has long been occupied with them, cannot bear a vacancy." Indeed it could not, and though neither Washington nor Madison could know it yet, his work in Annapolis over that Christmas holiday would have consequences beyond even his most optimistic dreams.

By the time Washington's work in Annapolis was done, Lafayette was on his way back to France, having taken his leave of Congress with a speech that went beyond the customary, mutually flattering pleasantries to plead one last time for a stronger central government. He spoke this time not only of the French-American friendship and commerce; he also made an impassioned argument on principle that few were making about this cause at this time. The American nation must do everything possible to secure its future and its power, he said, because the world relied on it now to "stand a lesson to oppressors, an example to the oppressed, [and] a sanctuary for the rights of mankind."

His remarks were published in full in newspapers throughout the United States, and they were eventually published abroad as well, but not in the *Gazette de France*. Vergennes, in his role as the nation's de facto chief censor, thought Lafayette's remarks about "oppressors" and the "oppressed" had gone a bit far.

.   .   .

The Potomac project consumed Washington during the early months of 1785. Guests at Mount Vernon complained that he talked of little else. "Were I disposed to encounter present inconvenience for a future income," he wrote Robert Morris, "I would hazard all the money I could raise upon the navigation of the river." At the time Washington was trying to raise money through subscriptions to the stock company, which he talked up to other wealthy friends as well, including Lafayette. "[M]en who can afford to lay a little while out of their money," he wrote, "are laying the foundation of the greatest returns of any speculation I know of in the world." Lafayette did not rise to Washington's obvious pitch but promised to "look out for subscribers when the matter comes to be a little better known."

Despite Washington's anxieties, the project sped forward as if predestined to succeed. With his prestige behind it, the Potomac stock company was quickly oversubscribed by a factor of two. In March a new bilateral commission, which met in Alexandria and finished its work at Mount Vernon, hammered out a pact between Virginia and Maryland calling for mutual non-interference, joint use of the waterway, and, most significant, annual meetings between them to review progress and problems. When the Maryland legislature debated this agreement, they decided to invite Delaware and Pennsylvania to the next annual meeting of the commission as well.

Before the next session of the Virginia Assembly adjourned, they resolved to invite any and all states interested in commercial cooperation to a convention in Annapolis set for September 1786. Though the states would obviously be free to decline, it was thought that most would send delegates if only to monitor the proceedings. James Madison, for one, saw immediately that any discussion of mutual trade agreements would lead to the discussion of a future mechanism for coordinating trade policy, and that any discussion of coordination would put the issue of central government authority squarely on the table. As he put it coyly in a letter to Virginia congressman James Monroe, such a conference "may possibly lead to better consequences than may at first occur." In fact, it would lead to the Constitutional Convention.

In May 1785, the Society for Universal Harmony blew up. Some time before, a royal commission had been established to settle the question of whether Mesmer's principles did or did not have scientific basis. Led by Benjamin Franklin, it included such eminences as the chemist Antoine Laurent de Lavoisier, the astronomer Jean-Sylvain Bailly, and the future inventor of eponymous medical-judicial appliances, Dr. Joseph Guillotin. Experiments were conducted. Several trees were mesmerized in the courtyard of Franklin's estate in Passy, and the wrong ones caused people to faint. Subjects were given different cups of water, only one of which had been doctored, and what convulsed the patients proved to be unmesmerized. On the basis of these and other experiments, the commission's report concluded that Mesmer's universal fluid, which was the basis of the theory of animal magnetism, did not exist, and that Mesmer's patients were cured, to the extent they were, by the power of their own imaginations. (A second, confidential report also raised questions about the propriety of the Mesmerist probing technique on women, which was said to be a threat to public morality.) Intriguingly, though, the report also suggested that their work on Mesmerism had pointed the way to "a new science, that of the influence of the moral on the physical." This would eventually lead to hypnotism, but before that it would provide certain nascent revolutionaries an important logical link between the natural and social worlds, between science and politics.

The commission's findings had the perverse effect of galvanizing support among Mesmer's most avid followers, whose outraged idealism now inspired a stance more virulently anti-establishment than ever. At the same time, certain of these hard-core Mesmerites, taking the commission's insight one step further, began to see in animal magnetism the basis of a decidedly provocative brand of politics. Nicolas Bergasse, founder and first spokesman of the Society of Universal Harmony, now postulated "a morality issuing from the world's general physics" and started talking about "artificial moral magnetism" and "moral electricity." He argued that one could extrapolate from Mesmerism "simple rules for judging the institutions to which we are enslaved, certain principles for establishing the legislation appropriate for man in all given circumstances."

Thus did the theories of Mesmerism and Mesmerists themselves make their way into revolutionary politics, which, however strange, was no stranger than other occult inspirations for revolution at the same time. In 1776, a certain Dr. Adam Weishaupt founded a sect within the Freemasons of Germany, who would come to be called the Bavarian Illuminati but who always called themselves the "Perfectibilists," because they were convinced that through certain gnostic mysteries grounded in radical rationalism (!), humankind was wholly perfectible. This would require the establishment of what they termed a New World Order, in which there would be no monarchs or religions or other such relics of superstition as marriage and private property, all of which were to be swept away by all means necessary. Two centuries later, there were still people (at the far margin) who contended that the Illuminati ran both the French and American revolutions. The evidence suggests at least that they would have if they could have. Just about the time when the Society of Universal Harmony was breaking up, however, the Illuminati were banned in Bavaria, and the group appears to have died out completely by 1789.

The Society of Universal Harmony moved more gently into radical politics, passing through a number of successor organizations that came to have less and less to do with Mesmerism per se and more to do with revolution. In the spring of 1785, the faction behind Bergasse and Kornmann was in effect excommunicated by the "orthodox" group led by Mesmer, for whom Mesmerist politics was a distraction and a sideshow. Bergasse and Kornmann took their meetings into Kornmann's home, where Bergasse was living at the time, and took with them many future figures of the Revolution, including one of the society's vice presidents, the parlementarian Adrien Duport, and of course Lafayette. Over the following year, others joined them who would become even more radically revolutionary, including Jean-Paul Marat, another scientist embittered by the Academy's rejection of his work, and his friend and admirer Jacques-Pierre Brissot de Warville, one of the Paris hacks who was trying very hard, without success, to be accepted as a *philosophe*. Soon Bergasse's ambitions were almost exclusively political. "Bergasse did not hide from me," Brissot wrote, "the fact that in raising an altar to Mesmerism, he intended only to raise one to liberty. . . . 'The time has now come,' he used to say to me, 'for the revolution that France needs. But to attempt to produce one openly is to doom it to failure; to succeed it is necessary to wrap oneself in mystery . . .

to unite men under the pretext of experiments in physics, but in reality for the overthrow of despotism.' "

Brissot was awaiting the guillotine when he wrote that, wishing to secure his place in history as a true revolutionary, but what he wrote comports with the facts as they unfolded. In the months and years that followed, the Mesmerist meetings at Kornmann's house would provide leaders and members for several other pre-revolutionary groups, such as the *Société Gallo-Américaine,* which was started by Bergasse and whose membership included Brissot and Lafayette; the *Société Française des Amis des Noirs* (Society of Friends of the Blacks), which included Brissot, Condorcet, and Lafayette; and, most important, the *Société des Trente* (Society of Thirty), which met at the homes of Adrien Duport and Lafayette, and which would take a strong position of intellectual and political leadership in the events leading up to July 1789.

D uring the rest of 1785 and all through 1786, Lafayette remained the staunchest ally in France for American trade, and the strongest voice in Europe for American union. On one day alone in the spring of 1785 he wrote eight separate entreaties, whose recipients included Patrick Henry, Richard Henry Lee, James Madison, Elbridge Gerry, and the president of Congress; and in July he began a tour of European capitals intended precisely to spearhead American trade.

Before he left, Lafayette wrote a letter to Washington, to be carried by young John Quincy Adams, on a subject that was becoming even closer to his heart, one "which I would not like to be ventured in the post offices of France." He used a cipher that he and Washington had agreed on so that they could keep each other candidly informed of events without worrying about prying eyes in America or France. Almost without preamble, he began: "102 [Protestants] in 12 [France] are under intolerable 80 [despotism]. Although open persecution does not now exist, yet it demands upon the whim of 25 [the king], 28 [queen], 29 [parlement], or any of 32 [the ministers]." This state of affairs was exactly one hundred years old, dating to Louis XIV's revocation of the Edict of Nantes in 1685. Since then Protestant marriages had not been recognized as legal, so all Protestant children were considered illegitimate and therefore without legal standing.

Most Protestants who had not left in the Huguenot emigration had become Roman Catholics. (One plausible explanation for Beaumarchais's relative radicalism is that, although he never advertised the fact, his father was Protestant, having "abjured the Calvinist heresy" eleven years before Pierre-Augustin was born. From the time he knew of his father's conversion, the *fils* Caron resented the fact that his father's legitimacy and his own were based only on a coerced and cynical oath, and all his life he paid very close attention to the cause of Protestant civil rights—including, not long in the future, those of Kornmann's wife.)

"I have put into my head to be a 1400 [leader] in that affair," Lafayette continued, "and to have their situation changed. . . . It is a work of time, and of some danger to me because [no one in government] would give me a scrap of paper, or countenance whatsoever. But I run my chance."

Washington replied to this letter from Lafayette with plainspoken advice. "My best wishes will always accompany your undertakings," he wrote, "but remember my dear friend it is a part of the military art to reconnoitre and *feel* your way, before you engage too deeply. More is often-times effected by regular approaches, than by an open assault; from the first . . . you may make a good retreat; from the latter (in case of repulse) it rarely happens."

Lafayette received this letter when he returned from his European tour, in late 1785. He answered it in February 1786 with the first letter of substance he had written Washington in months (one of the few periods in their relationship when Washington had been writing more than Lafayette, though not the last). He began by giving Washington a detailed account of his time in Europe, including long dinners with Frederick the Great, at one of which the famously sadistic king put Cornwallis next to Lafayette and then pointedly ignored him ("My reception . . . was not flattering," Cornwallis wrote, "there was a most marked preference for La Fayette"). More than anything else, Lafayette told Washington, his meetings with Frederick, the Austrian emperor, and other European leaders had deepened his conviction that America's greatness, its force in the world, depended on having a strong central authority, without which it would always be seen as a fickle trading partner and an unimportant ally. He also referred to America's failure to begin its debt repayments to France, which was becoming an increasing source of annoyance to the ministry. "By their conduct in the revolution, the citizens of America have commanded the respect of the world," he wrote, "but . . . unless they strengthen the confederation, give Congress powers to regulate the trade, pay off their debt or at least the interest of it, [and] establish a well regulated militia . . . they will lose it."

He told Washington he had finally begun his practical experiment at ending slavery in the French colonies by buying a 125,000-acre plantation in French Guyana, and he thanked Washington for his advice to calibrate more carefully his advocacy for Protestant rights. "I will improve," he promised, "and find that satisfaction in my prudence to think it is dictated by you."

The rest of the letter, though, cannot have set Washington's mind at rest. After predicting that in the following months "the affair of the Protestants will take a good turn," he said that the next stage of his work for French-American commerce would "not be an easy matter" because his aim was "no less than the destruction of the tobacco farm," among the most precious and closely guarded dominions of the Farmers-General.

Five days after Lafayette wrote this letter to Washington, Jefferson wrote to James Madison suggesting that Lafayette had gone down a path that could lead him into serious personal danger. Noting that the state of Georgia had recently made an honorary gift to the comte d'Estaing of 20,000 acres, he thought the state of Virginia should make a similar grant to Lafayette, not only as a mark of honor but because the day might be coming "when it might serve as an useful asylum for him." Lafayette's time in America had clearly made him incapable of accepting the injustices attendant to absolutism or tolerating life under its constraints, Jefferson wrote. "[I]t will need all of his prudence and that of his friends to make this country a safe residence for him."

XV

Forms of Bankruptcy

BOTH FRANCE AND the United States faced their inevitable reckoning with fiscal exhaustion in the summer of 1786. On August 20, Louis's controller-general Calonne brought him the news that the royal treasury was as good as bankrupt, which was the American Revolution's ultimate gift to France. Just as finance minister Turgot had warned in 1775, the 1.3 billion livres cost of that war (not counting interest on the new debt required to cover it) had delivered the final blow to the French financial system.

Nine days after Calonne delivered this news to the king of France, a violent tax revolt broke out in western Massachusetts. The protest and its attendant violence eventually spread throughout the Northeast, and Congress found itself unable to intervene because it was unable to find the money it had requisitioned for a federal force. "The Treasury," Rufus King wrote Elbridge Gerry that summer, "is now literally without a penny." Total revenue to the U.S. Congress in 1786 was less than a third of that year's interest on the national debt. In this way too George Washington shared the fate of his country. He started 1786 with a wearying load of debt and exactly £86 in cash.

In France, the financial crisis would precipitate a relentless, harrowingly eventful passage that led as if directed from reform to revolution. For the United States, the course of events was less dramatic, less violent, and more indirect, every step forward uncertain, but for all that another revolution: a seizure of authority from the thirteen states in a secretive, illegal, and arguably treasonous conspiracy that has come to be known as the Constitutional Convention.

B y the spring of 1786, the North American states were anything but united. New York was at sword's point with Massachusetts, which was claiming a large part of its eastern territory, and on the brink of civil war with its residents in the Northeast, who were seceding to form the state of Vermont. Civil war actually did break out in western North Carolina, where residents declared themselves a separate state, called Frankland. The depth of disunity was brought home with disturbing clarity by the attempt to negotiate with Spain for commercial access to the lower Mississippi and the port of New Orleans. In May, after more than a year of talks, Spain indicated that it was prepared to open Cuba, Puerto Rico, and its other island ports to American trade if the United States would give up any claim to Mississippi navigation rights for twenty years. This solution split the states in two. The Northern states were desperate to offset the loss of British trade by opening commerce with the Spanish islands, but the Southern states needed access to the Mississippi so that their western settlers could deliver their goods to market. A vote on the deal in Congress accordingly split by region, the seven Northern states against five in the South; and since nine states were needed to ratify any treaty, the only result was enmity on both sides.

Such conflicts among regional interests were paralyzing to Congress, which was unequipped to deal with either interstate commerce or foreign policy. This led to a widespread concern that the states were about to break up into three or four confederations of Northern, Southern, and mid-Atlantic states, with perhaps another in the trans-Appalachian West. Some of those who wished to avoid such an outcome began rethinking the virtues of monarchy. Frustrated by Congress's failure to deal with the colonies' debt to the Continental officers, one of them asked George Washington if he would take the throne. His reaction was to "view with abhorrence, and reprehend with severity" any such idea, and he encouraged the officer to "banish these thoughts from your Mind, and never communicate, as from yourself, or any one else, a sentiment of the like

Nature"; but the idea kept coming up, in part because there was such an obvious candidate for the job.

The causes of interstate friction lay both in the individual states' constitutions and in the Articles of Confederation. Given the prevailing distrust and antipathy toward both monarchy and aristocracy, several state constitutions had called for a greatly weakened executive and a strong popular assembly with no upper house, a unicameral legislature that would absorb all but the highest judicial functions of government and that would be tied tightly to the will of its constituents by frequent elections. Compared to the passionate and intellectually rigorous debate that took place during the drafting of state constitutions, the Articles of Confederation were drawn up with very little debate or deliberation, because it was understood that they would leave state sovereignty untouched. Indeed, many assumed that the Articles and the Continental Congress itself were simply wartime necessities that would expire with the peace. The people of Maryland called their state "the nation" as late as 1787, and in common usage, as it had been until very recently for George Washington, a man's "country" was still his state.

The unintended consequence of this system, in which state sovereignty was exercised by all-powerful popular assemblies that were held accountable in detail to the whims of local constituencies, was pandering politics and bad legislation. At the behest of constituents, state assemblies took over such minutiae as amending land titles, granting divorces, and adjudicating fines. They wrote laws to settle minor complaints and even passed legislation to end individual disputes that should have gone to court. Debt-relief legislation came in every conceivable variety, including more than one scheme that would allow people to pay their obligations in worthless paper money. Such legislatures did not attract the brightest and best candidates for office but rather a new breed of legislators, who considered themselves as servants not of a greater public good but of a constellation of narrowly construed self-interests, including their own. The system had an even more deadening effect on the Continental Congress, whose greatest lights from the revolutionary period had disappeared one by one as its authority declined. By the mid-1780s, Congress had all but given up trying to govern, rarely able to raise a quorum.

Despair over dysfunctional government by this time was general and deep, sharpened by the fear that the War of Independence had been fought for nothing and that the Revolution's republican ideals were baseless dreams. The civic virtue which was known to undergird all successful republics was plainly absent and had seemed to be declining ever since the initial patriotic fervor of 1774 and 1775. During the war years, the hope was that victory would inspire loyalty to the colonial collective that had won it. Clearly, that had not happened. The states would not give Congress even the money to pay the war debt. Washington was disgusted, he wrote Henry Knox, by the "contracted ideas, local pursuits and absurd jealousy [which] are continually leading us from those great and fundamental principles which are characteristic of wise and powerful nations, and without which we are no more than a rope of sand. . . ." He wrote that in February 1785.

Nine months later, when another congressional attempt to regulate interstate commerce had failed, he wrote in exasperation to James Madison, "We are either a united people or we are not. If the former, let us in all matters of general concern act as a nation. . . . If we are not, let us no longer act a farce by pretending to it."

Six months after that, he had even less reason for hope. On May 18, 1786, as he looked forward to the meeting of state delegates in Annapolis that had been called to discuss interstate commerce, he wrote John Jay: "Something must be done, or the fabric must fall. . . ."

Nowhere did the need for forceful government seem to be clearer in the summer and fall of 1786 than in western Massachusetts, where many of the men who had fought in Washington's army would be spending the tenth anniversary of independence in debtors' prisons, victims of a postwar depression in wages and prices that combined with rising taxes to create general misery, especially among farmers and laborers. Rising bitterness and resentment exploded into open revolt in late August, between haying season and the corn harvest, when fifteen hundred men marched on the Court of Common Pleas in Northampton, forcing it to close and thus preventing any pending land seizures for back taxes and prosecution of debts. A week later, hundreds more closed the debtors' court at Worcester, and the militia refused the call to move against them. Courts at Taunton and Great Barrington were closed the week after that, and from the 25th through the 28th, rebels occupied the courthouse in Springfield, threatening a large federal arsenal nearby. By then militia were deserting their posts all over Massachusetts.

Courts did not sit during the corn harvest, so the militants returned to their fields; but in November the uprisings started again, and by the end of the year they had broken out in every northeastern state but Rhode Island. All told, about a quarter of all men of fighting age in rural New England were involved in Shays' Rebellion, so called for one of its leaders, Daniel Shays, a captain in the Continental Army and a veteran of Bunker Hill and Saratoga. Many if not most of the rioters were veterans of Washington's army, and in their hats they stuck the same sprig of evergreen that Continental soldiers had worn before the Battle of Brandywine and that had appeared on the flag at Bunker Hill. In their view, they were fighting to overthrow a tyranny no less oppressive than that of the British. Among the rebels, as Henry Knox put it in a letter to Washington, the ideals of the American Revolution "seem to produce effects materially different from which they were intended," especially "the maxim that all power is derived from the people," which they had taken a bit far, in Knox's view. The irony in this did not interest the farmers' creditor-merchants and Massachusetts's seaboard elite, who feared that what the rebels really wanted was a general redistribution of wealth and property.

"For God's sake," Washington wrote to his former aide David Humphreys, "tell me what is the cause of all these commotions? If there were legitimate grievances, why had they been ignored? And if not, why had the government not deployed forces to put down the rebellion?" The explanation he received from Knox, then serving Congress as "supervisor of war," was frightening and somewhat overwrought. "The creed," Knox wrote, "is that the property of the United States has been protected from the confiscations of Britain by the joint exertions of all, and therefore ought to be the common property of all; and he that attempts [to disagree] is an enemy to equality and justice, and ought to be swept from the face of the earth. In a word, they are determined to annihilate all debts public and private." In fact, this was the view of only a radical minority among the Shaysites, but Knox was far from alone thinking otherwise and in believing that the very existence of the United States was threatened by the uprising.

By the time he heard of Shays' Rebellion, Washington had received news that was in a way even more discouraging: By any obvious measure, the convention in Annapolis on commercial cooperation among the states had been a disaster. It adjourned on September 14, after three days, by which time only twelve delegates from five states had showed up. At least two of them, however, had come with a clearly defined agenda which they managed at least partially to enact. New York delegate Alexander Hamilton, who as Washington's former aide-de-camp had been enraged by the states' chronic failure to support the war effort, had become an outspoken advocate of increased congressional authority as early as 1780. The like-minded Virginia delegate James Madison had come to Annapolis having prepared himself with two trunkloads of books on constitutional history and law that had been sent to him from Paris by his patron and friend Thomas Jefferson. Some historians have speculated that Hamilton and Madison got all they wanted from Annapolis with the call for a later, more wide-ranging meeting, this one with the power to go beyond interstate commerce and address the problem of a powerless central government; and it is indeed suggestive of intrigue that the delegates present unanimously issued this call and then hurriedly adjourned when they knew that two more states' delegates and thus a quorum were only two days' ride away.

Nevertheless, the news that Annapolis had resulted only in the call for another meeting was a sharp disappointment to Washington, particularly in the context of Shays' Rebellion. "What stronger evidence can be given of the want of energy in our governments than these disorders?" Washington wrote to Madison. "If there exists not a power to check [the rebels], what security has a man for life, liberty, or property?" As long as the separate states saw the Congress as simply their resort of convenience for particular interests and strictly local needs, they would never form a nation. "Thirteen sovereignties pulling against each other and all tugging at the federal head will soon bring ruin on the whole."

In early December, news from Massachusetts and everywhere else stopped coming to Mount Vernon, which was cut off by severe winter weather. When the mail resumed, Washington learned that the Virginia Assembly had approved sending a delegation to the convention of states recommended in Annapolis and had unanimously elected Washington to lead it. Letters from Madison and from the newly elected governor, Edmund Randolph, pleaded with him to let time pass and events unfold before he refused absolutely, as they felt he would be tempted to do—and so he would be, over and over again, in a months-long agony of indecision that was extreme even by the standards of a man who could exert himself over the purchase of a tea set. Clearly he was deeply pained by the quandary, but no one reading his correspondence would have been in much doubt about the outcome, even if he was.

"There are combustibles in every state which a spark might set fire to," Washington wrote to Knox the day after Christmas 1786. "We ought not therefore to sleep nor to slumber. Vigilance in watching, and vigor in acting, is, in my opinion, become indispensably necessary. . . . [T]he Spring will unfold important and distressing scenes, unless much wisdom and good management is displayed in the interim."

A s the thirteen states jealously guarded their increasingly awkward sovereignty and grieved separately over corrupt governance and shattered ideals, they might have taken courage in the attitude of the French, who were ever more wantonly inebriated by all things American. Vaudeville's biggest hit in 1786 was *L'Héroïne américaine* at the Ambigu-Comique, and its closest competition was *Le Héro américain*. Ladies at court sported coiffes styled *aux insurgents* and *à la Philadelphie*. At Latin Quarter bookstalls, there were works by *un bourgeois de New-Haven*, the pen name of Lafayette's friend Marie-Jean-Antoine-Nicolas Caritat, the marquis de Condorcet, and the *Lettres d'un cultivateur américain* (*Letters from an American Farmer*), whose author was in fact a native of Normandy. Images of America ranged from the Arcadian ("They say that in Virginia the members chosen to establish the new government assembled in a peaceful wood . . . and that in this sylvan spot they deliberated on who should preside over them . . .") to the heroic ("Every colonist is another Curtius, ready to leap into the gulf to save his country. His blood belongs to her . . .") to the entirely fictional:

The day when Washington resigned his command in the Hall of Congress, a Crown set with jewels had been placed on the Book of the Constitutions. Suddenly Washington seized the crown, broke it, and threw it in pieces before the assembled people. How petty does the ambitious Caesar seem before this Hero of America!

Understandably, Louis XVI could not wholeheartedly share in the American rapture. In later years, he said he never thought of the American Revolution except "with regret," and that change of heart was surely fixed on August 20, 1786, at the meeting in which Calonne told him that the cause of America had all but bankrupted France. The records of the royal treasury were so scattered and fragmentary that by the time Calonne felt he was ready to make this presentation to the king, he had been controller-general for more than two years. Even now, when he delivered the news that the deficit for the current year was 80 million livres, or 20 percent of the state's total revenues, he understated the actual shortfall by 32 million. Whether 20 percent or 25 percent of revenues, though, the deficit was clearly insupportable; and the plan that Calonne brought Louis to deal with it was, as it had to be, a blueprint for drastic reform. "I can easily show that it is impossible to tax further," Calonne told the king, "ruinous to be always borrowing and not enough to confine ourselves to economical reforms, and that . . . the only means of managing finally to put the finances truly in order must consist in revivifying the entire State. . . ."

In his presentation, Calonne portrayed France's system of revenues, quite accurately, as a hodgepodge of unevenly distributed privileges, self-defeating internal customs duties, and taxes that relied on those least able to pay them, among them the especially despised *corvée*, an obligation to do free work on the country's roads or pay a fee for exemption; the *gabelle*, a tax on salt; and the *taille*, a poll tax. The system placed the greatest burden on the peasantry and exempted from tax most of the nation's wealth, which was in the hands of the nobility and the Church.

None of that was new, of course, and the French government had been running a deficit for decades, but this time the usual levers were stuck. Debt service was already taking half of each year's revenues, so more borrowing could only be a stopgap; and such obvious targets for savings as the royal households, pensions, and public works amounted at most to 7 percent of the budget. The third and latest 5 percent (*vingtième*) tax, this one levied for the duration of the American war, was about to expire; short-term loans of 50 million livres would be coming due every year from now until 1794; and the state was already behind on debt repayment to the extent of six months' revenues.

If Louis was staggered by the enormity of the financial problem, he must also have been stunned by the magnitude of Calonne's solution, even if much of it had been contemplated at various times by his predecessors at the treasury. According to Calonne's *Précis d'un plan d'amélioration des finances* (*Summary of a Plan for the Improvement of Finances*), which he gave the king that day, all internal customs duties would be abolished, as would the *vingtième*. The *corvée*, the *gabelle*, and the *taille* would be phased out. There would be just a single tariff on imports and a single "land tax," based on a formula that would apply equally to all, including even the Church, which until now had reported no income from tithes, crops, rents from its lands, or anything else. The Church paid instead an annual *don gratuit* or "free gift," the amount of which was at its discretion. Under Calonne's plan, there would be provincial assemblies to supervise tax collection from all sources and to take over many functions of local administration from the parlements, and these assemblies would be made up of landowners whose votes would be weighted according to the extent of their property. Since peasants owned 30 percent of the land in France, the *bourgeois* another 20 percent, and the king about the same, the nobility would not dominate most such assemblies, and all of their special "considerations" and "liberties" would be canceled.

There being no chance that such a reform would be registered voluntarily by the Parlement of Paris, most of whose members were noble, Calonne proposed bringing together an Assembly of Notables, a gambit last played in 1626, when Cardinal Richelieu needed to get around the parlements. The delegates to such a convention, having been appointed by the king, would be more likely than any parlement to endorse the plan, and armed with such an endorsement the king could feel doubly secure in enacting it by force in a *lit de justice*. That, at least, was the theory.

·   ·   ·

Given his closeness to Calonne and the king, Lafayette probably got word of the reform program several weeks before it was announced; and were an Assembly of Notables to be convened, he had every reason to believe he would be called to it. Despite Jefferson's concern for his reputation at court and even for his safety, which would prove justified in time, Lafayette still enjoyed widespread favor, on both sides of the ocean.

His reputation in America, already great, continued to grow with news of his attempt to break the Farmers-General monopoly on tobacco. The *Pennsylvania Gazette* reported that despite a "bold attack [that] shamed the farmers but could not overthrow them," he had managed to get the American planters a price "much higher than what tobacco can be sold for in other European markets" and one that was "expected to become a standard. . . ." The whalers of Nantucket also had Lafayette to thank: Just at the moment when they had despaired of their disappearing market for oil and were preparing to take on other work, Lafayette made a deal for American whale oil to light the street lamps of Paris, which was no small victory at a time when Calonne was trying to reinvigorate the French whaling industry. To show their appreciation, the whalers decided to contribute one day's milk from one cow each to make him a giant cheese, and in late fall a 500-pound wheel arrived with a note declaring it to be "a feeble, but not less sincere, testimonial of the affection and gratitude of the inhabitants of Nantucket." As a mark of their esteem, both Massachusetts and Virginia made Lafayette an honorary citizen. North and South had at least an affection for Lafayette in common.

The "hero of two worlds" bridged a gulf equally wide in his own country by managing to become a favorite not only of the king and the ministry at Versailles but also of the *philosophes*, whose most recent works competed to flatter him. The marquis de Chastellux had just published his *Voyages dans l'Amérique septentrionale dans les années 1780, 1781, et 1782*, in which he recalled his visit to Lafayette's camp in 1780: "On seeing him, one is at a loss which most to admire, that so young a man as he should already have given so many proofs of ability, or that a man so well tried should still give hopes of so long a career." Another distinguished literary admirer was Voltaire's protégé Condorcet, a fellow abolitionist who had worked with Lafayette to formulate his early arguments against the Farm.

In the fall of 1786, Condorcet published a pamphlet *De l'influence de la Révolution d'Amérique sur l'Europe* (*On the Influence of the American Revolution on Europe*), a portrayal of America by the most rigorous of rationalists, whose transport suggests how infectious the American contagion had become:

> America offers the prospect of a vast land populated by several million men who, thanks to their education, have been made immune to prejudice and inclined to study and reflection. No distinction of rank or pull of ambition can deter these men from the natural desire to perfect their minds, to apply their intelligence to useful research, to aspire to the glory that comes with great works and discoveries. . . . America will in a few generations double the mass of knowledge. . . .

He dedicated the pamphlet, of course, "to the Marquis de la Fayette, who, at an age when ordinary men are hardly known to their own society, has earned the title benefactor of two worlds." Actually, it was four worlds now: America, France, the *philosophes*, and Versailles.

And in point of fact there was a fifth, a world in which his popularity spanned one of the deepest divides in pre-revolutionary France, between people like Chastellux and Condorcet, eminences of the French academies, and an increasingly embittered throng of second- and third-rate writers and self-proclaimed geniuses of science whose work had been scorned by the "despotic" establishment. Some of these men, like Jean-Paul Marat and Jacques Pierre Brissot de Warville, were the members of Lafayette's rump Mesmerism group, which was about to morph into the so-called Gallo-American Society, complete with Nicolas Bergasse and Guillaume Kornmann. Come the Revolution, when the reading public became democratized and literature took to the streets like everything else, these men and others with a certain talent for vivid prose and a taste for demagoguery—Camille Desmoulins, Jean-Louis Carra, Louis Mercier, and others—would finally have jobs and avid readers; indeed, they would be stars. For the moment, though, they were consigned to outer darkness, getting by as ghostwriters for the ministries of Versailles and as pornographers and libellistes, profitably eviscerating figures of society and the court, Marie-Antoinette being a popular favorite.

There were several hundred such writer-*philosophes manqués* hanging out in the cafés of Paris, whom Louis Mercier described sympathetically as "famished scribblers . . . poor hacks," men who had been seduced to follow in the footsteps of *philosophes* only to discover that their erstwhile heroes had become the establishment. In his *Tableau de Paris*, Mercier described the moment when the would-be *littérateur* or visionary scientist, the next Voltaire or Franklin, "falls and weeps at the foot of an invisible barrier. . . . Forced to renounce the glory for which he so long has sighed, he stops and shudders before the door that closes the career to him." All sorts of doors could close: the Comédie Française, the Académie Royale de Musique, the Académie Royale de Peinture et de Sculpture—all were legal monopolies; and atop them all stood the daunting Académie Française, with its forty "immortals." Just as the Académie des Sciences had rejected the work of Mesmer, the Société Royale de Médecine ridiculed the theories of Marat.

Brissot, unable to feed his family on pamphlets attacking such cruelty to himself and his friends, freelanced in the writing stable of the prolific comte de Mirabeau, and at one point went to the Bastille for writing a *libelle* about Marie-Antoinette. His authorship for this was never proved, and he was released in two months. The evidence is somewhat stronger that he may have taken the extreme measure of becoming a police spy. If so, he was not alone among his fellow scribes, as extensive police files on the hacks of Paris strongly suggest:

> AUDOUIN: calls himself a lawyer, writes nouvelles à la main, peddler of forbidden books. . . . He does all kinds of work; he will be a spy when one wants.
> CHENIER: insolent and violent poet. He lives with Beauménil of the Opéra . . . beats her . . . she describes him as a man capable of any crime. . . .
> DELACROIX: lawyer, writer, expelled from the bar. He produces [judicial] *mémoires* for shady cases; and when he has no *mémoires* to write, he writes scurrilous works.
> FRÉRON: . . . generally despised. It is not he who writes *Année lit-*

téraire, although he has its privilege. He hires young unemployed lawyers. He's an insolent coward . . . connected with Mouvel, who was expelled from the Comédie for pederasty.

GORSAS: proper for all kinds of vile jobs. Run out of Versailles . . . on personal order of the king . . . for having corrupted children he had taken in as lodgers . . . produces *libelles* . . . suspected of having printed obscene works . . . peddles prohibited books.

MERCIER: . . . a fierce, bizarre man . . . wants to become attached to the police.

By such means did writers in Paris in the mid-1780s subsidize those occasions when they could turn up in print under their own names.

One such instance was the publication of Chastellux's book on his travels in America, which inspired Brissot to a small pamphlet objecting to its insults to the American idyll: "You wish, sir, to destroy this enchantment! Cruel man!" In fact, Chastellux's general view of America was very positive, but in passing he had made a few arch comments at the expense of Quakers, blacks, and the American common man. To Brissot, such witticisms constituted a detestable assault on American dignity, proof of Chastellux's general inhumanity, and the occasion for a declaration of rights: "The dignity of man consists in his liberty, his equality before the law, in his independence, in his subordination only to those laws to which he has given his consent. . . . I say that man in our societies does not have that dignity." The notion of popular sovereignty was not new, nor was it distinctly American, but America had enacted it, and its political purity could not be impugned.

Chastellux and Brissot were contemporary surrogates for an old and acrimonious battle between the Enlightenment rationalism of Voltaire, who hated the Church but had no problem with aristocracy, and what might be called the romantic rationalism of Jean-Jacques Rousseau, who would have started over on the whole project of society and government. It was in part the very rejection of Rousseau's ideas by *le monde*, the hacks' word for the establishment, that made him their patron saint. Voltaire, who was excoriated by Brissot and company as a *mondaine* and a sellout, would doubtless have taken Chastellux's side in this case, but it fell to one of Chastellux's other colleagues in the Académie Française, Jean-François de la Harpe, to lead the counterattack. He called Brissot's work "revolting, both by its bitterness and its grossness" and Brissot himself "one of those affected madmen, the extravagant souls who have made themselves into the monkeys of Jean-Jacques Rousseau and who, by repeating words like virtue and humanity over and over again, think they are as eloquent as he was." The same side was taken up by Thomas Jefferson's friend Filippo Mazzei in the *Journal de Paris*, whose essay prompted a rebuttal by the abbé Robin, chaplain of French forces in America, which prompted another essay by Mazzei, which was seconded by a pamphlet from Condorcet; and so the literary war continued, virtually until the Revolution, when the hacks would have their day.

And in this whole controversy, no one had a bad word to say for Lafayette, whom Brissot extolled, as Chastellux had done, as "the hope of our Nation . . . whose name will be cited forever beside that of his father and friend Washington in the annals of the United States." Like the American North and South, Lafayette gave Brissot and Chastellux something they could agree on, at least for the moment.

E ven against this backdrop of universal favor, Lafayette's close relationship to the king must be considered noteworthy and somewhat mysterious. In a sign of high favor, during the last two months of 1786, Louis invited Lafayette to play cards with him four times. He also invited Lafayette along on a trip to the new port at Cherbourg when construction had just begun. This could have been a public relations ploy. The journey came only two weeks after the close of a sensational trial in what came to be called "The Case of the Queen's Necklace." Marie-Antoinette had nothing to do with it, but she had recently bought the palaces and estates of Rambouillet and Saint-Cloud, enhancing a reputation for extravagance that the necklace scandal, despite her innocence, served to cement. The trial ended in acquittal for the defendant, but before it was over—thanks in part to the hard work of the hacks—it had managed to smear both Louis and Marie-Antoinette. Lafayette was asked to ride in the king's carriage not for the quick two-day trip to Cherbourg but for the four-day, crowd-pleasing return to Versailles, which suggests that perhaps Louis asked Lafayette along in case he needed some protective coloration. If so, it was unnecessary. Lafayette reported with pleasure and relief that the affair of the necklace seemed to have had no effect whatever on the king's popularity. The crowds greeted him with throaty shouts of *"Vive le roi!"* and the king answered them happily, *"Vive mon peuple!"* It may have been the last time Louis XVI would ever enjoy such an unmixed outpouring of affection.

The king's affection for Lafayette was, of course, situational. When Calonne put Lafayette's name on a suggested invitation list for the Assembly of Notables, the king initially scratched him off. Calonne persuaded him later to reinstate Lafayette, but Jefferson was pleased to spread word of the king's first impulse. "This shows that his character here is not considered as an indifferent one," he wrote to his friend Edward Carrington, "and that it excites agitation." Jefferson thought it was Lafayette's identification with the American cause that had "drawn on him a very jealous eye from a court whose principles are the most absolute despotism." Some French observers, on the other hand, thought that Lafayette, the youngest of the Notables, would be all too amenable to the court's proposals, whatever they might be. On the day Jefferson wrote to Carrington, Lafayette played cards with the king again.

On December 29, 1786, Louis announced publicly that in one month from that date he would convene twelve dozen of the realm's most prominent figures to consider the fate of the nation. Calonne had wanted to pack the Assembly of Notables with *bourgeois*, who would have been only too happy to deprive the nobles of their exemptions, but Louis insisted on observing the traditional hierarchy. The seven princes of the blood were put in charge of a profusion of aristocrats—all the expected hereditary dukes, marquises, and counts, as well as many holders of high municipal and judicial office. Second in prominence only to the princes of the blood were the realm's most prominent archbishops. Fewer than ten of the members on the final list of the one hundred forty-four Notables were *bourgeois* professionals of the Third Estate.

Lafayette was one of only twenty-two attendees who were invited to stay at the château of Versailles for the duration of the Assembly, which was either a sign that his support was expected or a means of encouraging it. In either case, he was misread. Two weeks after the king's announcement, in a letter telling Washington about the Assembly, Lafayette set forth a very bold agenda for himself—to "produce popular assemblies in the provinces, the destruction of many shackles of the trade, and a change in the fate of the Protestants," not to mention a close examination of all the money the monarchy "squandered on courtiers and superfluities." The first two ideas were central to Calonne's plan of reform. The latter two certainly were not. To all four goals, Lafayette promised Washington, he was committed "with all my heart," and so he would prove to be.

The expected start of the Assembly had to be delayed to February 7, then the 14th, and again to the 22nd, because Vergennes had earlier weakened himself through overwork. His illness proved fatal, and his loss at such a critical time was crushing to the prospects of the Assembly and to the king. Louis's last letter to him suggests just how important he had become:

> I am afraid that despite everything I have said to you, you are still working too hard. I exhort you even more strongly to look after yourself. I ask it selfishly because you know how much the good of my service depends on you.

Vergennes died on February 13, and when the king heard the news he broke down in tears, mourning "the only friend I could count on, the one minister who never deceived me." At least for the moment, apparently, he forgave Vergennes the occasional lapse, including the policy toward America that had impoverished his treasury.

Oddly, it was not until the day after Vergennes's death that Calonne summoned help for the presentation he was to give the Assembly, which in effect was a draft of the entire plan the Notables were convened to approve. On that morning in his office at Versailles, he gathered several of the best practical minds in the realm, including Vergennes's protégé Pierre-Samuel Dupont de Nemours; Lafayette's friend and fellow American veteran the duc de Lauzun; and Charles-Maurice Talleyrand, the very secular abbé de Périgord (who was called by his ecclesiastical title only by his friends, as a joke). When Calonne brought the meeting to order, he handed each of the participants a sheaf of documents tied in a ribbon, which contained the raw materials of his program's several provisions. As Talleyrand looked at what he had been given, he was appalled that so little preparation had been done. He admired Calonne, whom he described in his memoirs with characteristic circumspection and wit: "brilliant intellect . . . ugly, tall, nimble . . . dupe of his vanity. . . ." This lapse in preparation, though, Talleyrand found as inexplicable as it was infuriating, requiring him and his colleagues to accomplish in a week "a task which the presumption and heedlessness of M. de Calonne had caused him to neglect for five months."

Elsewhere, the Assembly of Notables was taken a great deal less seriously than that. The comte de Mirabeau complained that all he heard about it were jokes and puns, and Lafayette complained to Washington that it was being called a convention of "not ables." On the morning of the Assembly's first meeting, hawkers at the Palais-Royal featured a print in which a monkey addressed a gathering of chickens: "My dear constituents, I gather you here to determine the sauce in which you would like to be eaten." On the same day Thomas Jefferson, who in time would become the staunchest American champion of the French Revolution, wrote Abigail Adams that all the *bon mots* had only convinced him that France was "incapable of any serious effort but under the word of command. . . . When a measure so capable of doing good as the calling the Notables is treated with so much ridicule, we may conclude the nation as desperate, & in charity pray that heaven may send them good kings."

Perhaps for some of the jesters, such lightheartedness was so much whistling in the graveyard. The astronomer Bailly, a man whose revolutionary future would soon place him shoulder to shoulder with Lafayette, wrote that when he first heard about the Assembly of Notables, he prophesied "a great event . . . not a revolution but a change, which, although I could not define its nature, must be to the nation's advantage." The street-level view of the Notables' reason for being, at least that of a certain bookseller named Ruault, was quite a bit bleaker than Bailly's, however, almost as dire as some Americans would come to see their own predicament. "Money there must be, and there's an end to it. . . . There is nothing but speculating, finance, banking, discount, borrowing, wagering, and payment. Every head is glued to money, crazy with speculation. . . . A fearful revolution is imminent; we are very, very close to it, at any minute we are going to reach a violent crisis. . . . In the meanwhile, though, we must live and contrive not to be carried away by the coming debacle."

XVI

Two Conventions

O N FEBRUARY 21, 1787, the day before the Notables formally convened, the Continental Congress belatedly voted to authorize the convention that was to meet in Philadelphia "on the second Monday of May next," adding that it was to be "for the sole and express purpose of revising the Articles of Confederation." Congress had delayed as long as possible to do this and had construed the convention's mission this narrowly because of the fear the states would revolt against its intermeddling. In fact, however, Congress was required to initiate any amendment to the Articles, not merely to authorize them; and the Annapolis declaration, which after all came from only four states' representatives, had bypassed Congress completely, appealing directly to the states. For that reason, Jay wrote Washington, such a convention would be illegal. Washington admitted that "in strict propriety," the convention "may not be legal," but argued that the urgency of the need for it was overriding. In a letter to Henry Knox, he likened the nation to "a house on fire" and compared legal objections to a constitutional convention to being unsatisfied with the water brigade. More serious than Jay's objection, however, was the fact that since the Articles' fundamental tenet was state sovereignty, they would likely have to be abandoned rather than amended in order to achieve the necessary reforms. By setting out to defy Congress, the states, and the Articles of Confederation, the delegates would at least technically be conspiring to commit treason.

Interestingly, these dramatically controversial legal aspects of the convention did not figure at all in Washington's ordeal of indecision about whether to attend it. The misgivings he cited were personal, and there were a host of them: His rheumatism had flared mercilessly and might lay him up even if he were there; the disarray at Mount Vernon and in his personal business made his absence from home highly inconvenient; the threat to state sovereignty might mean the convention would be underattended or would fail; he had given his word, on resigning his commission in 1783, that he would never again return to public life. Finally, and most embarrassing, he had cited ill-health and the press of personal business in begging off from the general meeting of the Society of the Cincinnati, of which he was still president and which was to meet, also in Philadelphia, the very week before the convention.

He admitted "in confidence" to James Madison that there was "a political issue" involved in his withdrawal from the Society that further complicated the prospect of his attending the convention, a factor that "operates more forcibly on my mind than all the others." Several state chapters of the Society had balked at making the reforms he had insisted on at the last general meeting, which were aimed at relieving suspicions that the Society would become a de facto aristocracy that could not resist asserting itself as a political force. He could only have been chagrined that the Massachusetts chapter of the Society had recently expressed as a body, in a letter to the state's General Court, their "abhorrence" of Shays' Rebellion and their "determination to support the present government" in quashing it by force—as plain an insertion into politics as the Society's wariest critics could have imagined. None other than Washington's former comrade General Benjamin Lincoln, head of the society's Massachusetts chapter, had led a fund-raising effort among Massachusetts merchants to raise a mercenary force; and it was Lincoln at the head of four thousand such troops who had put down the rebellion, with at least ten of their officers drawn from the Society. At the time, no one seems to have reflected on the irony that most of them had been among the officers at Newburgh, New York, whose grievance over back pay had led them to the point of mutiny against Congress and Washington.

Washington sympathized with the position of the Massachusetts government, of course, but his support was circumscribed. It did not extend, for example, to legislation passed in the wake of the rebellion that barred former rebels from voting and from holding public office, a measure Washington characterized in a letter to Lafayette as "too extensive" and "pregnant with . . . much evil." He was surely even more appalled that the Society of the Cincinnati had put itself forward as the nucleus of a para-military force.

For all these reasons, Washington's refusal to commit himself as a delegate went on for months, almost until the day he had to leave for Philadelphia, and at times it had almost the quality of a tease. One day after he told Madison that his attendance in Philadelphia would be "out of my power," he wrote to congratulate Edmund Randolph on his election as governor and, making no mention of his hesitation to attend the convention, said: "Our affairs seem to be drawing to an awful crisis: it is necessary therefore that the abilities of every man should be drawn into action in a public line, to rescue them if possible from impending ruin." Did he mean to exempt himself as a potential rescuer of his country? On the same day he wrote someone else that, while "[t]he present constitution . . . totters to its foundation and without help will bury us in its ruins," his attendance at the convention was "impracticable."

Madison remained insistent that Washington's participation at the convention would be decisive not only for attracting other state delegations but for the convention's eventual success. In responding to Washington's first refusal, he pleaded that "at least a door could be kept open . . . in case the gathering clouds became so dark & menacing as to supersede every consideration but that of our national existence & safety." Meanwhile, Washington carried on a correspondence with any number of friends and advisers, describing the awkwardness of his situation (sometimes more than once in the same words to the same person) and asking them what he should do. Knox and David Humphreys at first told him not to go: The prospects of success were too remote for him to risk his reputation. Madison agreed that he should not lend his name to an effort that seemed likely to fail but urged him to wait and see how many states sent delegates. On March 25, Washington wrote to Lafayette informing him of the upcoming convention, but he made no mention of his own attendance. Three days later, he sent Governor Randolph a painfully qualified acceptance:

[A]s my friends . . . seem to wish for my attendance on this occasion, I have come to a resolution to go, if my health will permit, provided . . . the Executive may not, the reverse of which would be highly pleasing to me, have turned its thoughts to some other character; for independently of all other considerations I have of late been so much afflicted with a rheumatic complaint in my shoulder that at times I am hardly able to raise my hand to my head or turn myself in bed.

Not only was Washington unconcerned about the legality of the convention, he even urged Madison to think boldly, and said the convention would have to do the same. He would approve of "no temporizing expedient" but would insist that the convention "probe the defects of the Constitution [by which he meant the Articles of Confederation] to the bottom, and provide radical cures," an approach that he thought would "stamp wisdom and dignity on the proceedings. . . ."

Despite his letter to Randolph, he kept reconsidering his decision. On April 2, he wrote to Henry Knox that his reasons for and against going to the convention were "so near an equilibrium, as will cause me to determine upon either with diffidence," and he asked Knox to sound out "prevailing opinion with respect to my attendance." A week later, he must have startled Randolph with a letter listing once again his whole litany of reasons not to attend, and Randolph can hardly have felt entirely reassured when Washington concluded that he would "hope for the best."

As late as April 27, Washington wrote to Knox to say he did not think he could come to Philadelphia after all because his mother was sick and he had to go to Fredericksburg immediately. He enclosed with this letter all the papers he thought would be needed at the general meeting of the Society of the Cincinnati, including a scathing note he had just received from Jefferson in Paris about how the Society was viewed in Europe. He left it to Knox how to handle this, and especially whether to tell them the note was from Jefferson or not.

Finally, just before dawn on May 9—two days after the Society's general meeting was gaveled to order—Washington left Martha standing at the door of Mount Vernon and set off in his carriage for the Constitutional Convention in Philadelphia. His mother had not been as unwell as he had been led to believe, but at least she had made it impossible for him to open the Society's meeting, for which he had every reason to be grateful.

Jefferson's letter about the Society, particularly by the standards of Jeffersonian prose, was beyond blunt. "I have never heard a person in Europe, learned or unlearned, express his thoughts on this institution, who did not consider it as dishonorable & destructive to our governments," he wrote, calling it "the germ whose development is one day to destroy the fabric we have reared." He had not been able to see this quite as clearly in America, he said, but having lived in Europe for two years now, he was thoroughly convinced that the Society would inevitably "produce an hereditary aristocracy which will change the form of our governments from the best to the worst in the world. To know the mass of evil which flows from this fatal source, a person must be in France. . . ."

The Hôtel des Menus-Plaisirs, on the avenue de Paris in Versailles, was the Bourbon monarchy's property department, a warehouse filled with the partitions, candelabras, curtains, costumes, rugs, tapestries, paste jewelry, and other gewgaws that had furnished the court's ballets and masked balls since the days of Louis XIV. To accommodate the first Assembly of Notables to be held in more than two hundred years, Louis XVI decided to add on to this building the one facility his illustrious ancestor had not thought necessary (or perhaps desirable) when he drew up the plans for Versailles: a large meeting room. On the brilliantly sunny winter morning of February 22, 1787, this latest addition—still smelling of fresh paint and cut wood, heated by two large stoves disguised as columns, and enlivened by several enormous tapestries of hunting scenes taken out of storage—was to be the theater for one of the most remarkable political dramas in the history of Western civilization, and yet another candidate for "the start of the French Revolution."

Sometime before ten o'clock that morning, the king went over final details for the meeting, checking the seating arrangements he had himself made by hand several days before and going over the last details as to ceremony and rank, including forms of dress. At about ten thirty he left his chambers, "in coat and mantle," according to the minutes of the day, which were kept by the grand master of ceremonies. Preceded by the princes of the blood, "also in coat and mantle," and preceded also by "his great and lesser officers and mace bearers," the king went to his chapel for a low mass. It fell to the grand master of ceremonies, the marquis de Dreux-Brézé, to arrange the king and his fellow worshippers for the service, while his subordinate masters of ceremonies, a father and son named Nantouillet, took the king's seating plan to the Hôtel des Menu-Plaisirs and began to place the Notables, whose rank was made plain by the costumes the king had prescribed for the day: the prelates "in cassock, rochet, cape, and square hat," the nobility "in coat and mantle with cravat and plumed hat," the presidents and attorneys of the parlements in "black gown and square hat," and so on.

At eleven o'clock, the king left the château for what would otherwise have been a very short walk, "in his ceremonial coaches . . . escorted by detachments of his military Horse Guard." Outside the hall, he was greeted by the appropriate dignitaries with the appropriate formal flourishes. Informed by the masters of ceremonies that the Notables were properly seated, he was escorted to a throne at the front of the hall, on a platform that was raised three steps from the floor and "covered with a carpet of velvet strewn with innumerable fleurs-de-lis." A violet canopy over the throne was decorated with more fleurs-de-lis. At the king's right, two steps below him but still on the platform and still one step above everyone else, was his younger brother, Monsieur, the comte de Provence. On his left, at the same level as Monsieur, was his youngest brother, the comte d'Artois. The other princes of the blood were seated beside them on the same step of the platform, but their chairs were off the carpet.

After giving the traditional signal that he was ready to begin by removing and replacing his hat, the king—seated, while everyone else remained standing—gave a short, anodyne speech. When he was finished, he signaled to the mace bearers, master of arms, and pages of arms, who were supposed to remain kneeling until the meeting was over, that they could stand, a small gesture signifying the king's magnanimity. Then the keeper of the seals approached the throne, "making three deep bows: the first before leaving his place, the second after making a few steps, and the third upon the first level below the throne; he then knelt and received His

Majesty's instructions." Only when the keeper of the seals returned to his feet did the Notables know that they could be seated.

Normally, it would then fall to the keeper of the seals to elaborate the king's instructions, but today that was the job of another man, whom he introduced as "Messire Charles Alexandre de Calonne, Grand Treasurer, Commander of the Order of the Holy Ghost, Minister of State and Contrôleur-Général of Finance." Calonne saluted, moved to take his seat at a table where he had placed his papers, and then, having removed and replaced his hat, began to speak.

What he said, after a throat-clearing tribute to his own stewardship of the royal treasury, was what he had told the king in their meeting on August 20, though not in quite such plain terms. After laying out what he was careful to describe as a plan the king had adopted as his own, one which he expected to be approved in all its details, Calonne gave the floor back to the keeper of the seals, who announced that the Assembly would now be divided into seven "bureaus," each of them chaired by one of the princes of the blood and each of them responsible for particular aspects of the plan. Lafayette, for example, was put in the second bureau, run by the comte d'Artois, which was charged to consider the composition of the new provincial assemblies, then the issue of new taxes.

After ten sessions, the Assembly was called together again, and despite the fact that all seven bureaus had suggested changes and discovered areas of disagreement with Calonne's plan and with each other, Calonne thanked them for their unanimous support of the measures they had considered so far and gave the seven bureaus new assignments.

This, of course, was infuriating. Each of the bureaus demanded that the king be told of their positions and reservations, and after that they in effect turned their backs on all of Calonne's recommendations and set to work devising their own.

Despite the fact that the Assembly's work was supposed to be held secret, the pamphleteers were hard at work from the beginning, no doubt encouraged by various Notables with private agendas. One member of Lafayette's second bureau, Etienne Charles de Loménie de Brienne, archbishop of Toulouse, was known to be after Calonne and his job, and when the hacks got word of Calonne's inept attempt to force the Notables' compliance, they went to work on him. The comte de Mirabeau, prince and patron of the hacks, weighed in with a very sticky charge of inside and otherwise illicit stock trading.

Lafayette worked to influence the Notables' deliberations from outside as well. Just as the second bureau came to the question of customs reforms, a book was published that addressed the most controversial issue involved, the role of the Farmers-General. The book was written by Brissot and his financial backer and friend Etienne Clavière, both of them Lafayette's colleagues in the Gallo-American Society and the Society of Universal Harmony, and their book tracked his arguments against the Farm so closely that it was clear he had collaborated with them.

With the pamphlet war intensifying and the Notables all but completely out of control, Calonne decided to go public himself, publishing the memoranda of the first and second bureaus as well as an introduction that priests were asked to read from their pulpits on April 1, which was Palm Sunday. Calonne's statement was sweetest reason itself. On the subject of taxes it read in part: "People will doubtless pay more—but who? Only those who were not paying enough; they will pay what they owe according to a just proportion, and nobody will be overburdened. Privileges will be sacrified! . . . yes, justice demands it and need requires it. Would it be better to put more burdens on the non-privileged, the people?" The message was clear, correct, and crowd-pleasing; but the messenger by that time had been so thoroughly discredited that the move was considered the last desperate cry of a dying man.

Just as the Assembly began, Thomas Jefferson left Paris on a tour of the South of France. For all his proclaimed interest in and support of the French Revolution, then and especially later, Jefferson did not seem much concerned with it while he was there. Never a fan of the Parisian French, at least, he seemed now more interested in getting back to America than in staying close to his mission. Before he left for the South, the author of the Declaration of Independence and notorious king- and Britain-basher told Lafayette to be moderate in his ambitions for the Assembly. "Keeping the good model of your neighboring country [Britain] before your eyes, you may get on, step by step, towards a good constitution." He never imagined and did not then hope that the Notables would turn rebellious.

Lafayette followed Jefferson's advice up to the point that Calonne went public, but at the next meeting of the Notables, he rose in his bureau to question several egregious examples of real estate ventures that had been disadvantageous to the king. There was a simple if unspoken explanation for them: Dissent years before over the many courtier pensions the king had awarded required him to curb the practice, which he replaced by buying and selling royal lands at favorable prices. Perhaps Lafayette was unaware of that, or perhaps he just chose to ignore it, but for whatever reason, in the first major political speech of his life, Lafayette took up a cause that put him directly at odds with the king and his closest advisers, including Calonne. In rhetoric that clearly had been sharpened for effect (anticipating Winston Churchill, no less), he decried "dissipated millions . . . granted to corruption or selfishness [which] are the fruit of the sweat, the tears, and perhaps the blood of the people." At that point d'Artois, shocked by the tone of his attack on Calonne (from whose sweetheart deals d'Artois had himself benefited), tried to silence him, but support for Lafayette in the bureau forced d'Artois to back down. Lafayette continued the attack, at the same time appealing to "the justice and goodness that we know to be the natural sentiments of His Majesty." He called for a full investigation. After that, he wrote Washington proudly, "it was thought proper to intimidate us. . . . M. de Calonne went up to the King to ask I should be confined to the Bastille."

Two days after that speech the Assembly adjourned for the Easter holidays, during which Calonne was sacked, not because of the corruption charges but because he had become a liability to the attempt to raise revenues. After a short interregnum, Brienne was named to replace him, "a man equally great by his abilities and his uprightness," Lafayette assured Washington. Since then, he added, "we have got the King to make reductions and improvements to the amount of forty millions of livres a year. We are proposing the means to insure better. . . . The walls of Versailles have never heard so many good things."

When the Notables reassembled, Lafayette returned in full stride, presenting two "memorials" almost as incendiary as his speech. The first argued that no new taxes should be levied until all economies possible had been made and that even then, given the "squandering and luxury of the court and of the highest classes of society," more taxes would be inhumane: "Follow these millions [of taxes] as they are demanded among the rural huts, and you will recognize them as the widow's and orphan's mite, the final burden that forces the farmer to abandon his plow or a family of honest workers to take to beggary"—a statement that, for all its inflamed rhetoric, was literally true. His second memorial prescribed economies the court could make. He proposed cuts in the military and in the royal households, including those of the king and queen. He proposed selling off unused royal property, including many of the king's hunting lodges. For good measure, he demanded prison reform, a system of regular audits for the royal treasury, and punishment of those who made undue profits from speculation in government loans. Only when all this had been accomplished, he declared, should the Notables consider new taxes: "All would be lost, even honor, if the king were not determined upon every saving and improvement that may relieve an already overburdened people of new exactions." Not surprisingly, Lafayette told Washington, "the King and family and the great men about Court, some friends excepted, don't forgive me for the liberties I have taken."

The wonder perhaps is that such defiance had so much support in his bureau, where Lafayette had clearly become a leader, in part due simply to his fearlessness. Some of that support dissipated with an even more radical third memorial, in which he called for "a new order of things" based on "the constitutional rights of the state." By this time, his thinking had clearly been influenced by his more radical colleagues in the Gallo-American Society. The Notables actually would never be able to sanction taxes, he said now, because that "imprescriptable right . . . belongs to the representatives of the nation alone"—in other words, he was asserting the principle that there could be no taxation without representation. He went on to attack the tax privileges of the Church and the nobility, and ended with the most revolutionary proposal anyone had ever made for the record, at the Assembly or anywhere else in France. "It seems to me," he said, "that we have reached the point where we ought to beseech His Majesty once more to assume responsibility for all measures and to assure their happy outcome forever by convoking a *national assembly*" (emphasis added).

After a stunned silence, d'Artois asked Lafayette if he was suggesting a convocation of the "Estates-General," a representative convocation of the three estates from all the provinces of France and a body that had not been called together since 1614. D'Artois knew the answer when he asked the question and may even have suspected the rest of his response: "Yes, monsieur, and more than that." The word "national" meant "popular," a group that would represent not the three estates but the nation as a whole. Lafayette thus became the first public official in France to utter the term "National Assembly" and the first to assert out loud, by denying the king the right to impose taxes even by fiat, that absolutism in France was dead. This time no one rose to second him.

Although the king continued to treat him cordially, Lafayette never had the trust of the queen again. Three days after this speech, on May 25, Brienne called the Notables together, thanked them for their work, and closed them down. "I had the misfortune to displease their Majesties, royal family, and a set of powerful men and courtiers," Lafayette wrote Washington, "while that conduct of mine . . . made me very popular among the Nation at large. . . ." In that he had a great deal of help from the pamphleteers and freelance orators in the Palais-Royal, who were becoming increasingly adept at the increasingly dangerous game of arousing an indignant public.

XVII

First Blood

O N THE DAY THE ASSEMBLY of Notables met for the last time,
May 25, 1787, the Constitutional Convention finally got under
way. Thanks to a wet spring that had turned the roads to mud,
delaying the arrival of a quorum, Washington had some time to work with
Madison on what would be presented, during the convention's first week,
as "the Virginia Plan," which contained many elements of the Constitution that would ultimately emerge. First, however, the convention would
take two decisions of enormous consequence: That it would deliberate in
secret, and that Washington would chair the convention. Everyone knew
the convention held the potential for a radical change of government—
that was why Congress was so late in recommending it, and the states so
focused on their instructions to delegates—but especially having worked
on the Virginia Plan, Washington knew exactly how critical secrecy would
be. After Governor Randolph presented it, on the fourth day of the convention, he candidly admitted that it would leave the states "nearly annihilated," and if any hint of that had got out, the convention would have
been finished.

Washington himself would be virtually silent during the four months
of the convention, and he would use a heavy hand to enforce the public
silence of what came to be known as "the dark conclave." Among other
things, he insisted that meetings take place on the second floor of the
State House (now known as Independence Hall) with windows shut. The
summer of 1787 was not among Philadelphia's hottest, but the atmosphere

could not have been comfortable for the delegates in attendance, most of them obese and all of them heavily clothed. Despite Lafayette's freedom with details of the Notables' deliberations, Washington observed the strictest confidentiality even with him. "You will I dare say be surprised . . . to receive a letter from me at this place," he wrote, explaining that despite his pledge to retire to private life, "the public voice was so loud, I could not resist the call. . . . What may be the result of the present deliberation is more than I am able, at present, if I was at liberty, to inform you, and therefore I will make this letter short. . . ."

By the time he read that, Lafayette had already heard from Henry Knox about both the high promise of the convention and Washington's decision to become a delegate to it. "Secure as he was in his fame," Knox wrote, "he has again committed it to the mercy of events. Nothing but the critical situation of his country would have induced him to so hazardous a conduct."

Here was a signal difference between Washington and Lafayette: As much as he cared about "fame," and he certainly cared no less about it than Washington, Lafayette never seemed to think twice about putting himself "at the mercy of events," retaining the intrepid optimism of a man who seemed to be leading a charmed life. Washington found this quality in Lafayette both attractive and mystifying. When he responded to Lafayette's account of the Notables, he gave to Lafayette's charge of abuses in the royal budget the not exactly rousing adjective "interesting," although he did call it a demonstration of "patriotism." By then he would have been made aware of the full fury of Lafayette's attack on Calonne by an account in the *Pennsylvania Gazette*, which ran his "sweat, tears, and blood" speech in full, including the charges of corruption against well-placed nobles whom he actually named.

It is perhaps overly tempting to imagine that Washington winced as he read this. He admired Lafayette's courage and initiative, and he had no illusions about the evils of absolutism. Still, as later correspondence confirms, he was worried about the extent to which Lafayette seemed willing to endanger himself and so, by extension, his cause. In his letter reporting on events in the Assembly, Lafayette told Washington he had been sick

during part of it (a flare-up of what appears to have been chronic lung disease, perhaps tuberculosis). In the context of warning him against overwork, Washington subtly suggested he might do well to avoid making
"application too intense . . . [which] may disqualify you for the laudable
pursuits to which zeal for the good of your Country and the honor of
human nature may prompt you."

Washington's self-imposed silence during the convention and his
successful enforcement of secrecy were only some of the more obvious
contrasts with Lafayette and the Assembly of Notables. Though the
Notables and America's framers were dealing with many of the same
issues, as any thoroughgoing reform of government would have to do—
where the power to tax should reside, the relative power of local and central government, the nature and relationship of the executive, legislative,
and judiciary functions—the differences between the two deliberative
bodies and their work were much more stark than the similarities. The
Constitutional Convention, as radical as its intentions may have been,
had a firmer basis and a narrower scope than the Assembly of Notables,
which threw open every question about French governance at once,
many of them issues that America had already settled (taxation by representation, freedom of religion, and the vices of absolutism, for example). In contrast to the disciplined agenda and decorum of the
Constitutional Convention, the Notables' vast self-designated agenda
was negotiated virtually in public and in the rude, raucous style of
French legislative debate. The Assembly of Notables became so unruly
that someone actually moved that only four people be allowed to speak
at once.

That the Notables failed to accomplish much of anything, then, is not
surprising; but even had their starting point been clearer, their scope more
limited, and their debate more composed, no group of Notables could
have accomplished the practical compromise necessary to accomplish
their task since virtually no one in France, thanks to absolutism, had any
experience in governance. Even the ministers were experienced mainly in
the intramural politics of Versailles. The best guidance available was from
its cadre of enlightened intellectuals, perhaps the best-read group of people on earth, but one with no experience at all in the management and
peaceful resolution of political conflict. Given the framers' collective expe-

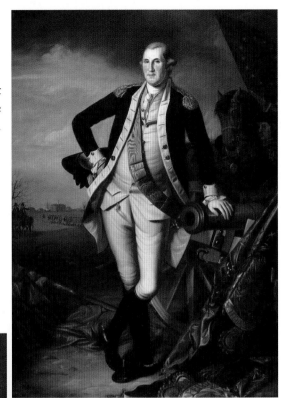

Charles Willson Peale's portrait of Washington after the Battle of Princeton, January 3, 1777.

Captain Lafayette in the uniform of the Noailles regiment, in a painting by Louis-Léopold Boilly.

Marie-Antoinette, archduchess of
Austria, in a portrait by Joseph
Ducreux, looking older than her age
(14) in 1769, the year she married
Louis XVI.

The lately crowned Louis XVI, in a
portrait by Antoine-François Callet.

The architect of Louis's policy toward
the American colonies was his
foreign minister Charles Gravier,
comte de Vergennes.

Charles-Henri-Victor-Théodat,
comte d'Estaing, led the first French
expeditionary force to America.

The decisive French force in the American Revolution was commanded by Jean-Baptiste-Donatien de Vimeur, comte de Rochambeau (left). His ground forces and the fleet commanded by François-Joseph Paul, comte de Grasse (above), combined with Washington's Continentals for the climactic siege of Yorktown (below, the signing of surrender terms).

Washington imposed secrecy on the Constitutional Convention by the force
of his personality. At the end of one day's deliberation, he brandished a copy
of resolutions that someone had left behind, warned the delegates to be more
careful, and barked, "let him who owns it take it." No one ever did.

The Republican-Federalist conflict, whose chief protagonists were Thomas Jefferson (above, left) and Alexander
Hamilton (above, right), became a war over the meaning of
the French Revolution. Because John Adams (left) was
closer to the Federalist view, his long friendship with Jefferson was abruptly severed. Even when Jefferson was
Adams's vice president they never spoke, and they did not
explain themselves to each other until both were old men.

Washington did not let accusations of regal display get between him and his love of dancing, with Martha and others.

Before the Assembly of Notables was convened, a cartoon appeared in the Palais-Royal, whose caption read: "My dear constituents, I gather you here to determine the sauce in which you would like to be eaten." When the assembled fowl objected to being eaten at all, the presiding monkey said, "You're avoiding the question."

The Tennis Court Oath, by Jacques-Louis David.

The Storming of the Bastille and the Arrest of Joseph Delaunay, by Charles Thevenin. Delaunay, the governor of the Bastille, had ordered fire down on the besiegers, and on the way to the Hôtel de Ville he was decapitated by the mob. His body was later cut in pieces by a cook's assistant and carried through the streets on pikes.

Three days after the Bastille fell, Louis XVI came to Paris, where he was received at the steps of the Hôtel de Ville by the new mayor, Jean-Sylvain Bailly, and (to Bailly's left) the city's new commandant-general, Lafayette.

An artist's rendering of Lafayette at the *Fête de la Fédération*, which marked the first anniversary of the fall of the Bastille and starred the commandant-general at the height of his power and popularity.

Another rendering of Lafayette at the time of the *Fête de la Fédération* shows him hand-in-hand with the French motherland, having slain the monster Despotism.

Lafayette's indictment of the Jacobins was answered in August 1792 by the storming of the Tuileries (here in a painting by Jean Duplessis-Bertaux) and the imprisonment of the royal family. Eight days later, to avoid certain execution at the guillotine, Lafayette gave himself up to France's enemies. He spent the next five years in prison.

An artist's rendering of what passed for courts of justice during the September Massacres of 1792.

rience in writing state constitutions and in local politics, no body ever delegated to the task of rethinking government had ever been better prepared than the ones who gathered in Philadelphia in May of 1787, whose greatest achievement, perhaps, was that they left Philadelphia united in their commitment to a document of which virtually none of them entirely approved.

No signatory to the U.S. Constitution left unhappier than the man who is always called its "father." James Madison detested especially the so-called Great Compromise, which balanced the rights of large states against the fears of small ones. The compromise was to give small states the same number of senators as large ones but to give the exclusive right to originate money bills to the House of Representatives, where more populous states would dominate because of proportionate representation. Madison felt very strongly that both houses should be proportional to population. He felt even more strongly that giving the national government an absolute veto over state legislation was critical, and he was desolate when that was voted down. Many delegates were horrified by other aspects of the Constitution, notably its compromise on slavery, which only deferred the issue to another generation (while delicately managing to avoid use of the word in the Constitution, which refers to slaves as "such people"). The convention's two most powerful delegates, Washington and Franklin, both had important reservations about the final draft, and both implored the convention to vote for it anyway. "I confess that I do not entirely approve this Constitution at present," as Franklin put it, "but sir, I am not sure I shall never approve it: For, having lived long, I have experienced many instances of being obliged . . . to change opinions even on important subjects. . . ." Given the array of competing interests that any body of men would bring to such a deliberation, Franklin said, he was surprised it was as close to perfection as it was. "I consent, sir, to this Constitution because I expect no better, and because I am not sure that it is not the best." That spirit of pragmatic compromise would be wholly absent in revolutionary France.

Washington's silence was, as it were, constitutional—he was never noted for eloquence or public speaking—but in the context of the convention that was a providential virtue. Never was the weight of that silence felt more forcefully than when the powers of the presidency were discussed, since everyone knew who the first president would be. It took the stature of Franklin just to get the conversation started.

Washington undertook a positive effort to make himself felt at the convention only twice. The second time was on the last day of the convention, when he sided with those who felt there should be a representative for every thirty thousand citizens rather than every forty thousand. The measure had been previously defeated, but once Washington declared himself, it was promptly and unanimously approved.

The first occasion had come some time before that, at the end of a long day's deliberation, when he rose, brandished a copy of resolutions that someone had left behind, warned the delegates to be more careful, slapped it down on the table before him, and barked, "let him who owns it take it." Then, according to William Pierce of Georgia, "he bowed, picked up his hat, and quitted the room with a dignity so severe that every person seemed alarmed; for my part I was extremely so, for putting my hand in my pocket I missed my copy of the same paper." Pierce was relieved to find his copy later in his room, in the pocket of another coat. No one ever claimed the one that Washington had found.

The vote on the Constitution was not unanimous, thanks to Elbridge Gerry of Massachusetts, Governor Randolph of Virginia, and Washington's old friend and mentor George Mason, whose opposition here and during the ratification debate ended their friendship. The night the vote was taken, those delegates who felt like celebrating adjourned to the City Tavern, after which Washington retired, as he wrote in his diary, "to meditate on the momentous work which had been executed after . . . sometimes seven hours sitting every day except Sundays . . . for more than four months."

Next day, September 18, he sent a copy of the new Constitution to Lafayette as he had promised he would do, along with a short, weary note which said only that the document "must speak for itself. . . . It is now a child of fortune, to be fostered by some and buffeted by others. What will be the general opinion on or the reception of it is not for me to decide, nor shall I say any thing for or against it: if it be good I suppose it will work its way good; if bad, it will recoil on the Framers." He left Philadelphia for Mount Vernon later the same day.

.   .   .

When Lafayette received the copy Washington sent him, his first reaction was alarm. He was well aware that he and his American friends were trying to solve very different problems—France was trying to break the stranglehold of executive authority in the interest of greater liberty, while America needed more energy in central government. Still, his greatest hope was that, as he wrote Washington only a few weeks before reading it, that the new Constitution would be able to "give solidity and energy to the Union without receding . . . from the principles of democracy, for any thing that is monarchical, or of the aristocratical kind is big with evils." He feared most what he knew best.

The Constitution as drafted did not allay his concern. Above all—and especially awkward given his relationship with Washington—he was troubled by the power of the executive, specifically that the president would be eligible for reelection indefinitely. He rushed his copy on to Jefferson with a note, the first sentence of which told him what was enclosed, the second of which read: "What do you think of the powers of the President?" In his opinion, "our friends are gone a little too far on the other side." Jefferson's reply to Lafayette is unknown, but he made his feelings known to Madison immediately and in no uncertain terms, calling the president under this Constitution de facto "an officer for life." Once elected, a president would never relinquish the office, Jefferson said, but would play foul, fix elections, whatever it took to keep himself in power. "Reflect on all the instances . . . of elective monarchies, and say if they do not give foundation for my fears." Throughout that summer and fall of 1788, while the Constitutional Convention debated in Philadelphia, the monarchy of France had been demonstrating to Jefferson, Lafayette, the Parlement, and the people of Paris all the many ways in which a too powerful executive could abuse its authority and all the many weapons it could wield against a popular will for reform.

When the Assembly of Notables failed, the king took unilateral action, lifting the *corvée* and establishing provincial assemblies; and still the Parlement of Paris refused to register new taxes. Finally he resorted to one of the absolute monarchy's bluntest instruments: On August 6 he called the Parlement to a *lit de justice*. This one did not end as they usually did.

"Gentlemen," he said, after removing and replacing his hat, "it is inappropriate for my Parlement to doubt my power. . . . It is always painful for me to resolve to make use of my full authority and depart from the ordinary usages; but my Parlement compels me to do so today and the safety of the state makes it my duty." With that, the keeper of the seals, in vastly more than so many words, informed the Parlement that there would henceforth be a stamp tax levied on every legal agreement in the kingdom, and the previously proposed land tax was to replace the expiring *vingtième*. As the keeper of the seals spoke, the king loudly snored. The meeting was taking place after lunch, and the king's lunches had become more and more plentiful. "The body is thickening," the Austrian ambassador wrote to Joseph II, "and the returns from the hunt are followed by repasts so immoderate that they provoke periods of irrationality alternating with a sort of abrupt unconcern, which are most trying for those who have to endure them."

The day after the *lit de justice*, the Parlement debated its response and settled on outright defiance, declaring the king's enforced registration of the taxes to be illegal. Against such emphatic resistance, Brienne and his fellow ministers convinced the king, who was easily persuaded of most things by this time, to suspend the Parlement and exile its members to Troyes, which he did with absolutism's more targeted club, the *lettre de cachet*.

Weeks and months of pamphleteering, demonstrations, and mob rioting in Paris followed, and word of similar protests came in from the provinces. Versailles responded by tightening censorship, warning bookstores against selling unauthorized publications, and banning political clubs. Finally, the king and the Parlement of Paris reached an informal agreement—or thought they had—in which the king agreed to drop his demand for a new system of taxation in return for an extension on some of the old taxes and registration of a huge new loan with a five-year term, at the end of which he would convoke the Estates-General. The king was to certify this agreement at a different sort of meeting with the Parlement, called a *séance royale*, or Royal Session, which would differ from a *lit de justice* in that parlementarians were permitted to express their opinions. Since there was agreement on the result in advance, this seemed to the king's ministers a meaningless concession.

The Royal Session, held on November 19, began with a two-hour lecture by the keeper of the seals that summarized and asserted for the last time the core tenets of absolutism:

That [the king] is accountable only to God in his exercise of supreme power.

That the bond between the King and the nation by its nature cannot be severed. . . .

That it is in the nation's interests that the rights of its leader should not be adulterated or weakened. . . .

Lastly, that legislative power lies unconditionally and completely in the person of the king.

The keeper of the seals then discussed the subject of the loans, and when he was finished, the president of the Parlement opened the floor to comments, which were expected to be brief and positive.

Seven hours later, after one more magistrate had suggested one more compromise—that they allow the loans only until 1789, and that the Estates-General would be called at that time—the king, long past bored and increasingly irritable, motioned for the keeper of the seals and whispered something in his ear.

"After hearing your opinions," the keeper of the seals announced for the king, "I find that it is necessary to institute the loans. . . . I command that my Edict be endorsed."

The king was on his way out the door when the duc d'Orléans rose, uncalled upon, to speak. He pointed out that this was not a *lit de justice*, and that the king therefore had no right to impose his orders upon the Parlement. "Sire," he said, "permit me to place at your feet my protest against the illegality of your orders."

There was a stunned silence. Talleyrand, for one, would never forget the moment. "It is necessary to revert to the ideas then ruling in France," he wrote in his memoir, to understand the shock "produced by the first instance of a prince of the blood making a protest . . . and attacking as null and void, in the presence of the king himself, the orders he had just given."

Like most others in the room, Louis was stunned. "I don't care," he said first. Then, "You're certainly playing the master." And then came the really last outburst of the Old Regime: "Yes it is! It is legal because I wish it."

The king left the Parlement through a quiet crowd outside the Palais de Justice, which exploded with joy when the Parlement voted, three hours later, to condemn the king's action as illegal. Next day, by *lettre de cachet*, the duc d'Orléans and two other leaders of the rebellion were sent into exile, and in the absence of further action the king's ruling stood, sparking more weeks and months of demonstrations in Paris and around the country.

Lafayette missed all the excitement in Paris to attend the meeting of his provincial assembly in Auvergne, where there was excitement enough. To the king's request for a 50 percent increase in tax revenues from the province, the assembly sent a petition, much of it written by Lafayette, asking the king to consider the "deplorable and truly critical situation of this province . . . the picture, frightening but accurate, of abandoned estates, deserted shops, unhappy farmers reduced to the alternative of begging or permanent emigration." Against that backdrop, the assembly resolved "that it would exceed its powers . . . if it required a figure beyond the already excessive and disproportionate sum of the existing *vingtième*." Its members based their decision, they said, on "the justice of His Majesty" and, pointedly, "the protection of the laws." Their plain implication was that the king had no power to impose taxes. Taxpayers alone could do that, through their representatives in the Estates-General.

Having sent off their petition, the assembly members continued their work and made good progress on specific reforms. Then they received another missive from the king that invited them to take reform even further, calling for the assembly to find ways to distribute the tax burden more fairly, build new roads and canals (a particular need for the farmers of rural Auvergne), and institute better methods of farming. Finally, the king asked that they consider how to reduce the number of deaths caused simply by accident and ignorance.

Emboldened by the king's obvious ambition for reform, the assembly took up the last mandate with special vigor. Members called for better training of midwives, free hospital care, traveling smallpox inoculators, and other specific measures, and they addressed the fundamental cause of most such problems, which was simple poverty—"poverty that crushes, hunger that oppresses"—and the attendant explosion of itinerant beggars. "We know that we must attach the poor man to his village by work suited to his strength, provide for the old and sick, and be definitely certain that the beggar has enough to eat if we are to dare refuse him alms. . . . [I]t is beggary, Gentlemen, and not the beggars that you must destroy. . . . We have no right to forbid them their sorrowful trade until we have assured them other means of support."

On December 6, Lafayette read this report to the assembly, whose members asked for only minor modifications before voting to send it on to the king. Just as they had finished their deliberations and were about to adjourn for the day, a message came by courier from Versailles. Apparently the king's call for additional reforms had been sent before he had received the assembly's earlier objection to new taxes, because the decree accused the assembly of Auvergne of having forgotten "the only purpose of its existence," which was to raise taxes. The king viewed its unwillingness to do so "with as much astonishment as disapproval and will never tolerate [it]." Arguing that conditions in Auvergne were not as bleak as they had been portrayed, and that in fact the king knew very well who had been evading their fair share of taxes all these years, the assembly was told that it "had exceeded the powers that the king had granted to it . . . and that it should hereafter devote greater attention and effort to earning [the king's] confidence and that of the province whose true interests it might have represented better." Finally, the notice set a deadline for the assembly to adjourn that left it with only four working days.

Lafayette was put on a committee of six to draft the assembly's response. In three days they came back with a direct challenge to the king's power and authority, beginning with an expression of "profound consternation" at the latest message from Versailles. They owed it to king and country to "persist in the sentiments that lay behind their resolution," the letter read, because the tax, which was "illegally assessed," would "augment the number of abandoned farms and migrant farmers, would result in detriment to His Majesty's finances and would wring his heart as well." The members said they took consolation in the fact that each of them had "listened only to the voice of his conscience." The king, of course, was not likely to find that consoling in the least.

When Lafayette got back to Paris at the end of the year, he found a city in open revolt over the king's exile of his opponents in Parlement and his reversal of their ruling. "[S]eeing that the power of the crown is declining," he wrote Washington, the ministry was trying to "retrieve it by an ill-timed and dangerous severity." Whatever they did, however, he was convinced that the "spirit of freedom in the people . . . will occupy the stage until it is filled by a National Assembly."

He was right, and events unfolded rapidly, though for the moment there was little he could do but watch and tend to his private causes. He helped Jefferson in their continued efforts for Franco-American commerce. He threw himself into various philanthropies. With Brissot, Bergasse, Clavière, and other Mesmerists who had migrated with him to the Gallo-American Society, he founded a new abolitionist group in Paris called *Société des Amis des Noirs* (Society of Friends of the Blacks), and he joined its parent organizations in London and New York. He also continued in his campaign for Protestant rights, which were finally confirmed at the end of January 1788. "You can easily imagine," he wrote Washington proudly in February, "that I was well pleased . . . in introducing to a ministerial table the first Protestant clergyman who could appear at Versailles since the revolution of 1685." Jefferson was less than impressed with what amounted to very limited legal protection for them. "It is an acknowledgement . . . that protestants can beget children and that they can die & be offensive unless buried. It does not give them permission to think, to speak, or to worship. . . . What are we to think of a country where such a wretched thing as this has thrown the state into convulsions?"

Protestant rights were not the greatest of the state's convulsives. On January 4, 1788, when demands that d'Orléans and his fellow parlementarians be freed from their exile were ignored, the Parlement of Paris ruled all *lettres de cachet* to be illegal. The king then demanded that this declaration be rescinded in his presence, which it was, after which the Parlement declared its recision to have been illegal as well. Meanwhile, the provincial parlements were becoming if anything more defiant than Paris, refusing to renew any expiring taxes or recognize any new laws, and deferring all new business to a convocation of the Estates-General.

The government won a limited reprieve when the first loan of those the king had registered by fiat in the Royal Session was subscribed within days, thanks to egregiously generous terms. During a suspicious quiet from Versailles after that, rumors spread that the ministry was plotting a drastic reform of the parlements, and by the spring, in the absence of any announcement from Versailles, rumor verged on certainty. In preemptive self-defense, the Paris Parlement, on May 3, set forth certain laws that it said were fundamental and overriding, including the right of the people to be taxed only by the Estates-General and the freedom from arbitrary arrest by *lettres de cachet*. Even more incendiary than the rights they claimed, the parlementarians swore an oath to resist any attempt by the king to impose a judicial reorganization. The next day, the king ordered the arrest of the two ringleaders of this manifestly revolutionary move, but the Parlement, true to its word, remained in session so that the king's order could not be carried out.

The standoff had continued for the better part of two days when, at eleven o'clock on the night of May 5, two hundred Swiss and French guards marched to the door of the Great Chamber in the Palais de Justice with bayonets fixed. When their commander demanded that the Parlement turn over the two men, by order of the king, the parlementarians refused to identify them and challenged him to arrest them all. At that he withdrew, ordering his troops to encircle the Palais de Justice and to let no one out. Finally the two wanted men decided to spare their colleagues and turn themselves in, after which they were lavishly but technically imprisoned. Everyone else was called to a *lit de justice* set for May 8.

There and then the king's men played their last gambit, joining some commendable prison and criminal code reforms to exactly the wholesale reorganization of the judiciary that the Parlement had feared was coming. The power to register the king's decrees was to be given to a new Plenary Court, which would be appointed by the king. The parlements would become simple courts of appeals, and their authority would be further undermined by the upgrading of subordinate courts. While the king thus attempted to silence the Parlement of Paris, provincial governors, protected by royal troops, made the same announcement throughout the nation. All of the courts of France were immediately suspended, to remain so indefinitely. The parlements' ensuing cries for the Estates-General were silenced in many places—Toulouse, Dijon, and Metz, among others—by exiling their parlementarians with *lettres de cachet*.

In the stunned aftermath of this brute repression, Lafayette wrote Washington to tell him that "the affairs of France are come to a crisis. . . ."

He was gratified to report that, despite the king's threats, magistrates were refusing to sit on the new Plenary Court. "Discontents break out everywhere," he wrote. "The clergy . . . are remonstrating. The lawyers refuse to plead. [Royal] commandants have been in some parts pursued with dirt and stones. And in the midst of these troubles and anarchy the friends of liberty are daily reinforced, shut up their ears against negotiations and say they must have a National Assembly or nothing. Such is, my dear General, our bettering situation, and I am for my part very easy when I think that I shall before long be in an Assembly of the Representatives of the French Nation or at Mount Vernon."

Washington knew even before he read that how grave the situation was that Lafayette faced. "I like not much the situation of affairs in France," he had written on June 19. The combination of the "bold demands of the parliaments" with "the decisive tone of the King" suggested that very little would be necessary "to blow up the spark of discontent into a flame . . . that might not easily be quenched." Urging "great moderation . . . on both sides," he advised Lafayette personally to tread very carefully, the bluntest advice he would ever give his friend. "Let it not, my dear Marquis, be considered as a derogation from the good opinion that I entertain of your prudence when I caution you . . . against running into extremes and prejudicing your cause." The king may, as Lafayette had said, be "good-hearted," but if he were to be "thwarted injudiciously in the execution of prerogatives that belonged to the Crown," he might "disclose qualities he has been little thought to possess."

O n June 7, two weeks before Washington wrote that warning and months before Lafayette received it, the king's *lettre de cachet* was served on the Parlement of Dauphiné, in Grenoble. It was a Saturday, market day, so an audience was ready when the *basoche*, Parlement's caste of young, poor, and chronically unruly law clerks, raised the alarm, passing out leaflets and posters, pleading with the people to prevent the exile of their parlementary champions, prompting shoppers to stop, shops to close, and crowds to mobilize. One group shut the city's gates, another unharnessed the coach horses that were to carry the parlementarians away, another gathered at the house of the provincial governor. Others began haranguing the regiments of grenadiers that were trying to enforce the Parlement's exile, and who faced them with bayonets fixed.

Trusting in the soldiers' unwillingness to shoot, the crowd surged. At that, the grenadiers charged and fired. Many people were injured and several were killed, including a twelve-year-old boy. After regrouping, the crowd, holding aloft the bloody clothes of the victims like flags before a charging army, turned on the grenadiers, pummeling them with cobbles torn up from the streets, then scrambling onto adjacent rooftops and tearing off tiles to throw at them. Meanwhile another crowd gathered up the leaders of the parlement, dressed them in their ermine-trimmed red robes, and escorted them—as they supposed, triumphantly—to the Palace of Justice, where they insisted on a special session. The parlementarians, unsure whether to feel vindicated or kidnapped but plainly unsettled by the ambiguity, left town as soon as they could.

A five-year-old boy named Henri Beyle watched out his grandfather's window as a hatter's assistant, who had been bayoneted in the lower back, "walked with great difficulty, supported by two men who had passed his arms over their shoulders. He had no coat on, his shirt and white trousers were full of blood, I can see it still, the wound from which the blood was pouring was in the lower part of his back, about level with his navel. As is natural, this is the sharpest memory that has stayed with me from that time."

June 7, 1788, would go down in French history as "the Day of the Tiles," and the boy at his grandfather's window, whom the world would come to know as the author Stendhal, would always remember this as the day when he saw "the first blood shed by the French Revolution."

XVIII

Experiments in Democracy

I N EARLY 1788, Beaumarchais was enjoying one of the great triumphs of his life with his first and only opera,* a libretto he had started working on more than a dozen years before, about the time he was waltzing the chevalier d'Eon and trying to sell Louis XVI on supporting the American Revolution. Gluck had turned down Beaumarchais's offer to write the music and suggested his student, Antonio Salieri, whose score for Beaumarchais's politically bold but otherwise well-forgotten *Tartare* appeared a year after the opening of Mozart's politically bland but otherwise unforgettable opera version of *The Marriage of Figaro*. With the audience of Paris at the time, though, Beaumarchais's opera was an enormous hit. An allegory about despotic power and religious bigotry, *Tartare* did to kings and priests what Beaumarchais had done in *Figaro* to the aristocracy, which was of course the ultimate subversion: He made them laughable. Perhaps subconsciously inspired by the chevalier and wishing for political reasons to sink his barbs into only non-European monarchs, his first characters were a eunuch and a Sultan.

*Beaumarchais had nothing to do with Mozart's *Marriage of Figaro* beyond providing the inspiration and story line for it. He did not even hear it until 1793, by which time he was hard of hearing and using an ear trumpet, which helps to explain why he said he did not much like the music. He was long dead by the time Rossini wrote his *Barber of Seville*.

THE SULTAN (*to the Eunuch*): If I'm not happy tomorrow, I shall have your head cut off.

THE EUNUCH: And why not, indeed! Injury to injury! Chop, chop!

It was not very funny in the final version, when Beaumarchais was taking himself and his message more seriously, but as the Baron Grimm reported in his *Correspondance littéraire, Tartare* overtook even the tumultuous street politics of Paris as "the only topic of conversation. . . . [N]otables, dismissal of the ministers, provincial assemblies, everything disappeared before this great phenomenon." Four hundred guards could not contain the crowd on opening night, and by February 1788 the opera had been performed no fewer than thirty-one times.

Thanks to *Tartare's* success at the box office, Beaumarchais decided to build himself a grand establishment, "a house of note," and so it was. The property he bought for the purpose was not in the chic Faubourg Saint-Honoré but in a working-class neighborhood, "a quiet spot" right by the Faubourg Saint-Antoine, with a wonderful view of the Bastille. The architect's estimate was outrageously low even by the standards of architects' estimates, off by a factor of six, and as his bills mounted, Beaumarchais appealed to Lafayette to help him try to collect the debt he was still owed for the weapons and supplies he had sent to the Continental Army. Happy to oblige, Lafayette took Beaumarchais's problem to Jefferson, who was appalled: Eight years before, he had written to Beaumarchais's agent and nephew Francey to apologize for Congress's delay in payment, promising that it would be coming soon, and bemoaning the fact that the depreciation of the Continental currency would unfairly punish "M. de Beaumarchais, who has so proved his merit to us and inspired our highest admiration by his love for the rights of man, his genius, and his literary reputation." This time surely, Jefferson assured Beaumarchais, Madison and Monroe would quickly untangle the issue in Congress.

When the house and grounds were finished, Beaumarchais sold tickets to picnickers and gawkers—the place was that spectacular, and Beaumarchais was that much impoverished by it. The gates gave onto a path through a sylvan idyll dotted with vaulted trellises and waterfalls, past a colonnaded Temple of Bacchus, a statue of Eros, and busts of famous men. There was a tunnel of love and, crossed by a Chinese bridge, a lake with small painted skiffs for children. The house itself was equally splen-diferous, a vision in marble and mahogany bathed in the light of two hun-dred windows, with such infrastructural innovations as indirect lighting, a central heating system, and an ingeniously camouflaged door to an under-ground passageway with a back street exit, without which, one day in 1792, Beaumarchais would have become one more victim of the French Revo-lution. By then his earlier reputation as a man of the people would be entirely forgotten.

The forgetting began even as the house was being built, when one of his many moneymaking schemes put him afoul of the comte de Mirabeau. Beaumarchais had become the principal shareholder of a company run by two brothers, both engineers, who had devised a system for bringing fil-tered water to the city. When a group of speculators caused the price of their company's stock to drop sharply, Beaumarchais took countermea-sures that raised it just as sharply, threatening the speculators' ruin. One of these speculators was the banker and Lafayette's fellow Mesmerist Eti-enne Clavière, who persuaded the chronically insolvent Mirabeau, in return for a large loan, to write one of his notoriously effective pamphlets against Beaumarchais's enterprise. Beaumarchais's arch reply to the attack infuriated Mirabeau, who answered it accordingly. Beaumarchais tried to end the fighting by choosing not to respond, but his silence suggested he felt beaten, and the smell of blood drew out other enemies, the most important of them being Nicolas Bergasse and Guillaume Kornmann, who were associates of Clavière in finance as well as Mesmerism.

The scandal that enmeshed all these players was worthy of a plot by Beaumarchais. Kornmann had had his wife imprisoned on a charge of adultery. She was unquestionably guilty, but her friends had good evidence that her husband had known and approved of the affair. Her lover had been an official in Strasbourg whose connections put him in a position to do a financial speculator a world of good, and Kornmann's wife was in effect given in exchange for services rendered. Only when the man lost his post did Kornmann seem concerned about his wife's infidelity and then only, it was said, so that he could get his hands on her fortune. This was a case that the chivalrous Beaumarchais could not ignore, perhaps especially because Mme Kornmann was also a fellow Protestant.

His intervention with powerful friends managed to get Kornmann's wife out of prison and protect her fortune, which of course enraged Korn-mann, reminded Clavière of his previous run-in with Beaumarchais, and engaged Bergasse's already inflamed imagination. Like the many hacks of Paris who felt they had been touched, as Mesmer had been touched, by the dead hand of a despotic, monolithic cultural establishment, Bergasse had written many pamphlets full of rage at the injustice and corruption of an exclusionary world, and Beaumarchais was a perfect case in point. Not only had he ridiculed Mesmer on occasion, he had committed the crime, unforgivable to Bergasse's fellow hacks, of becoming famous and wealthy through his writing, therefore clearly part of the aesthetic tyranny that had victimized so many embittered would-be *littérateurs*.

Over the next two years, Bergasse published dozens of pamphlets on "*l'affaire Kornmann*." Perhaps lulled by the inferiority of Bergasse's prose, Beaumarchais answered with only three. That a writer as bad as Bergasse could do so much damage to one as good as Beaumarchais seems funda-mentally unjust, but with lines no better than "Wretch, you reek of crime!," Bergasse was able to triumph decisively in the court of public opinion by painting Beaumarchais as a social-climbing pimp who curried favor by slipping Mme Kornmann into the bed of every aristocrat in Paris. ("This type of ridiculous cant has always had a following [in France]," Beaumarchais's biographer Frédéric Grendel amiably explained. "Inside every Frenchman there is a public prosecutor waiting to be let out. Go into a bistro, listen, and you're at the Inquisition.")

In April 1789, the libel case Beaumarchais had long before brought against Bergasse and Kornmann finally ended with his complete vindica-tion, but the damage was done. Figaro, the dashing, anti-aristocratic hero, was revealed as no better than the corrupt, lecherous Count Almaviva, and the verdict was taken as yet another proof that people with the right con-nections could get away with anything.

Beaumarchais was one of the first champions of the people to become their scapegoat, but he was far from the last. Lafayette must have observed this transformation at close range, since his associates were the agents of it, but apparently he watched without seeing, and small wonder. Who could then have imagined that the same thing would happen to him and so many of the revolutionary leaders who came after him, that every front rank would face as much danger from behind as from the ostensible enemy, and that one after another, the heroes of the revolution would be led, sometimes quite literally, to the slaughter?

Beaumarchais's libel case took as long as it did to play out because of the parlements' suspension, a move that sparked rebellions like Grenoble's "Day of the Tiles" all over France. In that pre-revolutionary summer of 1788, the parlementarians' assaulted dignity made them underdog heroes, despite the fact that almost all of them were noble. But at this stage, the incipient revolution was precisely, as historians have called it, a "revolt of the nobles." The parlements had popular support because they were perceived to be the people's last bastion against the tyranny of an absolute monarchy; but the nobles as a class, parlementary and otherwise, were in fact fighting for ancient "considerations" and "liberties," some of them already long lost, others perceived to be in danger.

No revolutionaries at this point were more convinced than the aristocracy of Brittany, who objected to the king's peremptory intervention against their parlement as a violation of their special ancestral privileges. Lafayette, whose property in Brittany made him one of them and led them to seek his support, wholeheartedly gave himself to their cause, not to protect the perquisites of fellow aristocrats or an historic privilege of Brittany but simply to oppose what he considered an assertion of despotic power. He knew exactly how badly his advocacy for the Breton nobles would be taken at Versailles, but despite the fact he knew it could cost him his freedom, he made his position more than plain, decrying the king's assault on the rights of "the nation in general and . . . Brittany in particular."

Louis refused to read a petition brought to him by a delegation of twelve Breton nobles, saying he did not wish to know the names of those he would have to punish for such impertinence. When reports reached Versailles of sympathetic public defiance in Brittany, however, his ministers persuaded him that he had to clamp down. The twelve nobles were sent to the Bastille by *lettres de cachet* and four others were stripped of their posts, including Lafayette, who lost his command and was lucky to keep his rank. "The Marquis de la Fayette . . . is dis-graced in the ancient language of the Court," Jefferson reported to Secretary of Foreign Affairs John Jay, "but, in truth, honorably marked in the eyes of the nation. The

Ministers are so sensible of this, that they have had separately private conferences with him to endeavor, through him, to keep things quiet." Brienne was one of those who tried to win Lafayette's support by drawing him into close confidence, but he told others he considered Lafayette to be rash, hotheaded, and, given his popularity, "the most dangerous man in France."

Just then Brienne and the French economy received a blow greater than any revolutionary leader could have delivered. On July 13, 1788, on the very eve of the harvest, a massive storm ravaged the Paris basin from Normandy to Champagne, raining down hailstones large enough to kill farm animals. Two thousand square miles of crops, already decimated by a severe spring drought, were flattened, including France's best corn fields. The loss was estimated at 25 million livres, but the cost was a great deal higher than that. In addition to the prospect of famine, the storm meant that French farmers and peasants would be unable to meet their tax obligations for the year, plunging France into a full-blown credit crisis, complete with a panic-driven run on government notes. In early August, to restore a measure of public order and confidence, Brienne convinced the king to set a date for the Estates-General the following spring.

With that concession, Brienne also convinced Lafayette to get his friends and friendly parlementarians to cease their protests and support the king and his ministers. Jefferson was dubious, describing the hailstorm as "the coup de grace to an expiring victim." If by the expiring victim he meant the French economy, he was right. Only a few days after getting Lafayette's promise of support, Brienne announced that he was suspending cash payments to the king's creditors and replacing them with interest-bearing government notes, a clear harbinger of bankruptcy. Within days Louis was forced to dismiss Brienne, whom he had come to trust, to make way for the return of Jacques Necker, whom he loathed, but whose credibility with bankers was higher than that of Brienne, perhaps higher than that of France itself.

Lafayette was livid at the betrayal of his good faith, but he was even angrier about the damage done to the prospects for reform. "This damnable suspension [of debt repayment] undoes all the good of the decision to hold the Estates-General," he wrote to Mme de Simiane. "Paris is thunderstruck; the guards have been doubled and orders prepared."

Sparked by fury at Brienne for his legacy of hunger and unemployment (weather being an unsatisfying object of vengeance), mob violence broke out across the country and was as usual especially fierce in Paris. On August 29, rioters looted the guards' stations on the Pont Neuf and burned them to the ground. That night, guardsmen shot into a crowd of several hundred demonstrators in the place de Grève, killing seven or eight of them. A week later, according to the memoir of the bookseller Hardy, fifty more were killed when guardsmen intervened to save their commander from another angry crowd.

Finally, on September 22, the king signaled retreat by calling back the parlements. That very day, amid riotous rejoicing at the good news mixed with continued fury at the bad, there was another clash between guardsmen and demonstrators that left none dead but many injured. As soon as the Paris Parlement reconvened, it called in the heads of the guard to chastise them for abusing fellow citizens, a highly popular move by the newly emboldened parlementarians but one that the forces of order would remember when called upon to control demonstrators the next time, and the next.

At this point, the French monarchy was as good as dead. Forced to surrender every time he attempted to regain control of the country, the king had lost his chief minister, his judiciary, his initiative, and his authority. Necker, the putative godsend, announced that he would do nothing beyond ensuring the government's temporary solvency until a comprehensive reform program was recommended by the forthcoming Estates-General. With that, the job of governance passed from the king and his ministers at Versailles to a formless convention of people yet to be named and nine long months in the future.

After chastising the guard, the first order of business for the Parlement of Paris was to register the king's call for the Estates-General and to determine the procedures by which it would be convened. On September 15, its members ruled that the Estates-General would be governed by the same rules as those of its last convocation, in 1614. Those procedures gave each of the three orders an equal number of representatives and called for them to deliberate and vote in their separate estates ("by order") rather than as a single body ("by head"). That would mean, as it did in 1614, that the Third Estate could always be outvoted by the privileged orders. Very quickly the pamphleteers, freed from censorship (and some of them from prison) by order of the ever more popular Jacques Necker, began to drum up the opposition.

No one was more diligent in purveying the insidious import of this decision than a group of dissident young parlementarians known as "the Americans," whose leader was the twenty-nine-year-old Adrien Duport, one of Lafayette's fellow Mesmerists. Some months before, Lafayette, Duport, and others had formed what came to be known as the "Patriot Party," a coinage taken originally from America's revolutionary "patriots" and applied later to the rebels of Holland, Belgium, and Geneva. The Patriot Party was at first just a loose alliance whose nucleus comprised the parlementary "Americans" and a group of liberal nobles, including Lafayette and some of his comrades-at-arms in the American Revolution, all of them brought together by their common commitment to bring an end to absolutism and to establish a constitutional monarchy that would guarantee fundamental rights to all citizens. Their initial agenda was simply to help others of like mind get elected to the Estates-General. With the Parlement's call for the "forms of 1614," however, the need to take more precisely targeted political action became urgent.

Duport, Lafayette, and their allies immediately undertook a campaign of posters and pamphlets to publicize the implications of the Parlement's decision; and thanks in large measure to their work, it was as if a mask dropped: The noble magistrates in Parlement had never been using the privilege and power of their high offices to fight despotism for the sake of the people after all, but only to gain power and privileges for themselves at the expense of the people and the king. They were no better than those "ministerial despots" who were always blamed for the king's repressive moves against reform. As that perception took hold, the Parlement of Paris came to be as execrated as it had been so recently hailed; the "revolt of the nobles" was shown for the reactionary movement it had always been; and the line of battle changed radically. No longer would it be the people and their magistrates fighting off the arbitrary rule of an absolute monarch and his ministers. Now it was a benevolent king, with the support of beloved and grateful subjects, making a stand against the depraved and corrupt power of an entrenched, self-dealing aristocracy.

To deflect public anger over the Parlement's decision, Necker decided to refer the question of procedures to another meeting of the Assembly of Notables, which reconvened in the first week of November. In the end, not surprisingly, it only reaffirmed the decision of fellow nobles in the Parlement of Paris. Patriot pamphleteers lost no time denouncing this outcome for what it was. In the words of one pamphlet that came out just as the Assembly adjourned: "Twice the king has gathered [the Notables] around himself to consult them on the interests of the throne and of the nation. What did the Notables do in 1787? They defended their privileges against the throne. What did the Notables do in 1788? They defended their privileges against the nation. The only friend of the throne, then, is the nation, and the only friend of the nation is the throne."

Lafayette and his party colleagues had expected nothing else from the second Assembly. Even as it began to meet, a small, self-selected group of Patriots began to hold a series of long meetings every Tuesday, Friday, and Sunday night, sometimes at Lafayette's home on the rue de Bourbon but usually at Duport's house in the Marais. They formed the nucleus of what quickly became a very potent coalition. In the ultimate reconstitution of the breakaway, political Mesmerists, this new core of the Patriot Party, which came to be known as the Society of Thirty (*Société des trente*), put the fortunes of some of Paris's richest liberal nobles and bourgeois financiers (Lafayette, Clavière) behind the work of avid propagandists (Bergasse, Brissot), with the goal of transforming a hodgepodge corporation of variously privileged orders and provinces into a constitutional monarchy in which the citizens' collective will rather than the king would be sovereign. Eventually the Society of Thirty would have almost twice that many members, including Mirabeau, La Rochefoucauld, the vicomte de Noailles, Talleyrand, Condorcet, the abbé Sieyès, and the Lameth brothers, Charles and Alexandre. As Mirabeau put it in a recruiting letter to the duc de Lauzun, the Society of Thirty was determined to push reform "as far as the public welfare, truly understood, would permit. . . . I believe you will not regret falling in with our wishes," he added, "for this conspiracy of reasonable men will go farther than anyone imagines."

So it did. At the end of 1788, on the day of the Assembly's last meeting, five of the seven princes of the blood wrote a cautionary memorandum to the king that minced no words: "Sire, the state is in peril . . . a revolution in the principles of government is being prepared." It was a populist, anti-aristocratic revolution in which Lafayette and the Society of Thirty were deeply implicated. By January 1789, the bookseller Ruault would write, "Each day it rains pamphlets and brochures," and he cited specifically the writers in the Society of Thirty. Such work turned up collectively in the princes' declaration to Louis labeled as "writings . . . memoirs . . . demands" that amounted to "a system of reasoned insubordination and scorn for the laws of the state. . . . Who can say where the recklessness of opinions will stop?" Virtually overnight, the king received some eight hundred petitions from various reform groups around the nation, all of them calling on him to double the representation of the Third Estate and to let the Estates-General vote by head rather than by order.

On December 27, the king announced to the nation that he was going to ignore the recommendation of the Notables and the princes, whose declaration had by then made its way into the press. The Third Estate's representation in the Estates-General would be doubled, he declared, because "its cause is allied with generous sentiments, and it will always obtain the support of public opinion." Having given the Third Estate the political force it sought, he also effected a leveling in the First and Second estates. The nobles' assemblies, he decreed, would include all those with inherited or transmissible titles, including the old-line provincial nobility, most of whom were entirely new to politics and who as a group would greatly outnumber the wealthy courtiers of Paris and Versailles. Similarly, high church officials would be numerically overwhelmed in the First Estate's assemblies because Louis insisted that they include all parish priests, "because good and useful pastors are daily and closely associated with the indigence and relief of the people" and are thus "much more familiar with their sufferings."

He went even further in the report of his deliberations which accompanied the announcement. In it was recorded his intention to become a constitutional monarch, to convene the Estates-General regularly, to give them control of taxation and the state budget, including the king's own, and to seek their guidance on *lettres de cachet* and freedom of the press. In a word, said the duc de Luxembourg, he gave them "more than the Estates-General on bended knees would have dared to hope for." The royalist comte de Bouillé ran into Lafayette on New Year's Day and ruefully congratulated him on all the king had conceded. He wrote in his memoirs that he was shocked by Lafayette's reply: "Oh, we'll take him farther than that."

Louis went further by himself a month later, on January 24, 1789, when he prescribed how delegates to the Estates-General were to be elected. With a few exceptions to account for special circumstances, each of France's 234 discrete political entities was to have an electoral assembly for each order. All nobles and all clergy could participate in these assemblies, but for the vastly more numerous Third Estate, male taxpayers over twenty-five years of age would vote for electors, who would then vote for delegates to their assembly. Each of the three estates' assemblies was to choose two delegates to the Estates-General and were furthermore to compile lists of grievances, so-called *cahiers de doléances*, so that "everyone, from the extremities of the kingdom, and from the most obscure of its hamlets, should be certain of his wishes and protests reaching [the king]."

Not surprisingly, this invitation to protest was widely accepted, and the following months were an experiment in democracy whose like would not be seen again in France for almost a hundred years, spreading the activism that had so far taken root mainly in a few large cities to every corner of the nation.

All through 1788, in each of the thirteen states, Americans debated the strengths and weaknesses of their new Constitution, whose agenda was in some ways identical to the one emerging from the "Americans" in the Paris Parlement and the Society of Thirty: to merge a collection of assertive localities into a single nation with an executive, a representative legislature, and a government whose power was derived from and bent on preserving the rights of a sovereign people.

Ratification of the U.S. Constitution was not a great deal more certain than the outlook for success in the Estates-General, pitting pro-Constitution Federalists against those who feared the abridgement of states' rights and the consequences of a powerful executive. They were called "Anti-Federalists" during the ratification process, after which many of them would comprise the core of the party that came to be known as Jeffersonian Republicans.

For the most part, Washington stood aloof from the ratification debate, in part because addressing the issue of executive power in public would have been exceedingly uncomfortable for the man everyone assumed would hold the office. Though he allowed his name to be invoked by those arguing for ratification and wrote many letters in support, all of his statements on the subject were intended to be private and advisory. On one occasion only did he intervene directly in the process. At the point when six of the nine states necessary had already ratified, he heard that Maryland was going to postpone its convention to await the outcome of debate in Virginia, where the Constitution had such oratorical powers against it as Patrick Henry and George Mason. At that, Washington wrote to both Maryland governor Thomas Johnson and Lafayette's former aide James McHenry, who had represented Maryland at the Constitutional Convention. He pleaded with them not to suspend their convention, arguing that delay would encourage the Constitution's enemies and raise the chances of a rejection in Virginia that could sway other states as well.

In the event, Washington's argument was moot: Maryland overwhelmingly approved the Constitution on the day after he wrote those letters, a full month before Virginia even convened. But the debates at the convention in Williamsburg turned out to be just as vigorous as Washington had predicted. Patrick Henry set the tone with his opening question—Why did the Constitution begin with "We, the people" instead of "We, the States"?—and George Mason was even more virulent in opposition than he had been at the convention. Even with Washington's prestige behind the Constitution and James Madison working the pro-ratification forces on the floor, the vote to ratify was close, 89 to 79. Nevertheless, on June 26, 1788, Virginia became the ninth state Washington knew to have ratified it, which allowed him the satisfying thought that his home state had had the deciding vote.* In a rare outburst of optimism even before the vote had taken place, Wash-

---

*New Hampshire was actually the ninth and deciding state to ratify, but Washington did not know that for three days.

ington wrote to Lafayette that he could envision a day "[w]hen the people shall find themselves secure under an energetic government . . . when the burdens of war shall be in a manner done away . . . when the seeds of happiness which are sown here shall begin to expand themselves, and when every one (under his own vine and fig-tree) shall begin to taste the fruits of freedom. . . ."

That Fourth of July was celebrated throughout the country by calls for Washington to be elected president, an office he was assigned by everyone but himself. "Knowing me as you do," he wrote to Lafayette, "I need only say that it has no enticing charms. . . ." The potential charge of sour grapes prevented him from preemptively declining the office, he said, but he insisted he had no ambition beyond "living and dying an honest man on my own farm."

He was saved from having to declare himself a candidate by the new Electoral College system, which in its original iteration allowed electors to vote for whomever they wished, declared candidate or not. In letters to friends, Washington debated whether or not to accept the office as if he might actually decline it. Against his accepting the job, he said, were the unknowns of a new office, the concern that he would never gain the support of the Anti-Federalists, the possibility that others could do the job as well as he, and the fact that he had promised in 1783 not to return to public life. Arguing for acceptance were variations on the fact that it was his duty; that his "glory" would suffer if he were to turn it aside; and that if he accepted the office he could always quit, return to Mount Vernon, and realize his fondest wish, so he said, "to pass an unclouded evening after the stormy day of life." He rarely admitted to feeling any optimism about the job at all, though once, as the election neared, he wrote to Lafayette: "I think I see a path as clear and as direct as a ray of light which leads to . . . permanent felicity to the Commonwealth."

More commonly, right up to the election, that path appeared to be buried in undergrowth. "May Heaven assist me in forming a judgment," he wrote to his friend the artist John Trumbull in December 1788, "for at present I see nothing but clouds and darkness before me." As results of the 1788–89 election began coming in to Mount Vernon, though, everything seemed bent on a Washington presidency. The people being elected to both the Senate and the House of Representatives were of a high caliber, and the great majority of them were Federalist supporters of the Constitution. Of all the senators elected by the end of December 1788, only Virginia's were Anti-Federalist; and on February 2, 1789, even James Madison, whose election as a senator from Virginia had been masterfully foiled by Patrick Henry, managed to be elected by a comfortable margin to the House. Anecdotal evidence, moreover, suggested that even the Anti-Federalists favored Washington for president, including Patrick Henry himself.

"My difficulties increase and magnify," Washington wrote to Lafayette at the end of January 1789, "as I draw toward the period when . . . it will be necessary for me to give a definitive answer." Still, he described the election results so far as "vastly more favorable than we could have expected," and said he thought the incoming Congress would be the equal of "any Assembly in the world." All that was necessary to make America "a great and happy people," he said, were "harmony, honesty, industry and frugality . . . the four great and essential pillars of public felicity."

Six days after he wrote that letter, in the first week of February, the College of Electors met in their respective states, where each of them was to cast a ballot for two presidential nominees. The result was as predicted. Washington received the vote of all sixty-nine electors. John Adams was second, with 34 votes, and was thus elected vice president.

After Washington learned the results, nothing further was heard about his refusing the job, only about his dismay at accepting it. "[M]y movements to the chair of government," he wrote Henry Knox on April 1, "will be accompanied by feelings not unlike those of a culprit who is going to the place of his execution. . . ."

At midday on Tuesday, April 14, 1789, Washington's dreaded fate knocked on the door of Mount Vernon in the person of Charles Thomson, secretary of Congress. Thomson read from a prepared statement that did not require or even request Washington's acceptance. Obviously, those who wrote it knew their man,* so Washington's painfully inverted reply

*"Sir, . . . I was honored with the commands of the Senate to wait upon your Excellency with the information of your being elected to the office of President of the United States of America. . . . I have now, sir, to inform you that the proofs you have given of your patriotism and of your readiness to sacrifice domestic separation and private

would not have surprised them. "[W]hile I realize the arduous nature of the task which is conferred on me and feel my inability to perform it, I wish there may not be reason for regretting the choice. All I can promise is only that which can be accomplished by an honest zeal."

Two days later, at ten o'clock in the morning, Washington once again said good-bye to Martha, who was more vexed by this sacrifice of her domestic felicity than she had been by any of the others, and left by carriage for his ineluctable destiny. In his diary for April 16, Washington wrote: "I bade adieu to Mount Vernon . . . with a mind oppressed with more anxious and painful sensations than I have words to express. . . ."

---

enjoyments to preserve the liberty and promote the happiness of your country did not permit the two Houses to harbour a doubt of your undertaking this great, this important office to which you are called not only by the unanimous vote of the electors, but by the voice of America. I have it therefore in command to accompany you to New York. . . ."

XIX

Acts of Defiance

IN EARLY 1789, while Washington was still brooding over whether to take on the presidency of a nation with a solid Constitution and a sweeping popular consensus behind him, Lafayette was fighting to be elected to the Estates-General by the nobles of his native Auvergne, having told them plainly that if elected he would vote to rescind their privileges. But, as the adopted motto on his sword read, *Why not?* He had faced worse odds and won, even against the express will of the king.

Lafayette had visited Auvergne exactly twice in the past decade, and many other nobles from Paris and Versailles were likewise turning up at ancestral estates they had not visited in years to stand for election, only to find themselves resented by the titled provincials, many of them of modest means. Greatly outnumbered in their assemblies, many of these absentee nobles had more than a little trouble getting elected. Working against Lafayette as well were his liberal politics, common enough for nobles in Paris, much less so in the provinces. His colleagues in the Society of Thirty saw him at times as all too moderate (Condorcet once asked a mutual friend to visit Lafayette and "take along in your pocket a little vial of Potomac water and a sprinkler made from the wood of a Continental Army rifle . . . to exorcise the devil of aristocracy . . ."), but many of his fellow nobles in Auvergne saw Lafayette as a dangerous radical.

Questions about his politics elicited from Lafayette a response that had not been characteristic of his life to date. "I shall do my duty and shall be moderate," he wrote at the time. "My conscience and my public standing are my two supports. If I lose the latter, the former would suffice me." He could not credibly have said that some years before, but his actions now and in the future seconded him. He proved that when he chose to cast his lot with the Second Estate, deciding to use his influence to moderate the conservative nobility of Auvergne from within rather than accept certain election in the province's Third Estate.

Early on, his fellow nobles decided to discuss what grievances they wished to bring to the king's attention before electing delegates, and Lafayette was named to a committee of four to draft their *cahier de doléance*. His influence on the result is obvious. Before the Assembly, he had been working on what he intended to propose to the Estates-General as a declaration of citizens' rights, and the Auvergne nobles' *cahier* takes key passages from his earliest draft virtually verbatim. It began with the declaration that "nature has made men equal," and allowed that while distinctions of rank were proper in a monarchy (this was a *cahier* of the nobles, after all), they must be "founded upon the general welfare." Like *cahiers* from all orders across France, many of which were based on models circulated by the Society of Thirty, it called on the Estates-General to draft a constitution providing for a government of three branches. It also joined in a widespread call for comprehensive legal reform, including freedom of speech, freedom from arbitrary arrest (*lettres de cachet*), the right to counsel, trial by jury, and equality before the law. More problematical, the draft *cahier* also joined the Third Estate's call for the nobles to renounce their pecuniary privileges and for taxes to be "proportionate to true needs . . . and to true ability to pay." Predictably, this feature of the *cahier* inspired fierce and persistent opposition; keeping it in the final *cahier*, Lafayette observed at the time, was as difficult as it had been to put it there in the first place. The *cahier* reflected its conservative provenance in its demand that nobles have the exclusive right to carry weapons and preferment in the officer corps, however, and when Lafayette made a long speech in favor of voting by head rather than by order in the Estates-General, he found himself virtually alone. The final *cahier* required all of Auvergne's noble delegates to oppose it. Lafayette could find justification for his wish to do otherwise only in another clause that exhorted delegates to follow their consciences.

He left Auvergne deeply unhappy with the final *cahier*, which "oppresses me," as he wrote to a friend in April. "[I]t is a composite of great principles and petty details, of popular ideas and feudal ideas. . . . There are two hundred years between one provision and another." The fact that it had so many progressive elements, though, was thanks in no small measure to his efforts, and his defense of them might easily have cost him the election. In the end he was elected to the Estates-General with just one vote to spare, receiving 198 of the 393 votes cast.

S ince most peasants and workers could not afford the time or expense to attend the electoral assemblies, they ended up sending very few representatives to the Estates-General. The fervent populist protest articulated in pamphlets like the abbé Sieyès's widely heralded tract *What Is the Third Estate?* reflected a frustration over lack of influence in government that was shared by the most successful and affluent men of the *bourgeois*, many of them as affluent as any noble. A memorandum from Nantes declared: "The third estate cultivates the fields, constructs and mans the vessels of commerce, sustains and directs manufactures, nourishes and vivifies the kingdom. . . . It is time for a great people to count for something." The authors of that statement were municipal officers, however, not cultivators of fields; and most such Third Estate protests in the name of the peasantry were similarly exercises in ventriloquism, since with few exceptions only nobles and *bourgeois* wrote pamphlets. Almost half of the representatives of the Third in the Estates-General were holders of venal offices. Two thirds of them had legal qualifications, as advocates, notaries, and magistrates. Historians have struggled to find a few peasants and artisans among the more than thirteen hundred elected delegates. Despite the ambition and reach of the democratic process of 1789, then, the vast majority of French people were not represented in the Estates-General.

The common folk made themselves heard in other ways. If their complaints in the *cahiers* were sometimes muted by drafters of a higher social order, their rage is not hard to find—for example, against feudal privileges, like the one that protected nobles' hunting rights and allowed rabbits and other foragers to devour the farmers' crops. There were many others, ranging from expensive to degrading. One *seigneur* claimed the right to take his vassals along when he hunted in winter and to "make them open their bowels so that he might warm his feet in their ordure." Most such relics

of earlier feudalism had been replaced with fees, which were another subject of widespread complaint. Peasants were charged for milling their
wheat, for crossing the lord's stream, for taking their produce to market.
But the most common target in the peasants' and workers' *cahiers* were
taxes and tax collectors ("those bloodsuckers of the Nation who quaff the
tears of the unfortunate from their goblets of gold"), and their deepest
wish was simply for relief from hunger. Since the fall of 1788, the price of
bread had steadily risen; by the beginning of the winter of 1788–89 the
four-pound loaf had risen from 9 sous to 14, higher than it was at the outbreak of the Grain War of 1775.

As Simon Schama has noted, the *cahiers* demonstrated that there really
were two revolutions going on, one driven by the political ambition of the
Third Estate and Enlightenment ideas about citizens' rights and constitutional government, the other by a powerful fusion of anger and hunger.
Peasants and laborers were not interested in the physiocratic ideal of free
trade; they wanted wheat regulated and the price of bread fixed at a "rate
the poor can afford." They wanted more and stronger government, a heav-
ier hand from their father-king against the aristocrats and their bullies
who were taking the food from their children's mouths, not constitutional
protections to bind him.

The problem of hunger presented itself to the king less forcibly in
writing than in the rioting that broke out all over France in this election
and *cahier*-writing season, which was the worst winter France had seen
since 1709. By the end of December, the Seine was frozen all the way to
Le Havre. Commerce that relied on rivers and ports came to a dead stop,
as did the jobs of dockers, boatmen, log-drifters, and many others. Water-
mills froze, and grain soured. Small-parcel farmers who could not pay
their taxes, thanks to the hail- and drought-ruined crop of the previous
season, had a choice of selling out—sometimes infuriatingly, having to get
permission from the local lord to do so—or being evicted. Three quarters
of the farmers in Normandy ended up landless, and the story was the same
if not as extreme elsewhere.

Thousands of the dispossessed flooded the cities in search of jobs
that were not there, by some estimates thirty thousand of them in
Paris's Faubourg Saint-Antoine alone, but even decent jobs no longer
offered relief from desperation. In some towns a large part of the pop-

ulation was reduced to beggary. Untold groves of olive and chestnut trees were killed by the long deep freeze, as were thousands of square miles of pasture crops. Much of the grain still left over from the previous harvest was spoiled, and as winter turned to spring even that began to run out.

By February, the official price of bread was allowed to rise to 14 ½ sous—half the high end of a well-paid laborer's daily wage, and two loaves were needed for a family of four. Market days in the cities became scenes of bedlam, and in the towns and villages mobs wielding hatchets, knives, stones, and pitchforks ransacked warehouses for wheat and corn, raided the stores of monasteries and convents, tore apart private homes searching for imagined "hordes," extorted wheat and bread from merchants at far below market prices, and waylaid convoys of grain being sent to other towns for famine relief. There were widespread tax strikes, and defiance of the game laws to protect crops that spring resulted in the killing of several gamekeepers. There were more than three hundred violent incidents across France in the four months leading up to the storming of the Bastille. Where local forces either could not or would not restore order, merchants and others formed so-called *gardes-bourgeoises* to protect their interests and themselves from the restive masses, who were driven by a wish less for political reform than for survival. Politics was reducible in many minds to a simple, in fact simplistic, calculus of hunger: Their misery was caused not by weather or free-market economics but by "aristocrats" and a powerful coterie of other unfeeling and unseen conspirators who were making huge profits from their hunger by hording flour and grain—the insidious *pacte de famine*, a suggestive play on the Bourbon kings' *pacte de famille*, though in truth the people were still loath to blame the king, their *père-nourricier* (father-provider).

As sympathetic as they might have been with the peasants' plight, the *cahiers* that spoke of political reform, even of a revolutionary change in government, were speaking another language. What use was talk of liberty, as one perspicacious writer put it, "to men dying of hunger? What use would a wise constitution be to a people of skeletons?" In reflecting on the underlying causes of the French Revolution, it is instructive to note that the price of bread did not come down until the Bastille did.

The differences between the aspirations of common people and those of even the most ardent of their defenders in the three estates was nowhere more apparent than in Paris, where economic desperation was keen and concentrated. In February alone, no fewer than twenty-seven bakers were fined for exceeding the government-imposed ceiling of 14½ sous per loaf, and the general economic depression that had started in winter did not abate with the coming of spring, when there were reports of men giving up shirts for bread. With the return of warm weather, crowds of the jobless, hungry, and dispossessed came back outside, ready for whatever might arise.

This is the Paris to which Lafayette returned from Auvergne on April 13, which happened to be the day that the government finally made its announcement of special conditions that would govern long-postponed elections in the city. The new rules were clearly intended to blunt the forces of rebellion in an already restive populace. The Third Estate was to meet in sixty newly drawn electoral districts, gerrymandered so that none of them focused on any existing guild, parish, or other focus of prior loyalty. There was not enough time for Paris to draw up *cahiers*, according to the new regulations, and the electors were to be chosen on a single day, each district's election to be supervised by a government appointee. There were also new, more restrictive qualifications for voters that eliminated voters by the tens of thousands, nearly a quarter of all men over twenty-five, including not only the unemployed but also most journeymen, apprentices, and day laborers. Recognizing the volatility of the situation, the government preemptively moved arms from the Arsenal to the Bastille and redoubled the guard on other stores of guns and powder.

How to pinpoint the moment in 1789 when the Third Estate decided to revolt is a matter of long argument. Some historians date it to the opening of the Estates-General in the first week of May, others to June 20 and the famous scene on a tennis court at Versailles, when the Third Estate declared itself the National Assembly. Still others credit July 14 and the storming of the Bastille.

Another good argument has been made by the historian R. B. Rose, who maintains that the first "deliberate and sustained act of insubordination" by the Third Estate was on April 21, voting day for electors to the

Assembly of Paris. This defiance was actively encouraged and partially orchestrated by the Society of Thirty.

At a meeting on April 19, after much debate and despite strong opposition to the electoral regulations, the Society decided to support the process so that the opening of the Estates-General would not be delayed. They circulated pamphlets urging the election of their members and, despite the regulations, calling for each district to issue a *cahier*. Their model was clearly based on a draft of Lafayette's "Declaration of the Rights of Man and Citizen," which he considered his best legacy to the French Revolution and to history. Among its provisions:

1. That all men are born free and equal in rights and that all power derives from the People. . . .
3. That no citizen may be arrested without proper judicial procedure. . . .
5. That all citizens have freedom of thought, speech, writing, printing, and publishing. . . .
11. That these rights can neither be diminished nor modified nor alienated by the Estates General, that they must be the basis for the future Constitution.

The society's model *cahier* also called for freedom of assembly, the right of the people to bear arms, and regular meetings of the Estates-General.

Many of the districts adopted this model, and followed the society's advice for coordination as well, each of them sending representatives to the others with reports of their actions and plans. Despite the informality of their contacts, the result was that they acted in concert when they defied government regulations by exercising discretion about who should lead them, accepting some of the government's electoral supervisors, rejecting others, and they chose more than 400 electors instead of the 147 they were allowed. Those electors, working on their own timetable, did not finally elect delegates to the Estates-General until almost two weeks after it had started.

In the end, the Society of Thirty sent no fewer than twenty-five deputies to the Estates-General, six of them from the Third Estate (including the abbé Sieyès and the comte de Mirabeau). Five of Paris's ten nobles were also from the Society. Thanks to their lobbying and pamphleteering and cooperation among the districts, the government's attempt to muffle dissent from Paris was almost entirely unsuccessful.

A distinctly separate outbreak of defiance erupted in Paris that was in some measure directed against the electoral process itself and driven by those who had been deprived of any role in it. What came to be known as the Réveillon Riots may be considered a direct precursor of Bastille Day.

On April 23, the second day of debate on the *cahier* in one of the districts of the Faubourg Saint-Antoine, a successful wallpaper manufacturer named Réveillon pleaded for a dramatic decrease in the government-fixed price of bread, which he argued would start a virtuous cycle: workers' wages could be reduced, which would allow the price of goods to drop, thus increasing consumption and reviving the economy. In another district's assembly on the same day, a saltpeter manufacturer named Henriot made the same argument.

Réveillon had done less to arouse suspicion among workers than many other employers in the Faubourg Saint-Antoine. Since his business was a casualty of the general downturn, he had had to lay off many workers that winter, but he continued to pay them 15 sous a day and did not reduce his generous salaries (35–40 sous a day) for those he kept on. He did, however, present a large target for resentment. Taking advantage of the new vogue for printed wallpaper, which could be made to match draperies, Réveillon was at the forefront of a new industry and so ran a factory free from guild laws. This made him a magnet for job seekers from the countryside. It also made him wealthy, and he had certified his entrepreneurial success by buying a grand home. Standing on the triangle made by the intersection of the rue Montreuil and the rue du Faubourg Saint-Antoine, the house was called Titonville, after the financier who had ruined himself to build it. Réveillon had put his wallpaper factory on the ground floor and kept the rest for himself and his family, including its large formal gardens, furniture said to be worth 50,000 livres, and a wine cellar that was found to hold two thousand bottles even after it had been ransacked by the mob.

All that was reported of the speeches that Réveillon and Henriot had given to their assemblies on April 23 was that they wanted to reduce wages. Given the hardships already being faced even by those with good jobs, and given the ongoing heat of electoral politics, the working-class faubourgs erupted at this news in spontaneous demonstrations. One elector was stopped outside his assembly by a crowd that had been barred from entry. "They spoke with one voice," he wrote later. " 'Is anyone looking after our interests? Monsieur, are they thinking of lowering the price of bread? I have eaten none for two days. . . . They make us pay fifteen sous for it now! . . . Ah, monsieur, don't forget us, we will pray God for you.' "

The electors would not be allowed to forget. On the afternoon of April 27, a column of demonstrators left the Saint-Marcel district, where tanneries and breweries dependent on the waters of a frozen river had been closed all winter. They made their way toward the Faubourg Saint-Antoine armed with sticks and shouting, "Death to the rich! Death to the aristocrats! Death to the hoarders! We want a penny loaf!" And for good measure, "Throw the damned priests into the river!" They were led by a drummer and two effigies hanging from a gibbet, captioned: "By order of the Third Estate, Réveillon and Henriot are condemned to be hanged and burned in the public square." Tradesmen closed their shops as the demonstrators passed by, the crowd gathering strength as it moved toward Réveillon's house. Finding the route blocked by *gardes-françaises*, they marched to Henriot's instead and rampaged through the house, destroying everything they could not carry away. Henriot and his family narrowly escaped. Their furniture and other belongings were taken to the nearby marketplace and burned.

Next morning, a crowd gathered in the Faubourg Saint-Marcel and marched toward Réveillon's house by another route, picking up laid-off stevedores and log-floaters and the people who made their homes under the bridges along the Seine, so that by the time they massed around Réveillon's home and factory, the crowd was thousands strong.

One of several aristocrats who came upon the demonstrators that day was Mme de La Tour du Pin, whose father-in-law was the chief officer on duty the night the Grain War broke out in Dijon fifteen years before. "Never had people sought more after pleasure than during the Spring of 1789," she wrote years later in her memoir *Escape from the Terror.* "For the poor, the winter had been very hard, but there was no concern for the misery of the people. There were races at Vincennes. . . ."

This particular day at the races promised to be especially exciting, pitting the thoroughbreds of the duc d'Orléans against those of the comte d'Artois, a race between reform and reaction. To get to the track from the aristocrats' favorite neighborhoods, the Marais and the Faubourg Saint-Honoré, one had to pass through the heart of the Faubourg Saint-Antoine and drive past Réveillon's house. Mme de La Tour du Pin remembered that when d'Orléans's carriage came up the street outside Titonville, the crowd massed around him, crying, "Long Live Our Father! Long Live King d'Orléans!" D'Orléans stopped his carriage and tried to calm the crowd, telling them to have confidence in the coming reforms. "Happiness is in sight," he said, referring to the Estates-General, which would be convening within days.

"But monsieur," someone cried, "they've been promising us happiness for years now. Meanwhile we're dying of hunger, and those bastard bosses are talking about reducing our wages to fifteen sous a day!" Shocking some of the aristocrats lined up behind his carriage, d'Orléans responded by opening his purse and scattering money to the crowd, then rode on to great applause. "The Duke has come to review his troops," one of the aristocrats in a coach behind him muttered, according to the police report. "Now the big show can begin."

All the racegoers eventually got through the crowd, after being forced to make pledges of loyalty to the Third Estate, an odious obligation for many of those on the road to Vincennes that day. Though somewhat becalmed by d'Orléans's money, the crowd did not leave, and the *gardes-françaises* remained behind the barricades they had built with carts and rafters from the house, guns loaded.

On the way home that night, all of the racegoers found their way around the scene at Réveillon's house except for one, the wife of the duc d'Orléans, who demanded to be let through the barricade in front of Titonville.* The *gardes*, knowing they would be criticized no matter what they did, decided that the greatest danger for them lay in defying a powerful aristocrat. When they opened the way to let her through, however,

---

*There has always been speculation that she may have been part of the Orléanists' plotting, and that her appearance that night was no accident, but the truth of the matter is unknown.

the mob poured in, overwhelming the guard and Titonville. Réveillon and his family barely escaped through the garden. The crowd spent two hours destroying the house and everything in it, kindling huge bonfires in the garden with wallpaper and hangers' glue and burning everything in the house that was flammable. Trees in the garden were cut down, mirrors and windows smashed. When it was over, nothing was left of Titonville but ruins.

Belatedly, the lieutenant general of police called for reserves to mass in the place de la Bastille, a few hundred yards from Réveillon's house down the rue du Faubourg Saint-Antoine. But they did not begin to arrive for almost three hours. The first cavalrymen to arrive on the scene were pulled off their horses and into the crowd.

When the infantry came up behind firing blanks, the protesters scattered into adjacent buildings, ran up the stairs and onto rooftops, and began throwing pieces of slate, stones, furniture, and anything else they could find at the troops below. The soldiers were then ordered to load live ammunition and fire at will. When the shooting stopped, the *gardes-françaises*, supported by Swiss guards, returned to Titonville and killed whoever was left there, though many of them were too drunk to be shot in good conscience. By nine o'clock the faubourg was under complete control of the authorities, and, by one commonly accepted estimate, more than three hundred people were dead, only twelve of them soldiers.

Though not the most gruesome incident of the French Revolution, it was among the costliest in lives, in part because the forces of order would never again be so quick to turn on fellow citizens. The only people ever punished were a sergeant, who was demoted for opening the barricades to the duchesse d'Orléans, and a blanket maker and a porter, who were hung in the place de Grève for their role in instigating the riot. In fear of what the reaction would be to any official finding, no investigation of the riot was ever undertaken.

One week later, a caucus of delegates from Brittany met at a café near the château of Versailles to plot strategy for the Estates-General. Soon they were meeting every night and drawing others, including Lafayette and other leaders of the Society of Thirty—Duport, Mirabeau, Antoine Barnave, Charles and Alexandre de Lameth, the abbé Sieyès, and a provincial lawyer named Robespierre. It was here, a few weeks later, that Sieyès raised the possibility that the Third Estate should exclude the other two orders and declare itself the National Assembly; and it was here six weeks after that when the first proposal was heard to abolish all "feudal rights" remaining to the aristocracy. Later, this group would be joined by others in Paris, where they rented a hall from the nuns at the Jacobin convent on the rue Saint-Honoré. (The Dominican Order in Paris were called Jacobins because their first monastery was on the rue Saint-Jacques.) Calling themselves the Revolution Club, they later christened the group the *Société des Amis de la Constitution* (Society of Friends of the Constitution), but everyone called them the Jacobins, and it was they, with a membership increasingly militant and radicalized, who would eventually take over the Revolution.

XX

The Spring of 1789

O N THE DAY THE RÉVEILLON riot's two scapegoats were hung in the place de Grève, George Washington was inaugurated president of the first constitutional government of the United States. Thousands jammed the streets and every doorway, roof, and window facing the ceremony, which took place on a balcony of Federal Hall in lower Manhattan. After saying, "so help me God," he kissed the Bible on which he had sworn the oath of office, which was borrowed for the occasion from a local Masonic lodge. At that, his fellow Freemason Robert Livingston, who had administered the oath, shouted out, "Long live George Washington, President of the United States!" and to the sound of thirteen cannon the throngs of people who had been gathering since before dawn broke out in wild cheers. They could still be heard exuberantly celebrating as Washington gave his first inaugural address to the members of Congress, who were assembled in the Senate chamber.

Though he may or may not have had help with the speech from James Madison, it was pure Washington, baroque with self-deprecation. "Among the vicissitudes incident to life," he began, "no event could have filled me with greater anxieties" than agreeing to serve as president. He had been moved, he said, to a "distrustful scrutiny" of his qualifications, which "could not but overwhelm with despondence" one with such "inferior endowments from nature" and so "unpracticed in the duties of civil administration."

His first draft of the speech was seventy-three pages long. This one was only five paragraphs, 20 percent of which was more of the same. Most of the speech would have been entirely forgettable had it not been a first inaugural. What people remembered most vividly was how uncomfortable Washington was, how "grave, almost to sadness." He was noticeably trembling, the pages of his speech shaking in his hand. Senator Fisher Ames also noted how old he looked: "Time has made havoc upon his face." At some points he seemed to have trouble speaking. Despite the plainness of his address, Washington's unsettled demeanor so fitted the solemnity of the occasion that when he sat down, Vice President John Adams was in tears, and he was not alone.

Perhaps the most notable fact of the speech was how many times Washington made references to the deity—not the religious God of church worship, of course, but the Deist's non-denominational "Supreme Author . . . Almighty Being . . . Invisible Hand . . . benign Parent of the Human Race." Almost a third of the speech was given over to calling down the blessings of this vague but mighty force on what he plainly saw as an experiment in government whose success was extremely doubtful.

So it seemed when the Senate reconvened later that day to consider its reply to the speech. A small war broke out over whether or not to refer to the address as Washington's "*most gracious speech*," the phrase used when the British Parliament made its reply to speeches of the king. The debate was so hot it had to be continued to the next day, when Senator William Maclay of Pennsylvania and John Adams, presiding over the Senate, quarreled publicly, the first objecting strenuously to what could amount to "the first step of the ladder in the ascent to royalty," Adams countering that he believed the British model produced a wise and efficient government some of whose patterns were worth emulating. Years later, in his journal entry for that day, Maclay noted the coincidence that, as they argued, France was about to overthrow "every trace of the feudal system. Strange, indeed, that . . . an attempt should be made to introduce these absurdities and humiliating distinctions which the hand of reason, aided by our example, was prostrating in the heart of Europe." In the battle over what to call the first inaugural address (it was finally called an "excellent speech"), Maclay and Adams opened what would be a years-long debate between proponents of Britain and France for the soul of America, a battle that would soon be fought inside Washington's cabinet by Alexander Hamilton and Thomas Jefferson.

The next round took place the following week, when Congress took up the question of what to call the president. There was substantial support for "His Highness the President of the United States and Protector of Their Liberties." Adams's choice was even statelier: "His Most Benign Highness . . ." When Jefferson learned of that, he called it "the most superlatively ridiculous thing I ever heard of."

Deliberations over matters of form, style, and ritual occupied most of Washington's first months as president. There was little else for him to do. There were no national laws to enforce because none had yet been enacted, no appointments to be made since Congress had not yet authorized any executive departments, not even any federal prisoners to pardon, there yet being no federal prisons. Congressmen were still trying to figure out the proper way to handle official communications between the House and the Senate.

In the absence of any venerable precedents, national monuments, or a permanent capital, Washington himself was the best evidence Americans had that there was any national government at all, and so not surprisingly he found himself spending most of his time as a symbol. The President's House on Cherry Street was a magnet for gawkers emboldened by the egalitarianism of the American idea, which made each man the equal of the president. His house was their house. "From the time I had done breakfast," Washington wrote to a fellow Virginian, "I could not get relieved from the ceremony of one visit before I had to attend to another." When Washington asked what the house's former proprietors, the presidents of Congress, had done about it, he found out that they just went along, since visitors considered the residence a public place, "and every person who could get introduced conceived that he had a *right* to be invited. . . ." In such conditions, how could the president get any work done?

Washington's solution was to conduct a one-hour "levee" every Tuesday afternoon at which any man could come without appointment, if suitably dressed, to meet the president. When Martha arrived, about a month after the inauguration, she held teas for men and women alike, also unrestricted by invitation. Washington's only other social obligation was to be a dinner for officials on Thursdays at four o'clock; and to avoid having to field requests for invitations and assuage hurt feelings, officials would come to these dinners by regular rotation. Otherwise, Washington said in a public advertisement, he would accept no social invitations and feel under no obligation to pay return visits.

When consulted, Adams and John Jay both had advised an even more restrictive social calendar, but even Washington's was conceived by many members of Congress, especially the Anti-Federalists, as a sign of royalist tendencies; his public reticence was said to be that of "an eastern lama . . . offensive." Washington, conscious that he was setting precedents for future presidents as well as for himself, felt strongly that the executive should reflect the "character" of a powerful nation, and too much familiarity would not allow that.

Hamilton's suggestion that the first U.S. coins to be minted should feature the face of President Washington created a similar crisis of revolutionary conscience. "The devices of the coins are far from being matters of indifference," Hamilton explained in his first *Report on the Establishment of a Mint*, "as they may be made the vehicles of useful impression." Precisely, argued the naysayers. Nero and Caligula had their heads on coins, grumbled John Francis Mercer of Maryland, and Washington's fellow Virginia John Page said he would "cut off my hand" rather than agree to the one-cent coin Hamilton had sent up with his bill, which bore the president's bust and the motto "G. Washington." The House voted down Washington's likeness by 42 to 34 and replaced it with an image of Liberty that (after Jefferson's State Department took over the Mint from Treasury) came to resemble the famous French revolutionary figure known as Marianne, her long tresses set off by a liberty cap. When the Federalist Timothy Pickering took over the post-Jefferson State Department, the Mint's Miss Liberty lost her cap, but she got it back after Jefferson was elected president.

Everywhere Washington turned there was another precedent to be set, a few of which were actually substantive. How was he to obtain the "advice and consent" of the Senate on matters of foreign policy? After one strained visit to Congress in person, he had part of the answer: He would never do that again. Almost plaintively, he asked Adams and other advisers whether they thought it would be all right if he sometimes went to a public inn to meet a friend for tea. And how should he be introduced at his levees? At one of the first, his aide David Humphreys threw open the door for Washington to a roomful of visitors and loudly announced, "The President of the United States!" As Jefferson told the story, Washington was flustered at first, then furious. Afterward he stormed at Humphreys, "Well, you have taken me in once, but by God, you shall never take me in a second time!" After that Washington waited alone in the room until visitors were let in all at once.

As a Virginia gentleman whose social prominence had accustomed him to show a good appearance, on the other hand, Washington had cultivated a certain taste for the posh. Taking advantage of the fact that his old friend and colleague Gouverneur Morris was going to Paris on business, Washington asked him to find a set of mirrors that could work together as a top for his dinner table. He also requested that Morris find eight silver-plated wine coolers, some "neat and fashionable" ornaments for the table, and for himself "a good gold watch"—"not a small, trifling" one, nor one with too much ornamentation but "a watch well executed in point of workmanship."

Morris was an abject admirer of Washington, and the president loved Morris for his sharp wit and a shrewd candor that few others were comfortable enough to share with him. The letter Morris wrote to thank Washington for his letters of introduction to people in France helps to explain the nature and value of his relationship to the president, which would increase with the unfolding of the French Revolution. In it Morris recalled another favor he had said he would do, this one for the master of Mount Vernon:

> I promised you some Chinese pigs, a promise which I can perform only by halves for my boar being much addicted to gallantry hung himself in pursuit of mere common sows, and his consort to assuage her melancholy (for what alas can helpless widows do) took up with a paramour of vulgar race and thus her grunting progeny have jowls and bellies less big by half than their dam. Such however as I have, such send I unto you, and to piece and patch the matter as well as I may, in company with the pigs shall be sent a pair of Chinese geese, which are really the foolishest geese I ever beheld for they choose all times for sitting but the spring, and one of them is now actually engaged in that business.

No one else wrote Washington such letters, at least not letters that have survived.

All pigs and geese discreetly confined to Mount Vernon, Washington ran a household in New York that he felt would reflect well on the presidency, and he ran it himself, with the same nanoscopic attention he paid to provisioning his army, populating his barns, and matters of state. A coachman named Dunn was the subject of a long letter from President Washington to his secretary Tobias Lear. Dunn had shown "such proofs of his want of skill in driving" that Washington took him off the coach and put him on a wagon, which he promptly "turned over twice, and this morning was found much intoxicated." He told Lear that Martha liked a coachman named Jacob, whom Washington seems to have fired previously and about whom he still had "great . . . prejudices and fears," but since Mrs. Washington was partial to him, would Lear please find out if Jacob was available.

Washington had brought seven slaves to New York with him from Virginia, but in deference to Northern sensibilities he kept them in jobs out of sight, hiring fourteen white servants to fill the public roles. He also hired a French confectioner, as well as a French valet who made sure there was powder for his wig, silk bags for his queue, and "solitaires," black ribbons that held the queue in place. The carriage he rode in was made in England for the pre-revolutionary governor of Pennsylvania and was given as a gift to Martha (which allowed Washington to finesse his rule against accepting such "emoluments"). Decorated with his coat of arms and paintings of the Four Seasons, it was drawn by six cream-colored horses with white manes and attended by four liveried servants.

For all that, the coach was the same one he had used at Mount Vernon, and if some congressmen considered that or any of the rest of the president's accessories or style suspiciously regal, the French minister Moustier could have told them they were wrong. In one of his first post-inaugural dispatches to Versailles, he reported that life at No. 3, Cherry Street was actually quite grubby.

Three days after Washington's inauguration, Louis XVI received the Estates-General delegates from the first two orders in Versailles' Hall of Mirrors—the parish priests in their black habits and everyone else in all their official finery, the bishops in full episcopal regalia, the nobles in the fashion of Henry IV: white plumed hats, black satin suits and silk cloaks trimmed in gold, silver waistcoats, white lace cravats and cuffs, ceremonial swords in silver scabbards hanging from their belts.

The Third Estate were pointedly met elsewhere, and their dress, prescribed by the king's grand master of ceremonies, seemed almost punitively severe: plain black suits and tricorne hats "without trimming or badges." They had been kept waiting for more than three hours when they were finally allowed to file past the king, who stood between his brothers the comtes de Provence and d'Artois. None of the three spoke as more than six hundred men passed by, and the experience left a bitter taste.

Three days later, the Estates-General had its first session. A hall had been made out of an open coachhouse at the Hôtel des Menus-Plaisirs to accommodate the more than twelve hundred delegates, and seating everyone took hours. First the clergy were admitted to seats to the left of the throne, then the nobles to its right. Finally the Third Estate, once again as if intentionally snubbed, were jammed onto hard benches farthest from the king.

After a long wait the king arrived wearing a suit made entirely of gold, a huge diamond pinned to his hat. According to custom, he took the hat off before he took the throne, then put it on again. Also according to custom, the privileged orders did likewise, exercising their *droit du chapeau*. The deputies of the Third were to have kept their hats off as the king spoke, but whether in ignorance or as a premeditated act of usurpation—most likely the latter—they put their hats on again too. The king, surprised, resolved the problem by taking off his hat, which required everyone else to do so as well.

The king then gave a speech that said nothing more than what he had said before. Notably, he warned the delegates against radicalism, and failed to address the most pressing issue of the moment, which was whether the delegates were to vote by order or by head. As he spoke, the queen seemed irritated, nervously fluttering her fan. Gouverneur Morris, seated nearby with Thomas Jefferson, remembered thinking she resented being there at all. "She looks . . . with contempt on the scene in which she acts a part and seems to say, 'For the moment I submit but I shall have my turn.'"

.   .   .

For all the weeks and months of buildup, for all the hopes of the people that resided in it, the Estates-General succeeded only when it failed. In its original iteration, it never got past the first item on the agenda, which was how to certify the credentials of delegates. The Third Estate insisted on doing so as a single body, fearing that verifying credentials separately would concede voting separately later. The other two estates refused.

Lafayette was literally alone among the nobles in advocating joint certification of credentials; when the three hundred noble delegates voted for a president, he received exactly one vote. Jefferson saw instantly the bind that Lafayette was in. Ignoring the diplomatic injunction against meddling in the politics of a host country, he wrote Lafayette to tell him that, as soon as possible, he must quit the nobles and join the Third. "The Noblesse & especially the Noblesse of Auvergne will always prefer those who will do their dirty work for them," he wrote. "You are not made for that. They will therefore soon drop you." If he waited to make his move, Lafayette would be received in the Third Estate "coldly, and without confidence," whereas defecting now would "win their hearts forever." Lafayette loved nothing more than the grand gesture, especially in the pursuit of acclaim, but he told Jefferson he could not in conscience renounce instructions to which he was bound by his word. A few days later, Jefferson wrote Washington, "I am in great pain for the M. de Lafayette." Explaining the obligations upon him as a delegate for the nobility of Auvergne and the political benefit of switching sides immediately, Jefferson admitted, "I have not hesitated to press on him to burn his instructions and follow his conscience. . . ."

Only the king could have resolved the argument over certification of credentials, and he refused. Debate on the issue had lasted a full month when the duc de Nivernais appealed to the king and Necker. "[The Duc] strongly represented to [the King] the necessity of taking a line in the debates between the [Third Estate] and the other two Orders. . . . No reply from the King. The Duc insisted once more: still silence from the King. And finally Necker came in with: 'It's still too early.' "

That morning, Jefferson went to see Lafayette at Versailles and suggested another way to break the impasse. Once again stepping outside the bounds of proper diplomacy, he suggested that the king present the nation with a charter of rights, which would preempt the stalemate in the Estates-General and let them get on with the critical business of reforming the tax system. Back in Paris that afternoon, Jefferson drafted such a charter and sent it by courier to Versailles. Lafayette could only have been discouraged by the comparison between the draft he had been working on for a declaration of rights, which derived its authority from a sovereign people, and Jefferson's charter, which consisted of paternalistic concessions by an absolute monarch; but Jefferson's charter was never shown to the king in any case. The issue was mooted when, that night, the dauphin died at the age of eight, and the king went into seclusion, not to be heard from for more than two weeks. When pressed once more to intervene, he said only, "There are no fathers then among the Third Estate."

The timing of the king's loss was fateful. On June 10, the Third Estate made one last invitation to the other two orders to join it and was once more firmly refused by the nobles. At that, the Third—which had long since begun calling itself the "commons"—voted overwhelmingly to adopt the new title and role of "National Assembly," thus declaring itself the sole legitimate legislature of the nation and excluding the other two orders entirely. Its members resolved further that they alone could authorize new taxes but that they would permit the collection of taxes already "illegally established and levied" until a new system could be devised. This move galvanized the clergy, which now voted by a bare majority to join the Third, and shook the nobles, eighty of whom voted for joining the Third on their next vote, seventy-nine more than had voted for it before.

The news that the Third Estate had constituted itself as a National Assembly did not at first trouble the king ("it's only a phrase"), but his ministers were not so sanguine. They convinced the king to call for a *séance royale*, at which he would declare the Third Estate's action illegal. At the same time, he signed an order for troops to move toward Paris, which would be just the first of several such orders.

When delegates to the new, self-appointed National Assembly tried to meet again, they found the doors to the hall locked. In the first of his two notable contributions to the French Revolution, Dr. Joseph Guillotin suggested they remove to a nearby indoor tennis court, the *Salle du Jeu de Paume.** There they bound themselves by oath not to separate but to face opposition from every quarter and to deliberate for as long as it took to establish a constitution for France.

Word of the "Tennis Court Oath" reached the king and his ministers as they prepared for the *séance royale*, but it obviously did nothing to stay their hand. The program Louis presented there was a familiar mix of sharply limited reform and the threat of forceful repression. "The king wishes that the ancient distinctions of the three orders be maintained," his declaration began, "that the deputies . . . vote by each of the three orders, form three chambers, deliberate by order, and, upon the king's approval, deliberate in common," but only on a limited range of subjects, those *not* to include feudal and seigniorial privileges. He then specifically nullified the Third Estate's assertion of its status as a national legislature and ended with an unveiled threat: "If you abandon me, I alone will provide for my people's happiness. . . . I will consider myself alone as their true representative. . . . Remember, sirs, that none of your projects, none of your resolutions can have the force of law except by my specific approval. . . . I order you to separate immediately and meet again tomorrow morning, each in the chamber set apart for your order, to resume your discussions."

Even reading about it in the old, cramped pages of the *Archives parlementaires*, there is a vivid power in this moment when, "after the king left [and] the noble deputies and part of the clergy retired," the rest "did not leave their seats." As the journalist Galard de Montjoye reported the scene in his paper *L'Ami du roi*: "The people . . . remained silent in the presence of the king, and from the beginning of the monarchy, this day was the first time for this grim experience. It was the treacherous calm that announced a terrible storm."

The silence was broken when the grand master of ceremonies tried to enforce the king's decree by ordering the delegates to leave the hall, but the king's move and their reaction to it had been anticipated—no doubt at the nearby café where the Breton deputies and representatives from the Society of Thirty were now meeting every night. It was now that Mirabeau

*Originally the game of tennis was played without raquets, thus "game of palm."

famously declared, "We shall not move from our places here except at the point of a bayonet," and Sieyès rose to second him: "Gentlemen, you are the same today as you were yesterday. Let us deliberate."

When the king was told of their defiance, he buckled instantly. "Well, damnit, let them stay!" That night, Lafayette told Gouverneur Morris at dinner that he had decided to resign his seat in the Second Estate and had written to Auvergne for new instructions. But the very next day the three orders began to dissolve into one. The majority of the clergy came into the Assembly on June 24, and on the 25th they were joined by forty-seven nobles. Lafayette was still among them, and though he could not yet reconcile himself to voting until he had his new instructions, the king spared him the necessity two days after that by giving in again to the drift of events, exhorting the holdouts among the nobles and the clergy to join with the Third Estate. On June 27, despite obvious reluctance among many of the older nobility in particular, they did.

In anticipation of popular disturbances or in preparation for a crackdown, Louis signed another order for troops to move toward Paris, and he signed further such orders on June 29, June 30, July 1, and July 7. By July 14 there would be thirty thousand troops surrounding Paris, many of them Swiss and German mercenaries, who were considered more likely than French soldiers to follow whatever orders they might be given.

In his maiden speech to the National Assembly, Lafayette rose to second a rousing speech by Mirabeau, who had called for the obviously massing troops to be withdrawn. That night, Mirabeau and the other leaders of the forthcoming Jacobin Club met at Lafayette's house (he used the Noailles château when he stayed at Versailles) to draft a formal appeal to the king, which was sent to him the next day. Certain that a royal coup was in preparation, Lafayette thought to write Jefferson that night, too. In case he was arrested, he said, "you must claim me as an American citizen," which according to several of the states he was.

With the same sense that he was acting on the brink of a bloody counterrevolution, Lafayette decided that it was time to present what he had titled his "Declaration of the Rights of Man and Citizen"; that way, he reasoned, even if their movement was suppressed, there would be a record of the principles for which they had been fighting. In the same letter in which he asked Jefferson for asylum, he wrote that he was going to pres-

ent his Declaration in the National Assembly the next day. Sending along
the latest draft, he asked Jefferson to "consider it again, and make your
observations . . . I beg you to answer as soon as you get up and wish to hear
from you about eight or nine at [latest]. God bless you."

Jefferson had been advising Lafayette on his Declaration since its earliest draft, just as (more properly) he had been advising Madison on a
draft of the U.S. Bill of Rights. (Madison presented his draft to Congress
almost exactly one month before, on June 8.) The draft that Lafayette sent
to Jefferson on the night of July 9 laid considerably more weight on the
rights of individuals than earlier ones had, and it counted among these
rights the "resistance to oppression," perhaps reflecting the presence of
foreign mercenaries around Versailles and Paris.

Jefferson made a few small notations on this draft, and he may have
returned it in person the next morning, because no written response other
than his notations has been preserved. In any case, Lafayette took another
day to work on it, and on July 11 read to the Assembly what he later called
his "profession of faith, fruit of my past, pledge of my future."

When he had finished, the delegates burst into applause. One listener
said his speech had "the noble simplicity of a hero-philosopher." Another
gave Lafayette what he would have considered the ultimate compliment:
"It seemed as if we were listening to Washington speak to the people on
a square in Philadelphia."

The public was equally impressed. His speech and the Declaration of
the Rights of Man and Citizen was all over Paris the next morning. Someone brought a copy to the electors of Paris, who had never disbanded after
voting for their delegates to the Estates-General and were meeting in
emergency session at the Hôtel de Ville. After having it read out loud,
they voted to make it part of the official minutes of that day, which was
July 12, 1789.

That they took the time from the business at hand is remarkable, given
all they had to do. While the National Assembly considered the
rights of man in Versailles, the city of Paris was erupting. The price of
bread, stubbornly high at the official rate and subject to scalpers' prices,
made it difficult enough for workers to feed their families. For the many

thousands of unemployed and homeless the result was a constant, gnawing hunger, and they were ever available for a demonstration of rage. "The closer the 14th of July approached the greater grew the shortage," wrote Montjoye in *L'Ami du roi*, hardly a revolutionary publication. "Every baker's shop was surrounded by a huge crowd. . . . And yet the bread . . . was far from being wholesome food; it was generally black, gritty, and sour, causing sore throats and colics. . . . I have seen stores of flour of the vilest quality, heaps of it, yellow in color and foul-smelling, clotting in hard masses that could only be broken up by repeated blows of an axe." The customs *barrières*, where the duties imposed on bread and flour coming into the city added insult to injury, had become targets of mob violence that had to be beaten back by force.

The crowd was moved in part by the deep, long-standing suspicion that an official conspiracy was responsible for the shortage of bread and flour, perhaps to render the people harmless by starving them, perhaps simply to undermine the much-publicized efforts of Jacques Necker to bring down the price of bread. Necker's absence from the *séance royale* at which the king tried to bring the Estates-General to heel was widely hailed as evidence of his opposition to it. It was taken that way by the king and his ministers as well.

So concerned were the Paris electors and the municipal government about these disorders and others that they began to call for the mobilization of citizens' militias, so-called *gardes-bourgeoises*, to support the royal forces and in some cases to replace them. The old *gardes-françaises* were everywhere throwing away their weapons and throwing themselves into the arms of the adoring crowd.* Montjoye wrote that as soon as they reached Paris, "all the troops . . . rushed off to the Palais-Royal. . . . The general officers themselves said that if the King should try to interfere with the slightest action of the National Assembly, he would be unable to count on the loyalty of a single regiment." On July 10, eighty artillerymen leaped the walls of their barracks at Les Invalides and fled to the crowd in

---

*The *gardes-françaises* were an elite infantry regiment attached to the king, one of only two, the other being his *gardes-suisses*. The membership of the *gardes-françaises* had over the years become heavily Parisian, which helps to explain their sympathy with the Revolution. Many if not most defected in the summer of 1789, and the regiment was officially disbanded in September.

the Palais-Royal, who fed them wine and held a ball in their honor. The orator and pamphleteer Camille Desmoulins, who was just then taking up his prominent place in revolutionary Paris, wrote to his father exultantly: "Everywhere you see working-class people clinging to all the soldiers they meet: 'Come on, *vive le tiers état!*' and dragging them off to the tavern, to drink a health to the Commons."

When one commanding officer punished such a mutiny by ordering the ringleaders arrested and sent to the Abbaye prison, a crowd from the Palais-Royal extorted their release by threatening violence and brought them back for dinner. The duc d'Orléans kept the gates to the Palais-Royal open all that night to celebrate.

D'Orléans was surely not responsible, as Lafayette often suspected he was, for all the disorders that preceded the outbreak of the Revolution, but he was far from innocent. In the week leading up to July 14, Mirabeau, who was employable in any cause (including, it would develop, that of Louis XVI), attempted to recruit Lafayette's support for making d'Orléans the nation's "lieutenant-general," a kind of regent, essentially deposing Louis XVI. As Lafayette heard the proposal, "he [d'Orléans] would be my captain of the guards and I his." Lafayette did not take the bait. "Since we correctly wanted to keep a king," he told Mirabeau, "the actual incumbent seemed better than any other." More practically, he wrote to Mme de Simiane on July 11, "I shall . . . keep an eye on Monsieur le duc d'Orléans."

At virtually the same moment that news of Lafayette's speech and Declaration of Rights reached Paris, so did word that the king, fulfilling the crowd's darkest suspicion, had sent Jacques Necker into exile. Next, it was thought, would come *lettres de cachet* for the National Assembly and, with Necker's influence out of the way, an even dearer loaf of bread.

The reaction to this news on July 12, which happened to be one of those sunny Sundays when Parisians would be on the streets in any case, was predictably vehement. Inspired by the crush of a record crowd in the Palais-Royal, Camille Desmoulins climbed on a table and began his famous harangue (famous because he wrote it down for posterity): "Citizens, you know that the nation had asked for Necker to be retained, and he has been driven out! Could you be more insolently flouted? . . . After such an act they will dare anything, and they may perhaps be planning and preparing a Saint-Bartholomew massacre of patriots for this very night! ... To arms! To arms!" Spotting police (where none were allowed, but perhaps the crowd inspired an exception), Desmoulins said, or said he said: "The famous police are here; well, let them look at me, observe me carefully! Yes, I call on my brothers to seek liberty!" Then, with a hair-raising lack of discretion if there actually were police there, he pulled a pistol from his pants and raised it high: "At least they will not take me alive, and I am ready to die a glorious death!" He would have a chance to prove that, though not at the hands he thought.

Bands of demonstrators formed to heed the call, the largest of them carrying busts of Necker and d'Orléans before them that they had got from a waxworks. Three thousand swarmed through the Opéra, forcing the director to refund money for the performance that was about to begin. All other theaters were forced to close as well, in recognition of the gravity of the moment. A crowd five or six thousand strong in the place Vendôme overtook a detachment of dragoons, which had to be rescued by cavalry of the Royal-Allemand regiment, commanded by the prince de Lambesc, who was to have a busy day. The crowd swept on to the place Louis XV (now the place de la Concorde), where there was another skirmish with royal troops during which the temporary custodian of the bust of d'Orléans, a peddler named Pepin, was stabbed. (He was also shot later but survived to testify at the investigation.) The commanding officer ordered Lambesc and his men to clear the square in front of the Tuileries Gardens, fearing especially the many stones that were collected nearby for the Pont Louis XVI (now the Pont de la Concorde), which was under construction. Sure enough, when the Royal-Allemand tried to disperse the demonstrators, they were beaten back by a hail of stones. Meanwhile, a rumor having spread that the Royal-Allemand had committed a massacre of civilians in the Tuileries Gardens, detachments of *gardes-françaises* rushed from their barracks to oppose them. Several on both sides were killed that night, while some citizen groups raided armorers in search of weapons and others set fire to forty of the fifty-four customs posts that ringed Paris.

Parisians awoke on the morning of July 13 to smoke from the fires, occasional bursts of gunfire, and the sound of the tocsin ringing out from belfries all around Paris, alerting the city's sixty assembly districts of the need to restore order. While the districts attempted to mobilize a force of militia, calling up eight hundred men from each, the crowd continued in search of arms, flour, and wheat, along the way ransacking the monastery of Saint-Lazare and carrying off some 25,000 liters of wine and eight barrels of beer as well as fifty-three cartloads of corn that found their way to Les Halles to be sold. The later investigation could only conclude that the wine and beer, which never turned up for sale, had been consumed as the crowd moved on, overrunning prisons and adding the prisoners to their number. Finding the Arsenal empty, since its stores had been moved for safekeeping to the Bastille, they marched to the Hôtel de Ville and demanded the arms they knew to be kept there. The citizens' militia were in search of arms as well, but who was who? The crowds merged, at least in the perspective of those being besieged for weapons. One of these was the city's chief magistrate, who would later be murdered for trying to protect the Hôtel de Ville's small armory, despite the fact that he eventually concluded he had no choice but to hand out the 360 guns stored there. Later that night thirty-five barrels of powder seized from a boat at the port Saint-Nicolas were distributed to anyone with a gun to use it, citizen-militiaman or not.

With the first of the new *gardes-bourgeoises* on patrol, calm seemed to some extent restored by that night. Formed in large part to protect life and property from the unruly mob, they disarmed whatever obvious vagrants and troublemakers they found, arrested many professional criminals who were operating under the camouflage of anarchy, and presented the aspect of a force for order altogether friendlier (to most people, at least) than the troops gathered in and around the city.

That night in Versailles, Lafayette presided over an extraordinary session of the National Assembly, which had been dealing all day with the crisis prompted by Necker's dismissal. When frightening reports reached them at midday of rising disorders in Paris, they decided to send a delegation to the king to protest Necker's dismissal and to present a formal request to withdraw his troops and let the citizens' militia keep order in the city. If he consented, a delegation from the Assembly would carry the news to Paris.

As the Assembly awaited the delegation and the king's reply, Lafayette wrote to Mme de Simiane: "If the king appreciates the danger to which he has been exposed, if he leaves us free to act, we shall restore complete calm. . . . But if the ministers recover from the fear which they have at this moment . . . great misfortune may befall the state."

The king's response was a blunt rebuke: "I have let you know my intentions regarding the measure which the disturbances in Paris have forced me to take. It is for me alone to judge of their necessity." He declined to recall Necker, he forbade any delegation from the Assembly to leave for Paris, and he suggested they attend to their own business.

In response, the Assembly drafted quickly and endorsed unanimously a formal resolution calling on the king to withdraw his troops, asserting the king's responsibility for the enforcement of its decrees, and reaffirming its oath to remain in assembly until the enactment of a constitution. Speaking in support of the resolution, Lafayette remembered something that had been said to him that morning, that "the constitution will be or we shall be no longer." In fact, Lafayette said, the point of no return had been passed. "The constitution will be," he said, "*even if* we shall be no longer." The Assembly's decrees were ordered published and sent to the king, and with that, as Lafayette put it to Mme de Simiane, they had "drawn the sword and thrown away the scabbard."

Fearful that the suspected crackdown was only hours away—the rumor was that the king's troops were poised to occupy the Hôtel des Menus-Plaisirs and arrest the Assembly with *lettres de cachet*—the delegates decided to remain in session overnight and for the indefinite future. Their current president being old and already fatigued by the all-day session, they called for the election of a vice president, and Lafayette was chosen by 589 of the 711 votes cast. He gave an impromptu acceptance speech which was candidly un-Washingtonian: "Gentlemen, on another occasion I would have reminded you of my inadequacy . . . but the circumstances are such that my chief sentiment is to accept with enthusiasm the honor which you have done me."

Debate lapsed that night at about eleven thirty, when the hundred or so deputies who remained to occupy the hall drifted off to sleep in their seats and on the floor. After stretching out for a few hours on a bench, Lafayette awoke at 6:00 a.m., about the time the sun almost impercepti-

bly rose into a thickly overcast sky. In the quiet of that Tuesday morning—
July 14, 1789—he wrote another letter to his mistress, Mme de Simiane.
Everything had changed, he told her. There was no longer any ground for
compromise with the king and his ministers. Whatever the consequences,
he said, as if thinking out loud, "we must work without let-up for the public good. . . .

"There is nothing more singular than the situation in which we find
ourselves. This is going to be an interesting day."

XXI

Come the Revolution

JULY 14, 1789, was far more interesting in Paris than it was at Versailles. The king's entry in his diary for that day was the same as it had been the day before: "*Rien*—Nothing." Usually that would mean only that he had not gone hunting. In any case, Louis XVI did not find out until quite late that evening how grave the disorders in Paris had actually been. The National Assembly spent the day debating whether the Declaration of the Rights of Man and Citizen should appear as the preamble to a constitution or simply be incorporated in the body of the text. For Lafayette, July 14 would actually be the least interesting and most peaceful day in the course of his French Revolution.

Not until late afternoon did the Assembly begin to receive reports of the events in Paris. There were new rumblings of counterrevolution as well, made palpable for them by the fact that Marie-Antoinette and the comte d'Artois were emboldening two regiments of German troops at the Orangerie with financial and liquid inducements for whatever might arise. The news they were getting from Paris was fragmentary, hours old, and as much rumor as fact. There had been violent confrontations between the people and the king's troops the day before at the Tuileries and elsewhere (true), the people were marching on Versailles (false), the king was preparing to leave that night for Metz (not yet, if ever), and had given orders for the National Assembly to be arrested by the regiments then being entertained at the Orangerie (probably false but not baseless).

Finally, late that night, the vicomte de Noailles arrived from Paris with the galvanizing news that Paris was in a "general insurrection," that the Invalides had been overrun by crowds in search of weapons, that thousands of muskets and many cannon had been carried off, and that the Bastille was under siege. Another man arrived shortly after Noailles with word that the Bastille had fallen and that the head of the fortress's governor was being paraded through the city impaled on a spear. Finally, two electors arrived from Paris and explained that despite their attempt to negotiate, the governor of the Bastille had ordered fire down on the people. More than a hundred had been killed. The two men carried a message from the Paris electors to the National Assembly urging "the promptest possible action to spare the city of Paris from the horrors of civil war."

The Assembly immediately sent a delegation to the king, whose response was either stubbornly foolish or intentionally dismissive, in either case stunning. The city's chief magistrate and royal officials, Louis declared, should "make the necessary dispositions" to stop the rioting. Further, since a *garde-bourgeois* had been formed, the king ordered his general officers to take charge of it. Either no one had told him or he preferred to ignore the fact that protection from the king's generals was one of the principal reasons that the *garde-bourgeois* had been recruited, and that his city government had been supplanted by the electors of Paris. Clearly he did not know—no one at Versailles did—that his chief magistrate, who had refused to yield the weapons stored at the Hôtel de Ville, was dead. His head too was now being proudly displayed on a pike.

Incredulous at the king's message, the Assembly sent another deputation to the château. This time his tone was clearly one of rebuff: "You know what I said to your previous deputation. I have nothing to add." That left some members of the Assembly certain that a counterrevolutionary coup was imminent.

Among the Assembly's nobles still present at this late hour was the king's grandmaster of the royal wardrobe, the duc de La Rochefoucauld-Liancourt, who decided to take it upon himself to make one more appeal to the king. The famous scene, as purveyed in contemporaneous memoirs, has Liancourt awaking the king in the middle of the night to impress on him the importance of what had transpired in Paris that day.

"It's a revolt, then," Louis said.

"No, Sire, it's a revolution."

Perhaps it really was Liancourt who conveyed the gravity of events in Paris to Louis, but it seems likely that he was even more impressed by what his top general told him—that in the sort of bloody confrontation which would be necessary to take back control of Paris, he could not count on the fidelity of his troops, who showed only increasing signs of sympathy with the people.

Next morning, the king surprised the Assembly by coming to them in person and unguarded, with only his brothers Provence and d'Artois. In another abandonment of Old Regime protocol, he remained standing as he called on the Assembly's help in calming Paris. He assured them there were never any plans to disband the Assembly or take any violent action against it, and he promised to order the withdrawal of all troops at Paris and Versailles. He asked a delegation from the Assembly to take this pledge to Paris.

A few hours later, in the late afternoon of July 15, a procession of forty coaches left Versailles, with Lafayette, as ranking member of the delegation, in the lead. Word of the king's decision had preceded them, and the crowd lining their path became ever more ecstatic as they approached Paris. At the Hôtel de Ville, when Lafayette delivered the king's concessions, the response was delirious, the deputies crying *"Vive le roi!"* until they were hoarse.

Near Lafayette as he spoke was Houdon's bust of him, which had been donated to the city by the state of Virginia in gratitude for Lafayette's wartime service. Several hours earlier the Paris electors' core governance group, the so-called Permanent Committee, had been discussing the need to find a leader for the appallingly undisciplined civilian militia. Two generals had turned down the job, and the man in charge now was clearly inadequate to the task. As they deliberated on a replacement, someone had pointed at the sculpture of Lafayette and suggested he would be the perfect commandant-general, an idea that met with general acclaim.

Now, when he finished speaking, and in the heady spirit of the moment, there was a motion to name him to the post on the spot, and with one voice it was so acclaimed. Plainly surprised, and with outspoken reservations—he would have to get the approval of the Assembly, he said, and his choice would have to be approved in a popular election as soon as possible—Lafayette provisionally agreed. His acceptance speech drowned out by cheers, he signified his acceptance by raising his sword, prompting an even louder ovation; but a friend said that he had "never seen a man so embarrassed by his triumph." A moment later, in another fervent acclamation, the astronomer and National Assemblyman Bailly was named mayor of Paris, the city's first. After that, all present were invited by one of the electors, the archbishop of Paris, to solemnize these appointments with a *Te Deum* at Notre Dame, where Lafayette and Bailly took provisional oaths of office, Lafayette's being to "defend with his life the precious liberty entrusted to his care."

Embarrassment, which was not Lafayette's usual reaction to acclaim, was in this case more than justified. At the age of thirty-two, he had just been given charge of security for a city where the all-powerful lieutenant-general of police had fled into exile; the royal government was dispersed and literally beheaded; the *gardes-françaises* could not be relied on; the citizens' militia, joining forces with the crowd, were out of control; and the only municipal power behind him, which had been constituted by the king months before only to choose electors to the Estates-General, was now governing the city by no authority but its own. Whatever his failings, Lafayette was not a coward, but his courage was now to be put to the test every day, and in ways he could never have predicted.

Lafayette immediately named intimates as his top aides, among them La Colombe, his shipmate from *La Victoire*, as well as Jean-Baptiste Gouvion and Mathieu Dumas, who had also served with him in America. Several of his fellow deputies from the National Assembly agreed to stay behind "on mission" in Paris, including his Society of Thirty colleague Adrien Duport and the comte de Latour-Maubourg, another Continental Army veteran. For all that, as he struggled in the months and years that followed to enact his oath, he would most often stand alone as the symbol of order in a city that was chronically in open revolt, eventually rising to the kind of prominence his hero George Washington had achieved during the American Revolution, but in a role from which Washington would surely have drawn back in horror.

.   .   .

By the time Lafayette returned to the Hôtel de Ville after taking his oath and holding an initial round of meetings at Notre Dame, it was almost midnight. Having had almost no rest for three days, he could deal with only a few pressing police issues—to make a thorough search of the Bastille, for example, since prisoners were rumored (falsely) to be left in the dungeons underground—before exhaustion overtook him. He excused himself at 2:00 a.m., promising to be back by seven.

He left his house on schedule next morning, but on his way to the Hôtel de Ville he was detained by the earliest tests of his oath. First he had to save the life of a monk who had been mistaken for a counterrevolutionary "traitor" and was about to be lynched by a mob. Then he encountered a band of militia led by a young lawyer named Georges-Jacques Danton. They had in custody and were about to execute a man they identified as "the second governor of the Bastille," who was accused of trying to take back the fortress from the people. In fact, he had been put in place the night before by the Permanent Committee and charged to secure the Bastille against further incursions by the general population. Lafayette dismounted, walked up to Danton's prisoner, and led him away by the hand, saying that if the city government were not respected there could be no order. This appears to have been Lafayette's first meeting with Danton, who would be just the first of many nemeses from both right and left.

After hearings at the Hôtel de Ville, the monk and Danton's prisoner were released with armed escorts to protect them from the clamorous throng that seemed to have taken up permanent residence outside the Hôtel de Ville. With that, Lafayette turned to a bewildering array of issues related to the new citizens' militia, which he now christened the National Guard of Paris: How should it be organized? How could it be blended with the *gardes-françaises*? Who could serve, under what regulations and command structure? Who would pay for it? What would be its specific responsibilities? The role of policing Paris in 1789 went far beyond keeping the peace, encompassing sanitation, public lighting, standards of weights and measures, product pricing, oversight of publications, and the protection of provisions as they came into the city and at the markets. The police authority was also responsible for the hated customs posts, whose tax collections for the city, despite their unpopularity, were needed now more than ever, among other things to pay for the National Guard.

Superficially Lafayette's new position could be likened to that of Washington, creating government anew, his every move a precedent. For example: During Lafayette's first day on the job, the king was persuaded that in two days he should go to Paris himself, to demonstrate his unity with the people. How should he be received? The question perhaps reminded Lafayette that he had not lately thought to keep the king informed of his activities, as a court noble and a high military officer would be expected to do. In any case, he was inspired at that moment to a strange, untimely flourish of royal etiquette. He had had no time, he wrote to Louis, "to bring to His Majesty's feet the explanation of all that I have seen, thought, and considered necessary to risk," and now that the king was coming to Paris, he was only sorry he could not report in person, since he interpreted this news as "an order not to leave this city or a permit to await Your Majesty here."

Perhaps he was only being kind: After all, his king was about to humble himself before his subjects under the auspices of the "hero of two worlds," who in the same letter said that his newfound position "astonishes me more than anyone in the world," as perhaps it actually did.

Under the circumstances, the king could not simply come to Paris, as he might for a ball or an opera: This was to be a ceremony of state, specifically the Parisian royal entry ceremony, last enacted in 1660 by Louis XIV and choreographed by Cardinal Mazarin. Accompanied from Versailles by thousands of courtiers and government officials, the Sun King was shown into a reception theater built for the occasion and decorated with every sign and symbol of absolutism; all the officials of Paris, including the Parlement, had met him on their knees. With that as the latest model, and given the radically changed circumstances, it is no wonder that the city's new officials found themselves confused about how they should welcome Louis XVI. As mayor, Bailly would have to make the official greeting, and he had no experience of either municipal governance or life at court. As he wrote in his memoirs, "I was quite embarrassed . . . not having yet understood the rights that my place gave to me . . . not knowing all the forms." Somehow, though, one thing was very clear to him, which was that he must not kneel. "No power could have commanded me to speak other than standing," he wrote.

The king was told he could be received on the familiar ground of the Tuileries or Notre Dame rather than the Hôtel de Ville, the symbolic and legislative center of the city's revolt, but Louis was quite sure that City Hall had to be the venue. "When one does such things," he said, "it is necessary to go all the way." "Such things" had of course never occurred before in the history of the French monarchy, so how did he know what was necessary?

In the event, Lafayette met the king's party just outside the city and rode in front of his coach to Paris with an unsheathed sword upraised, a gesture reminiscent of the old French constabulary, a lifetime office that Louis XIV had abolished in the previous century because of its independence. Accompanied this time not by his courtiers but by rows of deputies from the National Assembly, Louis XVI rode to Paris in a plain coach, guarded by *gardes-françaises* and every member of the Versailles and Paris National Guards who could be spared, some of the on- and off-duty volunteers "armed with guns, pistols, swords, pikes, pruning hooks, scythes, and whatever they could lay hold of."

When Bailly officially greeted the king at the Hôtel de Ville, he presented Louis with a new "distinctive badge of the French," the tricolor cockade, which Lafayette had invented only the day before—an inspired combination of the white of the House of Bourbon with the colors of Paris. But no one created French symbols or conferred symbols on a king; the monarchy was based on the king's monopoly of such gestures. Then Bailly gave Louis the keys to the city, saying they were the same ones given to Henry IV when "he had conquered his people," adding pointedly, "Now it is his people who have conquered their king." He went on to call this "the most beautiful day of the monarchy . . . the occasion of an eternal alliance of monarch and people," but he had made his point: The monarchy had surrendered to the nation, whose sovereign now was its people, not its king. Louis himself acknowledged as much when, inside the Grande Salle, he asked Bailly to speak before him, a long extinct privilege that had been reserved for the Chancellor of France, yet another office the Sun King had eliminated.

As a piece of theater, the ceremony of the king's entry into Paris was eloquent, and its meaning, though various, was clear to everyone who witnessed it. The left-leaning press predictably exulted in the new order, and just as predictably the conservative *Ami du roi* portrayed the king leaving

Versailles as a wounded father undone by the grotesque, murderous children of Paris—"the descendant of sixty-five kings taking to the road without a suite, without *éclat*, in the middle of an armed populace, going toward a capital in delirium, in order to sanction an insurrection, and to show his enemies a stripped king." But each of the event's oddly antique and original gestures had to be intuited rather than reasoned or researched in old protocols, because the principals in these scenes had to replace the ancient language of ritual deference with an entirely new symbolic vocabulary for politics in a nation of sovereign citizens. This was an act of demolition and creation far beyond what Washington and Congress had to face, and it had only begun.

Perhaps because they were accustomed to the personal rule of an absolute monarch, the people of Paris seemed to be governable by personal charisma far more reliably than by persuasion. This often required Lafayette's physical presence, and from the beginning he was uncomfortable with that, knowing there would be a time when it would not be enough. As early as July 16, he wrote to Mme de Simiane that while he appeared able to control them so far, "this drunk and furious people will not always listen to me."

By then he had personally intervened to save six people from mobs intent on lynching them. By July 22 that number was up to seventeen, and on that day he found the limits of his influence when a seventy-four-year-old financier named Foulon was brought to the Hôtel de Ville by an inflamed crowd. A farmer-general whose crime was to serve in the ministry that succeeded Jacques Necker, he was also alleged to have said that if the people could not afford to buy bread, they could always eat hay. For a time the electors were able to hold off his accusers, who were clearly determined on his guilt and execution, but finally they decided to call Lafayette back from a tour of inspection he was making in the districts. Arriving just as Foulon was about to be swallowed up by the crowd, he made an impassioned plea to let justice determine Foulon's fate. The people who heard him began slowly to disperse, but Lafayette had to continue to make the argument to others who were pushing in behind them, who became so loudly aggressive that he could no longer be heard. Finally, at the top of his lungs, he ordered Foulon taken to prison; but before the order could be carried out, the old man was dragged into the crowd and hung from a street lantern in the place de Grève outside. Hay was stuffed into the mouth of his decapitated head, which was placed on a pike for general display.

A few hours later, another well-known prisoner, who happened to be Foulon's son-in-law, was being driven through Paris. Arrested in Compiègne as he tried to emigrate, Bertier de Sauvigny had been the Royal Intendant of Paris, a notorious grain speculator, and one of the officials widely held responsible for the shortage of bread. Lafayette had sent a heavy escort to bring him into the city and to the Hôtel de Ville, but the crowd identified him in his carriage and ran along beside him, holding Foulon's bloody head up to the window of his carriage and crying, "Kiss papa! Kiss papa!" When Bertier reached the Hôtel de Ville, he was immediately ordered to prison for his own safety, but on the way he was shot and the crowd overwhelmed his guard. Minutes later a man came to the Hôtel de Ville proudly carrying Bertier's bloody heart in his hands, saying that someone was right behind him with the head. In their horror, Lafayette and the president of the Assembly could only think to send out word they were too busy to receive anyone.

Every account of the French Revolution must deal at some point with the monstrous violence of the crowd, in Paris and throughout revolutionary France, a field of study with an impressive scholarly literature of its own. All the explanations are plausible—the incendiary combination of anger and hunger in a population of the unemployed and dispossessed, the intoxicating prospect of liberation mixed with fury at the memory of oppression, resentment for centuries of coercion and injustice boiling up in the disorienting psychology of crowds—and all are to some extent confounded by a lack of reliable documentary evidence about who exactly was present at what events and why. By no means all of them were victims of poverty and hunger; some had friends in high places.

What is known without question is that terrible atrocities did occur and were justified with artful but real enthusiasm by some of the leading journalists of Paris.* The French press began to explode with the fall of the Bastille and the collapse of whatever government censorship was left. Almost ten thousand pamphlets were published in the first three years of the Revolution. In 1789, 184 new periodicals were launched across France, and by the fall there were 27 daily newspapers being published in Paris alone, some of which were royalist or centrist, but the best known of which were avowedly radical and obviously targeted at the hunger- and privation-motivated mass that identified itself as "the people." In the *Révolutions de Paris,* for example, Elysée Loustalot justified the murders of Foulon and Bertier in the present tense for histrionic effect: "A man, O gods, a man, a barbarian tears out [Bertier's] heart from his palpitating viscera. How can I say this? He is avenging himself *on* a monster. . . . His hands dripping with blood, he goes to offer the heart, still steaming, under the eyes of the men of peace assembled in this august tribunal of humanity. What a horrible scene! Tyrants, cast your eyes on this terrible and revolting spectacle. Shudder and see how you and your kind will be treated. . . . Frenchmen, you exterminate tyrants! Your hatred is revolting, frightful . . . but you will, at last, be free." Future justifications of such horrors would be even less apologetic.

Differences over the question of violence as a basis for political legitimacy were at the core of the French revolutionary struggle, and very soon this question would find its way into American politics as well. Were the French courageous fighters for liberty and human rights (the Anti-Federalist/Republican view), or political naïfs and lawless, bloodthirsty goons (the Federalist opinion, which likened street rioters in Paris to Shays's rebellious "democrats," at a time when the word "democracy" could still have the force of an epithet).

Lafayette's two closest American advisers, Gouverneur Morris and Thomas Jefferson, gave him a close-up preview of that debate. Morris's terse diary entry of July 22, which records how the "mangled fragments" of Foulon and Bertier were paraded about with "a savage joy," makes his

---

*In fairness to professionals of a later date, the practice of journalism then seems to have been appreciated by its readers more for polemics than facts, and newspapers were proud of their revolutionary-advocate role. As Camille Desmoulins put it, "Today, journalists exercise a public function; they denounce, decree, judge, absolve, or condemn."

position on mob violence in the French insurrection more than clear: "Gracious God what a People!" Jefferson's was the Republican view, that popular violence was a price worth paying and in fact an inevitable cost of freedom. Shays' Rebellion had worried Jefferson not at all. "God forbid we should ever be 20 years without such a rebellion," he wrote. "We have had 13 states independent 11 years. There has been one rebellion. That comes to one rebellion in a century and a half for each state. . . . What signify a few lives lost in a century or two? The tree of liberty must be refreshed from time to time with the blood of patriots and tyrants. It is its natural manure." Elsewhere he wrote—in fact he liked the phrase so much he used it in two letters—that he thought "a little rebellion now and then" was a good thing, a necessary purgative, like "a storm in the atmosphere," as he put it to one of his correspondents, and to the other, "a medicine necessary for the sound health of government."

Still, the way in which Jefferson downplayed events in France in his reports to Secretary of Foreign Affairs John Jay seems more wrongheaded than ideological, perhaps influenced by the fact that he was waiting impatiently to be relieved of his mission and allowed to come home. Two weeks *before* the fall of the Bastille, he wrote to Jay: "[T]his great crisis now being over, I shall not have matter interesting enough to trouble you with. . . ." In a covering note, he added, "all danger of civil commotion here is at an end." When the events of July 14 proved him flagrantly wrong, he spent more space in his report to Jay on the danger of counterrevolution than the siege of the Bastille. He even seemed to commend beheading as a political tool: "The decapitation of [the governor of the Bastille] worked powerfully thro' the night on the whole Aristocratical party, insomuch that in the morning those of the greatest influence on the Comte d'Artois represented to him the absolute necessity that the king should give up everything."

Jefferson concerned himself less with the life of the streets than with factional conflicts in the Estates-General, the Declaration of Rights, and evolving political reform. He told Jay that the Réveillon Riots had nothing at all to do with the "great national reformation" going on in France but were the work of "the most abandoned banditi." Jefferson had been in Paris for five years by this time. Morris had been in France for only five months, but he made the connection between political reform and the price of bread immediately, and he forecast a cycle of revolutionary and reactionary violence. On July 1, two days after Jefferson had reported all danger "at an end," Morris, though a private citizen, took it upon himself to write his own report to John Jay, who must have wondered if Morris and Jefferson were living in the same country. France was on the verge of anarchy, Morris said. Royal troops "parade about the streets drunk, huzzaing for the [Third Estate]. . . . *Liberté* is now the general cry and *authorité* is a name, not a real existence." The king had completely lost control, his hopes now resting only on the queen, who was "humbled, mortified," and the comte d'Artois, who was "hated . . . a broken reed." While Morris commended the impulse for political reform, those fashioning it were in his opinion naive theorists bound on taking their country further than it could safely go: "Never having felt the evils of too weak an executive, the disorders to be apprehended from anarchy make as yet no impression." The best chance for a restoration of order, he added, was that "popular excesses may alarm."

At the end of July, Morris wrote Washington to bring him up to date on events, which he did in no uncertain terms. France, he wrote, "is at present as near to anarchy as society can approach without dissolution." He also conveyed Lafayette's apologies for not having written ("he is as busy as a man can be") and described him as exhausted, tiring under the weight of too much power. He told Washington that when the king came to Paris, he had been "completely within [Lafayette's] power. He had marched him where he pleased, measured out the degree of applause he should receive as he pleased, and if he pleased could have detained him prisoner." Lafayette took no pleasure from the fact, Morris said, but it was nevertheless true that he held more power than the king, who "does not know a single regiment that would obey him."

In the aftermath of his failure to save the lives of Foulon and Bertier, Lafayette tried to resign as commandant-general of the National Guard, but the urgency of the pleas for him to reconsider and the palpable threat of anarchy left him no honorable choice but to stay. This of course left him in an even stronger position. To a man, the assembly in

Paris signed a document pledging their "submission and obedience to all his orders," just at the time when the district elections he had called for were confirming him in office by an overwhelming margin.

As the central figure of the Revolution in Paris, Lafayette was probably also, next to the king, the most famous man in France. Plays were dedicated to him, babies named for him, and several newspapers were almost slavish in their coverage, particularly Brissot's *Patriote françois*. As a senior member of the National Assembly who was also in command of an army, he had grown so powerful he had to calm a delegation from Paris's Cordeliers district (led by Danton) who were worried that he might try to set up a military dictatorship. He never wished such a thing—he turned down offers of a virtual regency more than once—and he remained as scrupulous as Washington had been about reporting to and taking his orders from the civil authorities. Yet, for the moment, everything he did seemed to conspire in his aggrandizement. Nominally the second most senior official in Paris, he was awarded a salary twice that of Mayor Bailly, and received widespread acclaim when he turned it down because the money was needed desperately elsewhere. Even Jean-Paul Marat, editor of the radical *Ami du peuple*, commended Lafayette then as "an example for public administrators."

As he went about the city dispersing crowds, taming outbreaks, negotiating labor disputes (at various times among shoemakers, wigmakers, and domestics), and appearing in areas of poverty and hunger to divert the always incipient impulse to violence, he was received virtually everywhere with cheers and florid declarations of affection, as the man on the white horse that he literally was. (Called Jean Le Blanc, his mount was a huge and impressive stallion that had cost him 1,500 louis d'or, for which he could have bought a nice house.) He did, of course, wish to cut a fine figure, just as Washington did, and he clearly enjoyed being perceived in every sphere as "the indispensable man," a phrase the biographer James Thomas Flexner applied to George Washington. More than a perception, during the first weeks and months of the Revolution it was a fact. At the same time that Lafayette was facing the formidable logistical challenges attendant to organizing his paid army and deploying a force of 24,000 volunteers, he was also trying to hold the Patriot Party together.

. . .

In August, the National Assembly sent legislation to the king that abolished all feudal and seigniorial privileges of the nobility and defined
the basic rights of all French citizens, a draft of the Declaration of Rights
very close to the one Lafayette had introduced on July 11. At the time,
debate over the new constitution in the Assembly was focused on how
much power the king should have in a new government, and there were
roughly four positions: (1) monarchists; (2) monarchists who wanted a
constitution; (3) constitutionalists who wanted to retain a strong monarchy; and (4) constitutionalists who wanted a king with little or no power.
The problem was that the latter three positions were all represented in
the Patriot Party.

A key issue was whether the king would be given an absolute veto over
legislation or a "suspensive" veto closer to the one in the United States, a
veto that the legislature, with sufficient votes, could override. At a meeting in his home, Lafayette tried to broker compromise with the so-called
monarchiens, who insisted on the absolute veto, but the attempt failed, and
when a vote on the absolute veto was resoundingly defeated, the king
refused to sign both the Declaration of Rights and the abolition of feudal
rights. At that, the Patriot Party itself began to splinter, not only over the
nature of the suspensive veto but also over whether or not there should be
an upper house in the legislature, which the more radical Patriots saw as a
vestige of aristocracy. Lafayette favored an elected rather than hereditary
upper house (like the U.S. Senate) but felt it inappropriate as a military
leader to involve himself in the National Assembly's debate directly.

When the infighting threatened to break the party and the Assembly
apart, he called on Jefferson "for Liberty's sake" to host a dinner for himself and seven other deputies to help them reach a compromise. Jefferson
obliged as host; but with an unusual new respect for diplomatic bound-
aries, he claimed no greater part in the discussion than that of a rapt and
admiring listener. In his autobiography, he described what he heard at his
dinner table that night as "a logical reasoning and chaste eloquence, dis-
figured by no gaudy tinsel of rhetoric or declamation, and truly worthy of
being placed in a parallel with the finest dialogue of antiquity." In the end,
though, it settled nothing.

The king's refusal to grant citizens their rights or lift the burden of the
nobles' privileges made debate over the provisions of a future constitution

increasingly contentious, and the continued shortages and high price of bread made for a volatile mix. Orators in the Palais-Royal excited the crowd with concocted conspiracies by die-hard proponents of the absolute veto to put an end to the Revolution itself. The Cordeliers district, which was among the city's most activist because of its leader, Danton, actually suggested that the National Assembly should adjourn until there could be a national referendum on the veto, the upper house, and other constitutional issues, a suggestion that infuriated such proto-revolutionaries in the Assembly as the abbé Sieyès.

In the end, the National Assembly agreed on a unicameral legislature and a veto that would be binding on two successive legislatures but reversible by the third. The debate that led to that compromise, however, left the Patriots so fractionated it was virtually a spent force: The conservatives were alienated from Lafayette's centrist constitutional monarchists and even more so from a left-moving faction led by the so-called triumvirate of Adrien Duport, Antoine Barnave, and Alexandre de Lameth.

By every evidence, popular energy was moving to the left as well. Any veto at all came to be seen in some quarters as a betrayal of the Revolution, thanks in no small part to the hacks of Paris, who had by now found their true voice and public. Brissot's *Patriote français* would retain its moderate, Fayettist politics for a while longer; but Jean-Louis Carra's *Annales patriotiques* and Camille Desmoulins's *Révolutions de France et de Brabant* were leftist from the start. Jean-Paul Marat also emerged now from his years at the margin with the most radical newspaper of all, *Le Publiciste Parisien*, which quickly changed its name to *L'Ami du peuple*. Marat's first major cause was for his readers to take direct action against the representatives who had betrayed them by voting for the suspensive veto. "Open your eyes," Marat wrote, "shake off your lethargy, purge your committees, preserve only the healthy members, sweep away the corrupt, the royal pensioners and the devious aristocrats, intriguers and false patriots. You have nothing to expect from them except servitude, poverty, and desolation."

Clearly, he found an audience. More than once, Lafayette had to post strong forces on the bridges to turn back crowds of demonstrators bound for Versailles, including one group led by the marquis de Saint-Huruge (recent yardmate of the marquis de Sade at the mental hospital in Charenton), who tried to lead a crowd to the National Assembly to demand the expulsion of sixty "royalist" deputies. His plan included bringing the king and his family back to Paris by force. Forewarned by intelligence, Lafayette intercepted the demonstrators and placed Saint-Huruge under arrest.

A month later, Danton, in the name of the Cordeliers district, called on the other districts of Paris to join him in demanding that Saint-Huruge be tried or released from prison. By then, the protest was reasonable; Lafayette had been hounding both the National and the Paris assemblies for new legal procedures since the second half of July, and would soon implore the king directly. But it is noteworthy that even at this early date, Lafayette's critics were becoming bolder. One anonymous attack on Lafayette (apparently by Desmoulins) was so virulent that even Saint-Huruge distanced himself from it.

For all his power and popularity, Lafayette was keenly aware that his hold on the army and the city of Paris was far from secure, in part due to economic problems beyond his control. Good weather had provided a fine harvest, but a subsequent drought had stopped the mills, and the price of bread, which had begun to fall after mid-July, began to rise again. Grain riots broke out in the outskirts of Paris, groups of angry women began hijacking grain convoys in the city itself, and National Guard troops had to be stationed in bakers' shops.

At the same time, the Guard itself was troubled. Their pay was chronically in arrears, district leaders interposed themselves in the chain of command, dealing with the volunteers' twenty-four-hour tours of duty was a bureaucratic nightmare, and the zeal that had brought out an overabundance of volunteers during the crisis had dissipated. By mid-September, Lafayette still had no organized artillery unit or cavalry, nor even a complete officer corps. "For the good of the service," he left officer appointments up to a Military Committee that he had established, and they were slow to plow through a political minefield of applicants. No one could even tell the commandant-general at any given moment how many men were on duty in any of the districts, though he knew many were below their quota. There were also desertions and other signs of disloyalty in the paid corps, which would have been court-martial offenses had there been a new military code, but there was not. Lafayette had only moral authority to counter insubordination, at a time when privation combined with provocation seemed to be driving Paris to a replay of July.

At a farewell dinner that Thomas Jefferson gave for himself on September 17, Morris asked Lafayette if he felt confident of his troops' fidelity. "He says they will not mount guard when it rains," Morris wrote in his diary, "but he thinks they would readily follow him into action. I incline to think that he will have an opportunity of making the experiment."

B y then, Paris and all France were thick with plots and counterplots. The king had been forewarned several times of plans to take him to Paris by force, allegedly to protect him from the counterrevolutionaries around him. A spy at Versailles told Lafayette of a plot among royalists— the queen was involved, not yet the king—to "converge on Versailles, disperse the National Assembly, make off with the king to a military post, seize the duc d'Orléans, and cut Lafayette's and Bailly's throats." They would then form up at Montargis, sixty-five miles from Versailles, recruit an army of twenty-five thousand, and launch a civil war. Similar stories were being told at the Palais-Royal, where there were calls every day for an assault on Versailles to capture the king. For the time being Lafayette and Bailly, with the help of the Guard, managed to turn back such movements as they arose.

Then a large contingent of former *gardes-françaises* who had defected to the Paris National Guard began agitating to take back their old posts, saying they wanted to share once more the honor of protecting the king. Lafayette was deeply suspicious, unsure if their apparent resurgence of feeling for the monarchy was sincere or only a ruse to put them in position to keep the king in check or even in custody. He thought that d'Orléans might be behind the idea, since the plan seemed quite advanced once he heard of it: The National Guard's companies of grenadiers were being recruited by circular to go to Versailles with the *gardes-françaises* at a fixed date and time. Lafayette felt obliged to warn Versailles of a possible movement of troops from Paris, and though he eventually talked them out of it, the plan had been sufficiently concrete that the king by then had called for reinforcements.

The appearance of the Flanders regiment at Versailles in late September was widely noted and gave rise to even more talk of a counterrevolutionary coup. Danton's Cordeliers called on Lafayette to demand that the

Flanders regiment be sent away, and they seconded the notion that Paris guards be sent to share protection of the king with those at Versailles.

Then came news of a gala banquet that had been held to welcome the Flanders regiment to Versailles at which endless toasts were raised to the king, the queen, the House of Bourbon, and even the Austrian Habsburgs—and none "to the Nation." The fact of a lavish, drunken feast seemed by itself offensive to people on the verge of famine, but worse than that, the queen's ladies had reportedly passed out white cockades for the House of Bourbon and black ones for the Habsburgs to replace the tricolor. On October 2, the papers of Loustalot, Marat, and Desmoulins all reported on the banquet, playing up the counterrevolutionary tone of the affair and passing along the rumor (apparently untrue) that for good measure some Flanders guards had thrown the tricolor to the floor and trampled on it, an insult tantamount to treason of which the queen had supposedly approved. Desmoulins's paper called on Parisians once again to bring the king to the capital, out of the hands of the counterrevolutionaries, and Danton's Cordeliers demanded Lafayette deliver the king and his ministers an ultimatum to this effect.

By Sunday, October 4, the Palais-Royal was boisterously bellicose even by its own elevated standard. The story of the day (again) was that the king's men were plotting to starve the city, and there was no evidence to the contrary in the city's barren markets and bakeries. A baker was nearly hung that day in the place de Grève, accused of giving short weight. Most furious were the women, whose helplessness before empty tables and the empty stomachs of children and husbands had long since turned to rage. At the Palais-Royal that Sunday, more than one woman tried to rally a march on Versailles to get all the flour and bread that must surely be hoarded there, and apparently the idea caught on.

Early the next morning, alerted by the sound of the tocsin ringing from the belfry of the Church of Sainte-Marguerite and the steadily beating rolls of a drummer, long lines of women formed and marched from the Faubourg Saint-Antoine and from markets around the city toward the Hôtel de Ville, chanting the title of a new pamphlet: *When Will We Have Bread?* Other women and some men gathered behind them as they marched, bringing along pitchforks, broomsticks, pikes, swords, and muskets. When they reached the place de Grève at eight o'clock, they were already thousands strong and quickly growing stronger. By nine o'clock the square was nearly filled with demonstrators demanding bread and satisfaction from Lafayette and Bailly, who were not yet there. At ten o'clock, some grew impatient in their absence, and, denouncing their lateness as criminal dereliction, took off for Versailles. Others forced their way into the Hôtel de Ville through a guard that refused to fire on women. (To give them no excuse, some men joined the crowd in women's dress.) Inside, they overturned furniture, ransacked files, emptied safes of cash, broke open the prison, freed the prisoners, and carried away whatever arms they could find. Guard reinforcements had routed the crowd by the time Lafayette arrived (it had taken him nearly two hours to get there from his house on the rue de Bourbon because of the massing crowds), but the crisis had only moved elsewhere. The crowd had seized some seven hundred rifles and muskets kept for the defense of the Hôtel de Ville and were on their way to Versailles with them, behind the group that had already left. In a note to be taken by courier to the king and the National Assembly at Versailles, Lafayette warned them of the danger and told them that while Paris appeared pacified for the moment, the danger there too was "far from over."

He and other city leaders attempted, too late, to address the causes of the crisis—doubling guards for grain convoys; sending a strong force to protect a large shipment of flour in Mantes-sur-Seine; calling up twelve thousand men from the districts to hunt for whatever wheat they could find in the rural areas around Paris; and authorizing Lafayette to use "all the military means in his power" to see that it was promptly threshed, milled, and baked into bread. But the crowd in the place de Grève was growing ever larger and more animated, and worst of all, the National Guards were joining them now, in large numbers. A designated spokesman came to tell Lafayette that the guardsmen were going to Versailles on behalf of a starving people. When Lafayette objected, he was told, quietly but firmly, "General, we must go. All the people want us to." Certainly in the place de Grève, that was manifestly true. For a while Lafayette played for time, going back and forth from the square to his business in the Hôtel de Ville. When the men remained determined, he mounted his horse to take his pleas among them, calling on their patriotism, their martial duty, and their loyalty to the Guard, all but begging them to abandon their plan. It was finally worse than useless. Amid cries of "Bread!" and "On to Versailles!," some of the men to the rear actually pointed muskets at him. More ominously he saw a street lantern being lowered, clearly not to fill it with oil but for the darker purpose it had very recently served.

Lafayette's position now was exquisitely difficult: He had kept his men in the square so far, but many other armed men who were not in uniform and under no military obligation had tired of waiting for them. With scythes, pickaxes, and muskets, they were leaving in droves to join the women on the road to Versailles. Several thousand people were on that road by now, and his troops were increasingly mutinous. The assemblymen in the Hôtel de Ville, clearly aware of the personal danger Lafayette was running as he confronted his men in the square, were fearful that if he was killed no one could control the troops. Lafayette was concerned that if his men went without him it would mean the end of the National Guard and the end of any pretense of order in Paris. If he went with them, there was at least a chance he could lead them toward a protective role and prevent their becoming a mob themselves.

At length, he sent an aide to the Assembly requesting orders to do exactly what he had been trying to prevent: To send the Paris National Guard to Versailles. He and the city officials in the Hôtel de Ville knew very well that keeping order might or might not be what they did there, but sending them was finally the only alternative that did not signal abject governmental failure.

In late afternoon, a huge detachment of guardsmen—at least fifteen thousand of them—left the place de Grève, led by their commandant-general on his white horse, and began to march through a cold and windy October rain, on roads that were turning to mud. Morris wrote in his diary that Lafayette was "marched by compulsion, guarded by his own troops who suspect and threaten him . . . a dreadful situation," since he was "obliged to do what he abhors or suffer an ignominious death, with the certainty that the sacrifice of his life will not prevent the mischief."

When the first women began arriving in Versailles, the National Assembly had just sent back its impatient response to the king's latest niggling objections to the Declaration of Rights. It was now time, they said, for his "pure and simple" approval. Emboldened by a warm greeting from the National Guard of Versailles, the sodden and besotted multitude made directly for the National Assembly, where they spread out their wet, mud-soaked gear among the delegates, while Assembly president Jean-Joseph Mounier attempted to tell them that everything possible was being done to provision the city. Leaving for the château with their demand to see the king, Mounier gave the gavel to the bishop de Langres, whose cries of "Order! Order!" got nowhere. "We don't give a fuck for order—we want bread!" Some of the women, obviously drunk, gave their cheeks to the bishop, who was forced to oblige them with a kiss. Others vomited on the floor and seats of the hall.

By then the king had been urgently recalled from a shoot (his diary reads, "shot at the Porte de Chatillon. Killed 81 head. Interrupted by events"). He agreed to see a deputation of six women, who chose for their spokesperson a pretty, seventeen-year-old flower girl. "Sire," she said shyly, "we want bread." When Louis promised her they could have all the bread in Versailles, she fainted. The king himself revived her with smelling salts. When asked if she could kiss his hand, the king said, "She deserves better than that," and gave her a warm embrace. He then gave orders that all grain available be taken immediately to the city under armed escort.

At that he assumed the crisis was past, and the women's account of the king's generous reception did appear to appease the crowd for a time. Some left for Paris at that point. More, however, remained. Some of them accused the deputation of having been bribed. Others were simply out for blood. "No more talking!" someone was heard to shout. "We'll cut the Queen's pretty throat! We'll tear her skin to bits for ribbons!"

Lafayette's warning that he was coming with thousands of Paris guardsmen, which arrived several hours later, calmed no one. Given his and their unclear intentions, their approach presented a threat far greater than that of the women. After he got this news, the king lost no time giving "purely and simply"—some said in tears—his approval to the Declaration of Rights. Necker, whose popularity had forced the king to recall him some time before and who was with Louis at the time, wrote bitterly in his account of that night: "We had to yield, but posterity will never forget the moment that was chosen to consecrate the theory of the rights of man and to insert the corner-stone of the temple of liberty."

That done, some of Louis's most senior ministers advised him urgently to flee Versailles, apparently not accounting for the fact that the crowd would never have let him go. In any case, he said he could not face becoming a "fugitive king" or leaving those who stayed behind at the mercy of an outraged mob. He would stay, and he gave orders to his troops that they were not to fire on the people, under any circumstances.

At eleven o'clock that night, the vanguard of Lafayette's force arrived at Versailles and took up position in the place d'Armes, an enormous plaza that was the hub for all the town's main roads. Meanwhile Lafayette had halted the main contingent to remind them of their oath of loyalty to the king and their mission to ensure the royal family's safety and dignity. By then, Lafayette realized he would face little or no armed opposition at Versailles, having received a request for orders from the men of the Flanders regiment (though not from their officers). He sent back the request that they stay in their bunkers. He also received two notes, one from the National Assembly, which said that the king had given his assent to the Declaration of Rights, and another from the king himself, welcoming Lafayette and informing him that the nation was now to be governed under "his" bill of rights, a flattering gift of sole authorship that may well have been inspired by the circumstance.

The main force of the Paris National Guard arrived in Versailles near midnight and stationed itself along the length of the avenue de Paris. Then, for the first time since July 15, Lafayette went to the National Assembly, and he explained that the Guard was not hostile but that he hoped to persuade the king to send away the Flanders regiment, allow the former *gardes-françaises* to rejoin the royal bodyguard, and make some public gesture of affection for the tricolor cockade. He then went to the château, and he insisted on going alone, overruling the fear of his officers that a trap could be set for him inside. As he climbed the steps to the king's chamber he passed his father-in-law the duc d'Ayen, a captain of the king's bodyguard, and he overheard someone else saying, "Here comes Cromwell." As if the association had perhaps crossed his mind as well, he answered quickly, "Cromwell would not have come alone."

Exhausted and splattered with mud, Lafayette told the king that his guardsmen had no hostile intent, but Louis could hardly have been comforted by Lafayette's explanation of why he had come: "I thought it better to come here and die at the feet of Your Majesty than to die uselessly on the Place de Grève." The king asked what his men wanted, and Lafayette said he brought four requests: that the king allow himself to be guarded only by the National Guard of Paris and Versailles (in other words, that the Flanders regiment would be sent away); that the city of Paris be guaranteed provisions for the coming winter; that the king agree to a new court system allowing for speedier trials and otherwise cooperate with the National Assembly; and that he "would prove his love of the French nation" by making his residence "the most beautiful palace in Europe in the midst of the largest city of his empire and the greatest part of his subjects." Louis gave or implied his consent to all but the last, and Lafayette came out of the meeting hopeful that in the end he would come to Paris as well.

Tired as he was, he now shared responsibility with the comte de Luxembourg of the king's bodyguard for the security of the château. He also needed to see that the king's guard was relieved and his own guardsmen on station. Given the hour and his own uncertainty, he did not press the point of taking over the interior of the château but posted his own men only on the outer perimeter. After that, he went to the Assembly to tell them all was well and that they could safely retire for the night. He returned to the château to make the same report, but the king was already in bed. He went then to review security arrangements for the night and next day with the comte de Luxembourg. By the time he got to the Hôtel de Noailles, where he had set up his staff headquarters, it was nearly five o'clock in the morning.

After servants had brought food and taken away his filthy clothes, his thoughts turned to Paris. Having ordered his top aide Gouvion to ride there at daybreak and take over security of the city, he could finally lie down and close his eyes, only to be awakened very soon with a jolt.

The crowd, which had remained quiet in the night hours, rose with the sun. Later investigations never discovered how they got inside the château that morning, nor how they would have known where the queen's bedroom was, but once inside they went straight for it, shouting: "Death to the Austrian! Where is the whore? We'll tear her heart out!" On the way, the crowd killed and decapitated two of the bodyguards whose physical resistance (they were still under the king's orders not to fire) barely allowed the queen to escape in her nightclothes, screaming for help. It was said that the hair at her temples went white that day.

Awakened by sentries, Lafayette did not wait for a horse to be saddled but ran to the château. By the time he arrived, his guardsmen were holding off the people who were still trying to push their way into the château, while the crowd outside were proudly carrying the heads of the murdered guards about on pikes and abusing several others they had captured, clearly planning to finish them off as well. When Lafayette ran into the crowd and ordered them to stop, one of them called for the National Guard to kill him. In a fury, Lafayette grabbed the man and placed him under arrest, but when he ordered his grenadiers to come to the bodyguards' aid, they did not move. Stunned, Lafayette could only remind them of their sworn duty to obey his command and that his personal honor was at stake: "I have given the King my word that the bodyguard will suffer no harm." Finally, they complied, and no more bodyguards were lost that day; but clearly the Guards' obedience, at least for the moment, had become situational, a case-by-case matter of choice.

When Lafayette finally had time to go to the king's chambers, he found Louis with Marie-Antoinette, still in her dressing gown, and their children, all of them obviously distraught, but as grateful as anyone could be for having been saved by a man they had suspected the day before could be their kidnapper. The people filling the courtyard below had set to chanting, "The King on the balcony!" and "The King to Paris!" Knowing some were armed and murderous, Louis nevertheless felt he had no choice but to face them; not doing so would be to admit, to himself if no one else, that the people were his enemy and his reign was at an end. Lafayette, who was in much the same position himself, agreed to go with him, and together with the queen and the children they faced the crowd. After the cheering subsided, there were still scattered shouts against the queen, but when he could be heard, the king promised that he and his family would move to Paris that very day, and after that whatever animus remained was drowned out by cries of "*Vive le roi!*"

Before they went back inside, the king asked Lafayette to do something to convince the crowd that his bodyguard was faithful to the nation as well as himself, and Lafayette, inviting one of the non-commissioned officers to join them on the balcony, pinned his own tricolor cockade to the man's cap, raising cries of *"Vive la garde du corps!"* Thus prompted, guardsmen in the crowd began giving the king's bodyguards their own tricolor-decorated hats to wear. At that Lafayette told everyone that they should go home, that they had been deceived by "factious men" into believing the king opposed the Revolution, but that he would be coming to Paris with them.

Some in the crowd started to leave, but others set up a new call for the queen. Gathering the dauphin and his sister in her arms, her hair askew and still in her dressing gown, Marie-Antoinette went to the balcony. Meeting immediate cries of "No children! No children!" she took them back inside. Lafayette asked her what she wanted to do. She knew that the reason some of them wanted the children to be left inside was that they only wanted a cleaner shot at her. "Haven't you seen the gestures they make at me?" she asked him.

"Yes Madame," he said quietly and offered his arm. "Come."

Witnesses said later that there were indeed calls in the crowd to kill her then, and that muskets were raised, but no shots were fired. Lafayette tried to speak to the crowd, but he could not be heard above the roar. With his gift for the grand gesture, he thought to give a low bow and kiss the queen's hand. Suddenly the crowd's demeanor changed, and she heard a cry she had not heard from the people of France for some time: *"Vive la reine!"*

For the ever more indispensable man, there would be no time for sleep again this day. Along with overall supervision of arrangements for crowd control and security for the royal family's twelve-mile procession to Paris, there were a thousand details. Because of a legal technicality, for instance, he had to sign passports for all the courtiers who were moving to Paris with the royal family. He also had to make sure the château of Versailles was secure. That afternoon, Mme de La Tour du Pin remembered, "the only sound to be heard . . . was the fastening of doors and shutters which had not been closed since the time of Louis XIV."

The procession to Paris could not have been entirely dignified, accompanied as it was by a drunken crowd cavorting in the mud and sporting loaves of bread held high on pikes and borrowed bayonets. Along the way they chanted the singsong boast that they were bringing back to Paris "the baker, the baker's wife, and the baker's son." To Lafayette's credit, no injuries were reported, and the king's welcome to Paris was a dignified ceremony filled once again with improvised revolutionary gestures.

By the time the king's party arrived at their only half-prepared, underfurnished quarters at the Tuileries, it was after nine o'clock and the end of a harrowing day. The dauphin, not yet five years old, had ridden to Paris in the lap of his terrified mother, who sat on the floor of their carriage so that they could not be seen. Half asleep, he muttered, "It's very ugly here, Mother."

The more common reaction at the end of it all was that of William Short, Jefferson's erstwhile secretary, now minister pro tem, who reported to John Jay that Lafayette had acted his part brilliantly, had turned disaster aside, and was being hailed by "all parties" as "the guardian angel of the day." Short's praise was deserved. Given the ominous beginnings of the Guards' expedition to Versailles, one can only wonder what might have happened there without him.

Gouverneur Morris seemed by the evidence of his diary struck dumb by the denouement of the "October Days." His pithiest remark comes in an account of an orator he heard proclaiming a clear connection between the lack of bread and the king's veto, which had somehow allowed aristocrats to spirit tons of grain out the kingdom. "Oh rare!" Morris wrote. "These are the modern Athenians! Alone learned, alone wise, alone polite, and the rest of mankind barbarians."

Jefferson was in England waiting for the ship that would take him home when he learned what had happened. He read it in the English papers, which of course were not to be believed, he said, but if it were true that the king had been brought to Paris by a violent crowd, so be it. Maybe the French were having a real revolution after all. "The mobs and murders under which they dress this fact," he wrote, "are like the rags in which religion robes the true gods."

XXII

Front Lines

ON OCTOBER 14, 1789, Washington wrote to Lafayette complaining of "a long interval of silence . . . I have not received a line from you." He knew from newspapers about the fall of the Bastille, of course, but he had received no dispatches directly from France about it. He did not say so to Lafayette, but he had no illusions that the end of the disorder was anywhere in sight even before he heard about the October Days. In a letter to Gouverneur Morris the day before he wrote Lafayette, he predicted that the fall of the Bastille was just the "first paroxysm." It was impossible that the sweeping change being attempted could happen "with the loss of so little blood," and the people's "licentiousness" combined with the "sanguinary punishments" that would come in response were bound to prolong the conflict. Washington knew that Morris would agree with this assessment, of course, and if to another correspondent he wrote that news of France and Europe seemed to him as distant as "events or reports of another planet," that was surely true as well. In fact, it would help explain the decision he had already taken to make Thomas Jefferson, with whose view of events of France he plainly disagreed, the nation's first secretary of state.

In the fall of 1789, most Americans gave the French Revolution little thought. The unseemlier events that took place—heads on pikes, the king "kidnapped" and brought to Paris, Lafayette's sometimes problematic control of the National Guard and the people—were all covered by American newspapers, even in stories lifted whole from the decidedly anti-revolutionary British press; but the prospect for a successful resolution seemed good, and Americans, who knew very well that revolutions did not happen without bloodshed, were not deterred from their enthusiasm by the relatively little and distant violence that had occurred so far. Americans were not much distressed when they heard that the Roman Catholic Church had lost its monopoly in France, and they were elated to hear that the last vestiges of feudalism had been wiped out not long after the Bastille fell and later that nobility itself had been abolished. Even American Federalists who were sympathetic to monarchy could hope for the success of the French Revolution, since a constitutional monarchy was still the outcome most widely predicted.

It would be some time before the French Revolution had any real place on the national agenda, and in the meantime it was seen mainly as just a wonderful homage to the American one, starring their own Lafayette. The story was widely reported that Lafayette had sent Washington the key to the Bastille, "a tribute I owe as a son to my adoptive father, as an aide de camp to my general, as a missionary of liberty to its patriarch." In reply, Washington thanked him for the "token of victory gained by Liberty over Despotism," which he called a symbol of America's "triumph for the New World and for humanity in general."

Even though most of 1790, it seemed to be about that simple. Lafayette had persuaded the king to go to the Assembly and there express his apparently genuine support for a constitutional monarchy. He had even escorted Louis, Marie-Antoinette, and the dauphin to the most rebellious and needy districts of the city, the Faubourgs Saint-Antoine and Saint-Marcel, which greeted him with cries of *"Vive le roi!"* The king had very publicly reviewed the troops in the Champs-Elysées, and, proving he was not the prisoner of the Tuileries he was said to be, he began taking the family to Saint-Cloud for days at a time, attended only by National Guardsmen. The Paris crowd was largely becalmed, violence had slowed, and though Lafayette was coming under increasing criticism from the left primarily from suspicion of his growing popularity and power, every attack only seemed to leave him stronger. The king's ministers sounded him out on becoming a marshal of France or "lieutenant-general of the realm," and the Assembly at one point moved that he be named "generalissimo" of all the National Guards in France. Lafayette turned away all such overtures.

"Such an extensive power . . . in the hands of one man . . . could cause very great harm," he said to the Assembly. "No one man should have command of more than the National Guards of one department." Enthusiastically received and widely reported, this was a position for which even the most radical journalists, however grudgingly, had to commend him.

In the summer of 1790, virtually every American newspaper carried an account of the huge national festival that was held to mark the first anniversary of the fall of the Bastille. The Champs de Mars was transformed into an amphitheater for the occasion, an enormous feat of earth-moving alone that required the labor of thousands of volunteers for more than a month. Several Paris newspapers recorded the fact that Lafayette himself was seen at the site, working with pickax and wheelbarrow. Inspired by Guard units in various towns and provinces around France, who had been spontaneously gathering together in regional "federations" to celebrate the Revolution and affirm their loyalty to each other and the National Assembly, the *Fête de la Fédération* brought fourteen thousand elected *fédérés* from all over the country to join with the Paris National Guard to receive the thanks of a grateful nation. A crowd officially estimated at more than three hundred thousand turned out to salute them that day. There was a mass celebrated by Talleyrand (it is probably apocryphal that he said to an acolyte, "Don't do anything to make me laugh," but it would have been in character), after which Lafayette administered an oath of loyalty to all of the guardsmen at once—"to Nation, the Law, and the King"—to which they responded with a massive flourish of swords and a deafening "I so swear." Then the king himself, in full voice, took an oath to "maintain the constitution" and "attend to the execution of the laws," and the crowd exploded with cries of *"Vive le roi!," "Vive la nation!," "Vive l'assemblée!,"* and *"Vive Lafayette!"* A windblown rain that would not let up turned the field to mud (cynics called it "an aristocratic storm in five acts," optimists said it washed the nation's sins away), but people who were there, aristocrat and peasant alike, said they would never forget how glorious the celebration was. Even Paris's incendiary *Orateur du peuple*, which had already become harshly critical of Lafayette, called the occasion "sublime." One National Guardsman who had been on duty for twenty-four hours, soaking wet, called it "the most beautiful day of the revolution," and a National Assembly deputy agreed: "I believe there has never been a more beautiful spectacle on earth." As master of ceremonies and reigning military eminence, Lafayette presided over the entire day on horseback, idol of the hour. In a private letter to Washington, William Short reported that the *Fête de la Fédération* marked Lafayette "at the zenith of his influence."

F or many Americans, the first sound of alarm about the course of the French Revolution came at the end of 1790 from Edmund Burke, whose strongly cautionary view was shocking in part because he had been such an early and forceful British champion of the American Revolution. In his *Reflections on the Revolution in France*, Burke recoiled at the prospect of the French throwing out centuries of tradition seemingly without thought, and he saw in the prospect of a young queen subject to the insults of a French "mob" during the October Days the death of chivalry. In Britain, "we still bear the stamp of our forefathers," he wrote. "We fear God; we look up with awe to kings; with affection to parliaments; with duty to magistrates; with reverence to priests; and with respect to nobility." By the time most Americans read Burke's *Reflections*, the emigration of French nobles was in full flood, some of them perhaps prompted by a new line in the revolutionary anthem *Ça Ira*: "Let's hang the aristocrats from the lanterns!" By then, too, the National Assembly, motivated mainly by a ballooning public debt combined with rampant tax evasion, had seized all property of the Church for sale, ordered that all monasteries and convents be closed (contemplatives were social parasites), made all priests and bishops subject to election by the laity, and in general put the Church under the management of the state. In response to fierce and persistent opposition from the Church, the Assembly required all clergy to take an oath to the nation on pain of dismissal and the threat of worse. All this sickened Burke, who believed that those who would set out to correct the errors of their country should regard them as "the wounds of a father, with pious awe and trembling solicitude." He contemplated "with horror" the prospect of French citizens "prompted rashly to hack that aged parent in pieces, and put him into the kettle of magicians, in hopes that by their poisonous weeds, and wild incantations, they may regenerate the paternal constitution, and renovate their father's life." The revolution in France, he concluded, would end in "madness, discord, vice, confusion, and unavailing sorrow."

A few months later, Burke was decisively answered by "Common Sense," sometime pen name of Thomas Paine, who tore brutally through what he called Burke's "pathless wilderness of rhapsodies" with *The Rights of Man*. Dedicated to George Washington and featuring an almost embarrassingly complimentary portrait of Lafayette, Paine's book became a best seller in America, France, and England. Instead of Burke's complicated arguments about sovereignty and constitutionalism from "musty records and moldy parchments," Paine wrote, he would quote Lafayette's call "to the living world" in the speech he made to the National Assembly to introduce his Declaration of the Rights of Man and Citizen: "For a nation to love liberty, it is sufficient that she knows it," Lafayette had said, "and to be free, it is sufficient that she wills it." If Burke was appalled by the awful prospect of mob violence, Paine averred, he should consider the source. "They learn it from the governments they live under; and retaliate the punishments they have been accustomed to behold." He reminded Burke of the English custom of drawing, quartering, and cutting out the hearts of criminals. In France, "who does not remember the execution of Damien, torn to pieces by horses?"

> These outrages are not the effect of the principles of the Revolution but of the degraded mind that existed before . . . and which the Revolution is calculated to reform. It is to the honour of the National Assembly and the city of Paris that during such a tremendous scene of arms and confusion . . . they have been able . . . to restrain so much.

Paine concluded by quoting Lafayette again, this time the speech he made when he took his leave of the Continental Congress in 1784, the speech Vergennes would not allow the French press to publish. What Lafayette had said about the American Revolution then, Paine declared, applied as well to the French one: "May this great monument raised to Liberty serve as a lesson to the oppressor and an example to the oppressed!"

Burke and Paine defined the poles of American opinion, which would become increasingly and ever more bitterly divided between those who favored the British model of a mixed constitution, with king, lords, and commons, and the egalitarian model of French republicanism. No one found Paine's *Rights of Man* more pleasing than Secretary of State Thomas Jefferson, and no one found it more hateful than Vice President John Adams, who had been writing a series of widely read essays called "Discourses of Davila," in which he upheld the necessity of social distinctions and even thought monarchy was a good form of government for many nations, though he specifically exempted the United States. As for Paine, he said, "I detest that book and its tendency from the bottom of my heart."

Jefferson, who had ridiculed Adams's suggestion that the president be called "His Highness" and critized him for riding around the capital in a grand coach drawn by a large team of horses and attended by liveried servants, sent his copy of *The Rights of Man* to a printer with a note attached commending Paine for having finally exposed "the political heresies which have sprung up among us." Jefferson professed to be horrified that the printer used his remark as a signed "preface" to the book, but printers were editorialists then, as Jefferson well knew. Adams had every reason to believe the barb was aimed at him and his "Discourses," because it was, and a long friendship was broken. They would serve together but never even attempt to explain themselves to each other until both were old men.

At the expense of Adams's friendship, the controversy over the preface cemented Jefferson's reputation as the defender of the common man against the forces for aristocracy and as the foremost exponent of the people's ability to govern themselves. When the controversy had died down, Jefferson wrote to Paine himself to congratulate him for having turned Americans against the pernicious "doctrine of king, lords, and commons" and having "confirmed them in their good old faith."

As Burke and Adams were squaring off with Paine and Jefferson over the French Revolution, the most pressing issue facing America was the same one that the Estates-General had been convened to solve: a mountain of debt, with public credit dangling from a cliff. Unlike Louis XVI, of course, Washington had the support of a ratified constitution, an elected government, and a redoubtable new secretary of the Treasury in Alexander Hamilton. Even so, the search for a solution would be nearly as fraught as it was in France. The first letter Lafayette received from Washington after the *Fête de la Fédération* congratulated him on "so favorable an aspect [of politics] in France! Be assured that you always have my best and most ardent wishes for your success." As for the new U.S. government, Washington said, there was only one dark cloud on his horizon, and that was Hamilton's financial program, a source of much "anxiety and perplexity." In fact, Hamilton's plan and the ideological choices it implicated would threaten to tear the government and the country apart over the next two years and place in question the very principles for which the Revolution was fought.

Many years later, Jefferson still remembered the "wonder and mortification" he felt when he first arrived in New York and detected at dinner parties a decided "preference of kingly over republican government." Fresh from Paris, he was surprised that there would be even a casual flirtation with monarchy in the country that had inspired France's struggle against it—a struggle he was coming to believe was more serious than he had thought, not in spite of the violence but because of it. In a letter to Lafayette that he wrote as he took up his new duties in early April 1790, he said he was happy to see the Revolution proceeding "at a steady pace." While the October Days might be considered a "setback," he wrote, "we are not to expect to be translated from despotism to liberty in a featherbed." He hoped Lafayette would "never see such another 5th or 6th October," but only because of the personal risk he ran. While he was certain of the Revolution's ultimate outcome, "I am persuaded, were [France] to lose you, it would cost her oceans of blood, and years of confusion and anarchy." Jefferson's overriding concern was that the French Revolution might fail, and his even greater fear was that the ideals for which it was being fought would not prevail in America either.

Hamilton's view of the French Revolution was that of his friend and sometime business associate Gouverneur Morris. As he worked on his first *Report on the Public Credit*, Hamilton wrote to his old friend Lafayette in part to discuss the American debt to France (then more than $6 million, plus an arrearage in interest of almost $1.4 million, about 15 percent of the federal government's total indebtedness). He was happy to see the efforts being made in France for "mankind and liberty," Hamilton said, but he thought it was inevitable they would push too far: "I dread the reveries of your philosophic politicians." He could have been speaking of Jefferson. Far from worrying that the French Revolution would fail, Hamilton's deepest concern was that its model of direct popular action would actually catch on in America.

Jefferson and Hamilton, who would become the bitterest and most prominent antagonists in this conflict, had not met until the secretary of state took up his post in the early spring of 1790. By then the battle was already raging in Congress over Hamilton's plan for the federal government to assume the collective war debts of the states. Jefferson helped Hamilton reverse an early defeat of that measure,* but that was virtually the last time he cooperated with Hamilton on anything. After that, at every step, Hamilton and the Federalists faced relentless opposition from Jefferson and his fellow Republicans in what both sides would come to see as a struggle for the soul of America.

The first reaction to Hamilton's *Report on the Public Credit*, from both sides, was simply relief that the long overhang of doubt about the security of American credit might soon be over. Implemented as proposed, the program meant that vast amounts of depreciated government paper that had been issued to fund the war would be redeemed at face value. The speculators who packed the House gallery for the reading of the report were especially pleased, of course: Having bought the paper for as little as 15 cents on the dollar from Continental soldiers and widows who held it in lieu of payments due, they stood to make a great deal of money. Some objected immediately that the original holders who had cashed out at low prices were due better treatment, especially the soldiers and their families; but even James Madison, who along with Jefferson would become one of Hamilton's severest and most indefatigable critics, found the *Report on the Public Credit* at first blush "well digested and illustrated . . . supported by very able reasoning." Hamilton had counted on Madison's support to get

*The compromise appeased Southern opposition by placing the new national capital on the Potomac. Middle state opposition to that was overcome by moving the temporary capital from New York to Philadelphia. Proponents of that move were betting that, given the time and effort it would take to build a new capital from land that was nothing but undeveloped swamp, it would never leave.

the plan through Congress and had consulted Madison as he drafted it, in the latest iteration of a collaboration that dated as far back as the Annapolis convention and was memorialized in their co-authorship of *The Federalist* papers.

When Congress began grappling with specific elements of the plan, though, its scale and implications became increasingly clear. Among the most contentious issues implicated in Hamilton's plan was its basis in debt, both the federal government's assumption of the states' war debt and Hamilton's proposal to issue new federal securities. Hamilton got his ideas about the utility of debt from many sources (including Jacques Necker), but his chief model was Great Britain, which had profited enormously from funding its public debt, that is, pledging certain revenue sources to its repayment. This created a market for bonds by guaranteeing investors the promised return on their investment, and the bonds, which could then be used as security for loans, poured cash into the economy. But basing the economy on what would become a permanent federal debt raised for Republicans the issue of the relative power of state and federal government, since federal paper would come to dominate the bond markets and compete unfairly (so the argument went) with the states' access to capital. Perhaps even more palpably, the Republicans feared putting the federal government's finances into the hands of the relatively few individuals wealthy enough to loan the government money by investing in bonds.

Beyond that, Hamilton's program for the U.S. economy plainly favored a manufacturing over an agricultural economy—which, it was argued, would have the effect of drawing the population from the land to crowded industrial cities, concentrating wealth in fewer hands, and devaluing individual labor, all of which was true. Hamilton's program was, in a word, capitalism.

Some of capitalism's unpleasant side effects helped to consolidate the opposition to Hamilton's plan. Even before debate on it had begun, speculators and their seconds were trolling the rural areas of the United States, particularly the South and the trans-Appalachian West, looking to buy up old government paper as fast as they could from those who did not know it was about to be redeemed at par. Some of the nation's most prominent men were among those who stood to benefit from such exploitation of the ignorant poor, including even a few members of Congress.

The fight over Hamilton's financial system for the United States would eventually give birth to the two-party system in America, but the present conflict was a clash of worldviews neither of which would survive intact. The Republicans remained attached to the ideal of an agrarian society with the least possible government, where land was wealth and capital was what a man could produce from it. Hamilton and the Federalists believed the bulwark of the nation was its private wealth, for good or ill, and that one of the chief roles of government was to protect property, including private wealth, from an essentially licentious citizenry. This was the vision of democracy as anarchy, Shays's rebels out for your land and your money.

Both sides had surrogates: John Fenno, editor of the *Gazette of the United States*, did printing for the Treasury Department and ran Hamilton's pieces under pseudonyms; Philip Freneau, editor of the *National Gazette*, was paid as a French translator in the State Department and under names such as "Brutus" and "Caius" featured essays by himself and Madison. But everyone knew who the principals were. As time went on Fenno and Hamilton found themselves increasingly on the defensive with Freneau and Jefferson (and Madison), who painted Hamilton and the Federalists as the spearhead for an oligarchy of cutthroat financiers—"corrupt squadrons," as Jefferson put it, of "money-men" and "stock-jobbers" who aimed to profit off the back of honest working people. Hamilton, of course, accused the Jeffersonians of demagoguery: The speculators deserved their profits. He knew that his program would not benefit only the upright and the good, but if soldiers and widows sold their paper early for cash, perhaps they had not had sufficient faith in their government; and in any case those who bought it had hazarded their money and deserved something for taking the risk.

At the end of 1791, Hamilton proposed an excise tax on distilled liquor as one source of revenues to fund government debt and a national bank to serve as a federal treasury and clearinghouse. There was some heated debate, but given that Republicans were still in the minority, the measures passed easily and unchanged in February 1792. By then, however, Jefferson had already begun to organize for the 1792 congressional elections in the hope of creating a Republican majority in the House, and the Federalists, though they would not know it for some time, were doomed. Ninety percent of Americans then lived on farms; only 5 percent lived in the cities. Property qualifications still kept most men from voting (in New York City the figure was less than 10 percent), but enough Republican sympathizers had the franchise to make a difference; and as Shays' Rebellion had shown, and the French people were demonstrating even more vividly, the disenfranchised could make themselves felt in other ways.

Over the course of 1792 the animosity in Hamilton's *Gazette* and Jefferson's *Gazette* became so personal and vicious that even Washington's attempt to enforce a peace had no effect. For different reasons, both men decided to retire from government, which of course freed them for less covert warfare. Already the conflict's terms of art had begun to invoke issues and forces at play in the French Revolution, casting "Anglo-men" and "monocrats" who worshipped at the altar of Mammon and King George against "Gallo-men" and "Jacobins" who would turn loose a wanton populace against property rights and the forces for social cohesion.

Still, the French Revolution did not really release its full seismic force into American politics until its most violent phase, beginning with the execution of Louis XVI. The period known as "the Terror" would challenge even Jefferson's fervor, and it fulfilled all of Gouverneur Morris and Alexander Hamilton's darkest suspicions about the perils of the revolution in France.

It would have fulfilled Washington's worst fears for Lafayette as well, except that by that time, facing certain death at the guillotine, he had surrendered to the forces of Emperor Leopold II of Austria and Frederick William II of Prussia, who had formed a military alliance to invade France, restore the Bourbon monarchy, and so discourage other liberation movements in Europe. Lafayette's years of imprisonment would be unforgivingly hard—he was after all blamed for starting the Revolution that threatened the monarchs holding him captive—but he was at least alive.

The impossible ambiguity of Lafayette's role in the October Days prefigured his fall, and both were rooted in those principles to which he had long committed himself. He would be loyal to the king so long as the king was loyal to the notion of constitutional government; he would put the military and himself at the command of the civic authorities; and he would respect the rights of the people. Had he been willing (and it is surprising how many of his freedom-loving cohort and otherwise liberal historians have faulted him for refusing) to accept the virtually absolute power that was offered to him and to turn the force of his popularity and his army against the opposition to a constitutional monarchy, he might indeed have managed to "save" the French Revolution from the violence that was to engulf it, but in doing so he would have made himself more powerful than the king. In becoming Oliver Cromwell to Louis's Charles I, he would have broken his word and betrayed his ideals; but losers right or wrong are goats, in history as in life, which explains some of Lafayette's biographers' disappointment in him. Years later, Napoleon said that if he had been in Lafayette's place, "the king would still be sitting on his throne." If not, Napoleon surely would have been.

In the end, Lafayette's principles were as irreconcilable as they were good. In a period of revolution, how could he possibly have served the king, the municipal authority of Paris, and the nation's legislative assembly while honoring the sovereignty and rights of the people? Which rights? Which people?

More than any other issue, the Assembly's takeover of the Church assured the French Revolution a long and bloody road ahead, moving millions of French Catholics who might otherwise have taken the side of the "patriots" to stand instead with the forces of counterrevolution. For this they were labeled "royalists," and a priest's refusal to renounce his fidelity to Rome was called "fanatacism." But the supporters of these allegedly royalist fanatics included about half of all the Roman Catholics in France, and their opposition to the "patriot" position was adamant. Many communities kept their traditional priests close by to preside over special occasions and ignored their constitutional replacements, for whom "no one rings the bells, no one takes the trouble to dress the altar. . . . In the night his erstwhile parishioners devastate the garden of the parsonage, throw straw in the well, deposit refuse outside the door, put sand in the locks. . . . On his passage, farmers loose their dogs."

It was worse than that. On the "patriot" side of the question was the perfectly logical fear of an upsurge in religious intolerance, just after a century of harshly punitive discrimination had been ended; and with two such viscerally urgent causes in the balance, it is perhaps not surprising that sectarian rioting broke out all across the country, and that both Protestants and Catholics were the victims of massacre.

The disjuncture between Lafayette's belief in religious freedom and his responsibility to enforce the acts of the Assembly placed his exquisitely difficult position in sharp relief. Even his wife Adrienne was among those who refused to take mass from a priest who had sworn the civil oath. When the act took effect in late 1790, Lafayette felt obliged to receive the new constitutional bishop of Paris for dinner at his home, but Adrienne, pointedly, did not appear. The incident was widely noted, as was an exchange between Lafayette and the bishop as he left. The bishop had heard that people were installing chapels in their houses so that they could attend masses celebrated by priests who had refused the oath (known as "non-juring" and "refractory" priests). He said he hoped he could count on Lafayette's help in closing these chapels down. In one newspaper account,

> Lafayette replied . . . that he was astonished at being asked to per-
> secute in the name of the constitution citizens whose opinions did
> not happen to be the same as his own, and that if he [the bishop]
> intended to act in this manner he would always find in his path a
> general who would be firmly opposed to him.

At home he had to tiptoe around the subject. "I am deeply grieved to have to say this," he wrote to Mme de Simiane, "but when one is compelled to adjust the fervor of one's family to the ifs and buts of the various administrative bodies and the ecclesiastical commission, one is apt to get home a little later than usual." He was unlikely to get any sympathy from his mistress on this issue, however, since she too refused to attend any mass said by a refractory priest.

No issue gave more impetus to the Jacobin* clubs of France than the

*Though the word "Jacobin" eventually became virtually a synonym for "radical," until this time the Jacobin Club was warmly monarchist and solidly *bourgeois*, its membership restricted by design. Lafayette was officially a member of the Jacobins until 1791, although he rarely attended meetings after 1789, when his moderate position for the suspensive veto and other issues had alienated him from the leadership triumverate of Duport, Barnave, and Lameth. With some like-minded colleagues—Bailly, La Rochefoucauld, Mirabeau, Sieyès, Brissot, Talleyrand, and Condorcet—Lafayette act calling for the Civil Constitution of the Clergy. Membership soared, and affiliate clubs sprang up all over. Pro-Church "royalists" were purged, and many of the clubs became centers of fervent anti-clericalism. Everyone knew that the king opposed the act, even after he was forced to sign it, and some thought this issue might be the one that would finally prompt him to take flight or mount a counterrevolution or both. At the same time, the constitution-writing process was in sight of completion, and such a move would completely undo the new order. With such a tantalizing prospect so close to reality, the leaders of the Assembly—the "triumverate" of Barnave, Duport, and Alexandre de Lameth—began moving toward the center, which made room for new leadership on the left. In the case of Paris, that new leadership consisted of, among others, Maximilien-François-Marie-Isidore de Robespierre and Georges-Jacques Danton.

Pope Pius VI did not respond comprehensively to the various actions of the Assembly against the Church until March 1791, but when he did it was clear that his opposition was complete and unalterable. At that, Louis repented having enacted the law, and he made that repentenance part of his next confession, firing his constitutional confessor first so that his contrition could be ratified by a non-juring priest.

When word of the king's change of position became known, Danton's Cordeliers* pounced. Until now counterrevolutionary actions or proclivities were blamed on the king's conniving ministers or the often invoked

---

founded the Society of 1789, which at least at first was more of a social than a political club, featuring very high dues and lavish banquets and presenting no threat or implied opposition to the Jacobins, just a more congenial place to go.

*In an administrative reform of Paris in the spring of 1790, Paris's sixty districts were replaced by forty-eight sections, and the Cordeliers district disappeared. By then, however, it had formed its own political club called the Society of the Friends of the Rights of Man, which was and continued to be called the Cordeliers Club. Danton belonged to the Jacobins but was best known as the leader of the Cordeliers, who were the more populist and radical group. In contrast to the Jacobins, which charged 24 livres annual dues at this time, the Cordeliers Club charged only 1 livre, and it was specifically committed to including those who could not afford to join or were otherwise excluded from the Jacobins, including day laborers and women. There were many other so-called popular societies as well, but the Cordeliers was the largest and among the most radical of them.

specter of an "Austrian committee" inside the palace, led by the queen. Only a month before, Jacobin clubs all over France had prayed fervently for the king's recovery from an illness. Now Louis XVI was the target of outrage. A resolution of the Cordeliers, which was published on Palm Sunday, reminded the king that he was the "first subject of the Law" and that by openly defying the act he had himself signed, he had opened his people to "all the horrors of discord and the scourge of civil war." One like-minded newspaper now ridiculed the fuss made over Louis XVI's illness as grown men "going into ecstasies . . . over the state of the King's urine and his stools to the point of falling on their faces before his toilet as if it were the most resplendent throne."

On Palm Sunday, word spread that the king was to leave with his family the next day for Saint-Cloud, presumably to spend Easter week in the care of his refractory priest. By the time the royal carriage tried to pull through the east gate of the Tuileries Palace on Monday afternoon, a large and belligerent crowd had gathered to stop it, and the National Guard was behind them in force. Lafayette rode to the scene and ordered his men to clear the way for the king, but they simply refused, and as had happened in the place de Grève the previous October, he began to hear threats muttered against him. The standoff went on for nearly two hours, while the king and queen sat hunched in their carriage surrounded by the crowd, being pummeled by verbal abuse. At one point Louis tried to point out the irony that "he who gave the French nation its freedom should now be denied his own." He was cut off by a guardsman, who said, simply, "Veto."

Nothing Lafayette could say or do had any effect on the crowd or his guardsmen at the gate, and in truth his hold on both the National Guard and the popular imagination was by then worse than uncertain. Ever since passage of the Civil Constitution of the Clergy, Lafayette had been forced to lead his guardsmen against violent anti-clerical and anti-royalist demonstrations around Paris, and he won few friends in the process. The left-wing press turned on him viciously, one paper commending a guardsman's wife who extracted a renunciation of Lafayette while making love: "Stop! Stop! Nevermore shall you enjoy the tender caresses that I have so many times wasted on you until you abandon your infatuation with the Corrupter!" Most such attacks were not nearly so amusing.

Lafayette's last attempt to get the royal family through the crowd was to call forward a battalion inside the palace who remained under his command; but by then the king and queen had given up the idea of leaving and used the loyal guard only to protect them as they walked back to the palace. Lafayette met them inside and urged them to reconsider, promising he would support them if they would go to the Assembly and assert their freedom, but the king said, thank you, no. He had been advised by his confessor that "it would suffice for the salvation of his soul merely to refrain from making his Easter at a [constitutional] church." Furious, sick with disappointment in his Guard, and personally humiliated, Lafayette went to the Hôtel de Ville and submitted his resignation.

Adrienne was thrilled. When guardsmen turned up at the house to beg him to reconsider, she told them there was no use trying to talk him out of it, he was quite determined; and for three days he did turn away the most abject appeals and promises of loyalty among city officials, deputies of the Assembly, and the Guard, at the same time that he was being pummeled from the right and left in newspapers and pamphlets. "Is M. de La Fayette a demagogue or a royalist?" asked the conservative *Vie politique* of Rivarol. "Does he want to uphold or topple the throne? . . . Circumstances have produced in [him] a kind of prudence that looks very much like falseness. . . ." Meanwhile, Marat called for someone to assassinate Lafayette, whom he castigated as the "leader of the Austrian committee, generalissimo of the counter-revolutionaries [and] chief conspirator for the kingdom of France."

After four days of entreaties, though, Lafayette disappointed Adrienne and relieved city authorities by taking up his duties again. "Monsieur de La Fayette is treading a path between two abysses," the *Journal de la Cour et de la Ville* observed a few days later, "and sooner or later will be a victim of one party or the other. Retirement alone can save him. That solution may not be the most heroic one, but it is at least the safest."

A secret plan for the royal family to escape from the Tuileries and from Paris had been in preparation for months, under the supervision of Count Axel von Fersen, the queen's favorite. That pre-Easter Monday apparently persuaded Louis to act on it. The plan was postponed several times in the weeks that followed, but finally the date was set for June 20. That night Lafayette attended Louis's *coucher*, the nightly ceremony of putting the king to bed. In the courtyard of the Tuileries as he left, he nearly bumped into Marie-Antoinette, who was in a disguise and holding a passport identifying her as one Baronne De Korff. As Adrienne's biographer André Maurois nicely put it, when Marie-Antoinette passed Lafayette, she "treated herself to the pleasure of touching one of the wheels of Lafayette's carriage with her riding crop."

The royal family's destination was the thirteenth-century citadel at Montmédy, about 180 miles east-northeast of Paris on the border of the Austrian Netherlands, where they would be protected by a force of ten thousand French troops and situated a convenient distance from the army of Austria's Emperor Leopold, who of course was Marie-Antoinette's brother. Such a flight into such protection was precisely the scenario that had been predicted for so long by the conspiracy theorists of counterrevolution, and Lafayette had promised on his life that such a thing would never happen on his watch. Next morning, as the royal family ate breakfast with their fingers on the road toward the frontier, Marie-Antoinette remarked happily to the king how embarrassed Lafayette must be right now.

He was more than embarrassed. Among the first to hear the news, he consulted briefly with Bailly and the current Assembly president and with their consent drafted an order to stop the king (the French word for "stop" also means "arrest," a helpful ambiguity under the circumstances) and to bring the royal family back to Paris.

Paris spent the day in shock. When the president of the Assembly began the morning session that day by breaking the "afflicting news," the announcement met *"un silence profond,"* and that grave quiet spread with the news. Lafayette's order had said that the king had been kidnapped by "enemies of the revolution" and needed to be rescued, but if he or anyone else believed that even for a moment, they were quickly proved wrong. The king had left behind a letter saying all that he apparently had wished to say before. He had left, he said, because he had become a prisoner of the National Guard, the National Assembly, the political clubs, and the people of Paris, which of course was true. In the course of a thoughtful critique of how the acts of the Assembly had hobbled the monarchy—a critique with which Lafayette and the triumvirate would have substantially agreed—he also confessed that his compliance in signing the constitution and all the other reforms had been extorted from him by the threat to his and his family's safety. Perhaps most impolitic of all, he condemned the "anarchy and despotism" of the political clubs and the left-wing press, "incendiary newspapers and pamphlets, which increase daily." By not acting against behavior "so far removed from true liberty," he declared, the National Assembly "has lost its credit."

The king's declaration was in a way more devastating than the flight itself, and as word of it spread, the city's sense of confused sorrow turned to anger. The king had sworn an oath to the people, he had vowed that he was one with them and with the Revolution, and he had lied. "How could one ever again have confidence in anything the king might say?" wrote the editor of the moderate *Journal de Perlet*. The French had relied on the king's "honeyed words," wrote Brissot. "We were lulled to sleep. It seemed a crime even to doubt the king's promises. So now this 'patriot' king has fled . . . and is unmasked." Louis's likenesses, which had been in every shop and home, were everywhere covered up or destroyed, replaced by depictions of him in newspapers, pamphlets, and posters as a pig. His overweight, once thought cuddly, was now disgusting. A sign appeared on a wall at the Tuileries: "A large pig has escaped from the premises. Anyone finding him is urged to return him to his pen. A minor reward will be offered."

When Lafayette appeared at the Assembly a few hours after the king's escape was discovered, he was immediately attacked by Robespierre: "Traitor to the people! . . . Accomplice!" Barnave and others defended Lafayette with enough success that he was emboldened to go that night to the meeting of the Jacobins, where Barnave once more stood with him, and Robespierre was once more merciless: "You, M. Lafayette, will answer to the Assembly on the fate of the King with your head." Marat enthusiastically seconded him. Danton was inclined to be more lenient, calling Lafayette "either a traitor or an idiot. . . . In any case you have shown yourself unable to command us any longer. . . . You want to be great? Go back and become a common citizen. . . . France can win its freedom without you."

The king's flight gave all of the nation's political clubs new life but especially the Jacobins, whose affiliates had already tripled to nine hundred since the beginning of the year. The National Assembly suspended discussion of the king's flight for three weeks while a committee considered the appropriate response, but there was no suspension of debate among the public, and during those three weeks attendance at Jacobin meetings exploded. In many places, they had to be moved to public squares.

Opinion on how France should now be governed was far from uniform even in the left-wing press. Danton's Cordeliers called for the king's immediate dethronement, and they sent a petition to the Assembly "to declare here and now that France is no longer a monarchy." The next day, Brissot's *Patriote françois* also came out for a republic. "Louis XVI himself has shattered his crown. . . . Let us have no half-measures." But even after the king and his family had been brought back to Paris, the Jacobins were divided (their resolution waffled on the king's responsibility and intent, saying just that he had been "led astray by criminal suggestions"). Ten days after the king's flight, Carra's *Annales patriotiques* was still coming down on the side of monarchy, concluding that France had "not yet . . . attained that homogeneity and general strength of character" that were essential for a republic. The July 16 issue of the *Moniteur*, the closest thing to a newspaper of record in revolutionary France, featured a debate on monarchy between Tom Paine, who dismissed it as "that nullity," and the abbé Sieyès, who argued that decisions should be made by one accountable executive rather than "a majority discharged of all legal responsibility." Marat, on the other hand, came out for a dictator, somebody who could "lay hands on the known traitors," someone who could "rid you of your mortal enemies." This position, like many of Marat's positions, was singular. Most of those ready to give up on the Bourbon monarchy favored a constitutional republic. In the July 16 issue of the *Républicain*, Condorcet, a newly avowed republican for whom the monarchy had become ridiculous, published a satire, signed "a young mechanic," that proposed building a king machine. He was sure he could build an almost lifelike mechanical monarch, with "an inclination of the head full of grace and majesty." "My king would not be in any way a danger to liberty," he promised, "and if he were carefully repaired, he would be eternal, which is even better than hereditary."

On July 15, the Assembly moved to put a stop to all such republican talk with its final decision: Plainly impressed by the fear that deposing

Louis XVI would bring on war with Austria, the Assembly exonerated him of responsibility for his flight, sticking by the patent fiction that he had been abducted and that the sentiments in his manifesto had been forced from him by conniving, counterrevolutionary advisers, foremost the queen. That night, the meeting of the Jacobins was interrupted by a crowd of thousands, "men and women of all conditions," outraged by the Assembly's decision and demanding the king's dethronement. Perhaps under the inspiration of a crowd whose demonstration they had themselves inspired, Danton and Brissot were appointed to a committee responsible for drafting such a petition. Next morning it was read at the club and then taken to the Champs de Mars, where copies were distributed. As modified later in the day, it called on the Assembly to rescind its acquittal of Louis XVI and to admit that by his flight he had abdicated the throne. The Assembly was directed "to receive his abdication and to convoke a new representative body to . . . judge the guilty."

The events of July 16 moved swiftly. Unable to sanction defiance of the Assembly's decision, most of the deputies in the Jacobins, including Lafayette, the triumvirate, and more than three hundred others, noisily withdrew to form a more moderate club, which met in the former convent of the Feuillants. They tried and failed to take the name and archives of the Jacobins with them, but the Jacobins were left with only a few hard-core members, including Brissot and Danton, and the club leadership, Robespierre and Jérôme Pétion. Robespierre and Pétion tried at the last minute to withdraw the club's endorsement of the petition, but it was too late for that, and the next morning, families out to enjoy a summer Sunday combined with a crowd in the tens of thousands who had responded to the widespread call to come to a signing ceremony on the Champs de Mars.

As the day began, two hapless vagrants were found under the national altar that had been erected for the recent Bastille Day celebration. In the prevailing atmosphere of conspiracy and threat, they were suspected of some unspecified form of subversion and lynched. When this news reached the Hôtel de Ville, Lafayette asked Mayor Bailly to put out the red flag of martial law and permit him to bring order to the Champs de Mars. "There is a storm about, don't you feel it?" he said, and Bailly agreed. In fact, at a Cordeliers meeting the night before, members were told to anticpate such a repressive move by Lafayette and the Guard and advised to bring concealed weapons to the signing ceremony to forestall it. When Lafayette arrived with his troops, they were showered with stones, and someone fired a shot at Lafayette at point-blank range but unaccountably missed. After that, his men opened fire on the mostly unarmed crowd. Estimates of the dead ranged from thirteen to fifty, but as word of the incident raced around Paris the number ran into the hundreds, and what was left of Lafayette's support on the left after the king's flight was lost. Even Brissot, whose *Patriote français* had been among his last liberal defenders, now turned on him. What was thereafter known as the "Champs de Mars Massacre," Brissot wrote, was the responsibility of "a man who has told me a hundred times that he was a republican. . . . There is from now on nothing more in common between him and me."

A general crackdown followed. Arrest warrants were issued for "seditionists," which prompted Danton to go to London for two weeks and sent several radical journalists, including Desmoulins and Marat, into hiding. Failing to find Marat's press, Lafayette's guards tore up copies of his *L'Ami du peuple* wherever they could find them—a fact that could be said to have been in conflict with Lafayette's ideals except for the fact that Marat had started calling for various people to be assassinated, listing them by name in almost every issue, at first a few at a time, then by the dozens, then by the hundreds. The historian Alphonse Aulard, who was generally sympathetic to the revolutionary left, estimated that Marat eventually called for the murder of 270,000 people, placing *L'Ami du peuple* comfortably within the definition that Oliver Wendell Holmes articulated for speech that could be constitutionally suppressed, which was "shouting fire in a crowded theater."

Two weeks after the Champs de Mars Massacre, Washington wrote Lafayette to answer several letters. They had been arriving at Mount Vernon and at Washington's office in the new capital of Philadelphia with worrisome frequency all through that spring of 1791. In March, Lafayette had written that he was "tossed about in the ocean of factions and commotions of every kind," and he described the prospects for his "personal escape from amidst so many hostile hands" as "rather dubious." In April, after the Guard refused his order to let the king go to Saint-Cloud, he referred to "dark clouds. . . . The rage of parties, even among the patriots, is gone as far as it is possible, short of bloodshed. . . . I myself am exposed. . . ." Washington would no doubt have read all about the incident, which had been reported in several of the newspapers he took. Another letter from Lafayette in early June, even before the king's flight, spoke of "intrigues . . . licentiousness. . . . I stand the continual check to all interior factions."

In response, Washington admitted to "great anxiety" about "the danger to which you are personally exposed . . . and your letters are far from quieting that friendly concern." He confessed that he had little to say that would be much comfort. "Until your Constitution is fixed, your government organized, and your representative body renovated, much tranquility cannot be expected."

But tranquility was not forthcoming even then. On September 13, the king signed the new constitution; but by then the radicals in Paris had taken the lead, in part because of the Feuillants' arrogant refusal to fight a propaganda war with the newly hard-core Jacobins, whose determination was redoubled by their distress and who never lost the support of their friendly newspapers. Making much of their willingness to compromise with the Feuillants and of the Feuillants' refusal to do so, the Jacobins also moved toward greater inclusiveness in their membership and called for universal manhood suffrage, just as the Feuillants were releasing a constitution that limited their membership to "active citizens," meaning mostly *bourgeois* taxpayers. All of this was duly publicized by the newspapers of Brissot, Carra, Desmoulins, and others, who denounced the moderates of the Feuillants as traitors to the revolutionary cause.

That fall, a steady stream of such "traitors" called for the Assembly to recognize that the Revolution was at an end, its ends fully accomplished with the newly ratified constitution. Along with such calls came motions to rein in the political clubs. One particularly onerous proposal would have limited them to instructing their members on the acts of the Assembly; it forbade affiliation among clubs and such acts of protest as petitions, demonstrations, even critical analysis of the Assembly's work. "The time of destructions is past," argued the author of the proposed decree. "Everyone has sworn to the Constitution; everyone calls for order and public peace; everyone *wishes* that the Revolution be over; these, now, are the unequivocal signs of patriotism." Only "perverse and ambitious men" could possibly wish for the clubs to continue on the path of libel and sedition they had been treading for so long.

This was the moment Robespierre had been waiting for. The motion was raised on the penultimate day of the National Assembly, which was to give way on October 1 to a newly elected Legislative Assembly. No member of the outgoing body had been eligible for election to the incoming one, so this might have been Robespierre's legislative swan song, and he was clearly well prepared for it.

Perhaps he did not quite understand the previous speaker, he said: The Revolution is finished? Would that not mean that the constitution was an accomplished fact, its principles well understood and all its guarantees in place? By the evidence of the pending motion, this did not appear to be the case. By his reading of it, "the Constitution guarantees the French people the right to assembly peacefully. . . . The Constitution guarantees the French people the right to freedom of thought and speech. . . . The Constitution guarantees to the French people the right to do anything that does not conflict with the laws of the state." By the time Robespierre was finished eviscerating the very notion of limits on political speech, there was thunderous applause from the left, and his speech was of course covered lavishly by his friends in the press.

The next day, when the National Assembly met for the last time, the king issued a proclamation: "The end of the Revolution has come. Let the nation resume its happy nature." His appearance before the outgoing Assembly was greeted with apparently heartfelt outbursts of *"Vive le roi!"* But outside there was another demonstration waiting, "a truly moving spectacle" that was happily reported in the following day's *Révolutions de Paris*:

> The people were awaiting Pétion and Robespierre on the terrace of the Tuileries; they come out, and the people surround them, press about them, embrace them; crowns of oak leaves are set on their heads. . . . A woman pierces the crowd, her child in her arms; she places it in those of Robespierre; the mother and the two deputies sprinkle it with their tears. They seek to escape from their triumph, and to slip down a side turning; but the people follow; they are sur-

rounded anew; they are borne on high to the sound of instruments and of cheers. . . . [T]hey speak . . . the people listen to them; bless them; they are escorted home amid a gigantic crowd; and the names of *"chaste deputies,"* *"incorruptible legislators,"* joined to their own, were heard on all sides as they went.

On the face-saving premise that with the adoption of the constitution his mission was completed, Lafayette resigned his command of the National Guard, this time for good. In truth, he resigned before he was pushed; he had made many enemies, and his control of the Guard was marginal. In any case, he accepted lavish encomia from the city and the Guard, and in October, after losing to Jérôme Pétion in the race for mayor of Paris, he retired to Chavaniac.

He had cause to be proud of his role in accomplishing what by any measure was an extraordinary feat. Consider just the preamble of the 1791 Constitution, passed by essentially the same group of men who had been convened as the Estates-General two years before. In France, as of 1791, it declared,

> there is no longer any nobility, nor peerage, nor hereditary distinction of orders, nor feudal regime, nor patrimonial justice, nor any title, denomination, or prerogative. . . . There is no longer venality nor heredity in any public office, and for no section of the nation and no individual can there be any exemption from the common law of the French.

Especially given the centuries-old social and legal systems that were replaced, it was one of the most thoroughgoing works of national reformation that had ever been achieved.

All the same, Lafayette left behind him in the fall of 1791 a city in uproar and a nation on the brink, pushed from the left by a newly radicalized and populist Jacobin movement, from the right by the threat of a royalist counterrevolution, and from outside its borders by a military alliance between Austria and Prussia that seemed bent on reversing all that had been accomplished since 1789.

By now the king's émigré brothers Provence and d'Artois had established a counterrevolutionary headquarters at the castle of Schönbornlust in Coblenz, a fortified city on the Rhine, where they created a court society worthy of the Old Regime, complete with favorite mistresses, ladies and gentlemen of the wardrobe and bedchamber, grand marshals, court gossip, intrigues for position, and nuances of etiquette as painfully precise as those of Versailles in the time of the Sun King. Subsidized by most of the German rulers as well as those of Russia and Spain, they had even established a substantial independent military force, which was now as strong as it would ever be.

In early September 1791, Provence and d'Artois had sent an open letter to Louis XVI, attaching the recently signed Declaration of Pillnitz, by which the Austrian emperor and the king of Prussia declared their intention to use force as necessary to support the Bourbon monarchy, "an object of common interest to all the sovereigns of Europe." The princes declared the draft constitution illegal and denounced virtually everything else the Revolution had accomplished as well, including the abolition of orders. They warned the nation and the king that if he signed the constitution (as he did only days later), they would infer that he was a prisoner and, supported by all the monarchies of Europe, would mount an invasion to set him free. This was bluster; the signatories at Pillnitz had conditioned their support on that of the other major European powers, knowing full well that England would never join them.

Still, the new Legislative Assembly had to take the threat seriously, and as it did so the center of political gravity in France shifted dramatically. The Legislative Assembly had begun with almost twice as many Feuillants as Jacobins but with more than four hundred committed to neither club; and under the influence of the newly elected deputy Brissot and a new "Brissotin" faction of the Jacobins, the Revolution was energized by the patriotic spirit of a crusade: The counterrevolutionary enemy was at the gates, and all true French patriots—all defenders of human rights everywhere—had no choice but to heed the call to battle. Suddenly, the most pragmatic reason to support monarchy, which was to avoid mobilizing the forces of counterrevolution both within and without, was gone, and with it the practical basis of the moderate Feuillant position. The Brissotins worked assiduously to undermine the king's authority—and the

Feuillants' advocacy of constitutional monarchy—by forcing issues that were certain to invoke the royal veto. They proposed the death penalty for émigrés, for example, a group that prominently included the king's brothers; and they called for confiscating the possessions of émigrés' families, which threatened the property of the monarchy itself. They also proposed criminalizing opposition to the Civil Constitution of the Clergy among both churchmen and their supporters. At the same time, they persuaded the Assembly to deliver an ultimatum to the emperor that required him to desist in any aid to the émigrés or the counterrevolutionary cause and to honor the Treaty of 1756, which prohibited Austria from allying itself with an enemy of France. The deadline for a response was March 1. It came and went.

The king, while declaring that he would fiercely resist any invasion, plainly hoped for it to succeed and for the French army to collapse quickly. Virtually alone among the Jacobins, Robespierre perceived and argued strenuously that war would play into the hands of the king and the counterrevolutionaries; but his voice was drowned out by the bellicose rhetoric of the Brissotins as they led the cry for war in the Jacobin Club and in the Assembly. In addition to eloquent orators and journalists, the Brissotins also benefited from a terrible combination of boundless idealism and the recklessly optimistic belief that virtuous ends would somehow find the means. Intoxicated by his own vision of French revolutionary ideas sweeping Europe, Brissot foresaw a general European "war of the people against kings," a virulent appeal infectious with war fever; and any doubt that Louis wished the virus to spread should have been dispelled when, in March 1792, he replaced his entire ministry with men acceptable to the Brissotins. This was taken by the Austrian-Prussian alliance as a virtual declaration of war, and by April there were fifty thousand Austrian troops on France's northeastern frontier. "I do believe we are about to declare war," Marie-Antoinette wrote happily to Axel de Fersen. "The imbeciles!"

Lafayette, who was nothing if not a French patriot, had by then already been called out of his "retirement" to lead one of three armies that were being positioned against the presumed invasion. In the face of war, conditions could hardly have been worse. The new constitution tightly circumscribed the powers of the king, who was nominally commander in chief of the French forces. Louis could appoint his own ministers, but they served only until the legislature chose to impeach them, and if he left a fifty-mile radius of Paris, he would vacate the throne. To compensate for the lack of executive authority, the constitution gave the Legislative Assembly, almost all of whose 745 members were new to national politics, virtually every task of government, from taxes to diplomacy, along with a new judiciary function. Meanwhile, the French armed forces had been allowed to fall into disarray. By the beginning of 1792, six thousand officers, two thirds of the officer corps, had emigrated, fleeing mutinous troops and the bleak future of aristocrats in France. By new regulations, two thirds of all officer replacements had to be elected by the troops, which had served to favor candidates with a haphazard view of discipline.

When Lafayette arrived at his headquarters to find critical shortages of food and supplies, he put his American experience to work, enforcing strict discipline while gaining the favor of his men by improving their living conditions, their clothing, their equipment, and their food. "I am to have twenty thousand men to garrison the frontiers . . . and thirty thousand to take the field," he wrote Washington proudly. "I will send you an exact return of my army when it is finally arranged, for I always consider myself, my dear general, as one of your lieutenants on a detached command." In his worst moment, though, Washington never found himself in Lafayette's confused position.

On April 20, 1792, Louis signed a declaration of war, and despite an almost complete lack of preparedness a preemptive strike was called for at once, on the ludicrous basis that local populations would rise up spontaneously to support it. Lafayette's army was given the first order to advance, but on the date the king's war minister had assigned for his troops to march, he did not even have his entire force in place. His vanguard of three thousand men were turned back by the first cannon shots. They withdrew in panic, and their general was murdered, as were some Austrian prisoners of war they had captured. France at that point was vulnerable in the extreme and saved for the moment only by preparations of the imperial alliance, which were as elaborate and time-consuming as the French plan was not. "I cannot conceive how the war could have been declared," Lafayette wrote, "since nothing was ready." That, of course, was Louis's idea, and the Brissotins' lust for war played into it beautifully.

Against a backdrop of renewed food shortages and rampant inflation caused by the anticipation of wartime government spending (currency fell to about half its value even before war was declared), military defeat turned the crowd hostile and sent the politicians in search of scapegoats. "There can be no doubt that Lafayette is the head of the nobles who are allied with the tyrants of Europe," said Danton. In fact there was a kernel of truth in the charge. In May Lafayette wrote to the Austrian ambassador Mercy d'Argenteau asking that the fighting be suspended while he attempted to deal with the incendiary Brissotins in the Assembly and among the Jacobins. Nothing came of the approach, but a lull in the fighting that month raised suspicions among radicals in the capital, including Robespierre, who by now supported the war. "I do not trust the generals," he said, and he especially suspected Lafayette of counterrevolutionary plotting. "Strike Lafayette, and the nation is safe."

Brissot did not suspect Lafayette of actively opposing the war, but someone had to be blamed for the battlefield defeats. "We have need of some form of treachery," he said. Marat, though, now let his *Ami du peuple* loose on Brissot, who he said was "apprenticed to chicanery, became a would-be wit, a scandal-sheet writer, an apprentice-philosopher, a fraudulent speculator, a crook, a prince's valet, a government clerk, police spy, publicist, municipal inquisitor . . . and finally henchman of the despot," most of which was true, of course, but the fact that he said it was a sign of things to come.

Washington wrote a long letter to Lafayette on June 10, in response to Lafayette's news that he was in command of one of the French armies arrayed against the possibility of invasion. Like all his other letters since becoming president, it was diplomatically opaque, and given the tense circumstances it could hardly have been otherwise, but a certain prophetic wisdom shines through it nonetheless. He notes that the situation in Europe is "pregnant with great events" and says he hopes that war can be avoided; but he seems more worried about the domestic situation in France than about the foreign enemy, and he is relatively blunt about that, saying he hopes that "while despotic oppression is avoided on the one hand, licentiousness may not be substituted for liberty nor confusion take place of order on the other. The just medium cannot be expected to be found in a moment, the first vibrations always go to the extremes, and cool reason . . . is as little to be expected in the tumults of popular commotion as an attention to the liberties of the people is to be found [under] . . . a despotic tyrant." He knew, of course, that Lafayette could be going into battle at any moment, and in fact might already be dead as he wrote this letter. They had been at war together before, however, and this is the only time in their entire correspondence when Washington ever addresses the danger that Lafayette might not survive whatever it was he was facing. Like his other American friends, Washington said, he had been "not a little anxious for your personal safety, and I have yet no grounds for removing that anxiety." He consoled himself with the knowledge that Lafayette was fighting, as he himself had fought, for something more important than himself, and that "if you should fall, it will be in defense of that cause which your heart tells you is just." He concludes by committing Lafayette "to the care of that Providence whose interposition and protection we have so often experienced . . . trusting that he will bring order out of confusion."

Lafayette may never have read that letter. If he did, it was many years later, when he was released from prison, but he acted in its spirit now, undertaking at considerable personal risk to take one last stand against "popular commotion" and for the "just medium" of constitutional monarchy. On June 16, he wrote a long letter to the Assembly that was so straightforward and outspoken that some of the legislators thought it had to be a hoax. "The state is in danger," he wrote.

> Can you refuse to see that . . . the Jacobin faction has caused all the disorders? I accuse it of this emphatically. Organized like an empire in this city and through its affiliates [around the country], blindly led by some ambitious men, this sect forms a separate body inside the French people, whose power it usurps by subjugating its representatives and their initiatives. . . . As we must fight the foreigners intervening in our disputes, must we not also deliver our fatherland from a domestic tyranny? . . . Let the royal party remain intact, for it is guaranteed by the Constitution; let it be independent, for their independence is one of the mainstays of our liberty; let the King be revered, for he is endowed with the Nation's majesty; let him

choose a ministry free from the prior loyalty of faction; and if there
be conspirators, let them perish under the sword of the law.

Those who believed it actually did come from Lafayette must have considered it both brave and foolhardy.

Four days later, on the anniversary of the Tennis Court Oath, in "a contumelious reply to Lafayette's letter" that was orchestrated by Danton, the
Tuileries was invaded by an armed and angry crowd dragging cannon past
guardsmen who did nothing to stop them. They found the king in his
apartment and for several hours, while the National Guard stood by, they
held him at sword- and knifepoint, forcing him to wear a liberty cap and
drink toasts to the Revolution.

Furious, and again humiliated by his once beloved Guard, Lafayette
now rode to Paris and went to the Assembly in person. In case there was
any doubt of it, he wanted them to know that his letter of the week before
was absolutely genuine. "It is time," he declared,

> to protect the Constitution, to assure the freedom of the National
> Assembly and that of the king, his independence, his dignity. . . . I
> beg the National Assembly to order the instigators of the crimes and
> violent acts committed on June 20 at the Tuileries to be punished as
> criminals . . . to destroy a sect that invades the nation's sovreignty
> [and] tyrannizes its citizens . . . and to give the army the assurance
> that the constitution will not be injured by an attack from within
> while they are shedding their blood in its defense at the frontiers.

The speech won wide applause, since a majority in the Assembly supported his position, but the Assembly was no longer in control of events.
Hundreds of deputies, unwilling either to vote with the radical Jacobins or
to oppose them openly, had stopped coming to the Assembly by then. The
radicals—Brissot prominent among them—called for Lafayette to be put
on trial for deserting his post and for treason. Despite such pressure, this
rump Assembly voted against his indictment; but the view of the crowd,
influenced by a growing (and studiously fed) panic about the counterrevolutionary enemy, was increasingly against him. Gouverneur Morris wrote
Thomas Jefferson about this time, "I verily believe that if M. de Lafayette

were to appear just now in Paris unattended by his army he would be torn to pieces."

Talk of storming the Tuileries again, in conscious mimicry of Bastille Day, was building up as that July 14 approached, but Danton and other Jacobin leaders decided it would be best to wait until pressure was sufficiently great to ensure that this time such an action would result in their ultimate aim, the dethronement of the king. For that, they knew it would be necessary to inflame the mass of *sans-culottes* ("without knee-breeches"), people of the working-class faubourgs who identified their scorn of fine clothes with honest, down-to-earth patriotism.

The spark came on July 25, when Paris received an ultimatum from the frontier declaring that it was the intention of the allied armies to rescue Louis XVI from his "captivity." The message carried a special warning to "the city of Paris and all its inhabitants," who were directed to restore Louis XVI to his "full and complete liberty." If the Tuileries were violated again, it said, "their said Majesties declare, on their word of honor as emperor and king, that . . . they will inflict an ever memorable vengeance by delivering over the city of Paris to military execution and complete destruction, and the rebels guilty of the said outrages to the punishment that they merit."

Emboldened by such an open challenge, Danton, the *sans-culottes*'s hero, called for arming all Parisians and opening the sectional assemblies to all citizens, without distinction. His Cordeliers and other radical clubs then orchestrated a general call for the king to be dethroned and gave the Assembly until August 9 to comply or be preempted by the unilateral action of the people. The signal that the Assembly would do no such thing came on August 8, when it once more vindicated Lafayette. Next day four hundred deputies, most of them Fayettists but some Brissotins as well, simply stayed home in fear of what "the people" might be moved to do.

That night, representatives of about half of the Paris sections descended on the Hôtel de Ville and declared themselves the new Revolutionary Commune of Paris. Next morning, a crowd that included many guardsmen swarmed through the Tuileries again, this time slaughtering some six hundred of the king's Swiss Guards, as many as half while they tried to retreat, slashing off limbs, mutilating soldiers' genitals and stuffing them in their mouths, burning some of the corpses, carting off others to be thrown into lime pits.

Seeing what was coming, the king and queen were gone, having thrown themselves on the mercy of the Assembly, which voted to put them in prison and suspend the monarchy. Some of the deputies no doubt comforted themselves that they were acting in the interest of the royal family's safety. Danton was that day named minister of justice by the fewer than three hundred deputies in attendance. Later the same abject demi-legislature called for nationwide elections, to be held within the next three weeks, to choose delegates to a new government, to be called the Convention.*

Now in control of both the legislature and the Commune of Paris, the radical Jacobins could have their way with Lafayette. The wonder is not that he chose to cross enemy lines rather than face a show trial and certain death at the hands of a newly formed military tribunal. The wonder is that he waited nine more days to do it. He always denied being involved in any counterrevolutionary plot, but there is no question that he spent several days measuring the willingness of his fellow general Luckner and the army to take action to reverse the course of the Revolution, and sounding out the king on his preference. Finding no support for such a move ("Of course Lafayette will save us," Marie-Antoinette was quoted as saying, "but who will save us from Lafayette?"), he disposed his army against an attack should it come, and on the evening of August 19 crossed into Austrian territory with some of his fellow officers. That day, a committee of the Paris Commune went beyond charging him with treason and declared him guilty.

Later in the week a guillotine was erected for the first time in the place du Carrousel near the Tuileries, and Marat was named to the Committee of Surveillance, which was responsible, among other things, for prisons.

---

*The Convention was given its name because it was to draw up a new constitution in the aftermath of the king's dethronement, which made the 1791 Constitution obsolete. The elections were by universal suffrage of all males age twenty-one or older. The Convention, which lasted through three years of war, was both a legislative and a constituent body. It also drew the executive power to itself and temporary war powers as well, a "confusion of powers" that helped to make possible the Convention's most egregious domestic initiative, which was the Reign of Terror.

In mid-August, word reached Paris that French forces had been defeated at Longwy, and two weeks later that the Prussian forces had passed Verdun. Now no fortress stood between them and the capital. "If we are bold, bolder still, and forever bold, then France is saved!" declared Danton, who called for a house-to-house search for weapons and "suspects" in Paris, which resulted in three thousand arrests and a crush in the city's already overcrowded jails. Danton also called for thirty thousand patriotic volunteers from the sections of Paris to go to the front immediately.

As the new recruits were mobilized, they panicked at the thought that when they were gone, all the counterrevolutionaries now in prison could join forces with the invading Prussians and kill their families. "To prevent this," a British eyewitness wrote, "a large body of sans-culottes . . . proceeded to the Church de Carmes, rue de Vaugirard, where amidst the acclamations of a savage mob they massacred a number of refractory priests, all the vicaires de Saint Sulpice, the directors of the seminaries, and the doctors of the Sorbonne, with the ci-devant archbishop of Arles, and a number of others, exceeding in all one hundred and seventy."

Then they went to the prisons.

[H]aving demanded of the jailors a list of the prisoners they put aside such as were confined only for debt, and pulled to pieces most of the others. The same cruelties were committed during the night and continue this morning in all the other prisons of the town. When they have satiated their vengeance, which is principally directed against the refractory Priests . . . it is to be hoped the tumult will subside, but as the multitude are perfectly masters, everything is to be dreaded.

Attacks on the prisons and prisoners of Paris grew only more savage.

[E]arly on Monday morning a detachment with seven pieces of cannon went to attack the Bicetre. It is reported that these wretches charged their cannon with small stones and such other things, and fired promiscuously among the prisoners. I cannot . . . vouch for this, they have however not finished their cruelties there yet, and it is now past six o'clock Tuesday evening. To be convinced of what I could not believe, I made a visit to the prison of the Abbaye about seven o'clock on Monday evening, for the slaughter had not ceased. . . . Two of the Municipality were then in the prison with some of the mob distributing their justice. Those they found guilty were seemingly released, but only to be precipitated by the door on a number of piques, and then among the savage cries of *Vive la nation!* to be hacked to pieces by those that had swords and were ready to receive them. After this their dead bodies were dragged by the arms or legs to the Abbaye, which is distant from the prison about two hundred yards; here they were laid up in heaps till carts could carry them away. The kennel was swimming with blood, and a bloody track was traced from the prison to the Abbaye door. . . .

Nothing can exceed the inconsistency of these people. After the general massacre of Sunday night many of the dead bodies were laid on the Pont Neuf to be claimed, [and] a person in the action of stealing a handkerchief from one of the corpses was hacked to pieces on the spot, by the same people who had been guilty of so much cruelty and injustice. . . .

Over the course of five days, in what came to be known as "the September Massacres," some fourteen hundred people were murdered, while the new Revolutionary Commune not only did not stop the slaughter but helped to coordinate it, later voting to compensate the killers for lost wages. About half the population of the Paris prisons were executed as counterrevolutionaries during that week, some of them non-juring priests but most of them common criminals; and the Terror was still months away.

XXIII

Works of the Guillotine

LAFAYETTE'S INSISTENCE THAT he be treated as a neutral non-combatant was never taken seriously. The Austrian general who would have made that decision, reading a note sent by a subaltern to explain the situation, got only as far as his name. "Lafayette! Lafayette! Run quick, tell the Duke of Brunswick! . . . His Highness at Brussels! . . . Lafayette! Lafayette!"

His second thought was to claim American citizenship. He wrote to William Short, now minister at the Hague: "You will greatly oblige me, my dear friend, by insisting on seeing me. I am an American citizen, and an American officer. I am no longer in the service of France. In demanding my release you will be acting within your rights, and I have no doubt of your immediate arrival. God bless you."

Short wrote for advice to Gouverneur Morris in Paris, and on September 12 Morris tactfully replied: "I do not exactly see how the United States could claim him. If claimed and delivered up, would [America] not be bound to put him to death for having attacked a neutral power; or else, by the very act of acquitting him, declare war against those who had taken him?" Morris felt for Lafayette's plight, but his advice to Short was in perfect accordance with instructions he had received directly from Washington: "[T]he less we meddle in the great quarrel which agitates Europe the better it will be for us." Whatever their "private feelings," as diplomats they had "higher duties to fulfill." If Morris were in Short's position, he said, "I should (I think) confine myself to prayer and solicitation until I received express orders from the President of the United States."

Such orders would not be coming. No one would have wished more fervently to liberate Lafayette than Washington, but as the president of an infant nation among great powers, and one moreover that was already allied by treaty with France, his position was beyond ticklish.

His first reaction was to write Adrienne. Not knowing where a letter would find her, he sent it with a friend who was setting sail for Europe. His letter to her said all that he was in a position to say, which was not much.

> If I had words that could convey to you an adequate idea of my feelings on the present situation . . . this letter would appear to you in a different garb. The sole object in writing to you now is to inform you that I have deposited in the hands of Mr. Nicholas Van Staphorst of Amsterdam two thousand three hundred and ten guilders Holland currency, equal to two hundred guineas subject to your orders. This sum is, I am certain, the least I am indebted for services rendered me by Mr. de la Fayette, of which I never yet have received the account. I could add much, but it is best perhaps that I should say little on this subject. Your goodness will supply my deficiency.

The money was, of course, his own, since a gift from the United States to the family of a proscribed and convicted émigré, much less a Lafayette, would have been a scalding diplomatic insult.

In February 1793, he received a letter that Adrienne had written to him the previous October, which indicated that she had been hoping for a good deal more from her husband's hero and her son's namesake. "In this abyss of misery, the thought of owing to the United States and to Washington the life and liberty of La Fayette causes a ray of hope to shine in my heart," she wrote. "I expect everything from the kindness of the people in whose land he helped to form a model of that liberty of which he is now the victim." Washington passed this letter along to Jefferson with a pained request that he draft a reply that would contain "all the consolation I can with propriety give her, consistent with my public character and the national policy, circumstanced as things are."

Jefferson did his best, which was very good, but finally he just had to say it. Despite "my friendship for him, and with ardent desires for his relief, in which sentiment I know that my fellow-citizens participate . . . the measures which you were pleased to intimate in your letter are perhaps not exactly those which I could pursue." He said all he could when he assured her that he was "not inattentive to his condition, nor contenting myself with inactive wishes for his liberation. My affection to his nation and to himself are unabated. . . ."

In fact, Washington's affection for France was being sorely tested at that moment, and it helped matters not at all that his own senior advisers and diplomats were in open conflict over what American policy should be. Even before Lafayette's flight and the September Massacres, the American ministers closest to the scene—Morris in Paris and Short at the Hague—were in emphatic agreement that the French Revolution was insupportable and had gone utterly out of control. Morris's reports to Jefferson were modulated to suit his audience, but Short's were not. "Those mad and corrupt people in France . . . have destroyed their government," he wrote in one of his reports to Jefferson. Power rested now "in the hands of the most mad, wicked, and atrocious assembly that was ever collected in any country."

News that the Prussian army had been turned back with the victory at Valmy in September 1792 was thrilling to Jefferson, who boasted that his fellow Republicans were now proudly calling themselves Jacobins. Short, however, considered all French victories "unquestionably evils for humanity. . . . I should not be at all surprised to hear of the present leaders being hung by the people. Such has been the moral of this revolution from the beginning."

By January 1793, Jefferson had had more than enough of Short's negativity. Complaining of the "extreme warmth" of Short's views, Jefferson wished to let his former secretary know that "99 in a hundred" Americans supported the French Revolution. Then he let his rhetoric and his temper get entirely away from him, which is why this letter, apart from the Declaration of Independence, is perhaps Jefferson's most famous prose:

Was ever such a prize won with so little innocent blood? My own affections have been deeply wounded by some of the martyrs to this cause, but rather than it should have failed, I would have seen half the earth desolated. Were there but an Adam and an Eve left in every country and left free, it would be better than it now is.

He warned Short to moderate his tone in the future and to "be cautious" in what he wrote to Hamilton especially, since it amounted to giving him ammunition for his attacks on the French Revolution and its democratic ideals.

Hamilton did not need Short's letters to confirm him in his "dread" of France's "philosophic politicians" when he had the Brissotins, who were even then enshrining their exuberant plans for world conquest in instructions for France's new minister to America, Edmond-Charles-Edouard Genêt. "We cannot rest until all Europe is ablaze!" Brissot declared. "What puny projects were those of Richelieu . . . compared with the worldwide risings, the gigantic revolutions, that we are called upon to achieve!"

In the elections to the new government of the Convention, the Brissotins did well in the provinces, but Paris elected more radical delegates. Brissot himself was named to the Convention without receiving a single vote in the capital. The most radical contingent, who took over the highest benches in the assembly, were referred to as "the Mountain," or *Montagnards*, and in short order, led by Danton, Robespierre, and others, they took over the Revolution itself.*

In a way, the Brissotins became victims of their successful call to war: The Mountain were able to blame them successfully for early battlefield defeats and use the same defeats as a way to recruit the *sans-culottes* to the revolutionary cause at home and abroad. They could then take credit for the resulting victories.

---

*What separated the Brissotins from the Montagnards is an especially tricky aspect of French revolutionary history. Roughly speaking, some historians see it as a conflict between the *bourgeois* and the egalitarian *sans-culottes*, others as an intraclass struggle over power and self-interest. Neither view seems to be wholly satisfactory, but close study tends to dissolve certainty in a confusion of variables; except for the hard core, it is difficult even to know who was a Brissotin and who a Montagnard in the Convention. In general, it can be said that the Brissotins were perceived by the Mountain as moderate and eventually counterrevolutionary, and the Brissotins, or at least some of them, came to view the Mountain as dangerously *anarchiste*.

The recruits called out by Danton after the defeats just before the September Massacres had indeed made the difference on September 20 at Valmy, where the victory was won precisely by numbers and revolutionary zeal. In the defeated Prussian camp that night, the writer Johann Wolfgang von Goethe tried to console his comrades with a prophecy: "Here and today a new epoch in the history of the world has begun, and you can boast that you were present at its birth." A subsequent string of French triumphs on the battlefield seemed to suggest that he was right.

On the day of the victory at Valmy, the new government of the Convention met for the first time, and their first order of business was what to do with the king. The discovery of a hidden strongbox containing evidence of Louis's conspiracy with Austria assured his guilt. The only question was his punishment, and the only substantive question about that was whether or not he should be executed. The Brissotins favored exile, and making the debate over the king's execution a test of patriotism was one way that the Montagnards were able to push the Brissotins toward the soft, suspect center. Even with such pressure from the radical left, a decree for the king's immediate execution passed by the barest possible majority, 361 votes to 360.

The crowd that came to watch as he met his end in the place de la Révolution on the morning of January 21, 1793, seemed equally ambivalent. Louis XVI went to his death with composure and courage. He is said to have mounted the scaffold "with a firm step," and he was heard to declare in a loud voice: "I die perfectly innocent of the so-called crimes of which I was accused. I pardon those who are the cause of my misfortunes. Indeed, I hope that the shedding of my blood will contribute to the happiness of France and you, my unfortunate people. . . ." He said something more, but a roll of drums drowned him out, and the last that was heard of him was "a frightful cry as the blade fell." The executioner Sanson helpfully filled a bucket with the king's blood so that people could dip in their handkerchiefs and other items for souvenirs.

.   .   .

Jefferson and the Republicans took Louis's execution as a heartening sign of victory over despotism by a faithful revolutionary ally. Hamilton and the Federalists thought the French had gone completely mad. Washington, who was more than skeptical about national "friendships" and knew France had only acted in its own interest in supporting the American Revolution, was also mindful as perhaps no one else of what Louis's aid had meant at the end of winter at Valley Forge, at Yorktown, and for the outcome of the war. In any case, he did not write and is not recorded as having said so much as a word on the subject of Louis's death. Jefferson thought he seemed dejected by the news.

The first report of the execution came to Philadelphia on March 27, 1793, at the same time word came that France had declared war on England. This had been suspected, because no packets from France had arrived for the past three months. Even ships' captains were bringing no news into Philadelphia, which raised the suspicion that blockades might already be in place as part of a general European war. The news being less than definitive even now, Washington decided to leave for a respite in Mount Vernon that day as planned. The reports that reached him there on April 8, however, were clear and even worse than he had feared: France had declared war not only on England but on Spain and Holland as well. Washington immediately sped back to Philadelphia for urgent meetings with his cabinet about the U. S. response.

On the same day that news of war reached Mount Vernon, the new minister Citizen Genêt landed in Charleston to a hero's welcome. He carried with him the certainty of the French government that their revolutionary ally would be with them in this hour of need.

Washington was no less certain that America should remain neutral in the conflict. He had no problem convincing Hamilton or Jefferson of the wisdom of neutrality, though neither of them understood the logic or necessity of it as he did. Both thought it should be used as leverage with the belligerents, Jefferson wishing to place conditions on England that would offset a sense of betrayal in France, Hamilton hoping that the French Revolution and its like-minded friends in the United States would take American neutrality as a sharp stick in the eye and that Britain would be mollified by it.

Washington disagreed with both of them, wishing to show no tilt in the direction of either nation. By then, however, Genêt had already done a great deal to undermine the U. S. position. His instructions, which had been drafted principally by Brissot himself as leader of the Convention's diplomatic committee, were breathtaking in scope, and seemed to take for granted not only America's cooperation in France's vast ambitions but also France's right to construe for itself America's best interests.

The plan called for Genêt to issue commissions to American officers (they gave him 250 blanks) to lead an assault on any and all Spanish and British outposts in North America, including Canada, and in particular to invade and occupy Spain's Mississippi Territory, where they would "deliver our former brothers of Louisiana from the tyrannical yoke of Spain." While admitting that the language in the Franco-American Treaty of 1778 had been ambiguous, Genêt was instructed to insist on France's reading of it, which was that America's ports would be closed to all of its enemies, and that French ships could use American ports for any purpose, not to exclude commissioning American ships as privateers and outfitting whatever British vessels could be captured as French warships. Genêt was to get a new treaty signed that would eliminate any ambiguity on this score. He was also to insist on accelerated payment of the entire French war debt.

True to his mandate and warmed by his reception, Genêt got to work even before he left Charleston, signing up American recruits for the expedition against Spanish Florida and commissioning his first four American privateers. In no time at all they began bringing captured British ships into coastal ports from Charleston to Philadelphia. Genêt also set up a French Admiralty Court in Charleston to adjudicate disputes over captured prizes. His first report to his foreign minister was ebullient.

The rest of Genêt's mission to America was a wonderful demonstration of some of the differences between the American and French revolutions, but enacted as farce. It was as if Genêt took as part of his instructions that the world, at least the United States, was obliged to operate according to the rules of revolutionary France, and in fact his instructions did imply that. The title they gave him, for example, was "Minister Plenipotentiary to . . . the Congress of the United States" rather than "to the President," which is understandable only in the French context, where the Convention was all-powerful and there was now no executive at all. Such a small mistake was easy to overlook. Not so was his insistence that if any of his plans were thwarted, as virtually all of them were, he would simply go over the head of the president and the State Department and appeal directly to Congress and the people, whose sovereignty he never tired of invoking and who after all had always been the first recourse of reformers in France. The gala receptions given him on his way north and then in Philadelphia demonstrated to his satisfaction that the people were on the side of France, and it was a revolutionary axiom that the people would have their way.

Genêt was quickly informed that his Admiralty Courts were an infringement on the sovereignty of the United States and would have to be dissolved; that he could not commission privateers or dispose of prizes in American ports; and that Americans serving aboard French privateers were breaking the law by violating American neutrality.

"No one has the right to shackle our [privateering] operations," Genêt shot back, and, whatever Washington and Jefferson might think, he was quite sure Congress, when it reconvened, would agree with him since the "fraternal voice" of the American people had spoken. For the moment he would agree only to make sure his ships' captains were faithful to the "political opinions of the President, until the representatives of the sovereign [people] shall have confirmed or rejected them."

When two Americans serving aboard his privateers were subsequently arrested for violation of America's neutrality, Genêt exploded. He could not imagine their offense, he wrote to Jefferson, unless it was perhaps "the crime which my mind cannot conceive, and which my pen almost refuses to state . . . of serving France, and defending with her children the common and glorious cause of liberty."

The worst problem for Genêt was that Washington refused to accelerate the payment of America's debt. Hamilton told Genêt that giving France the wherewithal to purchase weapons of war—not to mention repaying the debt in war materiel—would by itself be a violation of American neutrality. Genêt was furious: He had counted on that money to fund his wars in Florida and Louisiana, and he attributed Washington's position to the fact that the president was in the camp of counterrevolutionaries, no better than a despotic monarch himself, driven by the "infernal system of the King of England, and of the other kings, his accomplices, to destroy by famine the French republicans and liberty. . . ."

By this time Genêt's view of Washington was coming to be shared by a large and growing number of Americans, who mistook the president's official formality for pretension and linked that to what seemed a tilt toward British monarchy and away from the republican values of the French. His motivation, however, had nothing to do with either country but stemmed, as the policy of neutrality did, from his understanding of the American situation: The country was young, its government brand new, and above all it needed to establish what he always called a national "character," by which he meant something more than a sense of its unity and strength. It wanted a reputation and stature in the world, and he took it as his highest calling as the nation's first chief executive to nurture that character and to embody it. The man who could at many times have become a dictator had he wanted to and in 1782 had viewed "with abhorrence" and rebuffed "with severity" an overt plea that he become "King of America" was nevertheless taxed with self-aggrandizement, evidence being the way he bowed instead of shaking hands at his levees, and the fact that he held levees at all. Benjamin Franklin Bache's pro-French newspaper, the *Aurora*, Washington's most reliably scathing critic, ran a satirical help-wanted ad for a national poet laureate addressed to "the Noblesse and Courtiers of the United States." The winning applicant's poetry, it said, would demonstrate the ability to put across "certain *monarchical prettinesses* . . . such as levies, drawing rooms, stately nods instead of shaking hands, titles of office, seclusion from the people, &c. &c."

Another satirical jab at Washington's pretension, which was brought up at a cabinet meeting where the Neutrality Proclamation was discussed, had Washington on the way to the guillotine. At this, his famous temper made one of its rare appearances, and Jefferson took wickedly careful notes. The president was

much inflamed; got into one of those passions when he cannot command himself; ran on much on the personal abuse which had been bestowed on him; defied any man on earth to produce *one single act* of his since he had been in the government which was not done on the purest movies. That he had never repented but once

having [lost] the moment of resigning his office, and that was every
moment since. That *by God* he had rather be in his grave than in
his present situation. That he had rather be on his farm than to be
made *Emperor of the World.* And yet they were charging him with
wanting to be a King. . . .

Knowing Washington's sensitivity to criticism and his lifelong concern
about living up to and leaving behind an honorable reputation, the fact
that he took so many decisions that invited such animus (and never made
a move to stop the criticism, as Adams would do with the Sedition Act)
must be marked a signal and even moving sign of his commitment to the
welfare of the new nation above all—a commitment that was never so
tested as it was by his policies toward France and Britain during his second term in office.

Although Washington has often been thought closer to Hamilton and
Britain than to Jefferson and France, the record suggests that he was party
to neither man and no country but the United States, whose neutrality he
sought so that it could recover economically from the war, discover its
"character" independent of any foreign influence, and exploit its land and
other resources so that it could achieve the prosperity that was the fount
of every nation's greatness. As long as America remained free of European
politics and free to trade with all nations, he said, Americans "shall be the
gainers, whether the powers of the old world may be in peace or war"—
and especially, added the realist, if they were at war, in which case "our
importance will certainly increase and our friendship be courted." Yet at
the time it was proclaimed, the policy of neutrality was popular with virtually no one—least of all of course with Citizen Genêt.

In part because Jefferson was initially so optimistic about Genêt's mission, he had tried to help him understand American politics and in the
process made matters incalculably worse. In trying to explain the policy of
neutrality and how Genêt's initiatives could be rejected in the face of such
evident popular support, Jefferson shared with him the division in the cabinet between the pro-British and pro-French forces, urging him to be
aware that feelings were running high on both sides.

After this Genêt actually redoubled his efforts, eventually leading to
Washington's exasperated demand that France recall him. Obviously

Genêt had assumed from what Jefferson said not that he should moderate his behavior to accommodate competing views, but that one side or the other was going to wind up defeated or dead, which was the way of things in France.

He would not know it for some time, but that is exactly what was happening then in Paris, as the man who had written his instructions, along with more than a few of his fellow Brissotins, having lost to Robespierre and the Montagnards, were in prison and on their way to the guillotine.*

Someone once said that wherever you find a philosopher you will find a long-suffering spouse. Perhaps the same is true of revolutionaries. It was certainly true of the Lafayettes. Even her deep religious conviction cannot explain how Adrienne could remain so devoted to a man who had sailed to war on another continent, leaving her at sixteen with one child and another on the way; who had had at least two very public affairs; and whose career choices seemed always to be both life-threatening and a complete surprise to her. This observation is no doubt somewhat anachronistic and overdrawn. His flight to America had made him a hero, after all; everyone had affairs in eighteenth-century Paris (which would have erased the social stigma if not her sadness and sense of personal betrayal); and as frantically worried about him as she often was, during the war in America and on the streets of Paris, she never asked him to change. On the contrary, she is often quoted as saying she loved him for his courage, never more than when he demonstrated the courage of his convictions, even when they were convictions she did not share. In any case, when her love for him and a great deal more than that was tested, Adrienne demonstrated an almost inhuman strength of character and an unmatched qual-

---

*Citizen Genêt never returned to France. Justifiably fearful for his life at the hands of the Jacobin regime, he sought asylum in America, which was granted. Having already married Governor George Clinton's daughter Cornelia, he took up the life of a gentleman farmer in an estate on the Hudson River, where they raised six children and where he died in July 1834, a few months after Lafayette, at the age of seventy-one. All he wanted, he wrote Cornelia in 1794, was "to settle in a country where a man who obeyed the law had nothing to fear."

ity of devotion. That test began on August 19, 1792, when he crossed into enemy territory from his even more threatening homeland.

When he left them for the war, Adrienne and the children had stayed at Chavaniac, away from the tumults of Paris. Knowing of his outspoken opposition to the Jacobins, she thought after the events of August 10 that he might have been arrested and even executed as a counterrevolutionary traitor. At the end of August she found out he had left the country, which at least meant he was probably still alive; and some weeks later she got her first letter from him, which had obviously been written the day after he was first stopped at the Austrian front line, by now almost two months in the past. "I cannot believe that our captors will have the dishonesty to confine [us] for long," he wrote. He was hoping to get to England, and then to America, where as a family they would "find the liberty which no longer exists in France, and my love shall try as best it can to console you for all the happiness you have lost."

Just days after he wrote that, however, Lafayette was separated from everyone who left France with him except for three fellow officers—Latour-Maubourg, Alexandre de Lameth, Bureaux de Pusy—and their servants (aristocracy still had its privileges, at least for the moment). They were sent first into Prussian custody and confined in the fortress prison at Wesel. A note from the duke of Saxe-Teschen, to whom Lafayette had appealed for safe passage, explained why the request was denied:

> As it is you who are responsible for the revolution that has overturned France, as it is you who put your king in irons, despoiled him of all his rights and legitimate powers, and kept him in captivity, as it is you who were the principal instrument of all the disgraces that overwhelm this unhappy monarch, it is only too just that . . . your master, after having recovered his liberty and his sovereignty, can, in his justice or his clemency, decide on your fate.

At Wesel, his servants and fellow officers were imprisoned separately. Lafayette was put in solitary confinement in a damp dungeon cell, and there he spent twenty-four hours of every day being watched by guards on two-hour rotation, deprived of exercise, sunlight, books, and mail. At first he found it difficult to sleep because of the guards' close watch and the rats

After the king's attempted escape, his overweight was no longer considered cuddly. A contemporaneous cartoon depicted him as a leashed pig with the horns of a cuckold.

LOUIS XVI. taking leave of his Wife & Family.

A British artist's cartoon (above) depicted Louis being separated from wife and family on his way to the guillotine. A French royalist's portrayal stressed the pathos of the moment.

On May 31, 1793, the Brissotins were purged from the Assembly. They went to the guillotine that fall, two weeks after Marie-Antoinette. Jacques-Louis David sketched her as she awaited her execution.

Many others were spared when, on July 28, 1794, Robespierre himself met death at the guillotine.

J'ai joué les Français et la divinité....
Je meurs sur l'échafaud je l'ai bien mérité

CIVIC FEAST

A contemporaneous cartoon showed the five-headed Directory extorting America's peace commissioners in 1798 in what was known as the "XYZ Affair," after which there were many fewer Francophiles in America.

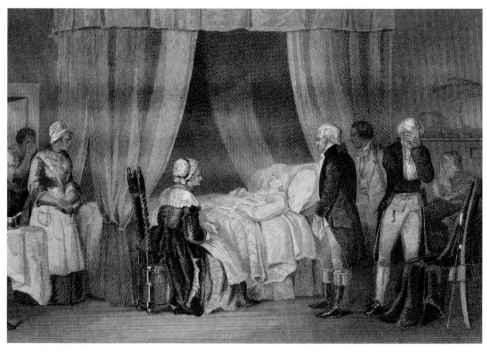

John Reuben Chapin's engraving of the scene at Washington's deathbed.

The Apotheosis of Washington, by Edwin David.

By the end of their captivity, Lafayette and his family were known simply as "the Prisoners of Olmütz" and were melodramatically commemorated on stage and in print.

Lafayette and Adrienne spent their last years together at La Grange, which was her inheritance from her mother. After she died on Christmas Eve 1807, Lafayette closed off her room to everyone but himself. He visited it often and wore Adrienne's portrait on a pendant until his own death twenty-eight years later.

In a portrait commemorating his visit to the United States in 1824–25, Lafayette was depicted as the last living general of the Revolutionary War.

In the final *beau geste* of his life, Lafayette wrapped the duc d'Orléans in a tricolor flag, embraced him, and kissed him on the forehead—coronation by a "republican kiss," as Chateaubriand described it later. The "July Monarchy" of Louis-Philippe lasted until the next revolution, which came in 1848.

Lafayette in the park at La Grange, in a portrait by Louise Adéone Joubert.

scurrying about in his cell. The damp cold brought on a fever and chest pain apparently caused by a recurrence of his chronic lung disorder. When he complained of trouble breathing, the prison doctor recommended exercise, but it was forbidden. He and his fellow inmates developed a crude form of signal communication. At one point Latour-Maubourg was convinced that Lafayette was going to die. Permission for a final visit with him was denied.

They had been brought to Wesel by coach. In late December, they were transferred to Magdeburg in a cart, in chains. The open air proved restorative despite the cold, as did their first conversation in three months; but at Magdeburg the cells were dark and damp, the walls thick with mold. Lafayette was once again placed in solitary confinement, and his fever and chest pain returned. He had still received no word of his wife and children, but he was able to bribe a guard for scraps of paper, and by improvising pen and ink with a toothpick and soot, he managed to get letters out. One of them was to be forwarded to the American consul in London, to whom he wrote of his ever more desperate hope that his adopted country would claim him as a citizen: "My physical constitution has almost as much need of liberty as my moral constitution."

In almost every letter he talked of his gratitude for American efforts for his release, but in fact there was still very little the American government could do. Through Jefferson, Washington did express to his ambassadors his "great and sincere" interest in Lafayette's well-being and asked them to do whatever they could, consistent with their responsibilities, to encourage his release. Gouverneur Morris drafted an appeal for Adrienne to send to the king, and William Short sent 10,000 florins, with which Lafayette was at least able to improve the food he and his companions received and bribe the guards to smuggle out his letters.

Finally, whether in response to an appeal by the American minister in London or Adrienne's letter or both, the Prussian king instructed the prison to inform Lafayette that his wife and children were alive and to allow him to write them a letter. Pen and ink were brought to his cell, and with the governor of the prison looking on, he wrote: "I am permitted . . . to certify to you that I am still living." He told her that "Chavaniac," the nickname of one of his servants, was being permitted to visit him during several hours of the day. "We talk of our village and our fellow-citizens.

Please give six louis to his father the tailor. . . ." Though he could not see his other servant, Felix, "I am assured that he is as well as such a situation will permit." At that, he said, "Monsieur le Commandant, who watches me write, must find the time long. I kiss you as tenderly as I love you." Adrienne probably never received this letter. By the time he wrote it, she was in prison herself.

Less than a month after Lafayette escaped to Austria, soldiers arrived at Chavaniac with orders from the Convention in Paris: "The woman Lafayette is to be arrested, together with her children if they are found with her, and confined in a house of detention." Making an excuse to get away from the soldiers for a moment, Adrienne managed to hide ten-year-old Virginie with one of the servants, but the men had already seen Anastasie, now fourteen, and Lafayette's aged Aunt Chavaniac refused to let Adrienne and her niece be imprisoned without her. (George, then thirteen, had already been sent to the mountains, disguised as a peasant, to live with a local priest.

The three women were taken to the nearby village of Le Puy and there, under custody of the municipal authority, were allowed to stay in the city hall rather than a prison. By appealing directly to Brissot, Adrienne managed to have her confinement changed to house arrest at Chavaniac and finally to have her arrest lifted completely at the end of 1792; but the authorities in Paris were not finished with Lafayette, whose fortune and property were confiscated. Adrienne would then have been virtually penniless but for the kindness of family and friends, including not only George Washington but also Gouverneur Morris, who made her a personal loan of 100,000 livres.

During 1793, her prospects continued to decline with the fall of the Brissotins and the ascent of the Mountain. After the king's execution and the declaration of war on England, Holland, and Spain that followed, the Montagnards worked relentlessly to consolidate their hold on power, notably with a wholesale purge of the Brissotin leadership, who were excoriated, then arrested, tried, and found guilty of counterrevolutionary treason. The Brissotin leadership, including Brissot, followed Marie-Antoinette to the guillotine by two weeks in the early fall of 1793.

With the Brissotin leaders dead and their faction discredited, the Mountain began to enact a rigorous agenda to take hold of both the Convention and the nation itself, a program that would lead to a despotism in the name of the people that was far more severe than any Bourbon king's. Its Committee of Public Safety set up nationwide "watch committees" to carry out "domiciliary visits" aimed at ferreting out "suspects" from their hiding places; they were to be "run to earth in their burrows by day and by night." Local authorities were instructed to arrest anyone who "either by their conduct, their contacts, their words or their writings, showed themselves to be supporters of tyranny . . . or to be enemies of liberty." This would include all former nobles "who have not constantly manifested their attachment to the revolution." Family members of the émigrés were especially large targets for suspicion, at a time when suspicion meant arrest, and arrest meant execution.

The Terror, which was declared "the order of the day" by vote of the Convention on September 5, 1793, did not arrive at Chavaniac until November. Aunt Chavaniac and the children were not arrested because of their age, but Adrienne was taken to a makeshift prison at Brioude, a few miles away. There she was informed that no appeal would be possible this time. She was at least able to see her children occasionally, however, and Virginie and Anastasie made an arrangement with the woman who did the prison laundry to smuggle in notes to their mother.

After six months there, in May 1794, just as the Terror in the capital was approaching its gruesome height, Adrienne received the terrifying news that she was to be transferred to La Force prison in Paris, one of several halfway stations to the guillotine. She said her final farewells to her children, making them promise to try to find their father if she was killed, as she fully and justifiably expected to be.

By the time she arrived at La Force, sixty people a day were going to the guillotine, and many more were pouring into the prisons every day. In part simply to make room for them by putting people more speedily to death, new judges and jurors had recently been hired and a new judicial code put in place that eliminated the need for witnesses and gave juries a choice between only two possible verdicts: acquittal or death.

Adrienne did not know it then, but her older sister Louise, her mother, and her grandmother were confined at the same time in the Luxembourg

Palace, one of Paris's many converted prisons. Two weeks after Adrienne arrived at La Force, they were moved to the Conciergerie, little more than a holding pen for the condemned. Before the guillotine, though, there was a circus trial at the Revolutionary Tribunal, where the ancient maréchale de Noailles, senile and profoundly deaf, probably did not even hear herself accused of being part of conspiracy "to dissolve the National Convention and to assassinate the members of the Committee of Public Safety."

When the judge asked her if she admitted her guilt, she pointed her ear trumpet at him. "What is that you are saying? You must forgive me, Citizen, I am extremely deaf."

"So, you were a deaf conspirator," he said, to great laughter from the court and gallery.

That was the end of her interrogation. Adrienne's mother and sister were not questioned at all. The jury dutifully declared that it was their "sincere and honest" opinion that all of the Noailles should be executed as traitors. They were held over until six o'clock that evening, when the tumbrels began the evening shuttle to the place de la Révolution.

Adrienne did not hear about any of this until some time later when the family confessor, a non-juring priest named Père Carrichon, visited her at La Force disguised as a carpenter. He had followed them to the scaffold, he told her, watching them from a discreet distance. The maréchale was in the first cart, writhing on the hard bench, trying to keep her balance as her hands were tied behind her. He could see that the back of her neck had been shaved. Adrienne's mother had a blue-striped shawl over her shoulders, and Louise was wearing a white dress. Despite the fact that it was evening, it was very hot, and then it began to rain. He told Adrienne that he had caught their eye as they got close to the guillotine, and that when they saw him give them absolution, he "was struck by their look of . . . serenity."

Forty-five people were to be killed that night, and they were formed up by the guillotine in rows. The maréchale was taken third, Carrichon remembered, and Adrienne's mother, who was tenth, looked "pleased to know that she was to die before her daughter." All he remembered beside a shocking amount of "bright red blood" spurting from heads and necks that night was that both Adrienne's mother and her sister Louise were wearing hats that were pinned in place. He noticed that because both times, when the executioner ripped them off, they winced.

XXIV

Between Scylla and Charybdis

ADRIENNE WAS SPARED the guillotine only because Robespierre's execution came not long after that of her grandmother, mother, and sister. The very citizens whom Robespierre, as president of the Convention, had encouraged the previous fall to undertake a Reign of Terror that would ferret out "hidden domestic . . . enemies of the state"—people who had suggested that France needed guillotines on wheels to wipe out nameless "monsters . . . these reptiles who corrupt everything they touch"—these very same men were found by Robespierre only a few months later to lack sufficient revolutionary "virtue" to be allowed to live. "In the system of the French Revolution," he intoned, "what is immoral is impolitic, and what corrupts is counter revolutionary. Weakness, vices, and prejudices are the high road to monarchy." In the spring of 1794, having become increasingly obsessed with wiping out the slightest taint of corruption among his co-revolutionists, Robespierre had sent even such former allies as Danton and Desmoulins to the guillotine.

When it was clear that no one would be safe from his revolutionary conscience, the demise of Robespierre was inevitable. Many of those who took part in the Thermidorian Reaction* were the accomplices of his crimes and showed no more concern for justice than he had. One day after he was denounced in the Convention, he and twenty-one of his associates

*So called for the date on the revolutionary calendar when the Convention turned against Robespierre, which was 9 Thermidor (July 27, 1794).

went to the guillotine without even the pretense of a trial. After that, hundreds of Jacobins were hunted down and murdered in the so-called White Terror. Once the Convention gave way to the new government of a five-member Directory, however, the domestic bloodletting, at least, was over.* By early 1795, most of the former "suspects" were released from prison.

Adrienne's fourteen months of imprisonment came to an end that January. Paper-thin and profoundly weak, she was nursed back to health by the new American minister James Monroe and his wife at their large house in Paris. Monroe had worked hard to gain her release, as Morris had before him. The president's letter congratulating her on her freedom was as diplomatically opaque about her husband as ever—"To touch on the case of M. de La Fayette in this letter would be . . . as unavailing as it would be inexpedient"—but Monroe explained to her the ways in which Washington had been trying informally to encourage Lafayette's release, and he persuaded her to send her son George into Washington's care in America. Monroe arranged for a passport, and George left that summer.

As for herself, Adrienne had long ago determined that if she survived, she and her daughters would try to join Lafayette in his confinement at Olmütz, a prison in Austria where he had been taken the previous spring. Since confiscated property was now being restored to the families of those killed in the Terror, she first needed to spend some time trying to secure her mother's estate. With loans from family, friends, and Monroe, she also managed to repay the many creditors who had supported her daughters and Aunt Chavaniac in her absence.

Finally that summer she could turn to plans for the journey to Austria. Monroe helped her get passports out of France, but the process was lengthy, and they did not leave until September. Even then, they left not knowing if they would ever actually reach Olmütz since their passports were valid only for passage to America, not Austria. In the end, Monroe managed to find an American packet leaving from Dunkirk that would make a stop in Hamburg, where the American consul could have new

---

*The government of the Executive Directory continued the French revolutionary wars in Europe in part as a way of maintaining itself in power, which eventually caused millions of casualties. The Directory's war policy also prepared the way for its successful General Bonaparte, who replaced the Directory and declared the Consulate in the coup of 18 Brumaire (Nov. 9, 1799).

passports made out to the Motiers of Hartford, Connecticut (one of the states in which Lafayette had been given citizenship). The consul there also gave them money for a carriage to Vienna.

"I am on my way to you," Adrienne wrote to her husband then. "Our little daughters . . . are with me. . . . Our son is in Boston. I have had news of his safe arrival, which makes me happier than I can say." She would wait until she saw him, she wrote, to explain her reasons for doing everything she had done and to bring him up to date on "all that has happened."

There was a great deal indeed to tell a man who had been out of contact with the world from the fall of 1792 until the fall of 1795—everything from the September Massacres and the execution of the royal family through the Terror to the fall of Robespierre—but some of the news was closer to home. This letter is one of the very few in all of her preserved correspondence that expresses displeasure with her husband. Though she did not mention it, she had formed a close friendship with Mme de Simiane, who had also emerged destitute from prison not long after Robespierre's execution. "I am persuaded that you have not always been fair to me," she said, and that vague suggestion of disquiet was all she ever said about Lafayette's long affair, at least in writing.

In Vienna, Noailles family connections among the Austrian nobility were able to get Adrienne an audience with Emperor Francis II, who was polite if not warm. "As far as his freedom is concerned . . . my hands are tied," he said, apparently meaning that he had made an agreement with the Prussian king to keep Lafayette captive, but he agreed to allow Adrienne and her daughters to join him in Olmütz. "You will find Monsieur de La Fayette well fed, well treated. I hope that you will do me the justice to agree. . . . In these prisons, inmates are referred to only by their numbers, but your husband's name is well known."

Lafayette was "Prisoner No. 2," and his imprisonment at Olmütz was the harshest yet, an eloquent expression of the European monarchs' common loathing for him. There was virtually no light in his cell, and nearby latrines and an open sewer thickened the still air with stench. His fellow officers and servants were kept separate from him and each other, and all of his possessions were taken away, including his watch, shoe buckles, and razor, despite his promise that he would never oblige his captors by killing himself. At one point when his health declined dangerously, he was allowed outside, but after a botched attempt to escape he was kept in his cell twenty-four hours a day. His door was opened only to deliver gruel crawling with insects, and he was not allowed so speak even to his guards.

Only when the driver of their carriage turned around to point out the towers of Olmütz in the distance did Adrienne break down at the prospect before them. Anastasie later remembered her mother saying to her and her sister, but mostly to herself, "How we will endure the ordeal before us I do not know."

Lafayette had been at Olmütz for almost eighteen months and in captivity for more than three years when his family arrived, and they barely recognized him. He had turned completely gray, his gaunt face was deeply lined, and he was beyond haggard. He had no shoes, and his clothes had turned to rags. After tearful embraces, the girls settled into the room they would share with their mother, and Adrienne began to tell Lafayette about what had happened since they last saw each other.

He had heard little beyond rumors, and of course he would have wanted to know everything, especially news of former friends and colleagues, whose various fates told the story of the Revolution from the time he had left it at the start of the war. Lafayette could not help cheering the French victories in the field, which were largely the result of huge nationwide mobilizations—by this time the French had an army of well over a million men in the field, three quarters of them fully trained and equipped—but he could only have been appalled at the cost of repressing opposition to the forced recruitments: a thousand dead in Toulon, two thousand in Lyons, more than three thousand in Nantes, ten thousand in the most rebellious departments of the Vendée, most of them killed while running away. Perhaps half a million people had been incarcerated as "suspects" at one time or another, and up to ten thousand may have died just from prison overcrowding. By comparison, the toll of the guillotine at the place de la Révolution in Paris, which took 2,639 lives between March 1793 and October 1794, was paltry. History recalls the violence in Paris more vividly perhaps because it took the lives of the royal family, high aristocrats, and so many of the principal players of the Revolution, but the vast majority of its victims were not famous, not noble, not churchmen, but so-called ordinary people.

Apart from those who had become émigrés, most of the people

Lafayette knew well from Versailles and Paris, friend and enemy, had either fled France or had been consumed in the Terror by the time Adrienne joined him in prison. Not all of the Revolution's victims died on the scaffold—Condorcet committed suicide in prison, La Rochefoucauld was torn apart by a mob—but most did die that way, from his nemesis d'Orléans to Revolutionary War comrades such as d'Estaing to his partner in government Bailly, for whom a special guillotine was built on the site of the Champs de Mars Massacre.* As discouraging as anything to Lafayette was the news that all the bloody spasms of revolutionary politics had resulted only in a massively apathetic electorate victimized by tiny, passionately antagonistic minorities, a recipe for repression that in fact took place not long after Adrienne and her daughters left Paris.

A s the violence of the French Revolution increased, American reaction to it became correspondingly more intense. Citizen Genêt's outrageous incursions on American sovereignty made him and his revolution a host of dedicated Federalist enemies, but his Republican friends were more demonstrative, sometimes violently so. Years later John Adams remembered the "terrorism" Genêt inspired with his crowd-pleasing appeals to republican egalitarianism, when "ten thousand people in the streets of Philadelphia day after day threatened to drag Washington out of his house," and Adams had guns brought over from the War Department so that he could defend his own house if necessary. Very consciously, and with an adeptness that even the Robespierrist government appreciated,

---

*One of the exceptions was his co-Mesmerist Nicolas Bergasse. After the king's flight to Varennes, he became an adviser to Louis XVI. His advice was to crack down hard: The king should, among other things, refuse to sign the Constitution. Later the same year Bergasse married into the old nobility, consummating his acceptance by the social hierarchy he had once so despised. After the king's dethronement, when his correspondence with Louis XVI was discovered, he tried to flee France. Captured and denounced, he was kept in prison for more than two years until his case was heard before the post-Robespierre revolutionary tribunal, which dismissed the charges against him. He went on to become an ardent supporter of the Bourbon Restoration and the most reactionary policies of both Louis XVIII and Charles X. After the Revolution of 1830, fearing for his safety because he had spoken out so forcefully against popular sovereignty, he withdrew from public life.

Genêt helped to bring the French Revolution into the heart of American politics and, precisely as he intended, to infuse it with popular energy. Beginning in Philadelphia, so-called Democratic-Republican societies sprang up around the country in sympathy. Washington was convinced that they were all the result of Genêt's subversive strategy, that they were even behind the violence of the previous summer's Whiskey Rebellion in western Pennsylvania, a tax revolt by distillers and their sympathizers that Washington put down by force. He may have been wrong about the source of that rebellion, but he was not alone. As an editorialist in the *Newark Gazette* put it, "Brissot begat the Jacobin clubs of Paris, the Jacobin clubs of Paris begat Genêt and his French brethren. . . . Genêt begat the Democratic Societies in America; and the Democratic Societies begat the Pittsburgh [Whiskey] Rebellion and its consequences."

Since to be pro-France was to be anti-Britain, the Democratic-Republican clubs inherited the revolutionary ardor and fighting spirit of 1776; and the British cooperated with the Republicans and confounded their Federalist friends with increasingly flagrant anti-American behavior, not only inciting Indian massacres of western settlers (from forts they were supposed to have vacated since the peace treaty of 1783) but also seizing American ships carrying goods to France and French possessions, which effectively eliminated all trade with the French West Indies. In no time hundreds of American ships were rocking at anchor in Britain's Caribbean ports, and thousands of American seamen were impressed into British service.

Washington's fury at such behavior was exceeded only by his determination to maintain the peace. To fierce and widespread scorn, he sent John Jay to London to negotiate a treaty. The negotiation was undercut by Hamilton, who was so intent on conciliation with the British and so convinced of the importance of British trade to the success of his fiscal program that he gave away the American positions in secret talks with a British diplomat. As a result, the treaty was so one-sided that Washington decided to keep its terms secret until it had been confirmed by the Senate. Inevitably there was a leak, and congressional debate, as Washington feared, was prolonged and complicated by bitter denunciations of the treaty as a humiliating surrender to America's old oppressor, a betrayal of the Revolution itself. Waves of mass demonstrations ensued in the months that followed, some of them violent. When Hamilton tried to speak for the treaty at a meeting in New York, he was hit in the head by a stone, and a group that peeled off from his audience ended up marching with a group of French sailors under a French flag to John Jay's house, in front of which they burned a copy of the treaty. Another mob in Philadelphia burned it on the front steps of the British minister's house, breaking a few windows for good measure. Jay later said that the whole East Coast was lit up every night by the blazes coming from his effigies. A parade in Philadelphia carried a life-sized figure of him captioned: "Come up to my price, and I will sell you my Country."

The connection between these popular uprisings and those in France was proud and explicit, as was American Francophiles' support for the street violence in France. The *North Carolina Gazette* was not alone in popularizing Joel Barlow's latest song, to the tune of "God Save the King": "God save the guillotine,/ 'Till England's King and Queen/ Her power shall prove:/ 'Till each anointed knob/ Affords a clipping job,/ Let no vile halter rob/ The Guillotine."

Washington seemed once again caught in the middle, because that is where he was. Francophiles accused him of being a monarchist and Anglophile, and (though less often and with less venom) Anglophiles accused him of being a Francophile. "This government, in relation to France and England," he wrote in the summer of 1795, "may be compared to a ship between the rocks of Scylla and Charybdis. There is but one straight course."

That course was made no easier to hold by the partisans in Washington's midst, only some of whom he knew about. Mutual suspicion among the advocates of France and Britain had turned executive politics rancid. "Our Jacobins mediate serious mischief to certain individuals," Alexander Hamilton wrote to his successor at Treasury, Oliver Wolcott, one day that summer. A letter from Wolcott that crossed in the mail told Hamilton of a suspected breach at the highest level: "Everything is conducted in a mysterious and strange manner by a certain character here. . . . Some curious facts . . . have recently come to my knowledge. I cannot but suspect foul play. . . ." Two days before he wrote to Hamilton, Wolcott had dined with the British minister, who handed him a packet of dispatches that the crew of a captured French vessel had thrown overboard and a British sailor had dived in to retrieve. In them Wolcott was shocked to read the French ambassador reporting to his minders in Paris on contacts with Edmund Randolph, who had replaced Jefferson as Washington's secretary of state. In reports that had obviously been prepared at the time of the Whiskey Rebellion, Randolph was said to have encouraged support for the Pittsburgh rebels by the Democratic-Republican Society of Philadelphia, "which in its turn influenced those of other states." Far more worrisome was the strong implication that Randolph had solicited a bribe to encourage further violent resistance among the rebels. "Thus, with some thousands of dollars the republic would have decided on civil war or peace!" the French minister boasted to his minders in Paris. He had refused the solicitation, he said, and was contemptuous of help from such quarters: "The consciences of the pretended patriots of America have already their prices."

Randolph resigned on August 19, and his guilt or innocence has been a subject of scholarly research and argument ever since. What has never been in question is that the poisonous acrimony between Anglophiles and Francophiles contaminated Washington's most intimate circle even after Jefferson and Hamilton were gone, not only costing him another secretary of state and one of his oldest friends but also leaving in place a host of other schemers whose behavior in another era would have been branded as disloyalty that bordered on treason.

A week after Randolph resigned, the ship carrying fifteen-year-old George Washington Lafayette weighed anchor in Boston Harbor. He could hardly have come at a worse time. The letter in which he introduced himself to Washington arrived in early September, and though Washington knew he was on his way, he was plainly thrown off by the news. "[H]ow can I be useful to him?" he lamented to the Federalist Senator George Cabot of Massachusetts, who agreed that Washington could not take him in at a time when the very word "Lafayette" was a synonym for revolution to the British and the worst sort of anti-revolutionary royalism to the French. Washington asked Cabot to take charge of the boy for the time being, to see that he was admitted to Harvard, and to send Washington the bills. He would undertake to be his "father, friend, protector and supporter," he promised, but for now Cabot should make sure that this remained confidential, since publicity would be "disastrous."

The thought of having abandoned the boy clearly gnawed at Washington, however, and when he heard in mid-November that George had not entered Harvard but instead had come to New York and was waiting for an invitation to Philadelphia, he wrote Hamilton that "unless some powerful reasons can be suggested to the contrary," he was going to take George in "at once." Hamilton replied immediately that it would be interpreted as a show of antipathy to the revolution in France at a time when Jay's Treaty was still weighing in the balance in Congress and needed all the Republican votes it could get. Washington took his advice and now wrote George directly, but carefully. "[L]et me begin with fatherly advice" he said, advising George to "apply closely to your studies. Your youth should be usefully employed. . . ." He also confessed that they were being kept apart by "considerations of a political nature," but promised to bring him to Philadelphia "as soon as they shall have ceased. . . ." Clearly conflicted, Washington wrote Hamilton again the day after he sent that letter off. "I am distrustful of my own judgment," he said, ". . . lest my feelings carry me further [than my] public character will warrant."

He could not get George out of his mind. In December, he told Hamilton the thought of young Lafayette "gives me pain . . . his sensibility, I fear, is hurt." Some time later, he was "continually uneasy. . . ." Finally, in late February 1796, he could no longer refrain from inviting George to join him, and a week after he extended the invitation he got political cover: A member of the House, having heard rumors that Lafayette's son was in the United States, moved that he be found and provisioned as necessary. Washington was deeply grateful. He wrote Madison that although he considered the matter so sensitive that no congressman before had ever "heard me lisp a syllable on this subject," he and young Lafayette had been in touch, his mother having sent the boy into his care. At the end of March, Washington's letter of invitation had apparently not reached George, so he wrote another, telling George to come "immediately to this city and to my house, where a room is prepared for you." His feelings for George's father were "too strong not to extend themselves to you," he said. "Therefore believe me to be, as I really am, sincerely and affectionately yours. . . ."

.   .   .

During the next two years, Washington's last years in office, George became almost as close to Washington as the boy's father had been. Always accompanied by the tutor who had come with him from France, George went to Mount Vernon when the president did and stayed with him in Philadelphia, their relationship untouched by continuing rancor between pro-French and pro-British Americans and a nearly complete breakdown in French-American relations. Other than Martha, George was in fact among the very few relationships Washington allowed himself in those rancorous times, when he was betrayed by some of the people he had once most trusted.

The month of July 1796 brought to light a string of such treacheries. Because of leaks that turned up in the Republican press, especially Bache's rabid *Aurora*, Washington had come to suspect that James Monroe was funneling confidential diplomatic dispatches from Paris to Madison and Jefferson that would be favorable to the pro-French cause in America; and now he learned that he was right. He had in his hands an essay that Monroe had written, the first of a planned series for the *Aurora*, to alert readers to the "actual state of things" in France. Monroe suggested to the editor that, to shield his identity, they might be made to seem to come from different people, one time "a gentleman from Paris," another "from Bordeaux, that it may not appear to be a regular thing." The first installment was about the furor that Jay's Treaty was causing in France. After a grace period that was inexplicably long, Monroe was recalled.

Later that month, Washington received a plaintive letter from Jefferson at Monticello swearing that he was not the source of a document recently leaked to the *Aurora*, an old memo from the president to his first-term cabinet listing the thirteen questions he wished to address before drafting the Neutrality Proclamation. One of them was whether the 1778 Treaty of Alliance with France could or should be abrogated, which would confirm Republicans' long-held suspicion that Washington had intended to favor Britain all along. Washington knew that only five people had ever had copies of that agenda, and he knew as well that Jefferson had never kept his sympathies to himself. Without addressing the leak, Washington bid Jefferson a not very roundabout farewell.

Until within the last year or two ago, I had no conceptions that parties would . . . go to the length I have been witness to; nor did I believe until lately that . . . while I was using my utmost exertions to establish a national character of our own, independent . . . I should be accused of being the enemy of one nation and subject to the influence of another; and to prove it, that every act of my administration would be tortured and the grossest and most insidious misrepresentations of them be made . . . in such exaggerated and indecent terms as could scarcely be applied to a Nero, a notorious defaulter, or even to a common pickpocket.

That was the last letter of substance from Washington that Jefferson ever received.

In the same month, Thomas Paine delivered perhaps the unkindest, certainly the most intentionally vicious cut of all. After publishing *The Rights of Man*, he had moved to Paris, become a French citizen, joined the Brissotin faction of the Jacobins, and was elected to the Convention. In a purge of second-level Brissotins, he was imprisoned with seventy others. After Robespierre's execution, they were released with all the other "suspects" in custody at the end of 1794. Paine credited Monroe with saving him from the guillotine and vilified Washington for not having claimed him as an American citizen (despite the fact that he was British). In a screed of several thousand words, all of them lovingly published in the *Aurora*, he attempted to discredit every aspect of Washington's career, going back all the way to the Jumonville massacre and moving slowly forward, charging Washington with having been a bumbling and mendacious failure as a general, as a founding father, and as president. The tone was so venomous that it probably won Washington as much sympathy as anything else, but it cannot have been pleasant for him to read, for example: "As to you, sir, treacherous in private friendship . . . and a hypocrite in public life, the world will be puzzled to decide, whether you are an apostate or an impostor; whether you have abandoned good principles, or whether you ever had any." Washington's vine and fig tree had never looked so appealing.

Washington's next annual address to Congress, which came in December 1796, was his last. He took the occasion of his final appearance before the Congress to plead one last time for two of his most cherished personal projects: a national university and a military academy. He called for subsidies for agriculture research and better pay for government officials so that public service would not "exclude . . . talents and virtue unless accompanied by wealth." He also proposed that America build a real navy, without which, as recent experience had shown, the nation could not defend its shipping and its neutrality at the same time. As to foreign policy, he was pleased to report a complete reform of British-American relations. Thanks to Jay's Treaty, the British had evacuated the western forts, British-American commerce was healthier than ever, and British ships once more respected the U.S. flag.

The problem now was with the French, who had begun violating American-flagged ships as brazenly as the British had before. Partially in response to Jay's Treaty but at least equally for the prize money, they were pursuing a "clandestine" war on American shipping, relying on technicalities in the Treaty of 1778 to justify the seizure of American merchant ships. "Our trade has suffered and is suffering extensive injuries in the West Indies from the cruisers and agents of the French republic," he said, and as badly as he wanted peace and friendship with France, it could not come at the expense of "the rights and honor of our country." The British minister's wife, a good friend of Washington's who was sitting near the lectern, recalled later "the extreme agitation he felt when he mentioned the *French*. He is, I believe, much enraged. . . ." Another close friend, Eliza Powell, wrote Martha that morning that she was sending over a strong stomach remedy, some "true Martinique noyan . . . I think it would not be amiss if my good friend the President will take a glass on his return from Congress."

Washington concluded this last address to Congress on a happier note, reflecting on the precarious beginnings of America's first constitutional government in 1789, "and I cannot omit to congratulate you and my country on the success of the experiment."

Given that his ultimate goal had always been the emergence of a uniquely American character, however—of a distinctive and respected American*ism* that was respected as such at home and abroad—he cannot have been sanguine as he left office. Thanks to the Electoral College system then in effect, the elections of 1796 had ended by bottling two scorpions in the executive branch, arch-Federalist John Adams as president with the arch-Republican vice president Thomas Jefferson. That divided executive reflected with painful precision the contending forces in the nation itself, which as Washington left office was being pulled apart by the opposing poles of France and England as never before.

By the time Washington spoke, French privateers had captured more than three hundred American-flagged vessels and had tortured at least one American captain to extract a confession that he was carrying legally proscribed (i.e., British) goods. As a result, John Adams had one of the shortest presidential honeymoons in American history. On May 16, 1797, only eight weeks after his inauguration, he announced to a special session of Congress that France had refused to recognize the credentials of Monroe's replacement as American minister, effectively breaking off relations. France's "depredations on our commerce, the personal injuries to our citizens, and the general complexion of our affairs," Adams declared, "render it my duty to recommend to your consideration effectual measures of defense." He urgently seconded Washington's call for a strong American navy at the same time that he appointed a new three-member commission to go to Paris in an attempt to divert the clear direction of events.

The peace mission sailed a few weeks after his speech, and Adams might actually have thought it a reason for optimism when he heard two months later that the ever dexterous ex-noble and ex-bishop Talleyrand, after years as an exile in America, had turned up in Paris again that summer as France's newly appointed minister of foreign affairs.

The conservative coup that spelled the end of Robespierre and ended the Terror had installed a five-man government called the Directory. It was barely more democratic than Robespierre's regime, paying only selective attention to a bicameral legislature consisting of the Council of Five Hundred and a smaller body called the Elders. It was relatively nonviolent toward the citizens of France, however, and represented a welcome change to many former exiles.

When they reached out for Talleyrand to be foreign minister, he could not believe his good luck. He had spent the last two years of his exile in Philadelphia, where he became friendly enough with Hamilton to know that one of his reasons for leaving Washington's cabinet and returning to his law practice in New York was to make money. He was shocked at the idea. In France, in his view, that of his fellow ministers, and most of its five-man Directory, making money was the best reason of all to sign up for government service, and he saw his appointment to the foreign ministry as the main chance. "I'll hold the job," Talleyrand told friends, "and I have to make an immense fortune out of it, a really immense fortune."

XXV

Farewells

NOTHING HAD YET BEEN heard from Adams's peace commissioners and Washington had been out of office for six months when the Lafayettes were suddenly released from prison, along with Latour-Maubourg, Bureaux de Pusy, Alexandre de Lameth, and their servants. They had all been in the same prison, but Lafayette had not seen them and they had not seen each other in more than three years. They were given no time to pack, but they had nothing to pack anyway, and Adrienne may have wished to spirit Lafayette out of Olmütz before he could change his mind. Two months before, they had been offered their freedom if Lafayette would agree to leave Austria and never return. His sense of honor and liberty offended, he refused.

His captors dropped the demand for a variety of reasons. Adrienne had written cleverly politic letters to the new government of the Directory that flattered them with hints that Lafayette might approve of the regime and assured them he knew that coming back to France would be premature even if he were to be released. At the same time the Directory may have felt somewhat embarrassed, with their victorious General Bonaparte virtually dictating terms of peace to Europe in the talks at Campo Fornio, at having one of their most famous citizens languishing in an Austrian prison. The "prisoners of Olmütz" had actually become something of a *cause célèbre* in Paris, where theatergoers were weeping to a new play about them in which the dashing Bonaparte rescues the enfeebled hero and his sacrificially devoted wife and daughters on the brink of death. From this combination of motives, the Directory instructed Bonaparte: "We desire to have these prisoners . . . freed without delay. All facilities must be given them to travel, if they wish, to North America, without, however, passing through France."

All of the prisoners of Olmütz were relatively unscathed by the ordeal of imprisonment except for Adrienne, who at the age of thirty-six was a very sick woman. She had been feverish for virtually all of the past three years, she suffered from varicose ulcers and edema, and eczema had opened sores on her legs, which had been stiff and swollen for so long she could barely move them. The prison doctor at one point said it was imperative that she be sent away for treatment, but the emperor ruled that if she left she could not return, and she could not be persuaded under those conditions to go. Because of Adrienne's health, the caravan of carriages that left Olmütz had to move very slowly across the Austrian countryside toward their destination, which was Hamburg.

From newspapers in Dresden they learned that there had been yet another change of government in Paris in recent days. Three of the five Directors had ordered the arrest of the other two, annulled recent elections, purged the legislature of suspected royalists, and closed down thirty right-wing newspapers. Even before the prisoners of Olmütz had reached Hamburg, a courier from two other would-be directors (one of them Lafayette's fellow revolutionary of 1789, the abbé Sieyès) arrived with the proposal that he return to France and take a somewhat vague but assuredly rightful place in French governance—"as if it were necessary for me to be advised of the ease with which I might have exploited popular enthusiasm, the devotion of the National Guard and all that." The man so often accused of a sentimental weakness for acclaim was prompted to reflect "that men of sentiment are not always as stupid as [more ambitious people] think."

Some time later he was asked officially for his opinion of the new regime and he was told that his answer would be reported back to Paris. Lafayette's precise language is not recorded, but the answer so infuriated the government that they ordered his estate in Brittany to be sold at auction, depriving him of the last property that still remained to him in France or anywhere else.

The prisoners of Olmütz were to be officially handed over from Austrian custody to the American consul in Hamburg, John Parish, who over many long hours had negotiated the details of their release and secured an asylum for them in Danish Holstein. On their way to Parish's house, they were followed through Hamburg by an increasingly large and enthusiastic crowd of well-wishers, so that by the time they arrived there in late afternoon, they had to struggle their way through a crush. Once safe inside, Lafayette embraced Parish—"Oh great friend! Our deliverer!"—while behind him, Adrienne collapsed on a couch. "Look at my poor, poor wife," Lafayette said to Parish, and sat down beside her; and only then did the family give themselves over to the psychological enormity of what had just happened to them. Lafayette broke down, then Adrienne and the girls, and for a long time they just sat on the couch speechless, crying and holding one another.

During the handover ceremony, the Austrian government made a point of saying that Lafayette had been released as a favor to the United States and not the French government. Lafayette politely declined to accept that, as much as he would have liked to believe it. He thought the Austrians were only trying to save face, and he was almost certainly right. Gouverneur Morris, who was at the handoff ceremony and was annoyed that the Lafayettes were late for it, "wasting their time and everyone else's," was even more irritated that Lafayette refused to give him the credit that he, certainly, felt he deserved for all the time he had spent in Vienna, most of it waiting for appointments that never happened. Still, when Lafayette wrote Washington on the day before he left Hamburg for Denmark, he expressed thanks for "your constant solicitude in my behalf" and his help in obtaining the release of "my two friends and that part of my family which was not under your immediate protection." Mainly, though, he just wanted to make contact with the man who plainly was still his polestar, in however forgotten English and with whatever jumbled emotions. "[I]n vain I would attempt, my beloved General, to express to you the feelings of my filial heart, when, at the moment of this unexpected restoration to liberty and life, I find myself blessed with the opportunity to let you hear from me—this heart has for twenty years been known to you—words that, whatever they be, fall so short of my sentiments would not do justice to what I feel. . . ." Sensitive to the "politics, so painful to me, although particulars are yet unknown," he also wrote agonized circles around the question of whether America might give asylum to himself and his family. He asked Washington if it would be "not unserviceable" for him to consider whatever "instructions you, or some members of government could perhaps think of sending over. What has been, can be, or is wished to be done I do not know. . . . I know only that my heart is just the same as it has ever been."

Two days after Lafayette wrote that letter, Washington unwittingly answered it. Young George, having got wind that his family were about to be released, insisted on leaving for Europe immediately, despite Washington's worry that he and his parents would cross on the Atlantic. Washington gave George a letter to give his father, which began with an almost guilty denial that he had anything to do with Lafayette's release. He also referred apologetically to "the delicate . . . situation" that had prevented him from taking George in when he first arrived in America. As for himself, he was pleased to report he was finally in "the shades of my vine and fig tree, where I shall remain . . . until the days of my sojournment, which cannot be many." Answering the question he did not know Lafayette had asked, he said that of course the whole family should come to America, where they would be welcomed into the fullness of freedom that had been denied them for so long. Lafayette had "never stood higher in the affections of the people of this country," Washington said.

This invitation, when it came, would be consoling; but as Lafayette considered his options, the truth dawned on him that even if he wanted to take his family to America, he could not afford to buy the tickets. What remained of his fortune after two revolutions had been confiscated by the government, and he was now worse than penniless: He was deep in debt and going deeper every day, living on borrowed money. As he surveyed the alternatives, they were pitifully few, and his current situation was bleak. Besides having no home or property, most of Europe was closed to him, including his native country, and his wife was gravely ill.

Lafayette and the other prisoners of Olmütz stayed for a while with Adrienne's aunt (her father's sister), the comtesse de Tessé, who had emigrated two years before. Having managed to bring her fortune with her in negotiable securities, she had bought a large estate in Holstein, and when Lafayette's party arrived, she was sustaining a fairly large group of émigrés, most of them royalists for whom Lafayette was the incarnate Satan.

Among them was Adrienne's sister Pauline, who remembered Lafayette as "so little changed that, listening to him, one felt oneself grow young again." It was as though he had just emerged from a time capsule, she said. "With him one was always at the Declaration of the Rights of Man and the dawn of the Revolution." Everything after that had been just a mistake. "He had the simple-minded faith and the calm fearlessness of those old navigators who in the sixteenth century set out to explore the world in ill-equipped ships with mutinous crews. He was prepared to go aboard again, should opportunity arise, on the four slightly readjusted planks with which the raft of 1791 had been constructed." After the first few days she tried not to talk politics with him, she wrote, "afraid of losing my temper, and also of hurting him." Pauline's father-in-law would not permit the name Lafayette to be spoken in his presence.

In a few weeks the Lafayettes and the family of Latour-Maubourg found an inexpensive house that they could rent together some distance away, and they were joined by Bureaux de Pusy and his wife and daughter. There, for the first time in his life, Lafayette's customary ebullience gave way to bouts of despair and self-doubt. "I have made many mistakes," he wrote to Mme de Simiane in December, recalling "painful wounds, public and private, that have torn my breast. . . . [M]y political life is finished. I shall be full of life for my friends, and for the public a sort of portrait in a museum or a book in a library." The concept of liberty, he said, "inflames me to-day as it did at nineteen . . . [but] my reason tells me that there will be nothing for me to do." To make money he began to write a memoir, but given his mood it turned not surprisingly into a score-settling exercise, and he wisely set it aside.

In February 1798, George Washington Lafayette finally caught up with his family. His father had not seen him in five years, and George was nineteen now, the age Lafayette had been when he first sailed to America. George came bearing what should have been encouraging news from Paris. He had tried to see Napoleon Bonaparte when he was in the capital. The general, who would soon be with an invasion force on his way to Egypt and was already so much the national hero that the Directory would be pleased to see him go, was not in the capital at the time. His wife Joséphine had given George an audience, however, in which she said, "Your father and my husband should make common cause." George was even more excited by the letter he brought with him from Washington inviting the family to come to America; but by then Lafayette knew very well what a hopeless dream that was, and the thought of Bonaparte's openness to an alliance must have been at least somewhat hopeful.

What otherwise sustained Lafayette in this difficult time was the warmth of his connection with family and friends, and in the spring there were unions of both to celebrate. Joining Lafayette and his group of exiles was Mathieu Dumas, who had served with him in America and had been among his staunchest supporters from the first days of the National Guard to his last days in France. Dumas's brother Delarue had asked to marry the daughter of Beaumarchais, who had pledged the debt America still owed to him as an important part of the bride's dowry. The last time the debt to Beaumarchais had been brought up in the U.S. Congress by Madison on behalf of Jefferson, it was sent for further investigation to the Treasury Department, so Lafayette took the occasion only a few months after his release from prison to write his old friend Hamilton to look into the affair about which "for twenty years I have often heard, yet I know very little." He did not ask for the debt to be repaid but only for the status of the case.

The other wedding that spring was between Latour-Maubourg's younger brother Charles and Lafayette's daughter Anastasie. Although some of the émigrés at Mme de Tessé's were horrified since neither of them had any money, Lafayette and Adrienne were entirely thrilled, and the wedding, coming so soon after the family were free and all together once more, seemed to restore Adrienne's mood and strength.

In prison and as Lafayette nursed her back to health, she and her husband had drawn closer than they had ever been, and Lafayette never felt this fact more keenly than after they agreed, not long after Anastasie's wedding, that she had to leave him and go to Paris for the summer. There was no proscription on nobility by then, and that on her husband did not apply to her. It was critical now that she move to take possession of the estate she had inherited from her mother, a farm called La Grange-Bléneau about forty miles east of Paris, since that was the only home remaining to them in France. Her former housekeeper offered to give Adrienne a room in her small apartment in Paris for as long as she needed. What was happening in the capital when she arrived, however, gave very little grounds for hope that they would be moving back to France any time soon and put going to America out of the question entirely.

O n the first anniversary of Adams's inauguration, when there still had been no word from the peace overture to Paris, Washington wrote to Secretary of War James McHenry: "Are our commissioners [to France] guillotined, or what else is the occasion of their silence?"

As it happened, on that very day, March 4, 1798, five dispatches from the commissioners were delivered to the State Department, four of them in code, a fifth in language plain and disturbing enough for Secretary of State Timothy Pickering to walk it over to the President's House himself.

Adams sent the open dispatch to Congress but kept the coded ones confidential, fearing they would start a stampede toward war. The pro-French Republicans in Congress were infuriated by the statement Adams wrote to accompany the dispatch, which renewed his request for a major increase in defense spending. Jefferson called Adams's response to the dispatch "insane." This had to be some kind of Federalist plot to bring on the war they had wanted all along, he said; the administration had to be hiding something. The Republicans in Congress demanded that Adams show them the rest of the dispatches, and so he did.

The first dispatch said that the French government had rebuffed the commissioners and had declared as official policy that any ship carrying British goods was subject to seizure. All French ports were now closed to ships carrying the flag of neutral nations, in clear violation of the French-American Treaty of 1778. That news was bad enough. The other dispatches were explosive. Three agents representing Talleyrand, identified only as X, Y, and Z in the commissioners' reports, had demanded a *douceur* (bribe) of $250,000 for themselves and Talleyrand and a $10 million loan to the French government to compensate them for President Adams's "insults" in his speech before Congress the previous May. One of the three French agents was quoted as having tried to blackmail the Americans to accept these demands based on "the diplomatic skill of France & the means she possesses in your country . . . to enable her with the French party in America to throw the blame which would attend the rupture of the negotiations on the Federalists. . . . And you may assure yourselves this will be done." After reminding the commissioners also of the military "power and violence" of France, they demanded an answer immediately.

"No!" one of the commissioners blurted out. "No! Not a sixpence!"* Clearly, the peace commission was going nowhere, and one by one the Americans came home.

It took a while for the full impact of the XYZ dispatches to sink in across the country, but once it did, the American Francophiles seemed suddenly to disappear, not so much because they had gone into hiding but because they—not all, but many, if not most—had turned their sense of outrage and betrayal at France's insolent treatment of U.S. diplomats into a fervent American patriotism. All they had tried to argue away or justify before—Citizen Genêt's plan for global domination, his attacks on Washington, the revolutionary Terror, the attacks on the Church and Christianity itself, the privateering, the torture of an American captain—could no longer be ignored; and revulsion at the XYZ Affair united Americans as nothing had done since the Revolution. Adams received "addresses" from 290 groups of merchants, state legislators, fraternal orders, state militias, and small cities and towns pledging their solidarity and readiness to defend the honor of America against the depredations of the French—and they came from every corner of the country, 108 from the mid-Atlantic states, 106 from the South, and 70 from the already strongly Federalist Northeast. They came from farmers and merchants, from cities and from the backcountry. A writer in the *New York Gazette* said people were wrong to think there were only two parties in America, those of Britain and France; there was a third now, stronger than the others, "consisting of principled Americans" who only held in contempt "attachments to any nation" except the United States. A Boston militia captain, quoted in the *City Gazette* just weeks after the XYZ dispatches were made public, spoke for many: "Fellow soldiers, the English have treated us damn'd badly—the French have used us a damn'd deal worse—Now let us take the field and drive them both to hell."

---

*Demonstrations over the XYZ Affair later inspired a more eloquent version of the response: "Millions for defense, not one cent for tribute!"

As Adams had feared, the XYZ Affair made the rush toward war all but unstoppable. Congress, while not yet ready to declare war, passed no fewer than thirty-three defense bills, authorizing spending of more than $10 million. The states followed suit. New York alone voted $1.4 million for armaments and coastal fortifications; private donations of $115,000 were pledged by the citizens of Boston for ships; and similar collections were taken up in communities from Portsmouth, New Hampshire, to Charleston, South Carolina. Volunteer militia units popped up everywhere, including one company of patriotic young women calling themselves the "Federal Amazons" of Baltimore. Young men wrote Adams to explain that their love of liberty had misled them to the French cause but they were no longer deceived. Their fathers got out their old Continental Army uniforms.

The dark side of war fever showed itself soon enough in passage of the Alien and Sedition Acts, disreputable legislation drawn up so that the president could deport French citizens at will and prosecute his critics as traitors. The vortex pulled in Washington as well, leading to an unfortunate coda to his presidency. Among its other reactions to the XYZ Affair, Congress called for raising an army, and Alexander Hamilton wrote Washington to say he hoped he was ready to lead Americans into battle one more time, not incidentally volunteering to be his second in command. Washington agreed, and Adams sent a commission to Mount Vernon in July, saying he only wished he could appoint Washington president. In a letter of gratitude for the confidence Adams had placed in him, Washington said he wanted Hamilton to be his top general. Adams's reply gently reminded Washington that appointments at that level were made by the president. Washington responded that if he could not have Hamilton, he would resign, which forced Adams to give in.

Adams had to give in to a great deal as president, surrounded as he was by a cabinet of like minds that were often unlike his—men who were willing to place their own notions of good policy ahead of their president's. Good Federalists, their notion of sound policy toward France seemed to be reducible to war, or the preparation for war, or whatever best served an alliance with Britain.

That fall he learned from the last commissioner to return from France that Talleyrand had heard about the reaction to the XYZ Affair in Amer-

ica, was appalled by what had happened, and sincerely wanted to negotiate an end to the hostility. Adams's cabinet would have none of it. Secretary of State Pickering and Treasury Secretary Wolcott drafted Adams's
annual address to Congress that year, and their draft reflected the cabinet's
unanimous view that France would have to prove its commitment to
friendship with more than words.

Adams made few changes in the speech, but one of them was critical
both to the United States and his presidency: He said he would send
another mission to Paris if he received the French government's assurance
that they would be received. Hamilton's fellow Federalists were appalled
that Adams, after such an insult to the national honor, would demand so
little. The reactions of Hamilton and Washington, both of whom were in
the gallery and in uniform for Adams's speech, are not recorded, but
Hamilton's mission for his army had in any case moved beyond mere
defense against France. His ambition now was offensive: to add to the territory of the United States by taking Florida and Louisiana from Spain.
Washington had from the beginning limited himself to little more than a
figurehead role in the new American army, and to the extent he gave much
thought to Hamilton's plans at all, his concerns seem to have been more
tactical and administrative than strategic.

In mid-January 1799, Adams's son Thomas returned from abroad with
assurances from his brother John Quincy, then minister to the Netherlands, that Talleyrand was indeed serious about negotiating an end to the
problems with America. That was enough. For once, Adams did not listen to his cabinet. He did not even give them a chance to speak. In the
single most important, courageous, and wise act of his presidency, Adams
drafted a statement, wrote it out in his own hand, and sent it to Congress
by courier. His vice president, Thomas Jefferson, with whom he had not
spoken in a year, was presiding at the time, and opened the message while
the business of the Senate proceeded. Clearly stunned by what he read, he
called an immediate halt to discussion of the matter on the floor to read it
aloud. Based on the receipt of preliminary indications that France was
willing to negotiate, the president declared, "I nominate William Van
Murray, our minister resident at The Hague, to be minister plenipotentiary of the United States to the French Republic." Adams promised that
Murray would "not go to France without direct and unequivocal assur-

ances" that he would be received; but the decision to proceed with peace talks was explosive all the same.

Jefferson saw it immediately for the masterstroke it was, calling it "the event of events. . . . It silences all arguments against the sincerity of France and renders desperate every further effort towards war."

Secretary of State Pickering was aghast. "The honor of this country is prostrated in the dust," he wrote Washington. "God grant that its safety may not be in jeopardy." Washington's reply gave him no satisfaction: "I hope the measure communicated . . . will eventuate beneficially for this Country."

In the months following Adams's peace initiative, Pickering threw every possible roadblock in its way. First he tried to poison Murray against the idea, in an attack on Adams's policy that was as vicious as it was transparent. Murray minced no words, saying that he was pained to lose Pickering's friendship but that his "harsh and ungenerous terms . . . have helped me to bear it." Pickering then told Adams he needed to work out instructions before the commissioners left, something that would take time. A month later, he said Talleyrand's message assuring that the commissioners would be properly received was not sufficiently explicit; and the instructions were still not quite finished. Then he told Adams that a royalist uprising in France had introduced an instability that would surely call for "a temporary suspension of the mission."

Finally Navy Secretary Benjamin Stoddert could stand by no longer and wrote Adams to warn of "artful designing men" who were attempting to thwart his peace initiative. He suggested a meeting of all parties in Trenton, New Jersey, temporary seat of government during a yellow fever epidemic in Philadelphia. Adams, who had been in Quincy, Massachusetts, all summer, agreed and called the meeting. Still undaunted, Pickering sent Adams news from Europe that he said required a postponement of the peace mission, so that "the trouble of your journey may be saved." Adams was not deceived. He had announced the peace initiative in February 1799, almost a year after the XYZ scandal broke. It was now October. Adams went to Trenton. There Hamilton tried one last time to stop him from sending the peace mission, arguing that the British were going to win the war with France and end up restoring the Bourbon monarchy, and that in any case revolutionary France would always be a dangerously unstable ally. Having heard him out, Adams ordered the peace mission to sail without further delay.

Hamilton replied to Lafayette's query about Beaumarchais with a letter that his old friend must have been pained to receive. After saying that he had left the Treasury before the inquiry was finished but was certain the matter must have been resolved by now in Beaumarchais's favor, Hamilton addressed a gulf that he said had come between them. "I frankly confess, I have differed from you," he wrote. Events as early as the September Massacres and the dethronement of the king had "cured me of my good will for the French Revolution," he said. Furthermore, he had "never believed that France can make a republic" and thought that the attempt to do so could only "produce misfortunes. . . . I hold with Montesquieu that a government must be fitted to a nation as much as a coat to the individual . . . that what may be good at Philadelphia may be bad at Paris and ridiculous at Petersburg." Relations between their countries being on the verge of war, the idea of Lafayette's coming to America was unthinkable: "It would be very difficult for you here to steer a course which would not place you in a party and remove you from the broad ground which you now occupy in the hearts of all."

This letter prompted a long reply in which Lafayette defended his principles both from Hamilton and from the successive governments of France, and he wrote several such statements of self-defense to Washington as well. On Christmas Day, 1798, Washington sat down to answer no fewer than six letters from Lafayette, all of the correspondence he had received since Lafayette's release from prison. Most of them had said he would soon be on his way to America, which is why Washington had not answered them before.

The last two letters, which Washington must have just received, said nothing about coming to America. They were written within two weeks of each other and followed closely on his reply to Hamilton. Lafayette could no longer think of coming to America, he told Washington now, because his wife's health was still too precarious. (Her health was less than perfect, to be sure, but as he wrote she was renovating their future home at La Grange, and he was directing her by mail to be quick about it.) Such a delay was "painful" to him, he said, because he felt so strongly that "the beloved shores of America" were the "natural place of my retirement." He assured himself that Washington would explain to his friends why he had not returned already.

At the same time, he left no doubt which side he was on. French military victories were clearly thrilling to him—"every monarch on this continent trembles at the irresistible power of France." All eyes now were "fixed on the Mediterranean," he said, where the "abilities and power of Bonaparte," everywhere victorious, would surely prevail again. (News of Horatio Nelson's very recent victory at the Battle of the Nile had not yet reached him.) He admitted to Washington without apology that "the original plan of the French Revolution [was] to go around the world," and said he had not abandoned hope that this would still be the case, blaming any delay on Europe's monarchs and their "foolish contempt of our national military institution."

Lafayette told Washington he was sorry about the "lamented differences" between the United States and France, the solution to which would require "much liberality and prudence." As much as he respected and cheered the "independence and dignity" of the United States, he hoped the assertion of it in negotiations with France would be limited to whatever was required by "public honour and interest" and not be used as an excuse for "party spirit, personal prejudice, discontent, or pride. . . ." The French privateers had now been restrained, he averred, but he had also had it on authoritative report "that in the conduct of American captains at sea there have been real causes of complaint."

A few days later Lafayette wrote again, having heard in the interim that Washington had accepted command of the U.S. forces that were to be arrayed against France. Obviously somewhat surprised and chastened, he softened his rhetoric and swallowed his national pride enough to say that he hoped that Washington was "more than ever in a situation . . . to make up this unhappy quarrel" in a way that would deflate the "boasting hopes" of France and "leave America increased in her national character and political consequence."

Not surprisingly, Washington shot back a rocket. Getting quickly past his profession of friendship ("it would be a mere waste of time to assure you of the sincere and heartfelt pleasure" etc.), he said he was relieved that

Lafayette said nothing this time about a trip to America, because coming now would "place you in a situation in which [nothing] could free you from embarrassment. . . . [Y]ou would lose the confidence of one party or the other [or] perhaps both were you here under these circumstances." As for Lafayette's suggestion that France was ready to negotiate, "let them evidence it by actions, for words . . . will not be much regarded now." And as for his wish that Washington support a reconciliation, he had always supported and would always support a policy of neutrality, not confrontation, but "neutrality was not the point at which France was aiming. . . . Whilst it was crying peace, peace and pretending that they did not wish us to be embroiled in their quarrel with Great Britain, they were pursuing measures in *this country* so repugnant to its sovereignty, and so incompatible with every principle of neutrality, as *must* inevitably, have produced a war. . . ."

Lafayette's caution about the limits of American independence rang hollow, Washington implied, when France had inspired efforts to "oppose the government in all its measures . . . to subvert the Constitution," when America was being treated "outrageously in its commercial concerns by the Directory," and when "those whose sole view was to observe a strict neutrality . . . whose principles were purely American" were denounced as "monarchists" and "aristocrats." Yes, there were indeed still parties in America for Britain and for France; but "it is a fact on which you may entirely and absolutely rely, that . . . a large part of the people are truly Americans in principle," and that they would pledge "their lives and their fortunes . . . to defend their country [if] the French should attempt to invade."

Never before had Lafayette got a letter even remotely like this one from his "dear general." On the other hand, neither had Washington's "dear marquis," at least since Sullivan's insult of d'Estaing at Newport more than twenty years before, taken quite so high a hand in France's behalf against America.

That was the last letter Washington ever wrote to Lafayette, and Lafayette's last substantial letter to Washington was his reply to it, in the spring of 1799. Most likely he wrote it in English, like all of his other letters to Washington, but it is at least metaphorically apt that an English version has never been found, and that the sole letter in their extensive correspondence that exists only in French is in effect a declaration of independence.

"Happily, your good letter of 25 December 1798, has been received," he began. Referring to Hamilton's cautionary letter, Lafayette said he had considered all the arguments Washington made against coming to America in his "frank and affectionate letter," but he claimed the right to disagree, having remained strictly aloof from any partisan quarreling. His motives were pure and his conscience was clear, he said, and he took the occasion to remind Washington whom he was talking to.

"From my youth, my head, my heart and my arms were consecrated to American independence," he wrote. "I have served in Europe the cause and the friends of liberty." Using what Washington had taught him, he said, he had served for three years, "not without boldness and with some public acclaim," in the "great and stormy theater of the French Revolution," during which he defended precisely those principles "for which you so gloriously fought and in which you so proudly led us." When he found that these principles were incompatible with his position, he quit and then spent five years in prison being punished "for the services [I] rendered to liberty and legal order." Upon his release, "three fifths of my fortune had been used up in the cause of the people," he reminded Washington, and when he refused to be compliant with the current regime, he had lost the rest.

"Your opinion, my dear general, is for me, as it has always been, of enormous weight," so he would not come to America until Washington gave his permission—unless, that is, he decided to come without it. "In the improbable case that I suddenly arrive there, be assured, my dear general, that my reasons will be strong enough to convince you it was necessary. I am confident that at such a time the various parties will concede to an old friend his independence."

In telling Washington that the Directory was ready to negotiate in good faith, he said, he was pleading no special case but only stating a fact that he knew to be true—and "again, now I repeat, I believe firmly that the [the Directory] wishes a reconciliation. . . ."

In closing, he sympathized with Washington about "the activities of the Jacobin agents in America," which he said he had known about even before Washington wrote. He "deplored and abhorred all such intrigues," pointedly adding that they were exactly the sort of insidious subversions that the British government had practiced with such great success against France. "It is the old way of Machiavellianism," he said. "Who knows that better than you, my dear general? And I have the right to add, who knows that better than me?"

Lafayette was right. Peace between France and America was not long in coming after that, and by the time Washington read this letter he had long since put down his sword and spear for the last time and picked up his plow and pruning hook again.

As he did so, he realized that Mount Vernon was getting too big for him. Apparently it was too big now even for his manager James Anderson, who found himself in bad health partly because of overwork. In September 1799, Washington proposed that Anderson take over the mill and distillery for himself, giving Washington a bit for the lease of it but mainly to run it for his own profit and that of his son. Perhaps he should look after the meadows as well, Washington suggested, of course for a fee. Washington didn't think he would need a manager anymore, he said, because he was going to rent out the fishery and sell at least one of his farms, in order "to bring the concerns which would be under my *immediate* management into some narrow compass . . . to make the superintendence of them a mere matter of amusement."

At almost the same moment, Lafayette was warming to the idea of farming himself. On September 4, he wrote to Adrienne: "The day after tomorrow I shall enter on my forty-third year. It is high time that I thought of settling down." He was thinking about La Grange, which seemed certain to be their home for the indefinite future. "If we are destined to find our place of retirement in France, I am pretty sure that my activities will be in the way of agriculture, which I am studying with all the ardor which in my younger days I gave to other occupations." He asked her to give him information about the facilities at La Grange, "how many animals, large and small, we shall be able to keep, what the cost is likely to be, and how many hands we shall need to look after them." Also, could she send "a word or two about the park and the woods."

Two weeks later, Adrienne dispatched one of Lafayette's old military aides with a passport and breathtaking news: Bonaparte had overthrown the Directory! Two hours after hearing that, perhaps remembering Joséphine's overture to his son, Lafayette was packed and on his way to Paris.

For Washington, there was no longer anywhere else to go; and so, far from actually restricting himself to a small, amusing compass, he spent every day riding around his farms, which by then covered nearly 8,000 acres—giving advice, checking up on people and things, making sure what he had ordered was being done. His imminent arrival could be spotted from the other side of a hill by a bobbing umbrella attached to his saddle that protected his fair skin from the sun.

He must have spent the entire day of December 10, 1799, working on a schedule of rotation for all of Mount Vernon's fields for the next three years and into the indefinite future. Anderson had apparently persuaded him that he would need a new manager after all, because he called this plan "Instructions for my Manager (while it is necessary for me to employ one)." Here, then, is the General of Mount Vernon, giving orders that were to be "*strictly*, and *pointedly* attended to and executed," because

> a system closely pursued (although it may not in all its parts be the *best* that could be devised) is attended with innumerable advantages. The conductor of the business in this case can never be under any dilemma in his proceedings; the overseers and even the negroes know what is to be done and what they are capable of doing, in ordinary seasons; in short every thing would move like *clock work*; and the force to be employed, may be in due proportion to the work which is to be performed; and a reasonable and tolerably accurate estimate may be made of the produce. But when no plan is fixed, when directions flow from day to day, the business becomes a mere chaos: frequently shifting, and sometimes at a stand, for want of directions what to do, or the manner of doing it. These occasion a waste of time, which is of more importance than is generally imagined. Nothing can so effectually obviate the evil, as an established, and regular course of proceeding; made known to *all* who are actors

in it; that *all may*, thereby, be enabled to play their parts, to advantage. . . .

Washington's "Instructions for my Manager" began with Field No. 1, which was now in wheat and was to be sown with oats. No. 2 was to be dealt with in quarters, one quarter for corn and another for buckwheat, both to be sown in April, another quarter in wheat, the last for the moment to be left fallow. The wheat in No. 3 was to be harvested in 1800, the stubble then to be plowed in and the field sown with rye. No. 4 was to be corn and should be harvested in 1801.

The plans were of course vastly more detailed than that and covered Fields 5 through 8, as well as four clover lots, the meadows and pastures, the care of animals, including nursing mothers and calfs, maintenance of the stables and farm pens, fencing, and further instructions for "the years 1802, 1803, and so on." That was just for River Farm, which was one of five. Equally detailed instructions were written out for two of the others. Twelve thousand or so words later, Washington observed that "These observations might be spun to a greater length," but he considered this enough to think about for the moment. Almost. "There are many sorts of *indoors* work which can be executed in hail, rain, or snow. . . . The man of prudence and foresight, will always keep these things in view."

Finally, "there is one thing . . . I cannot forbear to add, and in strong terms; it is that whenever I order a thing to be done, it must be done . . . and after it has been supposed to have gone into effect, for me to be told that nothing has been done . . . that it will be done; or that it could not be done . . . is unpleasant and disagreeable to me, having been accustomed all my life to more regularity and punctuality, and *know* that nothing but system and method is required to accomplish all reasonable requests."

Two days after his "Instructions" were completed, Washington spent another long day on horseback, riding around his farms. The weather was cold that day, hail alternating with rain, and when he came inside and shook out his wet overcoat, his secretary Tobias Lear noticed that his hair was full of snow. Lear said he should change his clothes, but Washington said his coat had kept him dry.

Weather the next day was even worse, but despite that and the start of a sore throat, he ventured outside briefly to mark some trees between the house and the river that he wanted the woodsman to take down. "Morning snowing and about 3 inches deep," Washington's last diary entry reads. "Wind at northeast and mercury at 30. Continuous snowing till 1 o'clock and about 4 it became clear. Wind in the same place but not hard. Mercury at 28 at night."

Before he went to bed he mentioned that his throat had got worse, and Lear told him to take something for it. "You know I never take anything for a cold," Washington said. "Let it go as it came."

At two o'clock in the morning, he had trouble breathing. Martha wanted to send for help, but she had just been ill herself, Washington worried that she might suffer a relapse, and so they waited until dawn, when a servant went round the house to light the fires.

Washington died at about twenty minutes after ten o'clock that night. Forensic specialists have settled on a diagnosis of acute epiglottitis, possibly caused by a flu virus. The epiglottis is a flap of cartilage at the base of the tongue and at the entrance of the airway that passes through the larynx to the lungs. In cases like Washington's, it can swell to ten times its normal size and form the equivalent of a ball valve, which, especially when the patient is in certain positions, will close with every attempt to inhale. The result is slow strangulation. All that day Washington was changing positions. At one point his manservant Christopher got him dressed so that he could sit by the fire, but after a while he lay back down in bed, then sat up, then got out of bed, then lay down again. His condition was only aggravated by the standard treatments of the day. In four bleedings, he lost about five pints of blood. He almost suffocated trying to swallow a mixture of sage tea and vinegar, and various purgatives led only to "copious discharge from the bowels," weakening him further as he struggled for breath and tried to find a comfortable position.

At one point he asked Lear to help turn him in bed. After considering the problem, Lear decided the only way to do it would be to climb in beside him and use the length of his body to urge Washington to his side. As he did so, Lear wrote later, he was crying.

There are many ways Washington might have reacted to such a moment, and it is worth noting that the president known for his cold aloofness, the man who had picked Gouverneur Morris's hand off his shoulder, the general who advised his officers against fraternizing with their men, apologized for the trouble he was causing his secretary and comforted him, saying, "This is a debt we must pay to each other, and I hope when you want aid of this kind you will find it." He told the servant Christopher, who had been standing all day, who had never done anything but stand in Washington's presence, to sit down.

Washington said no good-byes to the people around him, including Martha, and he called for no clergy to attend him. He comforted no one including himself with the hope of reunion in the afterlife or any afterlife at all. "I die hard," he told his oldest friend Dr. James Craik late that afternoon, "but I am not afraid to go."

Before he did, not surprisingly, the man with as much patience for paperwork as any executive in the history of government asked that the preservation of his monumental collection of correspondence and private papers be carefully attended to and that the few last letters he had begun the day before be properly completed. Then he asked Martha to bring him two wills from his desk downstairs. When she did so, he gave her one and told her to burn it, which she did.

In the will that survived was Washington's last great act, a clause that called for the emancipation of all Mount Vernon's three hundred slaves. This will was written in his own hand, without the benefit of any "professional character" or "any Agency in the draught." Perhaps he thought someone might try to argue him out of it. His family surely would have, had they known; none of them found anything wrong with slavery. Some of those affected were Martha's "dower slaves," who had come with her when they married, so he could not legally free them, but he insisted that all her slaves be freed on her death. He also promised any elderly slaves who chose to stay that they would be fed, clothed, and cared for at Mount Vernon by his heirs for the rest of their lives. In a direct challenge to Virginia state law, which forbade the education of slaves, he stipulated that all of his slaves then under the age of twenty-five must be taught to read and write and "brought up to some useful occupation. . . . And I do hereby expressly forbid the sale or transportation out of the said Commonwealth of any slave I may die possessed of, under any pretense whatever." To foreclose any opposition, he ordered that this clause be enacted "religiously . . .

without evasion, neglect, or delay," and with certain exceptions taken by his family, it was.*

Washington can always be faulted for doing too little to fight slavery in his lifetime, but none of the other founding fathers did as much, including the man who wrote the defining American declaration, "all men are created equal." At his death, Thomas Jefferson freed only the children he had had with his slave Sally Hemings (though not Hemings herself), and he left almost two hundred men, women, and children in bondage to his heirs.

Washington had declared his legacy to America more than three years before, in what has been called the Farewell Address, despite the fact that it appeared in newspapers as an open letter to the American people almost six months before he left office. At the time, its most explosive message was that he had decided, despite urgent pleas, not to accept a third term as president.

Jeffersonian Republicans had a favorite conceit—used in part as a way of criticizing Washington's policies without implying criticism of him, which would have been political suicide—that "principles and not men" were what counted in public life. Beginning in the early 1790s, and especially after the Neutrality Proclamation, Republican toasts to George Washington became distinctly backhanded: "To Citizen Washington— May he remember that he is but a man." "To the President—May his former patriotism never be eradicated." Celebrations of his birthday were likened to offering up "incense of adulation" to a potentate, and described as cringing, crypto-monarchic rituals "inconsonant with republicanism" that "ought to be proscribed."

With the announcement that he was leaving, the claim for "principles and not men" was seen for the facile construction that it was. America without Washington was literally unprecedented, almost unthinkable, and

*Bushrod Washington sold fifty slaves despite his uncle's deathbed injunction. The rest were freed early, a year after Washington died, except for one whom Martha kept; and when she died on May 22, 1802, she left "my mulatto man Elish" to her grandson George Washington Parke Custis. Small wonder Washington was concerned that his will would not be faithfully executed.

almost as unsettling for Republicans as for Federalists. He had been the foremost figure in America for a quarter century, and he had been its leader for seventeen years, longer than almost any democratic leader in history. Now he was setting the precedent of a term-limited presidency, defying predictions that his seeming indispensability would turn it into a lifetime office. As always happened when Washington gave up power, his stature grew even greater, and the Farewell Address took on the aura of American scripture. "Bind it in your Bibles next to the Sermon on the Mount," exhorted William Cunningham of Massachusetts, "that the lessons of the two Saviors can be read together."

Washington had worked on it during the virulent press attacks and personal betrayals of spring and summer 1796, when his letters to friends spoke almost obsessively of "infamous [June 26 to Hamilton], exaggerated and indecent [July 6 to Jefferson] attacks [same day to Wolcott]," assaults on his character and policies that were "as indecent as they are void of truth and fairness [July 18 to Pickering]." Alexander Hamilton's editing took some of the personal animosity out of Washington's early draft of the Farewell Address, but not all of it. Taking his last shot, Washington denounced as traitors the "cunning, ambitious, and unprincipled men" who comprised an "artful and enterprising minority" and who "agitated in every direction" in favor of "ill-founded jealousies and . . . animosity of one part against another, occasionally [causing] riots and insurrection." The great danger, he wrote, was that "foreign influence and corruption" could be introduced "through the channels of party passions," so that "the policy and will of one country are subjected to the policy and will of another."

If his concern about French and British influence seemed to border almost on the paranoid, what he suspected was in fact truer than he knew: Monroe's subversion of U.S. policy in France and Hamilton's betrayal of negotiating positions to Great Britain were just two results of a rigorous program carried out by French and British agents, secret and otherwise, to shape U.S. policy, an endeavor they attended to daily, with great ingenuity, and in close detail. To call it a conspiracy was to call it by its name.

The Farewell Address is often spoken of in two parts, one about domestic politics, the other foreign affairs, but of course in the country Washington saw before him they could not have been more closely aligned: partisan politics opened the way to foreign influence, which led to a corrupted foreign policy, which would conflict with American interests, which would open the door to domestic disputes, which would lead to partisan politics, and so on. "The nation which indulges towards another a habitual hatred or a habitual fondness is in some degree a slave," he wrote. "It is a slave to its animosity or to its affection, either of which is sufficient to lead it astray from its duty and its interest." He learned that not from a book but on the frontier, on the battlefield, and in the presidency. He had written in almost identical terms to Henry Laurens when he quashed Lafayette's plan to invade Canada in 1778: "Hatred to England may carry some into an excess of confidence in France. . . . I am heartily disposed to entertain the most favorable sentiments of our new ally and to cherish them in others . . . but it is a maxim founded on the universal experience of mankind that no nation is to be trusted farther than it is bound by its interest; and no prudent statesman or politician will venture to depart from it."

Men too served their interests first, however lofty their principles or deep their patriotic feeling. "It is vain to exclaim against the depravity of human nature on this account," he wrote in 1778. "The fact is so. . . ." He made this argument to the revolutionary Congress in favor of inducements to long-term enlistments, and he demonstrated its truth in his own life. Washington's land interests motivated him all his life, from his opposition to the French as a young militia officer, to his advocacy for a strong central government as a delegate to the Constitutional Convention, to his violent suppression of Native Americans to protect the settlement and development of the West. At his death, he still held more than 45,000 acres in the trans-Appalachian West. John Adams and Benjamin Rush, concerned that Washington was going to get all the credit for the founding of America, took turns tearing him apart in their late correspondence, telling each other to burn their letters while carefully preserving them. In one of their more discreet comments, Rush observed "how much littleness is mixed with human greatness, how much folly with human wisdom, and how much vice with the greatest attainments. . . ."

And yet, as pragmatic and even perhaps self-interested as Washington's vision may have been, it served an idea of America that was wholly optimistic, even idealistic. He put that idea most succinctly, perhaps, in a letter he wrote to Lafayette in 1790, long before neutrality became an issue. The best policy "to keep in the situation in which nature has placed us," he said then, was "to observe a strict neutrality, and to furnish others with those good things of subsistence, which they may want and which our fertile land abundantly produces. . . ." In other words, embrace the commerce of all nations, welcome all immigrants, let them settle the western lands and multiply, let the fruit of their labors help America recover from the war and achieve the prosperity that its abundant lands and natural resources would inevitably provide, so long as it remained "unentangled in the crooked politics of Europe."

The philosopher Isaiah Berlin once divided politicians into foxes, who know lots of small things, and hedgehogs, who know one big thing. Washington, as the historian Joseph Ellis has observed, was the quintessential hedgehog, and this is what he knew. He discovered this America as a young man on the frontier, and he found it again on his trans-Appalachian expedition after the war, when Britain in the North and Spain in the South made him desperate for an American government strong enough to draw the trade and loyalty of western settlers to the east.

There were some things he never learned about America because he was a man of his age. Toward the end of his life, in large gestures like freeing his slaves and small acts of kindness toward his secretary and manservant, there is evidence that Washington was moving to embrace the principle of equality; but he could never have countenanced egalitarian politics because it seemed to him dangerously fractious at a time when the success of the American experiment was threatened more by disunity than a lack of freedom. For Washington there could be no loyal opposition, in part because of his personal abhorrence of criticism but also because he did not believe that democratic, party politics would ultimately be safe for the republic. He shared this with the Federalists, whose core suspicion was that people were basically licentious and that a sound society called most of all for strength in government and submission in the citizenry.

Washington's various funerals and memorial services gave at least anecdotal evidence to the contrary. The crowds were the largest the nation had ever seen, from "the most well-attended procession that was ever seen in Bennington," Vermont, to "the greatest concourse ever assembled" in Savannah, Georgia. Federalists just then "imagined themselves in a state of siege," in the words of their definitive modern historians, Stanley Elkins and Eric McKittrick. "They, the friends of order, were menaced on every side by the forces of sedition, Jacobinism and insubordination." They were obsessed with the idea of social cohesion, convinced that the nation was about to fly apart in an explosion of contending interests, just as the prospect of Thomas Jefferson's taking the White House from John Adams had them quaking in their knee breeches. What must have been their surprise, then, when newspaper reports were virtually unanimous on how well behaved everyone was at the Washington memorials, how, for all their differences, they just seemed to get along. A correspondent for the Newark *Centinel* commented on the "decorum and orderly conduct observed by every description of persons. . . . Not a single incident occurred but what will bear a pleasing retrospect" and would be "transmitted to posterity without a stain." In Williamsborough, North Carolina, "attention, sobriety, and good conduct" was reported on the part of "citizens of every denomination," and "men of all classes" in Hartford, Connecticut, as well as "citizens of every rank" in Lexington, Kentucky, and "all ranks of citizens" in Wethersfield, Connecticut. At least in the rituals of Washington's death, Americans demonstrated what it looked like to be a people of "all ranks" and one nation.

Federalists were on the way out then and Republicans ascendant, but neither would survive by the time party politics really took hold—and yet in the end they both proved to be right. Just as the Federalists feared, Americans turned out to be almost ungovernably licentious, as licentious as any relatively law-abiding people can be; and as Republicans feared, America became the most capital- and market-minded nation on earth, a raw frenzy of commercialism. Maybe Washington would not have liked what he saw, but more than two hundred years later these traits were recognized (and caricatured) around the world as an important part of the distinctly American character, which was what Washington wanted for the United States most of all.

By leaving as his legacy the Farewell Address, he was in a way pointing out to posterity the last best thing he did, which was to maintain American neutrality at a time of war abroad and conflict at home. The Farewell Address is, among other things, one of the strongest cautionary statements about the dangers of war in American history, and given its provenance surely the most credible one, at least until President Eisenhower's Farewell Address a century and a half later. Although no one recognized more clearly than Washington that the readiness to make war was prerequisite for a stable peace, no one was less eager to test that proposition. The man who had stated a decade earlier that his "first wish" was that war could be "banished from the earth," now exhorted his country never to "unsheath the sword except in self-defense." In striking contrast to Lafayette and other leaders of the French Revolution, he recoiled at the notion of exporting the American Revolution by force, as a matter of principle as well as pragmatism.

This posture of principled indifference toward the sanguinary politics of Europe was largely responsible for one of the most obvious differences between the American Revolution of 1776 and the French Revolution of 1789. The latter was demonstrated to be unfinished on a decades-long series of smoking, corpse-strewn battlefields across Europe. The American Revolution can be said to have ended one afternoon in early 1801 in a drawing room of the brand-new President's House on swamp-lined Pennsylvania Avenue in the new Federal City, which people were already calling Washington. There the newly elected president, Thomas Jefferson, came to call on his distraught, outgoing predecessor, John Adams, whom he found alone in his study.

"You've turned me out!" Adams cried before Jefferson had even taken a chair. "You've turned me out!"

Calmly, Jefferson explained that that was not what had happened at all. "This was no contest between you and me," he said. "Two systems of principles ... divide our fellow citizens into two parties. ... Were we both to die to-day, tomorrow two other names would be in the place of ours, without any change in the motion of the machinery. Its motion is from its principle, not from you or myself." Adams was crushed by this defeat—he left town in the middle of the night before the inauguration—but when Jefferson recorded his opponent's despair and this scene many years after the fact, in a letter to Benjamin Rush, he also remembered President Adams saying, "I will be as faithful a subject as any you will have."

The quietude of this moment, which represents the first peaceful transfer of power to a loyal opposition in the history of modern democracy, was proof that America was sufficiently stable and free to find its own direction, for good and ill. Washington's policy of neutrality toward the belligerents—and, perhaps even more important, his insistence on a posture of indifference and detachment toward all nations in everything but commerce—saved Americans not only from involvement in the war between England and France but also from seeing either of them as models of government.

One can only wonder how the young Washington, so consumed with thoughts of glory that he had found something "charming in the sound" of "bullets whirring past" during his first experience of combat, might have decided a policy that would lead the *Aurora* and others to charge him, however fallibly, with treason. In the course of years, Washington had found a greater glory, or something greater than glory, which allowed him to achieve his final victory in a war for peace, without which American independence might never have been won.

The day after Washington died, France's brand-new First Consul, Napoleon Bonaparte, issued a "Proclamation to the French People," which read, in its entirety: "Citizens! The Revolution has been established upon the principles with which it began. It is over."

The French were by then only too relieved to agree, and in short order they demonstrated their political exhaustion in a plebiscite that gave Bonaparte virtually dictatorial power. The vote was 3,011,007 to 1,562. (One of the "no" votes, of course, was Lafayette's.) Fourteen years and many wars later, after Napoleon's fall and exile to St. Helena, Byron wrote a long poem called *Ode to Napoleon*. He ended it as follows:

> *There was a day—there was an hour,*
> *   While earth was Gaul's—Gaul thine—*
> *When that immeasurable power*
> *   Unsated to resign*
> *Had been an act of purer fame*
> *Than gathers round Marengo's name,*
> *   And gilded thy decline*
> *Through the long twilight of all time,*
> *Despite some passing clouds of crime.*

But thou forsooth must be a king,
*   And don the purple vest*
As if that foolish robe could wring
*   Remembrance from thy breast.*
Where is that faded garment? where
The gewgaws thou wert fond to wear,
*   The star—the string—the crest?*
Vain froward child of empire! say,
Are all thy playthings snatch'd away?

Where may the wearied eye repose
*   When gazing on the Great;*
Where neither guilty glory glows,
*   Nor despicable state?*
Yes—one—the first—the last—the best:
The Cincinnatus of the West
*   Whom envy dared not hate,*
Bequeath'd the name of Washington
To make men blush there was but one.

XXVI

Epilogue

BEAUMARCHAIS DIED a few months before Washington, having had, if such a thing can be said, a much more agreeable death, a massive stroke after a long dinner at home with close friends. He had spent his French Revolution and his last years as he had spent the rest of his life, in a dazzling, antic flurry of passionate activity that was not quite revolutionary, certainly not reactionary, but somehow, as always, everything at once. Delighted and horrified, he had watched the taking of the Bastille from one of his home's two hundred windows and the next day hid one of the royal troops in his house to protect him from the crowd. The chairman of his electoral district, he signed himself "Caron de Beaumarchais, Citizen-Soldier of the Gardes-Bourgeoises," by which he identified himself as a revolutionary who could not bear to be separated from his borrowed claim to aristocracy, the now illicit "de." "What is to become of us, my dear?" he only half-joked to his wife (the third, who managed to outlive him). "Stripped to our family names! without coats of arms! without liveries! Heavens, what a ruinous condition! I dined the day before yesterday at Mme de La Reynière's, and we called her Mme Grimod to her face. My Lord Bishop of Rodez and My Lord Bishop of Agen were just plain *monsieur* to us. It was like the end of a ball at the winter opera house, when everyone is unmasked."

Revolutionary conditions tested everything about Beaumarchais—for example, his power of forgiveness, which was found wanting. After his house was vandalized and his life was threatened by partisans of

Nicolas Bergasse, who had by then become a formidable figure in the legislature, he immortalized his old nemesis in a savage caricature named "Bégearss" in his last play. He failed also at the challenge of ideological consistency: When the "de-Christianization" campaign became the revolutionary order of the day, Beaumarchais the Protestant activist went all-out to see that more high masses would be said in his district, by civil and non-juring priests alike. Invigorated by the politics of the street, he was also nostalgic for the old candlelit Paris, when the streets were "our boudoirs. . . . Where sighs of love were once heard, you now hear cries of 'liberty' and 'Live free or die!' instead of 'I adore you.' These are our games now."

The erstwhile man of the people barely escaped their wrath one day when a large and angry crowd came storming toward his house looking for sixty thousand rifles someone accused him of hiding. He thought of trying to talk them out of coming in, but his best friend, convinced he would be killed if he did, persuaded him to use his secret exit to a side street.

As it turned out, the invading crowd proved to be, like Beaumarchais, a bit of everything. They tore through his property and house, teemed upstairs and down, opened all the doors, peered in all the crevices, even fished through the cesspools, and when they left they took nothing and nothing was broken. A woman who picked a flower in the garden was nearly strung up. Afterward, Beaumarchais was moved by the evidence of "a natural justice that breaks through even in a time of disorder."

There actually were sixty thousand rifles; the people's informant had just got the story wrong. The rifles were in Holland, and a middleman who knew of Beaumarchais's history as a gunrunner—at a time when France was going to war and would need them—thought he might like to get back in the game, which of course he did. As with all the deepest secrets in Paris, a not entirely baseless rumor about this was out and about in no time, and Beaumarchais was either a daring and ingenious patriot or a depraved, mercenary arms dealer, depending on who was telling the story.

Obviously assuming the latter, the authorities came to his house one morning and took him away. He had nearly talked his way out of trouble when Marat himself came in at the last minute and whispered in the ear of the presiding judge. After that he was taken to the Abbaye prison and probably would have been killed in the September Massacres had he not been released three days before they started. (He had thought to send his wife and daughter out of Paris by then, but they were later caught and imprisoned and, like Adrienne Lafayette, only avoided the guillotine because Robespierre got there just ahead of them.)

For several days after his release Beaumarchais protectively went into hiding, but then, desperate to finish what he had started, he dared returning to Paris so that he could make his case to the current war minister. (There were fourteen war ministers between the declaration of war in April 1792 and Louis's execution eight months later, which was one of Beaumarchais's problems.) He then embarked on a race around Europe, trying various ruses to secure the rifles in spite of a Dutch pledge to France's enemies not to let them fall into the wrong hands. At one point one of his former arms deal go-betweens in London arranged a bond for him which he took to Holland, where he got nowhere. Finally, in order to get home, he had to go through London, where he found messages warning him off. His property and fortune had been confiscated again, they told him; he had narrowly escaped being arrested in Holland, and only the guillotine awaited him in Paris. Beaumarchais would have gone back anyway if it had not been for what was either a providential kindness or a vile plot on the part of his agent, who had him imprisoned as a debtor.

As ever, setbacks only got him angry. Given time to write in prison, he took on his accusers in Paris with a rage that made Lafayette's attack on the Jacobin leadership seem timid: "A hideous little man with black hair and a hooked nose—the great, the just, the (in a word) *merciful* Marat," he wrote, "these are the men who lead us, turning the government into a nest of vengeance, a sewer of intrigues, a load of nonsense." He actually published that when he finally returned to Paris, in a memoir titled *Six Epochs, or Narratives of the Most Painful Nine Months in My Life*. It was his last work.

Not surprisingly, the next stop for Beaumarchais was Hamburg, where he spent the following two years as a penniless émigré, living in an attic on bread, water, and scraps. For the last time, he pleaded with the American Congress to pay him what he was owed from the Revolutionary War—a debt that represented his only remaining asset—and once again, he heard nothing.

When he finally returned to Paris, his money and homes were restored to him, and in the end, he was able to leave a considerable legacy—200,000 francs, his property, and his war debt, for which, thirty-six years later, his daughter finally got about 20 cents on the dollar.* Her inheritance would have been more if only Beaumarchais had been successful in the last big deal he attempted in his life, which was trying to sell Napoleon his house ("Don't say no, general, before you have looked it over"). Napoleon was polite in his response but privately called the place "Beaumarchais' folly" and said it should be torn down. It was, shortly after Napoleon was, with the ascension of Louis's brother Provence as Louis XVIII.†

Years later, James Fenimore Cooper saw the last architectural vestige of Beaumarchais's life in Paris. He was in a carriage with Lafayette riding toward La Grange, where Cooper had been spending so much time he left a small library there. Passing by a garden on the road out of Paris, Lafayette pointed out the pavilion where Beaumarchais used to write. "The roof was topped by a vane, to show which way the wind blew," Cooper wrote, noting with amusement that in place of the weathercock he

*The whole sorry tale was summarized in February 1824 in a 124-page report on the matter from a Congressional Select Committee of the 18th Congress; and even so the debt was not dealt with until the 20th Congress, which finally passed H.R. 252 on April 1, 1828: "Be it enacted by the Senate and House of Representatives of the United States in Congress assembled, that the sum of one million livres, and the interest thereon, which was charged to the account of Caron de Beaumarchais, in the settlement of his accounts at the Treasury, in eighteen hundred and five, be restored to his credit: and that the sum be paid to his heirs, out of any money in the Treasury, not otherwise appropriated."

†Provence ruled as Louis XVIII because he had declared from his exile in Westphalia in 1793, when Louis XVI was executed, that Louis's eldest son should now be recognized as King Louis XVII. On taking the throne, Provence insisted on the title of Louis XVIII in recognition of the uninterrupted Bourbon monarchy. In the meantime, the boy had died of tuberculosis. Rumors persisted for years that he was not actually dead but had been spirited out of France by royalist sympathizers, giving rise to the legend of the "Lost Dauphin." In the years and decades that followed, many candidates came or were brought forward across Europe, some of whom continue to have adherents to this day. Some of the best known nominees include the naturalist John James Audubon; a Native American missionary to the Mohawks named Eleazer Williams; and Karl Wilhelm Naundorff, a German clockmaker.

had put an arrow in the shape of a large writing pen, "and there it stands to this day, a curious memorial equally of his wit and of his audacity."*

Lafayette lived another lifetime after Washington died—nearly thirty-five years. During that time, he continued his battle for French freedoms through the reigns of Napoleon and the kings of the Bourbon Restoration. Just a few years before his death, he managed to install someone he thought would be the constitutional monarch he had always wanted for France, a nephew of Louis XVI from the Orléans branch and the son of his old adversary the duc d'Orléans. An unpretentious man, this Orléans had spent part of his exile in Philadelphia, where he lived in a single room over a barber shop. He had met and admired George Washington. He spoke the language of republicanism fluently and in all apparent sincerity.

As king, Louis-Philippe I† lavished gratitude on Lafayette for supporting him until, in no time at all, he developed the Bourbons' old distaste for popular politics. From then on, he and Lafayette were at sword's point. When Lafayette died (like Washington after prolonged exposure to bad weather, walking in a friend's funeral procession through a cold rain), Louis-Philippe ordered his kingmaker laid to rest with a martial extravaganza that was meant less to enshrine his place in French history than to enshroud it behind a *cordon sanitaire*. Three thousand former members of his beloved, now decommissioned National Guard were permitted to accompany the tricolor-draped coffin to the cemetery so long as they did not carry any weapons, while the ranks of royal troops that lined the route of the cortège were heavily armed, and threatening outbursts of popular feeling were quickly smothered by force. Lafayette was "separated from the public by bayonets and sabers," as one indignant journalist put it, and another sarcastically exhorted, "Hide yourselves, Parisians! The funeral of an honest man and a true friend of liberty is passing by!" Louis-Philippe said not a word about the death of the man

*It is no longer there.
†1773–1850; reigned 1830–48.

who had put him on the throne only four years before, and he ordered that there be no eulogies.

Louis-Philippe could not quiet Parisians for long, however: In that spring of 1834, the memory of the Revolution of 1830 was still too fresh. Lafayette's role in bringing that revolution to a successful conclusion and then in attempting to hold the new king to his promises had not only won him widespread public affection but had also reminded the French public of all that he had done before.

Until the events leading up to the Revolution of 1830, Lafayette had not had a visible public role for years. He had stayed out of office for fifteen years after his return to France, working on his *Mémoires*, restoring the 800-acre property at La Grange, and building up his fields and herds, which alone was an enormous challenge. The medieval château had noble bones—its entrance gate was flanked by two round towers, the drawbridge led over a moat, there was a court of honor and a large park, and the house was grand—but it had not been lived in for years. Everything from the leaky roof to the chimneypieces needed work, and the outbuildings, like the fields, had long since gone to seed. Reading deeply in the new theories of agriculture, Lafayette began to breed Merino sheep, cows from Switzerland and Normandy, later Devonshires. He planted orchards of pear and apple trees, for which the local peasants laughed at him but which in time produced the region's finest pears and cider; and his wheat fields would eventually allow him to provide them abundantly with bread in times of famine.

Since the farm lost money for several years, he and Adrienne slid ever further into debt. Nevertheless, he parried all of Napoleon's efforts to win him over, as inoffensively as possible but giving no ground when anyone, including Bonaparte, asked him directly what he thought of Napoleonic rule. He was as proud as any Frenchman of Bonaparte's victories in the field and approved many of his legal and social reforms, but the autocracy on which those achievements rested was unacceptable to him. He turned down every form of patronage that was offered him, including a seat in the Senate, the U.S. ambassadorship, even the Legion of Honor. "Faithful to the habits of liberty," as the historian Augustin Thierry put it when he was still a young journalist, "he cultivated his fields like Washington and practiced in silence the genuine civic virtues, simplicity and industry." Less visibly, he was also heavily involved not only with anti-Bonapartist activists in France but also as a supporter of liberation movements all over Europe and the Americas. When he was solicited for money by whatever irresistibly worthy cause, heedless of the fact that he had none to give, he borrowed more.

The general public heard little of this or anything else about Lafayette until he was first elected to the Chamber of Deputies, in 1815, just in time to put the weight of his revolutionary credentials behind the Chamber's insistence on Napoleon's final abdication after Waterloo. Hearing that Bonaparte intended to disband the Assembly to prevent it from taking such action, Lafayette rose to warn against this, and an eyewitness never forgot the scene. "He spoke as conversationally as though he were in a drawing room. The silence in the Assembly was absolute. He proposed a resolution: 'Whereas the Chamber of Deputies declares that the independence of the nation is threatened, be it resolved that the Chamber declares itself to be in permanent session, and that any attempt to dissolve it is a crime of high treason.'"

His resolution was adopted unanimously, and when Napoleon's brother Lucien came to the Assembly to denounce the move as the act of a weak-willed, fainthearted nation, Lafayette, unforgettably, cut him off. "By what right do you dare to accuse the nation of . . . want of perseverance in the emperor's interest? The nation has followed him on the fields of Italy, the sands of Egypt, the plains of Germany, across the frozen deserts of Russia. . . . The nation has followed him in fifty battles, in his defeats as in his victories, and for doing that we have to mourn the blood of three million Frenchmen."

Lafayette had been so little thought of or written about up to this point that Charles Rémusat, co-editor of a liberal newspaper, was surprised to find out he was still alive. "I considered him a historic character," he wrote in his memoirs. "I rather appreciated what he did [to force Napoleon's abdication] and what I learned later about his role during the [1789] Revolution gave me an even better opinion of him."

Lafayette despised the alliance of European monarchs whose army defeated Napoleon, occupied France, and restored the Bourbon throne, but he held out hope that Louis XVI's brother Provence would in time agree to become a constitutional monarch. Provence refused to accept the constitution that was hastily drawn up by the Napoleonic Senate and presented to him as the price of their support, and Lafayette was unhappy with his alternative charter for many reasons, mainly because it was a concession by a sovereign king rather than the declaration of sovereign citizens. He was also disappointed and more than a little suspicious that the tricolor was proscribed. Still, he did not give up on Provence as Louis XVIII until a plain resurgence of autocracy forced him into opposition that was both open and covert.

In the years that followed, he subsidized liberal newspapers and supported the work of radical journalists, and when they were threatened with arrest for sedition, he harbored them at La Grange. He also allowed himself to be drawn into a series of failed conspiracies to overthrow the government that ended in death sentences for several of the plotters, whose loyal silence alone saved Lafayette from the same fate. By 1820 he was the acknowledged leader of the opposition in France, and Louis XVIII began referring to him as "that animal." The king's ministers worked against Lafayette's election so openly that his election became a *cause célèbre* and he himself once more became a significant figure on the public stage.

In early 1824, through various electoral maneuvers, the ministry succeeded in depriving him of election, but toward the end of the year Louis XVIII died and was succeeded by his brother d'Artois as Charles X. Once more, Lafayette's hopes for a constitutional monarchy were revived, though more for personal than rational reasons. D'Artois was even more conservative than Provence, but he and Lafayette had enjoyed an easy relationship going back to their days together in the *Epée de Bois* crowd, and even during their wrangles in d'Artois's bureau of the Assembly of Notables. Lafayette admitted that he liked d'Artois more than he should, and Charles X returned the feeling. "I know only two men who have always professed the same principles," d'Artois said once, "myself and Lafayette: he as the defender of liberty, and I as the king of the aristocracy. I have a high regard for M. de Lafayette, and if the circumstances ever allow it, I should enjoy seeing him." To a royalist ally shocked by this soft spot for so ardent an opponent, Charles X responded lamely, "Ah, but you see I know him so well. . . . We were born the same year, we learned how to ride together in the Versailles academy. . . ."

Inevitably, personal warmth gave way to political disagreement, which could not have been more fundamental. Charles, a believer in the divine right of kings, the sanctity of the nobility, and the rightful primacy of the Roman Catholic Church, surrounded himself with a ministry of extreme royalists, known as ultra ultras. The ministers' wrongheaded influence and his own myopia combined to produce such incendiary measures as raising taxes to compensate the émigrés for their confiscated property in a time of prolonged economic depression.

Harsh legislation and years of bad harvests made conditions for the working poor—which included most of the population of Paris and of France—even worse in July 1830 than they had been in July 1789. At a time when 80 percent of the population were living on no more than 11 sous per day, a four-pound loaf of bread cost 19 sous, 5 more than the price in 1789. Most people began to experience acute hunger whenever the price of bread rose above 12 or 13 sous, and by 1830 the price had been above that and rising for years. All that stood between life and death for many Parisians were special cards handed out by the police that allowed the poor to buy bread at subsidized prices, a humiliating form of relief that nevertheless had 227,000 applicants in July of 1830, in a city of 755,000. By one contemporary estimate, more than half of all Parisians—420,000—lived in conditions of extreme poverty. None of these people could vote, but the depression hit those who could as well, since fewer purchases meant declining profits, which meant rising unemployment and falling wages, which meant even fewer purchases, and so on.

Everyone but the royalists blamed Charles and his ministry for the disastrous economy, and by 1830 his failure to address the people's basic needs had consolidated and galvanized the opposition. In the most recent elections, the Chamber of Deputies had lurched hard to the left. Now, in the spring of 1830, Charles dissolved it and called for new elections. Despite the ministry's hamhanded efforts to skew the process, the result of the voting in June and July was an even larger liberal majority, which forced Charles to choose between a constitution and an absolutist crackdown. At that he acted as the Old Regime monarch he had wished to be all along, issuing ordinances on July 26 that annulled the election, dramatically reduced the size of the electorate, and imposed strict press censorship, all in blatant violation of the charter conceded by Louis XVIII.

.   .   .

Lafayette was at La Grange when he heard this news the next day, and that night found him at the gates of a capital acutely reminiscent of 1789, the smoke of spent gunpowder in the air and the shattered glass of lanterns in the darkened streets. Driving through the Faubourg Saint-Antoine toward his home at No. 6 rue d'Anjou, he heard the familiar sound of pickaxes digging up cobblestones and saw workingmen and shopkeepers working side by side to chop down trees and throw up barricades. Government armories had been looted that day, and royal troops had fired on the people. "The reign of law has been interrupted and that of force begins," wrote one journalist who refused to be silenced. "Obedience ceases to be a duty." Some time before, when Charles had protectively disbanded the never quite trustworthy National Guard, one of the guardsmen put out a sign: "Uniform for sale. The musket will be kept." Now the guardsmen were bringing their guns out of storage.

Lafayette learned all this from Charles Rémusat, who was on his doorstep soon after he got home. Three years earlier, Rémusat had married Virginie's oldest daughter, so he was now Lafayette's grandson-in-law. A prominent journalist in the reform movement, he had by this time got to know Lafayette at close range and had no illusions about him. "Monsieur de Lafayette was starting to grow old," he wrote years later. "He had never shown a great mobility of mind, and this was actually one of his best qualities. For the last sixty years his impressions and his ideas had been the same." If his advocacy of them seemed at times to have a copybook quality ("When one is a character, it's hard not to play the role"), Rémusat knew that as a symbol Lafayette had enormous evocative power for the French public and especially for the generation born after 1789. "A man who had met Turgot, Malesherbes . . . General Washington, and all the men of the Revolution, brought back to life times which seemed so far from us." As the young writer Alphonse d'Herbelot put it, Lafayette represented "the springtime of our liberty and those first days of the Constitution when our sky was blue and cloudless . . . the only one remaining from so much glory and virtue, which existed as if by magic in 1789." Lafayette was the Declaration of

the Rights of Man and Citizen, the French Revolution without the guillotine; and if he seemed to some extent frozen in time, that was in part
because his values actually were.

The morning after he arrived in Paris, he was up before dawn, awakened by students from the Ecole Polytechnique who were going to join
the insurrection and wanted his blessing. Lafayette more than returned
the affection of such young admirers, he reveled in it; and as he sent the
students to the barricades that morning, just as the tocsin began to sound,
he had every reason to reflect that he was being given a rare chance to
relive some of the most glorious days of his youth. Early that morning,
from one of the towers of Notre Dame, someone unfurled an enormous
tricolor flag—his invention of an inspired moment more than forty years
before, which had been banned by the Bourbons for the past fifteen years.
Soon the air was filled with the sound of gunfire and the shouts of a people rising.

At midday, about twenty of the staunchest deputies—even they filled
with fears and doubts about the proper course of action—gathered in a
house at the center of the insurrection; and the sight of the seventy-two-
year-old figure of 1789 tottering toward that meeting through the revolutionary crowd prompted an eruption of popular, street-level adulation that
he had not experienced in many years. The talk at the meeting was mainly
of the dangers inherent in solidarity with violent protest and the need to
restore legal order; but Lafayette had seen all this before. The king's
despotic initiative, the reaction to it he heard from the students that
morning, what he had seen going on outside—all this told him they were
beyond the point of thinking about obedience to authority. "These events
can no longer be confined within the limits of strict legality," he said.
"This is a revolution. A provisional government is necessary and should be
formed immediately."

Just then word came that the people had overwhelmed the defenders
of the Hôtel de Ville at a terrible cost in lives and that fierce fighting continued there. One of the deputies moved that they send an official delegation to the commander of the royal troops with the request for a cease-fire.
The commander was Marshal Marmont, duc de Ragusa, the man whose
surrender to the invading allies in 1814 had made way for the Bourbon
Restoration. Lafayette, who had literally broken down in tears the day the

occupation army marched into Paris, firmly opposed making such a request. "Let us rather *order* Marmont in the name of the law to cease firing on the people." When the more moderate motion was carried, Lafayette delivered his fellow deputies an ultimatum: If they did not form a revolutionary government by the next day, he would do so himself, setting up headquarters at the liberated Hôtel de Ville. The fighting only grew more intense as the day wore on—more than a thousand people died before it ended—and Day Two of what came to be known as *Les Trois Glorieuses*, July 27–29, ended for Lafayette late that night with another inconclusive gathering of the deputies.

At a meeting the next morning, they did as he required, naming an interim government committee and placing him at the head of a reconstituted National Guard, the position he had left almost forty years before. By this time, however, despite a few final skirmishes and sporadic bursts of gunfire, the war in the streets was drawing to a close, some of the troops having joined the insurrection, the rest in retreat.

The people were already celebrating their victory as Lafayette made his way through the densely crowded streets from the meeting of deputies toward his new/old station at the Hôtel de Ville, and along the way he was hailed as if he had been the Revolution's victorious general, showered with brand-new tricolor ribbons thrown from rooftops and windows, while shouts of "*Vive la liberté!*" alternated with "*Vive Lafayette!*" His secretary Bernard Sarrans clearly felt unequal to the challenge of describing what he called "one of the grandest spectacles which can be offered to the admiration of man . . .":

We may figure to ourselves an immense crowd of citizens . . . who, having been left for three days to themselves, see at length a generalissimo appear, bringing to their recollection fifty years of battles fought in the cause of liberty; we may imagine a hundred thousand men, women and children lining the streets, hanging out the windows, and crowding the roofs, while their handkerchiefs wave in the air, and the city reverberates with exclamations of hope and joy; our imagination may paint all this, and we shall still have but an imperfect idea of the popular delirium that saluted the passage of Lafayette.

When he reached the steps of the Hôtel de Ville, someone offered to direct him inside, an offer he declined with a smile. "I know the way," he said.

This was the best chance Lafayette ever had to assume the leadership of France. In fact it was thrust at him, not only by some of his fellow deputies but even more palpably by the students and workers in the place de Grève outside, who were loudly proclaiming the wish that he declare a republic with himself at its head. Lafayette himself foreclosed the possibility that Charles X would ever return to power when an emissary arrived at the Hôtel de Ville that evening with an offer to rescind the recent ordinances and reform the ministry. "Reconciliation is impossible," he declared in a written reply. "The royal family has ceased to reign."

Foreclosing that option really left only two others: a republic with himself at its head or a monarchy under d'Orléans. When someone raised a third, that Lafayette become king, he replied, "in the words of Marshal Saxe, when it was proposed that he should become a member of the French Academy, 'It would become me as well as a ring would become a cat.'"

Charles Rémusat, who had friends in both the Fayettist and Orléanist camps, came to the Hôtel de Ville next day to try and force a decision. "There is no middle ground," he said. "It is either the monarchy with the duc d'Orléans or the republic with you. Do you wish to be the president of the Republic?"

"No, certainly not," Lafayette said, but in fact he was far from having decided that. He argued it out with friends all that day and into the next. Among others, he talked to the banker Jacques Lafitte, whom he knew to be a partisan of d'Orléans. Lafitte laid out all the arguments against a republic—that France was not ready for democratic government; that a republic would inevitably collapse into a replay of the populist Jacobin insanity; that a republic would turn the monarchs of Europe resolutely against France; and that a republican government would be at a disadvantage in trying to fund and prosecute the war that would surely follow. "I am not trying to scare you, my general, but just open your eyes on the consequences." When Lafayette raised the American example, Lafitte scoffed: "A victory in the war was all they needed. . . . Let them come and help you get rid of our outworn aristocratic [traditions]."

"Fine!" Lafayette countered, "but [d'Orléans] is unknown to the majority of the people. France will never be willing to place herself in the hands of a newcomer." And why would Lafayette agree to turn over France to d'Orléans anyway? "What has he done to deserve that? He has done nothing for the country."

"So much the better," Lafitte said, reminding Lafayette of Napoleon. "God save us from great men!"

With Lafitte, Lafayette left it that perhaps the French should declare their preference in a plebiscite, but events were moving too quickly for that to be a realistic option. A member of the provisional government, Odilon Barrot, came to see him the next morning. "I still remember this conversation very vividly," he wrote in his memoirs. "The general was not feeling well and was lying in his bed. We considered every angle of the problem—the choice of the institutions as well as the personalities involved." Lafayette talked again about the success of the American model and told Barrot he could not forget "the corruption and perfidy of the monarchy."

Finally the new American minister, William C. Rives, came to call, and Lafayette thought to put the question to him: What would the American people say if France proclaimed itself a republic? The answer was probably not what he expected: "They will say that forty years of experience have been lost on the French." Whether that was what settled the question in his mind or not, it was after that meeting when he sent his aide to tell d'Orléans that on condition of his willingness to reign as king under a constitution, in "a monarchy surrounded by republican institutions," Lafayette would support him. Barrot was not alone in thinking the decision a remarkable display of self-restraint. In Barrot's view of Lafayette's final calculation, he disliked monarchy, but "he hated Jacobinism even more." He could forget that it was the Jacobins who had run him out of France, Barrot said, but "he could not forget that detestable party had caused France so much blood and ruins. . . ." In the end, Barrot concluded, Lafayette's "reason and sincere patriotism predominated over his feelings." He made the decision "from the noblest, most disinterested sentiments, and it is my duty to bear witness to this."

Charles Rémusat's view was more pragmatic. Lafayette may have entertained fancies of a French republic, but "like all men of action," he wrote, he "always reverted to realism and common sense when faced with a serious, urgent situation."

When his overture brought d'Orléans to the Hôtel de Ville later in the day, it was clear that the crowd in the place de Grève did not share Lafayette's faith in him. A loudly insistent chant went up immediately: "No more Bourbons!" Had all the blood of the past three days been spilled so that they could exchange Charles X for his cousin? Only a single aide accompanied d'Orléans as he made his way through the hostile crowd on horseback, and when he dismounted in front of the Hôtel de Ville, witnesses said the color had drained from his face.

Lafayette was there to meet him, though, and in the last *beau geste* of his life, he wrapped d'Orléans in a tricolor flag, embraced him, and kissed him on the forehead—coronation by a "republican kiss," as Chateaubriand described it later. D'Orléans began waving the flag, and by all accounts the mood of the crowd dramatically changed. D'Orléans's detractors were not all won over that day by any means, but he had enough support that what came to be known as the July Monarchy lasted until the next revolution, which came in 1848.

Lafayette's role in the July Monarchy did not last the year. Resenting the very popularity that had given him the throne, Louis-Philippe approved a reorganization of the National Guard that left Lafayette only an honorary position. He resigned with a bitterness that can only be imagined, because he never spoke of it. All he said, that New Year's Day of 1831, was that his last few days as commandant of the Guard had been "not very nice."

He retained his seat as a deputy and fought hard for some of the reforms d'Orléans had promised and failed to deliver, such as eliminating the hereditary qualification for the Chamber of Peers, a cause he eventually won; but far more of his time was spent on his continued advocacy for popular uprisings around the world, especially now the battles for independence in Belgium, Italy, and Poland. His continual agitation for France to intervene in these and other liberation movements was only an irritating embarrassment to Louis-Philippe, known as the "king of the barricades" to the monarchs of Europe, who associated him with their troublesome radicals. In fact, Louis-Philippe was mainly concerned to keep France out of suicidal wars, and the best way to do that was not to make enemies of those who were capable of igniting them. George Washington would have sympathized.

Lafayette more often lost than won the domestic political battles of his last years, but he never lost either his hope or his ebullience, a fact that both charmed and amazed his friends. In victory and defeat he was almost eerily the same. "His enthusiasm was an inextinguisable fire," as Charles Rémusat put it. At his homes in Paris and the country, "Monsieur de Lafayette reigned as a loved and loving despot [who] tempered authority with tenderness and sprightliness, insisting on his opinions, tastes, and habits without ever imposing them. He dominated over everything simply because in most cases everyone's heart belonged to him. Everything was affectionate, courteous, considerate and tranquil because this is the way he was." A young nineteenth-century man in an eighteenth-century household, however, Rémusat found such comfort not entirely comfortable. Lafayette's good cheer sometimes felt relentless. " 'I really feel sorry for you!' " he remembered saying more than once. " 'You are obliged to be affable!' " Finally, Rémusat concluded, "It was impossible not to admire his household. It was very possible to be bored to death." Families, of course, do not see everything.

After Adrienne's death and to the end of his life, Lafayette continued to demonstrate his devotion to intelligent, accomplished women and to women in general. The pioneer feminist and abolitionist Fanny Wright, the opera diva Maria Malibran, and the Princess Christina De Belgiojoso, a beautiful young divorcée and aspiring author, were frequent companions of his last days, and though their degree of intimacy with him was never quite defined, it was sufficient to cause talk and unease in his family.

In his *Memoirs of an Egoist*, Stendhal described the continual salon that went on nightly along the rue d'Anjou in those days. Saturday night was at the Princess Belgiojoso's, where regular guests included writers (Stendhal, Heinrich Heine, Victor Hugo, Alexis de Tocqueville), composers (Bellini, Rossini), and artists. Sunday night a somewhat more political group gathered at the home of the social theorist Destutt de Tracy, and Tuesday nights all these were welcome *chez Lafayette* to join a mix of political figures, society matrons, generals, debutantes, and serious-looking young men in mustaches, some of them leaders of political conspiracies, others simply looking the part. Some of Lafayette's friends complained of having to consort with "undesirables." An American magazine called *The Lady's Book* ran an anonymous writer's charming description of Lafayette's salon in 1834:

> I have a horror of drawing-rooms, soirées . . . they make me ill. Is this my fault? . . . There is, however, one house which I would not confound with the others . . . the house of General Lafayette, in the Rue d'Anjou. There reign liberty, ease, and cordiality—there you have no refinement of forms, no superlative proprieties of manner, no etiquette, no ceremonious introductions, nothing but simple politeness, and kind attentions. Lafayette's drawing-room is like a public saloon—it is a place of universal intimacy, where friends bring their friends, sons their fathers, and travellers their comrades. Every body goes there who likes—enters at any hour, and retires when he pleases. There, natives of all countries, citizens of all classes, and all the different varieties in human society, meet, mingle, and shake hands. Thither all France and the whole of Europe have sent their deputations. There, Americans come to pay their respects to the friend of Washington; and all the liberals and political outlaws in the world, to salute the High Priest of Liberty. . . .

In the midst of all this, Stendhal could only marvel at the old marquis, who at seventy-five seemed to him "a hero from Plutarch. He lived from day to day without too much thought, quite simply performing . . . the great actions that presented themselves. And meanwhile, despite his age . . . solely intent on squeezing from behind the skirts of some pretty girl." Both of them, he wrote, were smitten with a certain eighteen-year-old. For her and "for every other young woman," Stendhal wrote, Lafayette was an easily kindled flame. "He imagines that she notices him, he dreams only of her, and the funny thing is he is often right to imagine all this. His European fame, the innate elegance of his speech . . . his eyes that light up as soon as they find themselves a foot away from a pair of nice breasts, all this combines to help him pass his last years merrily. . . ."

Lafayette entertained close female friends at La Grange as well, but here the social life was more sedate, no doubt subdued by memories of Adrienne, whose room he had left untouched since Christmas Eve 1807, the day she died. Her health had never completely recovered from Olmütz, and doctors in Paris were no more successful in diagnosing her illness than the prison doctor had been. Lafayette was at her bedside virtually every day in the weeks before her death, when a high fever took her further and further into a world of delusions. In one of her last lucid moments, she asked him whether or not he was a Christian. He did not answer.

"Ah, I know what you are," she said with a smile. "You are a Fayettist!"

"You must think me very egotistical," he replied, "but aren't you something of a Fayettist yourself?"

"You're right," she said. "That's a sect I would die for."

Until his own death twenty-eight years later he wore a pendant enclosing her picture and a lock of her hair around his neck, and he went alone to her room each morning as if to a shrine. Nothing irritated him more than being disturbed in this daily ritual, and Christmas was the saddest time of his year. Whatever his other infatuations and affections, his devotion to her memory was impermeable. Their experiences together at Olmütz, in exile, and in the last months of her life vivified a relationship he had taken quite for granted during most of their married life, and by the evidence of his letters, her loss completely undid him. He did not write Jefferson about her death for several months. When he did, he remembered that when they had first worked together in Paris, Jefferson was still in mourning for his wife Martha. "I have long ago, from my heart pitied you, my dear Jefferson," he wrote now, "and yet, before this blow, I confess I did not know what it was to be unhappy. . . . I feel irresistibly overpowered." The last act of his life was to reach for her locket and put it to his lips.

In his last years, he spent more and more time at La Grange, enjoying the warmth of his extended and growing family. By this time he had more than a dozen grandchildren, and his homes were often filled with them and their parents. There were seldom fewer than twenty-five or thirty people at dinner (his dining room could accomodate up to fifty), and though meals and accommodations were spartan, thanks to his ongoing sponsorship of liberation movements all over the world, the atmosphere was warmed by the family's complete and sincere devotion to their patriarch. Even Rémusat had finally to admit there was great vitality in the life at La Grange, "dominated by honest sentiments, noble ideas, true affections, under the paternal rule of an elderly man, loved by his family, looked after with tenderness, and ready to sacrifice everything . . . for his own glory and that of his country. I would say that it was both touching and appealing."

Lafayette spent most of his working hours at La Grange in his tower office, reading newspapers, keeping up with his correspondence, and occasionally reaching for a megaphone to shout some direction to a farm hand below. Surrounding him as he worked were the mementoes of a long and illustrious career—valedictories from the National Guards of 1789 and 1830, revolutionary banners, portraits of old compatriots, and the two silver pistols taken from an English officer that Washington left him in his will. Houdon's bust of Washington watched over everything, including the colors of a U.S. frigate christened *Brandywine*, which had brought him home from the journey that, as much as the Revolution of 1830, was the summation and the most glorious time of his life.

I n early 1824, at the instigation of President James Monroe, the U.S. Congress extended an invitation for Lafayette to revisit the nation that he had helped to create, "to see for himself the fruit borne on the tree of liberty." Monroe as well as Jefferson and Madison had been trying to get him to come to America for years, sometimes as a guest, sometimes for his own safety, offering an asylum from the hostile government of France. Jefferson in particular had concerned himself with Lafayette's welfare, offering him the governorship of the Louisiana Territory he had just purchased from Napoleon and later interceding with his successors to get him a land grant there which would help him out of financial difficulties. Lafayette gratefully but decisively declined every invitation to come to America, citing the importance of his work in France not only to the liberalization of his own country but also to other liberation movements in Europe and around the world. Coming to America would mean abdicating his responsibility to the cause, he wrote Monroe in November 1823. "[A] voluntary absence from the political field of action . . . might be interpreted for discouragement. . . . Yet I more and more look forward to the day when, with a safe conscience, it shall be my happy lot to find myself on American ground."

Three months later, the outlook for reform in France had changed drastically. Louis XVIII's hold on power appeared now to be unassailable. In the elections of February 1824, he had finally managed to rid himself of the liberal majority in the Chamber of Deputies, including Lafayette. (Lafayette blamed electoral chicanery, but the liberal deputies were in the middle of a boycott of the Chamber when the elections took place, which cannot have encouraged voters to return them.) In this case, Lafayette considered it just possible that press coverage of a journey through the one nation in the world that had successfully made the transition to republican government might be the best possible way to reawaken a thirst for liberty in France.

The timing for such a trip was also fortuitous in the United States, which, far from being the peaceable kingdom of Lafayette's imagination, was facing as great a threat of sectional breakup as any since the Constitutional Convention. The North-South divide over slavery had deepened with the bitter debate over Missouri's admission to the union as a slave state. And the so-called Missouri Compromise of 1820, which by admitting Maine at the same time kept the balance of slave and free states equal at twelve each, set a geographical boundary on slavery that threatened only to define the line at which the nation would eventually split apart. "[T]his momentous question, like a fire bell in the night, awakened and filled me with terror," Jefferson wrote from Monticello in April 1820. "I considered it at once as the knell of the Union. It is hushed, indeed, for the moment. But this is a reprieve only, not a final sentence. A geographical line, coinciding with a marked principle, moral and political, once conceived and held up to the angry passions of men, will never be obliterated; and every new irritation will mark it deeper and deeper." Even as he wrote, the central government's assertion of its right to enforce such a determination on the states created an issue that would help define the election of 1824, fortifying the old Republican states' rights position while it gave energy to the nationalism of the nascent Jacksonian Democrats.

Once again, the fates of America and France were intertwined. At the same time Congress sent its invitation to Lafayette, it was debating what came to be known as the Monroe Doctrine, which memorialized in policy the fear that Europe's monarchs, having quashed revolution there, would turn to counterrevolution in Latin America, where Spain's colonial rule had been overthrown. How legitimate that concern was is unclear, but the fear was palpable. The Monroe Doctrine, in the interest of avoiding both entanglement in Europe and Europe's interference in the Americas, called for dividing the world into spheres of influence: The United States would not permit any European power to intervene in North and South America and in exchange would itself refrain from intervention in Europe. Since Americans still felt their revolution to be the progenitor of all others, the idea of cutting loose the liberation movements of an entire continent was a matter of bitter debate. The liberation movement in Greece, birthplace of democracy, was especially dear to American hearts. In January 1824, Congress debated a resolution that in effect would have recognized the insurgent government there, and its simultaneous invitation to Lafayette was in part a protest against the Monroe Doctrine's implied indifference to the Greek cause. The assumption was that Lafayette, as the embodiment of liberation movements worldwide, would be the best possible lobbyist for American intervention in support of European rebellions, in Greece and elsewhere.

Clearly, Louis XVIII and his fellow monarchs feared the same thing. In Le Havre on the eve of his departure for America in July 1824, demonstrations for "that animal Lafayette" were forcibly suppressed.

Only Lafayette's symbolic power and a determined effort by his hosts to invoke it can explain the manic expressions of joy that greeted his arrival in America the following month and that continued for more than a year thereafter. Virtually every day for thirteen months, large to enormous crowds of slavishly admiring Americans from Maine to South Carolina and points west turned out to hear him speak. Merchants planted his face on buttons, handkerchiefs, bowls, medallions, furniture, and fans. Songwriters and poets exhausted themselves pouring out their souls to him. Every city he visited held banquets and band concerts and parades and fireworks displays in his honor, and he loved every minute of it, working the crowds and shaking hands to the point of exhaustion, all the while perfecting a repertoire of crowd-pleasing banter. "Are you married?" one favorite gambit went, and whatever the response he would say, "Lucky man."

His itinerary was exhaustive and exhausting, but adoring crowds had always given him strength—or, as Jefferson would have had it, they were his weakness—and this trip was all about adulation. Schools, parks, and babies were named for him, as were new counties and towns. (Two centuries later there were still more than four hundred Fayettes, Fayettevilles, and Lafayettes on the map of the United States.) His every stop and speech were news, though in the journalistic coverage of Lafayette's trip, fact had little chance against myth. Almost sixty-eight years old, Lafayette walked with a cane and a bad limp, the result of a fall that left him with a broken femur. The accident, combined with a disastrous experimental "cure," had made him almost lame. That explanation having no metaphoric resonance, however, it was ignored. The limp was everywhere attributed to his famous injury at Brandywine, and Lafayette did not exert himself to set the record straight.

Since he was distinctly unpopular with the French government, his American apotheosis was the subject of daily gloomier dispatches to Paris from the French minister, one baron de Mareuil. "There is at the moment only one occupation in America," he wrote four days after Lafayette arrived in New York, manfully assuring his minders in Paris: "I am prepared for this hurly burly. I will show no concern. . . ." As Lafayette approached Washington for the first time, Mareuil told Paris that he had "agreed to refuse any invitation, even from the President, to any festivity for M. de Lafayette." A few days after Lafayette arrived, Mareuil could confirm his government's worst fears. "[E]very one of his words . . . is less an homage to America than an appeal to the revolutionary passions in Europe, a wish for their success and for the complete triumph of democracy." Back in France, however, the trip was not having the effect Lafayette wished. He had brought along a secretary whose job it was to supply friendly journalists with copy, but censorship kept much of his journey out of the papers.

His effect on the United States, however, was electrifying. The first months of his tour came during a bitterly divisive presidential campaign, which brought James Monroe's two-term "Era of Good Feelings" to a decisive close. The good feelings had derived largely from an absence of political strife, since the Federalist Party had completely collapsed. Now, however, competing sectional interests took the place of ideological differences in dividing the electorate. After the bitterness of the Missouri Compromise and thanks to ongoing tariff battles, the North believed the South would never again vote for a free-state president (John Adams, who had served twenty years before, was the only U.S. president so far not to have come from a slave state), and the South and West believed no president from the Northeast would ever serve their interests.

Henry Clay of Kentucky and William Crawford of Georgia were nominally candidates, but the main contest pitted Andrew Jackson of Tennessee against John Quincy Adams, the South and West against the Northeast. Virtually the only idea on which all regions seemed to agree was that the union was near collapse. A newspaper editor in Georgia was convinced that a political earthquake was on its way that would "bury our free governments in irretrievable ruin," an opinion with which the pro-Adams *Patriot* in Boston was in full agreement: "We shall soon separate into bitter and unextinguishable hostilities."

Lafayette had long been friendly with Adams and became friendly with Jackson during his time in Washington, where they stayed in the same roominghouse, but he maintained a strict silence about both of them during the campaign, and as someone identified with no section but with the nation as a whole, he was the ideal symbol of unity and a reminder of the common American cause. His very return forty years later seemed to give Americans a prideful sense of just how far they had come. "He left us weak, unorganized and tottering with infancy," wrote an editorialist in New York's *Commercial Advertiser*. "[H]e returns to us and finds our shores smiling with cultivation, our waters white with the sails of every nation, our cities enlarged, flourishing and wealthy, and our free government, for whose establishment he himself suffered, perfected in beauty, union, and experience." He also helped Americans to recall their ideological roots, applying some healing context to the nation's political wounds. His visit "turns this whole people from . . . our manifold political dissentions," as one political analyst put it, "[and] carries us back to that great period in our history about which opinions have long been tranquil and settled. . . . It brings, in fact, our revolution nearer to us, with all the high-minded patriotism and self-denying virtues of our forefathers."

At times his presence seemed to encourage a spirit of unity even among the warring candidates, which was never needed more than when the already bitter contest became deadlocked: At the end of the voting,

Jackson had a plurality of both the electoral and popular votes but not enough electoral votes to win, which threw the election into the House of Representatives. Nine days after the inconclusive vote, Lafayette made an appearance before a joint session of Congress, and all four candidates were there to hear him talk about "the principles for which we have had the honour to fight and bleed." All four also attended at a banquet in his honor on New Year's Day, where he toasted "the perpetual union of the United States."

On February 1, 1825, John Quincy Adams won the presidency thanks to Henry Clay's support and promptly named Clay his secretary of state. The Jacksonians denounced this "corrupt bargain" and threatened violence to prevent Adams from taking office. At the reception that Monroe held in Adams's honor a few days later, though, Lafayette could justifiably take paternal pleasure in the sight of his new friend Jackson reaching out his hand to Adams, whom Lafayette had first known as his father's young son. Also taking in the scene as Jackson congratulated and pledged his loyal support to Adams was James Fenimore Cooper, who had met Lafayette shortly after he arrived in the States and had been following his tour ever since. "I watched [Jackson's] manly and marked features narrowly," Cooper wrote, but Jackson betrayed only "great dignity and . . . perfect good nature. . . . He left us laughing." He was also determined even then to beat Adams in the next election, which he did.

Lafayette spent that winter in Washington and resumed his tour in March, extending his time in America so that he could visit all twenty-four states. After a spring tour through the Southern states to Louisiana, he proceeded up the Mississippi by steamboat from New Orleans to St. Louis, and then from the Ohio to the Cumberland River to Nashville, where he spent several days with Jackson at his homestead, The Hermitage. He continued on through Kentucky, Indiana, Ohio, and western Pennsylvania to Buffalo, where he marveled at the natural wonder of Niagara Falls and equally, as he embarked on a barge for Albany, at the man-made splendor of the brand-new Erie Canal. Arriving in Boston in time for the fiftieth anniversary of Bunker Hill, he stopped in Quincy to say what he knew would be his last good-bye to the elder John Adams, then went north through New Hampshire to Maine, south through Vermont, by boat across Lake Champlain to Albany, then down the Hudson to New York, where he began his Fourth of July by laying the cornerstone of a library in Brooklyn. A crowd of schoolchildren were brought out for the event, and one of them was the six-year-old Walt Whitman, who remembered Lafayette driving up very slowly in a canary yellow coach. When he arrived, "in the midst of the crowd, with other gentlemen, [he] assisted in lifting the children . . . to safe spots where they could see the ceremony," Whitman remembered as an old man. "Happening to stand near, I remember I was taken up by Lafayette in his arms and held a moment—I remember that he press'd my cheek with a kiss as he set me down—the childish wonder and nonchalance during the whole affair at the time,—contrasting with the indescribable preciousness of the reminiscence since."

Few who saw Lafayette during that long tour through America would ever forget it, heralded as he always was by the thought that in this last surviving general of the Revolutionary War was the embodiment of all that America had been through and accomplished and would become. He played his part tirelessly, a remarkable physical feat for a man who was nearing seventy. He also played the role brilliantly, his keen sense of theater sharpened by his thirst for acclaim and the sense that he was creating at every stop the story that would be told about him after he was gone.

Introducing him before his speech to Congress, then House Speaker Henry Clay had talked about how rare it was for a patriot to be able to return years later to see what his sacrifice had accomplished. "You stand in the midst of posterity!" he said. Lafayette did not write down the speech he gave that day (he had been making speeches about America for months at that point and hardly needed a script), but James Fenimore Cooper was on hand here too, taking notes in the gallery. "No, Mr. Speaker," Lafayette said. "Posterity has not begun for me, since, in the sons of my companions and friends, I find the same public feelings I have had the happiness to experience in their fathers." Posterity was a distant prospect, one that resided in the unknowable future and in the judgment of history.

As Lafayette continued his journey south from New York, a profound sense of final farewell settled over him. After a week in Philadelphia, he stopped to visit the battlefields of Germantown, Barren Hill, and Brandywine, gathering an ever larger crowd of the last Revolutionary War veterans as he went. At the place where he had been wounded, he waved off their huzzahs and told them to remember Washington.

John Quincy Adams, now the president, designated a new frigate, christened *Brandywine*, to take Lafayette back to France. A ship had been offered to bring him over as well, but Lafayette had declined it. This time he did not, burdened as he was with literally tons of mementoes gathered along the way, all of which were precious to him, from an enormous stuffed grizzly bear to Indian headdresses to sacks full of dirt from Bunker Hill and Brandywine, in which he wished to be buried. He also took home an unprecedented gift from Congress of $200,000* (they called it back pay), which saved him from creditors in France who were threatening to seize his property. If he was no longer the "hero of two worlds," he was assuredly the hero of one, perhaps even more so now than he had been when his hair was still a sandy red.

A week before his sixty-eighth birthday, for which Adams had scheduled a gala dinner that was to be the last event on his calendar before the official farewell ceremony at the White House next day, he made one last trip to Virginia to say his most difficult good-byes: first to Thomas Jefferson at Monticello, where he spent three days (after which, it was said, Jefferson's wine cellar required significant restocking), then to James Madison at Montpelier, then to Monroe in Loudoun.

Then he said good-bye to Washington. Lafayette had been to the tomb at Mount Vernon the previous fall, but what might have been a time for reflection had perhaps predictably turned into something of a circus, with cannons booming, bands playing, and Martha Washington's grandson George Custis coming up to him after his visit to the tomb, ready with a souvenir and an elaborate speech, hailing "you who alone of all generals of the army of Independence survive among us" and offering him, "at this solemn and touching moment . . . a ring which holds a lock of hair of the man you loved! The ring has always been the emblem of the union of hearts," etc.

This time Lafayette's visit was not for public consumption. His secretary did not take notes, and at the tomb Lafayette asked everyone to leave him, including George. He stayed inside for an hour. Virtually nothing was written about the visit, although someone who looked through a crack in the door said that he was kneeling.

*The equivalent of more than $4 million in 2007.

The lack of authentic detail left a void, something as much abhorred by the human imagination as by nature. A few months after Lafayette's death, an unsigned piece in the *New-England Magazine* titled "An Hour at Mount Vernon" included the following paragraph:

> It is said that at the time Lafayette visited the grave of Washington, in 1825, an eagle, one which might have been a fit model for our country's emblem, kept hovering over the spot as long as [he] remained there. On his departure, the noble bird rose proudly into the air, then swept downward and disappeared in the thick covert of woods which skirt the shore.

At Lafayette's birthday/farewell dinner a few days later, President Adams broke with executive branch protocol (established by Washington) to propose a toast himself: "To the 22nd of February and the 6th of September, the birthday of Washington and the birthday of Lafayette!" A man who was quick to tears at most times and now almost constantly on the verge, Lafayette collected himself to reply: "To the 4th of July, the birthday of liberty in the two hemispheres!"

The next day's farewell at the White House was even more emotional, and accounts of it were entirely in keeping with all the coverage of Lafayette's last journey in America. As one early twentieth-century biographer described his final departure, the new frigate *Brandywine* made its way across the Chesapeake "under full sail, traversing the centre of a brilliant rainbow, one of whose limbs appeared to rest on the Maryland shore, and the other on that of Virginia." It is of course possible that there really was a rainbow.

When Lafayette died, nine years later, Americans seemed to be far more distraught than the French were, in part because of his unique place in America's past and present, and in part because the American Revolution really was over, while the serial French Revolution was far from it. While the French revolutions continued to produce heroes and scapegoats, America got no more founding fathers or heroes of the Revolution. "One by one the lights of the American Revolution have become extinguished," as one of Lafayette's legion eulogists put it, "and now the last glorious star is blotted from the firmament for ever." In part no doubt because he was the last, President Andrew Jackson (now in his second term) ordered that Lafayette be given the same military honors as George Washington. Officers wore black crepe armbands for six months, during which period flags stood at half-mast. At every army outpost and naval station, twenty-four guns (one for each state) were fired at dawn. The nation's representatives dressed in mourning for thirty days, and former President John Quincy Adams delivered his funeral oration to a joint session of Congress: "Pronounce him one of the first men of his age, and you have yet not done him justice. . . ."

Most eulogies, in the gravity of the moment, tend toward hyperbole, and those for Lafayette, which poured forth all over the world, were no exception. One of the best was that of John Stuart Mill, because his praise, while generous, was thoughtful. "His was not the influence of genius," Mill wrote, "nor even of talents; it was the influence of a heroic character; it was the influence of one who, in every situation, and throughout a long life, had done and suffered everything which opportunity had presented itself of doing and suffering for the right." Mill said he thought it would be a long time before "such a union of character and circumstances . . . shall enable any other human being to live such a life." The same thought was echoed in one of the wonderfully economical epigrams of Chateaubriand, whose conservatism had put him more often against Lafayette than with him: "This man has lived."

It would seem hard to deny him that at least, but there have ever since been those who wished to minimize the importance of his life. During the tour that led to his masterwork *Democracy in America*, which followed Lafayette's U.S. tour by five years, Alexis de Tocqueville was pleased to find less hero worship for Lafayette than he expected among what he called "the enlightened classes. . . . Almost all think that the regime of the Restoration was the happiest combination for France," he confided to his diary, "and that the present revolution [the monarchy of Louis-Philippe] is a crisis, dangerous and perhaps fatal for the liberty of Europe. The middle classes, the masses, and the newspapers representing popular passions, have on the contrary a blind instinct which drives them to adopt the principles of liberty professed in Europe, and the men who foster them." As acute a political observer as he was and as sympathetic to American institutions as he came to be, Tocqueville was also the great-grandson of Malesherbes, who had finished his long and distinguished career by defending Louis XVI at his trial and was punished for it at the guillotine in April 1794. Tocqueville thought the French needed their Bourbon monarchy, and he blamed Lafayette for having allowed France to be deprived of it.

Many historians since Tocqueville have also faulted Lafayette for having "lost" the monarchy of France. As late as 1987, in the *Histoire et dictionnaire de la Révolution française,* the distinguished historians Jean Tulard and Jean-François Fayard allowed the entry on Lafayette to include Napoleon's last, slanderous saber-slash from his deathbed on St. Helena, a withering and demonstrably false denunciation of Lafayette that the conservative *dictionnaire* nevertheless characterized as "not too excessive." The dictionary entry went on: "An empty-headed political dwarf, Lafayette is one of the people most responsible for the destruction of the French monarchy." Marxist and liberal historians have faulted him as scathingly or simply dismissed him for a lack of revolutionary rigor.

Such are the vagaries of history and those who write it. Because France had so many different regimes after 1789,* and because every regime imposes, in addition to its manifest principles and reforms, a range of subtler imperatives, such as the selective reinterpretation of all that has gone before, Lafayette's reputation, as hard as he worked to shape it, proved far more mercurial in France than in the United States, at least among historians. The French people have been more generous. In a poll by French news organizations on the eve of the 1989 bicentennial, Lafayette was voted the most admired revolutionary figure by 57 percent of respondents. (Danton and Saint-Just, whose revolutions ended with martyrdom at the guillotine, tied for second with 21 percent each.)

With posterity so divided, the safest resort, finally, may be what can be posited as uncontroverted facts. One is that the people closest to Lafayette, leaving aside his family, loved and respected him with a devotion that has left an indelible record; and those who knew him longest never questioned the fact that the ideals with which he set sail on *La Vic-*

---

*Three monarchs, two emperors, five republics.

toire at nineteen were the same ones he carried up the steps of the Hôtel de Ville at seventy-two. He decided on his cause as a young man, and he did not change course.

Another inarguable fact is that he did not lack courage, which was tested on the battlefield and on the streets of Paris, in his youth and in his old age. As many times as he was defeated, he never left the field.

Someone said of Lafayette that he had one idea, and he was lucky that it was the best idea of his time. Fair enough: Like Washington, he was a hedgehog, filled with one great thought. "He never lost faith in the final triumph of his ideas," Charles Rémusat wrote in his memoir, though with as much despair as admiration. "The criticisms one may have heard about him appear pretty childish in view of the courage he showed," he said, and yet he had to admit that the critics had a point since "he served in a cause that failed. . . . If—as I fear—the future sheds an unfavorable light on the 1830 revolution, his image will suffer, because he contributed to the creation of something which did not last."

Rémusat was not surprised at the fact that Lafayette was virtually worshipped in the United States—"It seems to me that in America he made no mistakes"—but he blamed that very success for the mistakes he made in France. His good fortune in America had only spoiled him with the illusion that fate was the wind at his back, "that things are easier than they actually are, that great ideas always prevail . . . that it was easy to carry out a revolution, and that he was born to make and lead them. . . . Everything seems to indicate that if the French Revolution succeeds it will do so quite differently from what Lafayette thought," Rémusat worried. "He may not survive the stupid judgment of the Parisian salons."

There is one more irrefutable fact to consider, however, and that is the Constitution of the Fifth Republic, which has been in effect since 1958 and which begins with these words: "The French people solemnly proclaim their attachment to the Rights of Man and the principles of national sovereignty as defined by the Declaration of 1789. . . . The nation's emblem shall be the blue, white and red tricolor flag. . . . Its principle shall be: government of the people, by the people, and for the people. National sovereignty shall belong to the people."

Notes

ABBREVIATIONS

AAE   *Archives des Affaires étrangères, correspondance politique, Etats-Unis*

AP   *Archives parlementaires de 1787 à 1860: Recueil complèt des débats législatifs et politiques des Chambres francaises*

BnF   Bibliothèque nationale de France

Doniol   *Histoire de la participation de la France à l'Etablissement des Etats-Unis d'Amérique: correspondance diplomatique et documents.* Henri Doniel, ed.

JCC   *Journals of the Continental Congress 1774–1789.* Worthington Ford et al., eds.

LDC   *Letters of Delegates to Congress, 1774–1789.* Paul H. Smith, ed.

LFL   *Lafayette in the Age of the American Revolution, Selected Letters and Papers, 1776–1790.* Stanley J. Idzerda et al., eds.

LFM   *Mémoires, correspondance et manuscrits du Général Lafayette, publiés par sa famille*

LG   *Lafayette,* by Louis Gottschalk

PGW-RWS   *The Papers of George Washington.* W. W. Abbot et al., eds. Revolutionary War Series (1775–83)

PGW-CS   *The Papers of George Washington.* W. W. Abbot et al., eds. Confederation Series (1784–88)

PGW-PS   *The Papers of George Washington.* W. W. Abbot et al., eds. Presidential Series (1788–97)

PGW-RS   *The Papers of George Washington.* W. W. Abbot et al., eds. Retirement Series (1797–99)

PV   *Procès-verbale des séances et déliberations de l'Assembée générale des électeurs de Paris, réunis à l'Hôtel-de-Ville le 14 juillet 1789,* Bailly et Duveyrier, eds.

Sparks   *The Diplomatic Correspondence of the United States of America from the Signing of the Definitive Treaty of Peace to the Adoption of the Constitution.* Jared Sparks, ed.

TJP   *Papers of Thomas Jefferson.* Julian Boyd et al, eds.

TJW   *The Works of Thomas Jefferson.* Paul Leicester Ford, ed.

Wharton   *The Revolutionary Diplomatic Correspondence of the United States.* Francis Wharton, ed.

Writings   *Writings of Washington.* John C. Fitzpatrick, ed.

PART ONE

I

5 "men crippled with debts": Robin, *Voyage dans l'Amérique*, 26.

5 "wild conduct": Lovell to GW, July 24, 1777, Francis Wharton, ed. *The Revolutionary Diplomatic Correspondence of the United States* [hereinafter Wharton], II:366.

5 "I am under no small difficulties": Abbot et al., eds. *Papers of George Washington* [hereinafter PGW]: *Revolutionary War Series (1775–1783)* [hereinafter RWS], VI:498–599.

5 "You cannot conceive what a weight": PGW-RWS VIII:305.

6 "I shall be much obliged": John C. Fitzpatrick, *Writings of Washington* [hereinafter *Writings*], Feb. 20, 1777, to Richard Henry Lee.

6 The reply ignored his request: PGW-RWS VIII:455–56, Feb. 27, 1777, Richard Henry Lee to Washington.

6 "will save us much altercation": L. H. Butterfield, ed., *The Adams Family Papers: Diary & Autobiography of John Adams*, 4 vols. (New York, Atheneum, 1964), II:263.

6 which was very late and men-only: J. Bennett Nolan, *Lafayette in America Day by Day*. Cahier VII in *Historical Documents*, Institut français de Washington (Baltimore: Johns Hopkins University Press, 1934). See also the journal entry for this date in Octavius Pickering and Charles W. Upham, *The Life of Timothy Pickering*, 4 vols. (Boston: Little, Brown, 1867–73).

6 Washington saw immediately in the young marquis: PGW-RWS, XI:4–5.

6 "What line of conduct I am to pursue": Ibid.

7 news that Washington had received: Flexner, *George Washington: A Biography* [hereinafter Flexner], II:212.

7 the "melancholy truths": *Writings*, March 26, 1777, To the President of Congress.

7 he was riding at Washington's side: Stanley J. Idzerda, ed., *Lafayette in the Age of the American Revolution, Selected Letters and Papers 1776–1790* [hereinafter LFL], I:91.

7 watched over anxiously by the general himself: LFM I:116.

8 Suddenly, "tears fell": Chinard, *George Washington*, 77.

8 "the man I love": *Writings*, Jan. 4, 1782, to Lafayette.

8 "Never during the Revolution": Freeman, IV:462

8 Lafayette found in Washington his long-lost father: See, e.g., Bernier, 46; Chernow, 87.

8 "father of his country," a phrase first applied: Brookhiser, *Founding Father*, 12.

9 "two centuries of marriage counseling": Jean-David Lévitte, then ambassador of

France to the United States, recalled Powell's words in a speech at Stanford—
Stanford Daily, Oct. 28, 2005.

10 **"at this day serves"**: Edmund Burke, "Speech on Conciliation with America,"
March 22, 1775.

10 **"degenerate, small, cowardly"**: For early French views of the American colonies
see Chinard, "Eighteenth Century Theories"; Corneille de Pauw, *Défense des
Recherches philosophiques sur les Américains* (Berlin, 1770); and Echeverria, *Mirage*.

10 **"men had just climbed down from the rocks"**: De Pauw, 105–7, quoted in Fay,
appendix I:479.

11 **Alexander Hamilton once offered**: Farrand, ed., *The Records of the Federal Convention of 1787*, III:85.

12 **began a rigorous course in self-improvement**: Details of Washington's early
study are in Longmore, appendix, 213ff.

13 **the revolutionary period's "cult of antiquity"**: See Parker, *The Cult of Antiquity*;
Gummere, *The American Colonial Mind*.

13 **Some of the great lines**: I am indebted to Garry Wills's *Cincinnatus* for pointing
out the origins of these lines, and for his general discussion of the importance
and meaning of "glory" and "fame."

14 **"A Roman soul is bent on"**: Addison, *Cato: A Tragedy in Five Acts* (Edinburgh:
Oliver & Boyl, n. d.).

14 **Virtue was learned**: Wood, *Radicalism*, 190, cites Edmund S. Morgan, *The Gentle Puritan: A Life of Ezra Stiles, 1727–1795* (New Haven: Yale University Press,
1962), 167.

14 **"recalling the lost images"**: Samuel Stanhope Smith to Madison, in Hutchinson
and Rachel, eds., *Papers of Madison*, I:208–09; Wood, *Radicalism*, 190.

14 **"It was as if he was always onstage"**: Wood, *Radicalism*, 198.

14 **The same was said by Talleyrand**: *Memoirs of the Prince de Talleyrand*, ed. Duc de
Broglie, trans. R. Ledos de Beaufort, 5 vols. (New York, 1891–92), I:52–53;
Gottschalk, *Lafayette* [hereinafter LG], II:39.

14 **"You are wrong!"**: "A Diplomat's Wife in Philadelphia: Letters of Henrietta Liston, 1796–1800," ed. Bradford Perkins, *William and Mary Quarterly*, 3rd ser., XI
(1954), 592–632; Flexner, IV:493.

15 **"canine appetite for popularity"**: *Papers of Thomas Jefferson*, ed. Boyd et al. [here-
inafter TJP], XI:95, Jefferson to Madison.

15 **carried a picture of Francis Bacon**: For Jefferson and Bacon's hierarchy of glory,
see Adair, *Fame and the Founding Fathers*, 14ff.

15 **"virtue and worth"**: Ibid.

15 **those "unborn millions"**: See, e.g., Circular to the States, June 8, 1783, in *Writings*.

15 **As the historian Douglas Adair pointed out**: See Colbourn, ed., *Fame and the
Founding Fathers*, 3–26.

15 **The word "honor" comes up 3,952 times**: *Writings* (result of keyword search).

16 **"We forgot"**: Wood, *Radicalism*, 330; Adair, *Fame*, "Was Alexander Hamilton a
Christian Statesman?" (with Marvin Harvey), 147.

16 **Washington wrote to introduce Lafayette**: *Writings*, May 28, 1788, to Lafayette.

17 **in a psychic compensation for repressed frustration**: See Idzerda, "When and
Why," 11–12.

17 **"above the common run"**: See Longmore, 46ff.

17 the great "Fraternity of Spectators": Addison, "Uses."
18 **In this sense both the American and French revolutions were psychological**: For this insight and its development, I am indebted to Gordon S. Wood's *The Radicalism of the American Revolution*.

II

19 the best part of his name: Grendel, 13–15.
19 "too *drôle*": Loménie, I:82.
19 pronounced, roughly, *fee-karo*: Grendel, 141.
21 The price of a four-pound loaf: Manceron, I:171
22 "Nothing can equal the ease": Burke quoted in Trevelyan, II:15.
22 "kicked the door of a bakeshop": Manceron, I:183.
22 "with their knees, kick the victims": Robert Anchel, *Crimes et Châtiments au XVIIIe siècle* (Paris: Perrin, 1933), 166; Manceron, I:183.
23 "covering robes for the king": *Journal de Papillon de la Ferté*, ed. Ernest Boysse (Paris: Ollendorf, 1887): 370–73; Manceron, I:191.
23 Turgot . . . tried to talk Louis out of: Gruber, 88–102.
23 "It is both a surprise and a relief": *Correspondance Sècrète entre Marie-Thérèse et le Comte de Mercy-Argenteau* (Paris: Firmin-Didot, 1875), II:346; Manceron, I:201.
24 "General Washington rose from his seat": Rush, *Autobiography*, 112–13
24 "I beg it may be remembered": Flexner, I:341.
25 "so much martial dignity": Brookhiser, *Founding Father*, 114.
25 The brief but bloody engagement: The account of Jumonville relies on Anderson, *Crucible of War*, 50ff.
25 "I hear bullets whistle": *Writings*, May 31, 1754, to John Augustine Washington.
26 "took out [Jumonville's] brains": Statement of Private John Shaw, Anderson, 55.
26 Washington suggested that the French scalps: Hofstra, 129, in J. Frederick Fausz, " 'Engaged in Enterprises Pregnant with Terror': George Washington's Formative Years Among the Indians," 115–55.
26 "the most infamous a British subject": Longmore, 23.
27 because he asked "ardently": *Writings*, June 10, 1754, to Dinwiddie.
27 "I am much concerned": *Writings*, May 29, 1754, to Dinwiddie.
28 "If you think me capable of": *Writings*, Nov. 15, 1754, to Col. William Fitzhugh.
28 "a new road to the Ohio": *Writings*, Aug. 2, 1758, to Maj. Frances Halkett.
28 "in no ways like a soldier": Hofstra, 208, in John E. Ferling, "School for Command: Young George Washington and the Virginia Regiment," 195–222.
28 "That appearance of glory": *Writings*, Sept. 1, 1758, to John Robinson.
28 "the heroic spirit of every free-born Englishman": *Writings*, April 27, 1754, to Horatio Sharpe.
28 "I was employed to go": *Writings*, Aug. 2, 1755, to John Augustine Washington.
29 "You may believe me, my dear Patsy": *Writings*, June 18, 1775, to Martha Washington.
29 "Very warm in the forenoon": Jackson and Twohig, eds., *Diaries of George Washington*, June 19, 1775.
30 "Though this scene was almost horrible": Freeman, *George Washington, A Biography* [hereinafter Freeman], III:465.

30 to know that colonial soldiers could stand up so well: Ibid., 465n.

30 308 barrels, or about 16 tons: Ibid., 484.

30 "an unaccountable kind of stupidity": *Writings,* Aug. 29, 1775, to Richard Henry Lee.

30 "the greatest boasters and worst soldiers": Flexner, II:37.

31 "Between you and me": *Writings,* July 10, 1775, to Richard Henry Lee.

31 On August 1, he found out: Force, Ser. IV: vol. 3, 5. Letter dated Aug. 1, 1775, from Elbridge Gerry to Washington.

31 "For half an hour, he did not utter": Letter from Brig. Gen. John Sullivan to the New Hampshire Committee of Safety, Aug. 5, 1775, *Letters and Papers of Major-General John Sullivan,* ed. Otis G. Hammond, 3 vols. (Concord, NH, 1930–39), I:72–73; Flexner, II:36.

31 Franklin talked up the virtues of: Wharton, II:67–71.

31 "know no more of a rifle": PGW-RWS II:71, Sept. 30, 1775, to Samuel Washington.

31 "Remember, Mr. Henry": Flexner, II:9.

III

32 a fine time with local girls: Description of life at Metz is from Ségur.

32 "Bliss was it in that dawn": William Wordsworth, "French Revolution" (1809) in *The Complete Poetical Works* (London: Macmillan & Co., 1888). Bartleby.com, 1999.

32 If you never lived in that time: Talleyrand paraphrased in Becker, 136.

33 "The women here are pretty": Feb. 28, 1777, to Adrienne, LFL I:23.

34 "In my blood is the hot lava": Holbrook, 5, cites *Mémoires, correspondance et manuscrits du Général Lafayette, publiés par sa famille* [hereinafter LFM].

34 When he was eleven: The facts of Lafayette's childhood and background in the following paragraphs are taken from LG I.

34 the most prestigious school, the Collège du Plessis: Information on the Collège du Plessis is taken from LG I; Compère; Palmer, *School;* and Parker, *Cult.*

35 Every morning was spent at the *Manège:* "Souvenirs d'un page de la cour de Louis XVI" by Felix, comte de France d'Hézecques (Paris: Didier, 1873), 121.

35 seeing that Lafayette got private lessons: Taillemite, 16.

36 "Remember to tell Noailles": *Correspondance entre le Comte de Mirabeau et le Comte de la Marck pendant les années 1789, 1790 et 1791,* ed. Ad. de Bacourt (Paris, 1851), 63–64 ; LG-I:6.

36 Mme Aglaé d'Hunolstein: The account of this relationship is from Gottschalk, *Lady-in-Waiting.*

36 Ségur could only laugh: Ségur, I:25.

36 and "disguised vanity": LFL I:"Memoir of 1779," 3.

36 he had never heard anything . . . worth remembering: LFM I:7.

36 "My awkward manner": LFL I:"Memoir of 1779," 3.

37 "Everyone knows that memory": LG I:47–48; Maurois, 39.

37 a dinner in Metz: *Histoire de la participation de la France à l'Établissement des Etats-Unis d'Amérique, Correspondance diplomatique et documents* [hereinafter Doniol], I:98; LFM I:8–10; LG I:50.

37 "When I first heard" LFL I:"Memoir of 1779," 7.

38 "sufficiently strong, energetic, and determined": Maurois, 44.
39 "male organs of generation": Grendel, 149.
39 Louis kept the chevalier on his pension: Loménie, II:183–84.
39 "All the king wishes to know": Loménie, II:163.
39 "I can give [the king] the most accurate": Grendel, 148
40 "We met," the chevalier explained: Loménie, II:195.
40 "When it is thought": Kite, II:18–19.
40 "Everyone tells me that this mad woman": Loménie, II:214.
40 a new favorite card game called "Boston": Ségur, I:87.
41 $5 million worth of arms: Manceron, I:364.
41 "The humiliating peace of 1763": Doniol, I:2.
41 "thirty-eight thousand armed": Loménie, III:110.
42 "inexpressibly distressing": *Writings*, Sept. 21, 1775, to the President of Congress.
42 "Essential points . . .": Loménie, II:208.
42 to "retake and wear the costume": Kite, II:24.
43 "If ever a question was important": Ibid., 53.
43 "strict and rigorous duty": Durand, 59–73.
43 "the Ministerial Troops": *Writings*, May 31, 1775, to George William Fairfax.
43 "Those who have too long": *Proceedings, Papers, and Debates of the House of Lord and the House of Commons, on Measures Relating to the American Colonies, During the Second Session of the Fourteen Parliament of Great Britain.* Documentary History, series four, vol. 6, from Force, VI:1, Oct. 26, 1775.
44 "You are to be drawn on hurdles": Flexner, II:14.
44 "many an uneasy hour": PGW-RWS III:87, Jan. 14, 1776, to Joseph Reed.
45 "fifteen minutes with the king alone": Doniol, I:251; Tower, I:99.
45 "a faithful account of events": Doniol, I:156; Tower, I:84.
45 "They asked me if France": Wharton, I:334–35.
46 "As the season is fast approaching": *Writings*, General Orders, Feb. 20, 1776.
46 "Peace or War": Durand, 74–85; Tower, I:118–24.
46 "Peace or War" was by all accounts critical: Corwin, 79 and n41.
47 The only minister at the meeting: Wharton, I:339–40.
47 the shortfall was almost 50 million livres: Parker and Brown, *Major Themes*, 350.
47 "The first gunshot": Schama, 87.
47 Turgot actually supported the republican ideals: For the irony of Turgot and Vergennes's relative positions on the American Revolution, I am indebted to Price, 49–50.
48 "if experience brings to light": Manceron, I:283–84.
48 "We have maintained our ground": *Writings*, March 31, 1776, to John Augustine Washington.
49 "the opposition and the ministry": Kite, II:72.
49 "but [the news] was so bad": Ibid., 72–73.
49 "Are we going to let them perish?": Ibid., 67.
49 "Do not suppose that because your plans": Doniol, I:385–86.
50 "On your part, do not fail": Wharton, II:97.
50 "we ought to do all in our power": Ibid.
50 "send out the supplies": Ibid., 98.

IV

51 **Deane did not receive official notice:** The date is in his letter to the Secret Committee of Nov. 28, 1775, Wharton, II:196.

51 **with instructions to obtain an array:** Franklin's instructions to Deane, March 3, 1776, ibid., 78ff.

51 **Vergennes promised Deane nothing:** Deane to the Secret Committee, Aug. 18, 1776, ibid., 112ff.

52 **inspired by the same dinner with the Duke of Gloucester:** Lasseray, *Treize Etoiles*, 20. Wharton, I:316, cites an article by Dr. C. J. Stillé in the January 1888 issue of *Pennsylvania Magazine of History*.

52 **thanks to a spy they had placed very close:** For details of Bancroft's activities, see Abernethy, "Commercial Activities," and Boyd, "Silas Deane."

52 **"well-nigh harassed to death":** Deane to Secret Committee, Nov. 28, 1776, Wharton, II:198.

53 **"My aim is simply to find":** *Archives des Affaires étrangères, correspondance politique, Etats-Unis* [hereinafter AAE], I:304–07, Manceron, I:393; also see Maurois, 43.

53 **"a man fitted to carry the weight":** Wharton, I:392–93, letter from Broglie to Kalb, Dec. 11, 1776. Wharton takes his translation from Kapp, *Kalb*.

53 **When he first approached Broglie:** LFM I:110.

53 **"Good!" Broglie said:** *Mémoires de Théodore Lameth*, ed., Eugene Welvert (Paris, 1913), 107; LG-I:74.

54 **"I find several vessels here":** Wharton, II:222.

54 **"I have procured for you":** Ibid., 129.

54 **"52 pieces of brass cannon":** PGW-RWS, IX, 244–45, cites the invoice for cargo on the *Amphitrite* Beaumarchais sent with his letter to Congress.

55 **displeased with a local production:** Kite, II:115–16.

55 **ordered the chief of police in Paris:** Memo to Lenoir, lieutenant-general of police, Versailles, Dec. 10, 1776, AAE I:396; LG I:79.

55 **"I am deeply touched":** Tower, I:160.

55 **"Before this you have only seen":** LFM I:12.

55 *La Bonne Mère,* **a 22-ton ship:** All details on *La Victoire* are in LFL I:84 and n4.

56 *"Vis sat contra fatum":* Buckman, 35.

56 **"London is a delightful city":** LFL I:26–27.

56 **"Don't worry," he wrote:** LFL I:51.

56 **"You will be astonished, my dear papa":** LFL I:28.

57 **"I am too guilty":** LFL I:32.

57 **"My heart is broken":** LFL I:47–49.

57 **a long, fervid shipboard letter:** LFL I:56–60.

V

59 **ships rats sold for a shilling:** William T. Parsons, *Pennsylvania Germans, A Persistent Minority* (Collegeville, PA: Chestnut Books, 1985), 47–60.

59 **a commercial convention:** Ibid.

59 **"I have been in the most tedious":** LFL I:58.

60 **"a new Olympus, a new Arcady":** Echeverria, *Mirage*, 31.

60 Lafayette had read Raynal: LFL I:116.

60 "I was in no position to be choosy": Mauroy's memoir is translated in LFL I:53–56.

61 "My fellow passengers were in a laughable state": Ibid.

62 At midnight on Friday, June 13: The account of *La Victoire*'s arrival is taken from LFM I:16ff., and Tower, I:171ff.

62 "The manners of the people here": LFM I:191.

62 "it was love at first sight": LG II:7.

62 "like beggars and brigands": Quoted from Dubuysson's memoir, trans. in LFL, 73ff.

63 One of the French volunteers wrote: See Echeverria, *Mirage*, 83.

63 In the days that followed: Lafayette's activities in Charleston are described in LG II:8–9.

63 to whom he donated clothing and arms: Alexander Garden, *Anecdotes of the America Revolution*, 3 vols. (Brooklyn, NY, 1865), II:200; LG II:9.

63 the "unsupportable" heat: De Kalb quoted in LG II:4.

63 "horrible lodgings" . . . "very sullen": *Journal par du Rousseau de Fayolle*, trans. in LFL I:68–72.

63 "as likable as my enthusiasm": LFL I:60ff.

64 In a few days the carriages had fallen apart: LFL I:66–67.

64 "On the whole, people are not very obliging": *Fayolle*, LFL I:68–72.

64 "vast forests and immense rivers": LFM I:15.

64 "The farther I advance": LFL I:67.

64 Finally, on the morning of July 27: Details of Lafayette's arrival and reception in Philadelphia are in *Dubuysson*; LG II:14–23.

65 on the *Amphitrite* alone . . . there were men representing: PGW-RWS IX, 244–45, cites *New-Hampshire Gazette*, April 26, 1776.

65 no fewer than fifty-seven French officers: Lasseray, *Treize Etoiles*, 73–79.

66 "injure our cause abroad": PGW-RWS IX, 497, May 17, 1777, Richard Henry Lee to Washington.

66 "Ought not this weak or *roguish* man": *Letters of Delegates to Congress, 1774–1789* [hereinafter LDC], VII, Lovell to Whipple, July 29, 1777.

66 "No one has been more backward": PGW-RWS X, 386–89, July 24, 1777, Lovell to Washington.

66 "his high Birth, his Alliances": Sparks, *The Diplomatic Correspondence* [hereinafter Sparks], I:99, Deane to the Secret Committee, Dec. 6, 1776.

67 "When I presented myself to Mr. Deane": LFL I:8, "Memoir of 1779."

67 "Not thinking that he can obtain": Sparks, I:99.

67 "[W]e are satisfy'd that the civilities": LFL I:51, Franklin and Deane to the Secret Committee, May 25, 1777.

67 "*brillante folie* de La Fayette": LFL I:44, Stormont to Weymouth, April 9, 1777.

67 "it does not do him discredit": Rosenthal, 41.

67 "All he seeks is glory": LFL I:52, Deane to Morris, May 26, 1777.

68 to "cross the Delaware": *Writings*, General Orders, July 31, 1777.

68 he knew he was in no position to fight: See, e.g., Morgan, *Genius*, 8–10.

68 "in a most extraordinary manner": *Writings*, June 13, 1777, to James Mease.

68 "Although he was surrounded": LFL I:91, "Memoir of 1776."

68 Washington . . . struck Lafayette as open: 1828 interview with Jared Sparks; see LFL I:100–101 n1.

68 taking Lafayette aside after dinner: Tower, I:214–15; LG I:29; LFM I:71–72.

69 When he was Lafayette's age: Flexner, I:52–53.

69 "The first rule": Cornélius de Witt, *Histoire de Washington et de la fondation de la république des Etats-Unis* (Paris: Didier, 1859) 99; Manceron, I:509.

69 "I do most devoutly wish": *Writings*, July 24, 1778, to Gouverneur Morris.

70 "eleven thousand men" . . . "not to teach": LFL I:91, "Memoir of 1776."

70 "we should be embarrassed": Ibid.

70 "The times are critical": *Writings*, July 22, 1777, to Maj. Gen. Philip Schuyler.

70 These two plans were never reconciled: See W. J. Wood, *Battles*, 134–35; also Edgar, *Philadelphia Campaign*.

71 a fact "so unaccountable": *Writings*, July 30, 1777, to Horatio Gates.

71 "a very disagreeable dance": *Writings*, June 29, 1777, to John Augustine Washington.

71 exhausted by all their futile marches: Flexner, II:212ff.

71 the fourteen thousand soldiers on board: Buchanan, *Road*, 219.

71 "the pitch [was] melting": Capt. John Montresor quoted in Edgar, *Philadelphia*, 9.

71 "appear as decent as circumstances": *Writings*, General Orders, Aug. 23, 1777.

71 "a fine appearance": LFM I:21; LG II:40.

71 The lineup after that: Freeman, IV:463.

71 During the two hours: Buchanan, 225.

71 "Our soldiers have not yet quite": John Adams quoted in Freeman, IV:463–64.

72 Disease was rife: *Writings*, General Orders, July 13, 1777.

72 the currency . . . was depreciating fast: Freeman, IV:456.

72 Howe's army disembarked: The account of Howe's arrival and subsequent movements are from Buchanan and Edgar.

72 "Dear man," she said: Edgar, 17.

72 In fact, he had only 6,800: Buchanan, 236.

73 "My life for it, you're mistaken": Edgar, 24.

73 "At half after four o'clock": *Writings*, Sept. 11, 1777, to the President of Congress.

73 the Third Pennsylvania Brigade was led: Details of the battle are drawn from *Mémoires*, I:24ff; LG II:44ff; Freeman IV:4771ff; Flexner, II:220ff; and W. J. Wood, *Battles*, 92ff.

74 "our left wing still had not been able": Capt. Münchausen quoted in Buchanan, 247.

74 "a steady, stubborn fight": Capt. Johann Ewald quoted in ibid.

74 "cannons roaring muskets cracking": Entry of Sept. 12, 1777, Elisha Stevens, *Fragments of Memoranda Written by him in the War of the Revolution* (Meriden, CT, 1922), 2; Royster, 225.

74 "Congress must be written to": W. J. Wood, *Battles*, 112.

74 "Sir: I am sorry to inform you": *Writings*, Sept. 11, 1777, to the President of Congress.

75 "disorders of the American army": Rush, *Autobiography*, 132–33; Flexner, II:226.

75 "a passive spectator": Wharton, I:278.

75 "I have since seen nothing" . . . "does want decision": Edgar, 54.

75 "Oh! Heaven grant us": *Adams Diary*, II:265; McCullough, 273.
76 Many years later John Jay: Washington Irving, *Life of Washington* (New York, 1857), III:346; Wharton, I:273.

VI

77 Kalb reported to Broglie on the fiasco: Kapp, *Kalb*, 123.
78 The victory actually belonged to his second in command: See W. J. Wood, *Battles*, 162–70.
78 Benjamin Rush, in a letter describing: Flexner, II:238.
78 "passive . . . miserable": Ibid., 241 and 243.
78 "It is with exquisite concern": Kapp, *Kalb*, 155.
79 "For God's sake, do not suffer": Flexner, II:241.
79 "My dear general . . . I do not do myself": LFL I:121–23, Oct. 14, 1777.
79 the "happy and glorious success": LFL I:125.
79 A few days later he wrote the president: LFL I:125, Oct. 18, 1777, to Henry Laurens.
79 the West Indies, or Mauritius, or India: LG II:65.
79 wrote about his ambitions in the West Indies: LG II:69.
80 "will one day end up selling the furniture": LFM I:28; LG II:71n.
80 "I . . . can but gratefully remember": LFL I:150.
80 "[I]f there is any truth in a report": *Writings*, Oct. 17, 1777, to Richard Henry Lee.
81 Gates had not even bothered to notify him: Freeman, IV:545.
82 "successes have raised him": Flexner, II:247.
82 " 'Heaven has been determined' ": Ibid., 248–49.
82 "Sir, A letter I received last night": *Writings*, Nov. 9, 1777, to Conway.
82 "What pity there is but one": Buchanan, 294.
83 "[Y]ou are a brave man": Freeman, IV:556,
83 "who had never seen a line of battle": LG II:65.
83 "whilst it is likely to produce": LDC, Oct. 20, 1777, Richard Henry Lee to Washington.
84 "[Y]ou have saved our Northern Hemisphere": LDC. See n5 to letter from Richard Henry Lee to Samuel Adams, November 23, 1777, which quotes Mifflin's to Gates.
84 "Gen. Mifflin has been here": LDC, Nov. 23, 1777, Richard Henry Lee to Samuel Adams.
84 No one had the nerve: PGW-RWS XIII:330ff.
84 a list of documents that were being forwarded: LDC, Nov. 30, 1777, Henry Laurens to Washington.
84 bore news that may have been: Ibid.
84 "Good God! What a situation": LDC, Nov. 27, 1777, Lovell to Gates.
85 "The project . . . seems to me attended": LFL I:"Memorandum on a Winter Campaign," 173ff.
86 "a thousand tender compliments": LFL I:182.
86 congressmen like Adams, Rush, and Lee were deeply suspicious: Wharton I:273ff.
86 "worship the image & pay an undeserved": LDC, Nov. 23, 1777; see n5 to letter from Richard Henry Lee to Samuel Adams.

86 "The list of our disgusted patriots": Ibid.

87 "a subject very sickening": LDC, Dec. 20, 1777, Lovell to S. Adams.

87 "a reform may take place in the army": LDC, Dec. 10, 1777, Robert Morris, Elbridge Gerry, and Joseph Jones to Washington.

87 his "delicacy in exerting military authority": Ford et al., eds., *Journals of the Continental Congress* [hereinafter JCC], Resolution of Dec. 10, 1777.

87 "essential to the promotion of discipline": Ibid.

88 "this being the third day": Diary entry for Dec. 18, 1777, in *Revolutionary War Journals of Henry Dearborn, 1775–1783*, ed. Lloyd A. Brown and Howard H. Peckham, quoted in PGW-RWS, XII:621n.

88 Washington ordered the regiments to be divided: *Writings*, General Orders, Dec. 18, 1777.

88 "We had neither bread nor meat": Boyle, "The Diary of Lt. Samuel Armstrong," *Pennsylvania Magazine of History and Biography*, 121 (1977), 237–70, quoted in PGW-RWS, XII:621n.

89 Congress asked Washington to send specific plans: JCC, Dec. 19, 1777.

89 "Three days successively we have been": *Writings*, Dec. 22, 1777, Varnum to Washington, quoted in note to letter of that date from Washington to the President of Congress.

89 "It would give me infinite pleasure": *Writings*, Dec. 22, 1777, to the President of Congress.

89 "I can assure those gentlemen": *Writings*, Dec. 23, 1777, to the President of Congress.

90 a little mutton: From Caleb Gibbs's account books, cited in Fitzpatrick, *Spirit*, 90ff.

90 Four days later, Conway came: Flexner, II:262ff. Flexner puts the date at the end of November, but Conway did not receive his appointment until Dec. 13, and both Lafayette's *Mémoires* and his letter to Washington fix the date as Dec. 29. The meeting itself is reconstructed from subsequent correspondence between Washington and Conway.

90 "Greatly disappointed and chagrined": Flexner, II:263–64.

91 "depend upon my attachment": LFL I: 182, Dec. 14, 1777, to Gates.

91 his "superiority over General Gates": LFL I: 188ff, Dec. 16, 1777, to the duc d'Ayen.

91 "I don't need telling you": LFL I:204, Dec. 30, 1777, to Washington.

92 "dirty arts and low intrigues": *Writings*, Dec. 31, 1777, to Lafayette.

VII

93 "This thought was an obsession": P. A. Roth, *Masonry in the Formation of Our Government* (Milwaukee: Masonic Service Bureau, 1927), 33–34. Maurice de la Fuye and Emile Babeau, *Apostle of Liberty*, trans. Edward Hyams (New York: Thomas Yoseloff, Inc., 1956), 41–42; see also LG II, appendix III:338. Gottschalk raises good questions about this story, but he may have mistaken a reference to the Canada expedition for one about Lafayette's previous promotion. Lafayette seems to have taken more pride in leading an expedition with a detached army under his sole command than in getting his division, and if so he would have been more likely to call the Canadian venture "a very important command-in-chief."

94 "The conduct of our soldiers": LFL I:156–57.

94 "The marquis is determined": Greene, *Life*, I:528; also LFM I:33.

94 "military ardor": *Writings*, Nov. 26, 1777, to the President of Congress.

94 and again in 1779, in 1780, 1782, and 1783: LFL I:244.

95 "They will laugh in France": LFL I:239.

95 On January 27, 1778, Lafayette received the news: LFL I:249–50, Jan. 24, 1778, Gates to Lafayette.

95 "I can only sincerely wish": *Writings*, Jan. 27, 1778, to the Board of War.

96 "Poor food—hard lodging": From the Diary of Albigence Waldo, digital edition at www.let.rug.nl/usa/D/1776-1800/war/waldo00.htm.

96 Charles Royster has written: See Royster, 192–93.

96 "The General is . . . well worn": Benson Bobrick, *Angel in the Whirlwind: The Triumph of the American Revolution* (New York: Simon & Schuster, 1997), 291; Chernow, *Hamilton*, 107.

97 "secret enemies . . . base and villainous": PGW-RWS XVIII:160, Jan. 6, 1778, Craik to Washington.

97 "there may possibly be some scheme": Ibid.

97 "The northern army [under Gates] has shown": Ibid., 610.

97 "Thoughts of a Freeman": Ibid., 364–66

98 He declared that he would refuse: LFL I:260, to Henry Laurens.

98 later he reported to the board and to Congress: PWG-RWS XIII:361.

98 He recorded proudly in his memoirs: LFL I:245, 248.

98 "I go on very slowly sometimes": Ibid., 287.

98 "the blunders of his youth": Ibid., 298.

98 in fact four generals warned him: See ibid., 308n.

98 Even Conway advised against it: Ibid., 312, Feb. 20, 1778, Conway to Lafayette.

98 "Men will have the right to laugh": Ibid., 295ff, to Laurens.

99 "I confess, my dear general": Ibid., 299ff.

99 "dispel those fears respecting your reputation": *Writings*, March 10, 1778, to Lafayette.

99 "I am very far from making complaints": LFL I:347ff., March 12, 1778.

100 "a few ounces of gunpowder": Flexner, II:269.

100 A civilian member of the Board of War: Edgar, 153.

100 Cadwalader finally called out Conway: The best account is in ibid, 156.

100 "the best friend he ever had": Flexner, II:269.

100 he would let the whole matter drop: *Writings*, Feb. 24, 1778 to Gates.

101 On the morning of December 4, 1777: Deane Papers, II:269; Schiff, 109.

101 so hard that his carriage overturned . . . a story for the newspapers: Isaacson, *Franklin*, 343.

101 two letters dated December 11: The letters are compared in Corwin, *French Policy*, 121n.

102 "If all monarchies were governed": Schiff, 142–43.

VIII

103 He had adopted these names: Royster, 213.

103 made a baron by the prince . . . also gave himself a fictional promotion: Ibid.

103 "hardworking people": Flexner, II:45–46.

104 "A coward when taught to believe": *Writings*, Nov. 9, 1776, to the President of Congress.

104 "no regular formation": From notes of a meeting of officers quoted in Stoudt, 157–58; Buchanan, *Road*, 303–4. (Also in Tower, I:322–23, but misattributed.)

104 "my rhapsody": Royster, 200. This account of Steuben's training and its effect draws heavily on Royster's study of the Continental Army, *A Revolutionary People at War*.

105 "The genius of this nation": Royster, 219, cites Baron Steuben to Baron de Gaudy, 1787–88, "Memorials of Baron Von Steuben: Unpublished and Forgotten Papers," *Deutsch-Amerikanische Geschichtsblatter*, XXX (1930), 135; also see Flexner, II:287.

105 "[O]fficers of the Massachusetts part": Royster, 232; *Writings*, Aug. 25, 1775, to Richard Henry Lee.

105 "share the fatigue as well as danger": *Writings*, General Orders, April 17, 1779.

106 "I should have been pelted": Royster, 218.

106 "but to every soldier": Ibid., 223.

106 "The guests clubbed their rations": Chinard, *George Washington as the French Knew Him*, 15ff.

106 Lafayette grabbed him and kissed: LFM I:78; LG II:175.

107 "my poor little Henriette": LFL I, multiple letters to Adrienne.

107 but Lafayette could celebrate only halfheartedly: LFL II:77, June 16, 1778, to Adrienne.

107 "The Brigade Inspectors will": General Orders, May 5, 1778.

108 "wore a countenance of uncommon delight": *Army Correspondence of Col. John Laurens*, 169; Royster, 253.

108 "an allowance of brandy": Royster, 253.

108 who wrote the comte de Broglie all about it: Flexner, II:291.

108 "It was a fine day": Kapp, *Kalb*, 159.

108 "there was a universal clap": Flexner, II:291.

108 "We were favored with a day": *Pennsylvania Gazette*, May 7, 1778.

109 "proud to put a man of honor": Beaumarchais to Francey, Dec. 6, 1778, quoted in Joseph Beatty Doyle, *Frederick William Von Steuben and the American Revolution* (Steubenville, OH, 1913), 45; Royster, 233.

109 "a joke to think of keeping": Edgar, 173.

109 had already cost them several hundred British ships: Ibid., 174.

109 should move to Halifax: Ibid.

109 "I now look upon the contest as at an end": Ibid., 175.

110 Howe was an inveterate playboy, a heavy gambler: Ibid., 163.

110 for control of the Hudson River: Stryker, 41.

110 "You will remember, that your detachment": *Writings*, May 18, 1778, to Lafayette.

110 a "variety of entertainments": Stryker, 25–26.

110 "embarked in flatboats": Edgar, 169.

110 fourteen young women in turbans: Ibid., 170.

111 "The Knights of the Burning Mountain": Ibid., 172.

111 to come back the next day for dinner with the marquis: Stryker, 26.

112 the British "didn't leave—they vanished": Du Simitère to Col. Lamb, Nov. 24,

1778, in Leake's *Memoirs of the Life and Times of General John Lamb* (Albany: Joel Munsell's Sons, 1857), 213; Stryker, 49.

112   fifteen hundred wagons and hundreds of Tory exiles: Edgar, 185.

112   "one of the genteelest public rooms": Wharton, II:68.

112   "Mr. Lee's Plan, 29 March, 1777": Ibid.

113   he twice withdrew his hand from the Bible: Stryker, 14.

113   "weak . . . ruining the whole cause": Edgar, 198.

113   a baggage train that alone was twelve miles long: Flexner, II:299.

113   "it would be the most criminal madness": Edgar, 195.

113   "would have done honor": Chernow, 113.

113   "I would lay my fortune": LFL II:85, June 24, 1778, Lafayette to Washington; LFM I, 51.

114   "recanted again": Flexner, II:299.

114   "The young Frenchman . . . moves toward": Lengel, 294.

114   "[I]f it is believed necessary": LFL II:91, June 26, 1778, Lafayette to Washington.

114   "At the same time that I felt for": *Writings*, June 26, 1778, to Lafayette.

115   "Your uneasiness . . . fills me with concern": *Writings*, June 26, 1778, to Lee.

115   who had never commanded an important battle: Freeman, V:58–59.

115   "abdicated much of his responsibility": Lengel, 298.

115   a fifer he found going: Ibid., 26–27.

115   An eyewitness reported: Stryker, 180n.

115   "Yes, sir, he swore": Brig. Gen. Charles Scott quoted in Edgar, 212.

116   "I never saw the general": Ibid.

116   "General Washington seemed to arrest": LFM I:39.

116   "the officers of the army": *Writings*, July 1, 1778, to the President of Congress.

116   until they both fell asleep: LFM I:53.

117   Of the 72 Americans killed: Freeman, V:43n.

117   "It is not a little pleasing": *Writings*, Aug. 20, to Brig. Gen. Thomas Nelson.

IX

118   he sent three such letters: LFL II:99.

118   "the appointment of so many Foreign": *Writings*, July 24, 1778, to Gouverneur Morris.

118   "His Countrymen soon find access": *Writings*, Aug. 20, 1778, to Henry Laurens.

119   "May you defeat them": LFL II:102ff.

119   his warships drew too much water: D'Estaing's 64-gun ship drew 27 feet, the equivalent British ship drew only 22—see Freeman, V, 48n7, and Tower, I:419n. The British could also remove their cannon to make the crossing, something d'Estaing could not do in the face of the enemy.

120   "I . . . was a little uneasy": *Writings*, Aug. 10, 1778, to Lafayette.

120   "The information, my dear Marquis": *Writings*, Sept. 10, 1778.

120   "his private views withdrew": LG II:246, Aug. 22, 1778, John Laurens to Henry Laurens.

121   He even gave d'Estaing: LFL II:128–31 and 134–35 to d'Estaing.

121   "like women disputing precedence": LFL II:136, n1, Aug. 10, 1778, John Laurens to Henry Laurens.

121 "never been so proud": LFM I:214.

121 a violent and relentless storm: For the activities of d'Estaing's fleet, see Doniol, III:175–99, 233–56, and 321–94. Also LFL II:149–55, Lafayette to Washington.

121 "men are more hardy than horses": Greene, II:114.

122 Greene left with the distinct feeling: Ibid., 117.

122 but even some American pilots: Lafayette to Washington, quoted in ibid.

122 "To evacuate the Island": Greene, II:120, August 22, 1778, Greene to Charles Pettit.

122 "derogatory to the honor of France": LG II:254–55, quoting Sullivan to d'Estaing, Aug. 23, 1778, in *Papers of Sullivan*, II:264.

122 "the renowned Don Quixoto": LG II:258.

122 "best be decided when Admiral Byron": LFM I:245; also in LFL II:189.

122 "The Marquis' great thirst for glory": Greene, 127, Aug. 28, 1778. Greene to Washington.

122 "Frenchmen of the highest characters": LFL II:152.

123 "put the best face upon the matter": *Writings*, Aug. 28, 1778, to Sullivan.

123 "afford a healing hand": *Writings*, Sept. 1, 1778, to Lafayette.

123 to Bermuda, the West Indies, Newfoundland: LFL II:169–70 to d'Estaing.

123 "I begin to see that": LG II:259 n28.

124 "If you have entertained thoughts": *Writings*, Sept. 25, 1778, to Lafayette.

124 Congress was deeply riven just then: Henderson, "Congressional Factionalism"; see also Doniol, IV:1–47.

124 Franklin wrote a letter to Congress: Henderson, "Congressional Factionalism."

125 No fewer than ten of Beaumarchais's ships: Tower, I:300.

125 he was able plausibly to insist: For Idzerda's view, see LFL II:192n2; 196n3.

126 Gottschalk argued that Lafayette: LG II:309ff.

126 "the idea was not suggested by me": LFL II:195, Oct. 24, 1778, to Washington.

126 his "wisdom and dexterity": LFL II:192, n2.

126 "He could say more than": LG II:306, Oct. 26, 1778, Morris to Washington.

126 "our wants and our weaknesses": *Writings*, Nov. 11, 1778, to the President of Congress.

126 He put his deeper concerns in a private letter: *Writings*, Nov. 14, 1778, to Henry Laurens.

127 "General Washington came every day": LFM I:61.

127 "No one but himself has known": LFL II:199, Oct. 30, 1778, William Carmichael to Benjamin Franklin.

127 an "elegant sword with proper devices": LG II:198.

127 "You know, Monseigneur": LG II:301.

128 "I am sure you will approve the part": LFL II:152, Aug. 22, 1778, to Washington.

128 "One becomes accustomed": LFL II:202, Nov. 5, 1778, d'Estaing to Minister of the Marine, Gabriel de Sartine.

129 "The moment I heard of America": LFL II:180, to the President of Congress.

129 "May I beg leave to recommend": LFL II:222, Jan. 9, 1779, to the President of Congress.

129 "Farewell, my most beloved General": LFL II:217–19, Jan. 5, 1779, to Washington.

130 "has been laid aside": *Writings*, Dec. 29, 1778, to Lafayette.

130 "fresh toils and dangers": *Writings*, March 8, 1779, to Lafayette.

X

131 **The army was down to barely more**: Details of the conditions of the army in this paragraph are from Ketchum, *Victory at Yorktown*, 8.

131 **the twenty dollars . . . worth exactly 1.6 cents**: Fleming, *Beat*, 4, says one "hard" dollar equaled 1,200 Continental.

131 **"A country, once overflowing"**: LG III:57.

132 **"Here I am"**: LFL III:3, April 27, 1780, to Washington.

132 **he "kept you constantly in remembrance"**: *Writings*, Sept. 30, 1779.

133 **Americans seemed to have stopped caring**: I am indebted to Royster's *A Revolutionary People at War* for this discussion of the corruption of army suppliers and the increasing alienation of the army from the citizenry.

133 **"The rascally stupidity"**: Ketchum, 11.

134 **he was short of his objective of a 22,000-man army**: The figure is inferred from Ketchum, 8–9.

134 **"an Army that is reduced to nothing"**: This letter is not in LFL but is quoted in Ketchum, 9–10, which cites Freeman, V:166.

134 **found himself in the midst of a ball**: LG III:1–2.

134 **his first official meeting with Vergennes**: LG III:2; Tower, II:56.

135 **Lafayette wrote Louis a contorted letter**: LFL II:232–34.

135 **"réprimande douce"**: Tower, II:57.

135 **"I see much of [Lafayette]"**: Gottschalk, *Lady-in-Waiting*, 54.

135 **"When I arrived"**: Gottschalk, Ibid., 59.

135 **a promotion to *mestre-de-camp* . . . invited him to his levee**: LG III:7.

135 **He even gave Lafayette the right to purchase**: Ibid.

136 **There are no fewer than nineteen letters**: LFL II:229–364.

136 **"By the *end of February* we must be ready"**: LFL II:344–48, Jan. 25, 1780, to Maurepas.

137 **Fifteen thousand tons of powder**: LFL III:96–97, July 16, 1780, Rochambeau to Lafayette.

137 **"As a general officer I have the greatest"**: *Writings*, July 16, 1780, to Rochambeau.

137 **Rochambeau had had his fill of courtier-officers**: Bonsal, 16.

138 **"I embrace you, my dear Marquis"**: LFL III:96–97, Rochambeau to Lafayette.

138 **"there are only two things"**: *Writings*, July 27, 1780, to Lafayette.

139 **"He now proposes"**: LFL III:141–42, Aug. 14, 1780, Rochambeau to Luzerne.

139 **"of opinion that nothing"**: LFL III:117, July 31, 1780, Lafayette to Washington.

139 **"From an intimate knowledge"**: LG III:112, July 27, 1780, Lafayette to Rochambeau.

139 **"If I have offended you"**: LFL III:147, to Rochambeau.

139 **"Permit an old father"**: LFL III:155–56, Rochambeau to Lafayette.

140 **Washington's "flying army"**: Wright, 454–55.

140 **"distinguished by a black-and-red feather"**: LFL III:156–58, Sept. 2, 1780, to Vicomte de Noailles.

140 **"we will loose all our feathers"**: Gottschalk, *Letters*, 110.

141 **"of a perfect whiteness"**: LG III:122.

141 **When Chastellux visited the headquarters**: Chastellux, I:108.

141 **"bring the rascals back"**: Kapp, 232. Details on Camden are from Kapp, 230ff., and Ward, 722ff.

141 "Was there ever an instance": Letter to James Duane quoted in Ketchum, 39.
142 "The government without finances": *Writings*, Sept. 12, 1780, to Comte de Guichen.
143 "Redoubt No. 3, a slight Wood Work": Ketchum, 53.
144 "Who can we trust now?": LG III:137.

XI
145 "Treason! Black as hell!": Royster, 291
145 "Somehow or other": Ibid., 290.
145 Dr. Benjamin Rush discovered a disease: Ibid., 286–87.
146 "The great importance which it has seemed": Tower, II:227, Feb. 25, 1780, Rochambeau to Washington.
146 to "execute the punishment": *Writings*, Feb. 20, 1781, "Instructions to Marquis de Lafayette."
147 "seems to make a difficulty": *Writings*, March 1, 1781, to Lafayette.
147 "I very much apprehend": LFL III:386, March 8, 1781, to Washington.
147 "I have clapped on board": LFL III:389, March 9, 1781, to Washington.
147 British intelligence knew of their plan: Kaplan, 133.
147 This allowed Clinton to dispatch: Lengel, 239.
148 "contract the latitude": LG III:219.
148 other vaguely described "essential reasons": Tower, II:245. The chronology of this and preceding paragraphs is from ibid., 221–45.
149 "Many men have already deserted": LFL IV:30–32, April 14, 1781, to Washington.
150 "The particular messmates": Fleming, 5–6.
150 "The distance that the platoons stood" . . . "mute as fish": Ibid.
150 the Americans' "immense demands": Bonsal, 78.
151 "it is impossible to conceive": Wharton, IV:254–55.
151 "This is already the fourth campaign": Doniol, IV:537, Feb. 19, 1781, Vergennes to Luzerne.
152 he had solicited loans of no less than 520 million livres: Doyle, *Origins*, 48.
153 "So here I am prescribed": LFL IV:89, May 8, 1781, to Luzerne.
154 "I shall now proceed": LG III:238, May 26, 1781, Cornwallis to Clinton.
154 "Had I followed the first impulsion": LFL IV:130–31, May 24, 1781, to Washington.
154 "The command of the troops": *Writings*, July 10, 1781, to Joseph Jones.
155 "we shall be in a position": LFL IV:123, May 22, 1781, to Noailles.
155 "sorcery . . . a very necessary science": LG III:271.

XII
156 Washington admitted in his diary: Fleming, 91–92.
156 would "detach part of his force": *Writings*, July 25, 1781, to John Parke Custis.
157 "we have not a moment": *Writings*, Aug. 17, 1781, to Rochambeau.
157 "distressed beyond expression": *Writings*, Sept. 2, 1781, to Lafayette.
157 "of a natural coldness": Wharton I:256n, quoting le comte de Deux-Ponts.

157 "a child whose every wish": Chinard, *Washington*, 42–43, quoting Deux-Ponts.
158 "never seen a man more overcome": Flexner, II:443.
158 "with an ardour not easily": LG III:305.
159 "To speak truth I become timid": LFL IV:111, May 18, 1781, to Greene.
159 "the division I will have under him": LFL IV:395, Sept. 9, 1781, Lafayette to Washington.
159 all of them under command of Lafayette: For the disposition of the light infantry at Yorktown, see Wright, 461.
160 all of them in spotless white uniforms: Ketchum,165.
160 "The play is over": LFL IV:422, Oct. 20, 1781, Lafayette to Maurepas.
160 As Charles Royster has observed: See Royster, 295ff.
161 for between $4 million and $5 million: Lengel, 345.
161 "The army has its alternative": Freeman, V:421.
161 "My God! . . . Can he be": *Writings*, March 15, 1783, To the Officers of the Army.
161 "you will give one more distinguished proof": Ibid.
162 "magnify properly & show": *Writings*, Feb. 16, 1783, to David Rittenhouse.
162 "Gentlemen, you must pardon me": Lengel, 349.
162 "With what soldiers in the world": Ibid., 343.
162 "A desire of fame": Royster, 234.
163 "absolute freedom and Independency": *Writings*, Circular to the States, June 8, 1783.
164 "to free the Negroes": LFL V:90–93, Feb. 5, 1783, to Washington.
164 "is a striking evidence of the benevolence": *Writings*, April 5, 1783, to Lafayette.
164 "There is no man upon earth": *Writings*, April 16, 1783, to the Secretary of Foreign Affairs.
165 a letter to the abbé de Mably: C. F. Adams, ed., *Works of Adams*, V:491ff.
165 "States, like individuals": Chastellux, 434.
166 "They are no longer fashionable": Chastellux, 165.
166 "Take care, young men": Wharton, I:340n.
166 "Fortunate his country": Chastellux, 108.
167 "as one saying to himself": Hardman, 70, quoting diary of Sartines.

PART TWO

XIII

173 On December 8, 1783, a remarkable notice: For many of the details in this discussion of Mesmerism and popular science, and for the connection between Mesmerism and revolutionary ideology, I am indebted to Robert Darnton's wonderful book, *Mesmerism and the End of the Enlightenment in France*.
173 "given such a shock to the French": Schama, 124.
174 "Are you men or gods?" . . . "the gods of antiquity": Darnton, *Mesmerism*, 22.
174 "It is impossible to describe": Ibid., 20.
174 "An authentic narrative": LG IV:76.
174 "In all our gatherings": Darnton, *Mesmerism*, 22–23.
176 "was designed to produce a crisis": Ibid., 8.

176 "most absolute despotism": Ibid., 50.

177 "There is a satisfaction": Ségur, 25–26.

177 Even Benjamin Franklin . . . was surprised: Rosenthal, *America and France*, 106.

178 "that it is in the people" . . . "liberty, equality": Ibid., 108–9.

179 "The reception I have met": LFL IV:8–10, Jan. 30, 1782.

179 "through which the just and grateful plaudits": *Writings*, Jan. 4, 1782, to Lafayette.

179 "I am not a judge": *Writings*, Jan. 8, 1782, to John Tyler.

179 "reserved for heroes": LG IV:369.

180 and in a letter that made much of how resistant: Gottschalk, *Lady-in-Waiting*, March 27, 1783.

181 "the more remarkable": Abigail Adams, *Diary*, 49.

181 "My little family": Gottschalk, *Letters*, 253, June 29, 1782.

181 "There . . . you can see everything": Quoted in W. H. Adams, *Paris Years*, 56.

182 "On earth I respected you": Darnton, *Mesmerism*, 162.

182 "Soldier stealing a bracelet": Grendel, 187.

183 "This man mocks everything": Ibid., 211.

183 "If I had been the king": Ibid., 220.

184 "Every day you could hear people": Ibid., 214–15.

184 "on pain of His Majesty's": Schama, 143.

184 "This prohibition by the King": Kite, II:215.

184 "I again patiently replace": Loménie, III:84.

184 "intriguers of the lower class": Ibid., 90–91.

185 "the most trifling of plots": Grendel, 222–23.

185 "No, Count, you shall not": All translations from *Figaro* are by Greaves from Grendel, 225ff., and are used by permission.

186 "Strange blindness!": Schama, 143.

187 No other play in the history of French theater: Grendel, 220.

188 an "infernal machine": Schama, 73.

188 "gateways to the capital": Adams, *Paris Years*, 45.

188 Calonne also paid off d'Artois's personal: Sears, 312.

189 "make a proper use of them": Dec. 25, 1783, Franklin to Morris.

189 "Observations on the Commerce": *Résumé de mon avis au Comité du Commerce avec les Etats Unis lorsque la question des tabacs nous a été présentée*, in Gottschalk, "Lafayette as a Commercial Agent," trans. in LG III:39ff.

190 "as soon as possible": *Writings*, Oct. 30, 1783, to Lafayette.

191 "I have made a purchase": *Writings*, Dec. 4, 1783, to Lafayette.

XIV

192 "At length, my dear Marquis": *Writings*, Feb. 1, 1784, to Lafayette.

192 He decided to build a greenhouse: Washington's nervous first days back at Mount Vernon are covered well in Randall, 411.

193 "If you have any news": *Writings*, March 3, 1784, to Washington.

193 "I suppose the crippled state": TJP VIII:266, March 15, 1784.

194 "I am satisfied that not a moment": *Writings*, March 29, 1784, to Jefferson.

194 "be compelled to consider herself": McDonald, *E Pluribus Unum*, 108.

194 the appeal of nationalism was roughly aligned: For this discussion of the states'

view toward the benefits of stronger central government I am indebted to McDonald, *E Pluribus Unum*.

195 "against the letter": Ford, ed., *Works of Jefferson*, IV:323, April 16, 1784, to Washington.

195 discussed the issue with Jefferson by candlelight: Malone, I:415.

197 "What concerns me now": LFL V:235, Aug. 13, 1784, to Adrienne.

197 to "get leave to let you into the secret": LFL V: 216–18; May 14, 1784 to Washington.

197 "as it supports . . . the commercial wealth": LG IV:86.

198 "The reception given by the magistrates": Bernier, 159.

198 "Our meeting was very tender": LFL V:237, Aug. 20, 1784, to Adrienne.

198 "The General has adopted them": Ibid.

199 "Dear Washington, I hope": From the program of a Lafayette exhibit at Cornell, 1964.

199 "the general and I got a little tipsy": LG IV:89.

199 "very sweet hours": Ibid.

199 "a full & complete settlement": *Writings*, Feb. 24, 1784, to Gilbert Simpson.

200 "after traveling the whole day": *Diaries of George Washington* IV:9, entry for Sept. 5, 1784.

201 "very valuable" tracts: Ibid., Sept. 6, 1784; see 15n3.

201 "the Tenant not to remove": Ibid., 14, Sept. 8, 1784.

201 "a very good stand for a Tavern": Ibid., 18, entry for Sept. 12, 1784.

201 "I never hear of the Mill": *Writings*, Aug. 20, 1775, to Lund Washington.

202 by 1784 he had accumulated almost 35,000 acres: Hofstra, 181, in Philander D. Chase, "A Stake in the West: George Washington as Backcountry Surveyor and Landholder," 159–94.

203 who hoped to get French merchants . . . back into the fur trade: Barbé-Marbois, 725ff.

203 "who appears to be proof": LFL V:245ff., Barbé-Marbois's "Journal of Visit to the Territory of the Six Nations."

203 a coat made of gummed taffeta: Ibid., 247.

203 late great warrior Kayeheanla: Ibid., 260n2.

204 "I know the character": LG IV:96.

204 "one of the head warriors": LG IV:103.

204 "The great Onontio gives": LFL V:254ff. "Account of Lafayette's Meeting with the Six Nations."

204 "the grace and nobility that you know": LG IV:105ff., Oct. 17, 1784, Madison to Jefferson.

205 "The first two are dearer": Ibid.

205 "Though his foibles": TJP VIII:414–15.

205 "The flanks and rear": *Writings*, Oct. 10, 1784, to Gov. Benjamin Harrison.

206 "with a countenance mingled": Joseph Barrell to S. B. Webb, Oct. 21, 1784, in W. C. Ford, ed., *Correspondence and Journals of Samuel Blachley Webb* (New York, 1893–94), III:40; LGIII:115.

206 Tonight there were thirteen of them: LG IV, 115.

207 "whether that was the last": *Writings*, Dec. 8, 1784.

208 "meets our entire approbation": *Writings*, Dec. 28, 1784, to the General Assembly of the Commonwealth of Virginia.

208 "It is now near 12 at night": *Writings*, Dec. 28, 1784, to James Madison.

208 "The earnestness with which he espouses": Madison to Jefferson, Jan. 9, 1785; cited in Freeman, 27.

208 to "stand a lesson to oppressors": LG III:142–43 cites Paine's statement in *Rights of Man* that Vergennes kept his speech out of "the press."

209 "Were I disposed to encounter": *Writings*, Feb. 1, 1785, to Robert Morris.

209 "[M]en who can afford to": *Writings*, Feb. 15, 1785, to Lafayette.

209 "look out for subscribers": Gottschalk, *Letters*, 299, May 13, 1785, Lafayette to Washington.

209 "may possibly lead to better": Madison to Monroe, Jan. 22, 1786. cited in Freeman, 67n.

210 A second, confidential report: Darnton, *Mesmerism*, 64n.

210 "a new science": Ibid., 113.

210 "a morality issuing": Ibid., 114.

211 the parlementarian Adrien Duport: See ibid., 80n. Although Darnton found no definite evidence that Duport migrated with the schismatics, he concluded that he "almost certainly did," because he was missing from the membership list after the schism and associated with other members of the Kornmann set in the groups that evolved from it, including the Society of Friends of the Blacks and the Society of Thirty.

211 "Bergasse did not hide from me": *Mémoires of J.-P. Brissot (1754–1793), publiés avec étude critique et notes*, ed. Claude Perroud (Paris, 1912), II:53–56; Darnton, *Mesmerism*, 79.

212 "102 [Protestants] in 12": Gottschalk, *Letters*, May 11, 1785, Lafayette to Washington.

213 "I have put into my head": Ibid.

213 "My best wishes will always": *Writings*, Sept. 1, 1785, to Lafayette.

213 "My reception . . . was not flattering": Unger, 213.

214 "By their conduct in the revolution": Gottschalk, *Letters*, 306, Feb. 6, 1786, to Washington.

214 "when it might serve": Ford, TJW:182, Feb. 8, 1786.

XV

215 "The Treasury . . . is now literally": McDonald, *Novus*, 171.

215 less than a third of that year's interest: LDC, June 18, 1786, Rufus King to Elbridge Gerry; see also Flexner, III:91n; McDonald, *Novus*, 171.

215 He started 1786 with a wearying load of debt: Freeman, V:44.

216 the North American states were anything but united: For this discussion of the states' various views of federal government, I am indebted to McDonald, *Novus Ordo Secolorum* and *E Pluribus Unum*.

216 Some of those who wished to avoid: See, e.g., Flexner, III:105ff.

216 to "view with abhorrence": *Writings*, May 22, 1782, to Col. Lewis Nicola.

217 a man's "country" was still his state: See Wood, *Creation*, 354–56.

218 "contracted ideas, local pursuits": *Writings*, Feb. 28, 1785, to Henry Knox.

218 "We are either a united people": *Writings*, Nov. 30, 1785, to James Madison.

218 "Something must be done": *Writings*, May 18, 1786, to John Jay.

218 **when fifteen hundred men marched**: For the discussion of Shays' Rebellion, I am indebted to David P. Szatmary, *Shays' Rebellion: The Making of an Agrarian Insurrection*.

219 **All told, about a quarter of all men of fighting age**: Ibid., 59.

219 **"seem to produce effects"**: Ibid., 97.

219 **"For God's sake,"**: *Writings*, Oct. 22, 1786, to David Humphreys.

219 **"The creed . . . is that the property"**: Flexner, III:99.

220 **"What stronger evidence" . . . "Thirteen sovereignties"**: *Writings*, Nov. 5, 1786, to James Madison.

221 **"There are combustibles in every state"**: *Writings*, Dec. 26, 1786, to Henry Knox.

221 **Ladies at court sported coiffes**: Darnton, *False Teeth*, 119ff.

221 **Images of America ranged**: Examples are from Palmer, I:254.

222 **"I can easily show"**: Doyle, *Origins*, 51.

223 **the nobility would not dominate most such assemblies**: Population figures are from Palmer, I:439.

224 **a "bold attack [that] shamed the farmers"**: *Pennsylvania Gazette*, Aug. 8, 1986.

224 **The whalers of Nantucket**: LG IV, 163.

224 **"a feeble, but not less sincere"**: LG IV, 254.

224 **"On seeing him, one is at a loss"**: Chastellux, 108.

225 **"America offers the prospect"**: Cordorcet trans. in Darnton, *False Teeth*, 121.

225 **an increasingly embittered throng of second-**: For this discussion of the "hacks" of Paris, I am indebted to Darnton.

226 **"falls and weeps at the foot"**: Mercier, *Tableau de Paris*, VIII:59; Darnton, *Literary Underground*, 20.

226 **the extreme measure of becoming a police spy**: See Darnton, *Literary Underground*, 41ff. For a lively debate on Brissot's merits as a writer and career as a spy, see Darnton, "Grub Street"; Frederick da Luna's critique in "The Dean Street Style of Revolution: J.-P. Brissot, Jeune Philosophe," *French Historical Studies*, vol. 17, no. 1 (Spring 1991), 159–90; which is followed in the same issue by Darnton's reply, "The Brissot Dossier," and da Luna's reply to Darnton's reply in "Of Poor Devils and 'Low Intellectual History.' "

226 **"Audouin: calls himself a lawyer"**: These extracts from police files are in Darnton, "High Enlightenment."

227 **"You wish, sir, to destroy"**: Palmer, I:260.

228 **"revolting, both by its bitterness"**: Darnton, *False Teeth*, 131.

228 **"the hope of our Nation"**: *Examen critique des "voyages dans l'Amerique septentrionale de M. le Marquis le Chastellux"* (London, 1786), LG IV:247.

228 **Louis invited Lafayette to play cards**: LG IV:276.

229 **"This shows that his character"**: TJW, V:251–52, Jan. 17, 1787, to Edward Carrington.

229 **one of only twenty-two**: LG IV:287.

230 **"produce popular assemblies" . . . "with all my heart"**: Gottschalk, *Letters*, 318, Jan. 13, 1787, to Washington.

230 **"I am afraid that despite"**: Price, 228.

230 **"the only friend I could count on"**: Price, 240.

231 **"brilliant intellect . . . ugly"**: Talleyrand, I:79.

231 **a convention of "not ables"**: Gottschalk, *Letters*, 320, Feb. 7, 1787, to Washington.

231 "My dear constituents": Adams, *Paris Years*, 260.

231 "incapable of any serious effort": TJW V:262, Feb. 22, 1787, to Abigail Adams.

231 "a great event . . . not a revolution": Manceron, IV:391.

231 "Money there must be": Ibid., 395–96.

XVI

233 "for the sole and express purpose": JCC, Feb. 21, 1787, Resolution of the Continental Congress.

233 likened the nation to "a house on fire": *Writings*, Feb. 3, 1787, to Henry Knox.

233 "operates more forcibly": *Writings*, Dec. 16, 1786, to James Madison.

233 "determination to support": Szatmary, 87.

234 with at least ten of their officers drawn from the Society: Ibid.

235 "too extensive" . . . "pregnant with . . . much evil": *Writings*, March 27, 1787, to Lafayette.

235 "out of my power": *Writings*, Nov. 18, 1786, to James Madison.

235 "Our affairs seem to be drawing": *Writings*, Nov. 19, 1786, to Gov. Edmund Randolph.

235 "[t]he present constitution . . . totters": *Writings*, Nov. 19, 1786, to David Stuart.

235 "at least a door could be kept open": *Writings of James Madison*, ed. Gaillard Hunt, Dec. 24, 1786, to Washington. Available at the James Madison Papers, American Memory Project, Library of Congress. http://memory.loc.gov/.

236 "[A]s my friends . . . seem to wish": *Writings*, March 28, 1787, to Gov. Edmund Randolph.

236 "no temporizing expedient": *Writings*, March 31, 1787, to James Madison.

236 "so near an equilibrium": *Writings*, April 2, 1787, to Henry Knox.

236 "hope for the best": *Writings*, April 9, 1787.

237 "I have never heard a person": TJW V:220, Nov. 14, 1786, to Washington.

237 The Hôtel des Menus-Plaisirs: For the minutes of the opening of the Estates-General drawn from the notes of the master of ceremonies as well as for details of the Hôtel des Menus-Plaisirs, I am indebted to Manceron, IV:405ff.

237 "in coat and mantle": Ibid., 407.

238 "making three deep bows": Ibid., 408.

239 "Messire Charles Alexandre de Calonne": Ibid., 409.

240 "People will doubtless pay more": Doyle, *Oxford*, 73.

240 "Keeping the good model": Chinard, *Letters*, Feb. 28, 1787, Jefferson to Lafayette.

241 "dissipated millions": LG IV:299.

241 "it was thought proper": Gottschalk, *Letters*, 323, May 5, 1787, Lafayette to Washington.

241 "a man equally great by his abilities": Ibid., 325, Aug. 3, 1787, Lafayette to Washington.

241 "squandering and luxury": LG IV:308.

242 "All would be lost": Ibid.

242 "the King and family": Gottschalk, *Letters*, 323, May 5, 1787.

242 "a new order of things": LG IV:311.

242 "It seems to me": Ibid.

243 "I had the misfortune to displease": Gottschalk, *Letters*, 331, Oct. 9, 1787.

XVII

244 "nearly annihilated": Farrand, May 29, 1787. The plan was presented on May 28 and the phrase was used during discussion on the 29th.

245 "You will I dare say, be surprised": *Writings*, June 6, 1787, to Lafayette.

245 "Secure as he was in his fame": Flexner, III:111.

245 "interesting": *Writings*, Aug. 15, 1787, to Lafayette.

246 "application too intense": Ibid.

246 someone actually moved that only four: Dunn, 112.

247 no body ever delegated to the task: Dunn, 37, cites the observation by Rossiter.

247 "I confess that I do not": Isaacson, 457–58.

248 "let him who owns it" . . . "he bowed": Dunn, 128.

248 "to meditate on the momentous work": *Diaries of George Washington*, V:185, entry for Sept. 17, 1787.

248 "must speak for itself": *Writings*, Sept. 18, 1787, to Lafayette.

249 "give solidity and energy": LGIV:342.

249 "What do you think": Chinard, *Letters*, 123, undated letter from Lafayette to Jefferson.

249 "Reflect on all the instances": TJW V:372, Dec. 20, 1787, to Madison.

249 "it is inappropriate": *Archives parlementaires de 1787 à 1860: Recueil complèt des débats législatifs et politiques des Chambres françaises* [hereinafter AP], I:244.

250 "The body is thickening": Manceron, V:144–45.

251 "That [the king] is accountable": AP I:265.

251 "After hearing your opinions": Ibid., 269.

251 when the duc d'Orléans rose: Ibid.

251 "It is necessary to revert": Talleyrand, I:146.

251 "I don't care": Manceron, V:208.

251 "deplorable and truly critical": LG IV:352. Lafayette's reports in Auvergne are in LFM II:184–88 and 485–91. I have used Gottschalk's translations.

252 "poverty that crushes": Ibid., 358–59.

253 "the only purpose": Ibid., 360.

253 "profound consternation": Ibid., 362.

253 "persist in the sentiments": Ibid.

253 "listened only to the voice": Bernier, 182.

254 "[S]eeing that the power": Chinard, *Letters*, 336–37, Jan. 2, 1788, to Washington.

254 "You can easily imagine": Ibid., 338.

255 "the affairs of France": Ibid., 343, May 25, 1788, to Washington.

256 "I like not much": *Writings*, June 19, 1788.

257 "walked with great difficulty": Stendhal, *Vie de Henri Brulard*; Manceron, V:276.

XVIII

259 "THE SULTAN (*to the Eunuch*): If I'm not happy tomorrow": Quoted in Grendel, 242.

259 "the only topic": Loménie, IV:183–84.

259 "a house of note": Grendel, 251.

259 The property he bought: Details of the house are in ibid., 251–53, and Loménie, IV:213–17.

259 "a quiet spot": Grendel, 251.

259 "M. de Beaumarchais, who has so proved": The letter is not in either Boyd's or Ford's edition of Jefferson's papers but is in his *Oeuvres complètes*, where the letter is given in French translation from the original, as quoted in "Beaumarchais, Francy, Steuben."

260 The scandal that enmeshed all these players: For the origins and development of the Beaumarchais-Bergasse conflict, see Chaudhuri, 40ff.

261 "Wretch, you reek of crime!": Grendel, 240.

261 "This type of ridiculous cant": Ibid., 239.

262 "the nation in general": LFM II:183.

262 "The Marquis de la Fayette . . . is dis-graced": LDC II:174, Aug. 3, 1788, Jefferson to Jay.

263 "the most dangerous man": LFM II:95.

263 "the coup de grace": Peterson, *Writings*, 927, Aug. 9, 1788, Jefferson to Crèvecoeur.

263 "This damnable suspension": LFM II:234; Manceron, IV:313.

265 the "Patriot Party," a coinage: The formation and evolution of the Patriot Party is well developed in Wick, *Conspiracy*.

265 They were no better than those "ministerial despots": For this insight and others regarding the pre-revolutionary pamphlet war of the Patriot party and the Society of Thirty, I am indebted to Van Kley, "New Wine in Old Wineskins."

266 "Twice the king has gathered": Fitzsimmons, "Privilege and Polity," 278n33.

266 "as far as the public welfare": LG IV:416, Nov. 10, 1788, Mirabeau to Lauzun.

267 "Sire, the state is in peril": "Memoir of the Princes," in Beik, ed., 10ff.

267 "Each day it rains pamphlets": Wick, *Conspiracy*, 301.

267 the king received some eight hundred petitions: Doyle, *Oxford*, 91.

267 "its cause is allied with generous": Taine, I: Book One, 17.

267 "because good and useful pastors": Ibid.

267 "more than the Estates-General": Hardman, 142.

268 "Oh, we'll take him": LG V:11.

268 "everyone, from the extremities": Taine, I: Book One, 17.

269 He pleaded with them not to suspend: *Writings*, April 27, 1788, to McHenry.

269 "We, the States": Freeman, V:136.

270 "[w]hen the people shall find": *Writings*, June 19, 1788, to Lafayette.

270 "Knowing me as you do": *Writings*, April 28, 1788, to Lafayette.

270 "to pass an unclouded evening": *Writings*, Oct. 3, 1788, to Hamilton.

270 "I think I see a path": *Writings*, Jan. 29, 1789, to Lafayette.

270 "May Heaven assist me": *Writings*, Dec. 4, 1788, to Jonathan Trumbull.

271 "My difficulties increase": *Writings*, Jan. 29, 1789, to Lafayette.

271 "[M]y movements to the chair": *Writings*, April 1, 1789, to Knox.

272 "[W]hile I realize the arduous nature": *Writings*, April 14, 1789, to Charles Thomson.

272 "I bade adieu to Mount Vernon": *Diaries of George Washington*, V:445, entry for April 16, 1789.

XIX

273 only to find themselves resented: The difficulty of court nobles in their home provinces is covered by Doyle, *Oxford*, 99–100.

273 "take along in your pocket": LG IV:416.

273 "I shall do my duty": LFM II:240.

274 "nature has made men equal": On the relation between Auvergne's cahier and Lafayette's initial work on the Declaration of Rights and Citizen, see LG V:29ff.

274 "proportionate to true needs": LG V:29.

274 which "oppresses me": LG V:37.

275 "The third estate cultivates": Schama, 319.

275 Almost half of the representatives of the Third: See Doyle, *Oxford*, 101.

275 "make them open their bowels": Schama, 319.

276 "those bloodsuckers of the Nation": Ibid., 314.

276 the price of bread: For statistics on bread prices, see Rudé, 33.

276 the winter of 1788–89: Taine, I: Book One, 13.

276 a "rate the poor can afford": Schama, 318.

277 There were more than three hundred violent incidents: Taine, I: Book One, 18.

277 "to men dying of hunger?": Schama, 332.

278 in sixty newly drawn electoral districts: For the politics of the electoral regulations of Paris, I am indebted to Rose, *The Making of the Sans-Culottes*, 23ff.

278 There were also new, more restrictive qualifications: Godechot, *Taking*, 133.

278 "deliberate and sustained act": Rose, 24.

279 Their model was clearly based: See Wick, *Conspiracy*, 291ff.

279 In the end, the Society of Thirty sent no fewer than: Ibid., 354.

280 Titonville: For details, see Godechot, *Taking*, 137.

281 "They spoke with one voice": Ibid., 137

281 "Never had people sought more": De La Tour du Pin, 83.

282 "Happiness is in sight": Godechot, *Taking*, 143.

282 "But monsieur" . . . "The Duke has come": Ibid.

XX

285 "Long live George Washington": Freeman VI:192.

285 "Among the vicissitudes": *Writings*, April 30, 1789, First Inaugural Address.

286 "grave, almost to sadness": Flexner, III 188.

286 "Time has made havoc" . . . John Adams was in tears: Ibid.

286 A small war broke out: Maclay, 2ff.

286 "the first step": Ibid., 11.

286 "every trace of the feudal system": Ibid., 13.

287 "the most superlatively ridiculous": TJW, V:485, July 29, 1789, to Madison.

287 Congressmen were still trying to figure out: See Maclay, 2ff.

287 "From the time I had done": *Writings*, July 26, 1789, to David Stuart.

287 "and every person who could get introduced": Ibid.

287 "an eastern lama": Flexner, III:196

288 "The devices of the coins": Newman, 490ff.

289 David Humphreys threw open the door: Flexner, III:197.

289 some "neat and fashionable" ornaments: *Writings*, Oct. 17, 1789, to Gouverneur Morris.

289 "I promised you some Chinese pigs": PGW: *Presidential Series* [hereinafter PS], I:103 Nov. 12, 1788, Gouverneur Morris to Washington.

289 "such proofs of his want": *Writings*, Nov. 23, 1790, to Tobias Lear.

289 "great . . . prejudices and fears": Ibid.

290 the French minister Moustier: Flexner, III:209n.

291 "without trimming or badges": Bryant, 421.

291 the experience left a bitter taste: Ibid.

291 "She looks . . . with contempt": Morris, ed., *Diary and Letters*, I:71, Diary entry for May 4, 1789.

292 "The Noblesse & especially": Ford, ed., TJW V:472 May 6, 1789 to Lafayette

292 "I am in great pain": Ford, ed., TJW V:476, May 10, 1789, to Washington.

292 "[The Duc] strongly represented": Hardman, 149.

293 "There are no fathers then": Ibid.

293 "it's only a phrase": Ibid., 152.

293 Dr. Joseph Guillotin suggested: Godechot, *Taking*, 161.

294 "The king wishes": AP VIII:143. The *séance royale* of June 23 is in ibid., VIII:142ff.

294 "If you abandon me": Ibid., 145–46.

294 "The people . . . remained silent": Bryant, 428.

295 "We shall not move" . . . "Gentlemen, you are": AP VIII:146.

295 "Well, damnit, let them stay!": Godechot, *Taking*, 165.

295 "you must claim me": TJP XV:254; LG V, 80.

296 to "consider it again": TJP XV:255.

296 his "profession of faith": LG V:96.

296 "the noble simplicity": LG V:93.

296 "It seemed as if we were listening": Ibid.

297 "The closer the 14th of July": Godechot, *Taking*,182.

297 "all the troops . . . rushed off": Ibid., 183.

298 "Everywhere you see working-class people": Ibid., 184.

298 "he [d'Orléans] would be my captain": LFM II:312–13.

298 "I shall . . . keep an eye": Ibid.

298 "Citizens, you know that the nation": Godechot, *Taking*, 187–88.

300 With the first of the new *gardes-bourgeoises*: Ibid., 199.

301 "If the king appreciates": LFM II:308, July 13, 1789, to Simiane.

301 "I have let you know": Godechot, *Taking*, 202.

301 "the constitution will be": LG V:102.

301 "drawn the sword": LFM II:316, June 12, 1789, to Simiane.

301 "Gentlemen, on another occasion": LFM II:254–55.

301 "There is nothing more singular": LFM II:316, July 14, 1789, to Simiane.

XXI

303 The National Assembly spent the day debating: The chronology of events for July 14 in the Assembly and at Versailles is taken from Bailly, *Mémoires*, and from Duveyrier, *Procès-verbal des séances et délibérations de l'Assemblée générale des électeurs de Paris* [hereinafter PV], I:281ff.

303 were emboldening two regiments: Morris, ed., *Diary and Letters*, I:126–27; Godechot, *Taking*, 249.

303 fragmentary, hours old: *Mémoires de Bailly*, I:336–37.

303 Finally, late that night: Ibid., 363ff.

304 "the promptest possible action": Ibid.

304 "make the necessary dispositions": Ibid., 339; PV I:403.

304 "You know what I said": PV I:404.

305 he could not count on the fidelity of his troops: Godechot, *Taking*, 253.

305 Two generals had turned down the job: PV I:422.

306 "never seen a man so embarrassed": LG V:114

306 "defend with his life": PV I:460.

306 the all-powerful lieutenant-general of police had fled: Taine I: Book One, 8.

307 "the second governor": LG V:115.

307 The role of policing Paris in 1789: See Clifford, "National Guard," 859.

308 "to bring to His Majesty's feet": LG V:124ff

308 This was to be a ceremony of state: For the discussion of the king's entry into Paris, I am indebted to Bryant, "Royal Ceremony and the Revolutionary Strategies of the Third Estate."

308 "I was quite embarrassed": *Mémoires de Bailly,* quoted in ibid., 433.

309 "When one does such things": Ibid., 434.

309 "armed with guns, pistols": Jefferson to Madison, July 22, quoted in LG V:127.

309 "he had conquered his people": PV II:85–86.

310 "the descendant of sixty-five kings": Bryant, 445.

310 "this drunk and furious people": LFM II:317, to Simiane; LG I:123

310 a seventy-four-year-old financier named Foulon: Details of events surrounding the murders of Foulon and Berthier are taken from PV II:318–25.

312 The French press began to explode: Popkin, 31ff.

312 In 1789, 184 new periodicals: "Journals: The New Face of News," by Popkin, in Darton and Roche, 150.

312 "A man, O gods, a man": Schama, 446–47.

313 "Gracious God what a People!": Morris, ed., *Diary and Letters,* I:137.

313 "God forbid we should ever be": TJW V:360, Nov. 13, 1787, to William Stephens Smith.

313 "a little rebellion now and then": Ibid., 254, Jan. 30, 1787, to James Madison, and 263, Feb. 22, 1787, to Abigail Adams.

313 "[T]his great crisis now being over": TJP XV:223; O'Brien, 59.

313 "The decapitation of": TJP XV:288.

313 "the great national reformation": TJP XV:110–11, May 9, 1789, to John Jay.

313 "parade about the streets": Morris, ed., *Diary and Letters,* I:108, July 1, 1789, to John Jay.

314 "is at present as near to anarchy": Ibid., I:142–43, July 29, 1789, to Washington.

315 "submission and obedience": LG V:154.

315 "an example for public administrators": *Ami du peuple,* Sept. 25, 1789.

315 had cost him 1,500 louis d'or: LG V:278.

316 At a meeting in his home: Wick, *Conspiracy,* 318.

316 "a logical reasoning": TJW I:"Autobiography," 153–54.

317 "Open your eyes": Schama, 459.

317 recent yardmate of the marquis de Sade: Ibid., 455.

318 Danton . . . called on the other districts: "Brochures." *Extrait du registre des délibérations de l'assemblée du district des Cordeliers,* Oct. 7, 1789 (digitized version at the BnF Gallica site).

318 even Saint-Huruge distanced himself: LG V:320 and note.

318 still had no organized artillery unit: LG V:284.

319 "He says they will not mount guard": Morris, ed., *Diary and Letters*, I:156, Diary entry for Sept. 16, 1789.

319 to "converge on Versailles": LG V:296–97.

319 Danton's Cordeliers called on Lafayette: LG V:325.

320 Danton's Cordeliers demanded: Rudé, 72.

321 "General, we must go": LG V:333.

322 "marched by compulsion": Morris, ed., *Diary and Letters*, I:173, Diary entry for Oct. 5,1789.

323 "We don't give a fuck for order": Hibbert, 99.

323 "No more talking!": Ibid., 100.

323 approving "purely and simply": AP, IX, 348, Oct. 5, 1789.

323 "We had to yield": Hardman, 182, quoting Necker's *Sur l'administration de M. Necker par lui-même, 1791*, 328.

324 "Here comes Cromwell": LG V:357.

325 "I thought it better": Mme de La Tour du Pin, 104.

325 "would prove his love": Lacroix, II:183.

325 "Death to the Austrian!": Hibbert, 101.

326 It was said that the hair: Hardman, 172.

326 "I have given the king my word": LG IV:372

327 "Haven't you seen the gestures": Schama, 468.

327 "the only sound to be heard": La Tour du Pin, 110.

328 "It's very ugly here, Mother": Hibbert, 105.

328 "the guardian angel": LG V:385.

328 "Oh rare!": Morris, ed., *Diary and Letters*, I:173, Diary entry for Oct. 5, 1789.

328 "The mobs and murders": TJP XV:522, Oct. 14, 1789, to Thomas Paine.

XXII

329 "a long interval of silence": *Writings*, Oct. 14, 1789, to Lafayette.

329 the "first paroxysm": *Writings*, Oct. 13, 1789, to Gouverneur Morris.

329 "events or reports of another planet": *Writings*, April 29, 1790, to Luzerne.

330 "a tribute I owe as a son": Gottschalk, *Letters*, 348, Aug. 23, 1790, to Washington.

330 "token of victory gained by Liberty": *Writings*, Aug. 11, 1790, to Lafayette.

331 "Such an extensive power": LG VI:197.

331 Several Paris newspapers recorded: Ibid., 511.

331 called the occasion "sublime": *Orateur du peuple*, quoted at ibid., 549.

331 "the most beautiful day": Ibid., 550.

331 "I believe there has never been": Ibid.

331 "at the zenith of his influence": Ibid., 551.

332 "Let's hang the aristocrats": Doyle, *Oxford*, 128.

334 "I detest that book": Bowers, 84.

334 a grand coach drawn by a large team: Ferling, *Adams*, 50.

334 "the political heresies": McCullough, 429.

334 "doctrine of king, lords": Hazen, 160; Peterson, 992, June 16, 1792, Jefferson to Paine.

335 "so favorable an aspect": *Writings*, June 3, 1790, to Lafayette.

335 "preference of kingly": TJW I:171, from the preface to "Anas."

335 "at a steady pace": Chinard, *Letters*, 168, April 2, 1790.

336 "I dread the reveries": Syrett, ed., *Papers of Hamilton*, V:425, Oct. 6, 1789, Hamilton to Lafayette.

336 "well digested and illustrated": Bowers, 46.

337 Hamilton got his ideas about the utility: For this discussion of Hamilton's financial program, I am indebted to Chernow.

338 "corrupt squadrons": Peterson, 985, May 23, 1792, to Washington.

340 "the king would still be sitting": Buckner, 197.

340 "no one rings the bells": Kennedy, *First Years*, 175, cites La Gorce, *Histoire* I:416–20.

341 "Lafayette replied . . . that he was astonished": *Journal de la Cour et de la Ville*, April 13, 1791; Maurois, 186.

341 "I am deeply grieved to have to": Ibid.

341 No issue gave more impetus: For this and subsequent discussions of the history of the Jacobin clubs, I am indebted to Kennedy.

343 the "first subject of the Law" . . . "going into ecstasies": Schama, 549.

343 "Stop! Stop!": Ibid., 521.

344 "it would suffice": Whitlock, I:411.

344 "Is M. de La Fayette a demagogue": Bernier, 225.

344 the "leader of the Austrian committee": Charavay, 265.

344 "Monsieur de La Fayette is treading": *Journal de la Cour et de la Ville*, April 25, 1791, Maurois, 189.

345 "treated herself to the pleasure": Maurois, 191.

345 "*un silence profond*": AP XXVII:358, June 21, 1791.

345 kidnapped by "enemies of the Revolution": LFM II:79.

346 "incendiary newspapers": Beik, 158ff.

346 "How could one ever again" . . . "honeyed words": Tackett, *When the King*, 102

346 "A large pig has escaped": Ibid., 104.

346 "Traitor to the people!": Latzko, 203.

346 "You, M. Lafayette, will answer": Charavay, 269.

346 "either a traitor or an idiot": Ibid., 269–70.

346 whose affiliates had already tripled to nine hundred: Doyle, *Oxford*, 153.

347 "to declare here and now": Aulard, I:281.

347 "Louis XVI himself has shattered": Ibid., 280.

347 had been "led astray": Ibid., 278.

347 Carra's *Annales politiques*: Ibid., 276.

347 "that nullity": Sonenscher, ed., 165–73.

347 Marat, on the other hand, came out for a dictator: Aulard, I:280.

347 "a young mechanic": Aulard, I:295.

348 "men and women of all conditions": Ibid., 311.

348 "to receive his abdication": Ibid., 314.

348 "There is a storm about": Holbrook, 103.

349 "a man who has told me": Ellery, 180.

349 "tossed about in the ocean of factions": Gottschalk, *Letters*, 352–53, March 7, 1791, to Washington.

350 "dark clouds": Ibid., 353 May 3, 1791.

350 "intrigues . . . licentiousness": Ibid., 355 June 6, 1791.

350 "great anxiety" . . . "the danger to which": *Writings*, July 28, 1791, to Lafayette.

350 "The time of destructions": Schama 576.

351 The Revolution is finished?: AP LXVII:619–21, Sept. 29, 1791.

351 "The end of the Revolution": AP LXVII:688, Sept. 30, 1791.

351 "The people were awaiting": Aulard, I:337.

354 "I do believe we are about to declare war": Schama, 586.

355 "I am to have twenty thousand": Gottschalk, *Letters*, 359, Jan. 22, 1792, to Washington.

355 "I cannot conceive": Bernier, 237.

356 "There can be no doubt" . . . "Strike Lafayette": Ibid., 238.

356 "We have need of some form": Cobban, 194.

356 "apprenticed to chicanery": Ibid., 195.

356 "pregnant with great events": *Writings*, June 10, 1792, to Lafayette.

357 "The state is in danger": LFM, III:325.

358 "a contumelious reply": Dalberg-Acton, 198.

358 "It is time . . . to protect the constitution": AP, XLV:653.

358 "I verily believe": Morris, ed., *Diary and Letters*, I:566, Aug. 1, 1792, to Jefferson.

359 his "full and complete liberty": Mason and Rizzo, 168.

360 That day, a committee of the Paris Commune: Ellery, 293.

361 "To prevent this": Browning, ed., 213–28.

361 "[H]aving demanded": Ibid.

361 "[E]arly on Monday morning": Ibid.

XXIII

363 "Lafayette! Lafayette!": Whitlock, II:6.

363 "You will greatly oblige me": Ibid., 8.

363 "I do not exactly see": Morris, ed., *Diary and Letters,* I:587, Sept. 12, 1792, to Short.

364 "If I had words": *Writings*, Jan. 31, 1793, to Adrienne.

364 "In this abyss of misery": Maurois, 266–67.

364 "all the consolation": *Writings,* March 13, 1793, to Jefferson.

365 Despite "my friendship for him": *Writings*, March 16, 1793.

365 "Those mad and corrupt people": Freeman, VII:23.

365 "Was ever such a prize": TJW VII:203, Jan. 3, 1793, to Short.

366 "We cannot rest": Ammon, 20.

367 "Here and today": Doyle, *Oxford*, 193.

367 "with a firm step": Jordan, 219.

367 "I die perfectly innocent": Hardman, 232.

367 "a frightful cry": Jordan, 220.

367 The executioner Sanson helpfully filled: Hardman, 232.

369 His instructions . . . drafted principally by Brissot: Bowman, 42n.

369 "deliver our former brothers": Ibid., 42.

369 Genêt got to work: See Ammon, 45.

370 "No one has the right": Ibid., 68.

370 "the crime which my mind": Ibid., 70.

370 the "infernal system of the King": Ibid., 72.

371 "the Noblesse and Courtiers of the United States": Newman, 486.

371 "much inflamed": Ford, TJW I: "Anas," 252–54.

371   "shall be the gainers": *Writings*, Aug. 11, 1790, to Lafayette.

372 In part because Jefferson . . . made matters incalculably worse. For this insight, I am indebted to Ammon, *The Genet Mission*, 64.

374 "I cannot believe that our captors": Maurois, 215.

374 "As it is you who are responsible": Whitlock, II:11.

375 "My physical constitution": Ibid., 31.

375 "I am permitted . . . to certify": Whitlock, II:31.

376 "The woman Lafayette": Maurois, 219.

376 who made her a personal loan: Brookhiser, *Gouverneur Morris*, 133.

377 "run to earth in their burrows": Maurois, 240.

377 "the order of the day": Quoted in *Réimpression de l'ancien Moniteur* (Paris: Imprimerie Nationale, 1858–63), XVII:586.

377 and a new judicial code put in place: Doyle, *Oxford*, 275.

378 "to dissolve the National Convention": Maurois, 253.

378 "What is that you are saying?": Ibid.

378 "was struck by their look of . . . serenity": Ibid., 254.

378 "pleased to know": Ibid.

XXIV

379 "hidden domestic enemies" . . . "monsters": AP LXXIII:Sept. 5, 1793.

379 "In the system of the French Revolution": Ibid.

380 "To touch on the case": *Writings*, June 5, 1795.

381 "I am on my way": Maurois, 275–76.

381 "I am persuaded that": Ibid., 276.

381 "As far as his freedom": Lasteyrie, 355.

381 "How we will endure": Ibid., 353.

383 "ten thousand people in the streets of Philadelphia": Hazen, 186; Flexner, IV:63.

384 "Brissot begat the Jacobin clubs": Hale, 96.

385 Jay later said that the whole East Coast: Ellis, *Founding Brothers*, 137.

385 "Come up to my price": Hale, 115–16.

385 "God save the guillotine": Ibid., 102.

385 "This government, in relation to France": *Writings*, April 26, 1795, to the Secretary of State.

385 "Our Jacobins mediate": Flexner, IV:223.

386 "which in its turn influenced": Ibid., 225.

386 "Thus, with some thousands": Elkins, 429.

386 "[H]ow can I be useful" . . . "father, friend, protector": *Writings*, Sept. 7, 1795, to George Cabot.

387 "unless some powerful reasons": *Writings*, Nov. 18, 1795, to Hamilton.

387 "[Let] me begin with fatherly advice": *Writings*, Nov. 22, 1795, to George Washington Lafayette.

387 "I am distrustful": *Writings*, Nov. 23, 1795, to Hamilton.

387 "gives me pain": *Writings*, Dec. 22, 1795, to Hamilton.

387 "continually uneasy": *Writings*, Feb. 13, 1796, to Hamilton.

387 "heard me lisp a syllable": *Writings*, March 6, 1796, to Madison.

387 "immediately to this city": *Writings*, March 31, 1796, to George Washington Lafayette.

388 the "actual state of things": Flexner, IV:288.

388 "Until within the last year or two": *Writings*, July 6, 1796, to Jefferson.

389 "As to you, sir": Freeman, VII:428.

390 "exclude . . . talents and virtue": *Writings*, Dec. 7, 1796, Eighth Annual Address to Congress.

390 "the extreme agitation he felt": Flexner, IV:325.

390 "true Martinique noyan": Ibid.

391 France's "depredations on our commerce": McCullough, 484.

391 "I'll hold the job": Elkins, 562.

XXV

394 "We desire to have these prisoners": Bernier, 259.

394 "as if it were necessary": Whitlock, II:81.

395 "Oh great friend!": Ibid., 82.

395 "wasting their time": Ibid., 83.

395 "your constant solicitude in my behalf": Gottschalk, *Letters*, 363, Oct. 6, 1797, to Washington.

396 "the delicate . . . situation": *Writings*, Oct. 8, 1797, to Lafayette.

397 "so little changed that": Maurois, 323–24.

397 "I have made many mistakes": Whitlock, II:89–90.

397 "Your father and my husband": Ibid., 91.

398 "for twenty years I have often heard": Syrett, ed., *Papers of Hamilton*, XXI:325, Dec. 8, 1797, to Lafayette.

399 "Are our commissioners [to France] guillotined": Freeman, VII:496.

399 "the diplomatic skill of France": O'Brien, 246.

400 290 groups of merchants: Ray, 400.

400 "consisting of principled Americans": Hale, 145.

400 "Fellow soldiers": Ibid.

401 passed no fewer than thirty-three defense bills: Ibid., 186.

402 "I nominate William Van Murray": McCullough, 523.

403 "the event of events": Ibid., 524.

403 "The honor of this country": Ibid., 523–24.

403 "I hope the measure": *Writings*, March 20, 1799, to the Secretary of State.

403 "harsh and ungenerous terms": Bowman, 372.

403 "a temporary suspension": Ibid., 275.

403 "artful designing men": Ibid.

403 "the trouble of your journey": Ibid., 377.

404 "I frankly confess, I have differed": Syrett, ed., *Papers of Hamilton*, XXII:404–5, Jan. 6, 1799, to Lafayette.

405 "the beloved shores of America": Gottschalk, *Letters*, 373–78, Aug. 20, 1798, to Washington.

405 "every monarch on this continent": Ibid.

405 **"more than ever in a situation"**: Ibid., 378–80 Sept. 5, 1798, to Washington.

405 **"it would be a mere waste"**: *Writings*, Dec. 25, 1798, to Lafayette.

407 **"Happily, your good letter of 25 December"**: French version in Gottschalk, *Letters*, 381–85, April 19, 1799.

408 **"to bring the concerns"**: *Writings*, Sept. 10, 1799, "Instructions for My Manager."

408 **"The day after tomorrow"**: Maurois, 364.

409 **"*strictly*, and *pointedly* attended to"**: *Writings*, Sept. 10, 1799, "Instructions for My Manager."

411 **"Morning snowing"**: *Diaries of George Washington*, VI, Entry for Dec. 13, 1799.

411 **"You know I never take anything"**: "A True Copy, Made at Mrs. Lear's Request, from the Diary of Col. Lear: Saturday, Decr. 14, 1799," in Lear, 130.

411 **a diagnosis of acute epiglottitis**: Morens, "Death," 1845ff.

412 **"This is a debt we must pay"**: Lear, 133.

412 **"I die hard"**: Ibid.

413 **"principles and not men"**: Newman, "Principles or Men."

413 **"To Citizen Washington"**: Ibid., 498.

413 **"incense of adulation"**: Ibid., 495.

414 **"Bind it in your Bibles"**: Eulogy of William Cunningham, quoted in Kahler, *Washington in Glory*, 386.

414 **"infamous [June 26 to Hamilton]"**: These quotes are gathered together in Smelser, "George Washington and the Alien and Sedition Acts," 327.

415 **"Hatred to England may carry"**: *Writings*, Nov. 14, 1778, to Henry Laurens.

415 **"It is vain to exclaim"**: *Writings*, Jan. 29, 1778.

415 **"how much littleness"**: Schutz and Adair, 96, Oct. 31, 1807, Rush to Adams.

416 **"to keep in the situation"**: *Writings*, Aug. 11, 1790, to Lafayette.

416 **the quintessential hedgehog**: Ellis, *His Excellency*, 344.

416 **Washington's various funerals**: Quotes in this section are from Kahler, 179, to whose dissertation I am indebted for the substance of this discussion as well as its details.

416 **"imagined themselves in a state of siege"**: Elkins, 693.

418 **"You've turned me out!"**: Bowers, 489.

418 **"This was no contest"**: Peterson, ed., *Writings*, 1236–37.

418 **"I will be as faithful"**: Ibid.

419 **"Citizens! The Revolution has been established"**: Stewart, 780.

419 **The vote was**: Dunn, 17.

419 **"There was a day"**: Lord Byron, *Ode to Napoleon*, as quoted in Wills, 240–41.

XXVI

421 **"What is to become of us, my dear?"**: Grendel, 256–57.

422 **"our boudoirs"**: Ibid., 260.

422 **to use his secret exit to a side street**: Kite II:247ff.

422 **"a natural justice"**: Grendel, 266.

423 **"A hideous little man"**: Ibid., 273.

424 **20 cents on the dollar**: Morton, 959.

424 **"Don't say no, general"**: Ibid., 288–89.

424 **he left a small library there**: Jones, "Flowering," 389.

424 "The roof was topped": Cooper, *Gleanings*, 331–32.

425 in a single room over a barber shop: Smith, *Patriarch*, 163.

425 "separated from the public": Charavay, 516, quoting *Le National*, May 23, 1834.

425 "Hide yourselves, Parisians!": Whitlock, II:412.

426 "Faithful to the habits": Thierry, *Liberal Ideal*, 60.

427 "He spoke as conversationally": Holbrook, 163.

427 "By what right do you dare": Ibid.

427 "I considered him a historic character": Rémusat, *Mémoires*, II:221.

428 "that animal": Neely, "Politics of Liberty," 154.

428 "I know only two men": Victor Hugo, "Choses vues," in *Oeuvres*; Bernier, 298–99.

429 conditions for the working poor: Statistics in this paragraph are from Pinkney, "A New Look."

430 "The reign of law has been interrupted": Whitlock, II:314.

430 "Uniform for sale": Ibid., 293.

430 "Monsieur de Lafayette was starting": Rémusat, II:227.

430 "the springtime of our liberty": Alphonse d'Herbelot, *La Jeunesse libérale de 1830: Lettres à Charles de Montalembert et à Leon Cornudet, 1828–1830* (Paris: Editions Alphonse Picard et fils, 1908), 115–16; Kramer, 228.

431 "These events can no longer be confined": Whitlock, II:317.

432 "Let us rather *order* Marmont": Vaulabelle, VIII:232.

432 "one of the grandest spectacles": Sarrans, I:304–05.

433 "I know the way": Vaulabelle, XIII:306; Fuye and Babeau, *Apostle of Liberty*, 297.

433 "Reconciliation is impossible": Charavay, 473; Sarrans, I:317.

433 "in the words of Marshal Saxe": Sarrans, I:328.

433 "There is no middle ground": Whitlock, II:332.

433 "I am not trying to scare you" . . . "God save us from great men": Lafitte, 232ff.

434 "I still remember this conversation": Barrot, 254.

434 "They will say that forty years": Rémusat, II:234.

434 "he hated Jacobinism": Barrot, 265.

434 "like all men of action": Rémusat, II:234.

435 "a republican kiss": Chateaubriand, *Mémoires d'outre-tombe*, XXXII: 15, 1.

435 "not very nice": Whitlock, II:373, quoting an unpublished letter dated Jan. 1, 1831.

436 "His enthusiasm was an inextinguisable fire": Rémusat, II:245.

437 "I have a horror of drawing-rooms": *Godey's Lady's Book*, IX:183, edition at accessiblearchives.com.

437 "a hero from Plutarch": Stendhal, 33–34.

438 "Ah, I know what you are": Maurois, 448–49.

438 "I have long ago, from my heart": Chinard, *Letters*, 272, April 8, 1808, to Jefferson.

439 "dominated by honest sentiments": LFM II:227–28.

439 "to see for himself": Unger, 349.

439 "[A] voluntary absence": Neely, *Lafayette*, 246; see also Lafayette to Jefferson in Chinard, *Letters*, 398–99; Neely, "Politics," 155.

440 The timing for such a trip: For the background to Lafayette's U.S. tour, I am indebted to Neely's "Politics of Liberty."

440 "[T]his momentous question": TJW XII:158, Letter to John Holmes, April 22, 1820.

441 "Are you married?": Whitlock, II:225.

442 "There is at the moment": Bernier, 293–94.

443 "We shall soon separate": Nagel, "Election of 1824," 318.

443 "He left us weak, unorganized and tottering": George Ticknor in *North American Review*, January 1825; Kramer, 194.

444 "the principles for which": Cooper, *Notions*, II:142.

444 "the perpetual union": Unger, 357.

444 "I watched [Jackson's] manly": Cooper, *Notions*, II:183–84.

444 and resumed his tour in March: For details of Lafayette's U.S. tour, I am indebted to E. E. Brandon's two books on the subject, *Pilgrimage* and *Guest*.

445 "in the midst of the crowd": Walt Whitman, *Lafayette in Brooklyn* (New York: George D. Smith, 1905).

445 "You stand in the midst of posterity!": Cooper, *Notions*, II:141–42.

445 "No, Mr. Speaker": Ibid., 143–44.

446 "you who alone of all generals": LFM VI:178–79.

447 It is said that: "An Hour at Mount Vernon," *New-England Magazine*, vol. 7, no. 5 (November 1834), 399.

447 "To the 22nd of February": Charavay, 447.

447 "under full sail": Morgan, *The True Lafayette*, 436.

447 "One by one the lights": William C. Easton, *Eulogium on Lafayette* (Washington, DC, 1834), 18; Loveland, 133.

448 "Pronounce him one of the first": John Quincy Adams, "Oration."

448 "His was not the influence of genius": Robson, ed., *Works of Mill*, VI:236–37.

448 "This man has lived": Dunn, 16.

448 "the enlightened classes": Kramer, 189.

449 "not too excessive": Tulard et al., *Histoire et dictionnaire*, 920.

449 Lafayette was voted the most admired: Kramer, 5.

450 "He never lost faith" . . . "He may not survive": Rémusat, II:249–55.

Bibliography

Abbot, W. W., Theodore J. Crackel, Philander D. Chase, et al., eds. *The Papers of George Washington 1748–1799.* 47 vols. to date. Charlottesville: University Press of Virginia, 1976– .

Abernethy, Thomas P. "Commercial Activities of Silas Deane in France," *American Historical Review*, vol. 39, no. 3 (April 1934), 477–85.

Adams, Abigail. *Journal of the Correspondence of Miss Adams, Daughter of John Adams.* New York: Wiley & Putnam, 1841.

Adams, Charles Francis, ed. *The Works of John Adams.* 8 vols. Boston: Little, Brown, 1851.

Adams, John. *The Adams Papers: Diary & Autobiography of John Adams,* ed. L. H. Butterfield. 4 vols. New York: Atheneum, 1964.

Adams, John Quincy, "Oration on the life and character of Gilbert Motier de Lafayette." Washington, DC: U.S. House of Representatives, Dec. 31, 1834.

Adams, William Howard. *The Paris Years of Thomas Jefferson.* New Haven: Yale University Press, 1997.

Addison, Joseph. "Uses of the Spectator," *Spectator*, no. 10, March 12, 1711. In J. H. Fowler, ed., *Essays from Addison.* London: Macmillan, 1938.

Akers, Charles W. *The Divine Politician: Samuel Cooper and the American Revolutionary in Boston.* Boston: Northeastern University Press, 1982.

Ammon, Harry. *The Genet Mission.* New York: W. W. Norton & Company, 1973.

Anderson, Fred. *Crucible of War: The Seven Years War and the Fate of Empire in British North America, 1754–1766.* New York: Alfred A. Knopf, 2000.

Andress, David. "The Denial of Social Conflict in the French Revolution: Discourses Around the Champ de Mars Massacre, 17 July 1791," *French Historical Studies,* vol. 22, no. 2 (Spring 1999), 183–209.

Archives du Ministère des Affaires étrangères, correspondence politique, Etats-Unis, 1774–1800. 51 vols.

Archives parlementaires de 1787 à 1860: Recueil complèt des débats législatifs et politiques des Chambres françaises. Publiés sous la direction de Mavidal, M. J., chef de bureau des procès-verbaux de la chambre des deputés. 1st ser. (1787–1799), 73 vols. Paris: Société d'Imprimerie et Librairie Administratives et des Chemins de Fer, 1887.

Arendt, Hannah. *On Revolution.* London: Penguin Books, 1977.

Aulard, A. *The French Revolution: A Political History 1789–1804.* Vol. I. New York: Charles Scribner's Sons, 1910.

Babeau, A. *La Vie militaire sous l'ancien régime.* Vol. 2: *Les Officiers.* Paris: Firmin-Didot, 1890.

Bailly, J.-S., and Duveyrier, le baron Honoré, eds. *Procès-verbale des séances et délibéra-tions de l'Assemblée générale des électeurs de Paris, réunis à l'Hôtel de Ville le 14 juillet 1789.* Vols. I–II. Paris: Baudouin, 1790.

Bailly, Jean-S. *Mémoires de Bailly, avec une notice sur sa vie, des notes, et des éclairiesse-ments historiques,* par MM. Berville et Barrière. 3 vols. Paris: Baudoin Frères, 1821.

Bailyn, Bernard. *The Ideological Origins of the American Revolution.* Cambridge, MA: Harvard University Press, 1992.

Baker, Keith Michael, ed. *The French Revolution and the Creation of Modern Political Culture.* Vol. I: *The Political Culture of the Old Regime.* Oxford: Pergamon Press, 1987.

Balch, Thomas. *Les Français en Amérique pendant la Guerre de l'Indépendance des Etats Unis 1777–1783.* Paris: A. Sauton, 1872.

Banning, Lance. *The Jefferson Persuasion: Evolution of a Party Ideology.* Ithaca, NY: Cornell University Press, 1978.

Barbé-Marbois, François de. "Marbois on the Fur Trade, 1784," *American Historical Review,* vol. 29, no. 4 (July 1924), 725–40.

Bardoux, A. *Les Dernières Années de la Fayette 1792–1834.* Paris: Calman Lévy, 1893.

Barrot, Odilon. *Mémoires posthumes de Odilon Barrot.* Paris: Charpentier, 1875–76.

Becker, Carl. *The Heavenly City of the Eighteenth-Century Philosophers.* New Haven: Yale University Press, 1932.

Beik, Paul H., ed. *The French Revolution.* New York: Walker & Company, 1970.

Bemis, Samuel Flagg. "British Secret Service and the French-American Alliance," *American Historical Review,* vol. 29, no. 3. (April 1924), 474–95.

———. *The Diplomacy of the American Revolution.* Westport, CT: Greenwood Press, 1983.

Bérard, Simon. *Souvenirs Historiques sur la Révolution de 1830.* Paris: Perrotin Editeur, 1834.

Bernier, Olivier. *Lafayette: Hero of the Two Worlds.* New York: E. P. Dutton, 1983.

Betham-Edwards, M., ed. *Young's Travels in France During the Years 1787, 1788, and 1789.* London: G. Bell & Sons, 1915.

Blau, Alan L. *New York City and the French Revolution, 1789–1797: A Study of French Revolutionary Influences.* Unpublished doctoral dissertation, City University of New York, 1973.

Blum, Carol. *Rousseau and the Republic of Virtue: The Language of Politics in the French Revolution.* Ithaca, NY: Cornell University Press, 1986.

Bonsal, Stephen. *When the French Were Here: A Narrative of the Sojourn of the French Forces in America and Their Contribution to the Yorktown Campaign.* New York: Doubleday, Doran & Co., 1945.

Bosenga Gail. *The Politics of Privilege: Old Regime and Revolution in Lille.* Cambridge: Cambridge University Press, 1991.

Bowers, Claude G. *Jefferson and Hamilton: The Struggle for Democracy in America.* London: Constable & Co., 1925.

Bowman, Albert Hall. *The Struggle for Neutrality. Franco-American Diplomacy During the Federalist Era.* Knoxville, TN: University of Tennessee Press, 1974.

Boyd, Julian. "Silas Deane: Death by a Kindly Teacher of Treason?" *William and Mary Quarterly*, 3rd ser., vol. 16, nos. 2, 3, and 4 (April, July, and October 1959).

——— et al., eds. *The Papers of Thomas Jefferson.* 31 vols. to date. Princeton, NJ: Princeton University Press, 1950– .

Brandon, Edgar Ewing, ed. *A Pilgrimage of Liberty. A Contemporary Account of the Triumphal Tour of General Lafayette Through the Southern and Western States in 1825, as Reported by the Local Newspapers.* Athens, OH: Lawhead Press, 1944.

———. *Lafayette Guest of the Nation. A Contemporary Account of the Triumphal Tour of General Lafayette through the United States in 1824–1825, as reported by the Local Newspapers.* Oxford, OH: Oxford Historical Press, 1950.

Brissot, J.-P. *Life of J. P. Brissot, Deputy from the Eure and Loire to the National Convention, Written by Himself.* London: J. Debrett, 1794.

Brookhiser, Richard. *Founding Father: Rediscovering George Washington.* New York: Simon & Schuster, 1996.

———. *Gentleman Revolutionary: Gouverneur Morris, the Rake Who Wrote the Constitution.* New York: Free Press, 2003.

Browning, Oscar, ed. *The Despatches of Earl Gower, English Ambassador at Paris from June 1790 to August 1792, to Which are Added the Despatches of Mr Lindsay and Mr Monro and the Diary of Viscount Palmerston in France During July and August 1791.* Cambridge: Cambridge University Press, 1885.

Bryant, Lawrence M. "Royal Ceremony and the Revolutionary Strategies of the Third Estate," *Eighteenth-Century Studies*, vol 22, no. 3 (Spring 1989), 413–50.

Buchanan, John. *The Road to Valley Forge.* Hoboken, NJ: John Wiley & Sons, 2004.

Cappon, Lester J., ed. *The Adams-Jefferson Letters: The Complete Correspondence between Thomas Jefferson and Abigail and John Adams.* New York: Simon & Schuster, 1959

Charavay, Etienne. *Le Général Lafayette 1757–1834.* Geneva: Slatkine-Megariotis Reprints, 1977.

Chastellux, François-Jean, Marquis de. *Travels in North America in the Years 1780, 1781 and 1782*, trans. C. Howard Rice, Jr. 2 vols. Chapel Hill: University of North Carolina Press, 1963.

Chaudhuri, Nupur Dasgupta. *Pierre-Augustin Caron de Beaumarchais Views the French Revolution.* Unpublished doctoral dissertation, Kansas State University, 1974.

Chernow, Ron. *Alexander Hamilton.* New York: Penguin Press, 2004.

Chinard, Gilbert. "Eighteenth Century Theories of America as a Human Habitat," *Proceedings of the American Philosophical Society*, XCI (1947), 27–57.

———. *The Letters of Lafayette and Jefferson.* Baltimore: Johns Hopkins University Press, 1929.

———, ed. *George Washington as the French Knew Him.* Princeton: Princeton, NJ: Princeton University Press, 1940.

Claretie, Jules. *Camille Desmoulins and His Wife*, trans. Cashel Hoey. London: Smith, Elder & Co., 1876.

Clary, David A. *Adopted Son: Washington, Lafayette, and the Friendship That Saved the Revolution.* New York: Bantam Dell, 2007.

Clifford, Dale Lothrop. "The National Guard and the Parisian Community, 1789–1790," *French Historical Studies*, vol. 16, no. 4 (Autumn 1990), 849–78.

Cobb, Richard. *The Police and the People: French Popular Protest 1789–1820.* London: Oxford University Press, 1970.

Cobban, Alfred. *A History of Modern France: Old Regime and Revolution, 1715–1799.* Harmondsworth, UK: Penguin Books, 1963.

Colbourn, Trevor, ed. *Fame and the Founding Fathers: Essays by Douglas Adair.* New York: W. W. Norton & Company, 1974.

Compère, Marie-Madeleine. *Les Collèges français III, Repertoire Paris: 16e au 18e siècles.* Paris: INRP, 2002.

Cooper, James Fenimore. *Gleanings in Europe (France)* (1838). Oxford: Oxford University Press, 1928.

————. *Notions of the Americans: Picked Up by the Travelling Bachelor.* 2 vols. (1828) New York: Frederick, 1963.

Corner, George W., ed. *Benjamin Rush. Autobiography.* Princeton, NJ: Princeton University Press, 1948.

Corwin, Edward S. *French Policy and the American Alliance of 1778.* Princeton, NJ: Princeton University Press, 1916.

Dalberg-Acton, John Emerich Edward. *Lectures on the French Revolution.* New York: Macmillan, 1925.

Darnton, Robert C. *George Washington's False Teeth. An Unconventional Guide to the Eighteenth Century.* New York London: W. W. Norton & Company, 2003.

————. "The Grub Street Style of Revolution: J.-P. Brissot, Police Spy," *Journal of Modern History*, vol. 40, no. 3 (September 1968), 301–27.

————. "The High Enlightenment and Literary Low-Life in Pre-Revolutionary France," *Past and Present*, 51 (May 1971), 81–115.

————. *The Literary Underground of the Old Regime.* Cambridge, MA: Harvard University Press, 1982.

————. *Mesmerism and the End of the Enlightenment in France.* Cambridge, MA: Harvard University Press, 1968.

———— and Daniel Roche, eds. *Revolution in Print: The Press in France 1775–1800.* Berkeley: University of California Press, 1989.

Davis, David Brion. *Revolutions: Reflections on American Equality and Foreign Liberations.* Cambridge, MA: Harvard University Press, 1990.

Deane, Silas. *The Papers of Silas Deane, 1774–1790.* 5 vols. New York: Collections of the New-York Historical Society, 1885–90.

Denis, Gen. Pierre. *Garrison de Metz.* 7 vols. Metz: Ed. Serpenoise, 1995–2004.

Doniol, Henri, ed. *Histoire de la participation de la France à l'Etablissement des Etats-Unis d'Amérique: correspondance diplomatique et documents.* 6 vols. Paris: Impr. Nationale, 1886–99.

Doyle, William. *Origins of the French Revolution.* New York: Oxford University Press, 1992.

————. *The Oxford History of the French Revolution.* Oxford: Oxford University Press, 2002.

Dunn, Susan. *Sister Revolutions, French Lightning, American Light.* New York: Faber & Faber, 1999.

Durand, John, trans. and ed. *Documents on the American Revolution: New Materials for the History of the American Revolution.* New York: Henry Holt & Co., 1889.

Echeverria, Durand. *Mirage in the West: A History of the French Image of American Society to 1815*. Princeton, NJ: Princeton University Press, 1957.

Edgar, Gregory T. *The Philadelphia Campaign 1777–1778*. Bowie, MD: Heritage Books, 1998.

Elkins, Stanley, and Eric McKitrick. *The Age of Federalism*. New York: Oxford University Press, 1993.

Ellery, Eloise. *Brissot de Warville: A Study in the History of the French Revolution*. Boston: Houghton Mifflin, 1915.

Ellis, Joseph J. *American Sphinx: The Character of Thomas Jefferson*. New York: Alfred A. Knopf, 1997.

———. *Founding Brothers: The Revolutionary Generations*. New York: Vintage Books, 2000.

———. *His Excellency George Washington*. New York: Alfred A. Knopf, 2004.

Farrand, Max, ed. *The Records of the Federal Convention of 1787*. 3 vols. New Haven: Yale University Press, 1911.

Fausz, J. Frederick. " 'Engaged in Enterprises Pregnant with Terror': George Washington's Formative Years Among the Indians," 129; in Hofstra, 115–55.

Fay, Bernard. *The Revolutionary Spirit in France and America. A Study of Moral and Intellectual Relations Between France and United States at the End of the Eighteenth Century*. New York: Cooper Square Publishers, 1966.

Ferling, John. *Adams and Jefferson: The Tumultuous Election of 1800*. London: Oxford University Press, 2004.

———. "School for Command: Young George Washington and the Virginia Regiment," 208; in Hofstra, 195–222.

Fitzpatrick, John C. *The Spirit of the Revolution*. New York: Houghton Mifflin, 1924.

———, ed. *The writings of George Washington from the original manuscript sources*. Washington, DC: Government Printing Office, 1931–44. Digital version at http://memory.loc.gov/.

Fitzsimmons, Michael P. "Privilege and Polity in France, 1786–1791," *American Historical Review*, vol. 92, no. 2 (April 1987), 269–95.

Fleming, Thomas J. *Beat the Last Drum*. New York: St. Martin's Press, 1963.

Flexner, James Thomas. *George Washington*. 4 vols. Boston: Little, Brown, 1965–72.

Force, Peter. *American archives: consisting of a collection of authentick records, state papers, debates, and letters and other notices of publick affairs, the whole forming a documentary history of the origin and progress of the North American colonies; of the causes and accomplishment of the American revolution; and of the Constitution of government for the United States, to the final ratification thereof*. In six series. 1837.

Ford, Paul Leicester, ed. *The Works of Thomas Jefferson*. 12 vols. New York: G. P. Putnam's Sons, 1904–05. PDF version at http://oll.libertyfund.org.

Ford, Worthington, et al., eds. *Journals of the Continental Congress, 1774–1789*. Washington, DC, 1904–37. Digital version at http://memory.loc.gov/.

Freeman, Douglas Southall. *George Washington, A Biography*. 7 vols. (Vol. 7 completed by John A. Carroll and Mary W. Ashworth). New York: Charles Scribner's Sons, 1948–57.

French, Allen. *The First Year of the American Revolution*. Boston and New York: Houghton Mifflin, 1934.

Furet, François. *Interpreting the French Revolution*, trans. Elborg Forster. Cambridge: Cambridge University Press, 1981.

———, and Mona Ozouf, eds. *The French Revolution and the Creation of Modern Political Culture*. Vol. 3: *The Transformation of Political Culture 1789–1848*. Oxford: Pergamon Press, 1989.

Godechot, Jacques. *France and the Atlantic Revolution of the Eighteenth Century, 1770–1799*, trans. Herbert H. Rowen. New York: Free Press, 1965.

———. *The Taking of the Bastille: July 14th, 1789*, trans. Jean Stewart. London: Faber & Faber, 1970.

Golway, Terry. *Washington's General: Nathanael Greene and the Trimph of the American Revolution*. New York: Henry Holt and Company, 2005.

Gottschalk, Louis. *Lady-in-Waiting: The Romance of Lafayette and Aglaé de Hunolstein*. Baltimore: Johns Hopkins University Press, 1939.

———. *Lafayette*. 6 vols. (I: *Lafayette Goes to America*; II: *Lafayette Joins the American Army*; III: *Lafayette and the Close of the American Revolution*; IV: *Lafayette Between the American and French Revolutions*; V: *Lafayette in the French Revolution: Through the October Days*; VI: *Lafayette in the French Revolution: From the October Days Through the Fête de la Fédération*, with Margaret Maddox). Chicago & London: University of Chicago Press, 1935–73.

———. "Lafayette as Commercial Agent," *American Historical Review*, XXVI (1931), 561–70.

———, ed. *The Letters of Lafayette to Washington, 1777–1799*. New York: Privately printed by Helen Fahnestock Hubbard, 1944.

Greene, George Washington. *The Life of Nathanael Greene, Major General in Army of the French Revolution*. 3 vols. New York: Hurd & Houghton, 1871.

Greene, Jerome. *Guns of Independence: The Siege of Yorktown, 1781*. New York: Savas Beatie, LLC, 2005.

Grendel, Frédéric. *Beaumarchais: The Man Who Was Figaro*, trans. Roger Greaves. London: McDonald & Jane's, 1973.

Gruber, Alain-Charles. *Les Grandes Fêtes et Leurs Décors à l'Epoque de Louis LVI*. Geneva: Droz, 1972.

Guizot, François. *Mémories pour servir à l'histoire de notre temps*. Vol. 3: *La Révolution de 1830*. Paris: Editions Paléo, Sources de l'Histoire de France, 1858–61.

Gummere, Richard M. *The American Colonial Mind and the Classical Tradition*. Cambridge, MA: Harvard University Press, 1963.

Hale, Matthew Rainbow. *Neither Britons nor Frenchmen: The French Revolution and American National Identity*. Unpublished doctoral dissertation, Brandeis University, May 2002.

Hardman, John. *Louis XVI*. New Haven and London: Yale University Press, 1993.

Hazen, Charles Downer. *Contemporary American Opinion of the French Revolution*. Baltimore: Johns Hopkins University Press, 1897.

Henderson, James H. "Congressional Factionalism and the Attempt to Recall Benjamin Franklin," *William and Mary Quarterly*, 3rd ser., vol. 27, no 2 (April 1970), 246–67.

Hibbert, Christopher. *The Days of the French Revolution*. New York: HarperCollins Perennial, 2002.

Higginbotham, Don. *George Washington Reconsidered*. Charlottesville and London: University Press of Virginia, 2001.

Hofstra, Warren R., ed. *George Washington and the Virginia Backcountry.* Madison, WI: Madison House, 1998.

Holbrook, Sabra. *Lafayette Man in the Middle.* New York: Atheneum, 1977.

Hunt, Lynn. *Politics, Culture, and Class in the French Revolution.* Berkeley: University of California Press, 1984.

Hutchinson, William T., et al., eds. *The Papers of James Madison.* Charlottesville: University of Virginia Press, 1962– . 29 vols. to date.

Hyslop, Beatrice F. "The American Press and the French Revolution of 1789," *Proceedings of the American Philosophical Society,* vol. 104, no. 1, Feb. 15, 1960, 54–85.

Idzerda, Stanley J., ed. *Lafayette in the Age of the American Revolution, Selected Letters and Papers 1776–1790.* 5 vols. Ithaca, NY: Cornell University Press, 1977–83.

———. "When and Why Lafayette Became a Revolutionary," in Morris Slavin and Agnes M. Smith, eds., *Bourgeois, Sans-Culottes, and Other Frenchmen.*

Isaacson, Walter. *Benjamin Franklin: An American Life.* New York: Simon & Schuster, 2003.

Jackson, Donald, and Dorothy Twohig, eds. *The Diaries of George Washington.* 6 vols. Charlottesville: University Press of Virginia, 1978.

Jones, Howard Mumford. *America and French Culture 1750–1848.* Chapel Hill: University of North Carolina Press, 1927.

Jones, Russel M. "The Flowering of a Legend: Lafayette and the Americans, 1825–1834," *French Historical Studies,* vol. 4, no. 4 (Autumn 1966), 384–410.

Jordan, David P. *The King's Trial: The French Revolution vs. Louis XVI.* Berkeley: University of California Press, 1979.

Kahler, Gerald Edward. *Washington in Glory, America in Tears: The Nation Mourns the Death of George Washington, 1799–1800.* Unpublished doctoral dissertation, College of William and Mary, 2003.

Kaplan, Roger. "The Hidden War: British Intelligence Operations during the American Revolution," *William and Mary Quarterly,* 3rd ser., vol. 47, no. 1 (January 1990), 115–138.

Kapp, Friedrich. *The Life of John Kalb.* New York: Henry Holt, 1884.

Kates, Gary. *Monsieur D'Eon Is a Woman: A Tale of Political Intrigue and Sexual Masquerade.* Baltimore: Johns Hopkins University Press, 2001.

———, ed. *The French Revolution. Recent Debates and New Controversies.* London and New York: Routledge, 1998.

Kennedy, Michael L. *The Jacobin Clubs in the French Revolution: The First Years.* Princeton: Princeton University Press, 1988.

———. *The Jacobin Clubs in the French Revolution: The Middle Years.* Princeton: Princeton University Press, 1988.

Ketchum, Richard M. *Victory at Yorktown, The Campaign That Won the Revolution.* New York: Henry Holt & Co., 2004.

Kite, Elizabeth. *Beaumarchais and the War of American Independence.* 2 vols. Boston: Gorham Press, 1918

Kramer, Lloyd S. "America's Lafayette and Lafayette's America: A European and the American Revolution," *William and Mary Quarterly,* 3rd ser., vol. 38, no. 2. (April 1981), 228–41.

———. *Lafayette in Two Worlds.* Chapel Hill: University of North Carolina Press, 1996.

Lacroix, Sigismond. *Actes de la Commune de Paris pendant la Révolution.* 19 vols. Paris: L. Cerf, Charles Noblet, Maison Quentin, 1894.

Lafayette, Marquis de. *Mémoires, correspondance et manuscrits du Général Lafayette, publiés par sa famille*. 6 vols. Paris: H. Fournier et comp., 1837.

Lafitte, Jacques. *Mémoires de Lafitte (1767–1844)*. Paris: Libr de Paris, Firmin-Didot et Cie., 1932.

Lasseray, Commandant André. *Les Français sous les Treize Etoiles 1775–1783*. Paris: Protat Frères, 1935.

Lasteyrie, Mme de. *Vie de Madame de Lafayette, par Mme de Lasteyrie sa fille*. Paris: Techener fils, 1868.

La Tour du Pin, Mme de. *Escape from the Terror. The Journal of Madame de La Tour du Pin*, trans. and ed. Felice Harcourt. London: Folio Society, 1979.

Lavnay, Jacques de. *La Croisade européenne pour l'independence des Etats-Unis*. Paris: Albin Michel, 1988.

Latzko, Andreas. *Lafayette. A Life*. New York: The Literary Guild, 1936.

Lear, Tobias. *Letters and Recollections of George Washington*. New York: Doubleday, Page & Co., 1906.

Lee, Henry. *The Revolutionary War Memoirs of General Henry Lee*, ed., with a biography of the author, Robert E. Lee. Reprint of *Memoirs of the War in the Southern Department of the United States*. New York: Da Capo Press, 1998.

Lefebvre, Georges. *The Coming of the French Revolution*, trans. R. R. Palmer. Princeton, NJ: Princeton University Press, 1947.

———. *The French Revolution from Its Origin to 1793*. 2 vols. New York: Columbia University Press, 1964.

Lengel, Edward G. *General George Washington*. New York: Random House, 2005.

Lewis, Thomas A. *For King and Country: The Maturing of George Washington, 1741–1760*. New York: Castle Books, 1993.

Loménie, Louis de. *Beaumarchais and His Times*, trans. Henry S. Edwards. 4 vols. London: Addey & Co., 1856

Longmore, Paul K. *The Invention of George Washington*. Charlottesville and London: University Press of Virginia, 1999.

Loveland, Anne C. *Emblem of Liberty: The Image of Lafayette in the American Mind*. Baton Rouge, LA: Louisiana State University Press, 1971.

Lucas, Colin. *The French Revolution and the Creation of Modern Political Culture*. Vol. 2: *The Political Culture of the French Revolution*. Oxford: Pergamon Press, 1988.

Maclay, Edgar, ed. *Journal of William Maclay, United States Senator from Pennsylvania, 1789–1791*. New York: D. A. Appleton & Co., 1890.

Madison, James. *The Papers of James Madison*, ed. William Thomas Hutchinson, William M. E. Rachal, and Robert Allen Rutland. Chicago: University of Chicago Press, 1962.

Malone, Dumas. *Jefferson and His Time*. 6 vols. Boston: Little, Brown, 1948–77.

Manceron, Claude. *The French Revolution*. New York: Alfred A. Knopf, 1977–89. 5 vols.

———. *Blood of the Bastille 1787–1789*, trans. Nancy Amphoux. (Vol. V)

———. *Their Gracious Pleasure 1782–1785*, trans. Nancy Amphoux, (Vol. III)

———. *Toward the Brink 1785–1787*, trans. Nancy Amphoux. (Vol. IV)

———. *Twilight of the Old World 1774–1778*, trans. Patricia Wolf. (Vol. I)

———. *The Wind from America 1778–1781*, trans. Nancy Amphoux. (Vol. II)

Markoff, John, and Gilbert Shapiro. *Revolutionary Demands: A Content Analysis of the Cahiers de Doléances of 1789*. Stanford, CA: Stanford University Press, 1998.

Marshall, John. *The Life of George Washington.* 5 vols. New York: AMS Press, 1969.

Mason, Laura, and Tracey Rizzo, eds. *The French Revolution: A Document Collection.* New York: Houghton Mifflin, 1999.

Mathiez, Albert, ed. *Le Club des Cordeliers pendant la Crise de Varennes et le Massacre du Champ de Mars: Documents en grande partie inédits, publiés avec des éclaircissements et des notes.* Geneva: Slatkine-Megariotis Reprints, 1975.

Maurois, André. *Adrienne: The Life of the Marquise de La Fayette.* New York and London: McGraw-Hill Book Co., 1961.

McCullough, David. *John Adams.* New York and London: Simon & Schuster, 2001.

McDonald, Forrest. *E Pluribus Unum, The Formation of the American Republic 1776–1790.* Indianapolis: Liberty Press, 1965.

———. *Novus Ordo Seclorum, The Intellectual Origins of the Constitution.* Lawrence: University of Kansas Press, 1985.

———. *The Presidency of George Washington.* Lawrence: University of Kansas Press, 1974.

Mercier, Louis Sebastien. *The Pictures of Paris Before and After the Revolution,* ed. and trans. Wilfrid and Emilie Jackson. London: George Rutledge & Sons, 1929.

Michelet, Jules. *History of the French Revolution,* trans. Charles Cocks. Gordon Wright, ed. Chicago: University of Chicago Press, 1967.

Morens, Dr. David. "Death of a President," *New England Journal of Medicine,* vol. 341, no. 24 (December 1999), 1845–49.

Morgan, Edmund S. *The Genius of George Washington.* New York: W. W. Norton & Company, 1980.

Morgan, George. *The True Lafayette.* Philadelphia: J. B. Lippincott, 1919.

Morris, Anne Cary, ed. *The Diary and Letters of Gouverneur Morris.* 2 vols. New York: Charles Scribner's Sons, 1888.

Morton, Brian N. "Beaumarchais, Francy [*sic*], Steuben, and Lafayette: An Unpublished Correspondence or 'Feux de Joye' at Valley Forge," *French Review,* vol. 49, no. 6. Bicentennial Issue: Historical and Literary Relations between France and the United States (May 1976), 943–59.

Nagel, Paul C. "The Election of 1824: A Reconsideration Based on Newspaper Opinion," *Journal of Southern History,* vol. 26, no. 3 (August 1960), 315–29.

Neely, Sylvia. *Lafayette and the Liberal Ideal 1814–1824. Politics and Conspiracy in an Age of Reaction.* Carbondale and Edwardsville, IL: Southern University Press, 1991.

———. "Lafayette's *Mémoires* and the Changing Legacy of Two Revolutions," *European History Quarterly,* vol. 34, no. 3 (2004), 371–402.

———. "The Politics of Liberty in the Old World and the New: Lafayette's Return to America in 1824," *Journal of the Early Republic,* vol. 6, no. 2 (Summer 1986), 151–71.

Newman, Simon P. "Principles or Men? George Washington and the Political Culture of National Leadership, 1776–1801." *Journal of the Early Republic,* vol. 12, no. 4 (Winter 1992), 477–507.

Nolan, J. Bennett. "Lafayette and the American Philosophical Society," *Proceedings of the American Philosophical Society,* vol. 73, no. 2 (1934), 117–26.

———. *Lafayette in America Day by Day.* Baltimore: Johns Hopkins University Press, 1934.

O'Brien, Conor Cruise. *The Long Affair. Thomas Jefferson and the French Revolution 1785–1800.* Chicago: University Press of Chicago, 1996.

Palmer, R. R. *The Age of the Democratic Revolution: A Political History of Europe and America, 1760–1800.* 2 vols. Princeton, NJ: Princeton University Press, 1959.

———. "The Dubious Democrat: Thomas Jefferson in Bourbon France," *Political Science Quarterly,* vol. 72, no. 3 (September 1957), 388–404.

———. *The World of the French Revolution.* London: Allen & Unwin, 1971.

———, ed. and trans. *The School of the French Revolution. A Documentary History of the College of Louis-le-Grand and Its Director, Jean-François Champagne, 1762–1814.* Princeton, NJ: Princeton University Press, 1975.

Parker, Harold T. *The Cult of Antiquity and the French Revolutionaries.* Chicago: University of Chicago Press, 1937.

——— and Marvin L. Brown, Jr. *Major Themes in Modern European History.* Vol. II: *The Institution of Liberty.* Durham, NC: Moore Publishing Co., 1974.

Peterson, Merrill D., ed. *Thomas Jefferson Writings.* New York: Library of America, 1984.

Pinkney, David H. "The Crowd in the French Revolution of 1830," *American Historical Review,* vol. 70, no. 1 (October 1964), 1–17.

———. "A New Look at the French Revolution of 1830," *Review of Politics,* vol. 23, no. 4 (October 1961), 490–506.

Popkin, Jeremy D. *Revolutionary News: The Press in France 1789–1799.* Durham, NC: Duke University Press, 1990.

Price, Munro. *Preserving the Monarchy: The Comte de Vergennes, 1774–1787.* Cambridge: Cambridge University Press, 1995.

Randall, Willard Sterne. *George Washington. A Life.* New York: Henry Holt & Co., 1997.

Ray, Thomas M. " 'Not One Cent for Tribute': The Public Addresses and American Popular Reaction to the XYZ Affair, 1798–1799," *Journal of the Early Republic,* vol. 3, no. 4 (Winter 1983), 389–412.

Rémusat, Charles de. *Mémoires de ma vie.* 5 vols. Paris: Plon, 1958–67.

Roberts, J. M., ed. *French Revolution Documents.* Vol. I. Oxford: Basil Blackwell, 1966.

Roberts, Kenneth, and Anna M. Roberts, trans. *Moreau de St. Méry's American Journey: 1793–1798.* New York: Doubleday & Co., 1947.

Robin, Abbé Charles-César. *Nouveau Voyage dans l'Amérique septentrionale, en l'année 1781, et campagne de l'armée de M. le comte de Rochambeau.* Paris: Moutard, 1782.

Robitaille, Abbé Georges. *Washington et Jumonville.* Montréal: Le Devoir, 1933.

Robson, John M., et al., eds. *Collected Works of John Stuart Mill.* Vol. VI: *Essays on England, Ireland, and the Empire.* Toronto: University of Toronto Press, 1963–91.

Rose, R. B. *The Making of the Sans-Culottes: Democratic Ideas and Institutions in Paris, 1789–92.* Manchester: Manchester University Press, 1983.

Rosenthal, Lewis. *America and France: The Influence of the United States on France in the XVIIIth Century.* New York: Henry Holt & Co., 1882.

Royster, Charles. *A Revolutionary People at War: The Continental Army and American Character, 1775–1783.* Chapel Hill: University of North Carolina Press, 1979.

Rudé, George. *The Crowd in the French Revolution.* London: Oxford University Press, 1959.

Saint Bris, Gonzague. *La Fayette.* Paris: Editions SW-Télémaque, 2006.

Sarrans, B. *Memoirs of General Lafayette and of the French Revolution of 1830.* 2 vols. London: Richard Bentley, 1832.

Schama, Simon. *Citizens: A Chronicle of the French Revolution.* New York and London: Penguin Books, 1989.

Schiff, Stacy. *A Great Improvisation: Franklin, France, and the Birth of America.* New York: Henry Holt & Co., 2005.

Schutz, John A., and Douglas Adair. *The Spur of Fame: Dialogues of John Adams and Benjamin Rush, 1805–1813.* San Marino, CA: Huntington Library, 1980.

Sears, Louis Martin. *George Washington and the French Revolution.* Detroit: Wayne State University Press, 1960.

Ségur, M. le Comte de. *Mémoires, ou souvenirs et anecdotes.* 3 vols. Paris: Alexis Eymery, 1826.

Shackelford, George Green. "William Short: Diplomat in Revolutionary France, 1785–1793," *Proceedings of the American Philosophical Society,* vol. 102, no. 6, Dec. 15, 1958. Studies of Historical Documents in the Library of the American Philosophical Society, 596–612.

Shapiro, Barry M. "Revolutionary Justice in 1789–1790: The Comité de Recherches, the Châtelet, and the Fayettist Coalition," *French Historical Studies,* vol. 17, no. 3 (Spring 1992), 656–69.

Shy, John. *A People Numerous and Armed.* New York: Oxford University Press, 1976.

Slavin, Morris, and Agnes M. Smith, eds. *Bourgeois, Sans-Culottes, and Other Frenchmen. Essays on the French Revolution in Honor of John Hall Stewart.* Waterloo, Ontario: Wilfried Laurier University, 1981.

Smelser, Marshall. "George Washington and the Alien and Sedition Acts," *American Historical Review,* vol. 59, no. 2 (January 1954), 322–34.

Smith, Paul H., et al., eds. *Letters of Delegates to Congress, 1774–1789.* Washington, DC: Library of Congress, 1976–2000. Digital version at http://memory.loc.gov/.

Smith, Richard Norton. *Patriarch: George Washington and the New American Nation.* Boston and New York: Houghton Mifflin, 1993.

Sonenscher, Michael, ed. *Emmanuel Joseph Sieyès: Political Writing, Including the Debate Between Sieyès and Tom Paine in 1791.* Indianapolis: Hackett Publishing Co., 2003.

Sparks, Jared. *The Life of George Washington. Two volumes in one, abridged by the author.* Cincinnati: Henry W. Derby, 1855.

———. ed. *The Diplomatic Correspondence of the American Revolution.* 12 vols. Boston: N. Hale and Gray & Bowen, 1829.

Staël, Baroness de. *Considerations on the Principal Events of the French Revolution.* Duc de Broglie and Baron de Stael, eds. 2 vols. New York: James Eastburn & Co., 1818.

Stendhal. *Memoirs of an Egotist,* trans. Andrew Brown. London: Hesperus Press, 2003.

Stewart, John Hall. *A Documentary Survey of the French Revolution.* New York: Macmillan, 1951.

Stinchcombe, William. "A Note on Silas Deane's Death," *William and Mary Quarterly,* 3rd ser., vol. 32, no. 4 (October 1975), 619–24.

Stoudt, John Joseph. *Ordeal at Valley Forge: A Day-by-Day Chronicle from December 17, 1777 to June 18, 1778,* Compiled from the Sources. Philadelphia: University of Pennsylvania Press, 1963.

Stryker, William S. *The Battle of Monmouth.* Princeton, NJ: Princeton University Press, 1999.

Syrett, Harold C., ed. *The Papers of Alexander Hamilton.* 27 vols. New York: Columbia University Press, 1961–87.

Szatmary, David P. *Shays' Rebellion: The Making of an Agrarian Insurrection*. Amherst: University of Massachusetts Press, 1980.

Tackett, Timothy. "Conspiracy Obsession in a Time of Revolution: French Elites and the Origins of the Terror, 1789–1792," *American Historical Review*, vol. 105, no. 3. (June 2000), 691–713.

———. "Nobles and Third Estate in the Revolutionary Dynamic of the National Assembly, 1789–1790," *American Historical Review*, vol. 94, no. 2 (April 989), 271–301.

———. *When the King Took Flight*. Cambridge, MA: Harvard University Press, 2003.

Taillemite, Etienne. *Lafayette*. Paris: Fayard, 1989.

Taine, Hippolyte A. *The French Revolution*, trans. John Durand. E-text edition, Nalanda Digital Library, Project Gutenberg (page numbers refer to PDF).

Thomas, Jules, ed. *Correspondance Inédite de La Fayette 1793–1801*. Paris: Delagrave.

Tocqueville, Alexis de. *The Ancien Régime and the French Revolution*, trans. Gilbert Stuart. New York: Doubleday, 1955.

Tower, Charlemagne. *The Marquis de La Fayette in the American Revolution*. 2 vols. Philadelphia: J. B. Lippincott, 1895.

Trevelyan, Sir George Otto. *The American Revolution*. 4 vols. New York: Longmans, Green, & Co., 1905.

Tulard, Jean, Jean-François Fayard, and Alfred Fierro, eds. *Histoire et dictionnaire de la Révolution française, 1789–1799*. Paris: Robert Laffon, 1987.

Unger, Harlow Giles. *Lafayette*. Hoboken, NJ: John Wiley & Sons, 2002.

Van Kley, Dale K. "New Wine in Old Wineskins: Continuity and Rupture in the Pamphlet Debate of the French Pre-revolution, 1787–1789," *French Historical Studies*, vol. 17, no. 2 (Autumn, 1991), 447–65.

Vaulabelle, Achille de. *Histoire des deux restaurations jusqu'à l'avénement de Louis-Philippe*. 8 vols. Paris: Perrotin, Editeur de Béranger, 1844–54.

Wharton, Francis, ed. *The Revolutionary Diplomatic Correspondence of the United States*. 6 vols. Washington, DC: Government Printing Office, 1889.

Whitlock, Brand. *Lafayette*. 2 vols. New York and London: D. Appleton & Company.

Wick, Daniel L. *A Conspiracy of Well-Intentioned Men: The Society of Thirty and the French Revolution*. Unpublished doctoral dissertation, University of California/Davis, 1977.

———. "The Court Nobility and the French Revolution: The Example of the Society of Thirty," *Eighteenth-Century Studies*, vol. 13, no. 3 (Spring 1980), 263–84.

Wiencek, Henry. *An Imperfect God*. New York: Farrar, Straus & Giroux, 2003.

Wills, Garry. *Cincinnatus: George Washington and the Enlightenment*. New York: Doubleday & Co., 1984.

Wood, Gordon S. *The Creation of the American Republic 1776–1787*. Chapel Hill: University of North Carolina Press, 1998.

———. *The Radicalism of the American Revolution*. New York: Vintage Books, 1991.

Wood, W. J. *Battles of the Revolutionary War: 1775–1781*. Chapel Hill: Da Capo Press, 1990.

Woodward, W. E. *Lafayette*. London: Cresset Press, 1939.

Wright, John W. "The Corps of Light Infantry in the Continental Army," *American Historical Review*, vol. 31, no. 3 (April 1926), 454–61.

Acknowledgments

W hen I set out to write this book, I was surprised to find that although many scholars have addressed the relationship of the American and French revolutions, no one had ever treated them as a single, simultaneously unfolding narrative. I understand now why that is the case: Two revolutions and two large lives are too big for any reasonably sized book or any sensible author. I learned this early and have restricted this book to the limits of the possible and the patience of the general reader. I have not written a full history of the American and French revolutions nor complete biographies of the protagonists. Instead, I've tried to write a narrative that considers the revolutions in the light of the relationship between Washington and Lafayette, and considers the relationship in light of the revolutions. This approach was more effective in limiting the writing than the reading, since the primary sources are beyond rich, and the historians of this period make for wonderfully inspiring guides. For certain specific insights and their deep study of the subjects at hand, I owe a special debt to Robert Darnton, Susan Dunn, Durand Echeverria, Lloyd Kramer, Edmund S. Morgan, Marie Morgan, Sylvia Neely, Charles Royster, Simon Schama, Timothy Tackett, and Gordon S. Wood. Every student of Lafayette must acknowledge the scholarship of both Louis Gottschalk and Stanley J. Idzerda, just as every student of Washington must acknowledge the contribution of his biographer Douglas Southall Freeman as well as W. W. Abbot and his fellow editors of the University of Virginia's edition of Washington's papers. I would also like to acknowledge another notable Washington biographer, James Thomas Flexner, whom I was lucky enough to know many years ago, when we were both working in the Frederick Lewis Allen Room of the New York Public Library, and who was very generous with his time and support to an aspiring young author of historical non-fiction with little to recommend him but his enthusiasm.

Among the most important people in the making of this book have been librarians. They are too numerous to mention by name and so scrupulously interchangeable that to name a few who have taken the heaviest burdens would be to slight others who have only helped a great deal. Their dedication and ability make all works of history possible, and for this one I must mention especially those at the Archives nationales, the Mitterand branch of the Bibliothèque nationale de France, the New York Public Library, and the Library of Congress. I would also like to acknowledge the invisible hands who digitized and made searchable so much of the most important primary source material for both the French and American revolutions. Anyone who wrote a book thirty years ago knows what a difference such resources have made to scholarship and to the lives of authors.

As much as myself, these people have helped my research associates, both the very smart and enterprising John Okrent, who mined the vast treasury of footnotes to Washington's papers, and Maria Vincenza Aloisi, one of the most versatile and experienced research professionals I have ever had the pleasure to know. Her ingenuity and care are reflected throughout this book.

At W. W. Norton I must thank most of all Starling Lawrence, whose belief in this book gave it life and sustained me throughout the writing of it. His assistant, Molly May, was there at every step as this book made its way into the world; Ann Adelman was its conscientious and discerning copyeditor; and the production manager, Anna Oler, picture researcher, Stephanie Romeo, designer, Brooke Koven, and cartographer, Paul Pugliese, have made it beautiful. Once again, my agent, Liz Darhansoff, has supplied the moral and practical support necessary, while Louise

Brockett, Lynn Goldberg, and Angela Hayes have worked tirelessly to help the book find its audience.

For various other forms of support and insight, I would like to thank Amy and Cliff Aronson, Geraldine Baum, Steve Bennett, Peter Bonventre, James V. Calio, François Cruzet, Nicole and Gaylord Dillingham, Trudy Dixon, Geoff Dufresnes, Caroline Fitzgibbons, Alma and Marvin Glickman, Lisa Kasteler, Nancy and Mort Lipton, David Garrard Lowe, Jonathan Newhouse, Daniel Okrent (who, among other contributions, has the distinction of being John Okrent's father), Donna Olshan, Michael Oreskes, Leslie Palanker, Heidi and Philippe Rubinet, Tad Smith, Etienne Taillemite, and Robin Tate.

Throughout this book, Lafayette is spelled Lafayette, not La Fayette, or LaFayette, or De La Fayette, all of which occur in contemporary letters to and accounts of him. The reason for the variation is simple: Many people at the time did not know how to spell his name or simply did not worry about the spelling, since precision and consistency about proper names seems not to have been much prized in eighteenth-century France. Lafayette's most famous ancestor was the seventeenth-century novelist Mme de La Fayette, author of *La Princesse de Clèves*, which contributed to the confusion, as did his wife, Adrienne, who habitually wrote La Fayette (with the space); but so did his own handwriting, in which both the lower- and upper-case *f* look the same, so that his name can be read as either Lafayette or LaFayette (no space). His immediate ancestors always spelled the name Lafayette, however, and so did the editors of his *Mémoires*, who answered to the family. I have taken their lead.

For the spelling of other French names, I have relied on expert opinion, and consistency is not the result here either. Vergennes is Vergennes, never de Vergennes, but de Grasse is de Grasse, never Grasse. I am not sure why, perhaps because *Grasse* alone means "gross," and he is thought to deserve better. Similarly, though equally inexplicable, d'Eon cannot be Eon, or d'Ayen Ayen, or d'Artois Artois, even though his brother is Provence, never de Provence. This is just the way it is, despite the occasional contrary usage. *La* in a name is almost always capitalized because it usually refers to a place, but *de* is never capitalized—except in the name of the Princess De La Belgiojoso, because she was Italian.

Unless otherwise indicated in the text or notes, translations from the French are my own. When quoting contemporary letters, particularly of Washington, I have most often modernized spelling and punctuation. I have left some of Lafayette's early letters in English as they were written, to show his progress with the language, to demonstrate how hard he worked at it, and to make the point that he was willing to risk error and embarrassment in order to be accepted by his new American comrades. Except for such early letters and one letter that he wrote when he was released from prison, whose odd syntax conveys the confusion and high emotion of that moment in his life, I have modernized the spelling and punctuation in his letters too.

Finally, for the support that is overarching and undergirding, I thank my wife, Karen, to whom this book is dedicated; my children—in order of appearance, Allison, Nicholas, William, Lillian, Ben, Miles, and Hannah; and my parents, Robert W. Gaines, Sr., and Harriet E. Gaines. I'm not sure exactly what it is that they gave me and my brother, Dr. Robert W. Gaines, Jr., but whatever it was, they made possible whatever success we have managed to have, in our work and in our lives; and for that they will always have our gratitude and our love.

Illustration Credits

Insert following page 150

Marquis de Lafayette departs for America, 1777. Granger Collection.

The first meeting of General George Washington and French General Lafayette in Philadelphia, Pennsylvania, on 3 August 1777. Corbis.

George Washington. Engraved by A. Blanchard after a drawing by Couder, ca. 1840. The New York Public Library/Art Resource, NY.

Portrait of Marie-Joseph-Paul-Yves-Roch-Gilbert Du Motier, Marquis de Lafayette. Bridgeman Art Library International.

Baron de Kalb introducing Marquis de Lafayette to Silas Deane in Paris, November 1776. Bettmann/Corbis.

Pierre-Augustin Caron de Beaumarchais, 1790. AKG Images.

Chevalier d'Eon. Mary Evans Picture Library/Alamy.

Duel of Chevalier d'Eon with Chevalier de Saint-Georges in Carlton House on 9 April 1787. AKG Images.

Chevalier d'Eon (1810). Mary Evans Picture Library/Alamy.

George Washington and Marquis de Lafayette at Valley Forge, 1776. Bettmann/Corbis.

Washington at Monmouth. Bettmann/Corbis.

The Resignation of George Washington on 23 December 1783. ca.1822. Bridgeman Art Library International.

Constitutional Convention, 1787. Bridgeman Art Library International.

George Washington Inauguration. Granger Collection.

Washington and His Cabinet. Currier & Ives lithograph, 19th century. Library of Congress.

Insert following page 246

George Washington after the Battle of Princeton, 3 January 1777. Réunion des Musées Nationaux/Art Resource, NY.

Marquis de La Fayette, in a captain's uniform of the Noailles regiment, 1788. Réunion des Musées Nationaux/Art Resource, NY.

Marie-Antoinette of Lorraine-Habsburg, Austria. 1769. Réunion des Musées Nationaux/Art Resource, NY.

Louis XVI, bust-length portrait. Réunion des Musées Nationaux/Art Resource, NY.

Portrait of Charles Gravier, Comte de Vergennes. Art Resource, NY.

Charles-Henri-Victor-Théodat, Comte d'Estaing. Réunion des Musées Nationaux/Art Resource, NY.

Jean-Baptiste-Donatien de Vimeur, Comte de Rochambeau. Archivo Iconografico, SA/Corbis.

François-Joseph Paul, Comte de Grasse. Réunion des Musées Nationaux/Art Resource, NY.

Siege of Yorktown. AKG Images.

Constitutional Convention. Bettmann/Corbis.

Thomas Jefferson. Oil on canvas, 90.8 x 72.4 cm, 1786. Bequest of Charles Francis Adams. National Portrait Gallery, Smithsonian Institution/Art Resource, NY.

Alexander Hamilton, 1806. By John Trumbull. Archivo Iconografico, SA/Corbis.

Portrait of John Adams. Gilbert Stuart/Musée Franco-Américaine, Blérancourt, Chauny, France/Bridgeman Art Library International.

George and Martha Washington at a ball. (Print is entitled: *First in Peace,* by Percy Moran) The New York Public Library/Art Resource, NY.

Assembly of Notables, 22 February 1787. Bridgeman Art Library International.

The Tennis Court Oath, 20 June 1789. 1791. Bridgeman Art Library International.

The Storming of the Bastille and the Arrest of Joseph Delaunay on 14 July 1789. Bridgeman Art Library International.

Louis XVI meets the Mayor of Paris, 17 July 1789. The Print Collector/Alamy.

Lafayette at the Fête de la Fédération. Archivo Iconografico, SA/Corbis.

Marquis de Lafayette Slays Despotism. AKG Images.

The Storming of the Tuileries Palace, the Carrousel courtyard, 10 August 1792. Photo: G. Blot/J. Schormans. Réunion des Musées Nationaux/Art Resource, NY.

Prison Tribunal. 1792.Visual Arts Library/Alamy.

Insert following page 374

Cartoon of Louis XVI as a Pig. Library of Congress.

Caricature of Louis XVI taking Leave of his wife and family, 1793. Bridgeman Art Library International.

Louis XVI taken by the People from the Tuileries Palace on 20 June 1792 to his execution. Bridgeman Art Library International.

Overthrow of Girondins, Deputies leave National Convention Assembly. Visual Arts Library/Alamy.

Marie-Antoinette before her execution. Pen, brown ink. DR 3599 Coll. Rothschild. Art Resource, NY.

Maximilien Robespierre. Snark/Art Resource, NY.

Cartoon: "XYZ Affair." Bettmann/Corbis.

Death of Washington. The New York Public Library/Art Resource, NY.

The Apotheosis of Washington. National Portrait Gallery, Smithsonian Institution/Art Resource, NY.

Lafayette and family in Olmütz Prison. Bettmann/Corbis.

La Grange. Library of Congress.

Madame Adrienne de Lafayette. Skillman Library, Special Collections, Lafayette College.

Lafayette. Humanities and Social Sciences Library/Print Collection, Miriam and Ira D. Wallach Division of Art, Prints and Photographs, The New York Public Library.

The Duc d'Orléans embracing General La Fayette and raising the national colors on the terrace of the Palais-Royal, 30 July 1830. Bridgeman Art Library International.

Portrait of General Lafayette in the park of the Château de La Grange. 1830. Musée de l'Armée/Dist. Réunion des Musées Nationaux/Art Resource, NY.

Index

ABOUT THE AUTHOR

A native of Dayton, Ohio, James R. Gaines is the former managing editor of *Time*, *Life*, and *People* magazines and the author of several books, including *Wit's End: Days and Nights of the Algonquin Round Table* and, most recently, *Evening in the Palace of Reason*, a book that examines the conflict between faith and reason in the early Enlightenment through the music of Johann Sebastian Bach. He lives in Paris.